D0677942

The Bigger Picture
Elements of Feature Writing

Edited by Ivor Shapiro
Ryerson University

2009
Emond Montgomery Publications
Toronto, Canada

Copyright © 2009 Emond Montgomery Publications Limited. All rights reserved. No part of this publication may be reproduced, stored in a retrieval system, or transmitted, in any form or by any means, photocopying, electronic, mechanical, recording, or otherwise, without the prior written permission of the copyright holder.

Emond Montgomery Publications Limited
60 Shaftesbury Avenue
Toronto ON M4T 1A3
http://www.emp.ca/highered

Printed in Canada on 100 percent recycled paper.
Reprinted December 2015.

We acknowledge the financial support of the Government of Canada through the Canada Book Fund for our publishing activities.

Acquisitions and development editor: Mike Thompson
Editorial assistant: Nick Raymond
Marketing manager: Christine Davidson
Director, sales and marketing, higher education: Kevin Smulan
Copy editor: Claudia Forgas
Proofreader: Grace Cherian
Production editor: Jim Lyons
Indexer: Paula Pike
Text designer: Brian Grebow, BG Communications
Cover designers: Stephen Cribbin & Simon Evers
Cover photo: Courtesy of Sam Javanrouh / www.topleftpixel.com

Library and Archives Canada Cataloguing in Publication

The bigger picture : elements of feature writing / edited by Ivor Shapiro.

Includes index.
ISBN 978-1-55239-280-5

1. Feature writing.   I. Shapiro, Ivor, 1953–

PN4784.F37B53 2008   070.4'4   C2008-903445-7

To the feature writers and editors I have worked with, too many to name, who have taught me what journalism is for and how it's done. And to the students who have helped me believe that the best is yet to come.—I.S.

Words are but the images of matter;
and except they have life of reason and invention,
to fall in love with them is all one as to fall in love with a picture.
— Francis Bacon, *The Advancement of Learning* (1605), Book I, IV.3

Contents

Preface

To say that journalism is in a time of profound change is rather like saying that the earth's climate is changing. Practically everyone knows it; few deniers remain and their number shrinks daily. News is delivered in new and increasingly sophisticated ways, and those who report the news include many who are neither paid to do it nor even, in many cases, involved in journalism as a career. People are increasingly skeptical about what "the media" tell them, and while many place their trust in the "feeling lucky" Google draw, or in TV's satirical takes on public events, others feed their hunger for information by ignoring journalists' efforts and doing their own research using near-instant access to primary sources that could only have been dreamed of a decade ago.

In response, those who work in the media have been engaged for several years in adjusting how they think about producing the news, and how they understand news itself. The idea of a "reader" or "audience" now seems somehow old-fashioned; everyone is a "user" of news—someone not only to communicate to but interact with. Reporters no longer choose between writing, voicing, filming, or programming; if they like, they can do it all. The technology of cutting-edge multimedia journalism is as available, and nearly as easy to use, as an iPod. Suddenly, everything anyone knew about journalism seems up for grabs.

Everything except, maybe, one thing. What has not changed is what journalism is *for*. Journalists live to ask new questions and describe new things, to expose what's unseen and explain what's misunderstood, to describe how the world works. Sometimes, they do this by digging beneath the surface of public knowledge and, through stubborn and imaginative resourcefulness, discovering the underlying truth. Sometimes they conduct steadfast research and incisive interviews to understand the character of a person or organization that's in the public eye—or that should be. Sometimes, they simply respond to their own curiosity and in so doing satisfy the citizens who benefit from their work. Yes, facts are easier than ever to come by in this age of infinite information. But understanding the meaning of those facts, grasping how and why those facts came to be—that's as hard as, or harder than, ever.

This is what feature writers live for: to paint the *bigger* picture. Features shine light on the why and the how of events. They zoom in for close-ups, then pan back for context. They tell full stories whose various parts may have been told before but separately, their dots unconnected. The best feature writers are obsessive about the fundamental journalistic discipline of verification, rooting out explanations and pruning out distortions and lies. These writers also push at the edges of style to engage readers, touch them emotionally, and move them to think, to understand, to react.

Each of the ten feature articles reprinted in these pages represents a Canadian author's journey and invites us, the readers, along for the ride. With *The New Yorker*'s Malcolm Gladwell, we explore the vagaries of condiment marketing; with *The Globe and Mail*'s Stephanie Nolen, we venture into a violence-ridden African countryside. Elsewhere on the itinerary, we watch engineers saving a massive BC dam from collapse, Montreal doctors saving lives after a campus shooting spree, and ad-biz hotshots making a quarter-million-dollar commercial with a doomed fly in the starring role. We are transported through time and place to watch dubbed Hollywood classics in pre-revolutionary Iran, the start of lobster season in the Gulf of St. Lawrence, and a strange war against hostile beavers in rural Alberta. In

Glad You Asked! Editor's Note

Q: What in the world is a GYA?
A: I'm *so* glad you asked!

Good reporters ask good questions—as do good students. So, it's not surprising that the journalists and teachers who have contributed to this book have heard some really good questions over and over again. We decided to gather some of those questions—and, of course, the answers—in a collection of sidebars spread throughout this book under the common heading of "Glad You Asked!" Some, like "How do I keep up with new writing, ideas, trends, and news?" and "What's the cure for writer's block?" are asked all the time. Others are asked far too seldom—how to judge the veracity of information; how to work the collection's only memoir, Katrina Onstad stares down her own teenage years to paint a complex, anti-complacent hue on a sexual abuse case. In a scrupulously detached investigation, John Vaillant probes the puzzling story of a rare old Queen Charlottes tree and the strange man who willfully destroyed it before disappearing.

These ten feature articles are as diverse as they are exemplary—enlightening and mysterious, funny and sad, inspiring and ironic, thoughtful and touching. They are written in the third person and the first, and use a wide range of styles, tones, voices, points of view, and approaches to structure. Some were written for newspapers, others for magazines; one became the core of an award-winning book. (None in this collection was created for the web, but feature writers are rapidly coming into their own there, and the craft of the broadcast documentarian, too, builds on many of the values and techniques explored in these pages.) But, if you find these wide-ranging tales as riveting as we did, you'll probably agree that they all depend on three things—clarity of purpose, meticulous reporting, and evocative, crystal-clear writing.

In the chapter preceding each of these ten treats of storytelling, you will be guided into the world and craft of the feature writer. The ten chapter authors have made a living as reporters, writers, editors, and teachers for dozens of leading publications and six Canadian journalism schools. The essential elements of successful feature writing that they explore are those underlying all good journalism: recognizing and articulating a storytelling opportunity (part one); conducting careful and rigorous research, interviewing, and observation (part two); planning and writing with style (part three); and respecting the principles of truthfulness, independence, and originality while rising to complex real-world challenges (part four).

courteously and professionally with editors. Still others fall somewhere in the middle. For instance: "What's a fact-checking package?" and "How do I navigate the information laws?"

I would like to thank all the chapter authors who contributed to the GYAs (as we came to nickname them), and the other veteran feature writers who generously gave their time and expertise to contribute. Mostly, I would like to thank Ivor Shapiro, who came up with the idea for GYAs and gave me the opportunity to edit them. Most of the wisdom and good advice in these items belongs to my colleagues; any errors or omissions are mine.

Paul Benedetti
Editor of "Glad You Asked!"

The scrupulous reader may notice some, but not much, repetition among the various chapters. This is because each chapter is intended to be free-standing, so that a selection of chapters can be assigned, in any order, at the instructor's discretion. Indeed, although the book was written with journalism schools in mind, we know that many readers will come upon it independently, and the book is intended to be suitable for self-edification as well.

Inevitably, some things (especially Internet links) will go out of date during the lifespan of this book. For that reason, the authors have collaborated in creating a "Feature Writing" page at the Canadian Journalism Project's website, J-Source.ca (click on "J-Topics," then "Feature Writing"). There, you will find links to other exemplary feature stories, additional resources, updates, and the websites mentioned in this book.

Many people have contributed invaluably to this book. First and foremost, it has been a privilege to work with my nine fellow chapter authors, all of whom brought to the task not just their experience and expertise but a palpable dedication to the project and patience with its editor. Thanks are also due to the authors of the ten feature articles in this collection; to those who provided peer review for individual chapters; to Jim Meek (University of King's College) and Sharon Dietz (Conestoga College), who provided their feedback on the proposal; to Mike Thompson, who dreamed this book up and steered it with imagination and flexibility; and to copyeditor Claudia Forgas and several others at Emond Montgomery Publications, who all displayed impeccable professionalism and commitment throughout the production process.

On a personal note, I extend deep thanks for the help and support of Paul Knox, chair of the School of Journalism at Ryerson University; John Fraser, master of Massey College in the University of Toronto, and several other staff and fellows at Massey (where my work for this book, among other projects, was done while on a sabbatical leave); Moira Farr, Sue Ferguson, and Ernest Hillen, who provided editorial feedback on my own chapter (Ferguson also spearheaded the creation of the "Feature Writing" web page at J-Source.ca); my esteemed and ever-cheerful colleague Paul Benedetti, who gave advice and encouragement on several fronts in addition to writing his own chapter and editing the "Glad You Asked!" items; Peter, Gill, Anna, and Michael Lurie, who shared their home in Perth, Australia, with me while I completed the editing; and Louise Paul, my partner in life and steadfast cheerleader of my work.

Ivor Shapiro
May 2008

Contributors

Ivor Shapiro (Editor) is an associate professor in the School of Journalism of Ryerson University, and editor-in-chief of the Canadian Journalism Project (*J-Source.ca*). He teaches feature writing as well as law and ethics for journalists. A former contributing editor of *Saturday Night* and features editor and managing editor for *Chatelaine*, he has written feature stories for those magazines plus *Maclean's*, *Toronto Life*, *The Walrus*, *Report on Business Magazine*, and *Today's Parent*, among others, and has been honoured six times at the National Magazine Awards.

Paul Benedetti has been a professional reporter and writer for more than 25 years. He has published work in *The Globe and Mail*, *The Toronto Star*, *The Hamilton Spectator*, *Canadian Living*, *Homemakers*, *The Financial Post Magazine*, and many others. He is deputy editor of *J-Source.ca*, and a full-time faculty member in the Masters of Arts in Journalism program at The University of Western Ontario.

Aaron Derfel is the senior medical reporter for *The Gazette* in Montreal, specializing in investigative and narrative journalism. He won the 2004 Judith Jasmin Prize—Quebec's highest journalism honour—for an exposé on hospitals reusing disposable medical instruments.

Abou Farman is a writer and visual artist who has published and exhibited internationally. His writing has appeared in *Maisonneuve*, *Arc*, *Green Mountains Review*, *Books in Canada*, *The Globe and Mail*, *Transition*, *Al-Ahram Weekly*, and other publications.

Moira Farr is an award-winning writer and editor who teaches magazine writing at Carleton University. Her essays, reviews, and feature articles have appeared in numerous publications, including *The Globe and Mail, The Walrus, Toronto Life, Chatelaine*, and several writing anthologies. Farr has worked as an editor for magazines such as *Equinox* and *THIS Magazine*. Her first book, *After Daniel: A Suicide Survivor's Tale* (HarperFlamingo, 1999) was shortlisted for a number of awards and was also *The Edmonton Journal's* top pick for non-fiction that year. A chapter of *After Daniel* appears in *The Vintage Book of Canadian Memoirs* (2001). She is a faculty editor for the Banff Centre's summer Literary Journalism program, and a contributing editor for the *Ryerson Review of Journalism*.

Sue Ferguson is an assistant professor of journalism at Wilfrid Laurier University – Brantford Campus. Her journalism career began in the late 1980s, as a freelance fact-checker at *Maclean's, Chatelaine*, and *Canadian Living*. She joined the *Maclean's* staff as chief of research in the mid-1990s, eventually rotating through a variety of editing and writing positions. As associate editor and senior writer at *Maclean's*, Ferguson wrote and edited stories about history, education, families, and, when pressed into service, modern dance. Since taking up her position at Laurier–Brantford, Ferguson has developed her research and teaching interests in children, toys, and media. She keeps a foot in the industry, however, through writing the occasional freelance piece and by serving as a judge for national and regional journalism awards. She is also a contributing editor to *J-Source.ca*.

Don Gibb is a professor at Ryerson University's School of Journalism in Toronto. A 1968 Ryerson graduate, Gibb has taught newspaper reporting since joining the faculty in 1988. Before coming to Ryerson, he spent 20 years at *The London Free Press* as a bureau reporter, beat reporter, editorial writer, occasional columnist, assignment editor, and city editor. He conducts writing and editing seminars and coaches writers at daily and community newspapers across Canada. Gibb is a visiting writing coach at *The Globe and Mail* and a contributing writer to *Media* magazine, the publication of the Canadian Association of Journalists (CAJ). He was named Ryerson's Professor of the Year in 2001. In 2006, Gibb was honoured by the CAJ for his outstanding contribution to journalism. He wishes to dedicate his chapter in this book to all of his students who have inspired him to become a better teacher.

Malcolm Gladwell has been a staff writer with *The New Yorker* magazine since 1996. His 1999 profile of Ron Popeil won a National Magazine Award, and in 2005 he was named one of *Time* Magazine's 100 Most Influential People. He is the author of two books, *The Tipping Point: How Little Things Make a Big Difference* (2000) and *Blink: The Power of Thinking Without*

Thinking (2005), both of which were number one New York Times bestsellers. From 1987 to 1996, he was a reporter with *The Washington Post*, where he covered business, science, and then served as the newspaper's New York City bureau chief. He graduated from the University of Toronto, Trinity College, with a degree in history. He was born in England, grew up in rural Ontario, and now lives in New York City.

Bruce Grierson is the author of *U-Turn: What if You Woke Up One Morning and Realized You Were Living the Wrong Life?* and is the co-author of *Culture Jam*. He is a four-time Canadian National Magazine Award–winning feature writer whose work has appeared in *The New York Times Magazine*, *Popular Science*, *The Walrus*, *The Guardian*, *Marie Claire*, *Adbusters*, *The Utne Reader*, and many other magazines. He lives in Vancouver with his wife and daughters.

David Hayes is an award-winning freelance writer whose features, essays, and reviews have been published in *Toronto Life*, *Saturday Night*, *The Globe and Mail*, *Chatelaine*, *Reader's Digest*, *The New York Times Magazine*, and many other publications. A graduate of Ryerson University's School of Journalism, Hayes has written or co-written four books and teaches magazine writing at Ryerson.

Matthew Hays is a Montreal-based critic, author, curator, and university instructor. He has been a film critic and reporter for the weekly *Montreal Mirror* since 1993. His articles have also appeared in *The Globe and Mail*, *The Guardian*, *The New York Times*, *The Walrus*, CBC Arts Online, and *The Advocate*. He teaches courses in journalism, film, and communication studies at Concordia University, where he received his MA in communication studies in 2000. A 2006 nominee for a National Magazine Award, Hays received the Concordia Alumni Association Award for Teaching Excellence in 2007. His first book, *The View from Here: Conversations with Gay and Lesbian Filmmakers* (Arsenal Pulp Press), was cited by *Quill & Quire* as one of the best books of 2007 and won a 2008 Lambda Literary Award.

Linda Kay is an associate professor at Concordia University in Montreal. A journalist for over 25 years, Kay was the first female sports writer at *The Chicago Tribune*, and the winner of the Mary Garber Award as Best Female Sports Writer in America. Upon moving to Canada, she wrote a weekly Page 2 column on social affairs for *The Gazette* in Montreal. Her work has appeared in newspapers and magazines around North America, including *The Globe and Mail*, *Newsweek*, *Chatelaine*, and *Ottawa* magazine. In 2005, a division of Rowman & Littlefield published her memoir, *The Reading List*. She is also the author of a travel guide published by Connecticut's Globe-Pequot Press called *Romantic Days and Nights in Montreal*. At Concordia, Kay teaches classes in news writing and reporting, magazine writing, and gender and journalism. She served five years as the department's graduate program director, and in 2007, she received the Dean's Award for Teaching Excellence in the Faculty of Arts and Science. Kay is co-editor of the "First Person" section of *J-Source.ca*.

Susan McClelland is a freelance magazine journalist based in Toronto, where she also teaches magazine journalism at Centennial College. Her writing has appeared in *Maclean's, Reader's Digest, More, Canadian Living, Chatelaine, Toronto Life, ELLE*, and *The Globe and Mail*. She has won and been nominated for numerous investigative reporting and feature writing awards, including National Magazine and Society of Professional Journalist awards. She's also the recipient of the 2005 Amnesty International Media Award. McClelland is currently working on a documentary film chronicling the experiences of amputees of the Sierra Leone war. Her first novel, *The Bite of the Mango*, tells the story of Mariatu Kamara, a child victim of the conflict.

Anne Mullens is an international journalist and author who lives in Victoria, British Columbia. She writes for Canadian and international editions of *Reader's Digest* and many other Canadian and North American magazines and newspapers. She has won more than a dozen Canadian awards for her writing. She has also written two critically acclaimed books, *Missed Conceptions* (1990) and *Timely Death* (1996), which won the Edna Staebler Award for Creative Non-fiction.

Stephanie Nolen is *The Globe and Mail*'s Africa correspondent. She is a three-time winner of both the National Newspaper Award and the Amnesty International Award for Human Rights Reporting. She is also the author of *28: Stories of AIDS in Africa*, which was nominated for the Governor General's Award for Non-fiction, *Shakespeare's Face*, and *Promised the Moon: The Untold Story of the First Women in the Space Race*. She lives in Johannesburg, South Africa.

Katrina Onstad is a freelance writer. Her work has appeared in *The New York Times, The Guardian, The Telegraph Magazine, Salon*, and most Canadian publications. Katrina was a film critic at *The National Post* newspaper for several years, and has written on arts, culture and society for *Toronto*

Life, Maclean's, Flare, and numerous other magazines, earning her National Magazine Award nominations in the United States and Canada. Currently, Katrina writes the "Modern Times" column in *Chatelaine.* Her first novel, *How Happy to Be,* was published to critical acclaim in 2006 by McClelland & Stewart. She is at work on her second novel. Born and raised in Vancouver, she now lives in Toronto with her partner and two children.

Philip Preville was a latecomer to journalism, starting out at the relatively ripe age of 30. He served four years as news editor at the *Montreal Mirror* before moving to Toronto to kick-start his freelancing career, and—save for a year-long stint as a senior editor at *Saturday Night* magazine—has been surviving on his freelancer's wits ever since. In 2003 he was appointed to a Canadian Journalism Fellowship at Massey College in the University of Toronto. He won the 2004 National Magazine Award for travel writing for his article in *Saturday Night* on the Magdalen Islands, "Living on Lobster Time." He is currently the politics columnist with *Toronto Life* magazine, and writes the City State blog on torontolife.com.

John Vaillant has written for *The New Yorker, The Atlantic, Outside, National Geographic Adventure,* and *Men's Journal,* among others. He lives in Vancouver with his wife and children. The piece included here, "The Golden Spruce," became a best-selling book by the same name, and is published by Vintage Canada.

PART ONE

The Idea of Story

CHAPTER ONE

A World of Ideas:
The Birth of a Feature

Philip Preville

All veteran feature writers can recite the highlights of their work: the best story they ever wrote, or the most difficult subject they ever tried to tackle. But one of the greatest highlights of a freelance writer's career is the silliest, most improbable story idea he or she ever sold. One veteran freelancer I know likes to tell the story of how he sold a feature about greasy-spoon breakfasts, which underwrote his weakness for cheddar cheese omelettes. For what it's worth, I once sold a 1,500-word feature about concrete rubble. Here's how.

One day back in 2001, the local papers in Toronto were full of coverage about a large chunk of concrete that had fallen from the underside of an elevated expressway. Talk radio picked up on the story, interviewing politicians and others about the city's decrepitude. Commuters were gripped with fear of falling concrete. Months before, visiting another city, I had been looking at a demolition site and was struck by the twisted, rusted metal bars that poked out of the jagged concrete rubble. How is it, I wondered then, that metal could rust when encased in concrete two feet thick? Connecting that image in my mind to the story of the crumbling expressway, I happened upon the questions that had never been asked in all the blanket coverage: why and how does concrete decay?

I made a few calls and discovered that those rusting metal reinforcing bars—*rebars* to engineers—were the very source of the problem. Concrete, though it appears as solid as rock to the naked eye, is actually porous to water: it is replete with tiny cracks and fissures, all interconnected, that channel water throughout its interior. And as the rain seeps through, the rebar rusts, expands, and, like an explosion detonated in slow motion, breaks the concrete to pieces from within. What's more, while this was news to me—and I knew it would be news to readers—it was well known to civil engineers, who had been hard at work for years trying to solve the problem with polymer-coated or stainless-steel rebar, which most governments refused to purchase because it was too expensive. One Canadian university had developed fibre-optic rebar which was not only rust-proof but which, when hooked up to the Internet, could provide continuous stress-test results, allowing officials to check on the inner health of any structure at any time of day and predict when the chunks would start to fall. I pitched the story to the science page of a national newspaper. It was an instant sell.

As we wrapped up the final edit on the night it went to press, my editor told me he never imagined a story about rebar could sustain interest for 1,500 words—but there's a first time for everything. As I hung up the phone, I felt that sense of illumination that comes from finally grasping the honesty beneath an old cliché. It's true what they say: no idea is a bad idea. The trouble lies in knowing where to find them, and making the search for them part of your working life.

Ideas in Journalism

Let's begin by stating one of journalism's stark realities, the kind that writers and editors don't like to admit but that they all know to be true: in a great deal of daily journalism, ideas scarcely matter. Most stories published in newspapers or broadcast on all-day radio or television news—a political debate heats up on the campaign trail, a vehicle accident ties up rush-hour traffic, a judge sentences a murderer to a maximum sentence—are reports in the purest sense. They are summations of events. They impart useful and important information. They often contain characters, and sometimes the characters offer some analysis, in the form of conflicting perspectives on the events and the facts at hand. But the journalists themselves, whose names are prominently featured in the reports they file, offer little insight. Lateral thinking and personal reflection are not required of them. This is not a criticism; it's simply the nature of the beast. Most daily journalism is responsive rather than enterprising. The writer's job is to be precise, thorough, and balanced. Everyone who works in the trade is familiar with the intellectual and professional frustrations that arise from the limitations placed upon their craft. It's the most common complaint in any newsroom: "I could have done so much more with that story."

Columnists and commentators have more latitude to express themselves. But ideas are not the same as opinions, and—alas—most columnists tend to rely on the latter. The difference is a matter of scope. An opinion is a judgment based on the facts at hand: Politician X is a fool, there are too many bad drivers on the road, the judge made the right decision. These kinds of judgments, which are the columnist's stock-in-trade, require little imagination, which explains why so many columnists seem to hold predictable opinions, and why they so often agree with each other.

Ideas are bigger than that. They are born out of originality, creativity, and imagination. They defy conventional wisdom. They look beyond the facts at hand. They seek out atypical dimensions to typical situations. They search for linkages. They bring a sense of wonder to the everyday world, roaming the landscape in search of portents, omens, secrets, blessings, curses, and small miracles. Ideas have soul. Ideas also take up a lot of psychic space, not to mention a lot of time to write and a lot of column inches in print, which is why the formulae of daily journalism tend to suppress them.

Thankfully, daily journalism is not the only kind of journalism. A lot of outlets welcome ideas and, indeed, make ideas their very lifeblood. These include particular sections of newspapers (especially on the weekend), some magazines, and online journals. Readers turn to these outlets not to feed their daily routines, but to step outside of them: to feed their thirst for knowledge, information, debate, and discussion. These are the places where feature stories live.

Where Ideas Come From

In simplest terms, an idea is a connection: a link between one thing (a person, an event, a place, a situation, a battery of facts) and another thing (a person, an event, et cetera) that provides unique insight into their relationship to each other and to the world we live in. A traffic jam is not merely a traffic jam—it's a social dependency on automobiles; a hindrance to economic activity; an engineering challenge; an environmental catastrophe; a colossal waste of time, money, and gasoline; or all of the above. A murder sentence is the flip side to someone's tragic loss; it's also an expression of such values as justice, retribution, and forgiveness. Behind every political blunder lies a bevy of backroom strategy sessions—what to say, when to say it, how to react—all designed to shape the opinions and the behaviour of the voting public; and the strategies that are successful tell us something about how our minds work, and about how so many individual, independent minds think in unison and translate their thoughts into votes. Though daily news does a poor job of fleshing out the bigger ideas, those ideas are always lurking between the lines, which is why daily news reports are usually the first place writers turn to when they are searching for inspiration.

When I first became a freelance feature writer, nothing was more daunting than the fear of running out of ideas. Each month's rent depended upon coming up with a publishable one—actually, more like three or four publishable ones. I would scour three newspapers daily, scrounging for hidden dimensions, unanswered questions, or quirky characters. While any writer will tell you that newspapers can be a fertile source of ideas, I soon discovered the perils of dependency. I was reading under a great deal of pressure ("Gotta find a story in here somewhere or it's steamed rice for me again this week"), which drained all the fun out of reading, and out of writing too. In university I'd had a tempestuous relationship with my *Globe and Mail*: every day's edition I would praise, criticize, blame, love, hate, disagree with, overanalyze, underanalyze, laugh with, and scream at—all before 10 a.m. It was a vibrant conversation, with the *Globe* providing no end of grist for my brain's mill. I wanted to write letters to the editor about every story I read: whether it was a column by Robert ("Brain Food") Fulford about academic fraud, a report on Quebec separatism, or a story about the latest financial crisis of the Canadian Football League, I had something to say about it—

Glad You Asked!   Essential Reading

Q: How do I keep up with new writing, ideas, trends, and news?
A: Read, read, read.

Writers are dedicated readers. Read a variety of publications, as well as anthologies of great journalism. The kind of non-fiction we're concerned with can be found, with varying degrees of consistency, in magazines such as *The Atlantic, Canadian Business, Chatelaine, enRoute, Esquire, Fortune, GQ, Granta, Harper's, The New Yorker, The New York Times Magazine, Reader's Digest, Report on Business, The Walrus, This Magazine, Vanity Fair,* and other more regional or topic-specific publications.

Strong feature writing can also be found in newspapers, especially weekend something the story had overlooked. But once under pressure to earn a living from my own writing, the conversation between my *Globe* and me atrophied. I tried broadening my horizons, reading more magazines and spending more time in bookstores and online. But the self-imposed pressure was bearing down upon all of it. My reaction to everything I read became the same: "I wish I'd come up with that idea, but I didn't, and now someone else has already written it, so it's too late."

I finally found my way out of my conundrum in, of all places, a stationery store—a place full of paper and nothing to read. On a bottom shelf was a tiny, spiral-bound notebook, three by four inches, with the words *Bright Ideas* etched in black upon its deep red cover. I bought it, tucked it into my pocket, and took it everywhere I went. Whenever my imagination went off on a productive tangent, connecting things I'd read to things I was seeing, to my previous travels or to my own experience, I'd quickly jot it down. Within days Bright Ideas was full of thoughts, complaints, arguments, joys, and other whimsy. I got back in touch with my own sense of curiosity. With my inner dialogue revitalized, reading newspapers became fun again. I could see my surroundings for what they were, a city with millions of dramas unfolding every day, more than could fill all its newspapers and magazines; all I had to do was find a few to tell. I went back and bought three more Bright Ideas.

I still have them. Some of the notes went on to be stories, like the idea I had for Asian and Middle Eastern knockoffs of American consumer brands, born from seeing a photo of a Crend toothpaste tube from Iran, identical to Crest. (I sold that one to *enRoute* magazine). Other ideas have yet to be written, yet still remain viable years after I first came up with them,

editions, such as *The Globe and Mail, The Guardian, National Post, The New York Times, St. Petersburg Times,* and many other city papers.

Several online sources carry ambitious feature writing, most predictably *Salon* (www.salon.com) and *Slate* (www.slate.com).

Of course, you must also—consistently—keep up with the news. Read your local paper, watch the TV news, and visit national and international news sites such as www.cbc.ca, www.globeandmail.com, www.bbc.co.uk, and www.nytimes.com.

These are only suggestions. The list of potential information sources today is near endless and changing every day. What you choose is up to you, but the only way to stay current and be abreast of new ideas is to read.

David Hayes and Wayne MacPhail

like the one about Canadians who, fleeing what they claimed was political persecution at home, have successfully applied for refugee status in the United States—I just need to find the time to corroborate the stories of the person who first told me about it. Now that I've revealed the idea, some-one—perhaps you—might steal it. (If so, that's fine by me; there are plenty more where it came from.) What's most interesting is to see all the ideas I had before anyone else, but that other people wrote before I did. I'd wanted to write about putting collars with GPS locators on cougars in Canada's national parks after I met the people who hunt them down with the tranquil-izer-dart rifles, but put off writing the pitch; the story has since been written dozens of times over. On one page I wrote, simply, "stupid economics," though I didn't elaborate on my own train of thought, which is too bad; if I had kept writing, I might have ended up authoring *Freakonomics*. But when I flip through the pages I don't see missed opportunities. I see a stream of consciousness that is alive and attuned to the world, swimming in an idea pool of unknown depths. To this day I never leave the house without a small notepad that fits in the palm of my hand.

The lesson: inspiration comes from within the writer, from your reac-tions to the things you read, see, and experience. The trick lies in not forcing inspiration, and in recognizing it when it comes to you unbidden and asks for your attention. It rarely arrives in the form of a *eureka!* moment, with a fully formed idea just waiting to be committed to paper and published for all to read. More often than not, it arrives in your head half-baked, in one of the following forms.

A deeper curiosity. You have a discussion with friends and colleagues that lasts for days, taking unexpected twists and turns—whether it's about Canada-US relations, surviving office politics, or dealing with prying par-ents. People start to share their experiences, and your eyes are opened anew. You find yourself deep in thought about a subject, and it energizes you. Time to start writing.

A nagging question. You see a newspaper headline that grips you. You begin to read in earnest, expecting to find the answer to some question that's been lingering in the back of your mind for a long time—yet as you read, the story fails to answer it. When that happens, it means the story has failed to make a connection. See if you can make it yourself. The nagging question doesn't have to come from a news report either. It could be that, one day, you zip up your jacket and notice that the letters YKK are stamped on the zipper's pull tab. You then notice that YKK is stamped on all your zippers, and on everyone else's zippers. What do they stand for? Decades after that question first begged for an answer, I wrote about it in 2001. The company now answers the question itself on its website.

A gut reaction. You read, hear, or experience something that turns your stomach. Maybe you've had a similar personal experience to what you've read, and so you have insight others don't. Maybe you're convinced there's more to a situation than meets the eye. Maybe you're outraged at what you consider to be utter nonsense. Maybe you, like I, watch politicians on television and sometimes are stricken with that dirty feeling you get when you are approached in the street by a con man or dope dealer. If your intuition is trying to talk to you, take the time to listen.

A contrarian opinion. You find yourself at odds with everyone you know over a particular subject, issue, or person. You feel like you are fighting an uphill battle against a deeply ingrained conventional wisdom. Maybe you think Quebec *should* be a separate country, or that recycling is a *bad* idea. Do you see something others don't? What is their blind spot? What's yours? Why is everyone so intractable? Try to find out. Contrarian opinions can turn into great features for Ideas sections of weekend newspapers.

A bad day. You nearly get run over while crossing the street—twice. You spend an eternity waiting in line. You pay for a bad-tasting hamburger, then eat it anyway, just like everyone else in the restaurant. Ask why. Bad days are the source of inspiration for every one of the thousands of hangover-cure articles that ever appeared in any newspaper's Life section.

A good day. You land a job. You find your keys. You fall in love. Suddenly you are taking in all of life's rich pageant with an open mind and open heart. There is no better time to rummage through your brain in search of story ideas. My own relationships have spawned more than one article about the science of love, including stories about the existence of human pheromones (still theoretical) and the scientific basis for spring fever (it definitely exists). There's no better vantage point on the whole world than cloud nine.

A moment of keen self-awareness. Whatever you're doing at any given moment is fodder for a feature if you can think about it insightfully and productively. In 2007 and 2008, uncountable hordes of freelancers sold stories about Facebook, because that's where they were hanging out. And because so many people had Facebook profiles, editors never turned down a Facebook pitch. Even doing nothing can be fodder for an article. In 2004, American dance critic Joan Acocella wrote a beautiful essay about writer's block.[1] Though she never mentions herself in the piece, I am convinced she decided to combat her own case of writer's block by researching and writing about it. If what you're doing right now—namely, reading a textbook—

drives you bonkers, there's probably a good feature to be written about why textbooks are detrimental to learning.

It's rare that a week goes by without one of these things happening to each of us. If you can link these aspects of daily life into your work routine, you'll never run short of ideas. I now pay a mortgage, which is much more daunting than rent, and meeting the payment still requires me to sell numerous ideas every month—but coming up with them no longer fills me with dread.

Testing Your Idea: Asking Why and How

Once you've got the beginnings of an idea, you can start plumbing its depths. The best way to do that is to ask why and how. Of the six basic questions inherent in all journalism—who, what, when, where, why, and how—daily journalism puts a premium on the first four. As James Carey once wrote, "Why and how are what we want most out of a news story and are least likely to receive."[2] There's a good reason for this: why and how are more qualitative, subjective, and just plain messy. They can quickly lead a writer into depths that their time and word count simply won't accommodate. For feature writing, however, these two messy questions are pillars of the craft, since it's a feature's job to deliver "what we want most from a news story."

To illustrate the point, let's go back to the seemingly mundane example I mentioned on page 5: the traffic jam. Ask yourself why traffic jams happen, and you'll quickly find yourself falling down a bottomless pit of additional questions, all of which also begin with "why." Why do people get so enraged in their cars when they don't get enraged walking on busy sidewalks? Why are there so many cars on the road in the first place? Why do people drive so much when vehicle accidents kill so many people every year? Why do so many accidents happen on the same roads, in the same places? Similarly, you could ask a series of questions that begin with "how." How does road design affect driver safety? How do drivers behave on crowded roads compared with empty ones? How does the human brain cope with highway driving—hurtling at lethal speeds on crowded roadways—an activity for which human beings were never designed?

The answers to these questions help explain traffic jams, but they are not about traffic jams as such—rather, they have to do with social isolation, automobile culture, willful ignorance, stress management, and road design. In other words, they *make the connection* between traffic jams and human psychology, sociology, economics, urban planning, and engineering. Suddenly, something as routine as a traffic jam is food for thought, and possibly the topic of many fascinating feature stories.

Shaping Ideas into Features

Though the world of ideas is boundless, the world of feature stories is not. It may be okay if an idea comes to you in raw form, providing more questions than answers in its first moments of inspiration. But it's not okay for a draft feature story to land on an editor's desk half-baked. In order to shape an idea into a feature story, you need to figure out three things:

- a clear focus or purpose,
- an audience that would be interested in it, and
- a feasible approach for addressing the idea that will sate your audience's curiosity.

The best way to think about these issues is to use the basic diagram known as the "communication triangle," which looks like so:

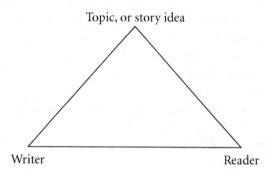

The triangle sets out the three essential ingredients in any act of communication: someone who communicates (writer), something the communication is about (topic), and someone to whom the communication is made (reader). For our purposes, think of the topic as your feature story idea, and think of the three sides of the triangle as the relationships between the things it connects. It's these *relationships* that matter most when you are trying to figure out how to turn a story idea into a feature.

Suppose, for example, that you've noticed how, over the last decade, fitness club memberships have risen dramatically and exercise tapes and gizmos are a staple of late-night infomercials, yet at the same time obesity has become a problem of epidemic proportions. The situation strikes you as a social paradox, and you think there's a feature story in there somewhere (in fact, there's almost certainly more than one). Use the triangle to figure out what it might be.

Explore your idea. The first thing to do is to gather a lot of basic information about your topic. What proportion of the population holds fitness club memberships? What proportion is obese? Suppose your hunch is that more people than ever are exercising and yet, simultaneously, more people than ever are *not* exercising—do the numbers bear you out? A few Internet searches can go a long way in this regard, bringing you up-to-date on the latest research and providing you with potential expert sources to interview.

Explore your relationship to your idea. The first thing to do is to sort out your own feelings and opinions about your idea. Is this just an intellectual curiosity, or have you been touched by the issue personally? Perhaps a friend or family member has been stricken with obesity. Perhaps you've noticed how everyone at your fitness club makes fun of the lone overweight regular and that, as a result, you've come to believe that he is the most courageous person in the room—others may have more muscle, but he's got more steel. Perhaps you know a sibling pair made up of one couch potato and one fitness freak, and you've noticed how their behaviours reinforce one another's anxiety, making one increasingly driven and the other increasingly lethargic. Perhaps you don't know any such people personally, but you know they exist, and if you could track them down they would breathe life into your idea.

Think about your reader's relationship to your idea. Next, take the time to think about who your target reader is, and what the reader's relationship to your topic might look like. It helps here to think in terms of specific publications, and to apply some basic knowledge of demographics. If a daily newspaper caters to a more affluent readership, its readers will be less prone to obesity and more likely to hold fitness club memberships. Another paper, relying more heavily on newsstand sales, may prefer a starker contrast. Magazines for young men (or "lad mags") love stories that feature fit bodies, and also stark polar opposites. Women's magazines will be more keenly interested in issues such as parenting and social networking. Either type of magazine would be interested in a story about odd-couple siblings or about a lone brave soul in a fitness club's social snake pit—though the stories they'd run would be wildly different.

Think about your relationship to your reader. How will you address your story in a way that hits home for them? For instance, if your purpose is to teach them something about living with obesity in a fitness-obsessed world, that's fine—but you don't want to be preachy.

You can see how this little intellectual exercise produces results. On the one hand, your idea is actually getting bigger, not smaller, because it is being shaped into many possible stories, not just one. And yet, at the same time, each story idea is becoming clearer, more focused, and more concrete.

Types of Feature

As a general rule, features tend to conform to a few basic structures. The trick is to figure out which structure provides the best fit. Once your story idea begins to take shape, it's time to consider which of the following story types would suit it best.

The profile. This is the most dependable and hoary of all features: the story that takes an in-depth look at a person, whether through a narrative or a simple question-and-answer format. The key is to use the person you're profiling as a conduit for ideas—and not merely for the ideas they want to talk about, but the ones you want to talk about. It's essential that you ask why your subject is worthy of a profile, and the answer should reach beyond the obvious ones, such as "they're in the news a lot." It is also essential to have an opinion about your subject so that, during the interview, you present him or her with a challenge. Needless to say, some profile subjects don't like to be challenged and might refuse to meet you. That's no deterrent—it's just an excuse to write an unauthorized profile, or what's known in the magazine trade as a "write around." The most famous profile of one of America's most famous celebrities, Gay Talese's "Frank Sinatra Has a Cold," published in *Esquire* in 1966, is a write around—not based on a single interview with Sinatra himself.[3]

The how-it-works story. This type of feature examines the behind-the-scenes machinations of some hidden aspect of everyday life. As its name implies, it relies more heavily than any other on the question "how." A perfect example is Michael Pollan's article "This Steer's Life" in *The New York Times Magazine*: to find out exactly how supermarket beef is made, he bought an ox. Ownership gained him access to the American beef industry, and his story traced the life of his livestock from stable to table, with stops at the auction house, feedlot, and rendering plant along the way.[4]

The riddle. All feature stories can be boiled down to a single question, but few questions are as compelling as the riddle. In "The Ketchup Conundrum" (reprinted following this chapter), *The New Yorker*'s Malcolm Gladwell seeks to answer a simple, silly, yet compelling question: why is it that there are so many types and flavours of mustard on the grocery shelves, but only one ketchup? It's the kind of question that could just as easily appear as a non sequitur in a stand-up comedian's routine, designed to do nothing more than get a laugh—in their song "If I Had a Million Dollars," the Barenaked Ladies crack an idle joke about "Dijon ketchup." But as Gladwell proved, getting to the bottom of the riddle can run thousands of words in length and be as compelling as the question itself.

The dramatic reconstruction. Editors sometimes call this "the tick tock," a moniker that evokes a race against the clock. But what makes the dramatic reconstruction work is the way in which the writer can suspend the action of the main narrative to explore related themes and issues that only heighten the suspense. Kim Pittaway's 1996 page turner for *Chatelaine*, "Borderline Babies," followed the first hours of triplets born after only 23 weeks of pregnancy, spinning off into the science of neonatal care and the innermost fears of parents—a quintessential reconstruction.[5]

The "being there" story. Like a dramatic reconstruction, only less dramatic, more anthropological. You find yourself in a strange place, or amid a culture or subculture, and you have the opportunity to see how others live and how their hierarchy of values leads them to make decisions the rest of us would consider foolish. David Hayes's "Die Hard," published in *National Post Business Magazine* and reprinted on pages 115–133 of this book, follows the making of a commercial which starred, of all things, a fly—managed, of course, by a "bug wrangler."

The investigation. This is often considered the pinnacle of feature writing: a work of classic journalism feature that exposes a hidden truth, or a series of hidden truths. It is thrilling work, but you need nerves of steel, not to mention the conviction that truth is being hidden and the determination to uncover it. In Canada, Marci McDonald has compiled a remarkable body of investigative work for *The Walrus*. Her exposé of Paul Martin's business holdings, "Blind Trust,"[6] was timed perfectly for publication just at the moment when he took over as prime minister. His public image never recovered from it.

The trend story. Popular trends and fads often have ripple effects that reach far beyond anything its originators had intended. In the summer of 2002, I noticed a gradual but substantial transformation in my neighbourhood supermarket: a proliferation of meat snacks such as beef jerky and pepperoni—the only things in the butcher's corner that weren't kept in some sort of cooler. I wondered: Why the spike in inventories of shelf-stable meats? The answer hit me the next day, when I read yet another story about the Atkins diet, the high-protein, low-carbohydrate nutrition regimen that had become a huge fad. Under the Atkins diet, potato chips were verboten, but Slim Jims would presumably keep you slim. Within a month I turned around 2,000 words for *National Post* on how health fads have influenced snacking trends for the last 30 years.[7]

The service feature. There's a part of every journalist's ego that strives to be considered an artist for their writing, and that part of our ego disdains service features. On the other hand, the part of our ego that is concerned with paying the rent loves service features, because they are an easy way to turn a favourite hobby—from backpacking to ultimate Frisbee to art history to stamp collecting—into some sort of gear guide or amateur's guide. But the best service features present useful information in artful form, like Duncan Hood's award-winning service feature for *MoneySense* magazine on the perils of personal debt, told in the form of his own successful attempt to borrow a cool million dollars.[8]

The big idea. An opinion does not a feature make, but an opinion backed by in-depth research, lots of interviews, and a trove of new and engaging information makes a great feature. It can be as simple as Judith Shulevitz's elegant argument on enforcing a mandatory day of rest in "Bring Back the Sabbath," published in *The New York Times Magazine.*[9] Or it can be as complex and nuanced as Ivor Shapiro's look at juvenile detention centres in an effort to answer the question, can troubled kids be turned around? in "High Fences," published in *Toronto Life.*[10]

In the end, there's no getting around the fact that it takes considerable effort to develop story ideas. But it's not so much about slogging hard work as it is about building good mental and intellectual habits: teaching yourself how to recognize the germ of an idea and sort through the possibilities of how it might bloom. Though you'll always need to do a bit of follow-up research, good habits will leave you more invigorated than drained by the process. You'll also spend less time testing your ideas and Googling your hunches because you'll have a keen sense of what will work and what won't. After all, you don't want to spend too much time researching the story's details until after you've sold the idea. But that's where the art of the pitch comes in, which is what the next chapter is all about.

Discussion Questions

1. Read "The Ketchup Conundrum" by Malcolm Gladwell (pages 17–28). How do you think Gladwell may have come up with the idea behind his story? (Hint: He lives on Manhattan's Upper West Side.)
2. Try to estimate how much ketchup you have eaten in your life. How often do you eat it, and on how many foods? When was the last time you had some? Can you describe the flavour of ketchup in 150 words? If not, why not, given how ubiquitous it has probably been in your eating habits?
3. What are your impressions of Jim Wigon as a businessman? As a personality? How does Gladwell use Wigon as a character in his story? Is Wigon the most compelling character in the story?
4. On the surface, the central conflict in the piece is World's Best versus Heinz. But other conflicts are much more crucial to the piece—and they are conflicts of ideas, not of people or organizations. What are they? Can you find a nature-versus-nurture debate lurking within the story?

Notes

1. Joan Acocella, "Blocked," *The New Yorker*, June 14, 2004.
2. James Carey, "Why and How?: The Dark Continent of American Journalism," in *Reading the News*, ed. Robert Karl Manoff and Michael Schudson (New York: Pantheon Books, 1987), p. 149.
3. Gay Talese, "Frank Sinatra Has a Cold," *Esquire*, April 1966.
4. Michael Pollan, "This Steer's Life," *New York Times Magazine*, March 31, 2002, 44.
5. Kim Pittaway, "Borderline Babies," *Chatelaine*, April 1996.
6. Marci McDonald, "Blind Trust," *Walrus*, October 2003.
7. Philip Preville, "Jerkish Delight: Fad Diets, Lazy Teens Lead Nation into Meat-Snack Madness," *National Post*, August 24, 2002, SP1.
8. Duncan Hood, "How to Borrow a Million Bucks," *MoneySense*, September/October 2004.
9. Judith Shulevitz, "Bring Back the Sabbath," *New York Times Magazine*, March 2, 2003.
10. Ivor Shapiro, "High Fences," *Toronto Life*, January 1999.

"The Ketchup Conundrum"

Mustard now comes in dozens of varieties. Why has ketchup stayed the same?

Malcolm Gladwell, "The Ketchup Conundrum." *The New Yorker*. New York: September 6, 2004. Volume 80, issue 25, 129. Reprinted by permission of the author.

Many years ago, one mustard dominated the supermarket shelves: French's. It came in a plastic bottle. People used it on hot dogs and bologna. It was a yellow mustard, made from ground white mustard seed with turmeric and vinegar, which gave it a mild, slightly metallic taste. If you looked hard in the grocery store, you might find something in the specialty-foods section called Grey Poupon, which was Dijon mustard, made from the more pungent brown mustard seed. In the early seventies, Grey Poupon was no more than a hundred-thousand-dollar-a-year business. Few people knew what it was or how it tasted, or had any particular desire for an alternative to French's or the runner-up, Gulden's. Then one day the Heublein Company, which owned Grey Poupon, discovered something remarkable: if you gave people a mustard taste test, a significant number had only to try Grey Poupon once to switch from yellow mustard. In the food world that almost never happens; even among the most successful food brands, only about one in a hundred have that kind of conversion rate. Grey Poupon was magic.

So Heublein put Grey Poupon in a bigger glass jar, with an enamelled label and enough of a whiff of Frenchness to make it seem as if it were still being made in Europe (it was made in Hartford, Connecticut, from Canadian mustard seed and white wine). The company ran tasteful print ads in upscale food magazines. They put the mustard in little foil packets and distributed them with airplane meals—which was a brand-new idea at the time. Then they hired the Manhattan ad agency Lowe Marschalk to do something, on a modest budget, for television. The agency came back with an idea: A Rolls-Royce is driving down a country road. There's a man in the back seat in a suit with a plate of beef on a silver tray. He nods to the chauffeur, who opens the glove compartment. Then comes what is known in the business as the "reveal." The chauffeur hands back a jar of Grey Poupon. Another Rolls-Royce pulls up alongside. A man leans his head out the window. "Pardon me. Would you have any Grey Poupon?"

In the cities where the ads ran, sales of Grey Poupon leaped forty to fifty per cent, and whenever Heublein bought airtime in new cities sales jumped by forty to fifty per cent again. Grocery stores put Grey Poupon next to French's and Gulden's. By the end of the nineteen-eighties Grey Poupon was the most powerful brand in mustard. "The tagline in the commercial was that this was one of life's finer pleasures," Larry Elegant, who wrote the original Grey Poupon spot, says, "and that, along with the Rolls-Royce, seemed to impart to people's minds that this was something truly different and superior."

The rise of Grey Poupon proved that the American supermarket shopper was willing to pay more—in this case, $3.99 instead of $1.49 for eight ounces— as long as what they were buying carried with it an air of sophistication and complex aromatics. Its success showed, furthermore, that the boundaries of taste and custom were not fixed: that just because mustard had always been yellow didn't mean that consumers would use only yellow mustard. It is because of Grey Poupon that the standard American supermarket today has an entire mustard section. And it is because of Grey Poupon that a man named Jim Wigon decided, four years ago, to enter the ketchup business. Isn't the ketchup business today exactly where mustard was thirty years ago? There is Heinz and, far behind, Hunt's and Del Monte and a handful of private-label brands. Jim Wigon wanted to create the Grey Poupon of ketchup.

Wigon is from Boston. He's a thickset man in his early fifties, with a full salt-and-pepper beard. He runs his ketchup business—under the brand World's Best Ketchup—out of the catering business of his partner, Nick Schiarizzi, in Norwood, Massachusetts, just off Route 1, in a low-slung building behind an industrial-equipment-rental shop. He starts with red peppers, Spanish onions, garlic, and a high-end tomato paste. Basil is chopped by hand, because the buffalo chopper bruises the leaves. He uses maple syrup, not corn syrup, which gives him a quarter of the sugar of Heinz. He pours his ketchup into a clear glass ten-ounce jar, and sells it for three times the price of Heinz, and for the past few years he has criss-crossed the country, peddling World's Best in six flavors— regular, sweet, dill, garlic, caramelized onion, and basil—to specialty grocery stores and supermarkets. If you were in Zabar's on Manhattan's Upper West Side a few months ago, you would have seen him at the front of the store, in a spot between the sushi and the gefilte fish. He was wearing a World's Best baseball cap, a white shirt, and a red-stained apron. In front of him, on a small table, was a silver tureen filled with miniature chicken and beef meatballs, a box of toothpicks, and a dozen or so open jars of his ketchup. "Try my ketchup!" Wigon said, over and over, to anyone who passed. "If you don't try it, you're doomed to eat Heinz the rest of your life."

In the same aisle at Zabar's that day two other demonstrations were going on, so that people were starting at one end with free chicken sausage, sampling a slice of prosciutto, and then pausing at the World's Best stand before heading for the cash register. They would look down at the array of open jars, and Wigon would impale a meatball on a toothpick, dip it in one of his ketchups, and hand it to them with a flourish. The ratio of tomato solids to liquid in World's Best is much higher than in Heinz, and the maple syrup gives it an unmistakable sweet kick. Invariably, people would close their eyes, just for a moment, and do a subtle double take. Some of them would look slightly perplexed and walk away, and others would nod and pick up a jar. "You know why you like it so much?" he would say, in his broad Boston accent, to the customers who seemed most impressed. "Because you've been eating bad ketchup all your life!" Jim Wigon had a simple vision: build a better ketchup—the way Grey Poupon built a better mustard—and the world will beat a path to your door. If only it were that easy.

The story of World's Best Ketchup cannot properly be told without a man from White Plains, New York, named Howard Moskowitz. Moskowitz is sixty, short and round, with graying hair and huge gold-rimmed glasses. When he talks, he favors the Socratic monologue—a series of questions that he poses to himself, then answers, punctuated by "ahhh" and much vigorous nodding. He is a lineal descendant of the legendary eighteenth-century Hasidic rabbi known as the Seer of Lublin. He keeps a parrot. At Harvard, he wrote his doctoral dissertation on psychophysics, and all the rooms on the ground floor of his food-testing and market-research business are named after famous psychophysicists. ("Have you ever heard of the name Rose Marie Pangborn? Ahhh. She was a professor at Davis. Very famous. This is the Pangborn kitchen.") Moskowitz is a man of uncommon exuberance and persuasiveness: if he had been your freshman statistics professor, you would today be a statistician. "My favorite writer? Gibbon," he burst out, when we met not long ago. He had just been holding forth on the subject of sodium solutions. "Right now I'm working my way through the Hales history of the Byzantine Empire. Holy shit! Everything is easy until you get to the Byzantine Empire. It's impossible. One emperor is always killing the others, and everyone has five wives or three husbands. It's very Byzantine."

Moskowitz set up shop in the seventies, and one of his first clients was Pepsi. The artificial sweetener aspartame had just become available, and Pepsi wanted Moskowitz to figure out the perfect amount of sweetener for a can of Diet Pepsi. Pepsi knew that anything below eight per cent sweetness was not sweet enough and anything over twelve per cent was too sweet. So Moskowitz did the logical thing. He made up experimental batches of Diet Pepsi with every conceivable degree of sweetness—8 per cent, 8.25 per cent, 8.5, and on and on up to 12—gave them to hundreds of people, and looked for the concentration that people liked the most. But the data were a mess—there wasn't a pattern—and one day, sitting in a diner, Moskowitz realized why. They had been asking the wrong question. There was no such thing as the perfect Diet Pepsi. They should have been looking for the perfect Diet Pepsis.

It took a long time for the food world to catch up with Howard Moskowitz. He knocked on doors and tried to explain his idea about the plural nature of perfection, and no one answered. He spoke at food-industry conferences, and audiences shrugged. But he could think of nothing else. "It's like that Yiddish expression," he says. "Do you know it? To a worm in horseradish, the world is horseradish!" Then, in 1986, he got a call from the Campbell's Soup Company. They were in the spaghetti-sauce business, going up against Ragú with their Prego brand. Prego was a little thicker than Ragú, with diced tomatoes as opposed to Ragú's puree, and, Campbell's thought, had better pasta adherence. But, for all that, Prego was in a slump, and Campbell's was desperate for new ideas.

Standard practice in the food industry would have been to convene a focus group and ask spaghetti eaters what they wanted. But Moskowitz does not believe that consumers—even spaghetti lovers—know what they desire if what they desire does not yet exist. "The mind," as Moskowitz is fond of saying, "knows not what the tongue wants." Instead, working with the Campbell's kitchens, he came up with forty-five varieties of spaghetti sauce. These were designed to differ in every conceivable way: spiciness, sweetness, tartness, saltiness, thickness, aroma, mouth feel, cost of ingredients, and so forth. He had a trained panel of food tasters analyze each of those varieties in depth. Then he took the prototypes on the road—to New York, Chicago, Los Angeles, and Jacksonville—and asked people in groups of twenty-five to eat between eight and ten small bowls of different spaghetti sauces over two hours and rate them on a scale of one to a hundred. When Moskowitz charted the results, he saw that everyone had a slightly different definition of what a perfect spaghetti sauce tasted like. If you sifted carefully through the data, though, you could find patterns, and Moskowitz learned that most people's preferences fell into one of three broad groups: plain, spicy, and extra-chunky, and of those three the last was the most important. Why? Because at the time there was no extra-chunky spaghetti sauce in the supermarket. Over the next decade, that new category proved to be worth hundreds of millions of dollars to Prego. "We all said, 'Wow!'" Monica Wood, who was then the head of market research for Campbell's, recalls. "Here there was this third segment—people who liked their spaghetti sauce with lots of stuff in it—and it was completely untapped. So in about 1989–90 we launched Prego extra-chunky. It was extraordinarily successful."

It may be hard today, fifteen years later—when every brand seems to come in multiple varieties—to appreciate how much of a breakthrough this was. In

those years, people in the food industry carried around in their heads the notion of a platonic dish—the version of a dish that looked and tasted absolutely
right. At Ragú and Prego, they had been striving for the platonic spaghetti
sauce, and the platonic spaghetti sauce was thin and blended because that's the
way they thought it was done in Italy. Cooking, on the industrial level, was consumed with the search for human universals. Once you start looking for the sources
of human variability, though, the old orthodoxy goes out the window. Howard
Moskowitz stood up to the Platonists and said there are no universals.

Moskowitz still has a version of the computer model he used for Prego fifteen years ago. It has all the coded results from the consumer taste tests and the
expert tastings, split into the three categories (plain, spicy, and extra-chunky)
and linked up with the actual ingredients list on a spreadsheet. "You know how
they have a computer model for building an aircraft," Moskowitz said as he
pulled up the program on his computer. "This is a model for building spaghetti
sauce. Look, every variable is here." He pointed at column after column of ratings. "So here are the ingredients. I'm a brand manager for Prego. I want to
optimize one of the segments. Let's start with Segment 1." In Moskowitz's
program, the three spaghetti-sauce groups were labelled Segment 1, Segment 2,
and Segment 3. He typed in a few commands, instructing the computer to
give him the formulation that would score the highest with those people in
Segment 1. The answer appeared almost immediately: a specific recipe that,
according to Moskowitz's data, produced a score of 78 from the people in Segment 1. But that same formulation didn't do nearly as well with those in
Segment 2 and Segment 3. They scored it 67 and 57, respectively. Moskowitz
started again, this time asking the computer to optimize for Segment 2. This
time the ratings came in at 82, but now Segment 1 had fallen ten points, to 68.
"See what happens?" he said. "If I make one group happier, I piss off another
group. We did this for coffee with General Foods, and we found that if you
create only one product the best you can get across all the segments is a 60—if
you're lucky. That's if you were to treat everybody as one big happy family. But
if I do the sensory segmentation, I can get 70, 71, 72. Is that big? Ahhh. It's a
very big difference. In coffee, a 71 is something you'll die for."

When Jim Wigon set up shop that day in Zabar's, then, his operating assumption was that there ought to be some segment of the population that preferred a
ketchup made with Stanislaus tomato paste and hand-chopped basil and maple
syrup. That's the Moskowitz theory. But there is theory and there is practice. By
the end of that long day, Wigon had sold ninety jars. But he'd also got two parking
tickets and had to pay for a hotel room, so he wasn't going home with money in

his pocket. For the year, Wigon estimates, he'll sell fifty thousand jars—which, in the universe of condiments, is no more than a blip. "I haven't drawn a paycheck in five years," Wigon said as he impaled another meatball on a toothpick. "My wife is killing me." And it isn't just World's Best that is struggling. In the gourmet-ketchup world, there is River Run and Uncle Dave's, from Vermont, and Muir Glen Organic and Mrs. Tomato Head Roasted Garlic Peppercorn Catsup, in California, and dozens of others—and every year Heinz's overwhelming share of the ketchup market just grows.

It is possible, of course, that ketchup is waiting for its own version of that Rolls-Royce commercial, or the discovery of the ketchup equivalent of extra-chunky—the magic formula that will satisfy an unmet need. It is also possible, however, that the rules of Howard Moskowitz, which apply to Grey Poupon and Prego spaghetti sauce and to olive oil and salad dressing and virtually everything else in the supermarket, don't apply to ketchup.

Tomato ketchup is a nineteenth-century creation—the union of the English tradition of fruit and vegetable sauces and the growing American infatuation with the tomato. But what we know today as ketchup emerged out of a debate that raged in the first years of the last century over benzoate, a preservative widely used in late-nineteenth-century condiments. Harvey Washington Wiley, the chief of the Bureau of Chemistry in the Department of Agriculture from 1883 to 1912, came to believe that benzoates were not safe, and the result was an argument that split the ketchup world in half. On one side was the ketchup establishment, which believed that it was impossible to make ketchup without benzoate and that benzoate was not harmful in the amounts used. On the other side was a renegade band of ketchup manufacturers, who believed that the preservative puzzle could be solved with the application of culinary science. The dominant nineteenth-century ketchups were thin and watery, in part because they were made from unripe tomatoes, which are low in the complex carbohydrates known as pectin, which add body to a sauce. But what if you made ketchup from ripe tomatoes, giving it the density it needed to resist degradation? Nineteenth-century ketchups had a strong tomato taste, with just a light vinegar touch. The renegades argued that by greatly increasing the amount of vinegar, in effect protecting the tomatoes by pickling them, they were making a superior ketchup: safer, purer, and better tasting. They offered a money-back guarantee in the event of spoilage. They charged more for their product, convinced that the public would pay more for a better ketchup, and they were right. The benzoate ketchups disappeared.

The leader of the renegade band was an entrepreneur out of Pittsburgh named Henry J. Heinz.

The world's leading expert on ketchup's early years is Andrew F. Smith, a substantial man, well over six feet, with a graying mustache and short wavy black hair. Smith is a scholar, trained as a political scientist, intent on bringing rigor to the world of food. When we met for lunch not long ago at the restaurant Savoy in SoHo (chosen because of the excellence of its hamburger and French fries, and because Savoy makes its own ketchup—a dark, peppery, and viscous variety served in a white porcelain saucer), Smith was in the throes of examining the origins of the croissant for the upcoming "Oxford Encyclopedia of Food and Drink in America," of which he is the editor-in-chief. Was the croissant invented in 1683, by the Viennese, in celebration of their defeat of the invading Turks? Or in 1686, by the residents of Budapest, to celebrate *their* defeat of the Turks? Both explanations would explain its distinctive crescent shape—since it would make a certain cultural sense (particularly for the Viennese) to consecrate their battlefield triumphs in the form of pastry. But the only reference Smith could find to either story was in the Larousse Gastronomique of 1938. "It just doesn't check out," he said, shaking his head wearily.

Smith's specialty is the tomato, however, and over the course of many scholarly articles and books—"The History of Home-Made Anglo-American Tomato Ketchup," for *Petits Propos Culinaires*, for example, and "The Great Tomato Pill War of the 1830's," for *The Connecticut Historical Society Bulletin*—Smith has argued that some critical portion of the history of culinary civilization could be told through this fruit. Cortez brought tomatoes to Europe from the New World, and they inexorably insinuated themselves into the world's cuisines. The Italians substituted the tomato for eggplant. In northern India, it went into curries and chutneys. "The biggest tomato producer in the world today?" Smith paused, for dramatic effect. "China. You don't think of tomato being a part of Chinese cuisine, and it wasn't ten years ago. But it is now." Smith dipped one of my French fries into the homemade sauce. "It has that raw taste," he said, with a look of intense concentration. "It's fresh ketchup. You can taste the tomato." Ketchup was, to his mind, the most nearly perfect of all the tomato's manifestations. It was inexpensive, which meant that it had a firm lock on the mass market, and it was a condiment, not an ingredient, which meant that it could be applied at the discretion of the food eater, not the food preparer. "There's a quote from Elizabeth Rozin I've always loved," he said. Rozin is the food theorist who wrote the essay "Ketchup and the Collective Unconscious," and Smith used her conclusion as the epigraph of his ketchup book:

ketchup may well be "the only true culinary expression of the melting pot, and ... its special and unprecedented ability to provide something for everyone makes it the Esperanto of cuisine." Here is where Henry Heinz and the benzoate battle were so important: in defeating the condiment Old Guard, he was the one who changed the flavor of ketchup in a way that made it universal.

There are five known fundamental tastes in the human palate: salty, sweet, sour, bitter, and umami. Umami is the proteiny, full-bodied taste of chicken soup, or cured meat, or fish stock, or aged cheese, or mother's milk, or soy sauce, or mushrooms, or seaweed, or cooked tomato. "Umami adds body," Gary Beauchamp, who heads the Monell Chemical Senses Center, in Philadelphia, says. "If you add it to a soup, it makes the soup seem like it's thicker—it gives it sensory heft. It turns a soup from salt water into a food." When Heinz moved to ripe tomatoes and increased the percentage of tomato solids, he made ketchup, first and foremost, a potent source of umami. Then he dramatically increased the concentration of vinegar, so that his ketchup had twice the acidity of most other ketchups; now ketchup was sour, another of the fundamental tastes. The post-benzoate ketchups also doubled the concentration of sugar—so now ketchup was also sweet—and all along ketchup had been salty and bitter. These are not trivial issues. Give a baby soup, and then soup with MSG (an amino-acid salt that is pure umami), and the baby will go back for the MSG soup every time, the same way a baby will always prefer water with sugar to water alone. Salt and sugar and umami are primal signals about the food we are eating—about how dense it is in calories, for example, or, in the case of umami, about the presence of proteins and amino acids. What Heinz had done was come up with a condiment that pushed all five of these primal buttons. The taste of Heinz's ketchup began at the tip of the tongue, where our receptors for sweet and salty first appear, moved along the sides, where sour notes seem the strongest, then hit the back of the tongue, for umami and bitter, in one long crescendo. How many things in the supermarket run the sensory spectrum like this?

A number of years ago, the H. J. Heinz Company did an extensive market-research project in which researchers went into people's homes and watched the way they used ketchup. "I remember sitting in one of those households," Casey Keller, who was until recently the chief growth officer for Heinz, says. "There was a three-year-old and a six-year-old, and what happened was that the kids asked for ketchup and Mom brought it out. It was a forty-ounce bottle. And the three-year-old went to grab it himself, and Mom intercepted the bottle and said, 'No, you're not going to do that.' She physically took the bottle away and doled out a little dollop. You could see that the whole thing was a bummer." For Heinz, Keller says, that moment was an epiphany. A typical five-year-old consumes about sixty per cent more ketchup than a typical forty-year-old, and the company realized that it needed to put ketchup in a bottle that a toddler could control. "If you are four—and I have a four-year-old—he doesn't get to choose what he eats for dinner, in most cases," Keller says. "But the one thing he can control is ketchup. It's the one part of the food experience that he can customize and personalize." As a result, Heinz came out with the so-called EZ Squirt bottle, made out of soft plastic with a conical nozzle. In homes where the EZ Squirt is used, ketchup consumption has grown by as much as twelve per cent.

There is another lesson in that household scene, though. Small children tend to be neophobic: once they hit two or three, they shrink from new tastes. That makes sense, evolutionarily, because through much of human history that is the age at which children would have first begun to gather and forage for themselves, and those who strayed from what was known and trusted would never have survived. There the three-year-old was, confronted with something strange on his plate—tuna fish, perhaps, or Brussels sprouts—and he wanted to alter his food in some way that made the unfamiliar familiar. He wanted to subdue the contents of his plate. And so he turned to ketchup, because, alone among the condiments on the table, ketchup could deliver sweet and sour and salty and bitter and umami, all at once.

Last February, Edgar Chambers IV, who runs the sensory-analysis center at Kansas State University, conducted a joint assessment of World's Best and Heinz. He has seventeen trained tasters on his staff, and they work for academia and industry, answering the often difficult question of what a given substance tastes like. It is demanding work. Immediately after conducting the ketchup study, Chambers dispatched a team to Bangkok to do an analysis of fruit—bananas, mangoes, rose apples, and sweet tamarind. Others were detailed to soy and kimchi in South Korea, and Chambers's wife led a delegation to Italy to analyze ice cream.

The ketchup tasting took place over four hours, on two consecutive mornings. Six tasters sat around a large, round table with a lazy Susan in the middle. In front of each panelist were two one-ounce cups, one filled with Heinz ketchup and one filled with World's Best. They would work along fourteen dimensions of flavor and texture, in accordance with the standard fifteen-point scale used by the food world. The flavor components would be divided two ways: elements picked up by the tongue and elements picked up by the nose. A very ripe peach, for example, tastes sweet but it also smells sweet—which is a very different aspect of sweetness. Vinegar has a sour taste but also a pungency, a vapor that rises up the back of the nose and fills the mouth when you breathe out. To aid in the rating process, the tasters surrounded themselves with little bowls of sweet and sour and salty solutions, and portions of Contadina tomato paste, Hunt's tomato sauce, and Campbell's tomato juice, all of which represent different concentrations of tomato-ness.

After breaking the ketchup down into its component parts, the testers assessed the critical dimension of "amplitude," the word sensory experts use to describe flavors that are well blended and balanced, that "bloom" in the mouth. "The difference between high and low amplitude is the difference between my son and a great pianist playing 'Ode to Joy' on the piano," Chambers says. "They are playing the same notes, but they blend better with the great pianist." Pepperidge Farm shortbread cookies are considered to have high amplitude. So are Hellman's mayonnaise and Sara Lee poundcake. When something is high in amplitude, all its constituent elements converge into a single gestalt. You can't isolate the elements of an iconic, high-amplitude flavor like Coca-Cola or Pepsi. But you can with one of those private-label colas that you get in the supermarket. "The thing about Coke and Pepsi is that they are absolutely gorgeous," Judy Heylmun, a vice-president of Sensory Spectrum, Inc., in Chatham, New Jersey, says. "They have beautiful notes—all flavors are in balance. It's very hard to do that well. Usually, when you taste a store cola it's"—and here she made a series of *pik! pik! pik!* sounds—"all the notes are kind of spiky, and usually the citrus is the first thing to spike out. And then the cinnamon. Citrus and brown spice notes are top notes and very volatile, as opposed to vanilla, which is very dark and deep. A really cheap store brand will have a big, fat cinnamon note sitting on top of everything."

Some of the cheaper ketchups are the same way. Ketchup aficionados say that there's a disquieting unevenness to the tomato notes in Del Monte ketchup: Tomatoes vary, in acidity and sweetness and the ratio of solids to liquid, according to the seed variety used, the time of year they are harvested, the soil in which they are grown, and the weather during the growing season. Unless all those variables are tightly controlled, one batch of ketchup can end up too watery and another can be too strong. Or try one of the numerous private-label brands that make up the bottom of the ketchup market and pay attention to the spice mix; you may well find yourself conscious of the clove note or overwhelmed by a hit of garlic. Generic colas and ketchups have what Moskowitz calls a hook—a sensory attribute that you can single out, and ultimately tire of.

The tasting began with a plastic spoon. Upon consideration, it was decided that the analysis would be helped if the ketchups were tasted on French fries, so a batch of fries were cooked up, and distributed around the table. Each tester, according to protocol, took the fries one by one, dipped them into the cup—all the way, right to the bottom—bit off the portion covered in ketchup, and then contemplated the evidence of their senses. For Heinz, the critical flavor components—vinegar, salt, tomato I.D. (over-all tomato-ness), sweet, and bitter—were judged to be present in roughly equal concentrations, and those elements, in turn, were judged to be well blended. The World's Best, though, "had a completely different view, a different profile, from the Heinz," Chambers said. It had a much stronger hit of sweet aromatics—4.0 to 2.5—and outstripped Heinz on tomato I.D. by a resounding 9 to 5.5. But there was less salt, and no discernible vinegar. "The other comment from the panel was that these elements were really not blended at all," Chambers went on. "The World's Best product had really low amplitude." According to Joyce Buchholz, one of the panelists, when the group judged aftertaste, "it seemed like a certain flavor would hang over longer in the case of World's Best—that cooked-tomatoey flavor."

But what was Jim Wigon to do? To compete against Heinz, he had to try something dramatic, like substituting maple syrup for corn syrup, ramping up the tomato solids. That made for an unusual and daring flavor. World's Best Dill ketchup on fried catfish, for instance, is a marvellous thing. But it also meant that his ketchup wasn't as sensorily complete as Heinz, and he was paying a heavy price in amplitude. "Our conclusion was mainly this," Buchholz said. "We felt that World's Best seemed to be more like a sauce." She was trying to be helpful.

There is an exception, then, to the Moskowitz rule. Today there are thirty-six varieties of Ragú spaghetti sauce, under six rubrics—Old World Style, Chunky Garden Style, Robusto, Light, Cheese Creations, and Rich & Meaty—which means that there is very nearly an optimal spaghetti sauce for every man, woman, and child in America. Measured against the monotony that confronted Howard Moskowitz twenty years ago, this is progress. Happiness, in one sense, is a function of how closely our world conforms to the infinite variety of human preference. But that makes it easy to forget that sometimes happiness can be found in having what we've always had and everyone else is having. "Back in the seventies, someone else—I think it was Ragú—tried to do an 'Italian'-style ketchup," Moskowitz said. "They failed miserably." It was a conundrum: what was true about a yellow condiment that went on hot dogs was not true about a tomato condiment that went on hamburgers, and what was true about to-mato sauce when you added visible solids and put it in a jar was somehow not true about tomato sauce when you added vinegar and sugar and put it in a bottle. Moskowitz shrugged. "I guess ketchup is ketchup."

CHAPTER TWO

Perfect Pitch, or How I Learned to Love Rejection

Matthew Hays

The following is, really and truly, an actual story pitch I received years ago while working as associate editor of the weekly *Montreal Mirror*.

Dear Sir, Madam,

Did some of your reporters just announce quitting you?

Did the summer vacation period make you made about finding enough people doing the right job? Don't worry, the helping hand is just around the corner. The only thing you should do is keeping this on a safe place and call me whenever you need me.

My name is ―― and I have 11 years of experience as a journalist in printed media and news agencies.

It's easy, don't look for other resumes, don't waist your time and money for job classifieds. Call me and you'll see that I'm the right person with the right services for you.

I appreciate your business and your time.

Best regards.

This is not a joke: that letter is exactly what came in. The reason you're reading it now, at the start of a chapter about how to create a perfect pitch (and yes, it's arguably a bit pompous to suggest there is even such a thing), is that it's a near-perfect example of what *not* to do. I'm sure you already know some reasons why I say that, and I hope that by chapter's end you will know the rest.

In my years of teaching experience in universities and community workshops and seminars, I've discovered that crafting the pitch often presents a tremendous roadblock for new writers. Daunting thoughts haunt them: *How do I put this idea together so it doesn't sound stupid? Editors get thousands of these—how do I make mine stand out? How do I close the deal and make that sale?* In this chapter I'll go over some basic steps, and then serve up some actual, successful pitches, winners that got several writers into the pages of the places they were aiming for.

Step 1: Get Over Yourself

One of the first things I tell any aspiring journalist is a lesson I still haven't quite learned myself. (Perhaps I keep repeating it in the hopes that it might actually sink in for me too.) When you're pitching, you must get used to the sensation of a door slamming gently (or not so gently) in your face. There are plenty of ideas floating around; there are loads of writers pitching them. Not every editor is going to see the sheer brilliance in your concepts the way your mother might. This is the way the business works, and you can't afford to take it personally. As an experienced freelancer once told me, for every ten pitches she sends out, approximately one will get the green light. The others, sadly, don't make it. You may think you've got the best idea for a story, ever. But if you can't find an editor who'll agree with you, there's a distinct possibility that no one will ever find that out.

Reasons for rejection may often seem mysterious to the writer, but it's extremely important that you sit down and ponder the role, responsibility, and workload of the average editor. In a funny and enlightening piece that was posted on Salon.com in July 2007, Gary Kamiya discussed the unique pressures involved in being a newspaper, magazine, or journal editor. In the piece, titled "Let Us Now Praise Editors," Kamiya went about exploring the role of the editor as gatekeeper and ego-tender, pointing out that "to people not in the business, editing is a mysterious thing." Editors, the author suggests, wear multiple hats, including those of "craftsmen, ghosts, psychiatrists, bullies, sparring partners, experts, enablers, ignoramuses, translators, writers, goalies, friends, foremen, wimps, ditch diggers, mind readers, coaches, bomb throwers, muses and spittoons—sometimes all while working on the same piece."[1] Kamiya makes some hugely important points in his piece, all of which you should keep in mind when you're approaching editors with your ideas. Editors are largely overworked, in situations where they are often handed additional tasks and chores for the same salary they were earning last year. Sometimes they're grouchy, but given the pressures they face this is fairly understandable, and it's best not to irritate them (unless you really don't want to be invited back). This sounds like an obvious pointer, but as one who was an editor myself for over a decade, I can tell you the skills of managing basic human interactions often seemed sorely missing where freelancers were concerned.

So, remind yourself that editors are human too and it's your pitch they have to accept or reject—not you as a person. Now you're ready for the next step.

Step 2: Do Some Advance Research

This being a highly competitive business, editors want to know they're getting something new. Make sure you've read your target publication and that they haven't covered this story (search their website or an online database). Then check their competitors: don't pitch a story that's "owned" by another venue in the same market. If they've covered it, you clearly need a new angle on the story, or fresh information. You don't want to end up pitching some kind of "exclusive" that, well, isn't.

It's extremely important that you assess the tone of the site, newspaper, or magazine you're pitching to. When I'm writing for an alternative weekly like the *Montreal Mirror*, for example, the rhythm, tone, and voice I adopt is quite different from, say, *The New York Times* or *The Globe and Mail*. They are different venues, and require different sensibilities. There's nothing worse than getting a pitch from someone who clearly has little or no knowledge of the outlet in question. Have a solid understanding of the venue's style, and know how you're going to reach their standards.

Many publications have writers' guidelines, often posted on their websites. Be sure to examine them carefully; some want detailed proposals, others like their pitches as short as a paragraph or two. Find out to whom it should be addressed, and "cc" it where necessary. Obviously, sending a pitch to the wrong person will be a waste of everyone's time.

Remember: an editor who feels that you're wasting his or her time will be that much less prone to open up an email from you in future. Alastair Sutherland is the editor-in-chief of the aforementioned *Mirror*, a journalist and university instructor with decades of experience as both an editor and writer. His advice: "The first thing I look for in a pitch is, how fresh is it? If we've already done the story, or done something similar, then most likely the pitch is no good for us. Plus it shows the writer doesn't know the paper too well. Alternately, if a writer says, 'I know you guys already covered this topic, but I've got a new angle on it,' I will be more interested."

Doing some preliminary interviewing is a good plan as well. When you write your pitch, you'll be able to indicate that you've already done some legwork. It shows that you've been thinking about this idea—it wasn't just a daydream you had on the way home from the ice cream shop.

And don't be afraid to go for the gold by trying for a big-name venue. If you've got a great story, how can it hurt? Most newspapers, magazines, and websites now rely on reporters in the field with their ears to the ground. On the other hand, don't be discouraged if you don't get into *The New York Times* the first time around. Have another place in mind to pitch right away. Persistence and perseverance are paramount in this business.

Step 3: Craft the Pitch

Here's some more sage advice from Sutherland:

> A good pitch should be well organized and to the point. If it's too vague, it will lose me. If there are too many mundane details, that will lose me too. Be snappy but not too glib. Ideally, the style the pitch is written in should be indicative of the style of the story to come.

Glad You Asked!   Before You Hit "Send"

Q: Is my pitch ready for an editor's eyes?
A: Before you send your pitch (also called a query), answer the following questions:

1. Will the query get the editor's attention straight away (for example, with a great lead that could come right out of the story itself)?
2. Does it clearly spell out the proposed story and your angle?
3. Does it contain enough content (for example, facts, an anecdote, a great quote) to entice the editor?
4. Have you included details that indicate you know the target publication and where your story might fit into it (for example, a specific section of the magazine)?

Let's unpack that a bit. First, since the editor's time is of the essence, succinctness is an iron rule. Pitches should be tight and to the point, without tangents or digression. Sutherland says: "A good pitch should take a few minutes to read, and by the end I should be able to already see most of the story." In other words, your pitch should be as focused and thoughtfully composed as the end-result article will be. Grab the editor's attention, be sharp and snappy in expanding on your theme, and then close it off briskly. This is no time for a Russian novel.

It's crucial that you show the weight of your research. Your letter must demonstrate what you know about the subject. Backing up your points with telling details, quotes, or a link or two will prove you've done your homework. When appropriate, include background material on trends, statistics, or items in the news that show how your idea is current or of interest to the readers of the targeted publication (but don't try to tell the editor what their readers should be interested in just because you say so).

And you should also let the editor know a thing or two about yourself that might help your case—your field of study or work, any connection you might have to the story (do you live around the corner from where the key events took place?), and links to any solid articles you have under your belt. But please, says Sutherland, no links to poetry or short stories, "unless a poem or short story is being pitched."

There'll be more tips for crafting the pitch when we look at some successful examples below.

5. Is it written in a style and tone that both suits the target outlet and reflects the way you would write the piece?
6. Does your query express how your story connects to the lives and interests of the publication's audience?
7. Does it provide a reason, whether explicit or implicit, why *you* should write this piece?
8. Is the spelling perfect? Are you sure?
9. Is the grammar perfect? Are you sure?
10. Is it directed to the right person and have you spelled his or her name correctly?

Matthew Hays

Step 4: Check Before You Send

If you were an editor and got a sloppy, grammatically inept pitch rife with mistakes and missteps, would you green-light it? (That was a rhetorical question.) What follows is a quick checklist to go over before you send off your pitch.

1. Reread your pitch. Is it entirely clear? Are there redundant sentences? If your pitch isn't well written or presented properly, then the editor reading it will almost undoubtedly assume the worst about your ability to pull off a solid story. Make sure it looks good and reads smooth.
2. Spell-check. I can't count the number of pitches I received that had careless spelling errors in them. At times, pitches crossed my desk that had my own name spelled wrong. I'm not all that sensitive about my name, but if a writer can't be bothered to do even that much checking, I get worried. It's easy to spell things wrong in an email—sometimes, you'll look back moments after hitting Send and think, *How did I miss that?* So don't miss it: check it.
3. Check your research. Review your facts and figures and make sure nothing careless has slipped by you. Is everything accurate? Is it up-to-date? If the research is flawed, then so is the pitch as a whole.
4. Proofread and spell-check, again. Did I mention that already? Yes, I did. Spelling or grammatical errors are the single best way *not* to get your foot in that door.

Step 5: Follow Up

It is a distinct possibility that your efforts will be met with a stony silence. In most cases, in fact, editors are so overwhelmed by pitches—some crappy; others, like yours, brilliant—that a follow-up contact will probably be in order. Don't nag, but it's okay to email back after a few days, asking politely if the editor received your pitch. If you still don't hear back, you can assume they aren't interested and try somewhere else. (If your story is time-sensitive, then you have licence to be a bit more pushy with it.)

Try to avoid using the phone; it is my experience that the best way to reach an editor is by email. When I was working a desk job, a phone call was often an unwelcome interruption—the person on the other end of the line was inadvertently getting in the way of the task I was busy on. An email, on the other hand, would be read when I had a down moment at the end of the day or off another deadline. That meant I was a bit more relaxed when I was looking at the pitch, and could ponder it while not under such pressure.

As an editor, I was very careful to reply to pitches, even if I thought they were dreadful, simply to politely say that we weren't interested in the idea. But many editors are now far, far too busy to offer such niceties. The drag is that many times you will simply have to gauge the level of interest from the overwhelming absence of response. In my non-scientific processing of anecdotal evidence, an increasing number of journalists have accepted that no response at all is a polite way for an editor to say "Thanks, but no thanks." If you want more sensitive responses, ditch your journalistic aspirations and go work in a morgue.

Step 6: Maintain the Relationship

Once in a while, you will find an editor who returns emails thoughtfully, replies conscientiously to your pitches and queries, and seems to like your concepts and perspective. After ensuring that you're not experiencing some kind of hallucination, make sure you maintain good relations with that editor. Editors tend to move around a lot, so you might have their ear for only a short time: savour it while you can. Editors who fit this description, though rare, are a welcome entry point into an outlet. I've fostered solid relations with a broad range of editors in Canada and abroad. When I vacationed in London, I emailed an editor I'd worked with at *The Guardian* and asked if we could meet for coffee. We did, discussing a few story ideas (plus he gave me a tour of the office). Same for editors at *The Globe and Mail* in Toronto and *The Advocate* in LA. Putting a face to a byline is always a good idea, and editors should appreciate the effort you've made to connect. Plus, these editors will often have great advice about what they're looking for and what the work environment is like on the inside of their outlet. (Keep in mind that this must be done on their schedule, and if they sound too frazzled to make time for a meeting, tell them it's fine and that you'll catch them on another occasion.) And when good, friendly, open editors do move on, they move on to *somewhere else*. That means someone who knows how good you are may contact you in future to have you contribute to another venue down the line. This is a business built on contacts, so try not to burn bridges.

Case Studies

What follows are some actual samples of pitches that got me, and a couple of my colleagues, into various publications.

The New York Times

In the fall of 1999, I learned that a TV production house in Montreal had managed to make a sale to American broadcasters. The show was *Dogs with Jobs*, in which episodes would focus on various canine friends who did things like help epileptics, autistic children, anti-terrorist squads, and lord knows what else. Sound strange? It was, just strange enough (the title alone deserves attention) that the *Times* bought the story. Here's the pitch that I sent the TV editor in the fall of 1999:

> Email to: TV editor, *The New York Times*
> Subject line: PITCH: *Dogs with Jobs* arrives on PBS
>
> *Dogs with Jobs* is an extremely odd half-hour TV series that has been running on Canada's Life Channel for close to a year, garnering critical praise and substantial ratings. Now the show has been picked up by PBS and will run on stations across the U.S. this January.
>
> Each episode of the show features two different canines with unusual vocations. I have seen all 16 of the episodes that have been created to date, and find the show quite charming, if at times a wee bit sentimental. Dogs profiled include anti-terrorist dogs, seeing-eye dogs, epileptic-seizure dogs, police dogs and dogs that sniff out survivors of earthquakes.
>
> I have an interview with the producer and creators of the series. Would *The New York Times* be interested in a review or interview related to this show?
>
> I have written extensively on TV and cinema for the weekly *Mirror*, where I have been a film critic for eight years. I write a column for *The Globe and Mail*, Canada's national newspaper. I have also written for *The Advocate*. If you need any samples of my work, I'd be happy to send them to you.
>
> Thanks for your time,
> Matthew Hays

Note a couple of things about this sample. I have kept the pitch short and sweet—don't waste a busy editor's time. And I write the word "PITCH" in upper case in the subject line, distinguishing it from the load of junk mail or spam that editors often get. The pitch worked beautifully, partly through a stroke of fortune. Though one editor emailed me to say she doubted they'd assign the piece, Oprah did a brief segment on *Dogs with Jobs* on her show. That meant it was on the *Times'* radar; they contacted me to commission the piece, and it ran in the *Times* in January 2000. (What can I say? People just love dogs, and there's nothing like inter-species bonding to make readers' hearts melt.) Since then, I've written several more articles for *The New York Times*, and having that name on your CV and in your portfolio immediately gives you serious added cachet as a writer. And that translates into more work.

Marketing Magazine

What follows is another short and sweet pitch, this one supplied by my colleague, the Toronto-based freelance writer and author Ryan Bigge. Note again how succinct the pitch is, and how appealing Bigge's to-the-point style is. It's an unusual story, but Bigge makes the case for its solid appeal.

TO: *Marketing* Magazine

I noticed that Labatt 50 redesigned its bottle recently, and is now advertising its product. This interests me because back in 1999, I was at a conference put on by D-code, and I got a chance to speak with someone at Labatt's. I told her how Labatt 50 had a kind of cachet because it had no cachet—cool because there was nothing cool about it. For example, I would sometimes bring 50 to a house party, knowing that no one else would, thereby ensuring that my beer would not get stolen.

Amazingly, Labatt's knew this—and she said that they were afraid of advertising 50 or leveraging this weird, anti-cool cachet because it might ruin the aura or whatever you might want to call it.

The other interesting thing about Labatt 50 is how it is viewed much differently in Ontario, than say Quebec (where it's still very popular with a certain demographic of older men). As well, it was discontinued in BC for a long time (sometime in the 80s) and then reintroduced in the late 90s.

So I guess the fact that 50 is redesigned and is being advertised is kind of a story, but perhaps a history of Labatt 50 might be a more interesting article. By looking at the history of the beer, and how its meaning and popularity has changed over time, we might learn something interesting both about marketing and about ourselves (as Canadians).

Please let me know what you think.

Thanks,

Ryan Bigge

Not only did the editors at *Marketing* magazine bite; this quirky pitch became their cover story.

ELLE Magazine (US Edition)

The following is a slightly longer pitch for an American magazine, *ELLE*. I find this pitch intriguing for a couple of reasons: it ties into a national scandal that was big in the news, after some women charged that they had been taken advantage of sexually when they were in high school two decades ago. This is a pitch of a far more personal nature, and it's also one for a more ambitious and longer story. Katrina Onstad, a Toronto-based author and journalist, actually had some ties to the very BC school that came into question. Note the way Onstad connects her own experience into this larger scandal, and by the nuances that run throughout her pitch. It's a complex story, and Onstad clearly wants to build on that complexity. You can savour the story as you read the pitch—much like an enticing movie trailer, it makes you want to read the entire thing.

TO: Editor, *ELLE* Magazine

Twenty years ago, as a 16-year-old in Vancouver (feel a San Francisco vibe), I took part in a one year Outward Bound-style program called BC Quest. Right now, one of the three men who led that program is in court on numerous charges—12 counts of gross indecency and four counts of indecent assault—and the other two are under investigation. The salacious details are getting huge press across the country (<http://www.theglobeandmail.com/servlet/story/RTGAM.20061011.wxsex-scandal11/BNStory/National>, or any search of Tom Ellison + Quest) and suddenly, it looks like I was a tenth-grade member of a cult. People who know me are asking, very delicately, how I'm doing. What I want to write is a reflection on my mixed feelings about that year, which extend to these allegations, particularly as the mother of a young daughter.

Before I did Quest, I was miserable, drunken, caked in black eyeliner and hostility. That year of snow-caving, canoeing, hiking, and most significantly, being physically separated from the social tyrannies of regular high school, changed me deeply, and for the better.

But Quest was also evil, and most of us knew it. Tom (Ellison, who is being charged), Dean and Stan, as we called "the boys," traded in military-style humiliations, sexual harassment and mind games. They were aging hippies and proud mavericks, reveling in anti-authoritarian shenanigans (pathetic badmouthing of "the man," etc.) while building a Rousseau-ian faux-utopia within this ultra preppy, upper-class public school. Far too skeptical to sign on to anything, I was liked, but never a full subscriber. I didn't give them foot rubs, like the hardcore Questers, and I only once joined the crew who visited Tom's boat—site of many of the alleged crimes—but left quickly when I learned we were there to clean it for him.

These were the final days before political correctness took hold. Today, a teacher who shouted "fat ass" at a female student, or placed a late student in a volleyball cage at the front of the classroom (for all the lefty idealism being pedaled, it felt like a frat: all hazing, all the time, all in the name of comedy) would be immediately, and fairly, chastened. But Quest was not part of any system, and that was its genius: for one brief year in high school, no rules applied. As the testimony proves, propriety did not exist in Quest.

But that borderless atmosphere was why I thrived. Though the teachers could be bullies, other times, in the most Edenic settings, they were adults who treated us like equals, who listened, who pushed us to conquer ice and snow and the limits of our bodies. Now, that climate seems suspect; a sexual trap of some kind. I never saw any actual sexual contact between the teachers and students, but everybody knew something was going on, and all three were dating ex-students only a few years older than us. Finally, after 15 years, the stink grew too strong to ignore, and the program was shut down. We were the last class to do Quest; the next year, the name was changed to Trek and a woman installed. The men who founded it soon disappeared into the school system.

So far, the court testimony suggests that the sex between teacher and student was consensual. One woman who took the stand had a relationship with Tom (I can't think of him as anything but Tom) for 14 years, into her 30s. There is no suggestion that Tom was aggressive or threatening with these girls—most of the complainants had sex with him several times, some for months—though, of course, his behaviour was utterly inappropriate.

And so I have been thinking about the wildness of that time—swimming in our underwear in the dark; days and nights in the mountains without clocks—and the power of teenage sexuality, the flush of strength a girl first feels under a grown man's gaze. And then—the regret in all of that. Doesn't every woman want to rewrite her first sexual experience? I find myself wanting to defend Quest, if not Tom. I think of Naomi Wolf's outrage over Harold Bloom's hand on her knee, and the persecuted professors who bedded their knowing students in Francine Prose's *The Blue Angel*, or J.M. Coetzee's *Disgrace*. I wonder about victim culture, and why we think we can smooth over every roughness in our past, culturally and sexually, in the courts.

People keep asking me if I would let my daughter do Quest, but I know that Quest could never exist now. For these women on the stand, whose stories I don't want to belittle in any way (the tricky part), that's progress. For me, it's something else.

Sincerely,

Katrina Onstad

This pitch not only led to Onstad writing a thoughtful, poignant 3,500-word feature, it also earned her an American national magazine award for 2008, on a shortlist that included articles from *Harper's* and *The Atlantic*. Not too shabby, as they say.

The Globe and Mail

I had interviewed a local filmmaker called Dimitri Estdelacropolis for the *Mirror* a couple of times over the years; he had made a name for himself on the festival circuit years earlier with his unusual, independent films. Then, on a trip to a film fest in Berlin, he had become hooked on heroin. This meant that his latest film, *Shirley Pimple in the John Wayne Temple of Doom*, had taken about 18 years to complete. Finally, the Vancouver Film Festival announced that it would screen the movie in 1998. I had my hook, and sent this email along to the arts editor at the *Globe*, a fellow I'd worked with before. With these pitches, I'm a bit more casual in my tone, as I'd already written a fair bit for the national Canadian daily.

Email to: Arts editor, *The Globe and Mail*
Subject line: PITCH: After 18 years in the making, *Shirley Pimple* to premiere

There's quite a funny story I've been following for a few years here. A filmmaker called Dimitri Estdelacropolis has been working on the same movie for about 18 years. He started it as a film student at Concordia University. Then he went to the Berlin Film Fest and was toasted as the latest hot up-and-comer. Then he tried heroin, and got hooked.

Now, after years of blunders, struggles with his addiction (including a stint in prison) and on-again, off-again shooting, the film, which has come to be known as the *Shoot from Hell* in Montreal film circles, is finally going to have its premiere at the Vancouver Film Fest next month. Its title is *Shirley Pimple*.

This is a very funny and odd story. And Dimitri is an exceedingly colourful character. Would you be interested in a profile for the *Globe* Arts pages?

Please let me know.

Thanks,

Matt

How could they resist? I wrote a 1,200-word story in the *Globe*, which they ran on the first page of the Arts section. It was a fun piece, and it ran in time to help pack the house at the film's Vancouver Film Festival premiere.

The Guardian

In the summer of 2006, I read about a show on Andy Warhol that filmmaker David Cronenberg would be curating at the Art Gallery of Ontario. Clearly, this story had huge potential; Warhol's name is universally recognized, while Cronenberg had just been hailed by every sensible film critic as having made the best film of 2005, *A History of Violence*. How would one cultural icon reflect on the work of another cultural icon? This would be a story that Canadian newspapers and magazines would undoubtedly already be reflecting on, but I suspected, correctly, that international publications like *The Guardian* might not have this story covered. This was the first pitch I sent to the Arts editor there.

Email to: Arts editor, *The Guardian*
Subject line: PITCH: David Cronenberg on Warhol, art exhibit in Toronto this fall

I am an experienced arts writer with publications in *The New York Times* and *The Globe and Mail*, among other places. I have a pitch that I think may be of great interest to *Guardian* readers.

This July, the Art Gallery of Ontario will unveil its new show on Andy Warhol. The intriguing thing here will be that the guest curator for the show is none other than celebrated filmmaker David Cronenberg.

Cronenberg, of course, made *A History of Violence*, a film many argued was the best of 2005. He is a director who has become renowned for his unique and disturbing treatment of violence and his complex approach to film genres. There are a number of questions to ask Cronenberg about his thoughts and feelings about Warhol.

Might *The Guardian* be interested in such an interview? Please let me know.

Thank-you,
Matthew Hays

Again, very short, very sweet. This one also got me into this paper, and I've since written a number of pieces for *The Guardian*.

∾∾∾

Everything I've written (and hopefully illuminated) in this chapter about the pitching process is merely a beginning. But what happens after the pitch is sold is equally significant: you want to get invited *back*. That means doing your job as a writer properly and professionally. Doing that, and remaining courteous (yes, even under sweat-inducing deadlines) will leave you remembered as someone who managed to get the job done to the satisfaction of your assigning editor.

That leads to the greatest reward: trust and respect of editors, who will then hear out your next pitch or, even better, call you with a new assignment. The task of pitching and writing stories is both simple and complex at once; it's about doing a good job, while conscientiously paying attention to every detail along the way.

Discussion Questions

1. Reread Katrina Onstad's pitch for "My Year of Living Dangerously" on page 38 above. Why do you think it succeeded? What were the keys to its success? Compare it to the other pitches reprinted in this chapter: what do they have in common and how do they differ?

2. Now read Onstad's story as published in *ELLE* magazine's US edition (pages 43–51). Clearly, Onstad succeeded not only in selling this story but also in delivering on its promise. But what if *ELLE* had said no? How could the pitch have been amended for submission to other publications? How might it have been tailored differently were it aimed at, say, a daily newspaper or another magazine of your choice?

3. Choose one of your own favourite feature stories—or a story reprinted in this book—and craft a pitch for that story, targeted at the publication in which it appeared. Then, amend the pitch for a different publication.

Note

1. Gary Kamiya, "Let Us Now Praise Editors," *Salon.com*, July 24, 2007, <http://www.salon.com/opinion/kamiya/2007/07/24/editing>.

"My Year of Living Dangerously"

He pushed girls to be strong, to be self-sufficient—and, according to some of his former students, he pushed them into sex. Katrina Onstad recalls a time of fear and freedom and wonders, in the frenzy of her teacher's prosecution, about what's been lost

Katrina Onstad, "My Year of Living Dangerously." *ELLE* magazine (US edition), August 2007, 212. Reprinted by permission of the author.

In the newspaper photos, my teacher looked changed, but just a little. He had grown very thin, so that when he attempted to out-walk the TV cameras, his knees jutted through his suit pants like wire hangers. But even at 63, standing in a courthouse awaiting testimony about what he had done—salacious details of fingers and tongues and a boat in the middle of nowhere and the teenage girls inside it—he was still handsome: his white hair boyishly thick, his body tree-tall. The creases in his face had deepened, but just with age, not shame, settling around a smirk that I instantly remembered. Twenty years later, I had a flash of recognition: *him.*

It was not the face of a contrite sexual predator, which is probably why newspapers across Canada chose to run that particular shot so often last fall. The hint of defiance suited the narrative of a smooth-operating molester facing 16 charges for sex crimes. According to reporters, Tom Ellison—always Tom to us—the leader of an Outward Bound–style program for high school students called B.C. Quest, handpicked the prettiest teenage girls from a pool of naive applicants and took them to the forest. The forest part made it irresistible copy.

Starting in the '70s and continuing until he retired from teaching in the mid-'80s, Ellison had been having sexual relations with present and past Questers, often on his sailboat, *Nostradamus,* moored in a harbor in downtown Vancouver. What went on there wasn't really contested in the trial, not even by Ellison. The crux was whether these liaisons were illegal at the time. Ellison faced four counts of indecent assault (using force during a nonpenetrating sex act) and 12 counts of gross indecency. To find him guilty of gross indecency, the court had to decide that Ellison's conduct was a marked departure from what the average Canadian at the time would have deemed decent. This silly standard was replaced in 1988 by a more clear-cut law prohibiting an adult in a position of authority from sexual contact with a person under 18 and in his charge. But all the complaints against Ellison predated 1988, meaning that at the time he was sexually involved with his students, there was no law against it. Unprofessional and unethical, yes, but not automatically criminal.

For more than a month, titillatingly graphic testimony fed enraged editorials and hang-him-high blogs: He performed oral sex but hardly ever penetrated! He thought he was some kind of sex coach! The families who handed over their daughters had no idea what was going on! At the victim-impact hearing (in which victims participate in the sentencing of the offender by explaining to the court and the offender how the crime has affected them) a woman addressed Ellison directly: "I have carried this burden of shame and guilt in the pit of my stomach. ... You may not think you did anything wrong, but you crippled me to the point that I was unable to have a healthy sexual relationship with a man. What kind of teacher did you think you were?" Another woman, deeply traumatized, told the court that after being involved with him at 16, she didn't date until she was 22.

People who knew I had done the program in the mid-'80s began to ask, Are you okay? How much do you hate him? They assumed damage, offering sympathy and outrage. But nothing had happened to me. With my androgynous looks and gangly body, I was hardly babe enough to have attracted his attention, and that year, I was untouched, and in a way, largely unnoticed. This seemed to surprise people, and even, I sensed, to disappoint them.

One day I read about a woman who testified, only when compelled to by the prosecutors, that she had sex with Ellison frequently over four years, beginning just before her eighteenth birthday. "He definitely, in my case, did not commit a crime, and he doesn't deserve to be convicted for a crime with respect to my charges," she told the court. "I told him that I really wanted him to be the first. And I begged him to be the first." Another reluctant witness said, "I would say I probably wanted to sleep with him, because everybody wanted to."

Those statements rang true to me. I saw an arrogant bully, but Ellison's image of macho woodsman in the city worked with many girls. He is not someone I want to defend, and I won't. Yet I can defend my memory of that time. Quest was the sole year of high school in which I didn't weigh myself daily, or fill journals with overwrought imaginings about boys who didn't know my name, or find myself in dimly lit basements with boys whose names I didn't know. It was a year in which I got muscles and I didn't drink and I felt alert to the world in a way that now, at 36, I keep trying to get back to.

It was also a year in which I observed that a number of the girls who went with Tom seemed pleased by whatever was happening on the boat or in the woods. But the girls' agency was rarely reported as the scandal heated up; it's still taboo for anyone to admit that teenage girls want sex, especially the girls themselves. Even as I don't doubt that most of Ellison's accusers sincerely felt abused, I loathe the way the press turned complicated stories into something reductive: She was a fresh young girl, he was a dirty old man. Ellison was lecherous, but no one described him as physically or mentally threatening. Though some of the encounters were brief, many went on for months and even years. One woman who pressed charges against him had been involved with him, on and off, for 13 years. Ellison's lawyer presented evidence at the trial that she brought charges only after he refused to have a child with her. (He does have a daughter with another ex-Quester, a pretty blond roughly 25 years his junior who has said publicly that she and Ellison got together long after she graduated from high school. Fourteen years later, they are still a couple.)

The trial, which dominated the Canadian media, made me think about how many women, looking back on their first sexual encounters, raw and stupid, want to erase their own desire from the story. So much of the indignation around Quest has a retroactive quality—the need to rewrite history, embarrassment about the people we were and the lenience we practiced in the past. In her book *Dilemmas of Desire: Teenage Girls Talk About Sexuality*, Deborah Tolman, professor of human sexuality at San Francisco State University, interviewed dozens of girls, almost all of whom admitted they did have sexual desires but found it socially unacceptable to cop to them. In dress and attitude, these girls mirrored the booty-shaking pop culture they consumed, yet they could never actually be sexual for fear of being labeled "slutty." They talked about their sex lives through what Tolman calls "cover stories"—"It just happened" being the most common how-I-lost-my-virginity recap. Of course girls feel the pull of desire, like everyone else on the planet. But is there still something in us as women that makes us ashamed to admit our lust, especially when it looks so bad from here?

One of the women pressing charges said that the births of her daughters had spurred her to speak out about her relationship with Ellison. I heard that comment while watching the news as my own baby daughter pulled every sheet of Kleenex from the box. The time in which we did Quest, just before the dawn of total political correctness, seems Paleolithic now: teenagers gone into the wilderness for days at a time without cell phones, injuring themselves on mountains, barely supervised. Ellison exploited the liberated atmosphere that made Quest so significant, especially for girls. He took the mental and physical freedom we were experiencing for the first time—that year in the outdoors I learned to be voracious, to be powerful, to be free—tossed in sex, too, and everything fell apart. My daughter will never do a program like Quest because it could never exist today. We will design our lives to keep her safe from all risk:

emotional, physical, and sexual. She will be electronically shadowed and chauffeured, all precautions taken to keep her away from threats like Tom Ellison and the great unknown. Such private experiments on the way from girlhood to womanhood won't be available to her. I suppose I should be comforted, yet I can't help but think that with all this safety comes a great loss.

I was raised in an upper-middle-class enclave near the University of British Columbia. Vancouver has now become a gleaming city of beachfront condominiums and gourmet organic supermarkets; a place so upscale I can't afford to live there anymore. But in the '70s and '80s, when I was growing up, our neighborhood still harbored a collection of draft dodgers, academics, and hippie moms who thrilled to send their kids to the alternative public high school I attended, a '70s experiment in decline. We called the teachers by their first names, designed our own curricula, and learned as little as possible.

In spite of all the enlightenment, when I recall who I was before I did Quest, I see a teenager manically trying to shape and reinvent herself every other week: a perm, then a geometric haircut; a love of Corey Hart followed by an all-consuming worship of the Velvet Underground. I was reading Ralph Ellison and discussing nuclear proliferation with my parents, then staying up late under a pink bedspread with a flashlight and Sweet Dreams romances.

My body was my biggest hobby. It seemed borrowed; it shocked me. My height skyrocketed and my weight plummeted within months, followed by binge-eating in the dark of night. Then back to exercise and deprivation, using teen novels on anorexia as how-to manuals. All this longing for food and thinness was matched by unspoken lust for boys. I was obsessed with the miasma of male sweat and unconcern at one end of the hallway. I wanted everything to happen to me, and on occasion, I would find some drunken boy-receptacle for all that wayward need. On weekends, my friends, a diseased group of cells always gathering and dividing, and I would drink wine coolers behind the 7-Eleven and ride the buses through the city, looking for something to do. Coming home from beach parties, late at night, I remember our attention only briefly diverted through the window by the mountains that surround Vancouver, melting down into miles of rough coast. We were 15, 16, 17, and inured to beauty.

The Questers, though, were something different. They would leave our little school for a semester in the Canadian wilderness and return happier and louder, having made it through a program rumored to be mentally and physically grueling. The girls, particularly, seemed like survivors of some grave, important experience. Though the fisherman's sweaters and makeup-free faces offended my black-eyeliner aesthetic, the Quest look secretly appealed to me: a clear uniform at last. A fixed identity.

The program was founded in 1973. Based in a giant room in a bigger high school in a richer neighborhood than mine, it attracted motivated kids from prominent families and was regarded by its supporters as a one-of-a-kind successful experiment in public education—it had even garnered the praise of world-renowned environmentalist David Suzuki. Students who were accepted did one semester of academics, cramming all of tenth grade into five months of intense classes in the regular school. In the nonacademic semester, they hiked, canoed, cycled, and cross-country skied, under the tutelage of Tom and his colleagues, Dean Hull and Stan Callegari. They were known as "the Boys," though all were in their forties by the time I did the program in 1986.

I do remember talk of military-style tactics and sexual improprieties, and to some at my high school, all those smiling, touching ex-Questers, linked together like paper-chain Christmas-tree ornaments, were suckers and followers. However, on the strength of a few stories told by the fisherman-sweater girls as they gave each other massages in the quad, I identified Quest as an adventure, the first piece of a future I imagined for myself. I would become fearless, a valued attribute in our family. My parents thought nothing of leaving my brother and me with friends and relatives for weeks at a time while they visited Nicaragua (where my dad went to help the Sandinistas rebuild their education system), China, Italy. They hosted supremely '70s slide-show parties upon their return, and I would find a place on the crowded purple corduroy couch, concentrating through the cocktail chatter on the Asian women in slippers and cafés in the shadows of cathedrals. There were keys to these places: legends and languages to help you navigate. I wished something similar existed for high school. I had a hunch that Quest would give me that, and I wasn't wrong.

I did all of tenth grade in an exhausting sprint through the regular school in the fall of 1985. After Christmas break, I felt giddy to be out from behind a desk. The gigantic Quest classroom was in fact an anticlassroom emptied of furniture, its walls hung with environmental posters and broken canoe paddles. My class of about 50 sat on the floor, no longer answering to the bells that rushed the other kids in and out of their paces.

Quickly, it became clear that the room was primarily a stage for Stan, Dean, and Tom. Dean had the true grizzly-man look, with a nimbus of frizzed hair and a beard halfway down his chest. He was the funniest of the three, and the most humane. Stan, a sniggering, younger jock, possessed a hard strain of aloofness.

Tom was the oldest, and so crippled by back problems that many days he didn't show up at all. He could usually be found at the marina fixing the boat from which he ran expensive sightseeing trips to the Queen Charlotte Islands, an archipelago off the coast of northern British Columbia.

On the first day, they summoned a few thick-necked hockey players to the front of the room and called them out as smokers. A long, jokey "scared straight" session began. One of the Boys asked the smokers if they were losers, if they could "keep it up." The tone for the year was set: a semiarticulated indoctrination into environmentalism (clear-cutting, acid rain = bad) and leftish politics (those opposed to clear-cutting, acid rain = good), mixed with fratty high jinks and boot-camp humiliations (teachers giving wedgies to teenagers = cool).

Our days were spent learning to rock climb on the city's North Shore or kayak in a nearby pool. We had a few silly academic assignments, presumably to satisfy the host-school's principal. (I did a presentation, using my father's slides, about the U.S.-backed war in Nicaragua.) And we trained for our trips. Jogging, sports, and weight lifting were punctuated by the Boys' macho idiocy. They poured buckets of water on students who weren't working hard enough. They made the slowest kids piggyback the heaviest up mud-slick hills in the rain, laughing from below.

If the Boys had an overarching philosophy, and I don't think they did, it might have been to return us to a state of nature, to let us choose good or bad without constraint. But they had been blithely degrading their students for years: We were rich kids who had skipped through life in a haze of clueless entitlement, and we deserved our comeuppance. One day, one of the three wheeled a cage that had been holding volleyballs and basketballs to the front of the room. A boy was put inside the cage in either his gym shorts or his underwear—it's unclear to me now. But I do remember Stan and Dean laughing as they told him to suck his thumb like the little rich baby he was. It was Tom who picked apart our bodies: "*Go* fat-ass!" I remember him yelling at a girl as she ran sprints. During the trial, an ex-Quester testified that the Boys would pinch girls' breasts and slap their butts.

Everyone talked about the skinny-dipping and pot smoking that went on during the Quest summer-reunion trips, but I never saw anything that overt. Instead, sex was a persistent undercurrent in the room. The Questers and Tom, Dean, and Stan were constantly massaging each other—especially Tom, with his bad back. Anointed popular Questers past and present hung out with the Boys in the equipment room. The two prettiest girls in our semester would emerge from amid the backpacks and camping stoves, seeming as happy and confident, as sly and smiling, as all pretty girls did in my 16-year-old eyes. They looked like they could handle anything.

Of course we speculated about what went on in there. The Boys were all either married to or dating ex-Questers barely older than we were. To me, this seemed like interspecies mingling; older men, tufted and expansive, looked repulsive next to the hairless boys in my grade. I was fascinated by the possibility that girls who had recently been more or less like me were flirting or even having sex with grown men. This spoke to my immediate future. Where was I on this spectrum of desire? How and who would I want to touch?

Quest was definitely a mental torture chamber, but the word "cult" isn't right; it presumes we weren't aware. Maybe some people bought into the games without question, but most of us were entirely conscious that year— consciously laying low in the classroom, totally conscious in the outdoors. The Boys, their arrogance and assholeness, were our favorite topic. We were young, but bright and precocious, and many of us were sexually active. When rumors started circulating that a girl in the semester before us had a breakdown under the Tom-Dean-Stan pressures and left the program, we talked about that, too, and empathized.

So if we knew it was creepy and corrupt, why did we stick it out? Why didn't we say anything to our parents, to the principal of the school?

In part, their contempt—for the authority of the regular school system, for us—was intriguing. They gave us our first taste of the routine indifference of adulthood, and not being of interest also meant we weren't being watched. There were no grown-ups around—we quickly ascertained that the Boys didn't count—and very few rules, except for how to survive in the outdoors (water bottle, sunscreen, hat). That's the trade-off, I see now; bad things happen to some girls while no one is watching. But for others, the slow walk toward some semblance of self requires freedom and privacy.

We were let loose for long runs through the city, and I recall how, during one grueling 10K run along the seawall, my eyes dropped back into my head and I felt a surge of adrenaline: My body could be a source of power instead of repulsion. I learned to be alone with myself, bicycling a painful hill on an island that peaked into a view of the Pacific. With a couple of other kids, I made a snow cave up in the Coast Mountains, digging until dark, sleeping in a hole carved into the side of an icy slope. I still think of the black silence of that night, the slick cocoon I had dug with my friends wet in the beam of the flashlight. "Do you remember that?" asks my old friend Christy, now an accountant. "I would never be that brave now."

These were the moments we stayed for. Somehow it was my least sexual year of high school. Boys weren't abstractions, but allies in situations where they needed me as much as I needed them. On a 10-day canoe trip through a difficult chain of lakes in the interior of the province, I told my male partner, a heavy-metal-head, that I would take the front of the boat, where less skill and strength is required. Dean overheard this and told me off: "I partnered you with that guy because you're a stronger canoeist. Why are you being such a wimp?" He was right; I took the stern and drove us through barely thawed water for much of those 10 days. Each night, collapsing in my tent, my wrists on fire with pain, I was thrilled.

The boys I knew all had informal initiation rituals, their Boy Scout Vision Quests and Tom Sawyer disappearances. Anthropologists have noted that for girls, most rites of passage have to do with menstruation, and therefore, with breeding and marrying. To become a woman in most cultures is to become a person on your wedding day or the day you become a mother. But in Quest (a word now synonymous in my hometown with the exploitation of girls), I had moments of feeling utterly singular and maximized. I didn't know it then, but I was outrunning the narrowing expectations waiting on the other side of my girlhood.

In the course of the trial, it emerged that Ellison had had close to 20 relationships with students between 1972 and 1982. Often, he performed oral sex on the teenagers, preferring to get them off rather than himself. Many of the women testified that Ellison saw himself as an educator, preparing inexperienced girls for future lovers. He positioned himself as the great benefactor. Of one former student, now a complainant, on whom he had performed oral sex, he said, "I'm not making light of this and I don't mean to be flippant, but it was the longest time I have ever made love to a person … [and] she really responded. She worked really hard at finally having an orgasm [and] she thanked me." He also testified, "I gave to them as much as I could."

I don't buy it; the Don Juan posture is just another manipulation that excuses his own turn-on and drive to dominate. But I can see why students— of both sexes—sleep with their teachers. Bell Hooks has written that teaching is infused with "erotic energy": Both teacher and student are caught up in the desire to impart, the desire to learn, the mutual desire to please. Nor does it surprise me that budding adolescent desire would sense a safe place in the bed of an older man, someone presumably at a distance from the vicissitudes of adolescent politics. I remember hearing anecdotes in school about students having sex with their teachers, *Election*-style. These girls (and one boy) survived and moved on. For some people, it's like that. For some, it's not.

In the end, the judge found Ellison guilty of two counts of indecent assault, one count of common assault, and four counts of gross indecency (two of which were stayed, or thrown out). He called Ellison's actions "a monstrous breach of trust." Ellison will spend two years under house arrest and has to provide DNA samples to authorities. Meanwhile, Stan Callegari and Dean Hull are under investigation by the Vancouver Police Department, says a spokesman.

When Ellison's sentence was announced, message boards and talk-radio phone lines lit up with fury. Editorials complained that the punishment paled beside the crimes. Maybe that's true. But for me the uneasily resolved case means that a freedom that mattered is now impossible to imagine for my own daughter. Quest as I knew it ended in early 1987, after Ellison had been pushed out of the program to defuse an approaching scandal (according to a recent article in *Vancouver* magazine, parents were beginning to call and complain that their daughters had been abused). Dean and Stan were gone soon after that. Later that year, Quest became a program called Trek. Trek still exists, staffed by both men and women, monitored by parents and officials. On the overnight trips, at least one female teacher is always present.

So now we watch our daughters, pretending that we can save them from themselves. As if they won't find their own ways into the forest.

"My Year of Living Dangerously" by Katrina Onstad has been nominated by the American Society of Magazine Editors for excellence in the Essay category.

PART TWO

Getting the Goods

CHAPTER THREE

The Great Quest: Researching Feature Stories

Sue Ferguson

Where is the knowledge we have lost in information?

Choruses from "The Rock" (1934)

T.S. Eliot, poet and author of the above lament, died in 1965—well before the dawning of the much-hyped information age. But the point he makes is critical to the theme of this chapter. Thanks to 24-hour news channels and satellite delivery systems, today's citizens regularly take stock of what's happening around the world within minutes of events unfolding. They also enlighten themselves daily on matters from the mundane to the sublime by typing a simple word or phrase into a search engine. With all this information literally at our fingertips, one might ask, why does a book on feature writing need a chapter on how to research? Because research is not simply—or even primarily—about getting information. It's about understanding.

The Fundamentals: Navigating the Information Age

Information is the guts, the raw material, of research, but it requires mindful and intelligent processing to turn it into understanding, knowledge, and insight. On its own, information can be unreliable. It can also be contradictory, irrelevant, or just plain wrong. It can, in fact, do more to hamper understanding than to promote it. So, while information is cheap (as anything so abundantly available usually is), research comes at a price. Mostly, that price is paid in journalists' time and intellectual energy. And that's what this chapter hopes to convey: how you can make the most of your time and energy as you mine the mountains of facts, figures, and ideas that await in our so-called information age, and how you can develop research habits that draw you—and your readers—to deeper levels of understanding.

Before we go any further, it's important to stress three research fundamentals:

1. **Start early.** Research takes time. Answers often come slowly, accumulating through circuitous and unplanned routes. Documents and interviews prompt new clues and questions that take you farther afield; the leading expert in an area may be inaccessible, or it takes three reminder voice mails before you get a call back; and when you finally connect, he or she refers to a book, article, or statistics that send you off to the library or museum archives. Meanwhile, the clock keeps ticking. The biggest mistake you can make is to procrastinate.

2. **Stay focused but open-minded.** As your research gathers steam, you'll be pulled in a variety of directions. New ideas and approaches will beckon, or interview subjects will steer you toward fresh, compelling themes, and the storyteller in you will be tempted to pursue them all. It's best to start with a firm idea of what your story is about. While good journalists always remain open to alternatives— especially those that challenge their angle on an issue—staying on track is vital. Pursuing the questions relevant to the story *you* want to write focuses your research, helping you judge when to stop researching and start writing.

3. **Research first, write later.** This maxim belongs among the fundamentals, even though journalists, quite rightly, ignore it on occasion. Sometimes only after you start writing will you realize you don't fully understand the nuances of your subject, or that you've neglected something important. At that point, it's best to hold up at

the keyboard and return to the digging. For the most part, however, research should come first. Precisely because research can shoot you off in various directions, a story only fully comes together when you've considered everything you've learned, and decided which elements are crucial, which are desirable, and which are expendable. Moreover, doing the legwork first is critical to developing the confidence to write with authority.

It's Not Always at Your Fingertips

Sometimes a phenomenal amount of time is spent getting to the bottom of a single fact. Patricia Treble, researcher-reporter at *Maclean's*, recounts the magazine's attempts to ascertain the date of Pierre Trudeau's brother Charles's death. The former prime minister had just died, and researchers were reluctant to call the family. They first consulted biographies, but these were of no help. A family friend confirmed Charles was deceased, but couldn't give a firm date. The Mormon Library in Salt Lake City, Utah (which tracks the births and deaths of millions of people) dug up his birthday, but a call to the Quebec provincial architect association (Charles's profession) brought up a different date. With the deadline approaching, Treble called Quebec's vital statistics office with the two birthdates, and asked for help. A fax of Charles Trudeau's death certificate landed on her desk by 7 p.m. that day—a full six weeks after the hunt began.

The breadth and depth of research is one of the two main qualities that distinguishes feature stories from news stories. (The other is writing style.) And while research is too creative and messy a process to be pinned down to a strict, never-fail methodology, writers tend to take a broadly similar path from conception of an idea to formation of a story. This chapter will take you down that path by shadowing the steps one writer takes, and pausing at moments to listen to what others say about landmarks along the way.

Our writer is Michael Valpy, an award-winning writer with *The Globe and Mail*. The story is "Mothers of Invention," a tale of how "two overweight boozing housewives" founded a Cape Cod religious sect that took control of a respected private eastern Ontario private school, Grenville Christian College, in the 1970s. The article, which ran on the first page of the *Globe*'s October 6, 2007, Focus section, fills in the background to a story Valpy broke earlier that year about psychological, physical, and sexual abuse of the school's students. (You can access it online through a library's Factiva or Canadian Newsstand databases: key in a title and author search for 2007.)

The Grenville scoop fell into Valpy's lap. "It was pure fluke," he recalls. A former student now living in Washington had asked a friend for help getting the abuse allegations into the Canadian media. The friend knew Valpy as a child, and gave the journalist a call. The former student related his experiences to Valpy, sent him school and cult yearbooks as well as Anglican Church documents relating to Grenville, and directed him to an Internet message board set up by some of the school's graduates.

There it was—a story waiting to be told. Now, it was just a matter of digging. But for what?

What's the Point? Research Goals

As juicy as his initial scoop was, Valpy needed much more to go to print. He needed, of course, the basics of any story: characters, concrete examples and scenes, and commentary from church officials and outside experts. He also needed to verify, to feel confident the abuse plausibly occurred (as is sometimes the case, certainty would be impossible to establish outside a court of law). This he accomplished within a week—a full week, he points out—of researching, and he went to print on August 31 with the breaking story.

So much for the news item. The feature came five weeks later, and to write that, Valpy needed more. He needed to connect the dots—to *make sense* of all the stories from former students, and of the Anglican Church's role in the affair. Feature writers not only collect information relevant to their story, they also interpret it. And for that, they need to know more than

Glad You Asked!   Making Sure

Q: What's a fact-checking package?
A: Many magazines employ fact checkers who will go over every line of every story, checking the accuracy and veracity of your facts. You can make their lives easier (and make yourself an editor's favourite!) by providing a comprehensive fact-checking package when you submit your article. While specific requirements will vary from magazine to magazine, the package should usually include the following:

1. A list of all sources interviewed, including the proper spelling of their names and titles as well as their correct phone numbers and email addresses.
2. Full reference information for books, magazine articles, journal articles, reports, and any other documents used or referenced in your piece.

just what happened, or what people are saying. They must master the history as well as the theoretical expertise and debates behind the facts.

The goal of feature-writing research, then, is twofold. On the one hand, you need to identify specific contacts and concrete examples that prove and showcase the story's theme; it's from this material that you build a *narrative arc*—your basic story-telling framework (see chapter 7). On the other hand, you need to develop a full understanding of and insight into the issue—an *explanatory arc* that reveals the story's deeper significance and meaning. The former goal can easily overshadow the latter: pressed to relate a compelling drama, journalists can underestimate the importance of explanation. But unearthing the connections between facts, and explaining how and why they came to be, lends a story both timelessness (because even if the characters and events are fleeting, the underlying meaning has staying power) and freshness (because readers feel they are arriving at a new understanding).

Valpy's research, for example, ultimately linked Grenville's abusive rituals to a US sect imported from Germany, situating the events in the broader context of the post-war growth in American evangelicalism, the failure of the Anglican Church to monitor the school, as well as the financial and religious motivations of the two sect "Mothers."

The story that is reprinted following this chapter, "The Golden Bough" by John Vaillant, also privileges explanation. The basic tale of a former BC logger cutting down a one-of-a-kind ancient spruce was old news. The well-publicized events occurred in 1997, five years before Vaillant's feature ran in *The New*

---

3. Clear and full citations (URLs) for websites used and specific page locations (you might consider printing out the pages you referenced and including them in the package).
4. Interview transcripts, with the sections used in your feature clearly highlighted for easy checking.
5. Studies, speeches, and other documents used, whether directly quoted or as background, with the pertinent sections highlighted or clearly marked
6. Business cards, brochures, and press kits from companies or institutions covered, and relevant photographs.
7. A note flagging any unusual names or spellings (Tommi Smythe instead of Tommy Smith) to save fact-checking time.

Sue Ferguson

Yorker. Yet no one had pulled the story's elements together in a narrative aimed at explaining how and why Grant Hadwin took a chainsaw to the exquisite tree. In delving into Hadwin's past, the history of logging in the Queen Charlotte Islands, and Haida Nation folklore, among other things, Vaillant brought a deeper level of understanding and new insights to Hadwin's actions.

The news reports, Vaillant says, "had written Hadwin off as a vagrant, an unemployed lunatic." Vaillant's story, on the other hand, reveals the logger as a man with an emotionally precarious background and uncanny backwoods smarts, struggling to lead a productive life working for an industry that was ravaging the land. We see how Hadwin's more rational attempts at protectionism (letter writing) and gainful employment fail, and how increasingly isolated he becomes. Woven among these threads of under-standing, Vaillant's research into the science and folklore of the spruce tree heighten the tragic significance of the story. As a result, the story both enlightens and engages readers at a deeper level than any news article could.

Testing the Waters

If you skimmed the part about research fundamentals at the beginning of this chapter, go back now and read the first point—the point about starting early.

Got it? Good. Let's continue.

Maclean's feature writer Brian Bethune usually writes about books, literature, and the ideas they spawn. You might think his first inclination would be to call the author of whatever tome he's chosen to expound upon. Not so. His first line of action "always, always, is the lead," he says. "If I can write the lead, that determines what I'm thinking the story will be, where I look and what I'm going to do next."

While Bethune violates research fundamental number 3 about not writing until your digging is complete, the principle behind his actions is in keeping with number 2, and is well worth underlining. Writers shouldn't start making calls or searching the web unless they first have some sense of what they're looking for. While there is no single correct way to begin research, you shouldn't dive in until you have a strongly focused idea of what you are writing about and what you need to find out. Bethune tests that by writing the lead; others like to have written a possible headline or a couple of theme-describing lines that they may or may not use in the final version. Still others just talk the story over with their editor, a friend, or their golden retriever. By articulating the theme, you shift your research from an amateur fishing expedition in which happenstance dictates where to drop anchor, to a professional one targeting the feeding grounds of specific schools of fish.

Where you go from here depends upon where the idea for the story comes from. But you want to be sure of one thing: that you cast the net widely. This first stage of research is really about gathering some basic information:

- What has (or hasn't) been written about the issue?
- Who's talking (or not) about the issue?
- Are there promising leads for telling the story?

There are only three possible lines of action:

1. **Pick up the phone and talk to someone close to the subject.** It could be an acknowledged expert, an author of a related report, a government official, a public relations person, or someone directly involved in the story. For Valpy, a tip led directly to a phone interview with the source who pointed him to that online community of fellow victims, further sources. With the help of a former Grenville student, he identified some of the usernames, and started phoning. In time, he had spoken with enough people to be convinced he could trust the allegations. "There's no magic to it," he says. "Find one person, and ask that person if they know anyone else. It's just plodding work."

2. **Pull up a search engine and type in a request.** "The net is easy," says journalist Sally Armstrong. "You can type in a term, and a whole conference about the subject will pop up." You could also check out a journalism resource site, such as J-Source.ca or www.journalismnet .com/canada. But remember, at this stage, you're looking for a sense of how significant your story is, who to contact, and where to go for further information. *Scan the offerings, and if you're not coming up with anything useful, move on.* Starting on the Internet is like sailing on the ocean—the landmarks can be difficult to see, and the waters hard to navigate. (See "Living on the Line" below for tips on honing these sailing skills.)

3. **Search the newspapers.** Online databases such as Factiva, Canadian Newsstand, and LexisNexis cover the major metro dailies here and abroad, as well as smaller North American community papers. "I don't start with Google because I'm always writing business stories," says *The Globe and Mail*'s Jennifer Wells. "I want my initial research to be sweeping and focused at the same time." That is, she wants a broad reach, but one tailored to her content needs. With Factiva, for instance, Wells can key in specific publications (especially helpful for stories with a strong local angle) as well as limit her search by word count. That way

she doesn't waste time wading through reports featuring only incidental mentions of her topic or person.

Whatever your first line of action, keeping an eye on the newsstands is essential. It is only by reading what *is* on the public record, that a writer can know what *isn't*. After all, it's filling out those gaps that you add depth and understanding to your story's topic.

Plunging In

The initial stage should tell you if you've enough information and contacts to proceed. Now is a good moment to sit back, take a few deep breaths, and think. Where are you heading? What do you know? What do you still need to know? What confuses you? Where can you find this information? Who do you need to talk to? About what, precisely?

It may be helpful at this stage to make a few notes about what the story will look like. Or you could take the advice of award-winning *Wall Street Journal* writer William Blundell, who believes outlines can dampen the creative flow of feature writing. Rather, he identifies six areas that can serve as research questions and focus your digging.[1]

- **Scope:** What happened? Who's involved? What time period and what locations are significant?
- **History:** What preceded this event? Has it, or anything like it, happened before? How did the situation evolve? How did the person get into her current position?
- **Reasons:** Why did this happen? What are the main political, economic, and/or social factors that can explain this? Who or what is responsible?
- **Impact:** Who or what is affected, physically and/or emotionally? Is the impact beneficial or not? Is it widespread or not?
- **Contrary forces:** Is anyone or anything opposed to the situation or person at issue? How and why?
- **Future:** What will come of this situation, or where will this person be in a few years?

Because feature stories need characters to carry the story's theme, locating these is one of the earliest challenges in research. In the case of "The Golden Bough," its protagonist was missing or dead, so Vaillant cast about for the next best thing: the family. "I became like a private eye," he says, describing how he phoned all the Hadwins in Vancouver, and then across Canada—to no avail (he later learned Hadwin's parents and brother were dead). The only other thing he knew about the logger's past was that he played tennis. "I called every single club in North Vancouver, looking for people who taught tennis in the 1960s," recalls Vaillant. Eventually, he found Hadwin's pro, now a 92-year-old man. "This guy knew the family, the father's sister," he says. "It took six months to get that name."

For Valpy's part, he had already developed strong sources and a firm grasp on the Grenville events. He wanted, however, to find out more about the history, reasons, and impact, in particular. Specifically, he says, that meant figuring out what a cult was, how this cult (the Community of Jesus) operated, how and why it gained influence at a Canadian school, who else knew about the abuse, and how involved the Anglican Church was. Those questions nagged him for 34 days straight, propelling him from source to source. Along the way, he conducted interviews with religious experts and church and school officials, tracked down US court filings, school and secret cult documents, unpublished news reports from a Brockville, Ontario paper, a book authored by a former cult member, and more. He spoke with dozens of people and, he recalls, "collected every piece of paper I could get my hands on." He estimates that for every hour of writing, he spent 20 hours researching.

The research process is also about finding those bothersome flies in the ointment—people, stories, and information that don't square with the story you want to tell. By digging into a subject, you are repeatedly testing the waters, making sure the evidence stands up. Coming across "inconvenient" facts or contrary arguments isn't necessarily a reason to abandon the story, but it is a reason to pause and either rethink or strengthen your theme *before* you spend more time pursuing it.

Resources: Where's the Beef?

Documents, people, and observation. Those are the raw material of research. Which specific resources you'll need depends, of course, on your story. This section directs you to some standard, information-rich sources that often serve as the first line of inquiry.

Public Records

The various branches of Canadian government, as in liberal democracies everywhere, operate (or are supposed to) on the principle of transparency. All government activities—from the decisions in the Prime Minister's Office to spend $50 on pencil sharpeners to debates in municipal committee meetings about which farms the new airport will expropriate—are recorded and filed, largely accessible to any member of the public to view. Such records can be invaluable to a journalist who wants to fully understand not only what government did or didn't decide, but how it arrived at the decision, under whose influence, and in consideration of what facts.

Governments also collect information on individuals. Many personal dealings leave a paper trail in birth, death, driving, property transfer, and other records. Valpy, for instance, unearthed a divorce affidavit filed in Massachusetts through which he learned cult officials had snatched the grandchildren of one of the cult "Mothers" from their mother. Vaillant got his hands on coroner and coast-guard reports, as well as police records. Business and legal dealings can also often be traced through SEDAR (the agency that tracks all publicly owned Canadian businesses), licensing offices, deeds, mortgages, and court records. "I often start probing court filings in the very early stages of research," says business reporter Wells. "And then I

Glad You Asked!   Gaining Access

Q: How do I navigate the information laws?
A: Most writers get their information from interviews and easily accessible articles and documents. But sometimes, they have to dig deeper.

The federal *Access to Information Act* (ATI) and provincial freedom of information (FOI) laws give all Canadians the right to petition government departments and agencies for specific public records. Filing a request involves submitting either a letter or a standardized form to the organization's information office. (A list of federal ATI coordinators can be found on each of the federal department websites; provincial information and privacy commissioner offices can direct you to their coordinators.) Here are some search tips from the experts:*

1. Ask first. The information you're looking for may be available without jumping through any ATI or FOI hoops. Also try an online search in a few different search engines: governments post numerous reports and documents online.
2. Learn the system. Figure out how records are stored and maintained, what terminology is used, and how the agency or department is structured. You can do this best by focusing on one or two departments you're keen to explore first, and calling staff to ask for help.
3. Cut to the chase. If you know what you're looking for, provide as many details and as short a time frame as possible in your request. Again, a call to someone working in the organization can help you zone in on the relevant details, but you can also check out directories of government information

cherry pick the stuff that might bear the most fruit," such as filings with names of people and businesses related to her story's main subject.

The treasure of public records is not located in one trove but scattered among various federal, provincial, county, and municipal offices, courthouses, and websites. You can link to some essential public records by checking the "Feature Writing" page at J-Source.ca (where you can also find links to other key Web-based research resources, and updates to links mentioned in this chapter). For a more complete directory, however, consult the investigative journalism text *Digging Deeper: A Canadian Reporter's Research Guide.*[2]

Just because it's in a government file doesn't mean you've got a right to see it. Public access to information *is* the default principle of Canadian and provincial legislation, and anything not widely accessible can be requested (sometimes for a fee) by contacting the appropriate government office (see page 64 for tips on filing requests). But individuals have a right to privacy,

such as the federal government's Info Source (www.infosource.gc.ca) or CAIR, the Coordination of Access to Information Requests system. A database of filed requests on CBC investigative reporter David McKie's website (www.onlinedemocracy.ca) takes you through the steps in searching the CAIR database (see also page 66).

4. Slice and dice. If your request is broad, consider breaking it up into a number of smaller requests, limited by shorter date ranges perhaps (the first five hours of ATI searches costs only $5, while the fee for longer searches increases exponentially).

5. Know your rights. Read the ATI or relevant FOI acts to learn what records you do and don't have a right to see; the length of response time permitted (generally governments must respond at least initially within 30 days); the fees and other processing details (such as your right to have documents shipped to the nearest government office so you can avoid hefty photocopying fees).

6. Be vigilant. Carefully track the dates of your request and their response, and file a complaint if and when the department misses a deadline.

7. Be patient and persistent.

Sue Ferguson

* These tips combine advice from two sources: Robert Cribb, Dean Jobb, David McKie, and Fred Vallance-Jones, *Digging Deeper: A Canadian Reporter's Research Guide* (Don Mills, ON: Oxford University Press, 2006), pp. 154–63; and David Pugliese, "A Handy Guide to Using Canada's Access to Information Law," *Media*, Spring 2006, 10–11. You can link directly to all online resources mentioned above, and others, from the "Feature Writing" page at J-Source.ca.

and the government has the prerogative of withholding some information. Provincial information and privacy laws deny access to most personal records (tax and health records, for example) and, depending on the jurisdiction, may exclude some public institutions (such as universities and hospitals). Moreover, any information jeopardizing national security is out of bounds.

What does and doesn't get released is, in the first instance, up to the bureaucrats administering the request. And the trend in recent years is to share less and less information with journalists: according to a Canadian Newspaper Association audit of the nearly 30,000 freedom of information requests made in 2006–7, only 23.1 percent disclosed all information in the document, down from 28.4 percent the year before.[3] In 2007, the government stopped publishing a monthly index that tracked all successful federal information requests. Journalists have been sifting through CAIR, the Coordination of Access to Information Requests system (available online through David McKie's website: www.onlinedemocracy.ca), since 1989 to help sharpen their own requests for information and to review and identify potentially sensitive information that may be already released but not widely publicized. It's important to point out that such reluctance to share information is built into the bureaucratic nature of officialdom. Citing a report by former federal information commissioner John Reid, the authors of *Digging Deeper* point out, "the test used by officials is: 'If in doubt, keep it secret.'"[4] Journalists, as a result, are often left with two options: either drop the ball, or kick it into a lengthy, sometimes costly, appeal process.

Other Researchers

Where better to look for a deeper understanding than by approaching another researcher—someone who has spent years reading, writing, and thinking about the very topic you're investigating? Canada has a rich research community, and most of its members are willing to share their knowledge with journalists free of charge. They not only provide insight, perspective, and information, they can be invaluable leads to further contacts, often people directly affected by the issue at hand.

Much publicly funded research is directly managed by government agencies and ministries. Studies are regularly posted on ministry or department websites (try looking under "Publications" or "What's New"), or a quick phone call to communications staff can point you in the right direction.

Statistics Canada maintains a deep archive of material online (as well as at a number of "depository libraries" across Canada). If you can't find what you're looking for, call its media relations office. Staff will work with you to develop a search, and run it on their in-house databases. While there may be a charge for this service, most searches for journalists are free.

Governments also fund other people's research. Agencies such as the Social Sciences and Humanities Research Council of Canada and The Ontario Trillium Foundation keep online records of successful grant proposals, and can be useful directories of research topics and experts.

Universities are another invaluable resource. Valpy consults frequently with what he calls his "little advisory group" of scholars—academics from a handful of universities that he's kept in touch with over the years and who, collectively, he says, represent a "huge personal knowledge base." But you don't need Valpy's personal connections: any university website or communications office can put you in touch with its experts.

Another place to look is publishing houses and journals. Usually a glance through the last few catalogues and issues (the titles are almost always available online) can offer up names of experts in defined areas or, in the case of journals, actual studies.

A lot of other professionals also have research expertise. Some, such as physicians, lawyers, and bankers may be hard to get on the phone, but if going through the relevant communications office doesn't work, try calling their office directly. You'd be surprised at how polite persistence with an executive assistant—and a promise not to take up too much time—can pay off. Other professionals are generally more accessible to the media. Investment firms, for instance, expect their analysts to speak with reporters. And professional associations for teachers, dentists, psychologists, and air-traffic controllers, among others, can usually scare up a warm body.

Charities, foundations, and other independent agencies also study social issues or fund research about everything from rare diseases to boreal forests. And then there are the gazillion smaller advocacy and citizenship groups such as Ontario's People for Education, or the British Columbia Childhood Cancer Parents Association. While not all of them have resources to carry out research, members are almost always well versed in the issues, and well enough connected to the community they represent to point to local examples and contacts. Beyond government and independent organizations, unions, corporations, and political parties regularly carry out research, although they may not always be willing to freely share the results. Check the "Feature Writing" page at J-Source.ca for links to online directories of experts and international research sites.

The Global Information Commons

Canada's research community is indeed vast. But that doesn't mean you shouldn't look outside its borders as well for research and experts. Here are just two places you can start looking:

1. **The United Nations** (www.un.org) and its many agencies—such as the World Health Organization, UNICEF, and the International Labour Organization—conduct studies on peace and security, economic and social development, human rights, and much, much more.
2. **The Organisation for Economic Co-operation and Development** (www.oecd.org) allows you to browse by topic or country, maintains a mountain of statistics, and includes a "Resources for Journalists" page.

Clearly, information coming from the private sector and political parties must be carefully weighed. Certain interests and agendas—to increase profits (business), bolster reputations (politicians), promote the welfare of their members (unions)—can get in the way of "balanced and objective" research. But it's important to be aware of the biases and social, political, and economic agendas informing *any* research organization or study. Sometimes you can figure this out by looking at the source of the funding: government-funded research is supposed to be carried out in the public interest, while independent foundations and institutes may serve a more particular interest, even those claiming to be "non-partisan." Check past references to them in the press (are they described as left- or right-leaning?) and poke around their websites. The Fraser Institute, for example, includes this pro-business statement in its mission statement: "Our vision is a free and prosperous world where individuals benefit from greater choice, competitive markets, and personal responsibility."[5] You can also check them out on SourceWatch, a US-based project of the Center for Media and Democracy that tracks corporate and independent organizations (www.sourcewatch.org).

Finally, one overlooked resource is the media themselves—both their products and their journalists. Newspaper, TV, and radio archives can be a gold mine—providing background and historical information. I've hunted around in the CBC archives listening to cookbook author and journalist Kate Aitken report on Hitler, Stalin, and Mussolini in between tips for decorating cakes and making nine-day pickles. For the Grenville story, Valpy spoke with a former publisher of the Brockville *Recorder and Times*. One of his reporters had looked into the school in the 1980s, and while he didn't publish the story at the time, he had held onto a copy of it, which he turned over to Valpy. The media can be excellent sources as well for local knowledge in the here and now. Sally Armstrong does a lot of her reporting on the road—in Afghanistan, Swaziland, and Iqaluit, for example. Her advice? "If you're in a place where you've never been before, go to the local reporters. They are an often ignored source that invariably has valuable information."

Google Schmoogle: Learn to Love Your Librarian

A search engine is a research tool with amazing reach—and we'll talk more about how to make the most of it in "Living on the Line" below. First, though, let's look at what it *cannot* do. It cannot tell you how the information within its grasp is organized; it cannot offer advice on how to find what you need; it cannot access all that many books, films, or music free of charge; it cannot take your request and connect it to a whole other area of research you've never heard about; it cannot automatically sort the reliable from the less reliable source; it cannot teach you how to use it and other electronic research media. In all these ways, search engines don't hold a feather to a living, breathing librarian.

Librarians are information *professionals*. And if ever there was a need for such a pro, it is now, in an age of information overload. Usually holding a master's degree in information science, librarians are experts in locating both scholarly and public knowledge—including, but not limited to, the books and papers that are the heart and soul of most libraries. They usually maintain strong reference sections, navigate and organize electronic resources using the latest technologies, keep current with what is getting published, and collect and manage rare special collections. And the best thing about librarians? They're hired to help you. "I've never mastered the library system," says Vaillant. "I kind of bumble through. But when I think of something I need," he adds, "I just ask."

Libraries house much more than books, of course. They have maps, photos, microfiche, official documents, and special collections such as the Northwest history holdings at Vancouver Public Library and the Drouin Collection at Montreal-based Jewish Public Library (a microfiche of Quebec's birth, death, and marriage records kept by religious dominations). Cruise a university or local library website, and you'll find free access to hundreds of info-rich databases of journal articles, news and magazine stories, reference material, and more. A sampling of such databases is posted, with links, on the "Feature Writing" page at J-Source.ca.

It's worth pausing to sing the praises of the lowly book, and for our purposes, the non-fiction variety especially. Books are big and comprehensive. Some, such as encyclopedias and directories, have the virtue of bringing together scattered bits of information in one place. Others, such as biographies and accounts of current or historical events, integrate information into a framework, an explanatory context. That's why Valpy, for instance, reached for the autobiography of a former headmaster of Grenville. More than anything else, the text helped him develop a more comprehensive picture, allowing him to understand the chronology of events, as well as providing him with names of priests who were advisers to the bishop at the time.

Pulling Teeth, or Getting Information from Reluctant Sources

Most people share information surprisingly freely. But you will inevitably bump up against some who won't. Sometimes you do have to simply walk away—but don't walk too soon. The power of persuasion is a skill—one that is mastered by practising both patience and respect.

Notice I use the term *persuasion*. Hostility, bullying, or sulking rarely works. To nail his story, Valpy needed to convince two very different groups of people to speak: those directly abused on the one hand, and those responsible for covering it up on the other. Both groups had plenty of reasons to keep quiet. Many of the former students blamed themselves, says Valpy. Some even had parents still living in the Community of Jesus compound and were concerned about straining already tenuous familial connections. Attentive to these psychological nuances, Valpy proceeded gently. He was, in some ways, their confessor, and he acted with the degree of confidentiality appropriate to that position. Valpy talked to the students both on and off the record, assuring them he would only publish their names with their agreement. "I didn't press them," he says. He did, however, ask some if they were considering launching a formal complaint against the church, which they eventually did. At that point, he says, "the floodgate opened."

For those who raise eyebrows at the ethics of Valpy's involvement in the story, he simply says, "I was a correspondent in Africa at the end of *apartheid*, and witnessed terrible police oppression. It occurred to me then that journalistic objectivity is a load of nonsense. You can't be objective about racism. And you can't be objective about child abuse." In other words, there are times when the nature of the story you're working on invites you to take a stand.

As for the church officials he interviewed, the local Anglican bishop was "very quick to stop talking," says Valpy. In dealing with higher church authorities, however, Valpy was confident he had the upper hand. "They needed me more than I needed them." That is, because Valpy and the *Globe* were already committed to the story, the church quickly realized it was in its best interest to put its side of the story in the public eye.

Getting reluctant sources to see their interest in sharing information is at the heart of the art of persuasion. It was the principle behind Carl Bernstein's and Bob Woodward's reporting in the 1972 Watergate scandal. It was how *Maclean's* magazine initially convinced all of Canada's 46 universities to take part in their 1991 rankings. (When 26 universities pulled out in 2006, the magazine sweet-talked some of them back in, and worked around others by using access-to-information requests and information from third parties, including government and educational granting agencies.) And it is how journalists operate every day.

But getting reluctant sources to speak takes trust, and trust is something you have to earn. Valpy has been reporting on religion in Canada for eight years, and has built that trust by striving always to be accurate and write knowledgeably about the issues. Students and people new to journalism don't have that luxury. So how else can you build trust? Vaillant likens the research process to an invasion. Journalists are outsiders digging around in other people's business. To be welcomed in, they must show respect. "You should always approach your subject with great humility, rather than with a sense of entitlement," he advises. It helps "to sniff around the edges" first— learn as much as possible about your subject or the issue you're reporting on before you reach for the fruit on the vine. If you've taken the time to inform yourself and develop a sensibility for the subject, you gain common ground with the interviewee: they sense that you too take the issue seriously. To gain the trust of the Haida elders, Vaillant spoke first with anglophones who, as he puts it "knew the scene." And to reach Cora Gray, Hadwin's Haida friend, Vaillant approached her son, and then her sister. "Finally," says the writer, "she received me." But even then, he needed to *earn* her trust. Initially claiming to have burned all of Hadwin's personal letters and papers, Gray eventually handed Vaillant a box stuffed with the valuable written records. Clearly, his research and patience had paid off.

Sally Armstrong suggests another trust-building method: if possible, spend time with your subject prior to the start of the official interview. That way the interviewee is more relaxed and has a better sense of who you are as a person.

At the same time, the journalist gets to know the subject better, size up her or his personality, and assess how far, and how quickly, to push.

And when her subject holds back? Armstrong starts gently negotiating. "I ask, 'Why does this make you uncomfortable?' and 'What if we were to approach it this way?'" She recalls a cover story on Barbara Amiel, columnist and former media baron Conrad Black's wife, at a time when the rumour mill was abuzz with reports of Amiel's health failing. Armstrong waited until she was well into her second interview with Amiel, when she felt she had established some familiarity and trust. Then, she asked: "How are you handling the gossip about your health?" Armstrong didn't, she stresses, ask, "What's your health problem?" Instead of a demand for information, she extended an empathetic question. When Amiel still refused to discuss it, Armstrong said, truthfully: "I can't ignore it. We can go with the gossip, or you can tell your story." The result? "She gave me the details," says Armstrong.

Living on the Line

The online universe is like our own physical universe: constantly expanding into a seemingly limitless void. You can't possibly expect to explore it thoroughly, but you can learn to explore it smartly.

The most well-worn Internet tool is the search engine. And the most well-worn search engine is Google—preferred for its ease of use and its commitment to sidelining (if not eliminating) advertising. But there are many others, with slightly different features. (Internet aficionado Julian Sher offers a directory to search engines and their capacities on his JNet site at www.journalismnet. com/search/best.htm.) One drawback of Google, for instance, is that it ranks sites primarily by popularity, which, if you're looking for information not already widely known, may not be a great place to start. Ask.com, on the other hand, ranks by the number of subject-related pages, while Yahoo! Search (<http://search.yahoo.com>) ranks by relevance (that is, how frequently the search term appears). Some specialized engines, such as Librarians' Internet Index (<http://lii.org>) and Google Directory (www.google.com/dirhp) pre-sort information into broad categories such as "Business," "Kids and Teens," and "Consumers > Advocacy and Protection."[6]

Almost all these sites offer either a choice between a simple search, in which you key in a relevant word or phrase, and an advanced search, where you limit the search by specifying such "operators" as domain name and suffix. (To access, for example, only Manitoba government sites, specify "gov.mb.ca.") Depending on the site, you can also search by document type (PDF or Excel, perhaps), title, region, date, and more. To paraphrase Bill Dedman, who maintains a *Columbia Journalism Review* site on web searching (www. powerreporting.com), rather than putting in a little and expecting a lot back, put a lot into your search engine, and get back specifically what you want.

On some sites, as well, simple searches yield clustered responses or related links. For example, if you type "phthalates" (a chemical used in many plastics in North America but banned in the European Union) into Ask.com, up pops (along with the usual grocery list of sites in the main part of the screen) a left-hand column with two complementary indexes: one that narrows the search (for example, "Phthalates in Cosmetics," "Phthalates in Toys," and "Asthma and Phthalates"); another that broadens it (for example, "Plastic Ingredients," "Chemicals in Plastics" and, illustrating the short-comings of broad-based searches, "Puerto Rican Girls"). On the right side of the screen, another column lists links to encyclopedic, video, and blog sites about this controversial chemical compound.

Search engines often adopt a few easy short-cut systems developed by librarians. The first, and most common, is to group search terms in quotation marks or round brackets, indicating you only want sites that include that particular phrase (as opposed to including both words in the phrase—for instance, "golden spruce" and not "golden" and "spruce"). Others include Boolean (a specialized terminology to combine or exclude certain words) and truncation (replacing word endings with a "wild card," usually an asterisk)—both systems are explained on most library websites, including www.collectionscanada.gc.ca (look under "Search Tips").

Rather than simply gathering information, journalists sometimes use online sources to *analyze* information. The term for this is *computer-assisted reporting* (CAR), and it refers to manipulating statistics (usually accessed online) by running them through such database programs as Excel. In so doing, journalists can add new meaning to raw figures—how the pollution index for various communities, for example, has changed between 1969 and 2009, or which universities attract the biggest or most grants in different areas. While it sounds potentially scary, especially for those of us who avoid number crunching at all costs, some of the simplest calculations can reveal intriguing, fresh information. To learn the basics of Excel and CAR, check out the "Microsoft Excel Tips" page at CAR*in*Canada (www.carincanada.ca), a site maintained by investigative reporter Fred Vallance-Jones.

Finally, remember: while the web *is* an amazing tool, it has a limited function for journalists. "The good stuff is out in the world," says Vaillant. "There's no substitute for the power of being there." On which point, you will read much more in the next three chapters.

Organizing Your Research

So you're done with the digging and delving. You're now staring at a stack of notepads, reports, and transcripts, and your mind is swirling. What do you do? If you're Michael Valpy, you pause and get some fresh air. "I go for long walks by myself to try to fit the information together," he says. It's a good idea, and one that's backed up by science: exercise and movement, studies show, can stimulate creativity and mental well-being.[7] What's more, shifting your environment helps you pull back from the myriad of details, and assess the totality of your work, helping you see how the pieces settle into place.

It's useful at this stage to recall your story's theme. Zoning in on the core of your story helps sort the essential from the extraneous. And an outline is like a map from which you can navigate your notes, slotting different bits of information and insights into defined categories. This is the moment, as well, to identify both what's missing and what's unclear or potentially inaccurate. Spend some time plugging these holes now, and the writing will flow more easily later. But don't research endlessly. "I used to never stop researching," says Bethune of *Maclean's*. "Now I know much better. There's probably some scientific formula like, you can make 3.6 good points per story. It doesn't do you any good to have your tenth insight." As for Vaillant, he stops, he says, "when I start boring myself."

The next step is to review your notes and organize them. "I like binders," says Jennifer Wells, especially if the story is complex. One story about the alleged theft of a Fabergé egg in Calgary involved compiling interview transcripts, news clippings, court filings, private investigation reports, and more. "It was so layered, I realized I had to start a formal filing system. By the end I had a three-inch thick binder of material, all tabulated." Others rely on cruder tools. Sally Armstrong calls her method of organizing "hideous," referring to how messy it looks to the outsider. "I have a certain way of turning pages down, asterisking some points, scratching three lines beside others," she says. "It means everything to me and nothing to anybody else." But that doesn't matter. The point is to have some sort of method that makes sense to you—so that when you return to your notes for that juicy quote someone gave you three weeks ago, you can find it easily, without having to read through the entire interview again.

Digging Takes Thinking

If, as T.S. Eliot admonishes, we have lost knowledge in the flood of information, it is the job of a feature writer to find it. And a strong research ethic and practice will set you off in the right direction. The methods and pace of research will vary from person to person, and from story to story. But the smart researcher will bear in mind the points emphasized in this chapter:

- Start early; research takes time.
- Know what you're looking for and stay focused, even as you remain open to other possibilities.
- Cast your net widely in the early stages.
- Learn your way around government records and the wider research community, and be attuned to their agendas.
- Respect your sources, and figure out how to woo or get around uncooperative sources.
- Appreciate what the Internet *can* and *cannot* deliver, and what a librarian can.
- When you're done digging, stand back, assess, verify, and organize.

Research involves not just doing; it involves thinking. Valpy recalls a profile he wrote of Michael Ignatieff, for which the Liberal Party deputy leader granted him a short one-hour interview. "I spent eight weeks researching," he says. "I spent as much time walking and thinking about what I'd been told as I spent interviewing and reading." Still, because research is a messy, creative process, enlightenment is often preceded by confusion. "I had a lot of anxious moments," he adds. "I'd come back from some walks with a *eureka!* moment, others frustrated." Those frustrations led him back to the phones, papers, and computer—back to the doing, the culling of information.

After all, information *is* the guts of the process, and knowing how and where to find it is essential. Yet the understanding, the knowledge gained and then reflected in the story you write, comes only through thinking carefully about what that information means. And it's in combining practical fact-gathering skills with thoughtful reflection that you will arrive at the insight and knowledge required to give your story depth, originality, and resonance.

Discussion Questions

1. **Goals of research:** Basic news reports summarize what happened and what others have said, but feature writing demands thoughtfulness, the cultivation of perspective, and deep understanding. Read "The Golden Bough" by John Vaillant (pages 77–89). Using a newspaper database, find one of the original stories about the destruction of the golden spruce in 1997, and compare it with Vaillant's treatment of the subject. How do

the stories differ? How does the additional research involved in writing a feature story expand and enhance your understanding of the issue?

2. **Story makers:** What details and characters in Vaillant's story make the feature particularly compelling? Why? How does the quality of his sources affect the overall quality and impact of the story?

3. **Learning leanings:** Every source has a potential bias, especially those associated with "think tanks" that double as lobby groups. How would you classify the following research organizations? Why?

- Canadian Centre for Policy Alternatives
- C.D. Howe Institute
- Canadian Automobile Association
- Frontier Centre for Public Policy
- Society for the Advancement of Excellence in Education
- CATO Institute (US)
- Canadian Coalition for Responsible Environmental Solutions
- David Suzuki Foundation

Notes

1. Blundell made these points in a 1982 interview excerpted in Roy Peter Clark and Christopher Scanlan, *America's Best Newspaper Writing: A Collection of ASNE Prizewinners* (Boston and New York: Bedford/St. Martin's Press, 2001), p. 131.

2. Robert Cribb, Dean Jobb, David McKie, and Fred Vallance-Jones, *Digging Deeper: A Canadian Reporter's Research Guide* (Don Mills, ON: Oxford University Press, 2006).

3. Canadian Newspaper Association, "National Freedom of Information Audit," <http://www.cna-acj.ca/Client/CNA/cna.nsf/object/ FOIAUDIT07/$file/FOI%20AUDIT%20REPORT-English.pdf> (accessed February 5, 2008).

4. Cribb et al., *Digging Deeper*, p. 153.

5. "Who We Are," *The Fraser Institute*, <http://www.fraserinstitute.org/ aboutus/whoweare/mission.htm> (accessed April 24, 2008).

6. If any of these links or strategies are out of date by the time you read this, you can find updates on the "Feature Writing" page at www.J-Source.ca.

7. See, for instance, David M. Blanchette, Stephen P. Ramocki, John N. O'del, and Michael S. Casey, "Aerobic Exercise and Cognitive Creativity: Immediate and Residual Effects," *Creativity Research Journal* 17, no. 2&3 (2005): 257–64.

"The Golden Bough"

Grant Hadwin got a chainsaw and did something terrible.

John Vaillant, "The Golden Bough." Copyright © 2002 by John Vaillant. Reprinted by permission of the Stuart Krichevsky Literary Agency Inc. This article originally appeared in *The New Yorker*. New York: November 4, 2002. Volume 78, no. 33, 50.

There was only one giant golden spruce in the world, and, until a man named Grant Hadwin took a chainsaw to it, in 1997, it had stood for more than three hundred years in a steadily shrinking patch of old-growth forest in Port Clements, on the banks of the Yakoun River, in the Queen Charlotte Islands. The Queen Charlottes, a blade-shaped archipelago that lies sixty miles off the northern coast of British Columbia and thirty miles south of the Alaskan coast, are one of a decreasing number of places in the Pacific Northwest where large stands of virgin coastal forest can still be found. Ecotourism is a growth industry here, and the golden spruce was a popular stop on visitors' itineraries. The tree was also sacred to the Haida Indians, two thousand of whom still live on the islands.

The golden spruce was remarkable enough to warrant its own scientific name: *Picea sitchensis* 'Aurea.' The tree, a Sitka spruce, lacked eighty per cent of a normal specimen's allotment of chlorophyll, and, as a result, its needles were golden yellow instead of green. Unlike a typical Sitka spruce, which sends its branches off haphazardly, the golden spruce was, for reasons no one can explain, perfectly coniform. It stood out in the deep, green forest like a giant yellow Christmas tree. Several other golden spruces are rumored to exist in the Queen Charlottes, but they reportedly lack their famous counterpart's distinctive shape and are smaller and less uniformly yellow than the Yakoun River specimen, which had been standing long enough to be named K'iid K'iyass (Old Tree) by the Haida people and to be incorporated into their oral history.

On the night of January 20, 1997, Grant Hadwin, then forty-seven, stripped off his clothes and plunged into the Yakoun River, towing a chainsaw behind him. The river was swift and the water was cold, but this was no problem for Hadwin, a self-described "extreme swimmer" who had alarmed local police in Whitehorse, Yukon, earlier that winter by spending a quarter of an hour in the Yukon River when the air temperature was thirty-five degrees below zero. The golden spruce was more than six feet in diameter, and Hadwin's chainsaw had only a twenty-five-inch bar, but Hadwin had worked in the timber industry for years, and he knew how to make falling cuts. Leaving just enough of the core intact so that the tree would stand until the next windstorm, he returned by ferry from the island to the mainland port town of Prince Rupert. Shortly afterward, copies of a letter he had drafted were received by Greenpeace, the Vancouver *Sun*, members of the Haida Nation, and MacMillan Bloedel, Canada's biggest lumber company, which had a timber lease on the land on which the golden spruce stood. The letter said, in part:

> I didn't enjoy butchering, this magnificent old plant, but you apparently need a message and wake-up call, that even a university trained profes- sional, should be able to understand.... I mean this action, to be an expression, of my rage and hatred, towards university trained profes- sionals and their extremist supporters, whose ideas, ethics, denials, part truths, attitudes, etc., appear to be responsible, for most of the abomina- tions, towards amateur life on this planet.

The golden spruce fell a couple of days later. Locally, the reaction was extraordinary. "It was like a drive-by shooting in a small town," one resident of the islands told me. "People were crying; they were in shock. They felt enor- mous guilt for not protecting the tree better." This was in part because, accord- ing to Haida legend, the golden spruce represented a person; and, later, a public memorial service for the tree, presided over by several Haida chiefs, was held "to mourn one of our ancestors." But beyond the mourning, some Haida, as well as residents of the mostly white logging community of Port Clements (where the tree had stood), wanted revenge.

Hadwin was located quickly by the Royal Canadian Mounted Police, and, after being charged and ordered to appear at the courthouse in Masset, which is close to the Queen Charlottes' two remaining Haida communities, he was released on his own recognizance. Hadwin, who was already known to—and suspicious of—the police, was offered no protection and did not request it. "They're making it as nasty as they possibly can," he told a reporter at the time. "They'll want me over there so the natives will have a shot. It would probably be suicide to go over there real quick."

Hadwin could have flown or taken a ferry from the mainland to Masset, but he chose instead to travel to court by kayak, leading people to believe that he was going to attempt a sixty-mile midwinter crossing of the notoriously dan- gerous Hecate Strait. In fact, Hadwin was last seen paddling north—bound, it seemed, for Alaska.

Throughout his turbulent and peripatetic life, Grant Hadwin demonstrated a level of woodsmanship and an imperviousness to the elements worthy of a character from the pages of Robert Service or Jack London. His wife, Margaret, from whom he has been separated for a decade, described him as "indestructible," an opinion shared by many who have known him. "Basically, you're dealing with a person who, with very few resources, could be dropped anywhere on earth and come up smelling like a rose," Cory Delves, one of Hadwin's former bosses, told me.

Hadwin always felt most at home in the forest. During his late teens and twenties, he worked as a lumberjack and gold miner and lived in the mining town of Gold Bridge, British Columbia, a five-hour drive north from Vancouver. It is a tough, marginal place that is now inhabited by fewer than a hundred people and is accessible only by rough logging roads lined with fatal drop-offs. When Hadwin first showed up there, in the mid-nineteen-sixties, the surrounding valleys were thick with virgin, high-altitude timber. Today, as in much of British Columbia, vast clear-cuts push outward in every direction, giving the mountains the appearance of enormous animals unevenly shorn of their coats. The Northwest coast is, for all practical purposes, a rain forest, and the tall timber it nurtures can live for a thousand years and grow to heights that rival California's redwoods. (A Sitka spruce taken from the same forest where the golden spruce stood left a stump seventeen feet in diameter.) It was Hadwin, in his most successful incarnation, as a forest technician, who laid out many of the roads that gave loggers access to the remote forest around Gold Bridge. In the end, he helped to raze the site of many of his happiest memories.

Hadwin was well known for outdoing his co-workers. Paul Bernier, a long-time colleague and close friend of his, told me, "He was in the best condition of any man I've ever seen." Bernier was with Hadwin when he outwitted a pair of charging grizzly bears by dodging across a stream and feinting upwind, where they couldn't smell him. In addition to consuming prodigious quantities of chewing tobacco, Hadwin was known for buying vodka by the case and going on spectacular binges that, even in freezing weather, would leave him unconscious in the back of his vintage Studebaker pickup or passed out in a snow-filled ditch, dressed only in slacks and shirtsleeves. There was a local joke: "Look, that snowbank is moving. Must be Grant."

Early photographs of Hadwin show a fine-boned, handsome man, slightly less than six feet tall and built like a distance runner. People who knew him during his Gold Bridge days likened his lean, sharp-eyed appearance and remote manner to Clint Eastwood's. Quiet and courteous though Hadwin usually was, he possessed an almost tangible intensity, a piercing, in-your-face conviction that some found alarming. "He always had to be the best, had to be first," his Aunt Barbara recalled. "It always had to be Grant's way. There was never any room for compromise."

The golden spruce wasn't discovered by scientists until it was almost three hundred years old. When the Scottish timber surveyor and baronet Sir Windham Anstruther stumbled upon it, in 1924, he was dumbfounded. "I didn't even make an axe mark on it, being, I suppose, a bit overcome by its strangeness in a forest of green," he told a reporter before he died. For years afterward, no one knew quite what to make of Sir Windham's arboreal unicorn. Some suggested that it might be a new species, unique to the archipelago; others thought the tree had been hit by lightning, or was simply dying. In fact, the golden spruce was alive and well; it was just fantastically rare. Only a chance mutation would ever produce another.

A tree with this mutation is called a "chlorotic," and although it is not uncommon to see a chlorotic branch or two on an otherwise healthy evergreen, it is in theory almost impossible for an entire tree to be chlorotic and survive. Because this condition causes a fatal intolerance to bright sunshine, no one knows why the golden spruce was able to compete so well against healthy trees for centuries, or why it was able to grow to more than a hundred and sixty feet tall. Some contemporary scientists believe the tree's success may have been due to the unique lighting conditions afforded by its location. The Charlottes are sometimes called the Misty Isles; they share southeast Alaska's weather (as much as twelve feet of rain per year), and direct sunshine is a rare occurrence. It is conceivable that the island's climate provided just enough light to facilitate photosynthesis and turn the needles yellow, while diffusing the light sufficiently to keep the needles from burning out and dropping off. D'Arcy Davis-Case, a forestry expert who lived in the Queen Charlottes for years before becoming a consultant to the United Nations on forestry issues, said that when she lived there botanists and dendrologists were always trying to explain the tree's golden color. When I asked what they had concluded, she smiled and rolled her eyes. "Magic!" she said.

To those who were lucky enough to have seen the tree in bright sunshine, Davis-Case's explanation sounds plausible enough. Many who saw the golden spruce spoke of its peculiar radiance, as if it were actually generating light from deep within its branches. Marilyn Baldwin, the owner of a sporting-goods store in Prince Rupert, saw the tree on a gray, foggy day in the early nineties. "A few minutes after we got there, the sun burned the fog off, and suddenly there it was in its golden brilliance," she recalled. "We called it the ooh-aah tree, because that's what it made us all say." Ruth Jones, a Vancouver-based artist, visited the golden spruce late one sunny afternoon in 1994. "It looked as if it were made of glowing gold," she said. "It was like a fairy tale. How can this be?"

The Queen Charlottes have always had a somewhat mystical reputation; even loggers and land-use planners employ the adjective "magic" to describe them. The hundred-and-eighty-mile-long chain comprises the most remote of all the West Coast islands, and, in many ways, they are a world apart, hosting species and subspecies that occur nowhere else. The Haida language, too, is an "isolate," unrelated to that of any other West Coast tribe, and the largest collection of historic totem poles in North America that still survive in their original, beachfront locations are situated here.

Haida warriors, who ranged widely throughout the North Pacific, became legendary for a ferocity and maritime daring comparable to that of the Vikings. One of their seagoing canoes—sixty-three feet long and hewed from a single log—is on permanent display at the American Museum of Natural History, in New York. During the nineteenth century, the Haida's numbers were reduced from as many as twenty thousand to fewer than six hundred by warfare and a biological holocaust of smallpox and venereal disease which accompanied British and American fur traders, settlers, and missionaries. Many of the survivors converted to Christianity and were absorbed into the nascent fishing and logging industries. Since then, these core industries have been practiced in a rapacious and indiscriminate fashion, and today the numbers of fish and old-growth trees have been reduced almost as dramatically as those of the Haida.

In the mid-sixties, MacMillan Bloedel had reluctantly set aside the few acres of old-growth forest remaining around the golden spruce. In 1988, after a long battle that pitted logging interests and the British Columbia government against a coalition of environmental groups and the Haida, the southern half of the chain was designated a national park reserve that includes a UNESCO World Heritage Site. The land is currently owned by the Canadian government ("the Crown"), which leases it to MacMillan Bloedel, which is now owned by Weyerhaeuser. Before long, tour buses began lining up to see the tree, and in 1996 the local tourist trade got an additional boost when an albino raven showed up, one of only two known to exist in the entire country. Between it and the golden spruce, Port Clements had cornered the freak-of-nature market in western Canada.

∾∾∾

Despite his mountain-man pretensions, Thomas Grant Hadwin could never wholly conceal his middle-class origins. He was born into an educated family from West Vancouver. His father graduated at the top of his class from the University of British Columbia's electrical-engineering program and became a senior engineer with BC Hydro, the province's biggest power company. Grant was the younger of two sons, who were brought up to be like their father— competitive and stubborn. Nothing, however, went as planned: Grant's older brother was given a diagnosis of paranoid schizophrenia, and Grant quit school and left home at seventeen.

Grant headed north, first working for a maternal uncle who owned a logging company that was engaged in clear-cutting the valleys above Vancouver. He was ideally suited to the work, and the isolated life style captured his imagination, not least because it flew in the face of his father's professional ambitions. But, even as Hadwin relished the bush life, he was horrified by what he saw. His paternal aunt, Barbara Johnson, recalls that Grant, who visited her as a teenager, described logging techniques that stripped the mountainsides down to bare rock. "Nothing's going to grow there again," he told her.

Meanwhile, his brother had become increasingly ill, and in 1971 he killed himself in a leap from the Lions Gate Bridge, in Vancouver. By this time, Grant had migrated to Gold Bridge, where he, too, with his excessive drinking, appeared to be well on his way to an early death. By the mid-nineteen-seventies, though, he seemed to right himself. He earned a forest technician's degree and, in 1978, he swore off alcohol and got married; Grant and Margaret, who was a nurse from Lillooet, about sixty miles away, had three children. In order to house his family, Grant built what would be the most imposing residence in Gold Bridge, two and a half stories tall and made entirely of hand-hewn logs. The capstone on the oversized chimney was a mattress-size slab of granite that weighed more than four tons.

Hadwin had also found his calling. After he had worked as a logger, a rock driller, a blaster, and a prospector, Evans Wood Products, in Lillooet, put him in charge of surveying "merchantable" timber in the deep wilderness and laying out roads to make it accessible. By most accounts, Hadwin was extremely good in the field, but this did not help him at the office. In 1983, Hadwin lost out on a major promotion. (He had been inserting critiques of the company into his written memos.) "He was out of time," Brian Tremblay, who has known Hadwin since they were teen-agers, recalled. "He was on his own trajectory. He was talking environment and proper forest management before anybody."

Hadwin believed in balance—in taking the good with the bad, the best with the bug-ridden—when it was standard practice to just skim the cream and move on. He quit Evans Products on bitter terms and went to work on his own. By this time, the impact of logging on the country around Gold Bridge had become painfully clear. According to Ecotrust, an Oregon-based conservation group, California, Oregon, and Washington have lost ninety per cent of their combined coastal rain forest, while British Columbia, which originally had twice as much forest area, has lost forty per cent. Hadwin was aware of this, and so is Al Wanderer, who worked with Hadwin in the early eighties. "We basically gutted the place," he told me last October, referring to some of the logging around Gold Bridge. "Good God," he went on, "I didn't think it was possible to log this much." Wanderer looked down into his beer and added, "I've made a good living, but sometimes you wonder if it's all worth it."

Hadwin struggled to find a way to remain gainfully employed in the woods without gutting them. For three years after leaving Evans, he ran his own logging operation outside Gold Bridge, where he made railroad ties by cutting selectively and salvaging trees that had been killed by a beetle infestation. "That guy worked hard," his neighbor Tom Illidge said. "It would have taken three normal men to do what he did up there." Despite his superhuman efforts, Hadwin couldn't make it pay, so he went into freelance consulting, where his increasingly pro-forest views and decreasing familiarity with contemporary practices worked against him.

In 1983, when Hadwin quit his job, he was in his mid-thirties. He was opinionated and eccentric, but he was also a family man, a strenuous provider, and a helpful neighbor. "He wasn't lazy and he wasn't crazy," Tom Illidge told me. Illidge is one of Gold Bridge's oldest and most successful residents, one of the few who stayed put and prospered there. He sympathized with Hadwin's disdain for the company men who wield so much power over the forest without knowing their way around it. "Half of those assholes have never been four feet from a parking meter in their lives," he said. But while Illidge, Al Wanderer, and Corey Delves were able to swallow their irritation and press on, Hadwin had become increasingly frustrated and bitter. He began writing letters to powerful political figures all over Canada and the world. To CNN, he wrote:

> Your focus appears to be Bosnia and O.J. Simpson. Your Native American problem, however, parallels our own and yet your coverage, appears to be non-existent. ... You would apparently go to *any* lengths to deflect the focus from the real issues, which discredit yourselves or your professional institutions.

In 1991, Grant and Margaret separated, and she got custody of the children. (She continued to pay Hadwin's Visa bills, with the help of a sizable inheritance from his father.) By 1993, Hadwin had begun to experience episodes of paranoia, one of which compelled him to seek refuge on a remote island off the coast of Alaska; his rented kayak was punctured en route, and he lived off the land for twelve days before he was rescued by the Coast Guard. Later that summer, Hadwin was stopped at the United States border with three thousand hypodermic needles in the trunk of his car. He talked his way through Customs and proceeded to Washington, D.C., where he distributed the needles on the street along with condoms, presenting himself as an advocate of needle exchange and safe sex. In July, with two thousand needles remaining, he caught a plane to Moscow; from there, he continued eastward, donating needles to children's hospitals as he went. He was arrested by the police in Irkutsk, Siberia, but apparently finessed the interview and parted on good terms. Hadwin wasn't simply on a good-will mission, however; he was also looking for work. Siberia is one of the few places in the Northern Hemisphere whose forests rival British Columbia's, and shortly before he disappeared he spoke of wanting to return there.

When Hadwin came back to Kamloops, a town of eighty thousand in south-central British Columbia, where his wife and children lived, people who knew him were alarmed by what they saw. The guerrilla-theatre dress he wore on his travels (running shorts, boots with spurs, and a baseball cap festooned with needles and condoms) raised questions about his mental state. After an altercation with a truck driver, he was sent to a forensic hospital for psychiatric evaluation. Hadwin was interviewed extensively by several doctors, and, although all of them found evidence of what one psychiatrist termed "paranoid reaction," the only diagnosis they could agree on was that he was mentally competent and fit to stand trial.

Hadwin's letter-writing campaign intensified, and within this raft of letters and faxes is what seems to be a last attempt to find acceptable employment. On January 12, 1996, in response to an ad for a Forest Renewal Project coordinator, Hadwin sent his résumé, along with this self-defeatingly honest cover letter:

> I do not like clearcutting and my philosophical differences, with the Forest Industry, run deep. If you are prepared to try a "gentler approach," to forestry, with less "short term profit," I may be able to help. I am not familiar with the new "buzzwords," such as Forest Renewal. All of Forestry and most of the Forests, appear to need "renewing," in some form or another.

Hadwin didn't get the job. Five months later, he left Kamloops after be-friending Cora Gray, an elder from the Gitanmaax tribe, in British Columbia's interior. Gray had a kindly, forgiving manner, and, from shortly after they met until the day that Hadwin disappeared, she served as his closest friend and confessor. He told her everything, it seemed, except his plan to cut down the golden spruce.

That fall, Hadwin moved to a hotel in Whitehorse, Yukon, and in November he persuaded Gray to join him there. She was watching when he swam in the Yukon River, despite the arctic temperatures. "The water was smoking," Gray recalled. "When he got out, there were icicles hanging off his eyebrows and hair. He ran back to the car, where I was waiting, and he said, 'I know I'm O.K. when you're there watching me.' I asked him, 'Why are you torturing yourself?' and he said, 'I'm training myself. I won't be around here next year.' I knew he was planning something."

Local natives took Gray aside and told her they had a bad feeling about Hadwin, that she should get away from him. "When I mentioned flying home," she said, "he cried like a baby, saying, 'I think you're the only one who's ever worried about me.'" Hadwin told her not to answer the phone when her sisters called. "Finally, I persuaded him that I had to go home, and he offered to drive me. He said, 'Don't tell your sisters you're coming home; surprise them.'"

Gray and Hadwin left Whitehorse at 4 a.m. on December 30th, setting out on a fifteen-hour drive, through extremely remote country, to Gray's home in Hazelton, British Columbia. At five-thirty that afternoon, two hours north of Hazelton, they reached the one-lane bridge that spans the Nass River. Hadwin headed toward it at full speed, and, despite the bright moonlight, he failed to register that a pickup truck was crossing from the other direction. The road was icy at the entrance ramp and, at the last minute, Hadwin hit the brakes. His car, a Honda Civic, skidded and went sideways, up onto the railing. Gray believed she had reached the end of her life.

In the end, they didn't go into the Nass; they hit the pickup head on. Gray's ankles were shattered, her cheek was broken, and both hands were bruised; Hadwin suffered only a cut lip. Gray's ankles had to be repaired with screws and plates, and now she must use a walker to get around. Hadwin visited Gray in the hospital every day until he left for the Charlottes on January 12th. "I've always wondered if Grant was trying to kill us both," she said to me shortly before I left for the Charlottes, "so he wouldn't have to be alone."

∾∾∾

Once Hadwin was in the Charlottes, he gave every impression of being a man on a one-way trip. While staying in a motel at the sparsely inhabited north end of Graham Island, he gave away all his possessions. "Take whatever you want, because I'm going to burn the rest," he told Jennifer Wilson, the twenty-year-old daughter of the motel's manager. Hadwin went on at length about university-trained professionals, referring to them as "an incestuous breed of insidious manipulators." He advocated terrorism as the most effective means of bringing about change, and he talked a great deal about trees. "I learned a lot from him about the forest," Wilson told me. "I got the sense he had found his purpose."

After buying a gas can, falling wedges, and a chainsaw, Hadwin relocated to Port Clements, where he checked into the Golden Spruce motel. The last time Wilson saw him, he was wearing earplugs; he had to wear them, he told her, because every word he heard felt like a direct insult.

Hadwin's chainsaw roared through the night of January 20th. In the morning, he gave the saw to an acquaintance and returned to the mainland, where he sent his final fax, the entire text of which was published in the local papers seven days after the tree was discovered. During the following weeks, Hadwin carried on a dialogue with infuriated locals through newspapers on both sides of Hecate Strait. "Right now, people are focusing all their anger on me when they should focus it on the destruction going on around them," he told a reporter for the Queen Charlottes' *Observer*. "They should see a person who is normally very respectful of life and has done a very disrespectful thing and ask why."

But this was asking too much. Hadwin had cut down what may have been the only tree on the continent capable of bonding loggers, natives, and environmentalists in sorrow and outrage. Meanwhile, newspaper and television reporters from across Canada were coming to the Queen Charlottes to cover the story, which also found its way into the *Times* and onto the Discovery Channel. "When society places so much value on one mutant tree and ignores what happens to the rest of the forest, it's not the person who points this out who should be labelled," Hadwin told a Prince Rupert reporter who questioned his sanity. Hadwin was charged with criminal mischief—damage in excess of five thousand dollars—and the illegal cutting of timber. There was no precedent for how a local judge and jury might compute the cultural damage to the Haida, the economic damage to Port Clements, or the loss to science.

With his belongings liquidated and his safety in doubt, Hadwin was down to the contents of a single suitcase and a Visa card. Among the last items charged were an expedition-grade sea kayak, a camping tarp, a cookstove, a life vest, an axe, and a shovel—everything one would need for a long trip up the West Coast. After notifying Cora Gray, his wife, Margaret, and Prince Rupert's *Daily News*, Hadwin set off across Hecate Strait late on the afternoon of February 11th, bound for his court date. Hadwin had told everyone that he was travelling this way because he was afraid he would be attacked by locals if he took the ferry or a plane. Both Cora and Margaret notified the Mounties, who intercepted Hadwin before he left Prince Rupert Harbour, but Constable Bruce Jeffrey, an experienced kayaker and one of the officers on the scene, was unable to dissuade him. "He wasn't irrational," Jeffrey told me. "He wasn't suicidal, but I could tell he was a few fries short of a Happy Meal. Unfortunately, you can't arrest someone for being overconfident or foolish."

At dusk, with his gear stowed in fore and aft compartments and an axe and a spare paddle lashed to his forward deck, Hadwin paddled out of Prince Rupert Harbour and directly into a storm. Weather reports for that night show waves over ten feet, winds gusting to forty miles an hour, and rain; the temperature was just above freezing, but the wind-chill factor would have driven it down to zero. Hadwin was not an experienced kayaker, but even if he had been, it was unlikely that he could survive a night in such weather—and yet, somehow, he did. At dawn, he found his way back to Prince Rupert. "He was waiting at the door when we opened," recalled Marilyn Baldwin, who co-owns SeaSport, where Hadwin had bought his kayak and equipment the previous day. Hadwin had returned to buy some warmer clothes and (on Constable Jeffrey's advice) emergency flares and a chart. When the topic of the tree came up, Baldwin recalled, "He wanted to argue. I think he wanted his day in court. He got very agitated; his muscles were vibrating like something taut, ready to snap."

Early on the morning of the thirteenth, with five days left to make his court date, Hadwin set off again. This time, he didn't come back.

When Margaret first heard that Grant was missing, she wasn't all that concerned; he had disappeared before, and he hadn't always been truthful about where he was going. The test would be whether he called his daughter on her birthday; when March 1st came and went with no phone call, Margaret began to fear the worst, and the Canadian Coast Guard began searching in earnest. No sign of him was found until four months later, in June, when large fragments of a kayak were discovered on an uninhabited island seventy miles north of Prince Rupert; the serial number matched that of the one Hadwin was known to have purchased. According to computer-generated scenarios, the boat could have drifted there from almost anywhere in Hecate Strait. This raises a host of possibilities, ranging from Hadwin's having capsized en route to Masset to the suggestion, by Blake Walkinshaw, a constable from Masset, that Hadwin "could have got a pumping" (been shot) out on the water; it is also conceivable that he was struck by another vessel—by accident, or intentionally. Equally plausible, though, is the theory that Hadwin paddled a short way up the wild, empty coast, gave his boat a push off the beach, and disappeared into the bush.

What is odd about the wreckage is that all the gear was in near-perfect condition. The fish biologist (and veteran beachcomber) who found it speculated that, based on its condition, the wreck was less than a month old. This complicates matters considerably, as does the fact that Hadwin charged three hundred dollars' worth of food on the day of his first departure. Corporal Gary Stroeder, the officer who was formerly in charge of the missing-person investigation on the Canadian side, is troubled by the location of Hadwin's axe. How, he wondered, did such a heavy object get above the high-tide line?

A number of alleged Hadwin sightings were made up and down the coast during the ensuing months, but none of them panned out, so rumors have filled the void: he was killed by Indians; he's doing time in the States for welfare fraud; he's running a trapline in Meziadin, British Columbia; he's in Siberia. Constable Walkinshaw believes that Hadwin could be alive: "The whole cop in me is saying there's something too neat about this." Constable Jeffrey, who has retired, thinks Hadwin drowned; Margaret Hadwin is trying to have her husband declared dead. But Corporal Stroeder isn't so sure. "If a coroner asked me to justify that he was dead, I wouldn't be able to," he told me, when we met in Prince Rupert. "There are too many loose ends."

One of them stretches all the way to California. Sometime during the Thanksgiving weekend of 2000, someone made a nearly fatal chainsaw cut in Luna, the massive California redwood made famous by the environmental activist Julia Butterfly Hill, who spent two years living in the tree's branches. As with the golden spruce, the cut did not fell the tree, but left it extremely vulnerable to high winds.

Port Clements, meanwhile, has suffered much; not only has the town lost its mascot (the tree is the centerpiece for the town logo) but, in November of the same year, its albino raven was electrocuted on a transformer. Yet the spruce may, in a sense, rise again; in 1997, eighty cuttings were taken from the tree as it lay dying by the Yakoun River. They were sent to a forestry-research station on Vancouver Island, where they were grafted to normal spruce seedlings and are now being held in trust for the Haida.

Last year, the Haida gave the town of Port Clements one of the grafts; it was planted in the town's millennium park, where it may be the safest tree in the Queen Charlottes. (The knee-high sapling is surrounded by a ten-foot chain-link fence topped with barbed wire.) Last June, in a private ceremony overseen by Haida elders, a second cutting was planted beside the stump of its parent tree. It is still green.

Meanwhile, Hadwin's case is still considered open by the Alaska State Troopers and the Mounties. No one has bothered to look for him in Siberia, but Cora Gray told me, "He talked about Russia a lot. He'd say, 'If I was going to choose a place to stay, it would be in Russia. Don't be surprised if you hear from me from there.' So now, when the phone rings late at night, I don't answer."

CHAPTER FOUR

Telling Pictures: Reporting and Reconstructing Scenes

David Hayes

Early in my career, I was assigned by *Toronto Life* magazine to write a story about pimps and prostitutes in Toronto. In their efforts to charge pimps—who, in addition to being brutal employers, are notoriously elusive—morality squad cops often target their "girls." I tagged along for a couple of nights with two undercover cops and at one point stood inside the tiny rented room belonging to a bespectacled young prostitute, nicknamed "Goggles," who, they knew, was being victimized by a pimp. (As one of the officers pointed out later, she was making several hundred dollars a night, yet neither her surroundings nor her clothing reflected a fraction of that.) Of course I'd been taught to "show, don't tell" in journalism school and it was obvious, at this moment, that the details of the young woman's life were telling:

> Goggles is sitting on a narrow cot in a room the size of a walk-in closet. A cracked mirror is propped above an old porcelain sink. A makeshift table is covered in bottles and tins of makeup. There are posters on the walls that might have been taken from the covers of pulp fantasy novels and several photographs of a graceless Goggles modeling department store fashions. A

tiny kitten named Minou squeaks querulously under the bed. The room is clean and very neat, as though someone is expecting guests.[1]

When you're in the middle of a scene, the heat of the moment can be distracting. Strangers may stare at you. People may ask why you're there. Resentment, even hostility, may be in the air. It can be hard to stay cool and do your job, and even the most experienced feature writers can miss things that they can never go back and retrieve. Sometimes I repeat a mantra in my head at moments like this: *take a deep breath, focus ... think ... focus ... think....*

When I was standing in Goggles's room, there was another detail that I sensed might be important. Later in the story, this is what I wrote:

> A piece of yellow paper is taped to the wall beside her closet. On it is a hand-written poem that includes the line: *Then love still taunts me with its thorny path.*[2]

The symbolism might have been too neat for fiction, but when you're writing non-fiction the things that really happen, and are really there, nearly always works. Afterward I always feel exhilarated, almost like a runner's high. It's what I call the thrill of the scene.

The Thrill of the Scene

"Show, don't tell," the fundamental rule in non-fiction writing as well as fiction, refers in large part to letting action and dialogue reveal information to readers through the use of dramatic scenes. This kind of narrative storytelling has long been published in magazines and used by writers of non-fiction books (not to mention documentary filmmakers). But in recent years there has also been a narrative revolution in newspapers in the United States and Canada as publishers and editors have come to realize that old-fashioned storytelling is the unique strength that print journalism has over other media. At the heart of this kind of reporting and writing is an ability to capture the essence of people, environments, and situations as they unfold.

If "show, don't tell" was as simple as it sounded, aspiring writers could transform themselves into working professionals without much effort. Although words can paint pictures that are rich in vivid detail, learning how to gather those details, *when* you've gathered enough raw material to tell your story, *which* details are most important, and *where* in your manuscript everything should go is what distinguishes the skilled craftsperson from the amateur. This chapter focuses on the gathering of details, both big and small, whether you're a witness at the scene—what Gay Talese calls "the fine art of hanging out"—or reconstructing events after the fact.

I think there is a kind of personality that takes to this aspect of journalism. New Yorker writer Susan Orlean once said that she "never cared … if I'm not the first one to write a story." My journalist-novelist-playwright friend David Macfarlane and I once agreed that we don't have the daily news reporter's obsession for the splashy front-page exclusive. As journalists, our obsession is learning about people's lives, exploring their worlds, seeing for ourselves how organizations or communities work.

As Macfarlane put it, so much of what we feature writers do these days is struggle to get access. He once wrote a profile on former Ontario premier Mike Harris which was a nightmare of negotiations resulting finally in a nearly useless face-to-face encounter with Harris in a boardroom accompanied by two of Harris's handlers, both armed with tape recorders. That kind of staged and artificial meeting is anathema to what makes feature writing interesting for Macfarlane. "I want to see people behaving naturally, in their element," he says. "I want to see the side of themselves they reveal to their family and friends."

When writers refer to "scenes," they mean it in the same sense as it was used in the theatre; it's action taking place within a physical setting, whether that setting is a bedroom, a ballroom, a boardroom, a ballpark, or the claustrophobic confines of a taxicab. Scenes emotionally engage readers; later, it's often these visual images and actions that readers remember.

When at a scene—whether it's 10,000 people at a demonstration or an individual interacting with one or two others in a workplace—interviewing may be involved, but a good deal of a feature writer's time is spent simply observing events as they unfold. Ted Conover, a superb literary journalist, describes this approach as "participant observation," which is the basic method used in both anthropology (his field of study in university) and qualitative sociology. "It means a reliance not on the interview so much as on the shared experience with somebody," Conover told Norman Sims for the introduction to Sims's 1995 anthology, *Literary Journalism*.[3] Conover added that he was drawn to "the idea that I could learn about different people and different aspects of the world by placing myself in situations, and thereby see more than you ever could just by doing an interview."

So the success of any feature lives or dies on a writer's ability to capture scenes in all their vivid, natural glory. And doing so is all about reporting. From the moment feature writers begin an assignment, they're thinking about how to tell the story. Most often this involves scene-by-scene construction. I suggest that you ask yourself the following as early as possible: *What are my scenes? Who are my characters?*

Here's a scene from my profile of pop crooner Michael Bublé, published in *Saturday Night* magazine. I knew from the beginning that Bublé, my profile subject, and his producer, David Foster, were going to be my main characters. I also knew where most of the scenes would take place: I'd negotiated with Bublé's management company for time with the artist in Foster's state-of-the-art recording studio on his property in Malibu, near Los Angeles, where Bublé was finishing the vocal tracks for his sophomore CD.

Glad You Asked!   A Feature Writer's Library

Q: What books should I own?
A: Well, that depends on whom you ask. But, not surprisingly, the feature writers we surveyed agreed on a list of "must-have" books in two general categories: books on how to write and books with great feature stories. Here they are.

Books on How to Write

William Blundell, *The Art and Craft of Feature Writing: Based on the Wall Street Journal Guide* (New York: New American Library, 1988)

Robert S. Boynton, *The New New Journalism: Conversations with America's Best Nonfiction Writers on Their Craft* (New York: Vintage Books, 2005)

Rene Cappon, *The Word: An Associated Press Guide to Good News Writing* (New York: The Associated Press, 1989)

Theodore A. Rees Cheney, *Writing Creative Nonfiction* (Berkeley, CA: Ten Speed Press, 2001)

Roy Peter Clark and Don Fry, *Coaching Writers* (New York: Bedford Books, 2003)

Jon Franklin, *Writing for Story: Craft Secrets of Dramatic Nonfiction by a Two-Time Pulitzer Prize Winner* (New York: Penguin/Plume, 1994)

Richard Rhodes, *How to Write: Advice and Reflections* (New York: Harper Paperbacks, 1996)

James B. Stewart, *Follow the Story: How to Write Successful Nonfiction* (New York: Simon & Schuster, 1998)

William Strunk and E.B. White, *The Elements of Style* (New York: Macmillan, 1999)

William Zinsser, *On Writing Well* (New York: Harper & Row, 2006)

Books with Great Feature Stories

Joan Didion, *We Tell Ourselves Stories in Order to Live* (New York: Everyman's Library, 2006)

In this scene, Foster, whose success with artists like Celine Dion, Madonna, Lionel Richie, 'N Sync, Whitney Houston, and Barbra Streisand makes him an authority, thinks the CD needs another sure-fire hit song, and wants Bublé to include Cole Porter's "I've Got You Under My Skin." Bublé, whose first CD was a multi-million seller and made him an overnight star, is like a teenager with his dad, testing the limits of his independence:

> Inside the studio, Foster, who looks as if he's just come off the tennis court in a blue fleece jacket, black shorts and white Nike runners, has gotten off the phone with Wayne Newton. He swivels his chair around to face Bublé, who's

Ira Glass, ed., *The New Kings of Nonfiction* (New York: Riverhead Books, 2007)

John Hersey, *Hiroshima* (New York: Vintage, 1989)

Kevin Kerrane and Ben Yagoda, eds., *The Art of Fact* (New York: Scribner, 1998)

Michael Lewis, *Next: The Future Just Happened* (New York: W.W. Norton, 2002)

John McPhee, *The John McPhee Reader*, ed. William Howarth (New York: Farrar, Straus & Giroux, 1982)

Susan Orlean, *The Bullfighter Checks Her Makeup: My Encounters with Extraordinary People* (New York: Random House, 2002)

David Remnick, *The Devil Problem: And Other True Stories* (New York: Vintage, 1997)

David Remnick, *Reporting: Writings from The New Yorker* (New York: Vintage, 2007)

Norman Sims and Mark Kramer, eds., *Literary Journalism* (New York: Ballantine, 1995)

Gay Talese, *The Gay Talese Reader* (New York: Walker Books, 2003)

Tom Wolfe, *The Purple Decades: A Reader* (New York: Berkley Books, 1987)

Tom Wolfe and Edward Warren Johnson, *The New Journalism* (London: Picador, 1998)

Any edition of *Granta* (a quarterly literary journal publishing fabulous non-fiction from English writers worldwide)

The series of writing anthologies from the Banff non-fiction writing program including *Word Carving: The Craft of Literary Journalism* (2003); *To Arrive Where You Are: Literary Journalism from The Banff Centre* (2000); *Taking Risks: Literary Journalism from the Edge* (1998); and *Why Are You Telling Me This? Eleven Acts of Intimate Journalism* (1997). All are published by and available through The Banff Centre Press (www.banffcentre.ca).

Don Gibb, Moira Farr, David Hayes, Susan Ferguson, and Linda Kay standing beside him. Bublé's mother and grandmother, who are visiting L.A., sit quietly on a sofa and chairs with [his fiancé, Debbie] Timuss.

"'Come Fly With Me' got more attention than any other song on the first record," says Foster, who has patiently gone over this argument several times since yesterday. He's now starting to sound frustrated. "There were two or three critics who didn't like it, but all the people loved it."

"My problem is 'Under My Skin' is so closely associated with Sinatra," says Bublé imploringly. "This is such a great record right now."

Foster snorts. "Yeah, and how many records have you made exactly?"

"It's a bonus track, right?" Bublé asks, trying to negotiate a face-saving compromise. Foster takes a call from Celine Dion's manager and husband, René Angélil, then continues the discussion.

"Sure, bonus track," says Foster. "We can't put this on the record without you wanting it on the record, you know. If it was up to me, entirely, though, if it was completely up to me, I'd still be looking for one more song."

Bublé looks stricken. "Why do you think we need another song?"

"Last night I was thinking, I wish there was just one more 'wow.' I was trying to think of what. 'Knock on Wood'? That old Tom Jones song, 'Delilah'? Neil Diamond's 'Sweet Caroline'? 'Brown-Eyed Girl'? Something so recognizable that everybody would go, yeah!"

"We don't need another song."

"Michael, did I ever tell you how many hit songs came at the last second?" says Foster. "'Hard to Say I'm Sorry' for Chicago came two days before the album was supposed to be out. Or Celine's 'Because You Love Me.' The album was being mastered, and we held things up because that song came along. Both those songs went to No. 1."[4]

This happened on the second of three days I spent hanging around the studio, and I'd been there for hours before this moment occurred. Sources had told me beforehand about a minor power struggle, and even Bublé himself had alluded to it when he told me over a lunch interview that he intended to exert more creative control over this recording. So I patiently waited, observing several small episodes when tension thrummed just beneath the surface until, finally, this moment happened without warning. Writers have to be attuned to what the great photographer Henri Cartier-Bresson called "the decisive moment," the one that separates great photographers from weekend snapshot-takers. But like professional photographers, writers record a great many potential moments to ensure they get the decisive one.

Much of the time I was visiting Foster's studio, I adopted the "fly-on-the-wall" approach to reporting. As I do in most circumstances, I tried to make myself as unobtrusive as possible so events would unfold naturally. It doesn't always happen, though, and the "observer effect," borrowed from science, is often invoked to explain why. Briefly, there are changes that the act of observing will make on a phenomenon being observed. For example, the tools used to measure electrons also alter the behaviour of electrons. There is, however, one thing you can do to help minimize the effect of your presence. No, it's not about hiding in closets or behind furniture, or equipping yourself with a hidden microphone and misrepresenting yourself as an innocent bystander.

It's about the time you spend on the job. In *The New New Journalism*, Robert S. Boynton's collection of interviews with top non-fiction writers, Ted Conover described the distinction between daily news reporters and long-form non-fiction writers as being like the difference between a *tourist* and a *traveller*. "The tourist experience is superficial and glancing," he said. "The traveler develops a deeper connection with her surroundings ... the traveler stays longer, makers her own plans, chooses her own destination, and usually travels alone."[5]

"Immersion" research or "saturation" reporting are two terms that describe it. You're *immersing* yourself in the world of your subjects; you're *saturating* all your senses with as much observable data as possible. You can't do this by parachuting into a scene to grab a few quick sound bytes and leaving in time for lunch. It's only over time that subjects get used to you, sometimes forgetting you're there and other times treating you with respect for the serious way you're approaching your job.[6]

Once, when I was alone in the studio with Foster, he turned from the console, leaned back in his chair and said: "This is really interesting. No one has spent so much time on an article. You're really seeing how the process works."

He sounded genuinely pleased and admiring. What's implied is that you're trying to understand things, get the story right. This reinforced my view that most subjects, no matter who they are, are flattered by the attention focused on them by ambitious feature writers.

Identifying and Negotiating Scenes

Even the most media-savvy people deal mainly with daily news reporters who conduct interviews over the phone or in one-hour-or-less sessions, generally in fairly formal circumstances. I call these "talking head" interviews, borrowing from the term used in broadcast that refers to those head-and-shoulder shots of people answering questions posed by an off-camera reporter. While they serve a purpose, and most of us have a least a few of them in every feature, they're also static, boring. There's no action. They're most effective for secondary characters, like expert sources (scientists, academics, or lawyers, for example, who provide a relevant quote but aren't part of the action). They're also effective for quoting a primary subject between scenes.

Don't assume subjects understand what your story is about, let alone your need for scenes. (When you've scheduled sessions with subjects through intermediaries such as executive assistants or PR reps, the subjects may have been given a vague, thumbnail version of your story.) Whether I'm negotiating meetings with subjects directly or through intermediaries, I explain that I'd like to see the subjects once for an in-depth, one-on-one interview in a setting where we'll be undisturbed. (Yes, this is often a "talking head.") But, I continue, I also want to see them once or twice more, where I can observe them doing what they do. I often say something like, "It's important for readers to see you in action, doing what you do, rather than having me interpret and explain what you do." Sometimes I add, "If you've ever been part of a TV documentary, you know that filmmakers need footage of you doing things. I need the same thing, although I'll be creating the pictures in writing." I find that if I patiently and respectfully explain why I need to spend time in their company, most people are agreeable. (Aside from being flattered, many also conclude that you must be genuinely trying to understand them and get the "real" story.)

I'll ask to sit in on a meeting they'll be attending or convening, or watch them interact with a client, or accompany them to a conference or seminar or university class where they'll be speaking. (The question-and-answer session at the end is usually better than the formal presentation, and it's useful to hover nearby when people approach your subject to talk to them after the event.) If you're profiling an entertainer, ask to attend rehearsals, accompany the person to an industry event, or tag along on a day of media interviews. Once, while writing a feature on efforts to boost Canadian country singer Michelle Wright from a respectable "B" level Nashville artist to the top tier, I asked Wright's manager about her upcoming schedule. I ended up attending a recording session; travelling with her in her car to her home for an afternoon wardrobe session with her image consultant; and observing the Country Music Association's "Fan Fair," an annual event where country artists meet fans, sign autographs, and mingle with radio station DJs. Everything tied into the theme of how critically important image and promotion is to the big leagues of the music industry.

If your story is about an athlete, ask to observe practice sessions, come into the dressing room, or join the team when they go out for drinks after a game. (A young student writer I knew, who had played a little lacrosse in high school, once asked Canada's top lacrosse player to play one-on-one with him at a neighbourhood schoolyard. The pro ran rings around the writer, but it was a terrific scene.) Even if your feature is as simple as profiling the owner of a local pet-grooming business, you can spend a morning or afternoon with the person watching them deal with customers and attend to pets. Nothing beats seeing your subjects in action.

Sometimes a scene can involve your subject as an observer. For a book I wrote on *The Globe and Mail* and the media in Canada, I wanted a scene for a chapter on *Globe and Mail* political columnist Jeffrey Simpson. You might think (correctly) that there isn't usually much action to be found when you're writing about a writer. In this case, Simpson said he was planning to attend (although not as a participant) an event in a university theatre at which several Canadian and international broadcasting and newspaper luminaries were taking part in a panel. That may sound like a static scene, but it worked quite well. I was able to describe the scene we were witnessing—the broadcasters in their expensive suits, impeccably groomed, able to tilt their head attractively into the light and dramatically present their image to the crowd in contrast to their relatively low-key and rumpled newspaper colleagues—and, sitting toward the back of the dark theatre, Simpson whispering comments to me like a colour commentator at a sports event.

For "Die Hard," the feature reprinted following this chapter, I wanted to observe every step in the making of a commercial. So I requested, and was granted permission, to sit in on almost every strategy meeting, the shoot itself, sessions to record music and voice-overs and screenings, including sensitive ones with the client. My principal subject, the president and founder of the ad agency, was delighted that a writer wanted to spend so much time with him and record the inside story of how his business works. But before I found him, I had pre-interviewed several ad agency presidents trying to find one that would grant me this kind of access.

So it's important to have a clear understanding of your story's theme. For a feature published in March 2002 in *National Post Business Magazine* on how jazz singer Diana Krall's managers had transformed her into a global "brand," I was told that I could hang around during a big charity concert she was giving in Vancouver or for part of a media junket in the United States. But neither of these events truly addressed the theme. Then I learned that her international tour was being launched with four nights at the Olympia Theatre in Paris. That was an expensive trip, but my editors at *National Post Business* understood that it was the obvious setting for the piece. (And no writer I can imagine would be disappointed by this assignment.)

In the case of Michael Bublé, his management company told me that I could hang around with him when he was beginning a Canadian tour in Vancouver or join him for a few days during a series of media interviews coming up in Ireland. But, as with the Krall example, neither of these scenes would speak to the theme of my story—the delicate, behind-the-scenes relationship between music artists and their producers. In a polite series of back-and-forths with a patient and helpful publicist, I confirmed the dates that Bublé would be finishing his new CD at Foster's studio in LA and was cleared to join them.

Despite your best efforts, you may not be able to observe your subjects in organic scenes, so you may have to create conditions in which a scene will occur. While reporting for "Listening to Khakis," one of many classic stories for *The New Yorker*, Malcolm Gladwell was in an interview with the three advertising agency executives who had taken over the successful Dockers line of men's khaki trousers. Understanding that he was in a room with three talking heads, Gladwell suggested they watch all of the TV ads from the original campaign, knowing that the men were likely to be more animated critiquing the ads amongst themselves than they would be in a formal interview.[7]

In 2000, I gave a seminar on feature writing at *The Hamilton Spectator*. During the Q&A, a woman told me that she was a feature writer assigned to interview the great urban thinker and community activist Jane Jacobs. She was wondering about scenes. I suggested she ask Jacobs, who has written so extensively on cities and neighbourhoods, to take her for a walk around her beloved Annex neighbourhood. There's a problem, the writer said. Jacobs had an injured knee and couldn't walk. The interview had to take place in Jacobs's living room where she couldn't even get out of her chair.

Thinking fast, I suggested that the writer could phone around and find an ant colony in a glass tank and borrow it for the afternoon. Yes, plunk it down in Jacobs's living room and ask her to talk about the relationship between the way ant colonies are organized and the way people organize themselves within cities, a theme close to Jacobs's heart. Many reporters in the room looked at me like I was crazy, but I figured Jacobs might be amused by the idea and enjoy the diversion. Weeks later, the writer emailed me to say that with some effort she'd found an art colony and that Jacobs became very animated as she referred to it to illustrate ideas about humans within urban life.

To summarize: once you've identified your characters and thought about potential scenes, don't be afraid to ask for access. But remember that as dramatic or unusual as a scene may seem, it must relate to your feature's theme. And be prepared to explain to your subjects—or their handlers—your needs and how it serves the greater good of the story. If no scenes are happening organically, think about ways to set up a situation that will serve your needs.

God Is in the Details

Architect Ludwig Mies van der Rohe's familiar aphorism, "God is in the details," referred to architecture, but it's equally true of almost any human endeavour, including feature writing. I try to gather as many details as possible when I'm doing on-the-scene reporting. Every young journalist knows that you're supposed to note the kinds of books, knick-knacks, and framed pictures a person has in their office or home but feature writers go much further than that.

When you're present at a scene, you should be working hard. You must be constantly alert while simultaneously appearing relaxed to your subjects, putting them at ease and carrying on seemingly casual conversations while, in fact, making sure you ask all relevant questions and simultaneously noting everything else going on in the environment. (Remember the mantra I mentioned earlier: *take a deep breath, focus … think … focus … think….*)

All senses should be active. You're recording sights and sounds, obviously, but you may also use smell, taste, and touch, depending upon the circumstances, and certainly instinct—the so-called sixth sense—is important. One reason I favour using a tape recorder a great deal of the time is because it leaves me free to write down other data, including drawing crude diagrams of a room's layout or the arrangement of people at a large gathering. I usually feel exhausted when I return from a few hours of reporting this way.

A key question to ask yourself—while you're at a scene and throughout the process of reporting a feature—is, *Have I captured a true sense of the characters?* Too often writers fall back on hackneyed and overly general descriptions ("tall," "burly," "petite," "brunette," "clean-shaven") and forget to think about what characteristics are the most interesting. For example, is a person's physical appearance what is most striking, or is it their body language or their speech patterns? Innocuous comments, or exchanges between individuals, often reveal character more effectively than a traditional "quote." How it's said may be as important as what's being said.

For example, in a profile of modelling agency owner Elmer Olsen for *Toronto Life* magazine, Katrina Onstad beautifully captured Olsen's personality by concentrating first on the way he speaks and his gestures, followed by a few physical details before returning to his speech. One thing that isn't present here is anything that much resembles an old-fashioned journalistic quote.

> Here is how Elmer Olsen gets excited. First, he releases a fast, stuttery can't-find-the-words sound—"oh ... ah ... ah ... ahh"—that turns to wind-whistling-in-the-trees—"Hooooo"—then his hand drops from his wrist and starts moving back and forth in the universal symbol for "hot." "Oh ... my ... gosh," he says, without ever resorting to profanity, which just wouldn't suit a man named Elmer. There is a lot of grabbing, too, and not lightly because though he is 57 years old, he is six foot two and fit, a high school baseball star back in the day, with a grip like an angry batter. "Katrina, Katrina, Katrina. Wait until you see Kate! Theeeee most beautiful, drop-dead ... Those legs, mmm ... Tiny ankles. A size nine shoe! Oh my *gosh*. To ... die!"[8]

Readers could be told about Olsen for pages without getting so vivid an impression of the man as Onstad manages in 127 words. That's the power of the scene. But you also may have to pay attention to more subtle mannerisms. When I interviewed City-TV founder and then-executive producer Moses Znaimer, I noticed that he had a quirky way of speaking that had never been mentioned in any of the dozens of articles I'd read about him.

> "You know, the great *sat-is-fact-shun* of City"—Znaimer enunciates each word in a near whisper, occasionally drawing out and stressing each syllable for dramatic effect—"was that it was a remarkably coherent idea from the start. It was of-the-moment. It's great to have been in the grip of *his-tor-i-cal* forces ..."[9]

Of course, I double-checked with other sources to determine whether this was typical of Znaimer's speech. (What if he'd just been putting on some kind of act for one journalist?)

But maybe the telling detail isn't the subjects themselves, but rather an object sitting on a table, a note stuck on a fridge, or something your subject has carelessly cast aside. Profiling musician Rufus Wainwright for *Saturday Night* magazine, I visited his home in Montreal:

> His loft is small and funky, and as messy as one might expect of a twenty-five-year-old who's rarely home. A fur coat lies on the floor where it apparently fell from his shoulders sometime in the early hours of the morning, along with a towel and assorted articles of clothing.[10]

I recorded a lot more detail about his apartment, but the image of Wainwright arriving home in the wee hours and letting his fur coat fall from his shoulders en route to bed symbolized the devil-may-care decadence he loved to project.

Feature writing isn't just about recording details, though. It also involves analyzing what is unfolding before you. One of my mentors, the great editor, writer, and educator Don Obe, believed that feature writing is about thinking at least as much as it's about writing. What is the dynamic in the room? What roles are people playing? Michael Lewis perfectly captures a moment like this in a 2001 story for *The New York Times Magazine*. Fifteen-year-old Jonathan Lebed had been charged with promoting stocks from his bedroom computer, and Lewis shows readers a tense back-and-forth between the boy's parents that could be a scene from an Edward Albee play. Then he writes: "They obey the conventions of the stage. When one of them steps forward into the spotlight to narrate, the other recedes and freezes like a statue."[11] That's not just recording what happened; it's placing action in a context to help readers understand all the dimensions of the scene.

When you're hanging out at a scene, it may be an off-the-cuff remark by a bystander that you realize—often later, as you go over material when writing the story—is a gem. During the commercial shoot in "Die Hard," with a dozen or so crew members milling around the scene, Jim Lovisek, the bug wrangler, is trying to get a fly to land on the table the way the director wants it to:

> Lovisek releases several more flies. A couple of them manage to escape. When another glances off the table and flies underneath, a crew member scurries after it. One of the techies whispers to another: "I've seen actors who can't perform much better."[12]

Crafting the Scene

A tip: you can learn how to craft scenes by watching movies and TV dramas. (The scenes unfold visually the same way you would write them, with logical entrance and exit points and a dramatic arc.) Here is an excerpt from a profile of a stock-car racer by one of the most cinematic feature writers of all time, Tom Wolfe:

> He comes tooling across the infield in a big white dreamboat, a brand-new white Pontiac Catalina four-door hard-top sedan. He pulls up and as he gets out he seems to get more and more huge. First his crew-cut head and then a big jaw and then a bigger neck and then a huge torso, like a wrestler's, all done

up rather modish and California modern, with a red-and-white candy-striped sport shirt, white ducks and loafers.[13]

It's easy to visualize this moment exactly the way it would have been filmed for a movie or TV show. First, a long shot of the white car speeding across the infield of the racetrack. The car comes to a stop in front of the camera, which closes in on the opening door and the head emerging, followed by the neck, the torso ...

Now let's combine a physical setting with some action and dialogue. In a 1993 profile of Leonard Cohen, Ian Pearson has just established where we are: on the set of a music video shoot in a rough-around-the-edges country-and-western bar in west-end Toronto:

> So many odd people were running around—women with platinum beehives, men with string ties and whiskey-veined faces, actors and dancers dressed to look like lowlifes—that the film crew was having difficulty getting its work done.
>
> Like over here, in the congested foyer beside the dressing room. The sign plainly said "Crew Only" above a catering tray of nuts, vegetables, and dip, just as a table bearing chips and Cheesies across the room was marked "Extras Only." It should have been perfectly obvious, but here was this guy with a lined face and slicked-back salt-and-pepper hair heading for the crew's tray. Actually, he was wearing a pretty nice dark double-breasted suit—it gave him a bit of dignity—but he was one of the oldest people in the room, clearly some geezer who supplemented his pension by working as a film extra.
>
> When the elderly gent raised a stick of the crew's celery to his lips, the production assistant had had enough. "Excuse me," he huffed officiously, "are you an extra?"
>
> "Yeah," replied an aged-in-oak baritone. "I'm an extra."
>
> "Well, would you *please* get your food from the extras' tray."
>
> Leonard Cohen kept a straight face and strolled over to the extras' tray, where he started wolfing down Cheesies. He liked Cheesies anyway and he was finding he didn't mind taking orders. This video business was a necessary evil of the music industry these days. After a gruelling couple of years trying to finish his new recording, Cohen found it relaxing to have someone else tell him what to do.[14]

It's a nice touch the way Pearson introduced the old gent as though he's going to be a small detail in the overall picture, then reveals that he's the subject of the story. Think about how this scene would appear on film. A long (or perhaps medium) shot establishes the setting: the crowded country-and-western bar with a colourful crowd of people milling around. Then the camera moves in on a table beside the dressing room just as an old man wanders over and begins to eat. When the production assistant confronts him, we see a two-shot of both men, perhaps from behind Cohen's shoulder. Then the camera follows Cohen as he ambles across the room to the "Extras Only" table, wearing a bemused expression. Also note the way Pearson integrates his own research into the scene—he knows what Cohen's thinking as he's eating the Cheesies.

How to Record a Scene

How do you remember all those details when observing a scene? Whether you use an audio recorder or notepad, what's most important is how you comport yourself. People don't want someone hanging around for hours who isn't well informed (that's where doing your background research comes in) or behaves like a cub reporter, standing stiffly, notepad poised, earnestly scribbling.

That's why I like using recorders. I often stand with my arms crossed or by my side, holding a small recorder under a notepad, its microphone aimed in the direction of my subject. (I always put a small piece of black electrician's tape over any blinking lights so attention isn't drawn to it.)

I try to keep things as conversational as possible. I do a lot of my scribbling when people are interacting with others, or when I'm able to slip away alone. (Yes, feature writers resort to trips to the bathroom to make notes, just like in the movies.) Generally, the longer you spend with people the less they pay attention to what you're doing anyway, as long as you lay back and respect the integrity of the scene.

Equipment check: Along with a recorder and steno notepad, I usually bring with me backup batteries (add tapes if you're using an analog recorder), one or two extra steno notepads (a one-hour interview might turn into three hours of hanging out), a couple of smaller pads, and many pens. And when I travel, I always bring along a backup recorder.

Here's one last example, the opening scene from a National Magazine Award–winning article by Susan Bourette. Unlike the previous ones, it's written in first person as a work of participatory journalism. Bourette signed on to work at a Manitoba meat-packing plant so she could write about working conditions in one of society's least-enviable industrial jobs.

We're deep in the shadows. In the bowels of a building with walls that sweat gristle and blood. A modern-day plant, more like Fritz Lang's Metropolis than Willy Wonka & the Chocolate Factory.

We're standing in a semi-circle on the kill floor at Maple Leaf Pork in Brandon, Man. Twenty-five fresh recruits, our mouths agape. Mike, a short, squat factory-floor veteran, stuffed into a bloody lab coat, is leading our tour. Hundreds of hogs swing by on a conveyer line; flayed and shackled up by their hind legs, their heads dangling by a flap of skin, they smack together like bowling pins.

We stare at the blank faces of the men who thrust in and out of the hogs' bellies with knives, yanking out glistening tubes of red and grey entrails, bowels, hearts and livers that will eventually be chopped, packaged and shipped off for the dinner table.

"We'd harvest the farts if we could," Mike offers with a certain morbid glee. "Yup. We use just about everything. Only 3% of the pig goes to waste around here."

My tongue suddenly feels like it's caked with the stench of sweat and scared animals. My head begins to swing like a seesaw.

"Don't you dare puke," Mike snorts, grabbing at my helmet to take note of my name, displayed there in bold lettering. "Suck it up, Princess."

I'm praying for a miracle. That I won't toss my cookies. Or worse, be tossed out tush over teakettle my first day on the job. "It's the smell," I respond weakly. And then with all the moxie I can muster: "I'll get used to it."

With that, Mike cocks his head and inhales deeply before he begins a spiel he's surely mouthed dozens of times before. "You know what that smell is?" he growls rhetorically. "That," he says, leaning in for emphasis, "that's the smell of money."[15]

Both Pearson's and Bourette's scenes function as mini-stories. There is a beginning, middle, and an end as well as a sense of action that rises and falls, building toward a resolution. It's a miniature version of your feature itself. Pearson's is more conventionally journalistic, and he crafted the ending of his scene himself by revealing Cohen's thoughts to readers. Bourette is a character in her scene, as she is in the story. The prose suggests sitting in a bar over drinks while Bourette spins a yarn that has everyone enthralled. Her use of Mike's quote ends the scene very effectively with the equivalent of a joke's punch line.

Reconstructing Scenes

Readers love feeling as though they are a "fly on the wall"—standing beside an investigator at a crime scene; crouched in the corner of a corporate boardroom watching a dramatic meeting; eavesdropping on a discussion between an athlete and a coach at the eleventh hour of a key game. What brings these kinds of stories alive is the skill of a feature writer who gets extensive access to the subject. But what about important stories that happened in the past—a few weeks, months, or decades ago, when the writer wasn't present? The term *reconstruction* is often incorrectly applied to any feature that provides a narrative account of an event that took place in the past. A true reconstruction seeks to do much more.

In the best reconstructions, writers make an event that happened long ago read as vividly as if they had been there witnessing it themselves; it has all the qualities of a "live" scene. I believe it's a technique that every feature writer should master, since these kinds of stories present themselves constantly. Writers on a long deadline enjoy the luxury of time to conduct the necessary research, reporting, and interviewing, but even deadline-driven daily news reporters can sometimes use these techniques to enliven some stories.

A few (among many) book-length examples that come to mind are John Hersey's *Hiroshima*, Tom Wolfe's *The Right Stuff*, Piers Paul Read's *Alive*, Kirk Makin's *Redrum the Innocent*, Mark Bowden's *Black Hawk Down*, Jonathan Harr's *A Civil Action*, and Sebastian Junger's *The Perfect Storm*. In the magazine world, reconstructions are very common in business journalism (think of all those behind-the-scenes tales of last year's corporate takeover or bankruptcy) and crime writing (the stories are triggered by the crime being committed, making it hard for journalists to have anticipated and been following events in advance). But any incident deemed worthy of an in-depth examination, regardless of the medium, may involve reconstruction.

In his foreword to *The Perfect Storm*, Junger wrote about the difficulties of reconstructing an event that took place several years earlier—in his case, one in which the six main characters all perished, without surviving witnesses to their end. "On the one hand," Junger wrote, "I wanted to write a completely factual book that would stand on its own as a piece of journalism. On the other hand, I didn't want the narrative to asphyxiate under a mass of technical detail and conjecture. I toyed with the idea of fictionalizing minor parts of the story—conversations, personal thoughts, day-to-day routines—to make it more readable, but that risked diminishing the value of whatever facts I was able to determine."[16]

As with any scene, your goal in the reconstruction is to gather

- physical descriptions of people,
- physical descriptions of the environment,
- actions, and
- dialogue.

And as with all good journalism, great effort needs to go into verifying the accuracy of these details. You can do so through interviews, documentation (everything from media reports and court transcripts to personal letters and diaries), visual aids (TV footage, amateur video, cellphone snapshots), and other research tools. To quantify the process, let's say that reconstructions can double the researching, reporting, and interviewing time. For example, if the basic information needed from a subject could be covered in a one-hour, in-person interview, feature writers may spend at least another hour going over details specific to the needs of a reconstruction, not to mention re-interviewing subjects later to clear up discrepancies or expand on information they've gathered.

Many years ago I reconstructed the story of how Peter Mansbridge, even then a prominent Canadian broadcast journalist, had been agonizing for months over whether to accept a $1-million offer from CBS in New York. (The story became public only when he decided to stay in Canada.) A key moment was a late-night visit to Mansbridge's apartment by three senior colleagues from the CBC—reporter Brian Stewart, Mansbridge's boss, John Owen, and Mark Starowicz, a legendary CBC producer. When interviewing each of these main players, I asked them conventional questions any reporter would ask. But I also told them that my goal was to reconstruct events in as detailed a way as possible, to make the scenes come alive for readers. Then I asked a series of apparently irrelevant questions about how they travelled to the site of the meeting, the colour scheme and furnishings in the room, where people sat (and whether people moved around during the meeting), what kind of food and beverages were consumed (if any), the tenor and tone of the discussion, etc. Brian Stewart introduced me to a useful expression I've since said to many subjects of reconstruction. He said, "Oh, I understand. You want me to 'play tape recorder.'" (*Who said what to whom? Can you remember exactly what was said at that moment? What roles did each person play in the discussion?*)

All four men had been physically described earlier in the story so I knew I probably wouldn't be describing their appearances, unless it was relevant to the events at hand. (I still asked everyone what they were wearing, of course.) Since the meeting took place in Mansbridge's apartment, I was able to observe the surroundings when I interviewed him there. I'd been told by two of his visitors that night that the phone had been constantly ringing but Mansbridge ignored the calls, letting his answering machine pick them up. One of them mentioned that the sound of the machine was "strange." While sitting in Mansbridge's apartment, the phone rang several times, and I noticed that his answering machine made an odd sound—like it was underwater. I could see where late at night it would have had a strange, haunting quality. That's the kind of detail that can reinforce the sense of verisimilitude feature writers strive for in reconstructions. (A tip: whether it's an answering machine, dining room table, or paint on the walls, remember to ask if things were the same at the time of your reconstruction, which may be weeks, months, or even years earlier.)

Here's part of the result:

> At 10 p.m., Owen and Starowicz arrived to find Stewart already there. Starowicz poured himself a scotch and Owen, who had not eaten, rummaged through the kitchen. "Jesus, Peter," he said, "Isn't there anything to eat in this place?" Mansbridge located two bags of microwave popcorn and Stewart managed to burn both of them. They finally settled down in front of the broad bay windows—Owen, Starowicz and Stewart on a pair of sofas; Mansbridge, looking like he'd not slept in days, hunched miserably in a Boston rocker. "Nobody understands how hard this is on me," he told them. "It's tearing me apart."
>
> The Popcorn Summit is destined to become a CBC legend. Throughout the evening, there were phone calls from friends and acquaintances—the mechanical burbling of Mansbridge's answering machine was haunting ...[17]

In this case, it was a great help to interview Mansbridge in his apartment, where a scene central to the story took place. If possible, visiting a scene is always to your advantage. My friend Kim Pittaway wrote a powerful story for *Chatelaine* about premature babies. Here is part of one reconstructed scene from it:

> In the neonatal intensive care unit at Barrie's Royal Victoria Hospital, the teams work against the backdrop of pink and blue walls, stuffed teddy bears and softly drawn pastel angels decorating walls and shelves. IVs are inserted into each of two Fearman babies' umbilical arteries and umbilical veins, not because other vessels are hard to find—the babies' skin is so translucent that veins are clearly visible—but because their bodies are so small that these two major vessels are the only ones large enough to allow the quick insertion of an IV catheter....
>
> There are low-tech touches, too: in an effort to stabilize their temperatures, both babies have been snuggled against latex gloves filled with warm water. The gloves are almost as big as they are.[18]

Pittaway, a thorough and exacting reporter, makes readers feel as though they're present in the unit. This happens largely because of the concrete details, all of which had to be reconstructed after the fact. She visited the hospital for interviews and asked to be shown around. She asked a nurse to retrace the route that would have been taken from the Fearmans' room to the neonatal intensive care unit. Pittaway paced off the distance herself, but also asked how long it would take a team rushing with preemie babies. (In the story, she notes: "At full speed, it's a 20 to 30-second journey.") She did floor diagrams of the neonatal unit and asked specific questions (Where would the babies have been placed? What would each team member be doing? Would all of this equipment I see in the unit be there at the time the Fearmans' babies arrived? Was some of it moved in and out at certain points?). Pacing around the perimeter of the unit, she tried to give herself a sense of how crowded and intense the small space would be in the heat of the moment.

But one key bit of information that she admits she might have forgotten to ask about was supplied to her when a nurse remarked that the delivery rooms had been redecorated recently. Fortunately, she was able to confirm that they had been pink and blue at the time the Fearman babies were born. (I can sympathize. While gathering the enormous quantity of data we need for reconstructions, it's possible for any of us to forget this kind of thing.)

If you can't physically visit a scene—which is often the case—you'll have to look into alternatives. If it was a newsworthy event, did the broadcast media cover it? (There may be video footage you can watch, or at least the sound captured for radio.) If it's a crime scene, the police usually have either video footage or still photographs. Was the event photographed, either by professional or amateur photographers? Did any bystanders or participants get cellphone footage or still photos? Was the scene described by the print media (newspapers, magazines, books)? Are there historical records that may include photographs or drawings? Are there blueprints?

Yes, it's a lot of work but there are ways to streamline the process. When faced with a reconstruction, it's critically important to ask yourself, what are the key scenes? There will be certain dramatic, pivotal moments that are crucial to what happened, and it's these that you're most likely going to use in a feature. So you can narrow your parameters by identifying the key scenes and gathering the extra layers of research only for these.

As a general rule, I like to talk to everyone who was present at a scene—or at least the principals. Sometimes, if one or two of those present were assistants, secretaries, or corporate lawyers, I'll focus only on the main subjects—though at times a secretary can be the best source. To reconstruct dialogue, I'll first identify several pivotal scenes, the ones I'm most likely to use in the story. Then I'll interview everyone who was present, asking each in turn what they remember of what was said. Where there's disagreement,

I'll often go back to the subjects and ask for clarification. If I can't satisfy myself within a reasonable doubt about what was said, then I'll paraphrase, reduce the size and importance of the scene in my feature, or discard it.

Here's a basic checklist to think about when you undertake a reconstruction:

Ask yourself why. Why am I reconstructing this scene? (Am I trying to convey an important event to readers, or simply trying to impress with my writing and research abilities?) It's so time- and labour-intensive to do an effective reconstruction that it's wise to choose only the most significant scenes, ones that are necessary to the storytelling.

Explain your intentions. Your goal is to write an anecdotal, richly detailed narrative. So you need a lot of rich details and revealing anecdotes, right? Explain that to your subjects so they'll understand why you're asking so many questions about seemingly irrelevant data. Most people, when they know what you're trying to do, will cooperate.

Ask for specific details. Here are a few examples: What time did you arrive at your apartment? Who were you with when you arrived? What time did the others arrive? What were you wearing that day? What were the others wearing? Describe the apartment. In what room did the meeting take place? Describe in detail the room. Where did everyone sit? Knowing that this meeting was going to take place, what were you thinking about before the others arrived?

Use silence. This is another general rule of interviewing that's especially important when reconstructing scenes. Silence is a natural response to a tough or perplexing question. When you're asking people to recall specific, seemingly irrelevant details about past events, pausing to think about them is a natural response. Don't be afraid of dead air; let your subject fill it.

Look for support materials. Your subject(s) may have diaries, journals, minutes, reports, tape recordings, email messages, etc., or perhaps a secretary took notes. (Police reports are unusually detailed. If the police won't share them with you, defence lawyers have often obtained them as part of their trial preparations.) Daytimers or phone bills can help establish precise chronologies. If your subjects use PDAs, ask whether they electronically archive the contents. Don't forget about other media reports (did local TV cover the story? local dailies or community papers?). What about photos or video footage? Need to know the layout of a place you can't visit? Ask for blueprints or check out articles in local papers or write-ups in obscure architectural journals.

Was the first Tuesday in January 1999 sunny or overcast? Consult a perpetual calendar to establish dates from years gone by. Check the weather reports in local papers or online history-of-weather sites to establish weather conditions. Use this information to "fact-check" your subject's recollections or help jump-start their memories. Draw up a timeline to help you figure out the chronology of events.

Is My Reconstruction True?

The best feature writers balance their ambition to produce dramatic narratives with the need to meet a high threshold of accuracy and authenticity. To test the level to which your reporting confidence is justified, ask yourself the following:

- How much time has passed since these events? Are my subject's memories credible? Have I tested the account against the memory of other participants, or others who might be in a position to know about it?
- Have I talked to all, or most of, the sources? (Or, in the case of a multi-character scene, the most significant players?)
- Have I taken into consideration vested interests, tendencies toward self-aggrandizement, etc.? Could I have been fooled by an unreliable source, or a source with a faulty memory or an axe to grind?
- Have I sought independent verification from documentary sources, such as public records, historical accounts, diaries?
- Will a lack of attribution (often present in reconstructions) undermine credibility?
- Does my reconstruction need an editor's or reporter's note to help readers understand how the incident was reported and sourced? (This is mainly used in non-fiction books, although occasionally in newspapers and magazines—either in print or on websites.)

There are many satisfying aspects to the craft of journalism, but the "thrill of the scene" is the one I love best. Scenes are the heart of feature writing, the building blocks upon which the story is constructed. And, for anyone with a true journalist's curiosity, they're the crack cocaine of our craft. Why are they thrilling? Because we're thrust into the action, becoming swept up in it at the same time as we're maintaining a distance, observing it. Back in 1969, in the appendix to his introduction to *The New Journalism*, Tom Wolfe wrote: "Often you feel as if you've put your whole central nervous system on red alert and turned it into a receiving set, with your head panning the molten tableau like a radar dish, with you saying, 'Come in, world!'"[19]

Well, okay, that was 1973 and Wolfe was cranking himself up to define the magazine feature writing of the era as "the new journalism," even though it was far from new. Today we understand that this kind of narrative-driven feature writing—with its heavy reliance on scenes—can be traced back to before the twentieth century and today is considered the norm.

Less adrenalin-fuelled than Wolfe, the self-effacing Adrian Nicole Leblanc, whose book *Random Family: Love, Drugs, Trouble and Coming of Age in the Bronx* is a tour de force of cinematic writing, has said that she works "up the courage to walk over and introduce myself to the people I'm reporting on, explaining as much as I understand of what I'm doing, and that I just want to 'be' with them, and not necessarily do anything. I draw the parallel with making a movie. 'Imagine I'm making a movie about your life. Show me the places that are most important to you: your room, the schoolyard, anywhere you'd like to be.' "[20]

Hanging out in people's lives and experiencing their worlds is great work if you can get it, but the thrill of the scene must not end with the writer. It's also what excites many readers, pulling them through a story that informs them or enriches their lives in some way. The words I most love to hear a reader say are, "You made me feel as though I was there."

Discussion Questions

1. Read "Die Hard" (pages 115–133). How do scenes drive the narrative in the story? (What kind of information is best communicated in scenes?)

2. Pick out three examples of background information being "smuggled" into a scene.

3. Several scenes are reconstructed: the opening; Rob Guenette brainstorming the brief; and the account of the sound specialist, Thomas Neuspiel, creating the sound effects (a reconstructed-scene-within-a-"live"-scene). What differences can you sense between the "live" scenes and the reconstructions?

4. Although "Die Hard" is written in third person, in what ways do you sense the presence of the writer?

Notes

1. David Hayes, "Tales from the Track," *Toronto Life*, January 1985.
2. Ibid.
3. Norman Sims, *Literary Journalism* (New York: Ballantine Books, 1995), p. 13.
4. David Hayes, "The Making of Michael Bublé," *Saturday Night*, April 2005.
5. Robert S. Boynton, *The New New Journalism: Conversations with America's Best Nonfiction Writers on Their Craft* (New York: Vintage Books, 2005), p. 8.
6. For more about the benefits and challenges of immersion reporting, see chapter 6.
7. Malcolm Gladwell, "Listening to Khakis," *The New Yorker*, March 17, 1997.
8. Katrina Onstad, "Bring Me Your Daughters," *Toronto Life*, March 2007.
9. David Hayes, "Moses Vision," *Toronto Life*, September 1987.
10. David Hayes, "The Chosen One," *Saturday Night*, May 1999.
11. Michael Lewis, "Jonathan Lebed's Extracurricular Activities," *New York Times Magazine*, February 25, 2001.
12. David Hayes, "Die Hard," *National Post Business Magazine*, September 1, 2001, 80.
13. Tom Wolfe, "The Last American Hero Is Junior Johnson. Yes!" *Esquire*, March 1965.
14. Ian Pearson, "Growing Old Disgracefully," *Saturday Night*, March 1993.
15. Susan Bourette, "Butchered," *Report on Business*, November 2003.
16. Sebastian Junger, *The Perfect Storm* (New York: HarperTorch, 1998), p. xiii.
17. David Hayes, "Peter and the Wolf," *Toronto Life*, March 1988.
18. Kim Pittaway, "Borderline Babies," *Chatelaine*, April 1996.
19. Tom Wolfe, *The New Journalism* (New York: Harper & Row, 1973), p. 52.
20. Boynton, *The New New Journalism*, p. 237.

"Die Hard"

He's the star of a $250,000 commercial for Cineplex Odeon. He's an adventurer, a romantic, a lover. He's Harrison Ford, John Wayne, Leo DiCaprio. But will Frank the Fly's big-screen debut—and comedic demise—deliver the buzz that advertisers are after?

David Hayes, "Die Hard." *National Post Business Magazine*, September 1, 2001, 78. Reprinted by permission of the author.

It's the afternoon of February 18, and Paul Lavoie, one of Canada's hottest ad guys, is on his cell. It's bad news. The talent for his new Cineplex Odeon Corp. commercial, he learns, has died. Lavoie is stunned. Now the production will have to be delayed, and all the necessary professionals—the editors, sound and music specialists, film colourists, digital technicians—will have to be rescheduled. All because several hundred flesh-eating flies, in pupae form, are sitting at the Toronto Nature Centre frozen in their packing cases. The bug wrangler, who had been guaranteed live delivery, isn't pleased. He will order more, Lavoie is told, this time from a more reliable insect supplier.

The bug wrangler is scrambling because Lavoie has built a quarter-of-a-million-dollar commercial around a fly. It's his latest solution to advertising's oldest dilemma: how to help a company solve a business problem while at the same time building an agency's reputation for creative genius. When the two come together, the result can be wildly successful. Last year, the "Rant," a commercial for Molson Canadian produced by a Toronto-based agency not previously known for its distinguished creative, featured Joe, a young man who became increasingly passionate as he described the differences between Canadians and Americans. The spot not only helped to reverse Canadian's decline, increasing its market share in the highly competitive beer industry, it won numerous awards and was both widely imitated and reported upon in the media: a genuine cultural phenomenon.

But today, Lavoie's mind is focussed only on the crisis at hand. His plan to help both himself and financially troubled Cineplex is on hold due to a box full of flies, the product of the same fanciful imagination that created an ad featuring disco-dancing ducks for Clearnet PCS Inc., which was recently purchased by TELUS Corp. He made that one work, despite major obstacles, but can he do it again?

The Business Problem

The story of a commercial always begins with a business problem. In the case of Cineplex, it was falling attendance due to increasing competition from elaborate home entertainment systems, video and DVD sales and rentals and other distractions, plus a perception that going to the movies has become too costly. To make movie-going more of an "entertainment experience," Cineplex and other chains throughout the 1990s built state-of-the-art megaplexes— with luxurious stadium seating, digital sound, wraparound screens, espresso bars and video arcades. But, at the same time, they were locked into long-term leases that prevented them from closing older, no-longer-profitable theatres. That left the chains with many more screens to serve roughly the same number of theatre-goers as half a century ago. As a result of these and other factors, by early this year, several chains, including Cineplex, had filed for bankruptcy protection.

Theatre chains traditionally do little advertising—they feed off the backs of film studios, which lavishly market each new release—and Cineplex, which doesn't even have a vice-president of advertising, was in no position to commission ambitious ads. So the origins of this commercial are some-what unorthodox.

Lavoie and several other ad people sit on a committee that tries to increase the Canadian industry's profile at the annual Cannes Advertising Festival. At a meeting at Cineplex Odeon on January 24, Lavoie and his friend Rob Guen-ette, an advertising director at Molson Companies Ltd. and a client of Taxi, Lavoie's agency, saw an opportunity. For Guenette, it was a chance to demon-strate his belief that advertisers would prosper if they took more risks and en-couraged exciting creative work. Not surprisingly, Lavoie agreed. In the ad business, agencies often do pro bono work, using the opportunity to make adventurous, attention-getting ads that burnish an agency's image. Cinema spots, which are longer than 15- or 30-second TV commercials and should have high-quality story lines and production values to compete with the Holly-wood films that follow them, are an adperson's dream. So, Guenette and Lavoie thought, why not donate their time and talents to help their colleague, Paul Bolté, Cineplex's director of national sales, by making a cinema commercial that would not only attract customers to the ailing chain but would also be a showcase for Canadian talent, a potential Cannes award-winner?

The Creative Brief

The first step in the making of an ad is to prepare a brief—a one- or two-page manifesto outlining the strategic goals the client wants the advertising to address for a product or service. Usually written by the client's senior market-ing executive, it provides a general direction for the agency's creative team.

Acting on behalf of Cineplex, Guenette took on the brief. He'd read research showing that, on average, people go to fewer movies than he'd imagined. So what would make them go more often? What is the one thing that is unique in the minds of consumers about going to the movies? What little advertising Cineplex has done focussed on gift packs of tickets or new, more comfortable seats, great sound or better cafés. But, thought Guenette, these are *features*, not *benefits*. Based on his experience with large corporations, he found it incomprehensible that a company wouldn't advertise its core competency. A movie chain's strength, he believed, is in presenting a film to an audience in a way that can only be duplicated in a cinema. For one thing, it's a social experience to laugh or to cry along with scores of fellow theatre-goers. For another, the experience can't be matched by even the largest TV screen, the best DVD player or the most expensive audio system. With all this bubbling in his mind, Guenette started the brief this way:

Exactly what do we have to do?
Convince and reward movie-goers: they are truly choosing the only real cinematic experience and anything less is a lot less by comparison.

What's the category need?
Get more people to see more movies at the cinema.

What are the mistaken assumptions that we can capitalize on?

- TV technology has caught up with cinema (e.g., DVD, surround sound, etc.)
- It's more comfortable and convenient at home
- Going to the cinema is really expensive

How can we do this in a surprising and memorable way?
Contrast the significant difference between the movie experience at home and at the cinema to illustrate that only the cinema provides the real experience.

With his buzzed hair, stylish black-on-black-on-black outfits and an assortment of narrow Armani glasses with frames of different colours, Guenette doesn't look like the stereotypical suit-and-tie client. But he's got the credentials: an economics degree and experience in retail banking and in a marketing division of Unilever. Nothing if not shrewd, Guenette knows that creatives—especially those who are visually oriented—usually don't read the entire brief. His solution, worthy of Pavlov, is to always include a sexy line that will push creative buttons. So, for Lavoie's benefit, he wrote:

What insights will make this communication truly surprising?
The difference between seeing a movie at home vs. at the cinema is like comparing watching pornography vs. having sex.

As Guenette expected, the line excited Lavoie, but how would the adman turn an arousing simile into an execution? Off and on throughout the rest of January, Lavoie toyed with ideas. He thought about running spectacular footage from effects-heavy films to dramatically demonstrate—especially to those theatre-goers who had only seen the movies on video—how stupendous they look on the big screen. But aside from being predictable and not much different from the high-impact trailers that precede every film, there was no glory in executing a spot that needed nothing more than a skillful editor. What about showing a tiny TV on the huge screen to demonstrate how much bigger the sound and visuals are in a cinema? No, thought Lavoie, I have to show something that is fantastic in the theatre but would die on a TV at home. *The boring made exciting.* Then, while on a business trip to Florida, Lavoie had a *eureka* moment: *A fly lands on a kitchen table. It gets swatted. It sings to its loved one. Like a Hollywood movie, it doesn't die.*

For such an audacious idea to work, of course, there are risks. The rules for cinema ads are somewhat different than those for TV ads. When people go to the movies, they expect to have a larger-than-life experience. To show a commercial on the big screen is no different. But what if Lavoie's approach backfired and consumers decided that instead of being a brilliant execution of the boring-made-exciting, the spot simply looked boring?

The Pre-production Meeting

February 7, 2:30 p.m. Eleven people are congregated around the boardroom table in the renovated warehouse that serves as Taxi's offices in downtown Toronto. The pre-production meeting is the first time the agency's creative team meets with everyone involved, including representatives from the production house and the editing studio, the cinematographer, a casting agent (if the spot involves actors) and wardrobe people, the sound specialist and, most importantly, the client. (It's at this stage that agencies, eager to move ahead, may push for approval from a still uncertain client, leading to potential conflicts later.) Although the key participants today are providing their services without a fee, in most ways the Cineplex commercial is like any other. Its value is about equal to an average Canadian spot—$250,000—and everyone is taking it seriously.

Standing up, Lavoie passes around Guenette's brief and a package entitled "Laura's Friend." It contains a working script and his pencilled storyboard for the visuals. With his partner, Jane Hope, Lavoie co-founded Taxi nine years ago and built it into an award-winning agency with $70 million in annual billings and a staff of 65. Although a relatively small player in Canada's $10-billion ad industry, Taxi has an impressive client list: Pfizer Canada Inc. (Reactine and Viagra), Molson Companies (Rickard's Red and the don't-drink-and-drive campaign), BMW Canada Inc. (the upcoming launch of the MINI Cooper), Krispy Kreme Doughnuts Corp. and TELUS (the ongoing campaign featuring ducks, frogs, lizards and ladybugs). When Taxi was an unknown start-up, Lavoie decided he didn't want category leaders. Instead, he preferred under-dogs—clients who were in second or third or fourth place—because they had less to lose and were more likely to take a chance on a new agency and edgier creative work. It was a strategy born of necessity as much as design, but one that remains in place today.

Lavoie is six-foot-three and broad-shouldered. With his shaved head and commanding presence, he looks a little like rock star Billy Corgan, leader of the Smashing Pumpkins. He is wearing a black sweater, black cargo-style Armani pants and black shoes that appear to have been outlined in white paint. Lavoie knows how to squeeze the juice out of casual. Acting out each step for his attentive audience, he explains how the commercial will look. It's meant to be a boring scene: a kitchen table, overturned glass, some spilled cola, a woman talking on a phone in the background who walks off-screen. Then, Lavoie says, you hear the sound of a plane that's so realistic the audience will think it's flying right over their heads. It does a loop, and flies by from another direction. After another loop it's even louder, right above the audience, as though it's coming in for a landing. Then a fly screeches across the kitchen table—"*Errrr, errrrrr,*" says Lavoie—and comes to a halt. Lavoie leans forward, his hands flat on the table, his shoulders heaving as he pants: "*Ah-huh, ah-huh, ah-huh ...*"

Looking up, Lavoie says: "Then he stretches. It's like he's just finished a long, hard run. ..." Lavoie stretches, loudly cracking his knuckles, groaning as though he's exhausted.

"Then he walks to the liquid. ..." Lavoie rocks animatedly from side to side, imitating the fly's gait. "He stops to drink. ..." Making animated slurping sounds, Lavoie swallows noisily. Everyone in the room is laughing at the performance.

"Then a door slams, someone's coming, he looks around. ..." Lavoie, his eyes wide open, glances nervously to the left and right, then in a stage whisper says: "*Whazz-that?*"

Raising his arm, Lavoie brings the palm of his hand down on the table with a dramatic *bang!*

"A big flyswatter comes down," he says. "And lifts up. The fly's stuck to it. Then he falls on his back. There's a pause. He looks dead...."

Al Jolson-style, Lavoie melodramatically spreads his arms and begins singing, with choked emotion, a song that he remembered listening to as a child and that seemed perfect for this spot. "Tell Laura I love her, Tell Laura I need her...."

Bang! He slaps the table again. Surely the fly must be dead this time. He sings: "Tell Laura not to cry...."

Bang! Bang! Lavoie weakly raises an arm, his eyes staring heavenward. "My love for her ... will ... never ... die...."

As the laughter subsides, Lavoie explains that theme music will follow, along with a superimposed title—known as a "super"—that reads: "Cineplex. Where movies come to life." Then he reads from a page in a handout entitled "The Buzz on the Fly": "He's an adventurer, a romantic, a lover. He's Harrison Ford, John Wayne and Charlie Chaplin rolled into one. The quintessential Hollywood hero who doesn't die."

Lavoie solemnly introduces Jim Lovisek, the bug wrangler who has worked with Lavoie on Taxi's TELUS/Clearnet spots.

"Jim, can you explain what kinds of things you can make them do?" Lavoie asks. "Like when the fly hears someone coming and looks up, startled, and says, *'Whazz-that?'*"

"For the movie *The Adventures of Sinbad*, I imported ants from Malaysia," Lovisek says. "If I blew a little puff of air toward the left side of the ant's head, it would move its head to the left. If I blew on the right side, it would move to the right. If I blew under its head, it would lift its head up. Flies aren't quite as responsive as ants, though."

"What about getting the fly to walk up to the puddle of liquid?"

"I'll have it on a harness. I can get it to walk up to the liquid, no problem. If you want the fly stationary, no problem. If you want it drinking, not a problem. The most difficult shot will be the landing. There's a lot of latitude as to where it can go."

The agency producer, Louise Blouin, a trim, striking blonde, asks: "What about close-ups?"

Lovisek furrows his brow. "Flies have large compound eyes. They're quite horrific, actually. I don't know if you'll want a close-up."

Later, while studying the director's storyboard, they discuss the swatter scenes. Michael Schwartz, the president and executive producer of Avion Films, the company that will be providing the technical staff and equipment to shoot the commercial, asks: "Will we be accused of abuse of flies? I'm sure there's an organization out there somewhere representing flies."

"They only live for 10 days to two weeks," says Lovisek. "I'll have lots of ones that died naturally. We can use those on the table for the swatting."

"Good," Lavoie says. "If it's on its back, it doesn't have to move at all. The digital effects guys can move a leg or arm in post-production."

Finally they discuss the length of the spot. Turning to Cineplex's Paul Bolté, Lavoie says: "We should aim for 60 seconds."

"Maybe it can go longer than that," says Bolté.

"So," Guenette concludes at the end of the meeting, "when consumers leave the theatre we want them to think, I'll never rent a film again."

The Bug Wrangler

February 28, 11 a.m. The offices of the Toronto Nature Centre are located in a nondescript suburban industrial park. Inside, the premises are filled with terrariums and aquariums containing snakes, lizards and other creatures. Upstairs, Jim Lovisek sits in a room about the size of a bachelor apartment cluttered with fossils, minerals, seashells and boxes.

Advertising is fond of using babies and animals, since consumers respond to them. It's not hard to find a dog or cat trainer, Lovisek explains, but who do you call if, as was the case with Taxi's TELUS/Clearnet commercials, you want a Nicaraguan red-eyed tree frog or a Madagascar giant day gecko or an Indian running duck?

As a boy, Lovisek obsessively collected frogs, snakes and other wild things. Later he became a zoologist, working on the remote coast of Hudson Bay and along the banks of Amazonian rivers in Colombia, Bolivia and Brazil. After a stint at the Royal Ontario Museum, he became a consultant in exotic creatures for the commercial and feature film businesses in the mid-1980s. He's a big man, over six feet, with a salt-and-pepper beard and moustache, an untidy thatch of dark hair and a soft-spoken, vaguely professorial manner.

Today, 10 days after the flies arrived frozen, Lovisek is staring intently into a wooden enclosure about the size of a large shoebox. It's screened on three sides and has fabric on the fourth so he can slip his hand inside, where there are dozens of live flies and, lying on a bed of pine chips, even more pupae, resembling grains of rice. This is the replacement shipment, which has just arrived.

"I ordered 6,000 greenbottle pupae," Lovisek says, explaining that flies are raised commercially in the U.S. for fishing bait as well as reptile and bird food.

Reaching into the box and removing several pupae, he rubs them between his fingers. "They'll hatch at about 25 degrees Celsius. I cool some of them, keep them at different temperatures, so they'll hatch at different times. That way I'll always have some.

"The biggest challenge with this job is the landing. I'll cool the flies down, so I'll have many of them at different temperatures. At a certain temperature, a fly won't fly much, but it will walk around a lot. This is important if, for example, you have a prosthetic of a decaying body for a horror movie and you want flies to appear to be feasting on it."

The Shoot

March 2, 8 a.m. The basement studio at Generator Productions, a facility affiliated with Avion Films, is crowded with people. The set is simple—a yellow Formica table with two chairs and, past that, a fridge, stove and another table against the back wall. The film camera is positioned just in front of the yellow table, and a fake wall with a realistic-looking window cut into it has been erected along one side, within camera view. With military efficiency, a production crew—the grips, gaffers, props experts, assistants and assistants to the assistants—is setting up lights, positioning portable reflectors (used to soften and diffuse lights), taping down cables and arranging props.

Just then, Jim Lovisek arrives, lugging two coolers and a toolbox. He opens a cooler and removes the wooden box, which is teeming with flies—the cool temperature keeps them less active. Coffee in hand, Lavoie walks by, looks inside and whistles in amazement. "This is a good yarn," he says. "Really, we can't worry about recreating the script exactly. The flies are going to do what they're going to do. We just need to shoot enough so that we have a lot to work with in post-production."

Lovisek sets up a small sheet of foam core on a nearby table and opens his toolbox. Taking a fly from the box, he anaesthetizes it with a blast of CO_2 from a portable canister. Placing it on the foam core, he puts two small pieces of cardboard over its wings and fastens the cardboard with entomological mounting pins. Then he begins the painstaking task of tying a harness around the fly's abdomen using a polyester line thinner than the thinnest fishing line. Explaining to Lavoie that he may use a drop of liver to attract the fly, Lovisek says: "I like my liver a little bit more rotten. I just took it out and put it on the heater. It's coming along, but it's not really foul yet."

Behind him, Lavoie is talking to production manager Greg Horton about swatting flies. For a brief pre-production session the previous afternoon, Horton had obtained an assortment of flyswatters: green, brown, yellow and red ones with white plastic handles; a purple one with a braided wire handle; and one with a child's flip-flop sandal on the end, which everyone laughed at but agreed was so weird it would take the viewers' attention away from the fly. "I love that big red swatter," says Lavoie. "It's going to look as big as a barn door on a theatre screen."

In the studio two hours later, after the woman has been filmed in the background, Stanley Mestel is sitting on the dolly, fine tuning the camera angle. The silver-haired Mestel, who's in his 60s and learned his craft in Britain, is a multi-award-winning cinematographer. He's using a camera that's capable of shooting at very high speeds—150 frames a second for some of the shots—to capture the rapid movements of an insect. He's also selected an 8mm lens, called a Boroscope, which gives an extremely wide-angle view, one that makes the saltshaker, fork and overturned glass on the yellow table look like a vista on some surreal landscape, especially with the dramatic shadows from a single, bright, carefully placed light. Staring at a video-playback monitor that shows an image of what the camera is focussing on, Lavoie says: "In my mind, it's a landing strip. That's the control tower." He points at the saltshaker. "That's the pond." He points at the small puddle of spilled liquid. "And that's the evil monster," he adds, as the man in charge of props—called the "key props"—brings the red swatter into view.

Lavoie tells Horton that the spilled liquid looks like it's drying out. Horton turns to the key props and asks him to touch up the puddle, which appears to be made of cola but is actually soy sauce. The man pulls a capped syringe of soy sauce from his tool belt and carefully adds some to the edges.

When they're ready to shoot the fly, Lovisek puts a drop of decomposing liver into the puddle and decides to try one without a harness. "Rolling," says Mestel. Lovisek removes a fly from the cooler and releases it. The fly lands very fast, almost straight down, and begins buzzing noisily. Lovisek tries to recapture it, but it flies away.

Lovisek gets another, picking one that's been kept at a cooler temperature so it will be less frisky. This time the fly lands on its back. Lovisek picks it up and releases it again. When it lands, it walks toward the liquid, pauses, turns around and walks toward the camera.

"That's okay," says Lavoie. "The more times he lands and walks around, the more they'll have to work with in post."

Lovisek releases several more flies. A couple of them manage to escape. When another glances off the table and flies underneath, a crew member scurries after it. One of the techies whispers to another: "I've seen actors who can't perform much better."

At one point, one of the bright lights, pointing straight up in the air, makes a sharp sizzling sound and there is a puff of smoke. "Is the light shorting out?" someone asks in a startled voice. There's a pause; then with a lazy drawl, the technician in charge of lights and electrical—the gaffer—says: "No, it's a fly."

Lovisek switches to the fly on the harness. "Action," says Mestel. For several minutes, Lovisek repeatedly places the fly on the table and yanks it up and away from the camera. Lavoie and Mestel coach him on how fast to pull. "It can't go too fast or we can't see its body, Jim, but it has to appear to have that runway speed."

Many takes later, Lavoie says: "That was interesting, Jim. It went right over the lens. That could be cool. Can we keep going?"

"Is the fly okay?" asks Horton. "Can I get him a soda?"

As Lovisek had predicted, getting the landing shot to look realistically like a small plane touching down on a runway is difficult. Hunched over the monitor, Lavoie says: "This is the most important shot. This establishes our credibility with the audience. If it succeeds, the rest will be fine." Finally, after another take, Lavoie leaps jubilantly from his chair. "Bingo! Great! We got it. Jim, you're a genius."

As the afternoon wears on, Horton carefully marks off each shot as it's completed. At around 5 p.m., Rob Guenette and Cineplex's Paul Bolté arrive. Sometimes the client's representatives are present for an entire shoot; with this one, Bolté's presence is relatively minor. Still, the client is on the set, and Lavoie defers to him.

"Hey, watch this," says Lavoie to Bolté, pointing at the fly on his monitor. "He walks sideways, stops a second, then continues. That could work for when he's walking, stops and says, "Whazz-that?""

There's a sizzling sound and a plume of smoke rises from one of the lights. Everyone stares at it silently until Mestel, without looking up from the camera, says: "At least we won't have to pay him residuals."

For the swatting scene, it takes many tries to get the fly sticking to the swatter, then dropping onto its back after a couple of taps on the table. Mestel shoots one of Lovisek's dead flies lying on its back for 10 seconds, then has the key props adjust its position slightly before shooting for another 10 seconds. These will be the shots in which the fly sings *Tell Laura I Love Her*. Finally, satisfied he has what he needs, Lavoie announces that the shoot is officially over.

Lavoie, who has an engaging, insouciant manner, can, like his friend Guenette, give the impression of trying to sell you something even when he's not, an occupational hazard, perhaps. Part of his charm is his absolutely sincere belief that advertising is a kind of contemporary popular art, rather than just cleverness in the service of capitalism, although he would cheerfully admit it's that as well.

Lavoie is determined that the fly spot will be a creative statement as well as good advertising, but will the final product create the buzz he's after?

The Rushes

March 5, 10 a.m. Three days after the shoot, Lavoie and Mestel sit with editor Gord Koch at Flashcut, an editing facility located on the floor above Generator. The film images have been transferred to digital videotape, so Koch can almost instantly bring onto the monitor any of the many hundreds of raw shots. Lavoie's task is to give Koch enough direction so he can put together a rough cut of the commercial—a version to show the client—with what seem to be the best shots in the best arrangement, without refinements, like digitally animated effects or the finished sound mix, which will come later. After they watch several sequences of the fly landing, Koch says he likes one in particular.

"See, it's that World War I feel, like one of those biplanes that hit the ground, and some of them landed clumsily. ..." Koch is wearing a faded check shirt, black jeans and yellow Converse All Stars. He has light brown, wavy hair, a wispy goatee and a silver earring in his left ear. He sticks out his arms and rocks from side to side, as though making a rough landing.

"Yeah, yeah," says Lavoie enthusiastically.

When they watch another shot, Lavoie points at the fly on the monitor and says: "See what he just did? He went up and down there. We can play that back and forth when he's panting. ..." Lavoie pants: "*Ah-huh, ah-huh, ah-huh.*"

"Go back to that other shot, Gord," Lavoie says. "Then cut to the one where he gets swatted. That's one option. Drinking, then walking back to get swatted. Option two: a slow dissolve from where he's drinking to the '*Whazz-that?*'"

Finally they study the swatting shots. Lavoie talks about the pacing: "Okay, there's two or three seconds, nothing happens. At this point, he goes ..." Lavoie sings: "Tell Laura I love her, tell Laura I need her. ..." Then he claps his hands together to indicate the swatter striking. "Pause. Tell Laura not to cry. Then, bam. ..." *Clap.* "Bam. ..." *Clap.* "Bam. ..." *Clap.* "You know, is it dead yet?"

Koch scribbles a few notes as Lavoie says: "So that's it. The Cineplex super comes up: 'Where movies come to life.'"

The Rough Cut Screening with the Client

March 8, 2 p.m. Paul Bolté is sitting with Lavoie, Guenette, Mestel and a couple of others in Koch's studio. In the best of worlds, the client screening is collegial and collaborative, with the client suggesting reasonable changes. However, it is at this screening that any cracks in the agency-client relationship will emerge. Sometimes, especially with large corporations, client representatives may be so aware of the chain of command above them that their reactions will be indecisive and vague, leaving the agency unsure how to proceed. Other times, as Gord Koch knows too well, the atmosphere can be toxic. He has sat with his nose inches from his monitor, listening to corrosive arguments rage behind him.

When everyone's settled, they watch the assembly. The opening super reads: "Mundane Productions Presents: A Really Boring Film," followed by "La Table de Cuisine (A Kitchen Table)," parodying an arty foreign film. Lavoie provides a running commentary, mentioning, for example, that the leash attached to the fly's harness will be digitally erased. Afterwards, everyone agrees that the fly singing the song—Lavoie's voice for now, until an actor has been recorded—is funny.

"About the super," says Guenette. "Instead of saying, 'This is a really boring film,' would it be better to say up front: 'This *could be* a really boring film'?"

Lavoie considers the suggestion, then says: "When you say it's boring, you'll get their attention."

Looking concerned, Bolté asks: "But is the first impression that it's boring on film? Not that it's boring on television?"

"I really feel strongly that we can achieve that at the end," says Lavoie. "Maybe we'll say something like, 'A boring film on TV is a boring film, but here in the cinema....'"

Bolté still seems worried. "What about saying, 'A boring film?' with a question mark?"

"Mmmm, I don't know," says Lavoie.

They watch it again.

"I'm still hung up on 'A boring film' with a question mark," says Bolté. "I think you're leading people to thinking, Oh no, it's a boring film."

Gord Koch, who's been listening to the discussion, says: "At the movies you always see trailers that say: 'Astounding,' 'Exciting,' 'Thrilling,' 'Explosive.' ..."

"Yeah," says Guenette. "It's like, I've heard that before.... Then, what's this? A *really boring* film?"

"It starts to make more sense," says Bolté uncertainly. "I start disagreeing with myself."

After they watch it again, Bolté asks: "What's the duration."

Koch glances at his monitor and says: "That version, with the Cineplex super at the end, was two minutes."

Bolté does a double take, his eyes bulging. "*TWO minutes?!*"

"Have a sale," suggests Lavoie. "Buy one ticket and get an extra film free."

Sagging weakly in his chair, Bolté says: "I knew it was longer than 60 seconds. We used to do up to 90 seconds. But with advertising, if you have three 90s, people would be, like, *When* does the movie start?"

Lavoie and Guenette exchange glances. A disturbed client is never a good thing. They discuss with Bolté whether Cineplex has an official policy on lengths of commercials, and whether the chain hasn't every right to go longer on a commercial for itself. Although worried, Bolté doesn't pull rank, which is characteristic of a good agency-client relationship, although in this case it also reflects the fact that Cineplex is getting the spot for nothing, defusing the client's authority, and that Bolté, who is a sales guy, is a bit junior compared to the senior marketing executives who often represent the client at these screenings. Clients, despite being the butt of jokes in the ad industry, often bring valuable insights to the process, however.

Shaking his head, Bolté says: "Well, I'll give it some thought." Pausing, he adds: "If it's under two minutes, that's okay."

Turning to Koch, Lavoie asks: "How long is it exactly?"

"Two minutes and four frames."

"Can you cut five frames?"

With comic timing, Guenette leans forward and says: "Cut out the Cineplex logo. That'd do it."

The room erupts in laughter. Even Bolté joins in.

The Visual Effects

March 14, 4:30 p.m. In a roomy studio at Toybox, a post-production company in Toronto, Lavoie is sitting on a sofa working on his Powerbook and taking calls on his cell. Across the room, Gord Koch sits beside Jeff Campbell, a visual effects artist whose credits include *Fight Club*, with Brad Pitt, and *The Cell*, with Jennifer Lopez. Campbell, who in his black ribbed T-shirt, black jeans and goatee looks like the part-time punk rock guitarist he is, has on his monitor the shot of the fly standing next to the puddle of soy sauce. During the shooting, the fly never walked up to the liquid in a satisfactory way, so Koch and Lavoie selected an overhead shot where the fly walked, paused, then walked farther and stopped. A partial image of the puddle from another shot was married to that, and Campbell digitally painted it in, adding reflections and tiny ripples when the fly appears to drink.

Now Campbell places a computerized web mesh over the fly's image, which allows him to isolate and digitally enhance individual features. Having just made the fly's head bob up and down as it drinks, he and Koch watch repeated playbacks. Koch tells him that Lavoie has talked about wanting the fly to look like "a little dog drinking at a puddle."

"If that was a dog, you'd believe it," says Koch. "But as a fly, you don't. A fly's head just moves from one position to the next—" Koch turns his head from side to side very quickly "—so fast you hardly see it. It doesn't swivel around—" he swings his head around in an arc "—like a dog, or like we do."

For much of the afternoon Campbell continues tinkering with the image. He puts the cursor on the fly's web mesh and stretches it, altering the way the head moves. Later, when Guenette arrives, he and Lavoie watch the entire sequence of the fly landing, walking to the puddle and drinking. Just after landing, the real fly did a small motion with a back leg that looked like a stretch. Campbell digitally extended both the leg and the shadow it casts on the table, making the stretch more obvious and human-like.

"Fuck, that's brilliant," says Lavoie. "When you see the whole thing coming together, it's like Christmas."

A Potential Crisis

March 14, 6:20 p.m. Shortly after Campbell and Koch finish their visual-effects work for the day, Lavoie and Guenette take advantage of one of Toybox's client services and order a bottle of Merlot. A waiter brings a cheese-and-cracker tray as well. Turning to Guenette, Lavoie says: "Paul Bolté called. He showed it to the powers that be. He said there may be some changes. "

"Oh, no," says Guenette, groaning. They both roll their eyes. Generally, people in advertising think clients are too cautious or present the work too early to decision-makers.

"He showed it to them without sound. They think it's too long."

Guenette shook his head. "The whole thing is: why not wait until you have the final production?" He pauses, then says: "If I single-mindedly turned a critical eye on it, we could reduce the length."

"It could be shorter," agrees Lavoie.

The two men sit in silence. Suddenly, a huge swarm of flies appears on the studio's wall-sized TV screen, which is tuned to Newsworld. It's a story about "The Bug Lady," a professor at Simon Fraser University's school of criminology who can, by studying insects that colonize human bodies, pinpoint with great accuracy the time of death.

"Well, that was symbolic," says Lavoie.

Guenette nods. "Forensic investigators go to flies for answers. Advertising people, like us, also go to flies for answers."

The Sound Effects

March 20, 11 a.m. Today, Lavoie and Louise Blouin are in a studio control room at Keen Music, Voice and Sound Design to oversee the recording session with the actor who will be the fly's voice. With them is Keen's owner, Thomas Neuspiel, a sound specialist who over the last few days has completed most of the effects and music, which will soon be cued to what Campbell has done to the fly. In addition to putting down some short segments of scored music, created by one of his composers, which add drama to the fly's movements, and a final theme based on the *Tell Laura I Love Her* melody, Neuspiel has recorded some sound effects. The *bang* of the flyswatter, for instance, was created by first recording the sound a real flyswatter makes, then combining it with the sound a thick book makes when smacked against a table and, finally, mixing it with the sound of a punch to the face, which was taken from a CD. The biggest challenges, though, were the sounds of the fly walking and the plane passing overhead.

For the fly walking, Neuspiel and an associate tried tapping twist ties and Q-Tips on a countertop. But they didn't like the sound it made so they tried lifting a Q-Tip off a piece of two-sided sticky tape, which sounded all right, though they ultimately used some cartoon-like pizzicato string music. The plane was much harder. The sound of an airplane changes constantly as it approaches a listener, and then as it recedes away into the distance. The sound is so complex that it's hard to digitally simulate it, so the live sound of a real plane was essential. In the end, Neuspiel found a recording of a Curtiss Jenny biplane that his team modified electronically to duplicate the flying pattern and sound Lavoie had wanted, then made intricate modifications to it electronically so it would work on the surround-sound audio systems in a theatre.

Through a window, Neuspiel, Lavoie and Blouin watch Frank McAnulty, a short, stocky actor who teaches at Second City's training workshops, as he prepares for his role, which Lavoie has dubbed "Frank the Fly." Activating the intercom, Lavoie says: "Don't hold back, Frank, or we'll swat you." With the help of a glass of water, McAnulty makes a variety of slurping, swallowing and burping sounds, then several exaggerated sighs. When they stop laughing, Neuspiel says: "Good choice, Paul."

For the next couple of hours they record the sounds of the fly panting after its landing, groaning when it stretches its leg and drinking from the puddle of liquid. Then it's time to record the nervous *Whazz-that* uttered by the fly moments before the swatter descends. McAnulty tries it, and Lavoie tells him it's too "big" for a little fly. McAnulty tries it a few more times, but Lavoie isn't satisfied, so McAnulty does a series of *Whazz-thats*, hunching his shoulders, drawing his arms close to his sides and curling his hands under his chin, making very small, almost spastic movements, each one tinier and more frightened than the last. After moving on to the singing, Lavoie decides he's satisfied with the assortment of takes.

"We get *paid* for doing this," says Lavoie, echoing a sentiment voiced by almost all advertising creatives. Lavoie is feeling especially upbeat having learned that Bolté's superiors at Cineplex Odeon have agreed to the two-minute length. "It's too much fun. We're just playing games. On this spot we didn't research it to death. We didn't have to fight through 33 layers of client to sell creative ideas."

The implication is clear: the unusual freedom of this Cineplex spot is going to translate into a superior creative execution and a highly successful commercial.

A Crisis Averted

March 22, 3 p.m. Two days later, Lavoie and Blouin are reviewing the sound mix in Neuspiel's studio. There's a problem. The closing theme is a sad, funereally paced rendition of *Tell Laura I Love Her* inspired by Frank McAnulty's anguished singing of the final line—"*My love for her … will … never … die …*" But as they listen, they realize that the closing super, "Even the mundane is *thrilling* on the big screen," isn't working with the music, a similar problem to the former closing line "Where movies come to life," which had been rejected because the contrast with the fly being whacked to death was just too great. "You know what my only worry is?" says Lavoie. "It's so sad at the end, but then the super says, 'Even the mundane is thrilling on the big screen.'"

As if reading his mind, Blouin slowly shakes her head. As she understands it, the digital master has been sent to the lab to be transferred onto film. Any change now will be very expensive. "We can't change the visuals," she says.

Neuspiel, suddenly worried that Lavoie might want to solve the problem by changing the music, quickly says: "I don't think the music should be thrilling there. It doesn't suit the sad mood of the story at the end."

Lavoie waves his hand distractedly. "No, the music's right. We've made an error." He pauses, thinking, then says to no one in particular: "Did we make the mundane *exceptional*? I think the word would be *dramatic*. Even the mundane is *dramatic* on the big screen." Turning to Blouin, he says: "What is the situation? Is it big?"

Blouin explains that it may be. For several tense moments Lavoie waits while she calls Gord Koch on her cell. "Hi, it's Lou. I have a Cineplex question. You know the super? If we need to change one word, can we? Are you serious...?" To Lavoie, she says: "They haven't sent it yet."

Lavoie shoots both arms above his head victoriously. The change can be made inexpensively.

"Paul's a happy man," says Blouin.

The Test Screening and Another Crisis

April 26, 6:30 p.m. The commercial is finished. Tonight, on behalf of Cineplex Odeon, Paul Bolté has invited the team that worked on the commercial to see it at a downtown Toronto theatre. There is a mix of advertising and production people in the audience, along with regular theatre-goers who have paid to see a 6:50 p.m. showing of *Blow*, starring Johnny Depp. If all goes well, Bolté plans to have copies of the commercial made and shipped to theatres across Canada.

Three commercials run first, each with its own crowd-pleasing qualities. The first, for the antihistamine Reactine, is a spot Taxi has just finished. Shot in South Africa and featuring a man with allergies shedding his clothes in joy as he frolics in the woods amidst the pollen, the ad draws many laughs from the crowd. The second, a hilarious series of clips of ordinary-looking people singing karaoke badly, turns out to be a Levi's commercial. Like the best cinema ads, the emphasis is on entertainment rather than hard sell. One viewer whispers to his companion: "Now that's what a commercial in a theatre should be like." The third, a car spot, is filled with fast cuts and the headache-inducing sound of a high-performance engine. These are followed by three trailers for upcoming films, each one characterized by dramatic editing and punchy sound.

Finally, the Cineplex spot runs. Lavoie himself is restless, anxious to see how it will look on-screen and observe how people will react. But as he waits to hear the dramatic sound of the carefully constructed biplane, he realizes something is wrong. The sound is so low that the spot, especially in contrast to everything that had come before it, isn't boring-made-exciting, it's just *boring*.

Later, a disappointed Lavoie says: "The spot is supposed to be really banal, but for it to work, it has to have big pictures and big sound. The sound was down so low that the impact was lost. So we're fixing that. Also, the spot was in the wrong slot. It should be with the group of commercials before the trailers. It's long, so if it doesn't come up until after all the commercials and trailers, people will be pissed off."

The Aftermath

June 22, 6:40 p.m. A Cineplex Odeon theatre in downtown Toronto is nearly three-quarters filled for a screening of the summer hit, *Moulin Rouge*, starring Nicole Kidman and Ewan McGregor. There are only two commercials before the trailers begin, the second one being "La Table de Cuisine." There is sporadic chuckling when the super: "Mundane Productions presents: A Really Boring Film" appears. After the now throaty roar of the biplane passes realistically overhead and the fly screeches onto the table, however, the crowd responds enthusiastically. When the swatter smacks the fly for the first time, there is surprised laughter, which grows in intensity when the fly begins singing. The credits are met with spontaneous applause. There are similar reports from other screenings.

The sound may have been solved and the response to the commercial positive, but the business problem that inspired the commercial had gradually begun to correct itself by the time the spot was in theatres. The latest box office numbers show a rise in movie ticket sales throughout North America, mainly because of a succession of hit films such as *Crouching Tiger, Hidden Dragon*, *Hannibal* and *Spy Kids*, as well as summer blockbusters such as *Pearl Harbor* and *The Mummy Returns*.

As Cineplex's fortunes improve, and because the firm has not commissioned market research, it's impossible to tell whether the spot's goal—to put more bums in seats—is working, or whether it's merely providing audiences with a bit of light entertainment before the feature presentation. Still, informal reports suggest that audiences are enjoying it and many are associating their enjoyment of it with the Cineplex Odeon brand.

What's more clear is that the spot succeeded as a vehicle to generate excitement for Lavoie and Taxi. Both agency colleagues and advertisers have been telling Lavoie and his associates how much they loved it, and it has been short-listed in the best cinema commercial and best direction categories at the prestigious Toronto Art Directors' awards, scheduled for November. In addition, when it was screened at Toronto's annual Worldwide Short Film Festival last June, the crowd heartily laughed and applauded. It may be telling that at a festival like this, where most cinema ads would have looked like what they were—commercials intended to sell a product—"La Table de Cuisine" looked more like a short film than a commercial.

Perhaps that's why, at the Cannes competition in June, reaction to the spot was neutral, although the industry crowd at Cannes is notoriously hard to please. More disappointing was that in a year in which a record 25 Canadian commercials had been shortlisted, "La Table de Cuisine" was not among them.

Lavoie, ever upbeat, says: "Our expectations were high there, but I honestly don't give a fuck. It's great PR for us, and as long as I know it's creative I'm happy, whether it wins awards or not. I would be more disappointed to think that people didn't get it. I know they feel fondly toward it, find it likable. Likability is a key element in how you feel about a company. At the end of the day, a commercial has to capture your imagination and say something interesting about the product or service. When you do that, you give something to the consumer in return for his or her attention. It's a more polite way of selling.

"Does it work 100% of the time? I don't know. But more often than not, great creative works better than bad creative."

CHAPTER FIVE

Anecdotal Evidence: Interviewing to Tell a Story

Don Gibb

"What's the weather like?"

Such a simple, conversational question, and yet it led *Globe and Mail* columnist Murray Campbell to a detail that provided a lead for his story on Julia Butterfly Hill, the woman who lived for two years in a 1,000-year-old giant redwood tree in California to prevent it from becoming lumber.

His simple question—along with follow-up questions—produced rich visual detail for readers. It was a cold, cold rainy day. The protective tarp was flapping in the wind. Butterfly Hill was shivering under layers of clothing. Seven, to be exact. And all of this happening on a platform the size of a double bed—yet another detail to let readers "see" the image in their minds.

He opened his story with this:

> It is beginning to hail, and Julia Butterfly Hill is shivering even though she is wearing seven layers of clothing. "It's extremely windy and it's extremely cold," she said, drawing out the syllables of "extremely" to underline the point that she has seen better days.

Ms. Hill was speaking on a cellular phone about halfway up a 60-metre redwood tree in northern California. She was huddled beneath rustling tarps on a platform about the size of a double bed.

Around her were her very few possessions: A single-burner propane stove and a bucket she uses as a toilet, some books and the cardboard on which she writes letters and poems.[1]

What's the weather like? What's your living space look like? What are you doing now? Such simple questions produce the details, anecdotes, quotes, dialogue, and scenes writers need to create the images readers need to "see" and to be part of a story. Good writers develop a built-in alarm that goes off every time one of their senses (see, hear, smell, touch, or taste) detects a moment worth capturing in more detail.

Like the father, his daughter abducted and murdered a year earlier, who cannot stand to hear the doorbell ring.

Why?

It was a year ago, as he made a pot of tea in the kitchen, that the doorbell rang. He walked past his daughter's high school graduation picture on the piano in the living room, opened the front door and faced a police constable.

What did the officer say?

"I looked straight into his eyes. He didn't have to say anything. I knew my daughter was dead. Every time I hear the doorbell, the image of the police officer—his eyes—flash back to remind me of my daughter's death." A single, simple detail of the doorbell allows the writer to capture a key moment—a telling anecdote—in the story of a father still grieving as police continue to search for his daughter's killer.

But keep going. *What did the father see in his eyes that told him she was dead? What were the first words the police officer said? Did he come in? Did he have tea with the father? Where was the mother of the girl when the officer arrived?* And then ... keep going.

The interview is the key that opens the door to great storytelling. Every interview should be an exploration for interesting, factual, informative, and visual detail. It is not simply a question-and-answer exchange or transcribing verbatim what someone says. When done well, it involves getting to the heart of an issue and to the very soul of a person.

Feature writing often offers writers a chance to do more research and more interviews. It gives writers more of an opportunity to see their interview subjects at work, at play, and at home—in other words, to go to the scene or several scenes. And that means the chance to gather more detail. It also offers the luxury of conducting follow-up interviews with key characters in the middle or at the end of the process, or after having talked to others.

To be an effective interviewer, writers need to know simple rules that form the building blocks of creating memorable features. Here are some of them.

Listen

Perhaps this is *the* most crucial interviewing skill. If you're too busy thinking of your next question or checking your digital recorder, you're not paying enough attention to the words coming from your interviewee. You have to be alert at all times to properly hear what people say and how they say it (emphatically, hesitantly, nervously, angrily, excitedly, abruptly, or clearly leaving out details). Such attention prompts important follow-up questions where the real story often lies.

The more distractions you have, the less likely you are to concentrate on the answers. Occasionally, you'll notice a television interviewer nodding in agreement to an answer from an interview subject, all the while glancing at an off-camera producer or looking at her notes for the next question. She never listened to or really heard the answer.

A single word can change the direction of your interview—even a slight hesitation by the subject can tip you off to asking another question: *Why the hesitation?*

Try to be less tied to your list of questions. Eventually, they should serve as a reminder of factual details you need, but should not form the backbone of the interview. They serve as a jumping-off point. The less you rely on your prepared list, the more the interview will evolve into a conversation and have a better chance to be spontaneous and stimulating, both for the interviewee and the writer.

Let the interviewee do most of the talking. The more you talk, the less information you get. Resist the temptation to interject to complete someone's sentence or to offer your own comments or opinions. Silence is a technique used by some writers. Often, the interviewee feels a need to fill the silence, so don't jump in immediately after someone has finished a sentence. Give the person time to elaborate. Often the best answers come in the aftermath of the original answer as the speaker reflects on what she said.

Stay in Charge

There is an art to capturing the images and anecdotes that take good reporting beyond the basics of who, what, when, where, and why. And that art can be developed over time as the writer becomes more comfortable with the process of interviewing.

A writer once described his best interviewing technique this way: "I throw out a question and the interviewee just talks on and on. I rarely have to ask a question." This writer was on cruise control. He wasn't interviewing; he was taking dictation. And he didn't lose control of his interview; he voluntarily gave it away.

Writers need to understand that everyone they interview has an agenda of some kind. It can be seeking good publicity, putting a positive spin on a

Glad You Asked!   Electronic Conversations

Q: Can I use the Internet to do my interviews?
A: The Internet is unquestionably as useful to journalists as a voice recorder, a video camera, or a cellphone. It offers instant contact through email, blogs, and social networking sites such as Facebook.

But it doesn't replace face-to-face or telephone interviews. To write a good feature, you still have to do the traditional legwork in researching and writing, including talking in person—whenever possible—to your sources. Internet communication, particularly email, can help you advance to the next stage—contact in person or by phone. The Internet gives writers the chance to make an easy first contact and to make a persuasive pitch to reluctant interviewees on why they should talk to you. However, communicating via the Internet does have its limitations.

Let's look at email for a moment. Recent research* identifies three major problems with email:

1. Email lacks cues, such as facial expressions and tone of voice, making it difficult for recipients to easily decode meaning.
2. The prospect of instantaneous communication creates an urgency that pressures email users to think and write quickly, which can lead to carelessness.
3. The inability to develop personal rapport over email makes relationships fragile in the face of conflict.

Because email gives us no clues about body language, and few indicators of tone of voice and facial expression, critics say it makes it almost impossible to interpret emotion.

Email changes the dynamics of the interviewing process. Email, like the traditional press release, gives interview subjects more control over content. Subjects have the freedom to make statements rather than expose themselves story, floating a new idea, hiding the embarrassing or negative side of a story, or self-promotion. Listen to them and listen to their agenda, but don't let them take control of the interview.

Being in control, however, means having your own agenda (what's in it for your readers?), looking for a story focus beyond the routine, asking questions readers might ask, keeping the interview on track.

The writer's agenda is to search for the truth and to ask questions readers might ask. Remember: You are not writing for the people you are writing about. You are not writing for your editors or fellow writers. You are writing

to the scrutiny of a face-to-face interview with the spontaneity of follow-up questions. In fact, some critics say an email Q&A is not an interview at all. Whatever your view, we can all agree that nothing replaces the face-to-face interview, particularly for the feature story, where the writer is seeking a deeper and richer understanding of the people in the story.

Email and other Internet-based communication demand the same level of transparency and due diligence as all other aspects of reporting. Writers, too, have to be alert to avoid being duped. Are you sure the email is written by the source and not an assistant or aide? Do you know the real name and identity of the blogger or the person posting on a social networking site? What assurance do you have that someone has not posted material using someone else's name? For example, the popular hand-held BlackBerry has made sources more accessible to writers, who also operate in the BlackBerry world, but the device can put too much control in the hands of the source. A cabinet minister's response, for example, could simply be a well-formulated response by her public affairs officer under the name of the minister.

Finally, you might ask, what are the rules around using Internet-based interviews? Do we need to inform the readers *how* we got our information? Yes. Whether or not the reader understands or appreciates the differences between live and virtual information sources, you do, and to omit the fact that information came via email, text message, or Facebook is to leave a false impression on its authenticity.

Internet communication is useful—for clarification or elaboration on a point previously obtained in a face-to-face or telephone interview, for a chance to get the cabinet minister on the phone, for a quick fact check. It's also good if there is NO other way to get the interview. But nothing replaces face-to-face contact.

Don Gibb

* Daniel Enemark, "It's All about Me: Why E-mails Are So Easily Misunderstood," *Christian Science Monitor*, May 15, 2006, <http://www.csmonitor.com/2006/0515/p13s01-stct.html> (accessed May 16, 2008).

for your readers. Keep reminding yourself of this as a way of trying to break through an interviewee's agenda and to keep you on track.

So writers have their work cut out for them. They have to be on the watch for "grey matter." Grey matter is what kills us most of the time: it's the stuff that leaves you frustrated after you've walked away from an interview, hung up the phone, or reviewed your notes. The notebook and tape recorder are filled with grey matter because your interviewee was pretty nimble at avoiding direct answers to your questions. And you let her off the hook. As frustrating as it can be, you need to soldier on in attempting to get better and more detailed explanations. Do not settle for the first answer if it is less than satisfactory.

Understand the Sequence of Events

For readers, nothing adds confusion to a story faster than not knowing where we are in time or place. Ask when something happened in relation to other events a person is talking about: Was it before or after she graduated from university? Was it before or after she moved away from home or moved to another community?

If it's relevant, find out the day, the month, the year, the hour, the minute, the location. Put it in natural sequence so readers can follow the timeline easily. At the same time, it will help you write the story in a more organized fashion.

Ask Open-Ended Questions

Why, how, and *what* questions are the most likely ones to get people telling stories that you could never have known are there to be found. These, plus the more fundamental *who, when,* and *where* are known as open-ended questions—that is, they won't get one-word "yes" or "no" answers, and open doors to details, though you may need to dig for them.

Probe for Graphic Details

A little girl in hospital with a feeble heart was chosen to present flowers to a visiting member of the British royal family. A writer covering that event settled for that simple, general fact. But had he asked follow-up questions, he might have produced a more compelling image for readers.

What kind of flowers?

Roses.

What colour?

Red.

Why red roses?

Well … after each of the five operations on this little girl's tiny, vulnerable heart, her grandmother placed a red rose by her grandchild's bedside.

Stop at a little girl presenting flowers to royalty and you never get to the heart and soul of the story. Those you interview don't purposely withhold such information, but they need the interviewer to draw it out. Always ask follow-up questions, and you will quickly discover that the answers generate better and more complete responses as well as added detail to bring more colour to your stories. They also help you understand your story better and lead to stronger, more specific questions.

Your own prepared script of questions may be fine, but rather than just writing down the pedestrian answers that they may evoke, venture into the more interesting areas raised by the interviewee. This leads to a conversation rather than a more formal and stiff interview. Writers who put a high premium on curiosity and listening will come up with their best material. And they won't be preoccupied with the thought—or sense of panic—of running out of questions.

Take One Thing at a Time

It's a good idea not to leave a topic until you believe you have explored it fully. Every detail leads to a possible anecdote or better angle for your story. If you move on to a different topic before clarifying the previous one, chances are you won't return to it. Later, you'll discover that your notes and tape recorder have documented a number of different topics or issues, but none fully.

Ask for Clarification

How often do you nod your head and mumble "uh-huh" to pretend you understand the point being made in a conversation? Don't do it in your interviews.

Follow this simple rule: do not move into a new line of questioning until you understand what has already been discussed. If you need to pull the interviewee back for better understanding, then interrupt. Forget unwarranted fears that somehow you have disrupted the natural flow of the interview, ruined a person's train of thought, or derailed the interview. Interviews do not follow smooth linear lines of thought. Your job is not to simply toss out a question and listen to some lengthy, complex answer. Your task is to understand what is being said and its relevance to your story and readers.

And here is a guarantee: if you ask more questions to understand what is being said, you will automatically ask better questions because you do understand what is being said. Your best material lies in the better questions. So, don't hesitate to ask, What do you mean? Could you be more specific? Do you have an example to illustrate the point? Leave these questions unanswered and you'll end up with a confusing story and confused readers.

Ask Tough Questions

Writers can twist themselves into knots just thinking about having to ask tough questions. How will the interviewee react? Will he respond with verbal or physical abuse? What if he abruptly ends the interview before you've got everything you need? You can get so worked up that the fear of confrontation or losing the interview overshadows everything else. Just go in prepared.

Personal questions—money, sex, and family, among them—can be sensitive, so know why you are asking a question. If a person responds to a tough or sensitive question by shouting, "Why would you ask such a personal question?" you'd better have a response ready or you'll stutter out something feeble and lose control of your interview because you now feel intimidated. The answer can be as simple or general as, "I think readers will want to know...." Unless you have uncovered some up-to-the-minute scandal about your interview subject that he or she knows nothing about—and you intend to confront your subject with the facts during the interview—chances are, he or she knows what tough questions might be asked and likely is prepared for them.

If you're listening carefully, you're likely to find the right spot to segue to your tough questions. A reporter wanted to ask a hockey player about his battle with alcohol. When the player made a reference to his "problem," it was the reporter's signal to move in: "Let's talk for a moment about your problem—your bouts with alcohol abuse." And he got his answers because of listening, timing, and asking in a tone of voice that wasn't intimidating or judgmental.

Some reporters will leave tough questions to the end. But they take a gamble. The interviewee might offer up some vague answers, then make a quick exit. If you have a problem blurting out the toughies, you can always preface a question by saying, "This is a tough question, but I think it's an important one." By doing so, you have given the interviewee a moment to catch his or her breath and prepare for your question.

Ask Dumb Questions

Some writers have turned this into an art. They say people are more than willing to explain things to a writer who knows nothing—and that leads to more and better questions. Reporters who are reticent to ask dumb questions risk the chance of failing to properly understand their story or explain it to readers. Too often, they allow a person's quote to substitute as a proper explanation. It doesn't work. Nothing replaces asking questions until you understand the story.

It's true that—as later chapters will emphasize—a feature writer should do as much research on a topic as possible before picking up the phone for an interview. But you can't turn yourself into an expert and no matter how much you prepare, your job is to find answers and to present them in a clear way to readers. You cannot do that without a willingness to clear up what you just don't understand. If it helps, open with this line: "This may seem like a dumb question, but ..."

Don't Accept "No" Too Readily

"No" is such a definitive word. Not much room for misunderstanding. However, it's important to get to the heart of a "no" answer. Why is the person saying no? Is there some concern or fear you can easily answer to make a person feel more comfortable? Is there a specific area of questioning the person doesn't want to get into? Is the person confused about his or her role in your story and how he or she will be portrayed?

Before accepting "no" as the final answer, your task is to try to determine what lies behind the rejection. Asking *why* gives you a chance to come to some sort of arrangement. Once, in attempting to do a story about a 17-year-old boy who hanged himself in a jail cell, I found his parents reluctant to talk. "Why?" I asked. They said they didn't want a "sob story" written about their only son. We sorted it out this way: I would ask my questions, and they were free to answer or not. They agreed—and I still managed to get details about their son that helped readers "see" the young man who had taken his own life. If you fail to convince an interviewee to talk to you, don't take the rejection personally.

When does refusing to take "no" for an answer become badgering? If a person continues to say "no," there is no point in persisting to the point of harassment. In the end, you may have to look for a more cooperative interview subject. Just don't give up too easily: try to explain to the person why she is important to your story.

And, just in case she has a change of heart after you have left, leave your business card. If you still believe she is crucial to your story, send her an email or note spelling out in detail what information you hope to get from her, and why. Never give up without exhausting—as politely as possible, of course—all avenues open to you. Maybe one of her friends, who has already spoken to you or agreed to talk to you, can convince the woman to speak to you.

Take Careful Notes

Some reporters rely too heavily on a voice recorder, using it as a substitute for note-taking. A recorder has its limitations and shortcomings—batteries running out, background noises, and hours spent transcribing. Use a recorder to supplement, but not replace, note-taking. A recorder can dull listening skills. Because it is doing the work of documenting, it allows the writer to be easily distracted and miss an answer to a question—an answer that could lead to the next question.

But a recorder can also be a feature writer's best friend, especially if you're doing many interviews over a long period. A recorded interview listened to days or weeks later can help writers recall and visualize what they heard and in what context—the laugh after a funny anecdote, the sigh as a person recalls some frustrating event.

As well, it is wise to record interviews that could be contentious or controversial. And today, for those writers required to produce online audio and video clips, a recorder is the modern-day pencil and notepad.

If you do choose to use a recorder, avoid getting locked into reviewing and transcribing the entire interview or interviews. Try to limit yourself to re-checking for a quote or a detail. But that, again, means you have to be a diligent note-taker as you record your interviews.

Go Somewhere

Columnist Jim Coyle, of the *Toronto Star*, offers this advice: "Go someplace. Pay attention. It's pretty simple advice, but like lots that's simple, it seems to work ... and it's often forgotten." This, too, is where the details lie.

Once while doing telephone interviews at home during a massive snowstorm, Coyle had to run an errand. Walking through downtown Toronto, he noticed how cheerful everyone was to each other. "People who normally would have bustled by each other, eyes down, shared a few words, a smile, stopped to chat, even if only to complain. People shovelled each other's sidewalks, helped elders across the snowdrifts, helped push stuck cars." So he started taking notes on all the exchanges and wrote a column on how snowstorms make people more human. And all because he went somewhere and paid attention to his surroundings.

Nothing beats a face-to-face interview. Nothing beats the opportunity to observe body language, nuances in speech, the chance to ask follow-up questions—not to mention observing emotions such as anger, laughter, sadness, frustration. A phone interview serves as the next best thing to a face-to-face interview for many of the same reasons—minus the face. In person, you get to see personality and body language, and get to engage in the natural spontaneity of a back-and-forth interview. Writers get to ask questions and see the immediate reaction from an interviewee. Did she raise her eyebrows, hesitate before answering, gaze out the window, tap her fingers? Did she sigh, laugh, cry, giggle?

You also get to experience the setting where a person works, plays, or lives. This allows writers to build scenes into their stories. And scenes are vital for telling stories. You don't need to know much about the story from which the following moving scene comes as a son is reunited with his mother:

> The van slows. A gaggle of villagers are waiting and waving as they pull up to the house.
>
> "He has come back!" shouts one of his nephew's wives, opening the passenger door.
>
> They usher him out of the van, and barrage him with handshakes and shoulder pats. Everyone is talking at once. "Do you remember Uncle So and So?" "This is Great Aunt such and such." Chester smiles and nods. "How are you?" he says over and over in the Hakka dialect.
>
> Slowly they move up the driveway, he like a rock star navigating a scrum of fans, through the stone gate and toward the house. Where she is waiting in the doorway.
>
> Xiong Chun Xi. Her name means "joyful spring." She is 88. Years of fieldwork and hardship have compressed her spine. She is just four feet tall, her back hunched. A wooden cane, almost as tall as she is, bears her slight weight. Her hair is soft, thin, white, as if spun by a silkworm, combed back from a far receded hairline, making her appear wise. As do the deep lines that score her face.
>
> She has been waiting for this moment, it seems, forever. Her eyelids droop slightly, but the eyes themselves, impossibly dark, nearly black, are sharp. They are locked on him. They are eager. When he finally notices her, they are filled with tears.

He ascends the few steps, and her delicate, bony hands move up to meet his. "I haven't seen you for a very long time!" she says, her voice wavering, high-pitched. She is smiling. Her words come from her throat.

He smiles, too. "Yes, it has been a long time."[2]

Such detail is not easily accessible when writers rely solely on the telephone or email. For her popular "Lunch With" column, *Globe and Mail* writer Jan Wong considered the setting for her interviews important. When she interviewed actor Mickey Rooney, she knew he liked to play the horses, so she chose a steakhouse with off-track betting. When she interviewed poet Susan Musgrave, whose husband was in jail for robbing a bank, she chose a bank-turned-restaurant—and booked a table in the vault.

Good writers know how much a sense of place can add to their story. You get this, as Coyle said, by going somewhere. Take the woman back to the scene of her near-drowning, and forgotten details may come flooding back. Take the company president through her factory, and you may witness personality-revealing encounters. Does she know every part of the operation? Do workers know her on a first-name basis?

Trust Your Senses

As the funeral train carried the body of former prime minister Pierre Trudeau from Ottawa to Montreal, *National Post* columnist Roy MacGregor, now of *The Globe and Mail,* had to rely on observation—on what he saw as the train passed through the towns and farmlands. Here are a few of the visual images he created in his column so that readers could get a sense of what it was like to be on that train:

> The railway worker at the side of the tracks, his yellow plastic coveralls smeared in grease but his hardhat cradled at his side as he held attention.

> The woman holding up the cherry paddle with the rainbow-coloured *voyageur* scarf wrapped around it.

> A farmer on the east side of the tracks just before Casselman, an older man in overalls and high rubber boots who stood dead centre in his field … at attention, his right hand raised in salute.[3]

Roy MacGregor captured wonderful images based strictly on observation. Just as writers record what people say, they need to quickly move into "observation mode" when necessary. They must record what they see in their notebooks rather than rely on their memory. And they must record the smallest of details—overalls *smeared* in grease; a *rainbow-coloured* scarf; *high* rubber boots.

MacGregor was watching people from a train, but relying on your senses is just as important when you are interviewing. Relax and take in your surroundings—the people and the places. What is your source wearing? What's that weird picture on her wall? Why does she have four empty Red Bull cans on her desk? Or that plastic fly? Slowly, the story takes shape as your questions get answered.

> Doug Lychak is explaining why a plastic housefly perches on his desk. The Surrey city manager said Tuesday it reminds him to confront problems before they become like pests buzzing around your head. To emphasize the point, he slammed his palm on the desk next to the bug.
>
> Striking city workers argue Lychak's confrontational approach to bargaining put them on the picket line.[4]

And this tiny but telling anecdote comes from asking a simple question to satisfy a writer's curiosity: "What's a plastic fly doing on your desk?"

A reporter interviewing Kim Phuc, who as a child was severely burned in a napalm attack on her South Vietnamese village in 1963, noticed a gold medallion around her neck and asked what it was. The answer: during a visit to a Veterans' Day service in Washington, DC, a pilot who had flown helicopters during the Vietnam War had come up to Kim, his eyes filled with tears, and given her a gold necklace with a medallion that says, "Helicopter Pilot, Vietnam."[5]

It was a tiny observation and a tiny, but telling detail. And here's a good follow-up question that the reporter might have asked: "Do you wear it every day?" This might have led to more questions about the exact significance of the medallion in her life today. What has it come to mean to her?

When he was reporting for The Canadian Press, Ian Bailey, now of *The Globe and Mail*'s Vancouver bureau, snagged an interview with Patrick Stewart, the star of *Star Trek: The Next Generation*—the only interview Stewart granted while in Vancouver shooting a movie. The two men were in that post-interview phase, "chatting about nothing," when Bailey noticed a Beavis and Butthead calendar on the wall showing those destructive, juvenile cartoon slackers obsessed with sex and destruction.

"That's an interesting calendar," Bailey said, asking Stewart why he liked Beavis and Butthead. Suddenly Stewart warmed up. "They make me laugh," he replied. "I know these guys. I went to school with these guys. I could so easily have been one of them—only in England. Just another shake of the dice." Stewart said he was a working-class lad and Beavis and Butthead plugged him into that side of his nature. Bailey had his lead.

The lesson, according to Bailey, is always to look for personal objects in an interview setting. Do not be afraid to ask about them. And a second lesson: don't hesitate to pull out your notepad and recorder for such a spontaneous continuation of the interview.

Phone with Your Eyes Open

A telephone interview is always second best to a face-to-face interview. Like piecing together a jigsaw puzzle, the writer wants to have a clear mental image before ending a telephone interview. It's a challenge, but it's worth the time and energy because of the pictures you can paint for readers.

Glad You Asked!   The Professional Skeptic

Q: How much should I believe of what I'm told?
A: In short, question everything. If your job was only to write down what people said and then reproduce every word in your newspaper, magazine, or online publication, life would be easy. But it just isn't that simple. Sometimes people get their facts wrong. Sometimes they lie. Sometimes they twist the facts to suit their cause. Sometimes they don't understand the facts.

It helps to develop a healthy skepticism. Ernest Hemingway said, "The most essential gift for a good writer is a built-in shock-proof shit-detector."
If something sounds too good to be true, it probably isn't true. If numbers or statistics seem improbable, they're probably wrong.
It's impossible in journalism to question everything, to challenge every fact. But it is always wise to double-check, or even triple-check, crucial information that serves as the foundation of a story. And remember one powerful question that can serve as a litmus test: *How do you know that?*
Being a professional skeptic is especially important for stories dealing with medicine, technology, the environment, and other science-related fields. Remember the big fuss over re-using plastic water bottles? Or stories about how cellphones may cause cancer? Or fears about overhead power lines? Reporters often mismanage stories like these because they don't ask the right questions before they write.
Highly respected medical science writers Victor Cohn (now deceased) and Lewis Cope advised journalists to ask the following questions:*

Charlie Gillis, formerly of the *National Post* and now with *Maclean's* magazine, once interviewed by satellite phone a man crossing Greenland by sled. Gillis talked until the man's phone died about 30 minutes into the conversation. Again, his questions were clear and simple: "How are you doing?" "How's your physical condition?" "Have you had any problems—any frostbite?" "Where are you right now?" "What are you eating?" Here's how he opened his story:

> Marc Fafard is huddled in his tent on a plateau of ice, safe from the Arctic wind and relentless sun, but painfully aware of what it will take to get to the other side of Greenland.
>
> His fingertips are blue from cold, and the tip of his tongue has been burned by the omnipresent sunlight. His lips are so swollen, he says, "they feel like watermelons."

1. How do you know?
2. Have the claims been subjected to any studies or experiments?
3. Were the studies acceptable ones, by general agreement? For example: were they without any substantial bias?
4. Have the results been fairly consistent from study to study?
5. Have the findings resulted in a consensus among others in the same field? Do at least a majority of informed persons agree? Or should we withhold judgment until there is more evidence?
6. Are the conclusions backed by believable statistical evidence?
7. And what is the degree of certainty or uncertainty? How sure can you be?

If your source can't answer these questions, there is likely a problem. So, find someone who can help you answer them. Phone the researchers directly. Call other experts in the field who had nothing to do with the study and get their views. Modern science is a team sport, not a solo act. Research is replicated and studies are done again and again to verify findings. Interview widely to find out what the consensus is in the field. And always be on guard for extreme views, outrageous claims, and dubious conclusions. Remember, as scientist and writer Carl Sagan said, "Extraordinary claims require extraordinary evidence."

If you believe everything you hear, your gullibility will show in your stories. Your job always is to check the facts.

Sue Ferguson and Don Gibb

* Victor Cohn and Lewis Cope, *News & Numbers: A Guide to Reporting Statistical Claims and Controversies in Health and Other Fields*, 2nd ed. (Ames, IA: Iowa State University Press, 2001).

With 10 days left in his cross-country ski trek across the giant, frozen island, he and his partner, Scott Smith, have just nine days' worth of food on their sleds.

"It's like a desert out here. Except it's a desert of snow, not of sand," he rasps over a satellite phone he has dragged behind him on a sled since they started the trip.[6]

Gillis worked to produce images readers could see and feel—the cold Artic wind chilling his bones. He could have taken an easier, routine route by simply writing

Marc Fafard, who continues his gruelling trip across Greenland, has 10 days left in his ski trek.

But that would not have been a feature story. Instead, Gillis shows his subject hunkered down in his tent away from the biting Arctic wind and the sun that has left his fingertips blue, the tip of his tongue burned, and his lips so swollen they feel like watermelons.

With telephone interviews, don't be afraid to ask for the simplest of details. If the description of a room is important, ask where someone is sitting, what she is sitting on, what colour it is, where it is in relation to other people or other fixtures in the room. No detail is too small as long as you have determined that the scene is important to your story. Unlike email, the telephone is at least a live conversation where you can still detect changes in the tone of voice, get a feel for personality, ask follow-up questions with ease, and get the subject to elaborate. You are still in control of the interview.

In the end, writers should maintain a healthy skepticism in any interview, but more so in those where they must rely on the subject to be their eyes and ears. They should also be aware that a telephone interview doesn't replace a face-to-face interview, just as contact by email does not replace a face-to-face or telephone interview.

Watch Out for Hazards

Every reporter will encounter many hazards in an interview, and the more complex the interview, the more hazards there are. Mostly, these are designed to intimidate and to wrestle control of the interview away from you. Here's a partial list of some of the more common issues.

Off the record. This is a phrase that can cause writers no end of agony. Some people drop it into virtually every sentence, others sprinkle it throughout their conversations, and some use it as a final blow to wrap up an interview. "Of course, all of this was off the record."

While this is a complex issue, if you agree to take information off the record, it means the information cannot be used in your story. However, one alternative open to the writer is to try to get a different source to provide the same information on the record.

Once "off the record" has been raised in the interview, the wise writer deals with it immediately. You need to stop and set the rules before proceeding with the rest of the interview. This might put you into negotiations, but you are clearly in charge. Will you accept anything or everything off the record? Is only her answer to one question off the record, or everything she said before and after? This all needs to be sorted out. If allowed to go unchecked, the subject who sprinkles the words "off the record" throughout the interview creates havoc when it comes time to write.

Are there times to take information off the record? Probably, but again you are in control—not the interview subject. It has to be on your terms. Don't be too quick to grant the request. Ask yourself, *How important is the information to my story? Is it important to get him on the record, even if he refuses to be specific? Can I get the information elsewhere? Can I convince him now or later in the interview that he should comment on the record?* You can always decide not to accept information off the record early in the interview and change your mind later in the interview.

However, taking off-the-record information shouldn't be a common practice. The writer's job is to get information on the record.

So what happens if you take information off the record, use it, and name the person who gave it to you? You won't go to jail, but you lose credibility with your source. Having given your word, you cannot renege without consequences.

And then there is the interviewee who waits until the interview ends and says, "But, of course, all this was off the record." More often than not, it has been a telephone interview where the subject couldn't see you furiously scribbling notes. To simply ignore the comment and hang up doesn't resolve the issue. As long as you identified yourself as a writer at the beginning of the interview, you are under no obligation—ethical or otherwise—to honour an interview-ending off-the-record statement. In a measured tone, tell the interviewee that you identified yourself at the beginning of the conversation, told the person why you were calling and proceeded to ask your questions that she freely answered. Tell her that her comments are an important part of helping readers understand your story. And tell her you intend to use some or all of those comments in your story.

You might want to determine why she doesn't want the information used, but you shouldn't feel obliged to review the interviewee's comments and engage in a discussion about what you will and will not use. During such a discussion, you may find out that the interviewee is concerned about a small part of your interview or how she will be portrayed, in which case it may mean putting her mind at ease.

Wanting to see the story before it is published. There's a simple response: "no." You do not surrender editorial integrity and independence to the person you interviewed. It is not a contact's job to give the story final approval or worse, to demand you remove information attributed to him or her.

If you need to check facts, you are free to call the person to clarify, but it would be considered a firing offence at many publications if you gave a completed story to contacts for their approval before publication.

"No comment." Someone has been watching too many old newspaper movies. Just as you shouldn't so readily accept "no" for an answer, you shouldn't take "no comment" without making your own comment.

Sometimes you only have one side of a story, so you need to point out the gap and tell the person his side is important to balance the story. Without making it sound like a threat, you can tell him you're writing the story with or without his comment (some people actually believe if they refuse to talk, no story will appear). Without his comments, rumour or speculation could be more damaging or embarrassing than answering your questions.

The person might also be saying "no comment" to a specific question or topic. Don't allow this to throw you off the interview. There are other questions the person might answer, and you can always return to the "no comment" again later in the interview when he might have changed his mind and is willing to answer the questions.

Snap ... Snap ... Snap

Your questions produce big pictures that are made up of little pictures. Questions generated to collect the details—macro and micro—are at the heart of every story. When Peter Cheney, a *Toronto Star* reporter at the time, but now with *The Globe and Mail*, produced his award-winning feature article on the death of 16-year-old Shidane Arone, who was tortured to death during a Canadian peacekeeping mission that went terribly wrong in Somalia in 1992, he gathered a wealth of powerful detail through interviews and documents.

One scene leading up to Arone's death captures part of the brutal beating—just like snapshots from a camera, frame by frame.

(Elvin Kyle) Brown had picked up a few Somali words. He said the word for thief, then punched Shidane in the jaw. Brown went outside and took off his rifle and shirt. When he came back inside, (Clayton) Matchee was kicking Shidane karate style, shooting his foot out sideways. Brown kicked Shidane too—two shots to the thigh.

Matchee was wearing heavy tan combat boots. He started kicking Shidane again, then punched him in the face. Brown crouched beside Shidane and told him he was "a stupid f----r" to come through the wire, then kicked him again.

Shortly after 10, Matchee stepped out and beckoned to a nearby soldier. Master Cpl. Jacques Alarie stepped into the pit. As he watched, Matchee kicked Shidane's drooping head. It wobbled back and forth like it was mounted on a spring.

For a moment, Alarie thought it was a joke. He thought Matchee was kicking a dummy. But then Matchee placed a lit cigarette against Shidane's left foot and he flinched in pain. Alarie realized it was a real person....

Matchee began kicking Shidane again. One kick hit him in the face and his nose began to bleed heavily....

Brown began to clean up Shidane with toilet paper and water, and untied the riot baton between his elbows. Shidane was whimpering softly.

Over and over, he said: "Canada ... Canada ... Canada."[7]

Notice how the pictures come one by one. A punch in the jaw: *SNAP*. A kick to the head: *SNAP*. A drooping head wobbling back and forth: *SNAP*. The pictures flow in such slow motion with such vivid detail that the reader is thrust into the pit to witness the blow-by-blow account. It could have been written in a clinical way, but it would be a vastly different account without the writer's skills to detail such an ugly scene.

The best writers collect the images detail by detail through questions designed to capture a story piece by piece. An *anecdote* based on a Beavis and Butthead calendar. A *key moment* captured by finding out why a distraught father cannot stand to hear the doorbell ring. A *scene* showing what it's like to return to your homeland and meet, after 60 years, the biological mother you never knew you had.

Attention to such detail takes stories beyond exposition—just the facts—and into the realm of storytelling. Writers shouldn't settle for less.

Discussion Questions

1. In this chapter, I have presented key techniques for becoming an effective interviewer. Read "The Fight for Their Lives" by Aaron Derfel (pages 155–163). Derfel's story illustrates the effects of using several of them. How many can you spot, based on the evidence in Derfel's story?
2. What scenes did the reporter show readers through his use of detail?
3. Find a compelling section of the story. What questions might the reporter have asked to capture the moment or scene?

Notes

1. Murray Campbell, "The Height of Commitment," *Globe and Mail*, December 10, 1999.
2. Andrew Chung, "The Letter," *Toronto Star*, April 23, 2006.
3. Roy MacGregor, "Touching the Train, Passing the Feeling," *National Post*, October 3, 2000.
4. Harold Munro, "Mayor, City Official Like a Pair of Duelling Gunslingers," *Vancouver Sun*, March 22, 1995.
5. Peter Cheney, "Vietnam Photo Girl Kim Now 'Smiles All the Time,'" *Toronto Star*, February 6, 1997.
6. Charlie Gillis, "Blue Fingers and Lips Like Watermelons," *National Post*, June 12, 1999.
7. Peter Cheney, "Canada … Canada," *Toronto Star*, July 10, 1994.

"The Fight for Their Lives"

Aaron Derfel, "The Fight for Their Lives." *The Montreal Gazette*, September 30, 2006, B1. Material reprinted with the express permission of Montreal Gazette Group Inc., a CanWest Partnership.

On Sept. 13, 11 gunshot victims were treated at the Montreal General Hospital. They came in three waves. The first patient arrived at 1:02 p.m., just five minutes after the hospital had been notified by Urgences Santé of the shooting rampage at Dawson College.

First wave ▪ 1:02 p.m. Leslie Markofsky, 22. He was unconscious, having been shot twice in the head. 1:06 p.m. Silvio Comanaci, 18. Shot in the left shoulder and right kidney. ▪ 1:12 p.m. Meagan Hennegan, 18. Shot in right forearm and right hip.

Second wave ▪ 1:25 p.m. Lisa Mezzacappa, 18. Shot in right knee and right arm. 1:26 p.m. Elizabeth Di Staulo, 17. Shot in both arms. ▪ 1:28 p.m. Catalin Ilie, 18. Shot in the stomach. ▪ 1:31 p.m. Yves Morin, 47. Shot in left shoulder.

Third wave ▪ 1:40 p.m. Hayder Kadhim, 17. Shot in the back of the head and in a leg. There were also fragments in the back of his neck. ▪ 1:43 p.m. Catherine Mandilaras, 17. Shot in the leg. ▪ Joel Kornek, 19. Shot in the left arm. ▪ Jessica Albert, 18. Shot in the chest.

꙾꙾꙾

At the precise moment that gunman Kimveer Gill began his shooting rampage at Dawson College on Sept. 13, the emergency room of the Montreal General Hospital was packed with patients.

There were 40 people lying on stretchers for various ailments, some in the hallways. The waiting room was full. A cyclist who had been hit by a car was in the adjacent trauma bay being patched up by doctors. So was another patient who had taken a bad fall.

The Montreal General, an imposing complex of brick buildings overlooking downtown, has one of the city's busiest ERs. It also doubles as a Level 3 trauma centre, specializing in saving the lives of those with the most life-threatening injuries.

Anne Thomas, the 64-year-old nurse manager of the ER, was striding through the acute-care section near the end of the lunch hour when one of her nurses called out to her.

"Urgences Santé is on the phone," Julie Robidoux said, holding the receiver. "There's a shooting at Dawson College. They have three patients for us now, and a possibility of five more. How many can I take?"

"Just tell them to send as many as possible," Thomas replied, referring to the ambulance paramedics. "Just tell them to keep sending them."

It was 12:57 p.m.—16 minutes after the start of the shooting spree that would trigger the largest trauma response in the history of the Montreal General.

Thomas—a veteran of another school shooting, the 1989 École Polytechnique massacre—wanted to declare a Code Orange, signalling an external disaster. It's the highest alert.

Hospital rules, however, dictate that only a doctor—and not an ER nurse manager—can activate a Code Orange, so the alert was not officially broadcast on loudspeakers until 1:12 p.m.

Still, Thomas didn't let the rules get in the way of preparing for a disaster, and she declared a trauma situation. She ordered her assistant nurse manager, Caroline McDonald, to move as many patients as possible out of the ER and into rooms on the floors above. Three were transferred to the ER of the nearby Royal Victoria Hospital.

Thomas scurried over to the trauma bay, a spacious room with overhead X-ray machines hanging from the ceiling. It was designed to accommodate up to three patients. Thomas informed the nurses of the shootings.

They were in the process of moving out the two trauma patients when they heard the scream of sirens as ambulances sped up Côte-des-Neiges Rd.

At around 1:02 p.m.—only five minutes after Urgences Santé first called—22-year-old Leslie Markofsky arrived by ambulance. He was unconscious, having been shot twice in the head. Orderlies shifted his body onto a hospital gurney and wheeled him into the trauma bay that had just been cleared.

Markofsky, tall and broad-shouldered, had dropped by Dawson that day for a lunch-hour pizza party. He had graduated from Dawson in the spring and was studying at the John Molson School of Business at Concordia University.

A hospital clerk entered Markofsky's name into a computer at 1:03 p.m.—a procedure that had to be done for each patient before they could receive treatment.

Three minutes later, 18-year-old Silvio Comanaci was rushed into the trauma room, fully aware of what was going on. He had been shot in the left shoulder and right kidney.

At 1:12, Meagan Hennegan followed Comanaci, also conscious. The 18-year-old psychology student had been walking with her mother on de Maisonneuve Blvd., in front of Dawson, when she was struck by two bullets. One hit her right forearm and the other went through her right hip.

These patients were part of the first of what turned out to be three waves of gunshot victims to pour into the hospital. Bruno Bernardin, an ER doctor who was the trauma leader that day, surveyed Markofsky, Comanaci and Hennegan quickly. Nurses attached two intravenous lines of saline solution to each patient to counter their blood loss.

Blood was dripping from their bodies onto the floor. Thomas spoke to Comanaci and Hennegan in her soft British accent, reassuring them that everything would be okay.

The nurses cut some of their clothing to get a better view of the injuries. Leo Boulanger, a kindly 75-year-old member of the housekeeping staff, threw a hospital drape on the floor to absorb the blood.

Despite his massive head injury, Markofsky's blood pressure was not dropping and he was not bleeding profusely. But he was having trouble breathing, so doctors stuck into his windpipe a tube that was connected to a ventilator.

Tarek Razek, the chief of trauma at the McGill University Health Centre, was carrying out his rounds in the intensive-care ward on the 9th floor when his pager sounded shortly after 1 p.m. It was a trauma activation, but he had no idea exactly what was going on. As he made his way down to the ER on the ground floor, a young doctor-in-training approached him.

"Dr. Razek," Amy Neville said, almost whispering. "I heard something on the radio. There's been a multiple shooting downtown."

Once in the trauma room, he traded his white lab coat for a surgical gown. After conferring briefly with Bernardin, Razek stood at the entrance to the trauma room so he could decide exactly where each incoming and outgoing patient needed to go.

The voices of the hospital staff were growing louder and louder by the minute. In contrast, the gunshot victims were relatively quiet.

"Get me an IV! Get me a dressing!" some of the staff said.

Suddenly, Bernardin yelled out: "Everybody, keep quiet!"

Staff throughout the hospital were beginning to trickle into the ER, some of them offering help and others simply curious. Security guards had to turn many away.

A surgeon sidled up to Razek. "Look, I'm here," the surgeon said. "Can I help? I have kids. I have two kids at Dawson."

Razek, the father of a 6-year-old girl and 4-year-old boy, guessed what the surgeon was hinting at—had the chief seen any patient with his last name there?

"I'll call you if I need you," Razek told him. "I'm not going to need you unless I absolutely need you because you're clearly stressed by this."

At 39, Razek had already seen his share of traumas, having volunteered for the International Red Cross to treat refugees from the war in southern Sudan.

He had undergone his fellowship training in Philadelphia, where multiple shootings are routine.

Still, the sight of a nurse's scrubs drenched in blood stunned him as more Dawson victims entered the trauma room.

At 1:25 p.m., 18-year-old Lisa Mezzacappa was wheeled into the hospital, her right knee and right arm bleeding from gunshot wounds. One minute later, Elizabeth Di Staulo arrived. The 17-year-old had been shot in both arms.

Catalin Ilie, 18, wounded in the stomach, followed at 1:28 p.m. And three minutes after that, Yves Morin, a 47-year-old Dawson carpentry worker, was brought in. He had been shot in the left shoulder after having stood in front of a girl to protect her from the gunman.

All four patients were conscious and talking. A couple of the victims suggested that there was more than one gunman prowling Dawson—a rumour that swept quickly through the hospital.

The nurses gave the patients morphine and fentanyl to ease their pain. They drew blood from their arms to be tested for matches should they require a transfusion. A couple of nurses, who have children going to Dawson, had tears in their eyes. One of the senior nurses was close to the parents of 18-year-old Anastasia De Sousa, who had died on the scene from nine gunshots.

By now, TV news helicopters were circling in the grey sky above the hospital. One of the trauma surgeons, Kosar Khwaja, ran across the parking lot to the ER. He peered up at the helicopters, and realized the enormity of the emergency.

When he stepped into the trauma bay, Khwaja saw six patients in the room—double its capacity. He threw himself into triaging the patients, making sure their airways were open, that they were breathing and that their blood circulation was in order. In trauma care, that's known as the ABCs—airway, breathing and circulation.

The doctors swung the overhead X-ray machine over the patients, snapping images of their injuries. After the ABCs, they examined their bodies a second time to check for any hidden injuries. The nurses helped them turn the patients on their sides to see if any bullets had penetrated from other angles.

As the doctors and nurses stood over the patients, Boulanger, of the housekeeping staff, snaked a mop around their feet to soak up the blood.

Of the patients who were in the ER by that point, Catalin Ilie required surgery right away because his intestines had been badly cut up. He was sent up to the 8th-floor operating room. David Mulder, the team physician for the Montreal Canadiens, operated on him.

Markofsky was still in the trauma bay and had lapsed into a deep coma. A CT scan revealed the extent of his injuries. There were bullet fragments stuck in his brain. One of the bullets had pierced through his skull from near one of his ears.

A doctor glanced at the images of Markofsky's head. "Ohh!" he gasped. "I hope we're going to be able to do something for this kid."

The trauma team summoned Jeffery Allan Hall from the Montreal Neurological Hospital. Hall, a talented neurosurgeon, was given the task of extracting the bullet fragments.

Since Markofsky's life was not in immediate danger, the doctors had time to plan the operation. They concluded that one bullet had to be left permanently in his brain. Removing it risked paralyzing him.

In addition to damage from the bullets, Markofsky's brain was swelling fast. That, in turn, could cause far graver injury than the gunshots. The orderlies transferred him to one of the 8th-floor operating rooms, where Hall and his team worked carefully for an hour and a half. Hall removed part of one bullet, with the other left intact.

After the operation, the doctors focused their attention on reducing the swelling. They performed osmolar therapy, which decreases fluid in the brain.

At 1:40 p.m., Hayder Kadhim arrived in the trauma bay, signalling the third wave of the gunshot victims. The 17-year-old had been shot in the back of the head and in a leg. There were also fragments in the back of his neck.

Fortunately, X-rays revealed that the bullet had not penetrated his skull. He was conscious and talking—but not for long.

"What's your name?" Thomas asked to assess how alert he was.

"Hayder Kadhim ..."

He was just about to say something else when he blacked out. His whole body shook violently and his legs kicked up and down. It was a grand mal seizure, probably caused by the bleeding in his head.

He was sedated with fentanyl and propofol, and doctors intubated him so he could breathe again. He was taken for a CT scan. Kadhim didn't have to undergo surgery that night. The doctors debrided—or cleaned out—his wounds instead.

For the first time during a major emergency, the Montreal General dispatched a team of psychiatrists to the ER to speak to the patients. Most were in disbelief as the doctors and nurses whirled around them.

"My friend! My friend! Is my friend here?" one of the victims asked.

"Yes, your friend is here and the other doctor and nurses are working with your friend and we'll let you know as soon as we can," Thomas responded. "But right now we want to look after you to make sure you're okay."

When family members of the victims showed up in the ER later in the afternoon, some of the psychiatrists sat down with them. The families huddled together in the waiting room, speaking quietly to each other, trying to avoid the mob of reporters.

At 1:43 p.m., two ambulances pulled into the ER parking lot. One of the ambulances was transporting 17-year-old Catherine Mandilaras, who had been shot in the leg.

In the other ambulance were 19-year-old Joel Kornek and his girlfriend, Jessica Albert. Kornek had been shot in the left arm. The bullet tore through his arm, skipped through his chest—millimetres above his heart—and whipped through his right arm.

But Albert, 18, was in mortal danger. The gunman, standing a metre away from her in the school cafeteria, had plugged a bullet straight into her chest. The projectile twisted as it sliced through her diaphragm, liver, two spots in her intestines, the spleen and the pancreas before exiting through her back.

But the doctors didn't know that then. What they saw was a waif-like young woman, ghostly-white, moaning in pain, whose hands were cold to the touch. Still, she was talking, advising the nurses that she was allergic to sulfa and amoxicil.

Kornek kept looking at his girlfriend, telling the doctors and nurses to pay attention to her, not him.

"It can't be happening to me," he told Thomas. "I shouldn't even be in here. I go to McGill. I don't go to Dawson."

One of the doctors had just finished reviewing an X-ray of Kornek's chest. He turned to him and said: "You're one lucky motherf---er."

Kornek burst into nervous laughter. There was a psychiatrist standing next to him.

"Go tell my parents what the doctor just said," Kornek told the psychiatrist. "Use those exact words."

Khwaja, also a critical-care specialist, was put in charge of Albert. The psychology student was the last patient to arrive, and at that moment, the closest to death.

Her blood pressure plummeted from to 50 over 20. A person's normal blood pressure is 125 over 80. Her core body temperature was 33.1 degrees Celsius, down from a normal of 37. And she was bleeding profusely. If

Urgences Santé had taken another four minutes to reach the trauma bay, Albert would not have survived.

Khwaja rushed Albert up to an operating room on the 8th floor so he could stop her internal hemorrhaging. She was awake and talking right until the anesthetist sedated her for the surgery.

Back in the trauma bay, Razek and Thomas were growing worried. They had tended to 11 patients, but Razek suspected they might have to deal with as many as 30 more. This was based on unconfirmed reports that there were up to four shooters roaming the college.

"How big is this going to be?" he asked himself. "How many more are we going to get here?"

In his mind, he went through a checklist of resources and tried to determine whether the hospital had a maximum load of trauma patients before it could receive no more.

Thomas was fearing the worst as well.

"Can we cope?" she asked herself. "Can we manage? Can we give them everything they need?"

During the École Polytechnique massacre, the Montreal General's trauma team had time to prepare for six out of the 13 wounded because police waited to secure a perimeter. The police did the same thing during the 1992 shooting rampage at Concordia University by a deranged professor.

But this time, the police didn't wait and burst into the building in search of the assailant. That strategy saved lives, but it left the Montreal General with little time to react and created some initial confusion.

Shortly after Albert arrived, Razek decided to phone a doctor at the scene to get an update. Francois De Champlain, an ER physician who also works for Urgences Santé, answered the phone.

"What are you looking at there?" Razek asked. "Do you have any more injured who are coming our way?"

"We don't have anymore right now," De Champlain replied. "The police are sweeping the building. We'll call you back in a little bit to see if we find anything and what the total numbers look like."

Although the lone gunman had killed himself after being shot in the right elbow by veteran cop Denis Côté, police swept the sprawling college a total of four times.

Razek called De Champlain a half hour later.

"Is it clean now? Are we off now?"

"I can't clear you yet," De Champlain said. "They've done one full sweep, and we don't have anything new."

By around 3 p.m., Razek surmised that the worst was over. Even if the police found a gunshot victim, there probably wouldn't be 10.

But at that same time, Khwaja was in the midst of surgery, scared that Albert would die on the operating table. He had slid a scalpel down her abdomen and discovered that her internal organs were spilling blood.

Assisted by medical resident Souad Gholum, Khwaja poked a hole through the sac enveloping Albert's heart. Good, the heart had not been punctured.

"Next, let's pack the liver," he told Gholum in a military-style clipped voice.

Short and stocky, the bespectacled Khwaja looks even younger than his 31 years. He stuffed the liver with gauze because it was bleeding copiously.

Next, he took out the spleen, blasted by the bullet. It, too, was bleeding terribly. He tied off the blood vessels going to the spleen.

The operation was going smoothly until he noticed that Albert's left lung had collapsed and air was leaking out and into her chest, expanding it. He inserted a tube in the left side of her chest to decompress the lung.

Khwaja then quickly stitched up the cuts in the intestines. It was a temporary measure to reduce the chances of infection. He left a tube in the pancreas to drain it, allowing it to heal on its own.

Khwaja suspected that Albert's aorta might have been hit. The aorta is the major blood vessel for all the organs in the abdomen. He pushed her intestines from one side to the other to gain a view of the aorta.

It was fine, untouched.

Khwaja held off closing the small hole in Albert's diaphragm until a second operation scheduled for the next day. He also refrained from closing her abdomen and instead placed gauze over her exposed organs.

The operation was a success. Albert had been transfused with great quantities of blood to bring her blood pressure back up. She was sent to the ICU for round-the-clock monitoring and for her body to be warmed up.

Despite a calm appearance, Khwaja left the OR tightly wound up. He wanted to meet the parents and to be the one to explain everything in detail to them. But they hadn't yet reached the hospital.

He waited until 8 p.m. when he finally saw the parents, Danielle Lachaine and Francois Albert. He described their daughter's injuries.

"I'm going to go over the list," he said. "Your daughter has been hit in the liver, in the stomach in two places, in the spleen, in the pancreas and in the diaphragm."

Francois Albert hung his head in his hands. Danielle Lachaine kept silent, but as Khwaja listed each damaged organ, she thought to herself: Stop! Stop! Stop!

Khwaja took his time with the parents, promising to give them detailed information the next day. Having worked 10 days in a row, he returned home at 11:30 p.m. It was only then that Khwaja burst into tears when he kissed his 26-year-old pregnant wife.

She had graduated from Dawson's nursing program a few months earlier.

Thomas, who has four grown children, was picked up at the hospital by her husband at 8:30 p.m. After eating dinner at home, she paced up and down the hallways, asking herself: "How could we have improved things? What could we do better for the next time?"

For one thing, the trauma team could have better handled the documentation concerning the patients, but that was a minor detail. Thomas, like many other nurses and doctors at the Montreal General, did not sleep well that night.

At least 85 hospital staff—including doctors, nurses, inhalation therapists, orderlies, security guards, among others—were involved in the care of the 11 gunshot victims. The hospital deactivated the Code Orange at 6:30 p.m.

In addition to the Montreal General, several other patients were transported to the Jewish General and Jean Talon hospitals. In total, there were 20 injured and two dead, counting the gunman.

On Sept. 13, doctors operated on five patients at the Montreal General. Over the course of the next two weeks, all but one patient were discharged from the hospitals. Some will face future surgery and lengthy rehabilitation.

Markofsky remains in the hospital. Albert, who has regained her appetite, was released on Thursday. She is walking on her own, talking and giggling with her boyfriend. She is expected to make a full recovery.

Markofsky's plight has attracted worldwide attention after Rabbi Mordecai Zeitz sent out emails calling for prayers. His mother and father are at the hospital every day to be by the side of their son, a prize-winning business student and expert golfer.

The swelling in Markofsky's brain has yet to subside completely. Doctors continue to take CT scans, and at this point, can't make a definitive prognosis.

But grandmother Lily Markofsky was full of praise for the medical attention her Leslie has received.

"I don't think you can get any better," she said. "The doctors are there for everything. The nurses are always on the floor, right in front of his room."

She paused for more words.

"We go day by day," she added. "There's a long haul ahead of us."

CHAPTER SIX

Going Deep:
Immersion Reporting

Linda Kay

I was a rookie reporter working for a family-owned daily newspaper in Paterson, New Jersey when I was drawn to the case of convicted killer Rubin "Hurricane" Carter. The former middleweight boxing champ, imprisoned for shooting to death three people in a Paterson bar in the late 1960s, had written a powerful autobiography from his prison cell proclaiming his innocence and accusing law enforcement authorities in Paterson of building a false case against him. Carter's book roused a number of celebrities to embrace his cause, among them Muhammad Ali and Bob Dylan, who later penned a song, "The Hurricane," detailing the boxer's plight. Carter's predicament also stirred writer Nelson Algren, author of the prize-winning book *The Man with the Golden Arm*, who moved to Paterson to investigate claims that Carter might be innocent and write the story for *Esquire* magazine.

I sensed that Algren's move to Paterson and his work on the Carter case might be an important story for me, a cub reporter. I was determined to meet the author and follow his path. It took me months to gain Algren's trust, but eventually, he took me into his confidence and ultimately convinced Carter to grant me an interview at Trenton State penitentiary, quite a coup since Carter detested the newspaper for which I worked. That jail-house interview then became the centrepiece of a three-part series I wrote for the (Paterson) *Morning News.*

Covering the Carter story was my introduction to immersion report-ing. The reporting yielded an in-depth interview with Carter in prison; it resulted in a profile of his co-accused, John Artis, a teenager at the time of the murders and a forgotten man then lurking in Carter's shadow; and lastly, it generated a sketch about the deepening friendship that had bloomed between Carter and Algren. What I wasn't able to discern through the reporting process, however, was the truth about Carter's innocence or guilt. Early on in my reporting career, I realized that finding the truth is a complicated quest.

As I dug into the reporting on the Carter case, multiple versions of truth emerged: from eyewitnesses, from law enforcement authorities, from Carter supporters, from Carter detractors—and from Carter. To this day, more than three decades later, the core of the case is still in dispute. Carter was re-tried in 1976 and found guilty again. He was ultimately released from prison in 1985 when a judge determined that given the racially tense climate in Paterson at the time of the murders, Carter could not have gotten a fair trial. Perhaps the whole "truth" will never come to light.

Journalists are trained to get the facts, defined in journalistic shorthand as who, what, when, where, why, and how. But finding the truth is another matter. Truth is often elusive. Truth is inexact. Truth is multi-faceted. Sources see truth from their own vantage point. Canadian journalist and cultural critic Robert Fulford, in his 1999 Massey Lecture Series entitled "The Triumph of Narrative," quoted novelist Vladimir Nabokov on a writer's inability to find truth, or, as he expressed it, reality: "You can get nearer and nearer to reality, but you never get near enough because reality is an infinite succession of steps, levels of perceptions, false bottoms—and hence, unattainable."[1]

So where does this leave the journalist? In my view, immersion reporting allows feature writers to come as close to the truth as possible. This means researching a subject thoroughly; collecting official documents and raw data; cultivating sources and patiently building their trust; interviewing extensively to gather many sides of a story; keenly observing a person or situation for days, weeks, or even months; not getting discouraged when sources refuse to speak with you; making absolutely certain that those you do speak with provide accurate information.

A journalist shoulders an important responsibility not to elicit a "truth" that may be elusive, but to construct the *truest* depiction of a person or situation through immersion reporting. Going deep into the reporting is exhilarating work. It brings great satisfaction to a journalist. It can uncover a flaw in the system, help right a wrong, illuminate a situation with long-term consequences—or simply touch readers in a deep and lasting way.

Taking the First Step

Immersion reporting requires an enormous amount of background research that can be compared to scholarship in some cases. Broaden your knowledge through wide and diverse reading. Read everything you can get your hands on, from books and journals to newspapers and magazines to circulars and even matchbook covers. Vital but unreported information can also be found in government reports, meeting records, court documents, real-estate transactions, and corporate publications. Investigative journalist I.F. Stone built his reputation on "reading the record," scrutinizing public documents and turning up scoops in his self-published *I.F. Stone's Weekly*. Though official documents can be intimidating in scope and may be written in arcane language, hidden in the jargon is often a valuable nugget of information. While researching a newspaper feature on Canada's air traffic control system for *The Gazette* in Montreal, I requested a report issued by the Canadian Aviation Safety Board. It was so heavy I almost needed help lifting it. But wading through it, I found confirmation of an alarming situation I'd learned confidentially from several sources. The report contained hints that the air traffic control system was a crisis waiting to happen because of a shortage of employees and a round-the-clock operation staffed by tired controllers. The board examined 217 of 710 "occurrences"—a buzz word for errors—recorded at airports in Vancouver and Toronto over a four-year span. It noted that "staffing considerations" played a part in 43 percent of the incidents—almost half. "The most serious shortcoming in the provision of air traffic services today," the report stated, "concerns the availability of sufficient qualified air traffic controllers to meet the increasing operational demand."[2] The information was deep in a text that had likely been read by only a few, but it confirmed what controllers were telling me in private conversations. I was thus able to write that the air traffic control system in Canada was short by perhaps as many as 400 controllers and that the deficiency had impacted the men and women controlling planes by causing a rash of health-related problems due to stress and fatigue.

Deep research not only allows you to uncover hard data, but also enables you to approach a source with a confident attitude rooted in knowledge, a crucial component in persuading someone to speak with you and in gaining his or her trust. The first "live" contact with a source generally occurs over the telephone, and that initial encounter is key to the success of the project. Go into it well informed. The more you know about a source and the subject matter in which he or she specializes, the easier it will be to convince that source to speak with you. When a young Alberta woman, Katrina Effert, was found guilty of second-degree murder and given a sentence of life with no parole for ten years for killing her infant, reporter David Staples of *The Edmonton Journal* wanted to understand the reasons for the harsh verdict and assess whether it was fair. As he quickly realized, he needed to understand the complex social history of infanticide in order to report the story. To do a proper job, he would have to talk to experts in Canada and around the world. He explains:

> Not being with *The New York Times*, or even a big Toronto paper, it's some-
> times difficult getting the top experts to call me back. My strategy here was
> to be as prepared as possible before I approached an expert. I first went to

Glad You Asked!   Character Sketch

Q: What do I need to ask a profile subject?
A: The personal profile is one of the most common feature stories assigned and written. Whether you are writing a quick 600-word snapshot of a local businessman or a comprehensive 6,000-word portrait of the prime minister, you need to cover the basics. Too many young reporters come away from a two-hour interview with a subject without some very basic facts. Here's a list of must-haves for a good profile:

1. First, last, and middle name. (Spelled correctly!)
2. Age: if your source refuses, get an approximate age or use other sources to confirm the date of birth. (D.O.B. is important especially if your story may not be published for several weeks or months.)
3. Birthplace: the city or town where they grew up; where they now live.
4. Schools they attended; degrees gained. (You may not need all this, but it's important to have it.)
5. Some information about family: mother's and father's occupations; number of brothers and sisters, etc.
6. Marital status: single, married, or divorced. Children? This may be crucial or tangential, depending on the kind of profile you are writing, but not knowing these facts is unacceptable.
7. Current job and job title—exactly. Check if there is more than one. Some people hold multiple jobs and have several titles (for example, Doctor Moira Jones, associate professor of Plastic Surgery at the Smithfield

the library and checked out a half-dozen books on infanticide and read them. I made sure to read at least an article or two either by or about each expert I planned to interview. If possible, I tried to get their main book on the subject, as well. I had to order a number of books to complete this part of my research, and the process took several weeks. But by the time I made first contact with each expert, I was able to portray myself, within a few sentences, as someone who had an adequate grasp of the main issues. Rather than just go over basic theories with an expert, I was able to explore areas of controversy and uncertainty. In addition, since experts often have strong political agendas, knowing the subject matter when entering a discussion means you won't get bowled over by their rhetoric or by their vastly superior knowledge of the topic.[3]

From his background research and in interviews with the experts, Staples discovered that the statute of infanticide had long been controversial. In Canada, he found, the legal community had debated the merits of the law since its inception in 1948. He found that many academic, medical,

University and head of the Reconstructive and Plastic Surgery Department at Mount Vernon Hospital).
8. Interests, sports, hobbies, etc. Again, this may not make it into the story depending on the length and focus, but if your subject just climbed Mount Everest in her spare time, you'll be happy you asked!

Sometimes, profile interviews are difficult. People are often guarded with their answers, fearful of how they will be represented in your story. Sometimes their answers are short, clipped, and colourless. Here are a few questions designed to kick-start a profile interview! Try them—you may be surprised at the answers you get.

- What's the most important thing your father/mother taught you?
- What will you be doing 10 years from now?
- If you weren't a doctor/CEO/teacher, what would you be?
- What's the worst thing that ever happened to you?
- What book(s) are you reading right now? What's the best book you read this year?
- What's the most important thing you've learned in life?
- Do you believe in God?
- What was your first job? What was your worst job?
- Who is the person who most influenced you? Why?
- What was the best day of your life?
- If you were reading your own obituary, what would you like it to say?

Paul Benedetti

and legal experts believed that the law was based on discredited science and an outdated notion that women are frail, irrational creatures, especially during pregnancy and lactation. He also found that, while many deemed the harsh sentence in the Effert case a radical departure, it was actually part of a trend where jurors and courts put a newborn's life ahead of any sympathy for mothers who kill their babies. This changing attitude had arisen from decades of progressive social change that improved the lives of single mothers, stripping away issues of poverty and shame that, in the past, might have justified infanticide to many people. Staples discovered that Canadian courts in the 1990s were reflecting this shift, and that prosecutors were taking a more punitive stance against women who killed their infants, charging them with murder and manslaughter, rather than the crime of infanticide. Staples won a National Newspaper Awards certificate of merit for Explanatory Work for his article "Revisiting Canada's Infanticide Law."[4]

Mining for Sources

To dig deep as a journalist, you must acquire sources. Remember that you'll need a range of sources for different reasons. You'll need sources to provide dependable background information on a subject, to supply tips that may lead to "scoops," and to confirm or deny information provided by a self-serving source or a source you suspect may be unreliable.

Before the advent of the BlackBerry—in the dinosaur age—I'd tell my students that a reporter is as good as his or her Rolodex. A Rolodex is a rotating filing system for organizing contact information. A desktop staple in the 1980s, today the Rolodex is an endangered species in newsrooms, much like the typewriter. But its function still stands. Whether a journalist uses a computer to log contact information or enters the data by hand in an old-fashioned address book, reporters are as good as their sources. My trusty Rolodex made me a valued employee in the newsroom. My source list was extensive and editors knew it. It came in especially handy one evening when editors on the city desk learned from the police scanner that an apartment building where a former star athlete lived was ablaze. Making the situation even more compelling, the athlete in question was disabled and confined to a wheelchair. Had he escaped the flames or was he trapped? A flip of my Rolodex and I retrieved the telephone number for his mother, who lived in another part of town. She knew he was safe and told me in detail how he got out of the building. I had a story. What's more, I had an exclusive news feature, thanks to my Rolodex.

Begin assembling a source list from your first assignment, even if you're a student covering an event for class or the school paper. Capitalize on the opportunity to collect names and phone numbers that might be helpful down the line when you're writing a feature. Don't be afraid to ask for a number where your source can be reached in off hours. When I worked as a sportswriter, I learned to ask for the number of an athlete's mother and/or mother-in-law. Athletes travel so frequently they're difficult to reach, but a mother or a mother-in-law generally keeps close tabs. Was I being intrusive by asking for the phone number of a close relative? I was being careful. Few sources turned me down when I explained that having the number enabled me to verify a fact or a rumour directly and thus ensure accuracy. I also promised to keep the number confidential—a promise I made certain to honour.

Once you've collected a precious phone number, tuck it away in a systematic fashion. Develop a method for gathering and filing contact information. When I freelanced for newspapers and magazines, I created two files for every story assignment: a computer file and a hard file. The hard version was actually a low-tech manila folder labelled with a story slug, which is a word or two describing the project. On the inside flap of the manila folder, I taped business cards gathered while reporting the story. Other contact names, titles, and phone numbers were handwritten on the same inside cover where I placed the business cards. The manila folder also contained my notes, handwritten and typed, plus a hard copy of the final story I submitted to the publication. In this way, all material was readily available if a fact-checker contacted me for verification or elaboration. In addition, I could return to the file months later and have important information at my fingertips if I wanted to recycle the story, take it in another direction or simply re-contact a source. Keeping meticulous files is imperative for another reason. Some publications want to see them. Consider this excerpt from the writers' guidelines issued by *Chatelaine* magazine:

> All finished stories must be footnoted or annotated to show the source of all quotations, statistics, studies, etc. In addition, you must submit a comprehensive fact-checking package that includes all documents, interview transcripts (or tapes), contact numbers, etc. *Chatelaine* rigorously fact-checks all articles, regardless of length, to confirm the accuracy to the best of our ability.[5]

Cultivating Sources

Now that you've begun to build sources, cultivate them. You can plant a tree in the ground, but it needs care to flourish. The same principle applies to your sources. Once you've established contact with a promising source, maintain it. Build a relationship. Drop by the person's office to say hello and ask what's new. Phone on a regular basis to chat about a topic of interest or to ask a question. Habitual contact initiates a trust-building process. In your eagerness to speak with people in high places, don't forget to cultivate people who work behind the scenes. Say hello to the mayor, but don't neglect the executive assistant or the receptionist. Those working for a politician or business executive or sports figure are crucial to your reporting effort. They can ease your way—or put up a roadblock. When I worked as a sports journalist at the *Chicago Tribune*, news broke that a powerful university basketball program would be sanctioned. I'd built a friendly relationship with the athletic director's secretary. I'd routinely chat with her a few moments before I'd ask to speak with the AD. When news of the sanctions came down, my relationship with the secretary paid dividends. Even though the sanctions were bad news for the university athletic program, the secretary nevertheless found her boss at my request. He was on a golf course with alumni, but I had a call back within minutes. Make sure to thank the people behind the scenes, as well as your more prominent sources. There's no replacement for a handwritten note when a source does you a favour by smoothing your way or sharing his or her time or expertise.

Casting a Wide Net

Good reporters never feel they've done enough reporting. They tap into multiple sources, never relying on only a single source for a feature story. As well, they are wide open to sources with contrasting opinions and competing interests. Jan Wong of *The Globe and Mail* asks a profile subject right up front to identify his or her enemies. Wong tells the subject she'll find the enemies anyway, so better get it out in the open from the start. Wong's method isn't a comfortable fit for every journalist. I've never tried her bold tactic, but the intent is sound. Gathering a full picture of a person means seeking out sources who don't necessarily like or agree with your profile subject. It also means gathering perspectives that don't fit your hypothesis, or contradict your own beliefs and convictions, when you're writing an issue-oriented feature. In the 1980s, I wrote a prize-winning piece for the *Chicago Tribune* on a burgeoning evangelical movement in major-league baseball dubbed Jocks for Jesus—athletes who prayed as a group inside the clubhouse and publicly credited God for their performances. I interviewed athletes whose views I deemed hypocritical and even repugnant (one athlete told me I was doomed to go to hell if didn't see it his way), but as a journalist you cannot overlook, dismiss, or ignore positions and opinions you don't like or support. These views must be part of your information-gathering process; otherwise, an incomplete picture emerges and your reporting is dishonest.

The reporting required for a feature story is often lengthy and complex. Organizational tools help keep the effort under control. At the outset, you might want to diagram your source pool in a way that resembles a family tree used in tracing a genealogy. Place the focus of your story at the top of the figurative tree, whether it is an issue or a person. Branching out from the centre on both sides are sources that can shed light on the focus of the story. For example, in profiling Canadian Olympic synchronized swimmer Sylvie Fréchette for *Chatelaine*, I set out to interview her family and friends, her fellow athletes and coaches, and the friends and co-workers of her late fiancé. Each of these categories became a branch on the tree, and hanging from the branch was the name of each individual I wanted to interview. This method is also helpful when conducting an issue-oriented investigation, such as a big grade-cheating scandal story that I'll describe later in this chapter. Place the issue you're investigating atop the diagram; sources that can clarify the issue hang from the branches. You can add or subtract from the diagram as you progress in the reporting.

Being There

It's fine to use the telephone and the Internet during the early stages of reporting, but reporters must get away from their desks and zoom in closely on their subjects. The public relies on journalists for information, but also to help them understand the meaning of an event, the story behind the story, or, in the case of a personality profile, the fundamental nature of an individual. A feature story in which all the reporting has been carried out from behind a desk is a pale imitation, a pretender. There's no substitute for being there. Develop your observational skills by being alert to sensory clues, by taking the time to really look and listen, by seeing and hearing with fresh eyes and ears, by noticing details you have not noticed in the past. As author William Ruehlmann emphasized in his book *Stalking the Feature Story*, reporters must attach themselves to their story, sniff it, poke it, and probe it. The best writing appeals to our five senses, says Ruehlmann, and your job as a reporter is to record the details that cause the reader to see, hear, smell, taste, and feel.

Start the observation process by going to the scene. It's important to see your source in his or her milieu. When I profiled gymnast Nadia Comaneci for *Chatelaine,* we met at a gymnastic practice facility at the former Olympic venue in Montreal. Comaneci triumphed in Montreal at the 1976 Games as a teenaged pixie who became the first to score a perfect 10 in Olympic competition. Now, 17 years later and far past her athletic prime, Comaneci was trying to get in shape again. She wanted to use her latent athletic skills to chart a bright future after escaping dictator Nicolae Ceausescu's Romania. I described a 31-year-old woman turning a back flip on the balance beam as she worked to reinvent herself. It was a powerful image. If you're profiling an athlete, go to the stadium. If you're writing about a doctor, visit the hospital. If you're profiling a chef, get into the kitchen. While observing, notice the small stuff. Look at the photos hanging on the walls when you're interviewing a CEO. Ask your subject for an explanation. It's an icebreaker. It gets the conversation going and also provides possible information for your feature. What about the signed baseball sitting on the CEO's bookshelf? What's the story behind it?

Power is conveyed by small images. Tiny details may hint at larger themes. The smallest fact could be crucial in developing the direction of a feature story. Scouring the Montreal Alouettes media guide while researching a story for the *Chicago Tribune* on the team's acquisition of running back Jarrett Payton in 2007, I learned that Jim Popp, then head coach of the Alouettes, had named his daughter Hayley Payton. That small fact allowed me to open up a line of questioning with Popp about his long-time emotional connection to the late Walter Payton, Jarrett's father, a legendary running back for the Chicago Bears. Popp's attachment to Walter Payton helped, in part, explain his willingness to reach out to Jarrett and bring him to Montreal while other executives in the professional football world had passed him by.

Building Trust

To fully depict a profile subject or any major character in your story often requires that you spend hours or even days with a person. Inserting yourself into the life of a stranger might seem like an awkward proposition, but careful planning and thoughtful behaviour will smooth the way.

What are the essential details necessary for success when you want to spend long periods of time with a subject? Here are some tips: Negotiate as much time with the subject as possible. Tell the subject up front that you'd like to spend an entire day or two with them. Let them know you want to tag along and see what a typical day is like. Ensure that there'll be action while you're there. You want to watch an athlete in training or a fashion designer preparing for an upcoming show, not someone watching television on a day off. Promise to be unobtrusive if your source expresses concerns that you'll interfere with their routine.

Initially, put away your notebook or recorder and just hang around and observe. Depending on the situation, you may not ask a single question for long periods of time. Just watch and listen. You'll be amazed at how much you'll see and hear. Your goal is to disappear into the woodwork so your source is less self-conscious and feels freer to behave as he or she normally would. But questions must be asked, of course, so reserve a specific time near the end of the day, over a meal, perhaps, or at another time when your subject is not occupied with other concerns. Then bring out your notebook. You'll have many more questions to ask now that you've observed the subject in his or her milieu. Things will have arisen during your time together that will generate new material, new ideas, and new questions. Though some journalists disagree, I tend to save the toughest questions for last— I don't want to be escorted off the premises prematurely.

The best way to build trust is by demonstrating your trustworthiness— your integrity. For a start, this means building a record of fair and accurate reporting. The most precious weapon in a reporter's arsenal is a reputation for impartiality, fairness, and precision. It must be carefully guarded. Readers will invariably catch even minor inaccuracies in your work, and your sources and their colleagues know when you've misrepresented ideas or taken information out of context. But when sources know your work is accurate and fairness is a priority, they will agree to speak with you—or even seek you out. Accuracy leads to access, so bulletproof your work through careful reporting.

On the simplest level, ensuring accuracy means checking and re-checking your work. It means never assuming anything, not even the spelling of a name. It means asking and re-asking questions if the answers are not clear in your mind or in your notes. It means posing difficult questions even when it's uncomfortable for you and the source. What does it mean to be fair as a journalist? I apply a simple rule: the golden rule. Treat a source as you would like to be treated. Respect their time. Understand they are doing you a favour by granting access. Let them fully respond to any question you pose. Give them a chance to confront an issue that might be controversial.

When I profiled Canadian Olympic medal winner Sylvie Fréchette for *Chatelaine*, I conducted dozens of interviews with fellow athletes to learn more about the synchronized swimmer. Fréchette's fiancé committed suicide shortly before the 1992 Games, and in the course of profiling the medal winner, I learned that some people close to her late fiancé held Fréchette

partially at fault for the tragedy. In fairness to Fréchette, it was my responsibility as a journalist to confront her with their accusations, however
uncomfortable I felt raising them. I'd already spent a great deal of time with
Fréchette at that point, but I needed to go back to her and put the allegations
forward for discussion. Much to my surprise, she was grateful for the chance
to respond to charges she somehow knew were circulating behind her back.
She was glad to set the record straight from her perspective. As hurtful as
she found the accusations, she wanted to address them. Not giving her the
opportunity would have cheated Fréchette. Not tackling the issue, on my
part, would have cheated the readers.

But even with those precautions, controversy is sometimes unavoidable
and often unpredictable. I spent two days at Ken Norton's training camp in
the California desert as the heavyweight boxer prepared for an eventual title
fight against Jimmy Young that would reportedly pay him $1.75 million. I
was writing a story on Norton for *The San Diego Tribune*. Like Rodney
Dangerfield, Norton felt he didn't get the respect he deserved. He'd spent
much of his career fighting in the shadow of Muhammad Ali. They'd fought
three times. The first time, fighting in San Diego, Norton broke Ali's jaw.
The victory stunned fight fans. But in both subsequent meetings, Norton
lost by decision. Many observers gave the third fight to Norton, however,

Glad You Asked!   When Sources Won't Talk

Q: What if someone refuses an interview?
A: *Maclean's* senior reporter Jonathon Gatehouse says that there are two categories of people who won't talk to reporters. The first and largest group fear
repercussions—in the workplace, their community, or the courts. The second,
smaller group won't talk because they are on the wrong side of the story.

In the first case, Gatehouse advises, be honest. Tell the source exactly what you
need from them and why you need it. Explain exactly why you need them to tell
their tale and why the public needs to know. No one is going to stick his or her
neck out if you can't provide a compelling reason.

Whistle-blowers in corporations, the police, criminals, government workers,
and others may all have reasons to remain anonymous or ask for pseudonyms.
Always try to get the information on the record with the source's real name.
But, if that is impossible, always check with your editors before making promises.
Remember that as a journalist in Canada, you can't offer absolute protection
to a source and that the courts can, and have, demanded that reporters reveal

and Norton himself wept when the judges picked Ali. When I interviewed him in the late 1970s, Norton brushed aside suggestions that he was almost an extra in a movie that starred Ali. "I'll make more money and kick his [ass] the next time," he told me. During the day, I followed Norton's regimen. I ran with him in the morning, watched him jump rope endlessly in the gym, saw him spar with various partners, sat at his training table for meals, and chatted with people in his entourage. I took out my notebook in front of Norton only when he relaxed at the end of the day. Immersion reporting enabled me to produce a more nuanced story about the fighter beyond his routine, although I did document in great detail what he termed a "light" breakfast: ham steak, sliced tomatoes, four eggs over easy, buttered wheat toast with jam, fresh orange juice mixed with raw egg, and tea with honey. Because of the immersion experience, I was able to catch a glimpse of the insecurity behind the outward confidence. Norton had been booed the previous year in San Diego while fighting a much lesser competitor. The fight was stopped in the tenth round with the competitor badly injured. Fans wanted the fight continued, and when it was halted, they booed Norton. He was still wounded by their behaviour because he identified with San Diego. He liked the town. But no more. He told me he would never forget the booing.

---

their confidential sources or face contempt of court charges and the very real possibility of fines or jail time. You can tell the source that you and your employer will not abandon them if things get messy. You can reinforce that you are an honest, trustworthy reporter. You should assure them, says Gatehouse, that if they are going to share a sensitive story, you are going to do them justice. Point to your past work; give them the name of someone who can vouch for you.

With those who are reluctant to speak because they're on the wrong side of the story, be polite and persistent—phone calls, emails, appeals via friends. Sometimes people will talk just to get you to stop bugging them. Use your leverage. Letting people know that a story is going ahead regardless, but that you want to include their viewpoint, is surprisingly effective.

Never bully. Never threaten. Never intimidate. It's wrong and as any good reporter will tell you, aggression is counter-productive. Finally, Gatehouse says, have a backup plan. Some people simply won't talk, but there are often other ways to put them on the record—through past interviews, court transcripts, web postings, friends, and family.

Linda Kay

Norton also was very touchy about his age, which caused a problem that I never anticipated. When I jokingly mentioned he'd been called the Jack Benny of boxing because he always gave his age as 29, Norton was deeply insulted. He vehemently insisted he was not a day over 31, period, although I knew he was just shy of 34. We argued over the veracity of his admitted age—and then Norton suddenly stopped talking to me. He got up and ended the interview. At the time, I thought that denying his age was pure vanity. I didn't realize at that moment that it was part of a larger theme: as an athlete, he was running out of time to prove himself a heavyweight champion. Norton calmed down later and we picked up our conversation, but needless to say, I didn't mention his age again. Except in my story.

Putting Issues on a Human Scale

A journalist, essayist, and writer for *The New Yorker*, E.B. White advised: "Don't write about Man, write about *a* man." That's a personal mantra I convey to my journalism students when they are writing issue-oriented features. White's overriding message: put issues on a human scale for the reader by tying them to specific human beings. To that end, it's important to locate a good "main character" that'll take the reader through an issue-oriented piece and illustrate your point. Whether you're writing a feature on the scarcity of affordable housing, depression in young children, or the validity of online college courses, you're dealing with issues and ideas that can seem remote to the reader. Bring the issues down to size by using a main character that exemplifies the situation you are describing. That main character then becomes a point of orientation for the reader within the text—a human link to take the reader through what might otherwise be a difficult story to navigate. The reader will want to know what happens to the main character and becomes invested in the outcome.

In a story about children who are caring for their aging parents, written for *Chatelaine* and reprinted in *Reader's Digest*, I sought a main character that would illustrate the poignancy of a complicated situation involving sacrifice, compromise, and frustration, but also compassion and love. I found that character in Lois Rhodes, a divorced mother of two sons. Then in her 50s, Rhodes worked as a speech language pathologist for the Vancouver School Board. Her mother, Helen, was a former violinist with the Calgary Philharmonic who, in her 80s, suffered from dementia. I used Lois Rhodes to illustrate the plight of a spiralling number of middle-aged Canadians juggling an already busy life with the added responsibility of caring for an elderly relative. In 1960, only 16 percent of Canadian women over age 50 had a surviving parent. But by 2010, that number would skyrocket to 60 percent. The statistics came alive through Lois Rhodes. She'd made the difficult decision to move her mother into her home. The reader saw Rhodes swell with pride as she watched one of her sons tenderly hold his grandmother's hand. The reader also saw Rhodes literally run away from an increasingly burdensome housekeeping routine by lacing up her running shoes and sprinting out the door.

Getting Specific

Generalizations don't work in journalism. Specifics do. Abstract ideas are hard for the reader to picture. The journalist must bring ideas to life by using concrete language and strong examples. Tackling the complex subject of neurosurgery for *Saturday Night* magazine, writer Jamie Findlay not only found a main character to bring the subject to life, but he also used concrete language and strong examples in this riveting scene-setter lead:

> Jean is now ready on the operating table, an intravenous tube in place, his head shaved and yellowish from a coating of iodine. He lies sedated on his left side, eyes closed and one hand outstretched. The surgeons have charted a course and identified the difficult spots. The x-ray photos on the walls of the operating theatre are topographical maps, displaying the deep terrain of the operation. It will take them eight hours to go in and come back.[6]

Every statement in a feature story should be bolstered with one of the following: examples, facts, quotes, anecdotes, and explanations. This material is the fabric of your story. It must be gathered in the reporting stage, which means the reporter is continually on the hunt for it. Quotes should be used judiciously in a feature. They must be meaty and they must resonate. Three decades after profiling Rubin "Hurricane" Carter's co-accused, John Artis, I still remember the quote I used to end the story. I'd asked Artis, a model prisoner who was earning a bachelor's degree in jail, how he dealt with the triple life sentence he'd been handed on the eve of his twentieth birthday. He said: "I just try to do the time rather than have it do me."[7]

The greater the scope of the feature story, the more muscle conveyed by well-drawn anecdotes. They enliven the prose and enlighten the reader. Anecdotes are small stories emblematic of a larger truth. They illustrate a point you're trying to drive home. Sometimes they contain quotes, but not always. You cannot ask sources to produce an anecdote for you on demand. But through detailed interviewing and observation, you can gather material for an anecdote. Follow-up questions are often essential to the process of building an anecdote, allowing you to flesh out the mini-story as it unfolded over time. Susan Schwartz, a veteran feature writer and weekly lifestyle columnist for *The Gazette* in Montreal, used a powerful anecdote to begin a story on whether standards for elderly drivers should be more stringent. The story was titled "The Dilemma: When to Take the Keys Away."

> Montrealer Connie Blatt Rothstein was leaning into the trunk of her car, parked in front of her apartment building, and unloading groceries when an older driver stopped a couple of metres behind her to drop off a passenger.
>
> Suddenly, his car was up against her, pinning her between the two vehicles. "Reverse!" she screamed at the driver. "Reverse!"
>
> Released, she fell to the ground, her right ankle broken in three places, her lower leg broken, ligaments torn in her right knee.
>
> It could have been an accident, a simple error in judgment, as the police officer who took the report observed that September day. But Blatt, who needed crutches, canes and intensive physical therapy to repair the damage, believes the driver hit her because he mistakenly stepped on the gas instead of the brake. And she believes it's an error he made because he was 91.[8]

Letting the Reporting Dictate the Story

You may start out with definite ideas about how your feature story will unfold, but set them aside as new information presents itself in the course of your reporting. A character you think central to the feature at the outset could fade into the background. Don't be married to the material. Go where the reporting takes you, even if it's in another direction. My mentor at the *Chicago Tribune* was a brilliant journalist who reported everything from Queen Elizabeth's coronation in 1953 to Muhammad Ali's banishment from boxing for refusing to serve in the military in the late 1960s. A long-time sports columnist when I met him, the late David Condon and I were asked by the *Tribune* to look into a grade-cheating scheme in college athletics. Valued collegiate athletes with poor academic records at universities such as UCLA, Berkeley, and Arizona State were nevertheless getting college credits and good grades from other schools in order to remain eligible to play basketball and football at their own institutions. The *Tribune* wanted to know how the scheme worked, who was behind it, how many schools were involved, and who in the academic community condoned it. Condon and I spent eight months tracking down a story that ultimately resulted in the publication of a three-part series.

True to the stereotypical picture of an old-time sportswriter, Condon was never without a cigar, but in the name of preserving his health, he did not light up. One day, as we were immersed in reporting the story, Condon chewed on his unlit cigar, rolled it around in his mouth, gazed over his bifocals, and then said dryly: "Investigate a story long enough and it'll blow up in your face." What was he trying to tell me? That a story is bound to take unanticipated twists and turns when you're reporting in-depth. And that's not necessarily a bad thing.

We had travelled thousands of miles to interview coaches, athletes, and officials with the National Collegiate Athletic Association, the governing body of collegiate sport in the United States. It had taken months to find only a couple of sources willing to talk about the grade-cheating scam. From the outset, we had hypothesized that certain coaches in our own Illinois backyard were involved because of connections they'd once had to schools already implicated. But after months of deep probing, we could not find a shred of evidence to back up that hypothesis. It forced us to focus instead on how the bogus credits were earned, rather than on who participated in the scheme.

We enrolled my colleague's four-year-old granddaughter Kate in one of the same courses that the athletes were taking. There were two requirements for the course: attendance at a series of lectures given over one weekend and submission of a paper analyzing the value of the material taught. Without attending the sessions, my colleague and I concocted a rambling nonsensical paper filled with misspellings and errors of grammar that had us in tears laughing as we wrote it. One section described a session taught by an Illinois basketball coach named Lou Henson:

> I did not attend much of Mr. Henson's lecture as one of the coaches who took my sister and I to Adolph's (restaurant) late Friday night said that Henson was giving lectures they had heard from Coach Myers [sic] at De Paul 20 years ago, but my sister says that Illinois and Henson were third in the MIT [sic] and that's pretty good so I listened to just a part of his lecture and have some notes.

We submitted the four-page paper by mail for a grade. A few weeks later, little Kate received a B for her effort along with a university credit from a small private college in southern California. Our story earned us credit, too: a national Associated Press award for Investigative Reporting in Sports.

By enrolling Condon's granddaughter in a course, we actually ended up with a better story than the one we were seeking in the first place. So while it's important at the outset to consider the probable direction a story might take, it's crucial never to preconceive the outcome. Let the reporting dictate the outcome. Tapping into multiple sources will gradually yield another layer of depth and perhaps a surprise you could never have predicted at the start. Tapping into multiple sources also allows you to become an authority on the topic or person. You've become the expert and can write your story from an informed point of view.

Immersing yourself in reporting gives you a chance to scratch beneath the surface. Seeing your sources in their milieu, you pick up details you could not get any other way. Events and situations unfold that you would never otherwise witness. You also get a chance to check your own perceptions against the perceptions you've gathered from your research. In planning my day with gymnast Nadia Comaneci, I suggested we go to lunch following her workout in the gym. I asked her to select the restaurant. She chose an unpretentious neighbourhood place where she knew the owner and some of the customers. For me, the restaurant proved a gold mine. The owner chatted with me and so did the customers. But before we even entered the restaurant, I picked up a telling detail about Comaneci.

As soon as I parked the car, Comaneci jumped out of the passenger seat and put money in the meter. It marked the first time in my reporting career that a source had taken the initiative to pay for parking, and it also flew in the face of a story I'd read about Comaneci in which she was depicted as selfish and self-absorbed. If I'd simply spent an hour asking her questions in the gym, I probably would have believed that myself. But going deep—investing substantial time with my subject—proved a path to deeper insight.

Discussion Questions

1. Read "Living on Lobster Time" by Philip Preville (pages 184–192). What are some strategies Preville may have used to research his story?

2. How would you go about gaining access to the fishermen that Preville interviewed in the story?

3. Preville met some obvious obstacles in reporting the story. What are they—and what obstacles might not have been obvious to the reader?

Notes

1. Robert Fulford, *The Triumph of Narrative*, audio tapes (Toronto: CBC, 1999).
2. Linda Kay, "Video Game in the Sky," *The Gazette* (Montreal), May 14, 1990, D1.
3. David Staples, "The Worst Murder of All," *J-Source.ca*, July 15, 2007, <http://jsource.ca/english_new/detail.php?id=1409> (accessed May 1, 2008).
4. David Staples, "Revisiting Canada's Infanticide Law," *Edmonton Journal*, November 12, 2006, E6.
5. "Chatelaine Writers' Guidelines," *Chatelaine*, <http://en.chatelaine.com/english/binary/pdf/writersguide.pdf> (accessed April 30, 2008).
6. Jamie Findlay, "Brain Storm," *Saturday Night*, July/August 1991, 13.
7. Linda Kay, "How to Succeed—by the Numbers," (Paterson) *Morning News*, September 24, 1975, A1.
8. Susan Schwartz, "The Dilemma: When to Take the Keys Away," *The Gazette* (Montreal), January 15, 2000, A1.

"Living on Lobster Time"

Entry Island has no hospital, no hockey rink, no swimming beach and no supermarket. But there's a good reason to live in the middle of the Gulf of St. Lawrence: the first Saturday in May, when the flare goes off to signal the start of lobster season

Philip Preville, "Living on Lobster Time." *Saturday Night* magazine, April 2003, 45. Copyright © 2004 Philip Preville. Reprinted by permission.

If history has a lesson to teach about the Magdalen Islands, it's that no one should be living on any of them. Jacques Cartier first stumbled across this archipelago of isolated islets north of P.E.I. on his maiden voyage, and the area quickly became notorious for the shipwrecks caused by its unrelenting gale-force winds—more than 500 since 1534. Two 17th-century colonization attempts saw settlers come safely ashore, look around, then pack up and leave. You'd pretty much have to be damned to live here, and in 1755 a group of Acadian families, fleeing expulsion from Nova Scotia, came here to hide in the one place they knew the British wouldn't come looking for them. They never left.

The first thing they did was hunt the region's walrus to extinction, which ought to have provided one more excuse to leave. But more settlers arrived, some Acadian, some English, many from the shipwrecks. Castaways became a godsend for the local gene pool. Sailors would be rescued from the waves, given "temporary" refuge for the winter, then pushed in front of a comely maiden. Soon they were calling the place home. Such as it was. All the islands' worthy timber was quickly felled to make houses and boats (wood and other materials were also regularly scavenged from the shipwrecks), and the long, harsh winters of wind and ice cut them off from the rest of the world for months every year.

For decades the islanders—Quebecers even if closer geographically to P.E.I. and Cape Breton—fished herring, cod and lobster. They also clubbed seals until Brigitte Bardot got wind of it, and her successful lobby for a European seal boycott put an end to that in 1983. In the aftermath of the controversy, the community built a Seal Interpretation Centre to preserve local history and curse Bardot for eternity. After that, they fished the herring to near-extinction, then the cod. Since then six of the seven inhabited Magdalens, fishing communities without fish, have reinvented themselves as a summer tourist destination.

The seventh, Entry Island, never really took to the tourist trade. The island is a tiny pimple of red sandstone, some four kilometres square, cut off from its neighbours and most amenities by an hour-long ferry ride. It has six kilometres of dirt roads; one canteen; two convenience stores stocked with beer, Viva

Puffs and tinned Vienna sausage; and one bar, the Lobster Trap, open only when there's enough of a crowd to warrant it, which is almost never. The island has no gas station, no street lights, no supermarket or drugstore, no street addresses, no swimming beach, hotel, hockey rink, hospital, doctor or police. Entry Island achieved a dreary milestone last year: with 130 residents and 150 tombstones, the dead now outnumber the living.

There's really only one reason left to live on Entry, and that reason is the first Saturday in May, the day lobster season begins. It's an annual ritual, marked by the firing of a flare at 5 a.m. and the ensuing stampede to the best lobster grounds. There's lobster around all the islands, but everyone knows where the good bottoms are, and the first fisherman to get there is first to lay his traps, leaving everyone else to fight for second best. Entry's harbour is closest to the best lobster grounds—by 45 minutes or so, depending on the speed of your boat—which makes Entry's residents lobster squatters, living here year-round so they can register their boats in this harbour, in anticipation of this one day.

"One time I got into a fight and someone gave me a hammer blow to the head, and that knocked me down. And when you're down, that's when you get the boot. That's how I ended up with this." Spencer Chenell takes out his front dentures and shows them to me. It takes him about 10 seconds to remove them, present them for my inspection and snap them back into place, grinning all the while. We met on the ferry ride from the local hub of Cap-aux-Meules to Entry Island. It's the only moment on our entire journey when he stops talking.

Most Canadians couldn't place the Magdalen Islands on a map—a forgivable sin, given that most maps of Canada are drawn to a scale that makes them disappear. But for francophone Quebecers "les Iles de la Madeleine" are a place of lore, Quebec's own private Cape Breton, a place where salty sailors tell tall tales awash in quaint regional accents.

"There's no police on Entry, so we settle our own scores," continues Spencer, his dentures back in. "The next day I woke up in the hospital off-island, and the policeman asked did I want to press charges. I told him, 'Hell no, I'll probably be mixin' it up the minute I get outta here!'"

Like so many fishing towns turned tourist magnets, the Magdalens have a time-warp quaintness about them. What's changed the most over the centuries, oddly, has been the geography. Winds, waves and currents have shifted the ocean floor so that, today, the six main islands are now essentially one island, connected by long, thin sand dunes into a 100-kilometre-long archipelago, with a paved highway linking them all together. Entry is the only inhabited island that remains separate and apart from the rest, the problem child of the Magdalen Islands, kept afloat by pluck, habit and subsidy.

"You're a journalist, are you? We had a journalist visit Entry Island some years ago, and people didn't take kindly to what he wrote. Three years later he came back and we were waiting for him, heh, heh, heh. Anyway, I'm *just*"—and here I fully expect Spencer to say he was just kidding—"I'm *just* telling you so you have fair warning."

Upon arrival I go for a stroll. A few people raise cattle, with the help of an inside-out land-tenure system: the homes are fenced in, leaving the cows to roam the rest of the island unencumbered. A bull decides to follow me around. I lose him by heading into the street amid the homes, where I'm quickly surrounded by three angry dogs. A brief standoff ensues until the owners finally call off the hounds from their windows. On an island of 130, any living beast can spot the stranger.

Folks smile when they learn that Spencer gave me the welcome-wagon treatment on the ferry. The local jaw-wagger, they say. Within hours I have half a dozen offers from fishermen willing to take me out on the water when the flare goes off. Even so, that reporter of Spencer's isn't the only writer stuck like a burr in local memory. Farley Mowat once likened Entry Islanders to Siberian convicts, I'm told. Mowat denies it. Still, the people are waiting for him to show up again.

"You'll have to forgive the mood around here," one lobster trapper tells me down at Entry's harbour. "The delays are making us all a bit squirrelly." Today is Wednesday. Lobster season was supposed to have begun last Saturday, but bad weather delayed the firing of the flare. The fishermen were then put on 24-hour notice for three days running until, finally, the Department of Fisheries and Oceans decided to simply postpone everything until the following Saturday. As if to confirm the DFO's folly, today is calm and sunny, a perfect day to be on the water.

The delays have coiled Entry Island harbour into a tightly wound spring. Most of Entry's 18 lobster vessels are ready to go, traps piled high on the decks. The cages were baited with herring days ago, and the harbour reeks of rotting fish. With nothing else to do, the fishermen gather down at the docks, overanalyze the weather updates and trade barbs to keep each other in good humour. Spencer Chenell can't stop yammering about a good fight.

Fact is, the countdown to the fishery makes everyone ornery, even when it starts on time. The Magdalens were once the herring smokehouse of the world, exporting crates of the stuff down to the Caribbean and points beyond. When the herring disappeared in the early 1970s, the DFO begged people to fish snow crab, but it was worth pennies and the licences had few takers. Today the Japanese can't get enough snow crab, and the five Madelinots who were fool enough to risk it are now millionaires. Instead, most fishermen turned to cod. Now, pretty much everyone is left fishing lobster. There are other fisheries in the Magdalens (some scallop and mackerel, a few herring and a bit of sealing once again), but they're mere income supplements. It's the lobster that trigger the big-money cascade into the region—$25 million annually, all of it pulled up from the ocean floor in nine short weeks, the weeks that will also qualify most of the community for Employment Insurance.

The fishery's gold-rush structure engenders a kind of mania that's never more intense than on its first day. The DFO calls it an "effort control" fishery: there are 325 lobster licences in the Magdalens, and each licence entitles you to 300 traps. The only quota is the time limit: 54 days of trapping (everyone— lobsters included—has Sunday off), which helps conserve the resource but also fosters competitiveness. Lobster season is essentially a 54-day battle royal among 325 fishermen, all crowding the same bottoms and trying to grab all the lobster they can. The total catch works out to about $75,000 per licence. The average fisherman can expect overhead of between $20,000 and $40,000—on boat payments, crew costs, fuel, etc.—so there is profit to be had. That is, so long as your traps are in the right spots. As the local DFO director says, fishermen are perfectly reasonable people during off-season town hall meetings, but they're crazy at the end of the pier.

Competition is equally fierce among harbours, of which there are nine in the Magdalens. Entry's isolation evokes resentment from the rest of the region's fishermen. In 2002 the DFO began $4.5 million worth of repairs to Entry's harbour—$250,000 per lobster licence—despite its being among the least busy of the nine. Last year, Entry's fishermen were accused of hoarding the undersized baby lobsters they caught around the rest of the archipelago, taking them home and returning them to the sea over by Entry's shores—a sneaky attempt to bolster the lobster population in their own backyard. The matter has not been resolved, and probably never will be. Entry Island is the much-maligned scapegoat of the Magdalens, with an aspersive eye cast upon it for as long as anyone can remember.

The fact that it's an English-speaking enclave in a predominantly French-speaking archipelago doesn't help. Entry's dirt roads are in desperate need of repair—the potholes are so deep, they'll soon be home to lobster themselves—and some folks say the municipality, unlike the DFO, won't spend money on the English island. While Entry isn't the Magdalens' only anglophone community, its offshore location naturally gives rise to suspicion. But no one really likes to talk about language politics anyway. "English and French get along fine round here," Spencer Chenell insists. "We eat together, sleep together, fish together, drink together. Fight together, too."

With less than 24 hours to go before lobster season, the DFO's decision to postpone is looking more foolish by the minute. The mid-week sun and calm have given way to rain and forecasts of gale-force winds. A few fishermen have gathered at Chez Brian Josey, Entry's lone restaurant. "Will you go out if the weather's bad?" "Have to wait and see. You?" "Forecast could change." "If I had a dollar for every time the weatherman was wrong." Then Brian Josey, Entry's lone restaurateur, chimes in: "Even if the weather's really bad, some idiot will decide to go out and drop his traps." Pause. "And once one of them goes, they'll all go."

Leave it to the man who doesn't fish to speak the truth about fishing. Whatever the DFO's rules might say, the lobster fishery is actually governed by a complex labyrinth of social pressures and rivalries. Though they are neighbours and in many cases brothers or cousins, fishermen keep their business to themselves, never revealing the amount or value of their annual catch. Over a lunch of salt mackerel and potatoes, two fishermen explain that, once their traps are in the water, they'll be going out the following morning at 1 a.m. to pull the lobsters out. Why so early? Because that's when everyone goes. But why doesn't everyone get a good night's sleep and go in the morning? Because 1 a.m. is when everyone goes. Brian adds his two cents' worth: "If you all wanted to go at a more reasonable hour, you could. You'd just have to decide to do it that way."

But it's not that simple. Some say the lobster are more active at night, some say they do it so they can empty their traps twice in a single day. It's also about keeping an eye on everyone else. If you're a lobsterman, you might prefer to make the rounds after sunup, but some other bastard will go out in the dark and empty the lobsters out of your traps while no one's looking, so you've got to go out same time as him, and you've got 300 traps dispersed around the islands and you've got to protect them all, so you might as well be the first guy out on the water, beat those other sons of bitches to the punch. Not that you would steal anyone else's lobsters, you'd never do that, but you got to protect yourself from pirates. And soon enough everyone is going to bed at 7 p.m. so they can fish lobster in the middle of the night.

Everyone, that is, except Brian Josey. Brian hates fishing and is prone to seasickness. Usually, in a place like Entry, that makes you the village idiot. But Brian took over his dad's store, opened the restaurant and also rents out two homes. Aside from his aunt, who owns Entry's lone B & B, Brian is pretty much the only resident of Entry who's equipped to pull money from tourists' pockets. Brian also raises cattle with his brother Ralph, and over the years has become Entry's biggest landowner. "A lot of people have left, and a lot of people have passed away," Brian explains. "When they go, I make an offer for the property." There aren't many other buyers in these parts, so people usually sell to him. Brian also owns the beachfront property beside the harbour and charges the municipality and the DFO to land their barges there.

This has been cause for some friction. The municipality once tried to expropriate some of his land. In the past he's had his restaurant windows broken. "He's land crazy," one fisherman told me, a seafarer's insult if ever there was one. Around here everyone owns a boat, a lobster licence and the roof over their heads. That's been the recipe for happiness for generations. But a community of 130 can support a merchant class of one; Brian is the first to fill the position. His landlocked store and restaurant, a stone's throw from the harbour, are a constant reminder: he's the only one who doesn't take orders from lobster.

Out the window, the rain has stopped and the harbour is quiet. All the boats are ready to go, save one. Alvin Dickson, the free spirit of Entry Island, is finally bringing his traps down to the pier, just as predicted. Last year he was still loading traps with 15 minutes to go before start time. I'm heading out on his boat tomorrow to drop traps, so I go down to the pier to lend a hand.

"If I had a dollar for every time the weatherman was wrong." It was pouring rain at 2 a.m., but now, 60 minutes from lobster time, it's clear and calm as can be. No one knows how long it will last. Five a.m. can't come fast enough now.

To avoid the bottleneck of the harbour's narrow entrance, most of the boats are idling offshore, jostling for position in open water. The flare flashes and all the boats are away. Except Alvin Dickson's. He's still trying to light his boat's heating stove. "Damn thing's brand new, won't light since the day I got it. I'm takin' it back!"

Alvin's not the least bit concerned about being slow out of the gate. His general temperament and lifestyle aren't prone to anxiety. Anyway, his boat, the *Daddy Ça* (pronounced "Daddysaw"), is among the fastest in Entry's fleet. His father, Donald, the dean of Entry's lobstermen, will captain the vessel.

Donald Dickson is 75 years old, recently had a kidney removed and is so hoarse from a lifetime of cigarettes that he's barely audible. As he climbs atop the lobster traps to reach the cabin, I fear he'll fall and break his leg. But he's never more sure-footed than when he's in rubber boots. The lobster keep him young. I ask how long he's been fishing them.

"Sixty-two."

"Nineteen sixty-two? That's quite a while."

"No. Sixty-two years."

Donald doesn't follow the crowd. While everyone else rushes to the prime lobster bottoms to pile their traps on top of one another and argue over who got there first, Donald takes us to his favourite bottoms, where we are alone.

The lobster trap is a remarkably low-tech contraption, essentially un-changed since the 1830s, a riddle easily solved even for a lobster. (According to video research, 94 per cent of all lobsters that enter a trap walk right out again.) So the lobstermen must outwit their prey. Lobster live among the rocks for shelter, and everyone agrees the trick is to drop your traps along the line where the rocks meet the sand, but not on the sand, because the lobster won't venture there.

Wisdom like this makes laying traps fussy work. Most ship captains slowly prowl the area, checking global positioning satellite, sonar and ultrasound readings to find a rocky seabed's edge at the right depth. Donald Dickson relies on the old magnetic compass, the visual landmarks of the islands to the extent his eyes can still make them out, the direction and strength of the tide and 62 years of thinking like a crustacean.

When Donald gives the signal, Alvin and his hired hand, Robbie Brymer, drop lines of traps off the back of the boat. Over two hours, 150 of Alvin's traps find the bottom. Then it's back to Entry for a second load.

For the next run I head back out with Blair Chenell, who talks and even looks like Jack Nicholson, though he wears the same large tinted glasses as his uncle Spencer. Blair spent the morning jostling for position alongside everyone else in the crowded areas, and decides to head over to Donald Dickson's favourite spot for this run. Blair makes extensive use of his electronic gad-getry, including a GPS system that tells him exactly where he dropped his traps last year. Even so, the currents push one of his trap lines off course as it falls to the bottom, forcing him to pull the line back up and start again. We come across Donald's trap lines, and Blair, checking his equipment, testifies that old Donald Dickson has dropped his traps with a precision that could not possibly be wrung from the technology. "He's got 'em right on the edge."

By noon, the weather is starting to turn, but everyone's traps are in the water and the day's work is done. Spencer Chenell is driving up and down the docks on his all-terrain vehicle, stopping to chat with everyone. Over whistle dogs and poutine at the restaurant, Brian Josey is mixing it up in conversation, arguing that fishermen shouldn't get pogey. They won't start pulling the lobster out until Monday. By then the buyers will have set up shop in the harbour. They'll ship most of the catch across Quebec, but the biggest lobsters will go to Boston and as far away as Japan.

For the next nine weeks the fishermen will work long hours, yap across the gunwales and risk their fingers applying blue elastic bands to lobster claws. The year's haul turns out to be a rich one: a record 4.4 million pounds of lobster at a record average price of $6.20 per pound. True to form, the Dicksons won't say how they fared.

Once lobster season is over, tourist season begins and the aspersions cast upon Entry will stretch from one industry to the other. On the summertime ferry to Entry, the smiling tour guide cheerfully describes Entry Islanders as the Magdalens' deformed hermits: they all have red hair, they keep to themselves, they surface once in a while for food.

Tourism authorities seem intent on keeping people at a safe distance from Entry's inhabitants, so that everything will remain picturesque. For years the government published Magdalens tourist guide never acknowledged Brian Josey's restaurant. The 2002 edition explains that, although there is a restaurant on the island, it's "agreeable" to plan a picnic and eat it atop the big hill. But tourism delivers a bum rap to communities like this, evaluating them on the song-and-dance routine they put on for fat-walleted strangers. The tourism industry is turning the six main Magdalens (and every other quaint rural outpost it can get hold of) into yet another Green Gables, and an accusing finger inevitably gets pointed at Entry for its refusal to dress itself up and sell key chains or googly-eyeballed seashells.

It's a laudable stubborn streak, but it could prove costly. Entry's population is shrinking faster than that of the rest of the Magdalens. The school has only 18 pupils. The harbour's $4.5-million facelift might be its last. The Magdalens' nine federally funded harbours are about seven too many for only 325 lobster licences. The DFO is trying to consolidate them, but progress is slow. Authorities left one wharf on the archipelago, Old Harry (that's its official name), to deteriorate until it was literally toppling into the sea, then condemned it. Old Harry's six fishermen, despite being only a 15-minute drive from two other harbours, tore down the barricades and continue to fish from there, even though it means they have to pull their boats out of the water and onto the landing every day.

To free-market economists, think-tank wonks and other eggheads with no sea legs, places like Old Harry and Entry Island are great Canadian ills, surviving only on welfare and subsidy. But no amount of policy tinkering or subsidy redirection can change the basics: lobster remains a lucrative resource, the people here are adept at exploiting it, and they call this place home. It will probably take some seismic economic shift, something that will shake Entry Island's way of life to its foundation—a natural gas discovery, perhaps (explorers have been drilling for years)—to drive the fishermen away. But like the fellas at Old Harry, they won't go gently. Most likely it'll take a hammer to the head and a kick in the teeth, and whoever eventually picks that fight had better be ready to get as good as he gives.

PART THREE

Writing It Down

CHAPTER SEVEN

Building the Beast: Approaches to Structure

Paul Benedetti

One of the big lies of writing is that great writers simply sit down and let the words flow out in a steady, brilliant stream—from a wonderful lead to a snappy closing sentence. Young writers particularly are excited by the now legendary story of beat author Jack Kerouac typing his whole novel *On the Road* on a giant roll of paper in a continuous white-hot writing marathon.

Even experienced writers and writing teachers such as William Zinsser, the author of the very fine *On Writing Well*, contribute to this myth when he tells young writers of non-fiction that the key is to start with a great lead and keep writing. "Continue to build," says Zinsser. "Every paragraph should amplify the one that preceded it."[1] That's actually good advice, as far as it goes, but it contains a misleading idea: that stories are built like races are run, by starting at the beginning and putting one foot in front of the other until you hit the finish line.

Don't believe it. That myth has done more to derail more would-be writers than low pay and nasty editors. In his book *Writing for Story*, two-time Pulitzer Prize–winning writer Jon Franklin confesses that this mistaken belief almost ended his writing career before it started:

I wasted five years of my writing career proceeding on the assumption that outlining could be avoided. Well, I'm here to inform you of a grim truth: It can't be. And even if it could be, no sane writer would want to because, believe it or not, once you understand what an outline is, it serves to make your writing much, much easier.[2]

Stories don't organize and write themselves. If the story is short, say a few hundred words, you can probably hold the story parts in your head. But, if the article is longer than that, several thousand words or more, most writers simply can't hold all the information they need in their working memory. The writing slows, you rewrite more and more, confusion sets in, and finally, the story falls apart.

Some writers produce feature stories without any real planning, but it's hellish work and at some point, it usually ends in disaster. To write a good major feature story, you need some sort of outline, however simple it may be. But first, you'll need to figure out what your story, and therefore your outline, is about.

Before You Write: Organizing Your Material

All successful feature writers, from *The Globe and Mail*'s Stephen Brunt to *The New Yorker*'s Malcolm Gladwell, spend hours, days, weeks, and even months organizing their notes before they write an outline or type one word of their story. This is the taking-stock-of-your-material phase of the writing. You must have a complete inventory of what you have before you can decide on a structure for your piece. If you haven't already done it, organize your notes, documents, clips, files, tapes, or digital recordings. You can do this on your computer with a series of carefully named files or, if you prefer, with hard copy and old-fashioned coloured file folders, or a combination of both.

Once you have done that, you must deal with what's probably the most important raw material you have—your interviews. Feature stories can contain detailed narratives, as does Anne Mullens's "The Sixty-Storey Crisis," which is reprinted following this chapter. Her award-winning story is a careful reconstruction of the events around the barely avoided catastrophic collapse of a huge British Columbia dam; to report it she had to conduct many detailed interviews. Other articles contain complicated science, medical, or business information (to name only a few areas), and the number and depth of interviews needed to produce this kind of article can take days, weeks, and even months to assemble. For medium-length and especially for long features, I recommend recording and transcribing your interviews. Handwritten notes have a limited shelf life; most reporters can barely read them even a few days after the interview. And transcribing an interview gives you a chance to familiarize yourself with the material again, helping you recognize the strongest parts of your story. Some writers transcribe every word of the interview, but most focus on potential quotes—you can just summarize the rest. Carefully mark your transcripts with the name of the interviewee, the location and time of the interview, and any other relevant information you need.

Many feature writers then reread their transcripts and other material, meticulously highlighting important sections. I like to use different-coloured highlighters to denote important quotes or to codify the material by topic, ideas, or sections. You can also tag the sections with coloured labels or sticky notes—whatever works for you. This may seem like a laborious process, but it pays off even if you are working on a short feature (a thousand words or less). It will save you time in the end, and it's an important part of the writing process because it demands that you *think* about your story.

Tips on Organizing Your Research

1. Organize all your notes, documents, clips, press releases, and tape or digital files.
2. Transcribe and arrange all interviews by source name, place, and date.
3. Mark sections and passages with coloured highlighter, and organize subjects by colour-code. If you do this on your computer, flag the subjects or sections any way you like, but make sure you can find your quotes and information easily.
4. Read over all your material. Read it again.

Story Forms

Features are real stories. Unlike the simplest kind of news story, they cannot be told by leading with the most important facts and then just adding stuff until you run out of material. Instead, they have a beginning, a middle, and an end. Though content should drive the story, the form you choose dictates what kind of story you will write. Let's say your story is about a Canadian cabinet minister's life-long battle with depression. Now, imagine that story as a novel, a film screenplay, a short story, or a piece of non-fiction for a magazine. Same content—many different stories.

Within each of those genres (film, for instance), there are many different story forms to choose from. Again: same genre—many different stories. But it's worth starting with a basic form that has evolved into what's sometimes called "the standard feature form." This classic template, widely used by newspaper and magazine writers everywhere, came out of *The Wall Street Journal*, a newspaper famous for its daily in-depth stories on a wide range of subjects. The stories engage readers with their lively mix of anecdotes and scenes and background information, statistics, and quotes. Here is the model for the typical story, as described by Cheryl Gibbs and Tom Warhover:

Glad You Asked!   "Great Hunks of Research"

Q: How do I know what to put in—and what to leave out?
A: We asked Stephen Brunt, a sports columnist for *The Globe and Mail*, a magazine writer, and the author of several books, including *Facing Ali: The Opposition Weighs In* and *Searching for Bobby Orr*, to tell us about his approach to the writing process.

On what to do before you start:

> I transcribe all my stuff. I'm usually a note taker, but I use a tape recorder when I'm working long form. The process of transcribing and hearing it again is really important. I've got to hear it again. I work my way back through everything I have. And, ideally, I like to have some time to let things percolate, so that whatever I have accumulated, I can let the ideas kick around in my head.
>
> I surround myself with paper. Or I have it in various screens on my computer. I have it all around me. I'm not super organized. I find the process is more about discarding stuff. I will have great hunks of stuff around me, most of which I am never going to use. Sometimes the mistake that people make, and I have made at various times, is trying to put all of the research on the page. You should have that stuff backing you, and you need to understand the story the best you can, but at the core of it, you have to have an idea. It has to boil down to something you can express in one line. Unless you understand the core thesis of your story, there is no point in writing anything. If it is a story you can tell somebody sitting over dinner, and you keep people engaged, then it is a good story.

1. Anecdotal lead
2. Nut graph that links the lead to the larger issue
3. Facts, quotes, and more anecdotes
4. Explanatory material, contextual information, and background
5. Return to the opening anecdote bringing the story full circle for a strong ending.[3]

Mark MacKinnon used this form for a short news feature in *The Globe and Mail* about the working children of Afghanistan. He opens with a short, descriptive story:

On getting started:

It's important for me to get the first leg right. I need my lead to be right. I generally know where it is going to end. I generally know in my head what the different legs are going to be, or what the scenes are going to be, where the exposition is going to be or where the nut graph is going to be. I just generally try to get that first leg of it down. If I am writing a magazine piece, there is a different rhythm. When I get the opening down, I like to walk away from it for a while, if I have the time.

I write out of order on a magazine piece. I might have the beginning and the end and work on the middle. Sometimes I will write a leg, where I know I have to get the material in there, and I will write that and get it ready to go ... But you have to know where your story is going. You have to bring them in for the big finish. Where a story loses momentum is where the writer loses focus, when they don't quite know where they are. The end is as important as the lead.

On keeping readers interested:

You want your article to "read short." That's what you want. I want someone to read 7,000 words and feel like they've read 2,000. You can't make people work too hard. So, you have to be a storyteller, and you have to understand attention span and the entertainment factor. It's not just exposition; people aren't going to read it for their own good. They are going to read it because you are pulling them through the story; you keep giving them something new.

Paul Benedetti

Nisar Ahmed wields the blackened set of pliers with what might be the world's smallest pair of grease-monkey hands.

First the six-year-old uses the pliers to tighten a nut on the motorized rickshaw he is repairing, then he effortlessly spins the tool around in his hand to wield it as a hammer, knocking a wheel cover back into place. Satisfied, Nisar wipes a dirty forehead and gets to work on the next wheel.[4]

After a few more paragraphs describing Nisar's working conditions, MacKinnon pushes the story toward a broader idea:

Most of the staff here—at least those doing the actual repairs—are children. Unlike Nisar, most of them will work until the sun goes down. The dozen or so adults and children on the Jalalabad sidewalk get through five or six rickshaws every day.

A year after the Taliban regime retreated from power, the country remains burdened by deep-rooted social ills, most of them caused by crushing poverty.[5]

Then MacKinnon ties the anecdotal lead to the current issue in a single focused sentence that contains enough facts and information to contextualize the lead:

There are an estimated 50,000 children between the ages of 5 and 14 working in Kabul alone, with many more believed to be working in other parts of the country. And the numbers have grown since the Taliban fled.[6]

MacKinnon continues his story by adding details, describing working conditions, and quoting UNICEF officials about the state of child labour in Afghanistan. He outlines the extent of the problem and the reasons for the situation before closing by returning to the scene he opened with:

Nisar, for one, sees little wrong with his lot in life.

Although he likes going to school, he also has many friends of his own age at the Jalalabad rickshaw repair yard.

And, unlike many people much older than he, Nisar already knows what he wants to be when he grows up. "A mechanic," he says solemnly.[7]

This basic feature structure can be expanded to accommodate a more complex story, one that has several important elements or ideas that need to be examined or explained. A good format is outlined by Catherine McKercher and Carman Cumming as follows:

1. Anecdote
2. Theme paragraph (theme and sub-themes)
3. Development of main theme
4. Development of sub-theme 1
5. Development of sub-theme 2
6. Other themes/other material
7. Return to main theme
8. Kicker[8]

These approaches can be used to build almost any feature. Although every story is unique, you still need to hook readers at the beginning with a strong lead, description, or anecdote, then move through the issues, ideas, themes, or questions you need to address before closing your story on a strong note, often coming full circle. You'll read more about the individual building blocks—the lead, the theme graph, and so on—in the next chapter.

Dramatic Non-fiction: The Elements of Storytelling

Great stories are built around four elements: character, conflict, change through time, and resolution. In fiction, think of Homer's *Ulysses*, Dickens's *Oliver Twist*, Hemingway's *The Old Man and the Sea*, and Steinbeck's *The Grapes of Wrath*. Powerful features often tell a single story in fundamentally the same way as riveting short stories and great novels. They tell human stories in a compelling way that is sometimes described as dramatic non-fiction.

The best explanation of structure in dramatic non-fiction, I think, comes from Jon Franklin in his book *Writing for Story*. He says all great features are composed of three parts, or foci:

- *The complicating focus* includes the lead or narrative hook, the introduction of character, and the major challenge or complication.
- *The development focus* usually consists of three foci, first a "flashback" or backgrounder and then two (or more) developments leading to the climax or moment of insight.
- *The resolving focus*, the shortest focus, describes the action the character takes and the outcome or resolution of the story.[9]

These foci, Franklin says, must be carefully plotted in a short outline that consists of simple sentences with action verbs and someone doing something. Say, for example, you are assigned to write a profile about Canadian wheelchair athlete Rick Hansen. Your focus statements might look something like this:

Complication: Hansen is paralyzed after a car accident.
Development:
  1. Hansen fights back physically and psychologically.
  2. Hansen battles stereotypes and takes physical education at university.
  3. Hansen becomes a champion wheelchair marathoner and launches the Man in Motion World Tour.
Resolution: Hansen uses his fame to help paraplegics worldwide.

Your outline has a person doing something. The verbs are action verbs and that action pushes the story forward to a conclusion. This looks easy, but many young writers miss the point. Imagine the same story outlined like this:

Complication: It's hard being a paraplegic.
Development:
  1. Hansen's life in a wheelchair
  2. The world of para-athletes
  3. Hansen as president of his foundation
Resolution: Hansen's ongoing work

None of this works because there is no action and no concrete reason for interest. The main character overcomes no obstacles and takes no action to provide forward movement for your story. Your story can start with a complication that affects your main character, such as a job loss, a divorce, or an illness. But, in order to have a story that holds people's interest, your main character should take some action and will likely change over the course of your story. Because this is real life and not fiction, these actions may not be wholly successful—jobs may not be regained, marriages may not be saved, and bodies may not heal—but your story should have some kind of resolution of the major problem presented, even if that resolution is uncertain or bittersweet.

Tips on Outlining Dramatic Non-fiction

Ask yourself the following questions as you write the outline of your story:

  1. Does each focus statement in the outline use action verbs?
  2. Is your main character in each focus statement of the outline?
  3. Can you illustrate the action described in each focus statement?
  4. Does your character take action?
  5. Does the resolution of your story respond to the complication?[10]

The outline process forces you to think through the main body of your story. Too many feature writers fix on a beginning and an end and then simply "fill in" the middle and hope for the best. Sometimes hard work and good writing keep the reader interested through a short feature, but often the story bogs down and the reader wanders off. The outline gives you a road map for each section of the story, ensuring that the forward momentum and the tension never flag.

Of course, full stories are not as simple as the outlines upon which they are based. Each of the developments listed above may include flashbacks, history, contextual material about places and people, even statistics and background facts. But, without a strong structural plan for all that material, your article will lack interest, momentum, and meaning. Having said that, I agree with Franklin's critics that his formula may be too simplistic and too rigid for all stories. Great feature stories have been written that do not conform to his rules of writing. Franklin's ideas will usually help you find your story and perhaps structure it, but feel free to improvise and create based on the information you gather, the people you meet, and the stories they tell you.

Okay, you may say, all that's great for profiles or stories about people, but my assignment is to write about the Toronto Argonauts, or Canadian Tire, or the drug problem in Vancouver's Downtown Eastside. In that case, that team, company, or place should become the "person" in your outline. All the rules still apply. The story of great companies, great (or terrible) teams, and even fascinating places are best told through people. If the focus of your story is a company (the rise and fall and rise of Linda Lundström) or an institution (what's wrong with the Canada Council?) or government (inside the Liberals' inner circle), it is, like all good stories, really about people. Nobody wants to read an article filled only with lifeless statistics or dry corporate history. For each of the stories listed above, a good reporter should try to find people whose experiences at the company or on the team help tell the overall story in a compelling and interesting—and human— way. And the way you tell those stories is the same way a filmmaker makes a movie—through the careful use of scenes.

From Outline to Article: It's All About Scenes

On *Esquire* magazine's 50th anniversary, the editors tried to decide on the best story the magazine ever ran. It was a difficult task, but they finally settled on the iconic story by Gay Talese called "Frank Sinatra Has a Cold," first published in 1966. This is how the story begins:

Frank Sinatra, holding a glass of bourbon in one hand and a cigarette in the other, stood in a dark corner of the bar between two attractive but fading blondes who sat waiting for him to say something. But he said nothing; he had been silent during much of the evening, except now in this private club in Beverly Hills he seemed even more distant, staring out through the smoke and semidarkness into a large room beyond the bar where dozens of young couples sat huddled around small tables or twisted in the center of the floor to the clamorous clang of folk-rock music blaring from the stereo. The two blondes knew, as did Sinatra's four male friends who stood nearby, that it was a bad idea to force conversation upon him when he was in this mood of sullen silence, a mood that had been hardly uncommon during this first week of November, a month before his fiftieth birthday.[11]

Notice how Talese puts the reader right into the bar beside Sinatra. We see the room, the women, the young couples; we hear the music, smell the cigarette smoke. Like a camera, the writer captures the scene—intimate, personal, and engrossing. This scene not only establishes that Sinatra is near 50 years of age and in a bad mood, but foreshadows many of the story's central themes: Sinatra's power, his essential loneliness, his nature, and his position in the entertainment world. Talese doesn't tell us these things—he *shows* us. That's the power of writing in scenes.

As you know by now, good feature writing depends on the development of scenes. These narrative sections are the building blocks of great feature writing. Like a good film (and a good film script), a feature story is composed of well-constructed, well-written scenes that use narrative techniques borrowed from the fiction writer's tool kit to establish the conflict or complication, introduce and develop characters, and show (not tell) action.

Does that mean that a great story is simply a collection of great scenes? No! A story consists of scenes that are organized in a meticulous order and that flow coherently, smoothly, almost seamlessly from one to another.

Using your outline as a guide, you can begin to identify and organize the scenes that will make up your story. Here is where your notes and your outline come together. As you carefully reread your notes, you will have listed a certain number of scenes or incidents or "actions" that you want in your story. Now, you have to organize them according to your outline, using the scenes to flesh out the basic sections or foci that make up your story. In a short feature, you can make simple notes listing the scenes under each section. In a longer feature article or in a book, you will want to write a fuller description of each scene within each section and use that as your guide. It might look something like this:

Complication: Judy gets breast cancer.
Scenes: (1) Doctor's office: Doc informs Judy. (2) Kitchen table: Judy tells husband. (3) At bedtime: Judy tells kids.
Development: Judy fights breast cancer.
Scenes: (1) Judy meets with cancer specialist. (2) Judy goes to alternative medicine meeting. (3) Judy argues with husband and friends about treatment choice. (4) Hospital: Judy starts chemotherapy.
Resolution: Judy goes into remission, but cancer could return.
Scenes: (5) Judy gets clear tests. (6) Judy goes to a cancer survivor group meeting.

You may juggle the order of these scenes, perhaps opening with the drama of Judy's surgery. Having a solid story outline will allow you to take risks and experiment with the form because you *know* your story. In the middle section, you may work in some of Judy's background and history and some exposition on the nature of breast cancer.

How to Organize Your Scenes

The first scene in your story will often be the lead (but not always, since not all features need to begin with a scene). Choosing that first scene has little to do with the choices you make for arranging scenes in the remainder of your outline. For instance, your lead scene can come from any part of your story, regardless of when that event happened chronologically. The inexperienced writer may gravitate to choosing, for the first scene, the first event in a chronology. But this is usually a mistake. Why? Because readers need to be hooked early in your story, and the writer must provide some sense of anticipation, even suspense, to keep readers engaged. A story that begins, "John Smith was born in a small, quiet town in 1927 ..." doesn't exactly grab a reader by the throat. By contrast, here's how Elizabeth Gilbert began a 2002 story for *GQ* magazine:

> Jim McLaren doesn't have any memory of the first accident. He can't tell you what it feels like to be hit by a New York City bus and thrown eighty-nine feet in the air, to have your bones shattered and your legs crushed, to have your organs pulverized and to be pronounced dead on arrival at the hospital, because he can't recall any part of it.[12]

Not only are we mesmerized by the stunning details of the accident, by the breathless pace of the opening sentences but, even if we don't quite notice it, we're utterly hooked by the first sentence where Gilbert expertly mentions that this is Jim's *first* accident. What reader on earth could resist finding out what happens to Jim in his *second* accident?

Your opening scene will often take readers right into the thick of the action—not to the climax because you must build to that, but close enough to it to hook him, and far enough away to allow you some room to develop the story. Here's how Jon Krakauer starts his award-winning 1996 story "Into Thin Air" for *Outside* magazine (which he later turned into a book with the same title):

> Straddling the top of the world, one foot in Tibet and the other in Nepal, I cleared the ice from my oxygen mask, hunched a shoulder against the wind and stared absently at the vast sweep of earth below. I understood on some dim, detached level that it was a spectacular sight. I'd been fantasizing about this moment, and the release of emotion that would accompany it, for many months. But now that I was finally here, standing on top of the summit of Mount Everest, I just couldn't summon the energy to care.[13]

In the next three paragraphs, Krakauer describes his few moments at the top of the world and ends the scene ominously: "To the south, where the sky had been perfectly clear just an hour earlier, a blanket of clouds now hit Pumori, Ama Dablam and the lesser peaks surrounding Everest."[14] Then, he hooks readers with two devastating sentences:

Glad You Asked! Kick Start

Q: What's the cure for writer's block?
A: Sometimes, the hardest part of writing is just getting started. There are many reasons for writer's block—anxiety, fear of failure, information overload, procrastination ... but the reasons are less important than the solutions. Here are some simple tips from the pros* for getting words on the screen.

1. Tell it to a friend. Move away from the empty screen or blank sheet and either meet or phone a friend. Tell them the story simply and directly. The process of marshalling your thoughts to explain the story to another person is often enough to get you going.
2. Forget the lead. Don't worry about the first sentence. Too many people spend hours labouring over the perfect opening. Write sentence number two. Write a piece in the middle of the story! It doesn't matter where you begin. Write whatever feels best and build around it.
3. Break it up. Don't let the whole story overwhelm you. Jot down words or notes for each section of the story. Break the article up into parts and

Days later—after six bodies had been found, after a search for two others had been abandoned, after surgeons had amputated the gangrenous right hand of my teammate Beck Weathers—people would ask why, if the weather had begun to deteriorate, had climbers on the upper mountain not heeded the signs? Why did veteran Himalayan guides keep moving upward, leading a gaggle of amateurs, each of whom had paid as much as $65,000 to be ushered safely up Everest, into an apparent death trap?[15]

Krakauer will spend the next almost 10,000 words answering those questions. Does he then proceed to retell the entire expedition story in chronological order? Not at all. He moves back and forth in time and across subject matter. But for Krakauer, knowing exactly what happened and exactly when it happened is crucial, and it is equally crucial for any story you are writing. If you do not understand the order in which things happened, the times and dates of events that make up the fabric of your article, you will get lost in the telling of it. More importantly, because you are writing a true story, you could get things wrong—events out of order; days, months, and years reversed or mixed up. So, no matter how you plan to write your story, you must know the chronology of events.

Having said that, chronology may not provide your story with its structure. Krakauer says, "I don't think about structure in terms of chronology.

---

then tackle a part. Just making notes will likely get you going.

4. Transcribe your interviews. Writers sometimes try to skip this, but working on your interviews gets you writing. You may find a great quote to inspire you or an interesting section of the interview that sparks your creativity.

5. Take a walk. Typing is not writing. Writing takes place in your head, not on the keyboard. Get away from the computer. Take a walk. Go to the gym. Make some soup. While you perform a simple task, your brain is free to process the story.

6. Talk it out. Say what you want to say *out loud*. (Try not to do this in a busy coffee shop or library!) Actually saying the words out loud can get them out of where they're trapped inside your head and on their way to the screen.

Paul Benedetti

* I don't remember where I got some of these ideas, and a few have been in so many writers' tool boxes for so long that they abound online. One excellent website—the Purdue Online Writing Lab (http://owl.english.purdue.edu)—contains some of the above advice on the writing process and much more.

Chronological order often means nothing to me. It can be a really stupid way to organize a book. I'm looking for whatever elements of story (character, dramatic events, the development of an idea) best propel my narrative forward—no matter what those elements are, or in what chronological order they occur."[16] Not surprisingly, his award-winning story moves seamlessly between chronological storytelling and background information, mini profiles of key characters, and fascinating sections where he explains technical matters such as how oxygen deprivation affects brain cells and impairs clear thinking. The key (regardless of your story's length) is to move smoothly between narrative and exposition, always propelling readers forward.

What's exposition, you ask? Glad you brought it up.

Exposition: Explaining Without Being Boring

So far in this chapter, I have talked mostly about one particular kind of feature article—that kind that is primarily a narrative, a dramatic reconstruction of events. In "The Sixty-Storey Crisis," Anne Mullens's day-by-day, sometimes hour-by-hour, reconstruction of events is fuelled by powerful narrative writing.

But even in a story like that, not all the material is narrative—some is explanation. How do dams work? Why is even a small hole dangerous? What would happen if the dam broke? Without understanding these issues, the story of the dam's near-collapse means little. The answers to questions like that—the places where you need to provide history, background, and sometimes difficult scientific and medical information—are called *exposition*. Clear, concise, and compelling exposition plays a part of most great features.

But how do you write good explanations, and how do you weave interesting expository sections into the narrative in a balanced way that does not slow the story, but rather, adds to the momentum? I suggest you bear in mind two keys to success: pick your moment, and watch your pacing.

Pick Your Moment

Do you want to start your story with an explanation about cancer cells, or how sailboats are built, or what goes into making greenhouse gas? Probably not. Who would read it? You know that your story must hook readers within the first few sentences, and that usually involves engaging them at a human level (with a human story). So, Anne Mullens opens her story with a suspenseful scene—a large hole has developed in a major BC dam. Great, but why should we care? Unless readers understand the implications of the complication you have presented, your story is meaningless, and consequently, uninteresting. That's why Mullens takes a deep breath, pauses, and explains clearly to readers what's important here:

> If the Bennett Dam should ever fail, catastrophe would follow in the shape of an unstoppable burst of water 135 metres high. Like a titanic fist, it would roar down the canyon and take out the smaller Peace Canyon Dam, 22 kilometres downstream. The combined force of two ruptured dams would then descend on the town of Hudson's Hope, a giant fury obliterating buildings, uprooting trees, tossing cars and trucks like Dinky toys, and likely killing any of the 1,200 residents unable to get out of its way.[17]

Without the knowledge provided in this expository passage, readers cannot fully understand the story as it unfolds, or its significance (Mullens goes on to explain how the dam failure could throw British Columbia's entire economy into turmoil). But it's not just in the lead that you need to ensure that readers are engaged in the events playing out in your story. And it's not just near the story's start that you'll need to maintain momentum while juggling necessary elements of background, context, history, and explanation. It is your job to provide readers with all the information they need to understand your story, and to provide it only and exactly where they need it and are ready for it.

Once Mullens establishes that there is a serious, potentially fatal sinkhole in the dam and has warned readers that there is "something very, very wrong," she pauses for a moment to explain that the "hole" was centred around a pipe in the dam and then provides some important scientific information in an interesting way. Notice how Mullens uses quotes, questions, and simple, clear images to make this section work:

> Stewart quickly calculated that the annular space of the corroded pipe extending 115 metres down to bedrock was roughly the same volume as the cavern at the top. Therefore, the cavity could be caused by silt and soil migrating to fill the space in the rotted pipe. But was that the only explanation? Did the softness go deeper? How many more unmarked survey pipes were in the dam? Would the earth be soft around them as well? Or was this internal erosion?
>
> Getting the answers meant drilling into the dam's core. Like slipping a needle into a living heart, it involved risk. "No dam engineer takes drilling into an operating dam lightly," says Stewart. "We knew we had to disturb ground and we knew we had to go ahead, but it was serious."[18]

Here, Mullens slips exposition so gently into her narrative you're scarcely aware it's there. She knows readers need this technical information and will stay with her to find out what happens next. But notice that the passage itself, while explaining the science of sink holes, does not sound like someone's lecture notes. It actually helps build suspense because now readers are even more worried about the hole and its possible effects! Remember, it's best to insert exposition precisely when readers are asking questions and where the story has aroused enough curiosity and interest that people will stay with you through the explanatory parts. Only then can you be sure they'll read your story to the end!

Watch Your Pacing

The key to writing explanatory sections is to do it tightly and engagingly. Go on too long and you will lose people. Stack explanation upon explanation and you will lose people. Misplace the explanation so that readers are confused and you will lose people. History, background, even scientific explanations are not "filler," and they don't have to be boring.

Take another look at Mullens's exposition paragraphs above. Notice her crisp, direct writing. Notice her use of images and how she translates measurements and dimensions into examples that we can all understand: "like slipping a needle into a living heart," "like a titanic fist," "like Dinky toys." This is good, clear writing that helps readers fully comprehend what is at stake in this tense drama.

In his award-winning story on Wayne Gretzky titled "Portrait of a Prodigy," writer and broadcaster Peter Gzowski wanted to compare the Great One to previous hockey legends and so had to provide a short backgrounder on six of hockey's greatest players. Boring biographies? Hardly. Here is Gzowski on Bobby Hull. Take note of the clean, conversational writing, the use of detail and anecdote:

> Bobby Hull was glamour. There was a purity about him. His sweater streamed in the wind. His slapshot could tear your hand off. Alone among the early members of the pantheon he won the Lady Byng Trophy as the most gentlemanly player in the league. He once sat out a game to protest the growing practice of physical intimidation. He was the ultimate hockey ambassador; when he left Winnipeg, a letter to the editor suggested the city should erect a statue of him, preferably with a coat slung over his shoulder as he signed autographs for a crowd of worshipping kids. Not long after that, his second marriage broke up, and in an ugly court case that was dragged across the front

pages of Winnipeg—there were two of them—he was sued for mental and physical cruelty to his wife.[19]

Ideas or Action? What Kind of Feature Are You Writing?

Some features are fundamentally narratives: How did Sydney Crosby break into the NHL? What happened the day Kimveer Gill opened fire at Montreal's Dawson College? For excellent examples of this kind of feature, take a look at "The Fight for Their Lives" by Aaron Derfel (reprinted on pages 155–163) and "The Golden Bough" by John Vaillant (reprinted on pages 77–89). These articles are essentially stories—they recount an event or series of events for readers. But not all feature articles are based on a particular incident. Some features are built primarily around an idea: Can renewable energy really power Ontario? Are Canadian doctors performing too many caesarean sections?

Both kinds of story usually require solid exposition as well as dramatic narrative to make them successful, but they are fundamentally different in terms of intent and, to some extent, structure. Why? Because the narrative story, although potentially complex, is based in the main on some kind of event—a near dam failure, the destruction of a rare tree, an emergency room's response to a mass shooting. But an idea story is about just that—an idea—and is therefore not constrained by time or place, and does not have the primary goal of using narrative to capture and relate a specific event or series of incidents. An idea story explores an issue or controversy or question, but remember it's not an essay. You still need interesting scenes, captivating narrative, and the human touch, though your idea story will very likely rely more on exposition than on narrative.

You've probably already read Malcolm Gladwell's "The Ketchup Conundrum" (see pages 17–28), an article written for *The New Yorker* on the science—and art—of flavour and how scientists and food industry specialists create the instantly recognizable trademark tastes of products such as Coca-Cola, French's mustard and, of course, ketchup. We'll look at the techniques Gladwell cleverly employs to make his idea story come alive—interesting narrative scenes, strong characters, and clear exposition—in a moment.

First let's figure out whether the story you are writing is basically a narrative tale or an idea piece. How do you do that? Well, let your research and your brain be your guide. Say you have been assigned a story on the use of pesticides on the lawns of Canadians. If your notes on pesticide use in Canada boil down to a few questions—Are they necessary? Are they dangerous? And are there viable alternatives?—then you likely have an idea or essay-like article on your hands. Your story will answer these questions using a logical thread of ideas instead of a narrative story line to structure your piece. You still need drama and scenes—activists picketing factories, children playing near warning signs, chemists tinkering with microscopes—but your article structure will be built around these central questions or ideas. You must carefully organize your ideas so that readers can follow your basic argument or thesis without becoming confused or bored.

Let's return to Gladwell's ketchup story to see how he keeps readers engaged. For now, let's look past the interesting characters and fascinating scenes that he uses to propel the article along. Instead, we need to ask: What is the central idea of this story? What other ideas are explored and explained along the way? You might come up with a list something like this:

Central idea: Mustard now comes in dozens of varieties. Why has ketchup stayed the same? (This is actually the subhead of the story).
Issues or ideas necessary to answer the central question:

- What is the history of ketchup?
- What is the history of mustard?
- How does the food industry create new products?
- How do they test them for taste?
- How does taste work in humans?
- What factors make something taste "good"?

I have not put these ideas in any logical order nor have I prioritized them. Once you have established that your story should deal with these ideas, your next job is to *organize* them in a way that is both coherent and engaging for the reader. Then you have to find ways to relate this material without writing 5,000 words of pure exposition to explain ketchup. Who would read that? Take a closer look at Gladwell's story and you will see that he does some interesting things: He opens a ketchup article with a story about mustard; he humanizes the ketchup question with the story of Jim Wigon, a man obsessed with creating a better ketchup. And you will see that he explains product development and the science of taste using a variety of interesting characters—Andrew F. Smith and Howard Moskowitz—as well as fascinating anecdotes, examples, and a dash of history.

It's difficult to prescribe to you the precise mix of these elements. It all depends on what you find, who you talk to, and what they tell you. But, like

Gladwell's wonderful story, your piece needs a balance between narrative and exposition. Too much narrative and you won't fully explain the issues; too much exposition and your article will read like a government report.

Remember to apply a basic structural analysis to the material by asking these questions:

- What is the essential issue or idea? OR What is the primary conflict or complication?
- What are the most important components or sub-ideas?
- What scenes, anecdotes, and characters can I employ to explore these ideas?
- What resolution or conclusions (if any) are inherent in the facts?

Final Thoughts

Once you have written a first draft of your story, you need to find a way to step back from your work and evaluate it. If you have time, let the story "cool off." Take a day if you can. If not, at least take a walk and come back to your story with fresh eyes. Try to approach it as an uninitiated reader; you know nothing about this subject or these people. What do you make of the story? Does the opening grab you? Can you follow the story? Is it clear and direct? Does it lag in parts? Are some sections too long? Too short? Is the chronology of events clear? Does the story have a satisfactory conclusion? In other words, is the end as powerful as the beginning?

These questions are unlikely to spotlight issues of style. Rather, any problems here point to issues of structure, and now is the time to fix them—before you begin to polish your prose. No amount of buffing the surface will make up for faulty design, so pay attention to the overall structure of your story before you focus on the finer points of writing.

Remember, if you build it right, they will read it.

Discussion Questions

1. Read "The Sixty-Storey Crisis" by Anne Mullens (pages 215–225). Mullens uses foreshadowing to create anticipation and suspense in the story. Take a highlighter and mark the points in the story where she creates suspense—sometimes with a single sentence!
2. Read "The Ketchup Conundrum" by Malcolm Gladwell (pages 17–28). Create a list of the scenes that Gladwell uses in the story. Then make a list of the characters he introduces and figure out what purpose they

each serve in the telling of the story. Finally, make a list of the main ideas he raises.

3. Compare the structure of Mullens's story to that of Gladwell's. What key planning choices helped each writer bring ideas—and people—to life?

Notes

1. William Zinsser, *On Writing Well: The Classic Guide to Writing Nonfiction*, 25th anniversary ed. (New York: HarperCollins, 2001), p. 56.

2. Jon Franklin, *Writing for Story: Craft Secrets of Dramatic Nonfiction by a Two-Time Pulitzer Prize Winner* (New York: Penguin/Plume, 1994), pp. 110–11.

3. Cheryl Gibbs and Tom Warhover, *Getting the Whole Story: Reporting and Writing the News* (New York: Guilford Press, 2002), p. 311.

4. Mark MacKinnon, "Six-Year-Old Repairman Cannot Fix Afghanistan," *Globe and Mail*, November 14, 2002.

5. Ibid.

6. Ibid.

7. Ibid.

8. Catherine McKercher and Carman Cumming, *The Canadian Reporter: News Writing and Reporting*, 2nd ed. (Toronto: Harcourt Brace and Co. Canada, 1998), p. 134.

9. Franklin, *Writing for Story*, pp. 102–8.

10. This outline checklist is adapted from Franklin's *Writing for Story*.

11. Gay Talese, "Frank Sinatra Has a Cold," *Esquire*, April 1966.

12. Elizabeth Gilbert, "Lucky Jim," *GQ*, May 2002.

13. John Krakauer, "Into Thin Air," *Outside*, September 1996.

14. Ibid.

15. Ibid.

16. Robert S. Boynton, *The New New Journalism: Conversations with America's Best Nonfiction Writers on Their Craft* (New York: Vintage Books, 2005), pp. 175–76.

17. Anne Mullens, "The Sixty-Storey Crisis," *BC Business*, January 1999, 27.

18. Mullens, "The Sixty-Storey Crisis," 28–29.

19. Peter Gzowski, "Portrait of a Prodigy," *Saturday Night*, November 1980.

"The Sixty-Storey Crisis"

The story behind BC Hydro's worst nightmare: the discovery of a hole in its massive Bennett Dam and the behind-the-scenes efforts to ensure the unthinkable—a breach in the dam—would never happen

Anne Mullens, "The Sixty-Storey Crisis." *BC Business* magazine, January 1999, 25. Reprinted by permission of the author.

Up until 4 p.m. on Friday, June 14, 1996, the day had been like any other in the 30-year history of the W.A.C. Bennett Dam. As one of the world's largest embankment dams, for years it had quietly straddled the Peace River in the northeast portion of the province, near Hudson's Hope. But then a tourist dropped into the tourist centre beside the dam, and nothing was to be the same again.

The tourist's name has been forgotten in the tumult of events that followed; nor is it known whether he had traveled by foot, car or bicycle over the road that runs along the embankment dam's crest. All that is known is that in the middle of the dam, he spied a hole in the asphalt and knew it ought to be reported. The tour guide thought so, too, and called the control building of the G.M. Shrum Generating Station nestled in the east shoulder of the dam.

Unless you've seen the Bennett Dam, it is hard to fathom its size. High as a 60-storey building and two kilometres wide, it's an enormous earth and gravel wedge that holds back 360 kilometres of Williston Lake, the largest reservoir in North America. In a word: massive—and with massive water pressure behind it.

And suddenly it had developed a small hole.

It was after office hours on a Friday; the control building was quiet. Peace River Generation manager Ron Fernandes, the regional boss for BC Hydro, had been in Vancouver on a business trip and was flying home. But operations manager Dennis Hunter was there and took the tour guide's call. He and another senior manager went to the crest to take a look, but not being civil engineers, they weren't sure what to make of it.

It was 4:30 p.m. when John Baker had the first inkling something was amiss. A civil engineer in BC Hydro's department of civil inspection, he was up from Vancouver for his yearly two-week check. So far, all the instruments seemed to show that everything was fine. He was in the office writing an e-mail when he picked up the tones of an intense conversation.

"Pothole …" He looked up to see Hunter and a manager of finances in serious discussion. They saw him and Hunter called over: "Hey, you're from civil, aren't you? Phew … Come with us."

The hole was just 455 mm in diameter, about the size of a large pizza. Baker lay on his stomach and stuck his head into it. Through the dim light he could see a small cavern, the size of a doghouse, with the top of a badly corroded metal pipe exposed at its base. He recorded the dimensions, drawing a cross-sectional diagram, noting time of discovery, location and size, and the position of the corroded pipe. "I knew it was something we had to deal with right away," Baker recalls. "I was apprehensive."

In dam engineers' parlance, the term "sinkhole" is akin to "cancer." So Baker told the others: "Right now, let's refer to it as a local surface depression."

As stipulated under the emergency preparedness plan, any event or incident which could potentially affect the integrity of the dam triggers a series of phone calls to about two dozen BC Hydro engineers, managers and government officials. One calls another, the word fans out. Hunter and his colleague returned to the control building to start phoning, Baker raced to the base of the dam to read the weirs—the drains that carry the natural seepage from the dam. "I was hoping against hope I didn't find dirty water or increased seepage or even worse, a crack opening up in the dam." He quickly walked the "toe" of the dam, looking for danger signs in the wall of gravel towering above. He found nothing.

"As we say, 'The vital signs were still good,'" says Baker. "It wasn't in imminent danger of collapse." But he didn't relax: "We didn't know how bad it was, but we knew we had a hole in the dam and that is not good."

If the Bennett Dam should ever fail, catastrophe would follow in the shape of an unstoppable burst of water 135 metres high. Like a titanic fist, it would roar down the canyon and take out the smaller Peace Canyon Dam, 22 kilometres downstream. The combined force of two ruptured dams would then descend on the town of Hudson's Hope, a giant fury obliterating buildings, uprooting trees, tossing cars and trucks like Dinky toys, and likely killing any of the 1,200 residents unable to get out of its way.

Unlike a tsunami, the destruction wouldn't simply peak and stop. The pent-up waters of Williston Lake would just keep coming, seeking to return to its natural elevation. The waters would flow for weeks, scouring away communities like Old Fort, Taylor, Peace River, Fort Smith and beyond. The onslaught would back up tributaries and inundate the entire Peace River Basin, flooding Lake Athabaska and Great Slave Lake. The floods could devastate northern Alberta, portions of Saskatchewan and the Northwest Territories all the way to the Arctic Ocean. The death toll could be high; the environmental and structural damage astronomical. Combined with the generating power of the dam, the unprecedented disaster would cost billions of dollars and throw B.C.'s economy into turmoil.

Dam failure isn't some unrealistic threat. In the last century, more than 70 major dams have failed worldwide, causing loss of life and untold millions in damage. In 1976, a town was devastated and 11 people killed when the Teton Dam failed in Idaho. In 1972, the small Kelly Barnes Dam in Georgia let go, and 39 bible students died while sleeping in a residence. The most famous dam failure in the United States occurred when the South Fork Dam collapsed on May 31, 1889, after a week of heavy rains. It sent 20 million tons of water, boiling with debris, crashing down on the community of 30,000 in Johnstown, Pennsylvania. The survivors reported hearing a roar like thunder as a 40-foot wall of water hit the town. More than 2,200 people were killed and almost the entire population left homeless.

Although the Johnstown flood remains one of the worst man-made disasters in North America, the collapse of the Bennett Dam would have unleashed a mountain of water 12 times larger.

"The failure of a large dam has the potential to cause more death and destruction than the failure of any other man-made structure," says Dr. Richard Woodward, an Australian dam engineer who maintains a Web page devoted to dam safety.

"The destructive power of water is phenomenal," agrees Jack Farrell. At the time of the Bennett Dam crisis, Farrell was comptroller of water rights for the Ministry of the Environment, a statutory position under the Water Act which gives him the legislative power to regulate and monitor dams in B.C.

That June 14, Farrell and his staff of dam safety officials and regional water managers were in the Lower Mainland for the department's annual golf tournament. They were having a beer at an outdoor patio when suddenly all their cell phones started ringing. A buzz quickly went around the table: "There's a pothole at Bennett Dam." Farrell and a few of his senior officials quickly retired to a quiet room to get more details.

"We said, 'Okay, it's a big dam and there's a little break in the asphalt and it dropped a couple of feet,'" recalls Farrell. "It could be nothing, but we'd better check it out." He decided to send a ministry dam safety engineer and engineering consultant up on the first flight to Fort St. John the next morning.

Meanwhile, a cadre of BC Hydro managers, engineers and executives had convened in a board room at BC Hydro's head office in Burnaby. The GM Shrum/ Bennett Dam combo was BC Hydro's largest power-producer, generating 2,730 megawatt/hours, or 30 per cent of all power in the province. A lot was at stake.

A conference call was made to the dam site, to where Ron Fernandes had returned from his trip and was back in command. In turn, Baker had faxed over the on-site measurements and drawings of the damage. The meeting was intense. Was this simply a small hole that signified nothing? Or was it the start of a larger problem such as internal erosion—a serious disease of an aging dam, one that could threaten its integrity, cost millions of dollars to repair, or perhaps even force the dam to be drained and decommissioned? If vital signs changed, how much time was there to alert the public? Although they agreed an actual dam breach was remote, the consequences would be horrendous. There was no question a full investigation must start immediately, and the repair undertaken as quickly as possible.

That night, Ray Stewart, an experienced dam engineer who at the time was manager of the geotechnical department of BC Hydro, was selected as the technical manager to oversee the investigation and repair of the hole. Arrangements were made to get equipment and gravel to the crest of the dam should it collapse further. The mayor of Hudson's Hope was notified, but as every indicator showed the dam was still performing normally, the town wasn't put on evacuation alert. Meanwhile, Fernandes was to recall a crew of workers to start round-the-clock surveillance of the dam and its weirs. Any change in the dam's vital signs would trigger an evacuation.

Confident that all was safe, for now, the meeting adjourned. "I don't think any of us slept well that night," recalls Fernandes. Before returning to his hotel room, Baker checked the weirs one last time around midnight. Meanwhile, all night long, shifts of three walked the crest, the middle and the toe of the dam. That same night, Ray Stewart packed a small bag, thinking he would be at most three or four days at the dam. It would be a year before he was able to finally return home again.

Saturday, June 15 dawned cold and grey. Fernandes, Baker and a small crew watched as a backhoe peeled the asphalt off the top of the pothole. One of the crew took a long metal rebar rod and began probing the cavern's bottom. The rod easily slid through what should have been hard-packed dam. "The ease with which that rod went down—that gave me the willies," shudders Fernandes. "It just kept going and going and going, I knew there was something very, very wrong."

By noon, Stewart, Farrell two men from the ministry and the mayor of Hudson's Hope, Lenora Harwood, had arrived. All afternoon they watched as the backhoe scooped out loose fill. Finally, the machine came to the end of its reach. The softness still stretched down, but it was feared any more digging would destabilize the top of the dam. Sand and gravel were pushed back into the hole and compacted, a marker placed to pinpoint the location of the corroded pipe.

They knew now that the pipe was a survey benchmark tube—a sighting marker used by surveyors as the dam went up. It consisted of a narrow steel rod, with a larger, hollow steel sheath surrounding it.

"The existence of the pipe was surprising to us because it wasn't on the plans," explains Stewart. "But at the same time, it was good news, because we had a cavity forming around some physical object—not just internal erosion developing on its own. It gave us a hypothesis of why the cavity was there."

Stewart quickly calculated that the annular space of the corroded pipe extending 115 metres down to bedrock was roughly the same volume as the cavern at the top. Therefore, the cavity could be caused by silt and soil migrating to fill the space in the rotted pipe. But was that the only explanation? Did the softness go deeper? How many more unmarked survey pipes were in the dam? Would the earth be soft around them as well? Or was this internal erosion?

Getting the answers meant drilling into the dam's core. Like slipping a needle into a living heart, it involved risk. "No dam engineer takes drilling into an operating dam lightly," says Stewart. "It was very much exploratory. We knew we had to disturb ground and we knew we had to go ahead, but it was serious."

The Vancouver office scoured B.C. and Alberta for an available drill rig. A Becker drill was located in Calgary. It and a crew set out Sunday afternoon by truck, arriving at the dam site just before noon on Monday, June 17.

A Becker drill is a large diesel-operated pile driver, or hammer. For this exploration, it was equipped with a closed sectional pipe and a computer to measure the number and back pressure of the blows needed to drive the pipe. "If it is very dense material, it will be a high number of blows per foot and the pressure will be higher," explains Baker. "We thought this would give us a good idea of how tightly packed the dam was."

The drilling began just after 1 p.m. At the surface, the dam was fairly dense from the new gravel compacted into the hole. But once the drill hit 18 to 20 feet, the ground began to lose density. The weight of the rig alone was enough to push the drill through the soil. For its hammer to fire, a Becker drill requires resistance; at 20 to 30 feet the ground was so soft the drill would not hammer. From 30 to 40 feet, some ground resistance was encountered, but the blows were low.

Every 10 feet, the crew added a new section of heavy, double-walled steel drill pipe. The drill string was becoming heavier and heavier. At 50 feet, the ground suddenly became so soft the hammer quit; its weight simply pushed through the soil. Baker's notebook attests to the alarming figures—from 50 to 100 feet, line after line of zeros. There was virtually no resistance in a portion of the core. As the drill neared 100 feet, Stewart returned to the control building for a pre-arranged conference call to head office. Baker stayed at the crest.

And then at 110 feet, it happened.

"I had turned away for a second, to do some adjustments to the computer, when the drill operator yelled: 'The hole is opening up!'" Baker says. "I turned and looked. The ground around the drill was starting to collapse inward, and the hole was getting wider, and the drill pipe being sucked down the hole."

Like some ghastly slow-motion nightmare, all 110 feet of drill pipe was disappearing into the dam as the walls caved in around it.

"I had no idea how long this process of collapsing would continue—for all I knew it might have been the start of the whole crest collapsing," says Baker. "The hole had gone, in 30 seconds, from nothing to four feet in diameter." He yelled to the drill operator, "Get the rig out of here!" fearing it was about to be swallowed. Then, in what was close to terror, he hopped in his rental car and raced to the control building.

Twenty years ago, the Teton Dam failed when a rift caused by internal erosion opened the way for a rivulet of water through the dam crest. In a film of the event, a bulldozer frantically pushed soil into the wound, but to no avail. The rift becomes a canyon. Then a huge wall of churning muddy water bursts free ... and devastates a small town downstream.

"I was thinking that the whole dam would breach," recalls Baker. "I really was. I was thinking the sides would continue collapsing to the point where the reservoir would enter the hole and then it would be game over. All the scenarios go through your head."

Heart racing, pale as a ghost, Baker ran into the control building where Stewart and Fernandes were conducting the conference call. As the two men spun around in alarm, Baker's face said it all.

"John is a pretty calm, collected guy and just to see him—it rattled us," says Fernandes. "We said to Vancouver: 'Something is happening, we'll call you back,' and slammed down the phone." Adds Stewart: "And all these senior managers in Vancouver are thinking: 'What the hell is going on?!'"

It takes time for a dam to fail. At the first signs of increased flow into the dam, it would take at least four hours before the Bennett Dam might give way.

Even with a catastrophic collapse of the dam core, it would still take 20 minutes for the wall of water to reach the Peace Canyon Dam and 30 minutes to reach Hudson's Hope. The men knew they still had time to assess the situation.

When they arrived back at the crest, the collapse had come to a halt. The vital signs remained healthy—no increased flow, no dirty water. One observation well did show a sudden increase in flow, but over the next two hours it returned to normal. What did it mean? One thing was certain: the little pothole was now a gaping maw 23 feet deep and eight feet across. They also knew the softness continued down for at least 100 feet, if not all the way to bedrock.

This was no longer a "localized surface depression"—this was dam cancer, a sinkhole.

"From that incident on, the safety status of the dam was uncertain," says Stewart.

In the minds of BC Hydro officials, the unexpected collapse and the coinciding response of the observation well marked the beginning of the sinkhole crisis at Bennett Dam. From that moment on, there would be no holding back. Whatever had to be done would be done, no matter what the cost.

Jack Farrell, the comptroller of water rights, was at home in Victoria that Monday night when the telephone rang.

"It was a shocker," Farrell recalls. "My first concern was for public safety. I knew that the snow pack was extremely high, one of the highest snow packs on record. And that time in June is when the melt really starts to flow into the reservoir. The water would be coming up very quickly. And here, the top of the dam is soft. We couldn't let the water get up here, because that's how dams fail."

As his staff gathered data about the rate of flow into the reservoir, Farrell knew he would soon have to order BC Hydro to spill water in unprecedented levels from the reservoir—a move that would have a huge cost to BC Hydro's bottom line and could even cause flooding and environmental damage downstream. However, he felt there would be no choice.

Meanwhile, down in Hudson's Hope, word of the collapse traveled fast—especially as almost one-third of the community had a family member who worked at the dam or generating station. That afternoon, some parents took their children out of school. Some even prepared to flee. The mayor and council held an emergency meeting that Monday night, and residents of the town's only nursing home were told to get ready for possible evacuation.

But still, the dam's vital signs remained good.

"It was such an anxious time. I think the worst part for us was the uncertainty," says Ron Fernandes. "We wanted to be sure we did the right thing. We didn't want to create havoc and panic everybody by ordering evacuation when it wasn't necessary, but we sure didn't want to wait too long, either. Part of me just wanted to say, 'What the heck, let's go to alert.' The responsibility I felt was enormous."

Ray Stewart and others started marshaling dam experts from all across Western Canada and beyond. Over the next six months, there were at times more than 60 experts, some from as far away as Sweden, working at the dam.

The teams doing 24-hour surveillance were immediately boosted to three inspectors and a shift supervisor. For the next 10 months, they walked the dam doing visual and instrument inspection. Nicknamed "Cresty," "Middleman" and "Toeboy," the men logged up to 20 kilometres a shift, even in the dead of night and the dead of winter when temperatures plunge below −40 degrees Celsius.

Wednesday, June 19. More than 400 people crammed into the Hudson's Hope school gym to hear Stewart, Fernandes and officials from the provincial emergency preparedness program speak about the dam.

"The meeting was intense," says Fernandes. "Some people were close to panic, but most were just really, really concerned and ready to do something like move. We did not tell them there was no problem. We told them we were concerned, too. We told them what we were monitoring and what vital signs we were looking for. I think there was acceptance that we were doing what we could and that there was no immediate danger."

In the months that followed, only one family moved out of the downstream area because of worries about a breach. As it was the family of one of the Hydro employees doing 24-hour surveillance of the dam, it sparked a flurry of worry among the downstream residents who heard of it. But Fernandes and others kept their families in the downstream path. Ray Stewart even moved his young family from New Westminster up to Hudson's Hope.

"When my wife was picking up the kids from school, moms would come and ask her what's going on at the dam," says Stewart. "I think they were quite reassured that I would move my family up there and we would rent a home in the downstream area."

Along with all the experts in dam safety and repair brought in to the site that first week, a BC Hydro communications team was dispatched from head office. It stayed for 10 months, commandeering the public relations arm of the crisis.

The strategy was straightforward: be proactive and give facts so that rumours don't proliferate; communicate immediately, even if tempted to wait for more or better information; be open and honest because people can handle bad news better than the feeling something is being withheld.

The policy of openness resulted in scores of news releases, daily fax bulletins, Internet updates, a toll-free line, site tours and briefings to any interested public, and even an explanatory video. The communiqués were rather technical and devoid of any emotion or drama, but they were accurate and correct.

Ironically, this openness not only increased the downstream residents' confidence and comfort with BC Hydro, it had another unexpected result: the major media, perhaps realizing there was nothing to hide, lost interest and over time ignored the story.

But the story was far from over.

Jack Farrell flew up from Victoria to attend the first on-site advisory board meetings June 21 and 22. Ray Stewart, who for the last week had barely slept or eaten, was so exhausted and stressed that when he tried to sum up the week's events, he was unable to speak. He had to leave the room to compose himself while a colleague briefly took over.

The two days of discussion centered on what could realistically be done to investigate the dam without further undermining the core. How much free-board is needed to safely work on the dam, and therefore how much water must be spilled from the reservoir? Farrell was adamant no further drilling and investigation could take place until the level was dropped by at least two metres. BC Hydro was worried that spilling that much water would not only risk flooding some downstream communities and farmland, but it could undermine the stability of bedrock on the downstream side of the Peace Canyon Dam.

"We were worried about something called the 'plunge pool,'" explains Fernandes. "When water is spilled from a dam, the force carves a pool in the bedrock. We were worried the Peace Canyon Dam's plunge pool hadn't stabilized yet. With the volume of water being spilled, the pool could carve itself either downstream or upstream. If it carved upstream it could weaken the foundation of the dam and threaten its stability."

A compromise was reached. The spill would be commenced, then briefly stopped so engineers could test the bedrock below both dams to confirm the plunge pools weren't carving upstream. Then the spill would be restarted.

On June 24, under order from the comptroller of water rights, BC Hydro began to spill 180,000 cubic feet per second; 70,000 through the generators and the rest down the concrete spillway. It was the biggest spill in the history of BC Hydro. Equal to the flow over the Canadian side of Niagara Falls, the spill plumed high into the sky and soon became a local tourist attraction. To BC Hydro, it represented an estimated $2 million a day in future lost power production.

While the spill created much-needed freeboard for repair work to begin, it also created problems downstream. Fish eggs and all that year's juvenile fish stock were wiped out. The rising waters cut off 200 deer fawning on one of the islands in the river. The does could swim through the current, but the newborn fawns were at risk of drowning. Knowing that news photos of dead, bloated fawns would be a public relations nightmare, BC Hydro orchestrated a helicopter rescue with help from the Ministry of the Environment.

Of greater concern was the risk of flooding in communities downstream, particularly a subdivision built on a flood plain in Taylor, a community of 1,200 people about 123 kilometres east of the Bennett Dam.

"We had to be on a continuous vigil, watching weather forecasts, seeing if any storms are coming in, to adjust the spill level so we wouldn't flood Taylor," says Fernandes. Since the water from the Bennett Dam took about eight hours to reach Taylor, all adjustments to the spill volume had to be anticipated. Sure enough, in mid-July, a record-breaking rain storm hit the region.

"It was very tense. We came not quite six inches from flooding the bank at Taylor," says Fernandes. (Last year BC Hydro bought all 40 houses in that particular Taylor subdivision and is removing them to eliminate future headaches.)

Seven weeks later, in the first week of August, the reservoir was down two metres. Crews began to use a number of new drilling methods to map the extent of the sinkhole and assess the health of the dam. Work continued night and day for months.

Then in early September, to BC Hydro's surprise and frustration, exploratory drilling revealed a second spot of major weakness in the core, smaller than the first, on the east side of the dam around another survey benchmark tube. "It seems that from that first day in June, everything just got worse and worse for months," sighs Fernandes.

Now the question, how to fix the weaknesses? Concrete wasn't an option: the material used must match the density and texture of the dam so as to distribute the water pressure evenly across the structure. But how to funnel rock, sand and gravel at high pressure to that depth? It had never been done before.

Through extensive research and modeling, "compaction grouting" was chosen as the best method to fill the holes. Widely used in North America in other construction, it had never been used to this depth in a dam. In mid-fall BC Hydro asked for bids from North America contractors, In a rare move for a Crown corporation, it would be a two-envelope bid system; technical details in one envelope, the price in a second. Once the best technical bid was selected, only then would its price envelope be opened. "We didn't want the price to influence our decision at all, only the technical merit," says Stewart.

For a month the successful team, Hayward Baker of Santa Paula, California and Foundex of B.C., practised on the Fraser delta at a spot where the soil consistency was similar to the dam core. Day after day they practised shooting the grouting material—a mixture of 20 per cent pea gravel, 50 percent gravel and 30 per cent silt—to deep levels. Only when the kinks were worked out did they finally, in March 1997, go up to the dam. By June, the repairs were finished.

The investigation and repair cost BC Hydro almost $40 million, not including lost power potential from the spill. By the end of the ordeal, Ray Stewart was appointed director of dam safety for all of BC Hydro's 61 dams. As well, the government ordered continued monitoring and surveillance of the Bennett Dam, status reports every six months and reinforcement of the structure's toe.

"It is easy to look back at it now, but at times I can recall the intense emotion and stress around the enormity of what we were dealing with," says Stewart. "It was like a war."

"We can be thankful that everybody did the right thing to avert a potential catastrophe," says Farrell, now a private consultant. "It worked out well. But I don't think any of us will ever feel completely comfortable with the Bennett Dam again. It must be watched very closely for the rest of its life."

CHAPTER EIGHT

Required Elements: Details of Structure

Susan McClelland

If you were writing a story about the former Pakistani prime minister, Benazir Bhutto, you might start with something like this:

> Islamabad—Pakistan rejected foreign help in investigating the assassination of Benazir Bhutto on Saturday, despite controversy over the circumstance of her death and three days of paralyzing turmoil.
>
> The Islamic militant group blamed by officials for the attack that killed Ms. Bhutto denied any links to the killing on Saturday, and Bhutto's aides accused the government of a cover-up.[1]

… or like this:

> Caesar is barking in the courtyard. When I pass him, he pulls at his chain, trying to reach me, and not for a pat on the head. He's not a big dog, but he's fierce and muscular, with a mouth full of long, sharp teeth. Caesar is Benazir Bhutto's dog. He's snarling in the background as I proceed on an afternoon in early September to the front door of one of Bhutto's houses, this one in a Middle Eastern country that she has asked me not to identify.

Caesar, it occurs to me, is a richly ironic name for the pet of someone who considers herself a freedom fighter and democracy advocate. But then, Bhutto's pets have run the gamut of appellations, and it is perhaps unwise to come to conclusions, ironic or not, based on what she chooses to name them. When she was a fiery opposition leader in Pakistan in 1986, two years before she was first elected prime minister, her cat was called Sugar.[2]

The first lead is from an Associated Press news story on December 29, 2007, the second from a feature story published in *MORE* magazine some months earlier. But the difference between the two leads goes far beyond the fact that one was clearly written after Bhutto's death, the other before. What readers see here—and see from the very first glance—is the difference between a "hard news" story, whose task is to provide key information about recent events, and a feature story, which promises context, explanation, understanding, and emotional connection to the people and events described.

The hard news story, and especially wire-service reports such as that from AP above, traditionally but not always follows a basic "inverted-pyramid" structure in which the most substantial, interesting, and important information is presented first followed by decreasingly important facts. The theory behind the inverted pyramid is that readers can take away the nugget or meat of the story quickly, gaining all they need to know about the subject in the first few lines without having to read the entire article. Some say this form was first employed during the American Civil War, when correspondents sent their stories to their respected news agencies via telegraph. The most important facts came first in case the transmission was interrupted and only a few lines of the story made it to an editor.

In 1941, *The Wall Street Journal*'s managing editor, Barney Kilgore, revolutionized non-fiction writing by introducing the "nut graph" method. Whereas the inverted pyramid is very much tied to time, anchored on the actual date on which an event occurred, Kilgore saw that news is more than just what happened on a particular day. The nut graph allows journalists to go back in time, to write about opinions and trends, to develop a point of view, and to go behind the headlines and write stories explaining in-depth why things happened the way they did. With the invention of this new reporting method, Kilgore also introduced the news feature, or the analytical feature story.

Think of a feature story as a body composed of distinct elements. If your reported facts are a story's bones, and your word choices its flesh, then a story's fundamental structure (see chapter 7) is its muscles. But for a body to stand up or move, it needs one more type of tissue: sinews, which connect muscles to bones. Each of the essential elements discussed in this chapter is like a tendon, the small but tough piece of fibrous tissue that connects a vital muscle to an equally vital bone. Without these essential elements, a feature story would be immobile, unable to carry readers from the beginning of the article to its end.

An Invitation They Can't Refuse: The Lead

The lead in a feature story should set the mood and tone of the entire piece, as well as arouse readers' interests and invite them inside the story. The lead can be based on a scene the writer has witnessed, a story that a source has relayed to the writer, or simply anything that draws readers in. There are no set-in-stone rules to writing feature story leads. Nonetheless, like the opening of a great documentary film, a lead in a feature story should be provocative and creative, drawing readers in with words so that they must know more and want to read further.

Here's a lead that does just that. It's from the opening story in a Pulitzer Prize–winning feature series by Sonia Nazario and published in the *Los Angeles Times*:

> The boy does not understand.
>
> His mother is not talking to him. She will not even look at him. Enrique has no hint of what she is going to do.
>
> Lourdes knows. She understands, as only a mother can, the terror she is about to inflict, the ache Enrique will feel and finally the emptiness.
>
> What will become of him? Already he will not let anyone else feed or bathe him. He loves her deeply, as only a son can. With Lourdes, he is a chatterbox. "*Mira. Mami.*" Look, Mom, he says softly, asking her questions about everything he sees. Without her, he is so shy it is crushing.
>
> Slowly, she walks out into the porch. Enrique clings to her pant leg. Beside her, he is tiny. Lourdes loves him so much she cannot bring herself to say a word. She cannot carry his picture. It would melt her resolve. She cannot hug him. He is 5 years old.
>
> They live on the outskirts of Tegucigalpa, in Honduras. She can barely afford food for him and his sister, Belky, who is 7. Lourdes, 24, scrubs other people's laundry in a muddy river. She fills a wooden box with gum and crackers and cigarettes, and she finds a spot where she can squat on a dusty sidewalk next to the downtown Pizza Hut and sell the items to passersby. The sidewalk is Enrique's playground.[3]

A good lead foreshadows what is to come as well as hints at the theme in the story. In her lead to "Enrique's Journey," Nazario has chosen a scene that particularly shows the bleakness of the family's situation. This lead fore-shadows that Lourdes will leave Enrique soon and why (to move to the United States for work), and that Enrique eventually will follow her, alone on a heart-wrenching journey that few children take.

Where you decide to enter a story is completely up to you. Novice feature writers, however, often make the mistake of choosing a lead from something they have witnessed first-hand, such as the scene in which they interviewed a source. You are not confined to writing only that which you have wit-nessed. The lead in my story, "Nanny Abuse" (see page 233 below), was chosen after several hours of interviews with Kristina, my main source. Kristina, a Filipino nanny, told me of the time she lived in the basement of a Vancouver mansion. I had Kristina describe the scene and what she did when she was alone in the basement at night. Although this scene took place years prior to my interview, I played with time and put the scene in the present tense. In feature writing, creative non-fiction techniques, such as using the "historic present" tense, are not only permissible but encouraged. Later on in "Nanny Abuse," I made the actual time sequence clear in my sentence, "It would be months before Kristina finally escaped her abusive Vancouver employer."[4]

A lead, as William Blundell writes in *The Art and Craft of Feature Writing*, should be simple, be relevant to the theme of the story, and provide focus.[5] Whether the story is a celebrity profile or the tracking of a trend, the lead

Glad You Asked!   Sidebar, Your Honour

Q: When should text be broken out?
A: That's not an easy question, because every story is unique, but here are some general guidelines.

A sidebar is generally, though not always, used to manage content that might interrupt the flow of your story; that adds another element to the story; or that more effectively stands alone. Let's look at each possibility.

If you have information that is important, but does not fit easily into the story you are telling—for example, historical background, legal explanations, or the terms of an agreement or treaty—it could go into a sidebar. Say you are writing a feature about the battle to preserve a famous local tavern. You may want to break out a list of the building's past owners so the names don't clutter up your story.

Content that adds another element can be as simple as a profile of a great will often paint a picture with words. By now, you are more than familiar with the phrase "show, don't tell." Feature writing is all about show. As writer Erik Larson puts it:

> Kill all the adjectives. If you simply assign yourself to go through your prose when you're rewriting and cut out all adjectives, and then read it over first before re-inserting the adjectives, I think you will find that your prose will be far, far cleaner.... When you try to write without adjectives, you say things in a very different way. You don't say, "He lived in a blue house"; you say, "He lived in a house that was the colour of the lake on a summer day." ... It forces you to come up with something vivid.[6]

John Vaillant does exactly this in his 2002 story "The Golden Bough" (reprinted on pages 77–89):

> There was only one giant golden spruce in the world, and, until a man named Grant Hadwin took a chainsaw to it, in 1997, it had stood for more than three hundred years in a steadily shrinking patch of old-growth forest in Port Clements, on the banks of the Yakoun River, in the Queen Charlotte Islands.[7]

David Sumner and Holly Miller have listed several lead styles that succeed and others that are sure to fail.[8] Successful styles include the following:

character or an anecdote that you don't want to lose but that doesn't quite fit your story. If you are writing about treating prostate cancer, you might have a short sidebar on one man's battle with the disease or a brisk profile on the doctor who perfected a specific treatment.

What kind of content is more effective standing alone, outside the frame of your story? A glossary of terms might be a great sidebar, particularly in a science or medical story. The actual text of a court ruling or a proposed government bill might be a helpful sidebar to readers. A list of the "players" in the story or a "who's who?" is often a good sidebar. A timeline of events may free you up from cluttering your story with dates. Lists, such as dos and don'ts, are often great sidebars because they distill the key messages of your story in a handy way for readers.

Finally, write a sidebar if your editor asks you to! Many feature assignments come with a request for a sidebar or two.

Paul Benedetti

Scenario lead: The opening of "Enrique's Journey" (see page 229) and of my "Nanny Abuse" story (see page 233) don't give a lot of information but paint pictures that reflect the backdrop, topic, or theme of the story to come.

Shock lead: The example from Vaillant's story, above, mesmerizes and hooks readers in the first line—this golden tree, which stood for 300 years, has been cut down!

Blind lead: A blind lead leaves out a key piece of information, like the identity of who is being written about, to rouse the reader's curiosity. The lead of Bruce Grierson's "When Animals Attack!" which follows this chapter, does just that.

Indirect quote lead: As I learned in journalism school, using a direct quote for the opening sentence of the story is often seen as the lazy writer's escape from being creative. But indirect quotes can work well, as in a 2002 story I wrote for *Maclean's* magazine:

> She always felt different from other kids. "I thought maybe I was adopted and my family was too ashamed to tell me," says Shelley Kreutz, a fine arts student at the University of British Columbia in Vancouver. For one thing, Shelley wondered why she was petite while her mother and grandmother had large frames.[9]

Anecdote lead: This type of lead uses a short self-contained story to reveal the major point of the entire article. Here's the lead of a feature by Clive Thompson in *Wired News*. Note that while it happens to be in the first person, an anecdote lead can just as easily be about a character in your story.

> In retrospect, maybe I shouldn't have looked.
> I was 10 days into playing *Dungeon Maker: Hunting Ground* ... and I was poking around the "settings" menu. I noticed that it had a "time played" option, which shows you how long you've been toiling away at the game. Curious, I clicked it.
> Thirty-six hours.
> Upon which my heart sank into a fathomless pit. Thirty-six hours? How in god's name had I managed to spend almost *four hours a day* inside this game? I should point out that this was not the only game I'd been playing during that time. I'd also been hip-deep in *BioShock* and *Space Giraffe*, so I'd been planted like a weed in front of my consoles for hours more.

This is a missing-time experience so vast one would normally require a UFO abduction to achieve it.[10]

Sumner and Miller also list 11 lead styles that should be avoided, including those that give too much factual information so the story sounds like an encyclopedia excerpt, or ones that ask too many questions ("Do you have a daughter who is of dating age? Are you worried she may have unprotected sex? Have you talked to her about it?").

If you're still in doubt about how to begin your story, try this. Ask yourself before writing your lead, *What did I see, hear, feel, touch or smell that moved me the most in reporting my feature story?* Chances are, your answer is your lead.

Elements of "Nanny Abuse"

The Lead

Throughout this chapter, I am going to quote key parts from one feature story to illustrate the various "required elements" I describe and how they fit together in a story's fundamental structure. The story I've chosen is one I wrote myself. It's called "Nanny Abuse," and it ran in the March 2005 issue of The Walrus magazine.[11] The feature is about the foreign women who supply Canada's working parents with a vast pool of cheap labour for child care—and about some nannies' demands for a quicker route to citizenship and protection from abusive employers. Here's how the piece began:

> Flickering candles cast a pale glow on the tiny, dark-haired woman kneeling in front of a small statue of the Virgin. "God give me strength," Kristina murmurs in front of the makeshift altar, her thumb moving unconsciously through a rosary dangling from her right hand. "Hail Mary, full of grace," she continues as a door slams shut down the hall. Her prayers interrupted, she turns on a bare overhead light revealing the gray concrete walls of her tiny room in the basement of a mansion in central Vancouver. Moving to her bed, she sits with her back against the cold wall, draws her knees to her chest, closes her eyes and runs through her chores for the next day—get five kids to and from school, take the youngest to the doctor, clean six bedrooms, do four loads of laundry, and prepare a casserole dinner for eight. "God," she begins praying again, "just help me get everything done."
>
> She tries to sleep, but the whir of the furnace just a few feet from her bed keeps her awake and finally she reaches for a half-finished blanket of red, yellow, and blue wool and knits late into the night.

What Your Story Is About ... and What It's *Really* About: The Nut Graph

The nut graph, which over the years has also come to be known as the "billboard" or "theme graph," almost always follows the lead. The nut graph is often the section that editors change or tinker with most to ensure that the writer's theme, which can also be thought of as the writer's argument or thesis, is well developed and easily understood by readers.

The nut graph tells readers what the story is about as well as why the story is important. In longer feature stories (2,000 words or more), the nut graph may be several paragraphs long. This element is called the "nut graph" because it contains the nut, kernel, or essential theme and facts of the story. Christopher Scanlon, of the Poynter Institute in St. Petersburg, Florida, writes that this vital section of the feature article has several purposes:

- it justifies the story by telling readers why they should care;
- it provides a transition from the lead and explains the lead and its connection to the rest of the story;
- it often tells readers why the story is timely; and
- it often includes supporting material that helps readers see why the story is important.[12]

A nut graph usually begins by telling readers the five W's—where, when, why, who, and what—as well as how, much like the inverted pyramid. But what distinguishes the nut graph from the top of the inverted pyramid in a news story is that it also tells readers why the story should be important to them. At *The Philadelphia Inquirer*, reporters and editors called the nut graph the "You may have wondered why we have invited you to this party?" section.[13] Simply put, there is a reason why you are writing this story, and the nut graph is where you tell readers what it is. And that reason will be one that resonates with the readers of your target publication, so they will read on!

Since the lead to a feature story often does not give much factual information, the first part of the nut graph often fills readers in on what they've just read. The nut graph begins to answer the unanswered questions someone will have after reading the lead. For instance, in the lead of "Nanny Abuse" (above), I show Kristina, a Filipino nanny, living in the basement of a Vancouver home. I know that my readers are now asking, for instance, Who is this woman? How did she get in the basement? Why is she there? While my lead is descriptive, I must now offer more detailed information in the nut graph, telling readers what they need to know so that they will want to stay and read on.

The second part of the nut graph is usually the place where the feature writer begins to lay out the theme, also termed *the argument* or *thesis*. For those schooled in the hard-news business, this idea of the writer's argument or theme might sound a lot like "slanting the news," which is a no-no. But point of view is inevitably present in a feature story, where the writer often lays out facts in a particular order precisely to support a specific line of argument. And it is in the second part of the nut graph where it often becomes obvious what the writer's position is on the topic, or what the theme or argument is.

Author Patricia Westfall has described the difference between the topic of a feature story and its theme. She asks, "What's the story about?" The answer to this is the topic. And then, "What's the story really about?" The answer to this is the theme.[14] In the text of the second part of the nut graph, you usually answer the second question. While "Nanny Abuse" is about a Filipino nanny named Kristina, it's *really* about the exploitation she suffers at the hands of her employers, and the Canadian and Philippine governments. The theme: exploitation!

Similarly, in "The Ketchup Conundrum," reprinted on pages 17–28, Malcolm Gladwell states his theme—struggle—in the very last line of the last paragraph of his nut graph:

> Jim Wigon had a simple vision: build a better ketchup—the way Grey Poupon built a better mustard—and the world will beat a path to your door. If only it were that easy.[15]

For another example, a 2001 feature in *The Globe and Mail* was in part about a man named Fred Dunn, who lived in the woods in a downtown Toronto ravine. In the lead, writers Margaret Philp and Patti Gower introduced Fred this way:

> Fred Dunn speaks in rhyme, bits of fractured wisdom tumbling from his mouth. When he stops talking, as he only reluctantly does, he runs. He runs like religion, sprinting up hills with an 80-pound timber hoisted on a shoulder, peeling off dirty wool socks and rolling up his trousers in sub-zero temperatures to race barefoot in the snow.
>
> He is a modern-day hermit. For 12 years, he has lived year-round in the woods—not in some remote corner of Canada but woods surrounded by the hustle of the nation's biggest metropolis.[16]

But in the nut graph, readers get to know what the story is *really* about. Fred Dunn, it turns out, is not just one man, but "one of many":

> Drivers are not oblivious to Fred's presence; his sprawling display of artifacts salvaged from city garbage cans—ski poles, soccer balls, plastic flowers—is clearly visible in the winter. But few would suspect that he is just one of many.
>
> Along the Don Valley from the lakeshore to the city's northern reaches, and in tributary ravines spreading to the east and west, people have staked a claim to public land, living under an uneasy, unspoken truce with the authorities.
>
> Their tents and precarious perches are undisturbed by works crews and parks employees who turn a blind eye. Still, they seldom light campfires, mindful that a skein of smoke above the treetops would give police an excuse to evict them.
>
> By nature suspicious, elusive, even deceptive, they are the lost ones.[17]

Publications may differ on how the theme is revealed in the nut graph, and that's why writers need to study the magazine or newspaper for which they want to write features. Some publications want the theme to be explicitly stated. Others, as lawyer and journalist James Stewart stresses, like the theme of the story to be foreshadowed, or hinted at.[18] For Stewart, the key role of the nut graph is to begin to establish suspense. Vaillant's story "The Golden Bough" provides an example of this. His theme, a mystery, is hinted at by the suspense built in the nut graph:

> The golden spruce was more than six feet in diameter, and Hadwin's chainsaw had only a twenty-five-inch bar, but Hadwin had worked in the timber industry for years, and he knew how to make falling cuts. Leaving just enough of the core intact so that the tree would stand until the next windstorm, he returned by ferry from the island to the mainland port town of Prince Rupert. Shortly afterward, copies of a letter he had drafted were received by Greenpeace, the Vancouver *Sun*, members of the Haida Nation, and MacMillan Bloedel, Canada's biggest lumber company, which had a timber lease on the land on which the golden spruce stood. The letter said, in part:
>
> > I didn't enjoy butchering, this magnificent old plant, but you apparently need a message and wake-up call, that even a university trained professional, should be able to understand.[19]

How you write or lay out your theme is up to you. There are no hard and fast rules. In her short feature story that appeared in *ELLE* magazine,

Liz Scarff used a quote from a source to reveal the story's theme. The story is about the underground ball scene for black gay and lesbians in Philadelphia. What the story is *really* about: kinship!

> This is the underground ball scene, which is experiencing a revival across the United States. Here, gay women and men—predominantly African Americans—band together in "houses" named after fashion designers such as Givenchy, Chanel and Balenciaga. They take the name of their houses as their surnames and, for recognition, compete with other houses in deliciously camp catwalk shows....
>
> "A house is just like traditional family," says Blahnik. "There's a mother, a father and the kids. A lot of the kids get thrown out when their parents discover they're gay. We make sure they have good role models and stay in school." The houses have regular meetings, where members can discuss anything from the latest Prada collection to advice about HIV. "The family isn't connected by DNA," he says, "but we all have a bond. It's community taking care of itself."[20]

Ken Wells, a writer and editor at *The Wall Street Journal*, described the nut graph as "a paragraph that says what this whole story is about and why you should read it." Other writers liken the nut graph to a movie trailer. A movie trailer sets out to show and tell viewers what a film is about, why it is interesting, and why they should want to watch it. A good trailer draws viewers in so that they just *have to* see the movie. A good nut graph does the same thing.

As with the first few paragraphs of an inverted-pyramid story, if readers care to read no further than the nut graph, they at least know what the story is about, what it is *really* about, and why they should care.

Elements of "Nanny Abuse"

The Nut Graph

The following extract is the entire nut graph for "Nanny Abuse," which hits on many of the above points.

> Kristina, twenty-six, came to Canada in 1999 under Ottawa's controversial Live-in Caregiver Program, an initiative that has lured tens of thousands of women to Canada from impoverished countries over the last twenty-five years. As so many in the developing world have done before them, these young women left, or, more accurately were forced to leave, the security of family for the promise of a more prosperous life in the West. If years of hardship can be

endured after their arrival, they may even reach their ultimate goal and be given citizenship and the right to rescue their relatives from poverty by bringing them to Canada.

Unlike wealthy foreigners who can purchase Canadian passports simply by making an investment in Canada or highly educated immigrants who receive landed immigrant status on arrival, women like Kristina are told to line up at Canada's back door. They will not be given landed status—essentially citizenship—on arrival and will be admitted only if they agree to work for a minimum of two years as live-in nannies. On the surface that may not seem so bad: two years of servitude in exchange for a Canadian passport. Even the low wages—about $700 a month after room and board—may seem adequate to many. And besides, don't nannies eat the same meals, watch television, and go on vacations with the family they're living with?

Many are no doubt happy doing just that, but after more than two decades in operation, according to politicians on both sides of the House of Commons, the Live-in program has a darker side, one that has exploited impoverished women from around the globe and must be reformed. It has now come under formal scrutiny by Citizenship and Immigration Canada, and several studies cast a disturbing light on the baby boomers—the richest generation in Canadian history—who employed most of the women. During a period when individual rights were enshrined in law and women, finally freed from the kitchen and the nursery, entered the workforce in numbers almost equalling their male counterparts, many of the nannies were suffering physical and mental abuse at the hands of the very people they had liberated from the routine drudgery of family life.

An advertisement placed by an Internet auction house in the *Montreal Gazette* in 2003 is an extreme case, but underscores both the vulnerability of the nannies and the contempt in which they are often held. The auctioneers wanted to offer up the services of three nannies to the highest bidder, generating a heated debate on the floor of the House of Commons where politicians called for a drastic overhaul of the Live-in program. At the same time, many nannies came forward with stories of abuse, and crushingly long hours of work with very little pay. Others compared attempts to auction the women to a more painful time in history. "Foreign domestic workers have become Canada's modern-day slaves," says Evelyn Calugay, of PINAY, a Montreal-based advocacy group for Filipina women. "I would call it trafficking in humans."

What Comes Next? The Essential Background

Now that you've set out your theme, argument, or thesis, you can move on to nail it home. Other chapters have and will cover most of what's needed in approaching the main body of your story, in which you show readers, using both facts and narrative, the truth of your theme—that the kinship in the underground ball scene is real (as per Scarff's "It's a Family Affair"); that nannies in Canada are exploited (as per "Nanny Abuse"); and that illegal immigration can be an act of desperation (as per Nazario's "Enrique's Journey").

Layer in essential background for your story, such as the political situation in the Philippines and Central America that drives mothers to abandon their children, or the plight of African-American gays and lesbians. You may have to begin by giving readers some history. In "Enrique's Journey," Nazario shows readers why the economic situation in Central America is so bleak that mothers move to the United States in search of money. In "Nanny Abuse," I write about the history of the Live-In Caregiver Program and the economic situation in the Philippines. In both articles, we did not repeat what was said in the nut graph. Rather, we expanded on it, backing up all the points we'd already made.

Elements of "Nanny Abuse"

The Essential Background

Here's what came after my nut graph:

In 1993, 57 percent of workers in the Caregiver Program were from the Philippines. That figure rose to 93 percent by 2002, an increase that can largely be attributed to the complementary relationship between Ottawa's determination to find a source of cheap labour to provide daycare, and the Philippines' draconian labour export policy, a controversial government initiative under which Filipinos are encouraged to work overseas and send money home.

The export of impoverished Filipinos to richer countries began in the 1970s as Manila looked for ways to reduce unemployment and diversify the economy beyond rice and sugar-cane farming. Banks were encouraged to loan individuals money to go abroad, and fly-by-night employment agencies promoting foreign contacts soon opened in cities and villages across the country. Today females are the principal export, and in 1998 Filipinas working abroad sent almost $8 billion home.

While the Philippines' economy improved with the inflow of foreign earnings, Ottawa in turn could boast that it had provided the baby boomers with a program to help them raise their families while allowing both spouses to work.

Take a Break: Line Spaces and Exposition

Feature stories are often long in word count, and highly textured. There is usually more than just one reason why an event is happening, why a trend is occurring, or why a celebrity feels a certain way. Line spaces can be used to introduce a new point, to start a new narrative, or to look at the topic and theme of your story in a different way.

Line spaces can also be used to introduce a new scene or a different time frame. As mentioned above, in feature stories time can be altered to make for better storytelling and support your topic and theme. In "Nanny Abuse," I chose an incident from the past for my lead, and put it in the present. As I moved through the story, developing my theme and then presenting my argument, I used more narrative from the life of my lead source, Kristina, to illustrate the phenomenon of abused nannies.

I divided up Kristina's narrative, weaving the narrative in and out of my facts and argument. Passages of argument or background are often called *exposition*, to distinguish them from elements of storytelling (such as scenes and transitions). Many writers like to separate an exposition passage from a narrative passage by using a line space.

My first line space in "Nanny Abuse" comes after my lead, nut graph, and some basic history about the Live-In Caregiver Program and the Philippines' economy. But there are no rules for the placement of line spaces. You can use line spaces to allow a breath of air at an exciting moment in your story, or to signal the end of exposition or its beginning. In shorter articles, line spaces might not be necessary at all.

Elements of "Nanny Abuse"

Line Spaces and Exposition

In the following extract, I placed a passage of exposition immediately before a line space and then returned to my main narrative ("A crowing rooster...") to show another face to Kristina's plight:

> Equally disturbing is what happens to many domestic workers when they finish the Caregiver Program and achieve permanent residence status. Many, without access to education and retraining, continue to work as low-paid nannies, and the cycle of abuse continues. Even more troubling: a recent study by the Philippine Women's Centre of British Columbia suggests that a growing number of nannies are working part-time as prostitutes so they can pay off bank loans and debts to unscrupulous immigration consultants. "Canada has designed a program to have a continuous supply of cheap labour," says filmmaker Florchita Bautista, whose 1999 documentary *When Strangers Reunite* follows the lives of three Filipina domestic workers who came to Canada. "The poverty these women so desperately tried to pull themselves and their children out of is only being transferred from one country to another."

ର୍ଷର୍ଷର୍ଷ

A crowing rooster announces the rising of the sun over the tiny farm that Kristina's parents own in the countryside outside of Cebu, a financial centre and popular tourist destination in the southern Philippines. As she does almost every day, Kristina's younger sister, Jan, rose early to feed the cows and goats before sitting down to a breakfast of rice and fish. This day would be different. After kneeling in prayer with her mother, Jan left on an hour-long walk along a dirt road to catch the bus that will take her into Cebu to register for university. Four hours later, as the bus finally approached the city, she watched the densely green landscape slowly turn urban, with posh new hotels and tourist cottages lining the white sand beaches.

In the evening, wealthy foreigners jam the city's discotheques, restaurants, and shops selling diving gear and beach wear. Jan hurries by these places. On her family's $500 annual income she can't afford to shop there anyway. But there are other businesses she visits that tourists never enter. Simple signs made from cardboard and paint and others of flashy neon, hang above these makeshift shops, enticing young people with information about immigration, passports, and overseas employment. Jan knows these businesses only too well. When she finishes university she will be pressured by her family to find a job abroad.

"My parents have been telling Jan that she will be responsible to pay for our brothers to go to university," says Kristina. "And my parents told me when I was in elementary school that I would be responsible for Jan's education." At first Kristina resisted, and when she finished high school she took a college secretarial course. But for more than two years, the only employment she could find was with a trucking company that paid only $100 a month—not nearly enough to help with the family's expenses, let alone pay for Jan's education.

Coming Back to Your Theme: Grounding

While an inverted-pyramid story can be viewed pictorially as an upside-down triangle, a feature story is more like a wavy line like this:

The part of the wave that touches the straight line is known as *grounding*, when you reiterate to your readers, in different words, your topic and theme. Your story takes off with the lead, and the wave begins to move outward. The wave then turns back toward the straight line as you present your argument. The wave touches the straight line at the point in the nut graph when you tell readers your theme. After the nut graph, the wave begins to move outward again, with a new scene, background information, the narrative of a new source, etc. Then, the wave turns back toward the straight line again as you ground your story before taking off again.

For instance, after Scarff wrote the nut graph for her story, she wrote about the history of the underground ball scene in Philadelphia. She then wrote about what some of the members personally got out of the scene. She ended this section of her story by reminding readers of her theme—kinship.

> Blahnik recently put up one member affected by Hurricane Katrina and also helps get members into shelters and support programs.[21]

Scarff also used quotes from sources to ground her theme:

> "I loved the creativity and energy of the show. They accepted me and gave me the support to get out there in the world and not be ashamed of who I am."[22]

Elements of "Nanny Abuse"

Grounding

Here are two grounding statements in my story—the first is an expository statement, the second a quote. Each returns readers to the story's central theme: exploitation.

> But critics charge that employers and the government are perpetuating a myth by claiming that women from the developing world do well by coming to Canada.
>
> ∼∽∼
>
> "At first I didn't believe what I was hearing because I just couldn't imagine employers dehumanizing the women looking after their children," says Rachael. "But then I saw the behaviour for myself when some of the employers at the park ordered their nannies around like servants."

He Said, She Said: Using Quotes

Quotes in news stories are often from sources who back up the facts written immediately preceding them. These quotes may give basic information, and are there to convince readers that yes, indeed, Benazir Bhutto has been assassinated, for example. Take the following quote from the *Toronto Star*:

> Sardar Qamar Hayyat, a leader from Bhutto's party, said he was standing about 10 metres away from Bhutto's vehicle.
> "She was inside the vehicle and was coming out from the gate after addressing the rally when some of the youths started chanting slogans in her favour," he said. "Then I saw a thin, young man jumping to her vehicle from the back and opening fire. Moments later, I saw her speeding vehicle going away."[23]

Notice how the quote provides vivid information, but not in a particularly compelling way. A feature article might use the exact same information, but the writing will likely be more descriptive and the quote used to add character or understanding, rather than information. For example, the writer might have preferred to find a more atmospheric quote and use it in something like the following way:

> As Benazir Bhutto got into her car, she was still wearing the colours of freedom: red and white leis, over her sea blue dress. Youth from the crowd that Bhutto had just addressed were chanting slogans in her favour. As her car began to move away, a thin young man moved out from the crowd and opened fire from behind. At the first shot, a supporter who had been standing nearby hid his face in the back of the man in front of him. "There were screams all round me, and people jostling, and I heard the car speeding away," he said. "Then we all started running."

In feature stories, quotes are not used to convey or reinforce basic information. They move the story along and drive home your theme, often by adding emotional identification and impact, as in Andrew Chung's story of a man returning to his native China to find his birth mother:

> It was five years ago, and Chester Wan was attending a nephew's wedding in Toronto, when someone—he can't remember who—passed him The Letter. It introduced some members of his family back in China whom he'd never met.

But more important, it told of Chun Xi, his biological mother. It said that ever since the woman Chester thought was his mother had died, she had wanted to tell him.

"It was a real shock to me," he says. "I never thought I had another mother."

The picture he had in his mind of this woman, whom he used to call ayi, or aunt, is still from the vantage point of a little boy—from below, her face turned down to him. He vaguely remembered her soft skin, and that she was slightly plump.

"She was very gentle," he recalls. "I used to like to sleep with her."

Her role in the family was to take care of the household and tend to his mother, Chester remembers.[24]

In a 2003 profile of then–*Us Weekly* magazine editor Bonnie Fuller, Marci McDonald used quotes to help establish the character of her subject:

Then *Advertising Age* handed Fuller sweet revenge. Last fall, it anointed her Editor of the Year, the only person to have twice copped a title that pays tribute to consumer savvy. "Love it or hate it—and we're not entirely sure on a day-to-day basis where we fall," *Ad Age* wrote, *Us* "is as undeniably compelling as … ripping the top off a gumball machine and stuffing fistfuls in your mouth."

Fuller's friend Lesley Jane Seymour, editor-in-chief of *Marie Claire*, agrees. "What Bonnie does so amazingly well is that she picks up the silly subconscious ideas that run through your mind and you're too embarrassed to voice," she says. "She goes for those secret thoughts, like what is Ben Affleck's underwear like? That's why it's such a guilty pleasure. She isn't bound by conventional editing."[25]

Quotes in feature stories should be lively, engaging, or disturbing. In fact, feature writers often use quotes to convey things that could never be adequately conveyed in another way. In this extract from a 1985 award-winning story about the teaching history of notorious anti-Semite James Keegstra, for instance, Robert Mason Lee uses quotes to provide a window on hate:

"Consider the atomic bomb, I told my students," Keegstra recalls. "Jewish scientists were involved in its creation. Why drop it on the two cities in Japan that were basically Christian? Was it an accident, or was it deliberate?"

Gwen Matthews, asked if she'd been taught to hate, replied: "I think we should be free to hate if we're free to love. If we love something, we must hate the opposite of it. If we love God, then we must hate the Devil."[26]

Quotes can also be dialogue—what was said in a scene that is described—as in "Enrique's Journey":

> But Lourdes cannot face Enrique. He will remember only one thing that she says to him: "Don't forget to go to church this afternoon."…
> She walks away.
> "*Donde esta mi mami?*" Enrique cries, over and over. "Where is my mom?"[27]

Almost always, you should identify the speaker after the first sentence of a quote or immediately preceding, as Nazario does above. Many novice feature writers string together many sentences in one quote, which leaves readers guessing, who is talking?

And never leave readers guessing as to the quote's meaning. The following extract from my story "Who's My Birth Father?" provides a good example of setting up your quote so that its meaning is clear:

> The Ontario university professor began donating sperm in 1976, at the age of 40, after a divorce. He didn't take a cent for his contributions. "When there is money involved there is a tendency to be less than honest about your medical and personal history by making yourself look better," Jim says of the procedure.[28]

Elements of "Nanny Abuse"

Using Quotes

The quote at the end of the following extract helps readers understand what precedes it—why the nanny stuck with her job under terrible circumstances:

> Her first assignment in Canada involved caring for a two-year-old girl in Victoria and looked promising. But within a month, Kristina was nearly raped when the child's grandfather, dressed only in his underwear and stinking of rum and marijuana, barged into the family's recreation room where she slept. He retreated after she threatened to break a window with a lamp, but came back later that night and tried to re-enter the room.
>
> Her frantic screams finally alerted the man's wife, who told him to sober up and go to bed. It took her eight months to find a new employer, and every day until she left he would whisper menacingly into her ear about having sex with her. "I felt completely vulnerable," she says. "I didn't know what my rights were in Canada and I thought if I called the police they would blame me. It was hell."

Final Curtain: The Ending

Endings in traditional inverted-pyramid news stories aren't particularly important. When the facts are presented in the order of most important to least important, the conclusion is the least interesting part of the story, and sometimes can be sliced right off to save space without anyone noticing, not even the author. Not so in feature writing!

According to Michael Bugeja, a feature story "takes a scenic route, presenting the same facts, perhaps, but with more levels of content and truth, more thorough research and observation, more drama or perspective, clearer focus and deeper tones or texture."[29] Bugeja says that a feature story should resemble a good road map: it should take the driver—your reader—through both the scenic and the factual, and arrive at the desired destination, your ending! And where is that destination?

Often your beginning or lead hints at the ending: it paints a scene, an image of your destination. The ending wraps up the theme and answers all the reader's yet unanswered questions. For Bugeja, an ending has a few basic requirements:

- it echoes or answers the introduction, fulfilling the contract promised in the title of your work;
- it has been foreshadowed; and
- it contains a final epiphany or peak experience for take-away value.[30]

One common mistake novice feature writers make is keeping readers guessing at the end. If your article features a source prominently, don't leave readers hanging on by not finishing his or her story. Bring readers up to the present, or wherever the story ended for that source. Remember Vaillant's lead in "The Golden Bough" (see page 77)? Note the way he closes:

> Meanwhile, Hadwin's case is still considered open by the Alaska State Troopers and the Mounties. No one has bothered to look for him in Siberia, but Cora Gray told me, "He talked about Russia a lot. He'd say, 'If I was going to choose a place to stay, it would be in Russia. Don't be surprised if you hear from me there.' So now, when the phone rings late at night, I don't answer."

Readers may be left wondering, *Where could Hadwin be?* but, at the same time, they know the story is over. This is all we know at the time of the article's publication as to Hadwin's whereabouts.

Here are two more great endings. Like Vaillant's, both are quotes, but as different in feel and approach as they are united in purpose: to leave readers filled with a final, evocative sense of character and theme. The first is from a portrait by Ian Brown of legendary 84-year-old stage actor William Hutt taking on one of theatre's toughest roles, Vladimir, in Samuel Beckett's *Waiting for Godot*:

> But it's opening night now, and the stage manager has called the half-hour to curtain. Mr. Schultz is making his sacred rounds of the dressing rooms. He finds Mr. Hutt on his cot, as still as a mummy. The old man already had a pre-show word with Jordan Pettle, his young Estragon. "I told him, 'Tonight,'" Mr. Hutt says, "'we're just going to go out there and talk to each other. They're just eavesdroppers.'"
>
> Mr. Schultz is closing the door when he hears Bill Hutt's question: "Is it a full house?"[31]

Jay Teitel, in a surprisingly tender profile of Don Cherry, ends with the hockey shock-jock talking about how coaches make a bad mistake if they send kids off the ice when someone gets badly hurt. Instead, a coach should get one or two players to stay with the injured kid ...

> "to hold his hand. Because he's all alone out there. His teammates are gone, and he's all alone.
>
> "I was one of those guys when I was playing who was always holding their hand.... And the funny thing is, the toughest guys, a lot of them, they call for their mothers. Not when it happens, on the ice, but when they're in the ambulance and it's quiet. They don't *yell*, 'Ma!'"
>
> Cherry pauses a moment. He's thinking about this. Getting it right is important. "It's soft. It's just, 'Ma!'"[32]

Though the possibilities for endings are almost infinite and there are no iron rules, there are two main approaches: open and closed.

An open ending leaves readers pondering the arguments, themes, and narratives of the story. An open ending suggests, rather than states, for example, the ramifications of the exploitation of Filipino nannies or where Hadwin could be. The goal of an open ending is to leave readers to draw their own conclusions and think through the story for themselves. An open ending is merely a suggestion of the outcome of the issue or trend about which you are writing. Readers know that the story might end in another way. Vaillant's open ending, above, is an excellent example.

In contrast, a closed ending states rather than suggests the outcome. Scarff's "It's a Family Affair," for instance, ends as follows:

The ball scene is attracting the attention of trendsetters like Patricia Fields, the stylist for *Sex and the City*, and *Kill Bill* actress Vivica A. Fox. In this world, the look is everything—fake or real.[33]

According to Sumner and Miller, a great feature story can "crash" in its closing paragraphs if the author either leaves key questions unanswered or repeats information already written in the story.[34]

As with a good movie or documentary, a feature story's ending is just as important as its beginning. Leave your readers at a place where they can walk away enlightened or thinking about your story and its theme, not scratching their heads saying, "I think I missed something." So, whether you choose an open or closed ending, don't miss the pivotal importance of a strong, creative, and original close.

Elements of "Nanny Abuse"

The Ending

At the close of "Nanny Abuse," I knew that readers would want to know where the woman in the basement ended up. I answered the question as best I could at the time of writing:

> It would be months before Kristina finally escaped her abusive Vancouver employer. With the help of a kindly lawyer she managed to get the $3,000 in back pay owed to her, and was finally able to apply for landed immigrant status and find her own place to live. She now rents a two-bedroom, subsidized apartment in downtown Vancouver, furnished with a couch, end tables, computer, TV, and nativity figures.
>
> Kristina also gave birth to a baby daughter, who coos happily in a playpen in the corner. The baby's father is the son of a domestic worker who came to Canada after being left behind in the Philippines for fifteen years while his mother worked in Canada. He has trouble holding down a job and has a gambling problem. As a result, she has decided to raise her daughter on her own—a move that has been criticized by some of her Roman Catholic friends. She blames the father's money and job problems on the fact that he was apart from his mother for so many years. "I can really see the impact the separation had on him," says Kristina. "He's lost and I don't want my daughter to grow up with that kind of uncertainty."
>
> When she arrived in Canada, she was not aware that she was part of the exodus of women from poor nations. But Kristina now plans to tell her daughter about everything she has been through. "People in the Philippines are in denial," she says. "It's like the money Filipinas earn in the West washes away the sacrifices and misery. I want my sister Jan and daughter to be aware of the

struggles of the Filipina women in Canada and in the Philippines." If any good can come out of her experience, she hopes it is that her sister and daughter can avoid the ordeal she has been through.

Discussion Questions

Read "When Animals Attack!" by Bruce Grierson (pages 251–255). Consider the narrative techniques Grierson uses under the following headings:

- The lead: Why do you think Grierson chose to begin the story where he did? Can you come up with other possible leads?
- The nut graph: Identify the nut graph. How effectively does it develop the topic and theme? What do you think the theme is?
- The essential background: As a reader, ask yourself, *Does Grierson answer my questions as they arise throughout the story?* If not, what should he have included? Do you have enough of a background to understand his topic and theme?
- The ending: Is Grierson's conclusion closed or open? Explain your answer.

Notes

1. Associated Press, "Pakistan Rejects Foreign Help in Bhutto Investigation," *Globe and Mail*, December 29, 2007.

2 Amy Wilentz, "The Exiles Return," *MORE* (US edition), December/January 2007, 144.

3. Sonia Nazario, "Enrique's Journey: Chapter One—The Boy Left Behind," *Los Angeles Times*, September 29, 2002.

4. Susan McClelland, "Nanny Abuse," *Walrus*, March 2005.

5. William Blundell, *The Art and Craft of Feature Writing: Based on the Wall Street Journal Guide* (New York: New American Library, 1988), pp. 127–40.

6. Ron Kovach, "Erik Larson: A Devil of a Good Writer," *Writer*, September 2003.

7. John Vaillant, "The Golden Bough," *The New Yorker*, November 4, 2002, 50.

8. David E. Sumner and Holly G. Miller, *Feature and Magazine Writing: Action, Angle and Anecdotes* (Ames, IA: Wiley-Blackwell, 2005), pp. 91–98.

9. Susan McClelland, "Who's My Birth Father?" *Maclean's*, May 20, 2002.

10. Clive Thompson, "Gamer Regret," *Wired News*, September 2007, <http://www.collisiondetection.net/mt/archives/2007/09/_battle_with_ga.html> (accessed March 3, 2008).

11. You can read the full story online at <http://www.walrusmagazine.com/articles/2005.03-politics-international-labour-migration/1> or <http://susanmcclelland.com/art_nanny.htm>.

12. Christopher Scanlon, *Reporting and Writing: Basics for the 21st Century* (New York: Oxford University Press, 2002).

13. Ibid.

14. Michael J. Bugeja, *Guide to Writing Magazine Nonfiction* (Boston: Allyn & Bacon, 1998), p. 39.

15. Malcolm Gladwell, "The Ketchup Conundrum," *The New Yorker*, September 6, 2004, 129.

16. Margaret Philp and Patti Gower, "The Disappeared Ones," *Globe and Mail*, March 31, 2001.

17. Ibid.

18. James B. Stewart, *Follow the Story: How to Write Successful Nonfiction* (New York: Touchstone, 1998), p. 152.

19. Vaillant, "The Golden Bough," 50.

20. Liz Scarff, "It's a Family Affair," *ELLE* (Canadian edition), March 2006, 102.

21. Ibid.

22. Ibid.

23. Sadaqat Jan and Zarar Khan, "Former Leader to Be Buried Friday as Anger with Musharraf Increases," *Toronto Star*, December 27, 2007.

24. Andrew Chung, "The Letter," *Toronto Star*, April 23, 2006.

25. Marci McDonald, "Queen B," *Toronto Life*, January 2003.

26. Robert Mason Lee, "Keegstra's Children," in *The Presence of Excellence: Twenty-five Years of Selections from the National Magazine Awards*, ed. Don Obe (Toronto: National Magazine Awards Foundation, 2003), p. 75. Originally published in *Saturday Night* magazine.

27. Nazario, "Enrique's Journey."

28. McClelland, "Who's My Birth Father?"

29. Bugeja, *Guide to Writing Magazine Nonfiction*, p. 148.

30. Ibid., p. 149.

31. Ian Brown, "Grappling with Godot." *Globe and Mail*, June 19, 2004.

32. Jay Teitel, "Peeling Grapes," *Saturday Night*, March 2005, 36.

33. Scarff, "It's a Family Affair."

34. Sumner and Miller, *Feature and Magazine Writing*.

"When Animals Attack!"

The lines are drawn and the battle begins: dam-building beavers versus a homeowner just trying to protect his damn building.

Bruce Grierson, "When Animals Attack!" *Western Living* magazine, September 2002, 26. Reprinted by permission of the author.

My brother-in-law, Dennis, has a heads-up, skeptical nature—some might call it paranoia—that I've come to tolerate and even respect. But I wasn't prepared for what he said to me when I visited him and my sister, Carol, last August: "I think the beavers are trying to do me in."

Every single summer for the past 19 years, the basement of Dennis and Carol's home in the Alberta countryside has flooded. Always the water laps up to within about a thumb's width of the top furnace pad, threatening to cause an electrical short, leaving them without power, or worse.

And every year Dennis develops a more sharply focused rage at the source of the problem. I should tell you that he is a psychologist in private practice. Rage is not in his nature. Rage isn't rational, and it isn't constructive—unless you happen to be fighting a war.

Dennis and Carol moved to their acre and a half to escape the frustrations and horrible mall culture of the city. To raise their kids in peace, in nature. And at first it looked like peace is what they'd found. I can remember how thrilled Dennis was to discover, on his first walk around the property, a lake—still and blue and big enough to canoe on. He actually said, "It doesn't get much more Canadian than this."

He was wrong. It did get more Canadian. The lake was home to beavers.

I should say at this point that the saga of my brother-in-law and the beavers has reached mythic status in our family. But until my last visit, most of us had bits and pieces of it. For some reason, on this particular night, Dennis was burning to tell the whole thing. My job was to listen.

The first beaver Dennis spotted was—ominously—dead. But soon he began to see the extended family, arrowing in across the water, "just as the day was coming to twilight."

The scene put Dennis in mind of Grey Owl, the professional Indian (who was really an Englishman), bonding with the animals in the prairie wilderness. In full Grey Owl mode, Dennis started sitting by the lake, perfectly still, giving off good vibes, until the beavers got used to him, or forgot about him, and came near. He watched their reflections in the lake. He looked at their dark eyes and stained yellow teeth from "as close as you are to me now." He felt a little bit of awe. No thoughtful Canadian can contemplate a beaver without thinking about its place in the chain of our colonial history: this country was built on the beaver's back.

"I was out there admiring them day after day," Dennis said. "Then the water started coming into my basement.

"I began connecting the dots." He hitched out a thumb. "Our house was in the middle of a flat field, yet there was a lake on it." Index finger. "The lake appeared to be getting bigger, yet it hadn't rained." Middle finger. "The beaver population seemed to be growing."

Sorry: I need to tell you a few things about beavers.

A beaver can take down a poplar as thick as an axe-handle in just one quick and easy bite.

Beavers are workaholics: You can destroy their dam in the evening, and a new one will be there to greet you in the morning.

Beavers are smart.

Beavers are territorial.

Beavers have a vestigial memory that they were here first.

Because he is a sensitive man, and because his daughter, Kerri, had made it clear no beavers were to be harmed in the making of this particular movie, Dennis decided he had to develop a way to deal with the problem that everybody could live with.

He'd read somewhere that beavers are repelled by mothballs, so he bought a big bag of them and he went to the creek. After he'd broken down the beavers' dam, he scattered the mothballs liberally on the bank. The beavers were undeterred. They showed up for work as usual and built their dam back up. There were actually footprints on the mothballs where the beavers had trudged over them.

"So I bought a length of plastic tubing. This is something a friend who's an animal-rights person had suggested. It's humane and it's supposed to be effective. You punch a hole in the dam and shove the tube in, the way a surgeon puts a drain in a wound. The water runs right through the dam. Or that's the theory."

"Didn't work?" I said.

He shook his head. "The beavers built a little peninsula of mud around the pipe. They plugged it."

Dennis called up the county for advice. It turned out the county had a beaver patrol department, and they sent a guy out with a trap.

A beaver trap is a sort of spring-loaded metal jaw that sits, cocked and open, in the predicted path of the beaver and snaps shut as the beaver swims through. The first trap the guy laid actually did catch a beaver. But it quickly became clear that the county's approach to beaver control was laid-back at best. "They treat beavers as a sustainable resource," Dennis said. "They never want to kill them all, because that would put them out of work. So they take a beaver here and a beaver there and then pat themselves on the back." In truth, it's doubtful the beaver-patrol guy could have caught many more beavers if he'd tried, because the beavers very quickly learned the ropes.

Less than 24 hours after the beaver-patrol guy laid his second trap, Dennis went down to the creek. The trap was gone. In its place was a fresh new dam. Dennis waded into the water and started breaking it up, "and then my shovel hit something metal." There was the trap, gleaming between the poplar branches. The beavers had simply incorporated it into their project. Dennis dug the trap out and flung it toward the creek bank. Just as it left his fingers—bang!—it snapped shut. A trap designed to snap the neck of a beaver could easily break the arm of a man; this one almost had. The implications sank in. Not only had they built the dam around the trap, they hadn't even sprung it. "That," said Dennis, "is when I began to get scared."

In his counselling work, Dennis often uses stories he hears as therapeutic aids, and the tale of man against beaver—internecine, interspecies stubbornness in the Canadian North (involving the national symbol, no less)—ought to be ripe with usable metaphors. But Dennis refuses to see the symbolism. This thing is too personal.

Dennis owns a gun—a .22 rifle. Perhaps it was appropriate, even necessary, to have a gun on the farm where he grew up, but it seemed stupid and un-Canadian to own one in the city, where he and Carol lived until they decided to start a family. He hadn't used it in ages. As he walked to the creek, it felt foreign in his hands.

He tried to psych himself up for the job. "You can do this," he said to himself. "Be the man. Be the hunter." From a distance, he could see a beaver dutifully working on a new dam. As he walked closer, levelling the gun at the beaver, "I thought of that story of the soldier in Nazi Germany who said, 'The hardest to kill was the first one. After that, the hardest to kill were the next 10. After that, the hardest to kill were the next 100.' "

I asked Dennis how Kerri had responded when she learned her father had put a bullet in a beaver. "She was in tears," he said. "She thought I was Attila the Hun." They named the creek Kerri Creek, after their daughter's Dian Fossey–like defence of the animals.

Dennis stepped up his patrols after that. Rain or shine he'd be out there in his green down vest and duck boots and rifle, mosquitoes eating him alive. The only thing missing from the picture was the Elmer Fudd cap. Over time, he wore a visible path through the woods to the creek.

People who study beavers find it remarkable that they almost always manage to cut down trees within falling distance of water, despite their poor eyesight. "They're looking up from ground level—it's amazing they're that accurate," Dennis said. If the whole tree doesn't fall in, at least part of it does. They never cut down trees anywhere else. Okay? Remember that when I tell you that I'm on my way to the creek, and there in the middle of the trail—nowhere near the water—three fallen trees have come down over the path." Not onto the path, but snarled in the branches and hanging precariously, like traps set by the Viet Cong.

At this point you may be feeling a surge of sympathy for the beavers. I confess that as Dennis reached this point in the story, I was. But I also know I'd feel differently if it were my home that were threatened.

Every year, the do-no-harm position adopted by Carol and Kerri and her sister Kathleen softens. Carrying soggy boxes out of the basement and wrestling with a pump compressor will do that to you. "With Kerri, it used to be, 'Dad, do you have no heart?'" Dennis said. "Now it's, 'Dad, did you kill the damn beaver yet?' Over time, they all got converted, every one of them."

To his credit, Dennis himself has come full-circle on the issue of nonviolence. His current system of beaver management is one of early intervention. Twice a day, he walks the creek. "A beaver will float a stick down the river and then come back later and see if it's got stuck anywhere. If it has, that's a good place to start building. So any twig that looks like it's been sitting there more than an hour, I scoop up.

"The whole key is to move fast. If you knock a beaver dam out within 24 hours, they'll fight for that spot for a day or two, and then they'll move away, downriver. But if you let them get a beachhead, they'll fight you for months."

I think it was good therapy for Dennis to talk about this. I know it was good therapy to hear it. But I must admit that, since arriving back home in Vancouver, I've been a little worried for the guy. As long as he and my sister live on that acreage, they will have no rest. I keep half-waiting for Dennis to tell me the beavers have been tapping his phone.

Postscript:

The droughts that have savaged northern Alberta this summer have reduced a lot of rural streams—including Dennis and Carol's—to a trickle.

But beavers are merely inconvenienced by conditions that kill lesser species. When the going gets tough, beavers don't die—they move. Like the Okies in the dust-bowl '30s, beavers all over Alberta have gathered everything they own (not much) and migrated to more hospitable ground, which is to say the rivers. Some have been killed by coyotes and some run over by cars en route; but on the upside, a lot of optimistic beaver families have come upon roomy, stylish dams abandoned by other beavers, and moved right in.

If it stays dry, the county beaver-patrol guy says, Albertans may have fewer beaver problems in the future, because, with food growing scarce, the litter size will probably decrease. Unless it increases, which beaver populations have been known to do when pressure has been put on them by, say, trapping (a kind of genetic "revenge of the cradle").

As for Carol and Dennis's beavers, they've departed, too, but not very far. They have waddled into the outstretched arms of the woman who lives downstream—a woman who happens to love beavers. Banking on rain, they have commenced to lower the property values of everyone in the area by building a dam out of the surrounding birch and poplar. The neighbours aren't happy about this, but what can they do? She won't let anyone on her land to blow up the dam. (My sister is sanguine about this woman's love. "It'll last until she loses all her trees," Carol says, "and then she'll move.")

Anyway, Dennis and Carol are glad to have the beavers out of their hair. Now they can give their full attention to the colony of carpenter ants that has established itself in their walls.

CHAPTER NINE

Doing It in Style:
The Feature Writer's Art

Moira Farr

You already know from preceding chapters that feature articles differ in structure from breaking news stories, and provide more lengthy, in-depth perspective on issues and events. Still, just like news stories, feature stories must be written in clear, precise language without jargon, clutter, vague generalities, or abstractions. Your starting point may be an anecdote, scene, or character (perhaps even yourself), and your aim, always, is to keep the reader interested. Your story may be more complex than the average news item, but that doesn't mean your language needs to be any less clear and simple.

Consider the following example from a reconstructed account of the violent 2004 hostage-taking that took place at an elementary school in Beslan, Russia and resulted in the deaths of 334 people, more than half of them children. Writer C.J. Chivers opens his story with devastating directness:

September 1
  Afternoon. The Gym.

Kazbek Misikov stared at the bomb hanging above his family. It was a simple device, a plastic bucket packed with explosive paste, nails, and small metal balls. It weighed perhaps eight pounds. The existence of this bomb had become a central focus of his life. If it exploded, Kazbek knew, it would blast shrapnel into the heads of his wife and two sons, and into him as well, killing them all.[1]

Of all the thousands of details Chivers had gathered in his research, when it came time to construct his story's lead, he picked this one scenario, for good reason. Immediately, we see the event from the perspective of one person, in this case a terrified father. A widely covered news story that lumped together hundreds of anonymous people immediately focuses our attention on the plight of a single human being with whom we can surely empathize. The words Chivers uses to describe the explosive device could not be more ordinary—their very simplicity only heightens the inherent, surreal drama of the scene. By referring to his lead "character" by his first name, Kazbek, on second reference, rather than opt for the standard journalistic use of the surname, he further humanizes him and brings readers closer to his horrible predicament. Who could not imagine his fear? It's a classic example of "show, don't tell." Chivers trusts his material, and his unadorned words, to convey the story's meaning and power. He doesn't have to clutter his lead with exclamation marks or commentary ("He was terrified!" "It was a horrible situation!"). The plain details speak eloquently for themselves, here and throughout the piece. The author's intent, of course, is to hook readers and keep them interested in reading on. He succeeded with this reader—I finished the gripping story (all 50 anthology pages of it) in one sitting, and had to wipe my brow of sweat, and my eyes of tears, at the end of it. No other story I read or saw on TV about the event had ever conveyed with such stunning immediacy the harrowing reality of what people endured inside that school.

That's good writing.

What Is "Style"?

"Every writer, by the way he uses language, reveals something of his spirit, his habits, his capacities, his bias. This is inevitable as well as enjoyable."[2] Reading this statement from Strunk and White's *The Elements of Style*, rightly considered one of the most concise and reliable guides to writing style in the English language, I think I can tell you something about the writers' bias. It's no surprise that the book was published in 1957—long before anyone would have judged it undesirable to use the possessive adjective *his* in a context that refers to a general group of people. Today, a writer (just as likely to be female as male) might hesitate to exclude an entire gender in this way. She could opt to even the score and use *her* instead, or, being entirely egalitarian, *his/her*, though most newspaper and magazine editors would reject that construction as too awkward a compromise for the sake of being "PC" (common jargon now for *politically correct*, but a term that hadn't been invented when Strunk and White first wrote their famous manual). An editor would recognize the problem and want to fix what might be considered the linguistic equivalent of duck-tailed hair greased back with Brylcreem.

Today's writer would be wise to construct the sentence in a way that avoids the *he/she* issue altogether. For instance: *All writers, by the way they use language, reveal something of their spirits, their habits, their capacities, their biases.*

The sentence expresses the original idea, as valid today as it was more than 60 years ago, but with a simple switch to the plural, it no longer jars the twenty-first-century reader who has become used to more gender-neutral language. In fact, that's just what the editors of the original manual have done in its most recently reprinted version: "This edition has been modestly updated ... with a light redistribution of genders to permit a feminine pronoun or female farmer to take their places among the males ..." writes Roger Angell, eminent writer and editor for *The New Yorker*, in the book's foreword.[3]

The Strunk and White example demonstrates an important point about writing style: the fact that a book first published more than 60 years ago has been steadily re-issued year after year tells you that there's much about popular language use that doesn't change—principles and practices that worked in the last century still work in ours. Yet linguistic anachronisms are inevitable—1957 wasn't quite a time when dinosaurs roamed the earth, but shark-finned Chevies did, the Everly Brothers were at the top of the pop charts, and poodle skirts were a must for stylish girls. I'm guessing you don't drive a big Chevy, don't have "Wake Up Little Susie" on your iPod, and would not wear a poodle skirt unless you were going to a serious retro party. In an age of hybrid vehicles, 50 Cent, and lululemon yoga gear, these references to past pop culture sound almost bizarre (as will those we now consider current, 60 years, or maybe even six months, from now).

Regardless of the era, we should all aspire to craft sentences with good bones and a lot of powerful, lean muscle. If you can provide these, editors and readers will love you. When the structure is sound, word usage clear, and flab minimal, the body of the entire piece of writing can flow with grace. The result may be smooth and effortless, but in reality, good writers, working with good editors, labour over their work, composing, strengthening, trimming, streamlining, and choosing precisely the right words until they are satisfied that the desired effect has been achieved.

Consider the difference between these two sentences:

The dog went across the road.

The poodle ran across the expressway.

Which one most makes you want to read the next sentence? The first statement is what we might call generic or bland, and though it isn't likely to elicit much curiosity, it does leave many obvious questions unanswered.

Glad You Asked! The Big Fix

Q: How do I maintain a good working relationship with my editor?
A: The short answer is simple: hand in clean copy on time, and behave professionally. For more detail, follow these tips:

- Do get to know your editor between assignments. If you live in town, ask to meet in person. Suggest a coffee, talk about journalism, reporting, and writing in general, rather than just about your piece. Get a sense of him or her as a person.
- Do make sure you fully understand your assignment. Talk through the story idea, focus, and approach thoroughly. Raise any questions that come to mind. If you get an assignment letter, read it several times over, highlight the main points, and post it on your bulletin board. If you are not sure you can deliver what the letter asks, call your editor and troubleshoot the assignment together. The time you spend clarifying the assignment is time saved on revisions and additional reporting later on.
- Don't agree to do a story you don't believe is true. Be clear and open with your editor. You may convince him or her to let you do the better story!
- Do listen carefully and note everything your editor says. If you don't understand something, say so! If you don't agree with something, politely raise it and discuss it. In all conversations with editors, do as much listening as talking.
- Do read your contract carefully. Understand what rights you are giving up, for how long and for how much.
- Do ask about resale rights and electronic rights.
- Do get in touch with your editor if any of the following situations arise:

  - you think you can't make your deadline
  - you find out things in reporting that affect or change the assignment's core premise

A dog (what kind of dog?) *went* (how?) *across the road* (what road? where? who cares?).

The second statement catches our attention much more forcefully. Poodles, we know, do not as a rule run across fenced highways. Why is this poodle in such a predicament?

By simply making two nouns (dog = poodle; road = expressway) and one verb (went = ran) more specific, we've punched up the impact of the sentence considerably. We could go further: *The poodle ran, bleeding and limping, from the wreckage of its owner's SUV, in between honking cars and trucks, until it made it onto the icy shoulder.*

- you find out things that could improve the story but change the focus
- you change your mind or get confused in any way

- Do make sure your editor is not surprised by developments that affect the nature or do-ability of the assignment. Troubleshoot problems right away.
- Don't call your editor to read him or her your lead or to ask for some quick writing advice. Editors are busy. Write the best draft you can, highlighting any missing facts or areas of uncertainty or potential problems (keeping these to a bare minimum).
- Don't waste your editor's time with questions you can solve on your own (for example, facts you can research online or at the library, emails or phone numbers you should be able to find).
- Do submit your draft *on time*. If that becomes impossible, do raise the alarm well in advance and set a new deadline with your editor.
- Don't take criticism personally. Remember, your editor is the only reader who will talk back to you, and readers—not you—are the best judges of your work. You are almost always too close to the story to assess it clearly without assistance. If your editor tells you that your story has lost focus, or is too short or too long, or muddled or unconvincing or poorly organized, or could be improved in other ways, she is right about 80 percent of the time. The other 20 percent of the time, you pretty much have to act as if she's right, unless you're asked to do something that is inaccurate, misleading, or dishonest.
- Do trust your editor (until he or she gives you a good reason not to).
- Do communicate clearly, completely, and undefensively. It's not just this story that's at stake—it's whether the editor will want to work with you next time, or you with the editor.

Ivor Shapiro

Used sparingly, additional phrases such as "bleeding and limping" sketch in the details, efficiently providing important information, perhaps evoking an emotional response, suspense even (will the poodle survive?), and enhancing the reader's understanding of the situation you are describing. The goal, always, is to keep your reader interested—and reading.

What's Your Style?

We all have a particular way of organizing words on a page. Ask 10 writers to report on the same event, and you will get 10 different versions. The same basic facts may form the frame, or spine, of each story, but every one will have a different rhythm, tone, and voice. Some might be full of colloquialisms and outrageously funny; others more subtly ironic; still others more formal, deadpan, or earnest. Assuming each story is to be published somewhere other than a personal blog, the writers must do more than please themselves; self-satisfaction is deadly in a writer. It's not just about entertaining and impressing yourself; your goal is to be read and understood by others. You may have a wonderfully unique way with words, and a smart, tone-sensitive editor will not strangle it out of you. On the contrary, a distinct voice is worth nurturing and celebrating. Nothing is more gratifying for writers than knowing that others enjoy reading their work and appreciate their boldness and originality.

Developing a unique style has been an aspiration of legions of feature writers since the 1960s, when people such as Tom Wolfe, Hunter S. Thompson, and Joan Didion began playing with language, inserting themselves into their stories, and applying fictional devices to non-fiction writing, creating a new form that was in fact dubbed "the new journalism." Their fearless breaking of convention fit the rebellious times and delighted literate audiences.

In "The Girl of the Year," a 1968 profile of a young New York socialite named Baby Jane Holzer (today's equivalent might be Paris Hilton), Wolfe perfectly captures the effervescent, almost breathless spirit of his subject and her milieu in an opening narrative burst:

> Bangs manes bouffants beehives Beatle caps butter faces brush-on lashes decal eyes puffy sweaters … ballerinas Knight slippers, hundreds of them, these flaming little buds, bobbing and screaming, rocketing around inside the Academy of Music Theater underneath that vast old mouldering cherub dome up there—aren't they super-marvelous![4]

Thompson was famous for entertaining readers with his own often shocking antics on the reporting trail. In "The Scum Also Rises," his 1974 *Rolling Stone* story about the resignation of disgraced President Richard

Nixon, he spends much of his time drinking in a hotel room or beside the pool, tracking events on a portable TV. There's no mistaking the tone of righteous anger or the fact that despite his wild persona, Thompson had done his research:

> The rats are deserting the ship at high speed. Even the dingbat senator from Colorado, Peter Dominick—the GOP claghorn who nominated Nixon for the Nobel Peace Prize less than two years ago—has called the president's 11th-hour admission of complicity in the Watergate cover-up "sorrowful news" ... Jesus, we need more ice and whiskey here ... The rain is still lashing my window, the dawn sky is still black and this room is damp and cold. Why is my bed covered with newspaper clips and U.S. Government Printing Office evidence books from the Nixon impeachment hearings?[5]

Didion, more understated but no less powerful a writer than Wolfe and Thompson, employs a novelist's technique in "Los Angeles Notebook" (1968), linking weather patterns to the city's—and her own—unsettled mood, in a vivid, diary-like format that moves from broad canvas to micro detail, and from one vaguely disturbing scene to the next:

> There is something uneasy in the Los Angeles air this afternoon, some unnatural stillness, some tension. What it means is that tonight a Santa Ana will begin to blow, a hot wind from the northeast whining down through the Cajon and San Gorgonio Passes, blowing up sandstorms out along Route 66 ... I have neither heard nor read that a Santa Ana is due, but I know it, and almost everyone I have seen today knows it too. We know it because we feel it. The baby frets. The maid sulks. I rekindle a waning argument with the telephone company, then cut my losses and lie down, given over to whatever it is in the air.[6]

These writers have had many imitators, for good reason if not always with good results. Writing well is harder than many who try it realize. A fine line separates brilliance and self-indulgence, crackling language and mere pretension. Getting caught up in your own thoughts or trying too hard to be profound or hilarious will backfire. You do not want to lose readers to complicated sentences that wander aimlessly around a fuzzy idea or undefined theme. Note that each writer quoted above writes perfectly understandable, if unique, sentences: Wolfe doesn't use punctuation in his opening riff, but the imagery, build-up, and subsequent information tells you everything you need to know about the unfolding scene. Thompson uses the dated term *claghorn* to describe a Colorado senator, but in the context, could we miss that it's a put-down? (I had to look it up: it refers to a 1940s radio character named Senator Claghorn, once described by *Time* magazine as "loud-mouthed, platitudinous, corn-cackling" … I think we get the picture.)

Simplicity, as much as daring, is a trusted tool of the most sophisticated writers. "The baby frets. The maid sulks." What could convey meaning more clearly than Didion's short, declarative sentences?

But before throwing out the rule book, it's best to get to know it well.

Style Basics

Editors will ask that you acquaint yourself with the style guides and general points of their publications before you write for them. No matter how distinctive your style, the way you write for a daily newspaper aimed at a wide general readership will differ from the way you write for a business publication, women's fashion monthly, literary quarterly, or web magazine. (And if you decide to freelance, versatility will be professionally rewarding.) Most publications have a style guide, detailing the basics of spelling and word choice you will be expected to follow. It's the job of copy editors to ensure that stories adhere to these rules consistently, but don't get lazy knowing this: you're more likely to be awarded future assignments if you put some effort into tailoring your prose to the publication's preferences. At the very least, learn what gets capitalized, what punctuation and abbreviations are acceptable, and what spellings the publication favours.

In Canada, we have long faced the linguistic challenge of choosing between British and American spelling and usage: *Colour* or *color*? *Centre* or *center*? *Cheque* or *check*? *Program* or *programme*? Metric or imperial? No definitive rules exist, which is why style guides are useful, if conflicting. For example, at *The Globe and Mail*, sources in the news pages—but not entertainment or fashion—are still referred to as "*Mr.* Smith."[7] Most other Canadian news organizations, which follow *The Canadian Press Stylebook*, have dropped honorifics and would refer only to "Smith."[8]

These may seem like niggling points, but they are worth your attention when you begin writing for a publication; after awhile, you will find yourself automatically adopting the spelling, grammar, and style each prefers. (And if you are unsure, look it up in the guide or ask your editor!)

Avoid Jargon

In the course of their jobs, journalists often find themselves reading government or corporate reports, and interviewing bureaucrats, politicians, scientists, and business executives. Many of these sources write and speak in what may seem to outsiders an incomprehensible code, filled with catch phrases, "buzz words," and abbreviations (such as *CMA, CMHA, CMPA, CMHC, CHEO*—it can get confusing) that clarify little. Do we really know what to make of a business claiming to offer *value-added* service, government *liaising* with stakeholders, or pharmaceutical companies and science labs boasting of their *synergy*? Some words are so overused that they've become almost meaningless: *grassroots, empowerment, sustainability*: you've no doubt heard passionate environmentalists, shrewd corporate leaders, and politicians (from the most liberal to the most conservative) utter these words, and wondered if they could possibly be talking about the same things, or if any standard definition could exist.

Those who rely on this kind of jargon may be guilty of mere linguistic laziness (which means you'll have to do some lifting for them and find comprehensible alternatives), or something more deliberate.

People who want to be journalists are, ideally, motivated to challenge governments and corporations on behalf of the general public, whose lives are affected by their actions. That's why it's critical to write in a way that readers can understand and that does not obscure the truth. In order to do that, you will no doubt find yourself decoding cryptic language, learning to pin people down when they rattle off a list of short forms, and translating jargon into plain English. *Collateral damage* equals dead civilians. Corporate *downsizing* means people losing their jobs. Be clear, even when your sources would rather you weren't. There's nothing wrong with asking someone point blank: What do you mean? If sources don't know and you don't find out, you merely pass on their undigested jargon in your written work, and readers remain unenlightened.

Avoid the Passive Voice

Just as jargon can muddy meaning, so too can the voice you choose for your sentences. Although the passive voice is not grammatically incorrect, most writing instructors will advise you to avoid it because sentences like the following sap energy from your prose and can reduce clarity.

It was decided that all the money would be kept in a personal bank account.

The tainted food was prepared on Monday.

We were told that the vehicle was safe.

In each of these sentences, a key party to the action is missing, and we are left (excuse me, the writer leaves us) with serious questions: Who decided that the money would be kept in a personal bank account? Who prepared that tainted food? And who told them the vehicle was safe? We could add this missing information and still have passive, possibly misleading and unnecessarily lumpy sentences:

It was decided by the prime minister that the money would be kept in a personal bank account.

The tainted food was prepared by the cut-rate catering company on Monday.

We were told by the used-car dealer that the vehicle was safe.

Instead, be direct:

The prime minister decided to keep the money in a private bank account.

The cut-rate catering company prepared the food on Monday.

The used-car dealer told us the vehicle was safe.

Not only will the active voice make your writing more effective from a technical standpoint, it will help you do your job as a journalist—that is, to expose wrong-doing; hold people accountable for their actions; and answer the questions readers are likely to ask.

Cut ~~the~~ Flab

Flab, clutter, extra verbiage, call it what you will, the fact remains that there's actually quite a lot of it around when it comes to the written word, and the bottom line is pretty much that writers really need to do whatever it is within their power to do, to make sure that, indeed, they make a habit of padding their prose with as little of it as they possibly can, if you get my meaning in the end.

The problem with the paragraph you just read is, of course, that readers may well have trouble discerning the meaning of such a blubbery sentence. (Feel free to turn it into an editing exercise.)

It's always a good idea to edit yourself. You can usually find places to trim and tighten a story. Both your editor and eventual readers will welcome your efforts to be concise. Do you need two adjectives to describe someone? Do you need any? Is your use of an adverb—"he says *resignedly*"—helping achieve or getting in the way of clear style? (Note: What he said in the quote should tell us he's resigned about something). Have you used a big, clunky word—*conceptualize*, for example—when a small, straightforward one—*think*, let's say—would do (better)? Have you repeated words unnecessarily? This is sometimes referred to as a word "echo" or "mirror," and will distract the reader.

> *The teacher told the students that the school's motto was To Thine Own Self Be True, but students at the school wondered if the teacher was following the motto's advice about being true to yourself. After school, teachers and students mingled and discussed the teacher's actions and decided that it was true—the teacher was a hypocrite and the school administration should confront the teacher about how she was not true to the school's own To Thine Own Self Be True motto.*

Help! You know that paragraph can be cut in half and still give us the necessary facts. Try it.

Bust That Cliché

Whose feisty brainchild was the first cliché? I'm cautiously optimistic that, at the end of the day, if we have the patience of Job, we'll know soon enough, and beat a path to that trailblazer's door. Chances are it will be a win-win situation.

Clichés are so abundant that it's hard to know where to start nipping them in the bud. I recently polled a group of freelance writers about clichés they would not miss if they never saw again. Here are some of them:

24/7	my bad
bells and whistles	nosh
brutally honest	paradigm shift
comic genius	proactive
critical mass	pushing the envelope
cut the tension with a knife	redonculous
drawing a line in the sand	rock the boat
face time	safety in numbers
fashionista	the bottom line
guru	there's a disconnect ...
'hood	thinking outside the box
_____ is the new _____	to die for
I was thinking to myself ...	touching base
leading edge, cutting edge, edgy	über
light at the end of the tunnel	voracious reader

Language can be viral; turns of phrase that once seemed fresh, funny, and original spread like wildfire (you see how easy it is to resort to them; and can you spot the twisted simile there too?), and soon everyone's writing is padded with them. The overall effect is never good.

Although it's difficult to avoid common or clichéd expressions entirely, alternatives usually exist. You can at least attempt to reduce them by scanning your written work for overused words or phrases, and replacing them with simpler, clearer, more original constructions.

See if you can improve on these examples of clichés and tired language:[9]

grind to a halt

seriously consider

in the wake of

The restaurant had a cool ambience.

It's a moot point.

The politicians were at loggerheads with each other.

Avoid Redundancy ~~and Unnecessary Repetition~~

From the Department of Redundancy Department—trim this paragraph of its clutter:

> When she got home at 12 noon, she went inside the house she lived in. While she'd been away, the husband she was married to had added on an addition. She circled around the house and found that one room was an exact replica of another. Irregardless, the work gave her full satisfaction and she was happy to show it off to invited guests.

Tensions Over Tense

It remains the general practice of newspapers to use the past tense ("he said") when quoting someone, while magazines more commonly use the present tense ("he says").

Apart from this rule, journalists have become more flexible in their use of tense, particularly in writing that we might put in the category of "literary" journalism or non-fiction. Traditionally, prose writers have used the past tense to tell their stories, but it has become more common for contemporary writers of both fiction and non-fiction to use the present tense as a means of lending immediacy to the action of their stories. The present tense can be extremely effective, but it is not necessary for every story, as C.J. Chivers demonstrates in the passage from "The School" (see page 257), which loses none of its impact by being told in the past tense. Whichever tense a writer chooses, it should always serve the story's intentions.

While it's possible to switch tenses within a story, it rarely works to do so within the same sentence or paragraph. Remember that it is your job to ensure that you never confuse readers.

> *Steve left the house at 10 and walked to work. He comes back home at 6, opens a beer and turns on the TV. Then he called his girlfriend, who says he said, why don't you order a pizza and I'll be over soon? "It was the last time I heard from him," she said in an interview. Now Steve was on the run, and he wasn't sure what to do next. "I just felt like taking a break," he says. He's not sure if he still had a job, or if his girlfriend ever wants to see him again.*

Huh? Try changing tenses so that this paragraph makes sense. One way to keep things straight, if you are going to mix your tenses, is to begin with the present, and make sure that all other time periods are either past or future relative to that initial present time.

Metaphors, Similes, and Analogies

Sometimes writers employ language techniques that go beyond the literal, and when they do it well, the result can be entertaining and enlightening.

Metaphors, you may remember from English class, are figures of speech in which one thing is used to signify another (*he was a bear of a man*). Similes are a kind of metaphor in which something is directly compared to something else (*the girls were like two peas in a pod*). Analogies explain something by noting and describing its similarity to something else (*listening to the guest speaker drone on, Bob thought of a foghorn in the night*).

In "The Persian Dub," reprinted following this chapter, author Abou Farman uses metaphors, similes, and analogies to great effect as he explores the deep cultural meaning of American westerns, dubbed in Farsi, that he remembers watching as a child growing up in Tehran, Iran: "John Wayne was not so much translated as he was alchemized by the wizards of the Persian dub into a new alloy" (metaphor). "The WASPy dryness of Katherine Hepburn dripped into Farsi like droplets of rose water" (simile). "Imagine [filmmaker] Akira Kurosawa giving Robin Williams a free hand at dubbing his masterpiece *Ran*" (analogy).

The use of metaphor, simile, and analogy is common practice in today's feature writing. See if you can spot these techniques in the passages below, taken from various stories that appeared in the Arctic issue of *The Walrus* (November 2007):

> In summertime, the two-metre-thick polar ice fractures into a kaleidoscope of floating floes, some as large as a city, others too tipsy to stand on. ("On Moving Ice," by Jon Turk)

> The maple top was whale blue, and abalone inlays shaped like flying birds dotted the rosewood frets. ("To Live and Die in Wales, Alaska," by Tony Hopfinger)

> It started like a nasty marital spat flaring up in a crowded hotel lobby. It turned into a long series of angrier spats heard around the world. The antagonists were loggers and environmentalists ... The decade-long shoving match made headlines from Washington to Tokyo. ("Hands Off," by Paul Webster and John Cathro)

> Far away, the ice makes a loud crack, like the sound of a gun going off. ("Paddling Back in Time," by Alison Pick)

> But a dead walrus, up close, is like a seagoing Jabba the Hutt. With a hide like an elephant, the colour of sand, it looks more like a protoplasmic waterbed ... This is the scary, refreshing thing about remote places like the wilderness ... they encourage the human chameleon's true colours to show themselves—not in the civil pastels of our daily lives, but in the primal blacks and whites and reds of undiluted self-interest. ("The Archetypal Walrus," by John Vaillant)

Obviously, in the right hands, figures of speech such as these serve to illuminate themes; paint vivid word pictures; make us laugh; and evoke time, place, sound, even smell. Used clumsily, they can also slow down a story, take away clarity, and make someone laugh for all the wrong reasons:

> *That goal really took the steam out of the Leafs' sails* (a mixed metaphor)

> *That goal really took the steam out of the Leafs' sails and throws them into the abyss of a losing streak* (a mixed and extended metaphor)

> *His eyes were as large as flying saucers* (a twisted simile)

By all means, be creative. But make sure you are in control of the language you use, and understand why your metaphor, analogy, or simile strengthens, rather than weakens, your story.

George Orwell's Style Rules

1. Never use a metaphor, simile or other figure of speech which you are used to seeing in print.
2. Never use a long word when a short word will do.
3. If it is possible to cut a word out, always cut it out.
4. Never use the passive where you can use the active.
5. Never use a foreign phrase, a scientific word or a jargon word if you can think of an everyday English equivalent.
6. Break any of these rules sooner than say anything outright barbarous.[10]

Break These Rules

I would not want to contradict the great George Orwell's unbeatable list of linguistic dos and don'ts above. He is right: on occasion, it's okay to break a few rules, as the writing of people such as Tom Wolfe and Hunter S. Thompson attests. Once you've mastered the basics and begin to develop your own writing style, there may well be times and places when it will work for you to do precisely that.

Writers must make many decisions when it comes time to put words on a blank page. This chapter has outlined some guidelines that should help you make those decisions as you craft words into a viable story. Spelling, grammar, and word usage are the building blocks of story composition, just as musical notes and time signatures are the basic tools of writing songs.

Yet, perfect spelling, impeccable grammar, and language clarity do not necessarily add up to a story that sings. The best writers have a sure and obvious command of the basic tools, but on another level, their ability to use language that delights and moves us is difficult to explain or deconstruct. Style isn't a matter of painting some "colour" onto a black and white canvas after the fact, or fluffing up a "serious" story with a few choice adjectives or descriptive phrases. The process of writing well is much more instinctive than that.

Style Success

You might compare becoming a good writer to learning to drive a car. In the beginning, you must work to memorize the rules of the road and consciously prompt yourself to perform all the motions of shifting gears, braking, turning, passing other cars, or parallel parking. Eventually though, a day comes when these actions are automatic and driving seems like second nature.

That sense of assurance and comfort behind the wheel probably won't come the day after you get your licence, any more than you'll feel like a fully confident writer after writing your first feature. The best way to get better is, of course, practise, practise, practise. Take the constructive criticism you receive from teachers, mentors, and editors, and incorporate it into your next story. And don't forget to read, read, read. You won't become a great or even good writer if you don't look to the masters, any more than a pianist can learn how to be an original instrumentalist without listening to those who have already achieved unique brilliance. First they imitate, then they create their own kind of music.

I could not possibly name every writer I admire here, but a favourite is Marni Jackson, one of Canada's wittiest and most intelligent non-fiction writers. She's received dozens of awards for her writing in magazines and books, and includes *The Walrus, The Globe and Mail, Rolling Stone,* and the London *Times* in her publication list. She wrote a much-loved bestseller about motherhood called *The Mother Zone,* and recently, *Pain: The Fifth Vital Sign.* What distinguishes Jackson's style is her ability to mix humour with serious intent.

Consider the tone and theme of Jackson's brilliant short essay "Veils for Western Women." It begins as follows:

> An Anglican school in England suspends a twenty-four-year-old teaching assistant for wearing a *niqab,* the Muslim head covering that leaves only the eyes exposed. France has banned the niqab in public schools. In Montreal, a YMCA clashes with its Jewish neighbours, members of a Hasidic synagogue; they want the windows of the gym frosted so their worshippers won't be exposed to the sight of skimpily clad young women mounting Stairmasters ... All over the world, there seems to be confusion about which parts of which women we ought to be able to see.[11]

Then she tips the entire debate on its head:

> But Western women have their versions of veils as well. Let us project these into the near future and imagine how Islamic cultural scholars might interpret the ruthless orthodoxy of high fashion, the pressure to expose the flesh, and the curious body coverings (and uncoverings) of the secular, middle-class, North American professional woman.[12]

What follows is a detailed description of various head and body coverings worn in this imagined near future by women of this cultural group, written in the earnest manner of an anthropology textbook, and with the same underlying satiric intent employed so famously by the eighteenth-century writer Jonathan Swift, in his classic essay "A Modest Proposal," in which he appeared to argue in all seriousness that starving Irish people should eat their own children. Swift was skewering the indifference and cruelty of the social order of his day; Jackson, in the most subtle and humorous way, is asking us to look at cultural practices that we take for granted and may not always examine with a critical eye. Among the "curious body coverings" Jackson describes is the "Niqkebab":

> A body covering for the active woman, this is an extreme high-top sneaker that extends up to the eyes, with a 146-hole lacing. The unusual feature of this garment is that while women wearing it can walk, run, and use the Stairmaster comfortably, they cannot speak clearly or carry things ...
>
> The Niqkebab has been traced back to the first woman's running shoe, invented in northern California, when women banded together in a communal effort to lose weight. They stripped tree bark from large sequoia trees, lined it with spongy moss, laced the objects to their feet, and discovered that they could run long distances in this marvellous new footgear. The word "marathon" may have derived from the term "mere-a-thong," which also come into use at that time.[13]

She also describes the "Lululemabab":

> This Western "active wear" with strong links to Eastern religions is worn by urban women who gather in "gyms" to practise yoga or Pilates. Their rituals are often accompanied by recorded chants or music involving Andean pipes. The coverings are monochromatic, highly pliable, and must not be buttoned. Lululem is thought to be the name of a Hawaiian god famous for his flexibility; some gyms display icons of Lululem in a backbend with all his toes in his mouth. Women wearing this garb often carry rolled-up rubber mats on which they kneel during their prayer sessions.[14]

Note that the writing itself is not self-consciously "funny"—the humour lies in the concept, and the way a perfectly plain description—women do gather in gyms to practise yoga and Pilates—suddenly leaps into something we know is a stretch—the Hawaiian god Lululem. A writer of Jackson's intellectual agility and linguistic finesse makes this kind of writing look easy; in reality, it's supremely difficult, a style and voice that takes years to craft and perfect.

When Jackson first began writing, she says she didn't receive a universally great reception from editors, who didn't always get her quirky interests and approach. But somewhere along the way, an editor noticed that this girl could write, and gave her the opportunity to do just that. Her hard work and willingness to take risks paid off. And now, in the pages of many magazines and books, we see the gloriously stylish results of a writing talent well nurtured.

So, be brave—put words on blank pages and see what happens. Learn the rules of the English language and, now and then, break them. That's the enjoyable part of being a writer, to which Strunk and White alluded. Write well—with care, passion, courage, and humility—and one day, you'll delight an eager audience of your own.

Discussion Questions

1. Read "The Persian Dub" by Abou Farman (pages 276–283). Farman opens and closes his essay with scenes constructed from his personal experience. How do these scenes relate to the overall theme of the story?
2. In what ways does Farman employ humour as a means of illuminating his theme?
3. What "elements of style" make this an effective piece of writing?

Notes

1. C.J. Chivers, "The School," in *The Best American Crime Reporting 2007*, ed. Linda Fairstein, Otto Penzler, and Thomas Cook (New York: Harper Perennial, 2007), pp. 131–86. Originally published in *Esquire*, June 2006.
2. William Strunk Jr. and E.B. White, *The Elements of Style*, 2nd ed. (New York: Longman, 1972), p. 59.
3. William Strunk Jr. and E.B. White, *The Elements of Style*, 4th ed. (New York: Longman, 2000), p. 67.
4. Tom Wolfe, "The Girl of the Year," in *The Kandy-Kolored Tangerine-Flake Streamline Baby* (New York: Farrar, Straus & Giroux, 1987), p. 204.
5. Hunter S. Thompson, "The Scum Also Rises," in *The Art of Fact: A Historical Anthology of Literary Journalism*, ed. Kevin Kerrane and Ben Yagoda (New York: Scribner, 1998), p. 304. Originally published in *Rolling Stone*, October 10, 1974.
6. Joan Didion, "Los Angeles Notebook," in *The Art of Fact: A Historical Anthology of Literary Journalism*, ed. Kevin Kerrane and Ben Yagoda (New York: Scribner, 1998), p. 480. Originally published in Joan Didion, *Slouching toward Bethlehem* (New York: Dell, 1968).
7. J.A. McFarlane and Warren Clements, *The Globe and Mail Style Book* (Toronto: McClelland and Stewart, 2003).

8. Patti Tasko, *The Canadian Press Stylebook* (Toronto: The Canadian Press, 2004).

9. Adapted from the clichés mentioned in Tasko, *The Canadian Press Stylebook*, p. 157.

10. George Orwell, "Politics and the English Language," in *Modern Classics Penguin Essays of George Orwell* (London: Penguin, 2000), p. 359. Originally published in *Horizon*, April 1946.

11. Marni Jackson, "Veils for Western Women," *Walrus*, February 2007.

12. Ibid.

13. Ibid.

14. Ibid.

"The Persian Dub"

In a memoir of 1970s Tehran, Abou Farman recalls John Wayne, Cowboy Bazi and the "genius club of dub" that remade the West in Iran's image.

Abou Farman, "The Persian Dub." *Maisonneuve* magazine, December 13, 2006, 32. Reprinted by permission of the author.

Growing up in Tehran, Iran, I spent a great deal of my time playing Cowboys and Indians. We called it Cowboy *Bazi*, or cowboy play, and I always played one of the Indians. They were the underdogs who lost battles on TV every weekend, whose defeat seemed as inevitable as bedtime, but who still gave their best with nothing but bows and arrows. In a bathing suit, with a pigeon feather in my arm band, I slapped my palms against puckered lips to ululate just as I had seen in the movies. I fashioned my own arrows, whittling straightness into willow branches, and aimed them up at crows perched on the bent peaks of cypress trees. I once charred a blanket trying to send up smoke signals, and my brother still remembers the time my arrow wobbled off course, almost taking out his left eye. I took the role seriously. When grown-ups asked, "Well, good little boy, what do you want to be when you grow up?" I would answer, "I want to be a Crimson Skin."

In Farsi, the Persian language, Native Americans are called "Crimson Skins." *Sorkh*—as opposed to *ghermez*, a shade of red that applies more to cherries and women's lipstick—has a positive connotation, representing the colour of good health, much like "rosy cheeks" does in English. When you jump over the Zoroastrian fires the week before Iranian New Year, you ask the flames to blaze the jaundiced pallor from your skin and burnish it instead with their crimson glow.

The slight slippage from red to crimson allows a little more romantic wiggle room. But still, the term, with its focus on skin colour, was probably an adoption of Victorian racial classifications. The peculiar tension between the Iranian sense of historical superiority and our diminished contemporary reality made a good nesting ground for these kinds of discourses—theories of the Aryan race, theories that group together Indo-European languages and myths, theories of civilization. Theories, in short, that lumped us together with Europeans and Americans took root quickly in the fertile soil of a once-grand empire that had little left to boast about. If the present did not say much in our favour, history was squarely on our side. And so we considered ourselves white, as opposed to black, brown, yellow or, for that matter, crimson. Anything to remove us from that miserable modern lump called the Third World.

∾∾∾

I may have preferred the more romantic role of Crimson Skin, but the central figure in our games was John Wayne. In the Iran of the 1970s, John Wayne was a household name. His swagger was adopted by tough guys in the street and his gunslinging was mimicked in school yards. For us he was neither actor nor fictional character; he was The Cowboy. But Wayne's place in Iranian culture is even more special and surprising, for the persona we really liked was not so much "John Wayne the Hollywood Hero" as "John Wayne the Persian Dub." Mention The Duke to anyone who lived in Iran during that period and you'll end up talking about Persian voice-overs.

It was the 1970s and Western icons were available for purchase and idolatry. Elvis, Sophia Loren, the Beatles—and later, Farrah Fawcett, Pink Floyd, the Eagles and the Bionic Man also figured on the list. You could buy their posters in little stores that sold Americana. This was also when Iran got its third television channel. Channels one and two broadcasted in Farsi; channel three, in English. But whatever the language, all three spoke the idiom of the state, the royal kingdom of Iran. However, the third channel—the Armed Forces Radio and Television Service—was commonly called the American channel.

It sounds naive to our ears today—accustomed as we are to corporate über-identities like MTV, Globo and CNN—yet the American channel was the perfect name for a network whose programming and purse were filled by the US government, the shah of Iran's best friend. Now, instead of just local sports, wrinkle-free news reports read in Farsi and bedtime children's stories intoned by a doe-eyed woman with a sleeping pill of a voice, we had *The Banana Splits Adventure Hour, Starsky and Hutch, Donny and Marie, The Mary Tyler Moore Show* and more—all delivered with the original twang of American English. It's hard to say what it was, but something about that twang resonated with us. Combining a rubbery tongue with nasal exhalations, we all "twanged"— usually not saying anything meaningful; maybe not even using real words. We "twanged" as a posture and that was meaning enough.

Mine wasn't much of a TV household. My mother, brimming with pedagogical urgency, lectured on everything she believed to be harmful in the universe, which included air pollution, sweets, neon signs, bad manners, corporal punishment as a child-rearing strategy, popular music and, of course, television. Our TV-watching time was restricted to an hour a day on school days and two hours on weekends. In the early days, the restriction didn't really matter: there was only so much worth watching anyway. And the black-and-white TV set—white plastic casing, metal knobs clacking into place, screen too small to please a group—was not seductive.

I have only a few TV-watching memories linked to that set—the most vivid being the 1974 World Cup finals. Gathered in our large living room, with a two-ton chandelier hanging above our heads and a collection of Iranian and Western art surrounding us, we rooted for Johan Cruyff and the Dutch side (wearing what appeared to be, in black and white, dark grey jerseys) against "Kaiser" Franz Beckenbauer and the West Germans (white jerseys with black shorts). A minute into the game, Cruyff was brought down in the box and the Dutch were up by one. With a start like this, we couldn't wait for the next eighty-nine minutes. Then with a merciless trill, the image was sucked out of the TV, slowly receding to a glowing white point at the center of the screen until even that faded, leaving us without a flicker of hope. It was a city-wide blackout and by the time the electricity was restored, the Dutch side was down 2–1. The good guys in dark grey seemed shell-shocked, and a little later the game was over. Just like that, our hopes terminated with another merciless trilling sound—the referee's final whistle.

A few years later, we got our first colour television. It was a Grundig and it seemed gigantic sitting on a black-and-silver stand, sleek and tubular like something from *The Jetsons*. The colour bar printed on the manual fulfilled its magic promise of red, green and blue as soon as we switched it on. The grass on football pitches was greener than any grass I'd seen, and the lipstick on the news anchors' lips glowed redder than a neon heart at the bazaar. On the Grundig, everything looked more real than reality.

To top it off, it came with a remote control. Action at a distance was a miracle. As soon as footsteps approached, we scrambled for the little red button, sinking the beautiful reds and greens into glassy darkness and restoring ourselves to innocence—mere kids leafing through a book or playing backgammon. Our TV-watching habits changed. When asked how many hours of TV we had watched, we mumbled our first lies.

John Wayne's popularity in Iran started in the late 1950s, a decade or so before I was born. But it was in the later context of the 1970s that his reputation really spread and, at least for children, became a part of everyday life. Every weekend we could bank on a western, from classics like *Bonanza* and *Rawhide* to the spaghettis. It was a time when television was blurring the border between traditional roles and fictional identities.

Wayne shot to stardom in Iran along with Sophia Loren in *Legend of the Lost*, but his status had little to do with sexy co-stars and even less to do with good cinema. It was, as I said, the "dub" that made the man. John Wayne was not so much translated as he was alchemized by the wizards of the Persian dub into a new alloy—a man who walked like a cowboy but talked like a dude from southern Tehran. The Cowboy was turned into a character you might meet in a kebab house, wolfing down a mountain of rice and a couple of lamb skewers, wiping his enormous moustache clean with the back of his hand.

The Cowboy's tough-but-tender talk was delivered as the slang of downtown knife-fighters and hero-thugs, an urban subculture known as *jahel*: men with a strict code of honour not unlike lonesome Wild West heroes. In keeping with the *jahel* tradition, the Iranian Wayne and his gang insulted the honour of parents and family members alike, swore by Ali and Allah and addressed each other with the most diverse, absurd and expressive range of epithets they could find. Every time an actor turned his back, the dubbers, freed from any obligation to sync the lips, grabbed the opportunity to throw in some slangy insults: corpse washer, stinking vulture. And during gunfights there was always time for *jahel* philosophies—while ducking bullets, Wayne looks over at a drunk on a porch and mumbles, "Lucky bastard. So totally oblivious to the world." In *Rio Bravo*, Wayne often addresses his partner Stumpy, the lame, old prison guard, as a "seedless fig." And when he and Dean Martin are alarmed by a creaking sound, only to discover a stabled mule, there ensues between the sheriff and his sidekick a repartee of donkey-related swear words—of which Farsi is particularly rich, the donkey being a key cultural trope. All this done with cheery disregard for the script and the authority of its creators.

Like many westerns, Wayne's films unfolded in a space where the modern state—the omniscient, abstract rule of law—was still struggling to establish its version of order over local power and authority. Wayne understood this in-between space, being neither entirely part of the order nor apart from it. Above the red shirt, brown vest and the bandana around his neck, he gazed boldly into the camera with a half-smile, subtle and clever. That uneasy sincerity sealed a pact between himself and his audience by showing his awareness of the camera, of fame made through the camera, of the pose as a pose. Rather than trying to cover up that crack in the fiction, as his contemporaries did, or ironizing it entirely (as our contemporaries might), Wayne sat on the fence, managing at once to be two types of people: himself and The Cowboy, present and past in one body. He was a pose that had become itself without entirely erasing what it was before—an appealing prospect to Iranians stuck halfway between authenticity and modernity, wondering how to transform one into the other.

The man who dubbed Wayne was a pharmacist by profession and, like many other dubbers, an aspiring actor. His name is Iraj Doostdar, and he and his team were the genius club of dub. Theirs was not the only good dub in town, but it was the best. A different crew employed a similar style of dubbing to create Peter Falk's brilliantly stuttered and goofy Columbo—a detective whose inner being found expression in the outer world only with great difficulty. Young viewers like myself and my friends—struggling to translate ephemeral inner selves into solid figures in a confusing and changing world—could relate. When I saw an episode of *Columbo* in English, years later, I was stunned at how boring and flat it was. The Persian-language version felt so perfect, it was the original that came across as the bad dub.

The art of the Persian dub has an unexpected lineage. When talkies came to Iran in the 1930s, distributors continued to treat them like silent movies, interrupting the films with occasional he-said-she-said text panels. But literacy was low, so professional reciters often paced up and down theatre aisles belting out reductive translations, in competition with sunflower seed vendors. Another strategy for domesticating foreign cinema was to splice local pop culture into imported films. When a cowboy entered a saloon, for example, the doors swinging in his wake might suddenly fade to a popular and sultry singer, belly dancing her way through a handkerchief-waving, song-and-wiggle routine as though she were a stage act inside the local Texan joint. Then the film would seamlessly wipe back to the western drama of cheats at the poker table. No one complained about incongruence or bastardization. The downtown audience was quite happy with the pastiche.

Alex Aghababian, an Armenian Iranian, put out the first successful Persian dubs in Italy. He and a handful of other artistically-minded Iranian students tackled the works of Italian neo-realist directors, and sent the films back to Iran for distribution. In their goal of matching lips and making voices belong in the bodies, their innovative strategy was to sacrifice true meaning. They replaced the original words with nonsensical, rhythmic syllables similar to the nonsensical American "twang" we had spoken as children. The sounds carried no literal meaning, but they matched Marcelo Mastroianni's lips perfectly and resembled the kind of mumbled inward conversation people often have with themselves. By careful repetition of the same sounds throughout the film, distinct character traits emerged. This style established such a precedent that as more and more studios in Iran began to make their own dubs, there was an entrenched obligation to ignore the integrity of the original.

In fact, when they stuck to the original, Persian dubs failed, regardless of genre. Jerry Lewis, already working an extreme slapstick angle to begin with, was amplified into unbearable silliness. In Laurence Olivier's version of *Hamlet*, the prince's existential crises poured out like complaints on a daytime soap; and the WASPy dryness of Katherine Hepburn dripped into Farsi like droplets of rose water—wet, scented and sweet.

We were clearly much better at stealing than imitating. When the three soldiers in Stanley Kubrick's *Paths of Glory* are being led out to execution, the Persian dub has them pleading for their lives—pitifully, comically—in the vernacular of downtown Tehran. They are begging to kiss the hands and feet of the colonel, to be his slave, his sacrificial kid. They ask him to "get down from his donkey" (stop being so stubborn) and spare their worthless lives. Imagine Akira Kurosawa giving Robin Williams a free hand at dubbing his masterpiece *Ran*.

What made the best dubs so good was that they added another register to the film, a metacommentary that created and revealed subtexts in the films. One classic sequence takes place in *The War Wagon*, an average film with two big stars, John Wayne and Kirk Douglas, as untrusting partners. Douglas is a womanizer and slick gunslinger who'd shoot his mother in the back; he has just left two Asian prostitutes to confirm a deal with Wayne. Like so many womanizers, there's a touch of dandyism in Douglas' obsession with his looks and the way he cares for his clothes. Here, he's wearing a shiny silk robe with an elaborate Asian dragon stitched onto the back, while Wayne, who is shaving, is in a plain, full-body undergarment with a holster buckled around his waist. Wayne explains that the gun is always with him because, these days, you can't trust anyone. It's the typical line—the most obvious and predictable comment that anyone could type into a script. But then, as Douglas turns to exit, showing us the dragon on his robe, we hear Wayne's off-screen Persian voice whisper something like, "Well, check out the dragon." Obviously not in the original, this is an under-the-breath, catty comment—a perfect subversion of the predictable, manly Hollywood line that preceded it.

Then it's Douglas' turn. In his own room, he stops for a moment to mentally register the deal and ponder Wayne's comment about trust. He is pensive and amused—represented through the usual raised eyebrow, wrinkled forehead and upturned corner of the lip. He doesn't say anything in the original. But in the Persian dub, when Douglas turns and takes off his robe, you hear his Persian voice say, in self-admiration, "Now that's what I call a great body." It's the beginning of what will develop into a very strong homoerotic relationship between the two half-outlaws, who keep addressing each other as "my love" in the Persian dub.

The dubs often reframed the films through a disembodied voice-of-the-spectator strategy. These are side comments that a viewer, rather than an actor, might make. For example, some secondary character always took note of Wayne's height, and the sexiness of heroines was occasion for playful remarks. As Dean Martin is being shaved by the delicate, razor-wielding hands of Angie Dickinson, a John Wayne-sounding voice from off-screen moans, "Oh, I'd die to be hurting like your beard, Dude." When I first heard lines like these (I feel utterly incapable of retranslating the translations and transmitting any sense of the rhetorical depths they plumbed), they seemed to float out of the screen with an ambiguous quality—part of the film, but also part of someone's reaction to the film. Those bits of dialogue, spoken in the dubbed voice of the characters but not from their mouths, sounded more like a running commentary by a comic friend sitting next to you on a weekend afternoon watching TV.

The Persian dub died a slow death in the late 1970s with the spread of corporate notions of ownership, stricter enforcement of copyright, a growing sense of loyalty to the original and a swelling class of globally aware consumers who demanded nothing but "VO" (*version originale*). The Islamic Revolution of 1979 hammered in the final unironic nail. During the ayatollah's early years, when films from the West were banned and unavailable and the dubs were locked up deep in the archives, a few enterprising people smuggled in westerns and other films, and found a way of overlaying a new dialogue track onto VHS cassettes. The result: on the streets of Tehran today, you can find bootlegged copies of *Rio Bravo* with credits and subtitles in Italian and flat, literal dialogue dubbed in Farsi.

The glory of the Persian dub, while it lasted, was that it did not hide the artifice of film or its theatrical, scripted elements. On the contrary; by showing that the original lines were made up just as much as the dubbed ones, it seemed to acknowledge something even more postmodern: that social roles, as much as acting roles, depend on artifice, and that perhaps all cultural forms develop through acts of mistranslation. There were countless invented lines per film, but none of them were meant to fool anyone. All we knew was that the original didn't matter. Seeing the Persian dubbers get away with one more side comment, one more joke, one more invented aphorism, brought us closer to the film in a conspiratorial kind of way. It allowed us to own it.

Running around an Iranian garden in six-gallon hats, pistols, feathers and war paint, we were reinventing cultures that had themselves been invented by television, piling layers of imagination overtop of the other. Our social identity was no longer an accumulation of our past, but rather a gleaning activity carried out by picking up stranded objects here and there—objects made not in experience but in studios, slowly eroding the notion that having a history was even necessary. Life itself was a Persian dub.

So many skins, so many roles. It is only now—years and continents away, separated by identities produced and patented by political and corporate fundamentalists—that playing Cowboys and Indians in a garden in Tehran appears odd, like something outside of the natural course of events, or an episode from a dream vaguely recalled in the morning. Now, with the voices of childhood filtered through the claims of history, I hear Montesquieu's famous question—How can one be a Persian?—echo in on itself: "*Comment peut-on être Persane?*" has always been the same question as "*Comment peut-on être Cowboy?*"

When I visit my mother in London, I find myself, heavy-footed again, in the silt of translation. On the console, she has placed a framed, black-and-white picture of me when I was about nine. I know the picture and remember its occasion. It was the day they dressed me up as a cowboy. The adults, all members of a Europeanized elite, decided at some point that my brother made a great Marcello Mastroianni. So they gave him a fake moustache and a cigarette. My cousin was cast as Gina Lollobrigida, and her brother as the most civilized of all self-invented Americans, Cary Grant. There wasn't much of a corner left for me in that love triangle, so they stuffed me into a checkered shirt and a cowboy hat. This was their fantasy world and my aunt took pictures. Down on one knee, my head cocked, I'm taking aim with a toy revolver. Despite everything I lived and imagined in my own world of Sioux and Cherokee, despite everything I care to remember now of those days, that picture is what has survived: a Cowboy, shooting a gun at someone outside the frame—possibly a Crimson Skin—way off in the distance, crouching somewhere inside an untranslatable segment of time.

PART FOUR

Rights and Responsibilities

CHAPTER TEN

Truth and the Storyteller: Ethics in Non-fiction

Ivor Shapiro

In the light of everything you have learned in the preceding chapters about interviewing, observation, and writing, consider now the following opening passage in a story written a century ago:

> I had the story, bit by bit, from various people, and, as generally happens in such cases, each time it was a different story. If you know Starkfield, Massachusetts, you know the post-office. If you know the post-office you must have seen the man drive up to it, drop the reins on his hollow-backed bay and drag himself across the brick pavement to the white colonnade; and you must have asked who he was.
>
> It was there that, several years ago, I saw him for the first time; and the sight pulled me up sharp. Even then he was the most striking figure in Starkfield, though he was but the ruin of a man. It was not so much his great height that marked him, for the "natives" were easily singled out by their lank longitude from the stockier foreign breed: it was the careless powerful look he had, in spite of a lameness checking each step like the jerk of a chain. There was something bleak and unapproachable in his face, and he was so stiffened and

grizzled that I took him for an old man and was surprised to hear that he was not more than fifty-two. I had this from Harmon Gow, who had driven the stage from Bettsbridge to Starkfield in pre-trolley days and knew the chronicle of all the families on his line.

"He's looked that way ever since he had his smash-up; and that's twenty-four years ago come next February," Harmon threw out between reminiscent pauses.

The "smash-up" it was—I gathered from the same informant—which, besides drawing the red gash across the man's forehead, had so shortened and warped his right side that it cost him a visible effort to take the few steps from his buggy to the post-office window. He used to drive in from his farm every day at about noon, and as that was my own hour for fetching my mail I often passed him in the porch or stood beside him while we waited on the motions of the distributing hand behind the grating. I noticed that, though he came so punctually, he seldom received anything but a copy of the Bettsbridge Eagle, which he put without a glance into his sagging pocket....

Every one in Starkfield knew him and gave him a greeting tempered to his own grave mien; but his taciturnity was respected and it was only on rare occasions that one of the older men of the place detained him for a word. When this happened he would listen quietly, his blue eyes on the speaker's face, and answer in so low a tone that his words never reached me; then he would climb stiffly into his buggy, gather up the reins in his left hand and drive slowly away in the direction of his farm.

"It was a pretty bad smash-up?" I questioned Harmon, looking after the man's retreating figure, and thinking how gallantly his lean brown head, with its shock of light hair, must have sat on his strong shoulders before they were bent out of shape.

"Wust kind," my informant assented. "More'n enough to kill most men...."

"He looks as if he was dead and in hell now!"

Harmon drew a slab of tobacco from his pocket, cut off a wedge and pressed it into the leather pouch of his cheek. "Guess he's been in Starkfield too many winters. Most of the smart ones get away."[1]

It's a vivid, evocative start to a sad, compelling account. Notice, for instance, how precisely the narrator describes his mysterious protagonist and the town of Starkfield; notice how some great tragedy—the "smash-up"—is foreshadowed but not explained. One must read on—and of course one does—to find out how the man at centre stage turned into a "ruin" through enduring "too many winters" but one tragic season in particular. It's an unputdownable tale, and it rests on an intriguing character and a gripping turn in the events of his life. In short, it's a terrific story. A *great* story.

But it's not journalism.

That's quite okay, because the passage you just read is from a work of fiction—a powerful short novel named *Ethan Frome* by the great American observer of her people and time, Edith Wharton.

And, by the way, I cheated, removing from the passage above the name of the novel's eponymous protagonist and substituting, in three places, "the man('s)." I did it to keep some readers on the hook and thinking it a work of journalism, until I chose to reveal the contrary.

That's okay, too, isn't it? After all, Wharton is long dead and her work long out of copyright, so no one will be suing me. And I did it for a good reason—to enhance the effect on you, my reader—and no one got hurt, so there's nothing wrong with my changing a word or two. Is there?

Welcome to the complicated world of chapter 10, where we will look at the sometimes tricky relationship between journalists' values and principles, on the one hand, and the art and craft of non-fiction reporting and writing, on the other. Up until now, this book has been mostly about technique, and for the most part the advice you've been given in it has been, intentionally, forthright and straightforward. Of course, almost everything in this book is a matter of opinion, but the views we've presented here have largely rested upon hard-won experience and careful research. So you can feel comfortable about placing a certain amount of trust in the advice we've offered. "Do all this," the book has seemed to be saying, "and you'll be okay."

And hey, maybe you will. Or not. Because there's a bit more to being a feature writer—more to being a journalist of any kind—than getting your technique down.

Let's take another, more lingering, look at the *Ethan Frome* passage above. If you didn't recognize it immediately, you may well have been fooled into thinking that it was a journalist's work, and a fine piece of feature writing at that. After all, from the opening line it's clear that the narrator (who later turns out to be a man visiting Starkfield to do some work) is a mere reporter, rather than a participant in the events he's about to describe. "Bit by bit," the reporter is piecing together Frome's story—or rather, "this vision of his story" (as the narrator, later in the novella, is modest enough to call it).

Piecing together visions of other people's stories, bit by bit, is exactly what a feature writer does. Some bare facts (a "smash-up" happened 24 years ago with a lifetime of consequences); some opinions ("Guess he's been in Starkfield too many winters," says local source Harmon Gow); some closely recorded details ("it was the careless powerful look he had, in spite of a lameness checking each step like the jerk of a chain"); a subtle but consistent authorial point of view ("There was something bleak and unapproachable in his face, and he was so stiffened and grizzled that I took him for an old man").

Glad You Asked!   Keep It Legal

Q: What must a feature writer know about the law in Canada?
A: Well, you need to know the basics, but it doesn't take a law degree to spot possible legal problems when researching and writing feature stories.

Here are some media-law tips on what to watch for—and what to avoid—to keep the lawyers at bay.

Libel. Does the story damage a person's reputation or tarnish someone's character and, if it does, is there evidence to back up the allegations being made? A libel is a false statement that tarnishes the reputation of a person or company—portraying someone as a crook, a liar, a racist, or incompetent at their job. The best way to spot a potential libel? Think about how you would react if the same things were being said—without justification—about you.

Truth is a defence if the target of a statement sues for damages, but bear in mind that the evidence must come from reliable and credible sources. And you're not off the hook if you simply quote someone else making a libelous statement—writers and media outlets are responsible for every word they publish or broadcast.

Contempt of court. When a criminal case is before the courts, journalists must take care not to imply the person charged with an offence is guilty. Judges have the power to fine those who reveal information or express opinions that could affect the outcome of a trial. The timing of the report, the potential damage it could cause, and whether the case will be tried by a jury are all factors to consider when assessing the risk of being cited for contempt.

There's less risk of prejudicing cases heard by a judge sitting without a jury. And timing is crucial. Reporting that a defendant has a criminal record when an arrest is made or many months before trial, for instance, is unlikely to undermine someone's right to a fair trial. The same information published in the midst of a jury trial could trigger a mistrial and a prosecution for contempt.

Publication bans. Legislation also restricts what can be published or broadcast about court proceedings. Routine *Criminal Code* bans are imposed on evidence presented at bail hearings and preliminary inquiries to prevent jurors from being influenced by media reports before a case comes to trial. There is also an automatic ban on reporting trial sessions held in the jury's absence. These bans are temporary, allowing journalists to report this material once the jury begins to deliberate or after a verdict as been reached.

It's a fine example of the seductive similarity between writing a feature work of journalism, on the one hand, and writing a short story of fiction, on the other. The best feature writing takes many lessons from the styles and conventions of literature. Take, for instance, the opening of the feature by Stephanie Nolen that is reprinted following this chapter:

Other *Criminal Code* bans protect the privacy of victims of crime and witnesses. They are common in sexual assault cases and prevent disclosure of names as well as other information that could reveal the person's identity. These bans are permanent. Only a judge can reverse the ban, so a journalist who interviews the victim of a sexual offence cannot use that person's name, even if the subject agrees to be identified. The victim can make a formal request to a court to lift the ban, and such requests are usually granted.

The *Youth Criminal Justice Act* protects the names of young people between the ages of 12 and 17 who are charged with an offence, as well as victims and witnesses under the age of 17. Those convicted of murder and other serious crimes can usually be named, and there are provisions for seeking permission to name both offenders and the victims of homicide.

Child protection hearings, public inquiries, and other proceedings may be subject to bans on evidence or the identities of those involved. Writers who suspect a ban could apply should consult the relevant legislation or seek legal advice. Judges also have the power to impose custom-made bans to deal with situations where the *Criminal Code* or other statutes do not apply. For example, if two persons charged with the same offence were tried separately, the judge at the first trial may prohibit the media from identifying the co-accused who has yet to stand trial. Bans like these must restrict the disclosure of as little information as possible to protect the constitutional right of freedom of the press.

Confidential sources. Be careful what you promise. Canadian law does not give journalists a blanket right to withhold the names of sources. While the courts recognize that sources may demand confidentiality to protect their jobs or even their lives, a journalist can be ordered to identify a source in order to solve a crime or resolve a legal dispute. A journalist who refuses to identify a confidential source in defiance of a court order may be fined or imprisoned for contempt. While such steps are rarely taken, journalists should consult their editors before promising to protect a source. It's prudent to negotiate an exit strategy requiring the source to come forward if the journalist is threatened with punishment. And make sure sources know that if they lie or provide false information, all bets are off.

Dean Jobb

Further reading: Dean Jobb, *Media Law for Canadian Journalists* (Toronto: Emond Montgomery, 2006), and the "Law" page at J-Source.ca.

KIPKELION, KENYA—With the sun barely over the edge of the valley, the colours on the hills were muffled. The banana leaves were dull green, the sugar cane stalks pale yellow. And so the flames, when we saw them flare in first one house, then a second, then streets and streets on fire, were shocking, vivid orange, more alive than anything around....

There were people all along the side of the road, but no one spoke. The only sound was the dull thud as they flipped over the fallen tin sheets that used to be roofs, looking for anything to salvage. The sight of the ruins seemed to stun people into silence.

I climbed through the rubble and held out a hand to a young man who stood in the smouldering remains of his small electronics shop. "*Pole, pole sana,*" I said, Kiswahili for "very sorry," a phrase I had been using incessantly in the past few days. There was nothing to save, no trace of the 300,000 shillings—$4,350—that Jose Muiruri, 25, had saved up and invested. Next door was the shell of his family's house.

Then it got worse: Behind it, he found the body of a young woman. She was so badly burned that he could not tell who she was; her skirt and sweater were reduced to ash. But the baby, perhaps a year old, whom she clutched to her chest, small head tucked beneath her chin, was still discernible. Mr. Muiruri looked, and turned away. There was no one to help, nowhere to take their bodies. He needed to gather his family and get out.[2]

For comparison's sake, here's the opening of a report by Jeffrey Gettleman in the news pages of *The New York Times* that same weekend:

NAKURU, Kenya—Nairobi, the capital of Kenya, may seem calm, but anarchy reigns just two hours away.

In Nakuru, furious mobs rule the streets, burning homes, brutalizing people and expelling anyone not in their ethnic group, all with complete impunity.

On Saturday, hundreds of men prowled a section of the city with six-foot iron bars, poisoned swords, clubs, knives and crude circumcision tools. Boys carried gladiator-style shields and women strutted around with sharpened sticks.

The police were nowhere to be found. Even the residents were shocked.

"I've never seen anything like this," said David Macharia, a bus driver.

One month after a deeply flawed election, Kenya is tearing itself apart along ethnic lines, despite intense international pressure on its leaders to compromise and stop the killings.

Nakuru, the biggest town in the beautiful Rift Valley, is the scene of a mass migration now moving in two directions. Luos are headed west, Kikuyus are headed east, and packed buses with mattresses strapped on top pass one another in the road, with the bewildered children of the two ethnic groups staring out the windows at one another.

In the past 10 days, dozens of people have been killed in Molo, Narok, Kipkelion, Kuresoi, and now Nakuru, a tourist gateway which until a few days ago was considered safe.[3]

There's nothing wrong with Gettleman's story in the *Times*: it is an important, rigorously reported stock-taking of developments in Kenya and has the same purpose as Nolen's in the *Globe*—to explore how things got so bad so fast. But Nolen's story is distinguished by an approach that reads like fiction—a fast-paced first-person narrative of descent into danger. Fear heightens with every passing paragraph, much as it clearly did with every passing mile covered by the writer and her travelling companions. The piece rests on keenly observed facts and sensitivity to style, tone, and pacing. This kind of narrative creativity is part of what distinguishes the feature-writing form from even the best news writing.

But it's risky, too.

There are many similarities between the best fiction and the best journalism; both are rooted in careful observation, research, sympathy for the human condition, and careful thinking. Both are characterized by writing that paints pictures and draws the reader inward and onward by means of scenes, plot, character development, voice, tone, and point of view. And both operate and succeed at two distinct levels—that of narrative (where the audience asks, in the literary critic Northrop Frye's words, "How will this story turn out?") and that of theme ("What is the point of this story?").[4] But there are important differences, too—the most obvious of which is that good journalists don't make stuff up. Wharton's *Ethan Frome* can itself be read as a meditation on the conflict between the need to compile a coherent narrative—a "vision" of a story—and the need for scrupulous accuracy.[5] The narrator in *Frome* clearly wants more than facts—he wants interpretation, he wants to see how characters formed, he wants to understand the sequence of events that led to Ethan Frome's present condition and circumstances. He wants truth, you might say—truth in its fullness—not merely a collection of truths.

But telling the truth is harder, even, than collecting truths. "Bit by bit," a journalist or historian may harvest facts and assemble them into something that seems like a story, with each fact connecting to, affecting, and perhaps effecting the next fact.[6] But the resulting patchwork will always comprise only one of several possible stories or "visions," a fabrication of intuitions and conclusions. And the more narratively coherent it seems, the more likely it is to reflect the writer's will and subjective interpretation as much as, or more than, the objective facts of the case.

If Edith Wharton had come to Starkfield, Massachusetts as a reporter—a feature writer—she'd have had to talk to a lot of people before someone made a cogent, light-shedding remark such as, "Guess he's been in Starkfield too many winters. Most of the smart ones get away." This is a very important quote because the work's central theme paints lower-class small-town life as a prison, and winter as its malicious guard, a ravisher of youthful passion and of human freedom and power. "When I had been there a little longer," the narrator says soon after the introductory passage,

> and had seen this phase of crystal clearness followed by long stretches of sunless cold; when the storms of February had pitched their white tents about the devoted village and the wild cavalry of March winds had charged down to their support; I began to understand why Starkfield emerged from its six months' siege like a starved garrison capitulating without quarter. Twenty years earlier the means of resistance must have been far fewer, and the enemy in command of almost all the lines of access between the beleaguered villages; and, considering these things, I felt the sinister force of Harmon's phrase: "Most of the smart ones get away."[7]

So our hypothetical feature writer really would need to find a quote something very like that sinister foreshadowing thing about winter and the smart ones that get away. But what if, in dozens of interviews, no one said it? What a pity that would be for the theme—the angle—implanting itself more securely in the reporter's mind with every passing day. What if you, for instance, were that reporter and your interview with Harmon Gow went something like this:

You: Frome looks a lot older than 52.
Harman Gow: Seen some tough times, has Ethan.
You: You mean the smash-up?
Gow: Mm.
You: How bad was it?
Gow: Wust kind. More'n enough to kill most men. *[Trails off, looks at town-hall clock.]* I got to go get my horse shod.
You: What was that winter like, when the smash-up happened?
Gow: Seen worse. Seen better.
You: Remember anything about that winter, specifically?
Gow: Nope. Guess I been in Starkfield too many winters. *[Looks at clock again.]*

You [increasingly desperate]: And Ethan Frome?

Gow: Him too. Ethan and I sh'ld have gone south years ago. Most of the smart ones get away. Like you, f'r instance. *[Chuckles, slaps you on the back.]* Guess I got to go now. *[Gets on horse and rides away.]*

Well, now. After all those interviews, all those days in Starkfield questioning dozens of people with little to say, all those nights eating dried-out beef and mashed potatoes in the single hotel's dining room, couldn't that steadfast reporter, "you," after all your hard work, feeling so in command of the facts of the case and so convinced of the story's deeper purpose, be forgiven for making a teeny adjustment to a quote? Just a little cutting and pasting of fragments from the Gow interview, such that he himself would surely never notice, would be enough to frame that all-important quote for the story's theme passage: "Guess he's been in Starkfield too many winters. Most of the smart ones get away."

Who would ever know?

No one would get hurt, after all.

When I was a struggling and younger reporter, an editor told me to write a lie, and, of course, I did.

I had written a travel piece for a national magazine, which mostly consisted of profiling a hotel and its eccentric owner in a far-away land. When I came home to Canada and filed the story, the travel editor told me he'd like to print it, but could I please amend the part where I first described the hotel, to show me checking in? It would be so much more effective that way.

"But," I said, "I didn't stay in that hotel. I stayed with a friend in town to save money."

That, he responded, was okay. This kind of thing was done all the time in travel pieces—just "tweaking" at little details that don't change any of the basic facts. No one would ever know. No harm would be done.

"You may do it all the time," I said, "but I don't." Well, actually, if I said it, it was under my breath. I might also have mentioned, equally silently, that in calling something non-fiction, a writer engages in an unwritten contract with readers that invites those readers to place reliance on accuracy. What I said aloud was words to the effect of, "You're the boss." And I squirmed. And then I wrote the lie, and the story was later selected for an anthology of travel writing, and though I keep the book on a shelf and sometimes enjoy looking at my name on the cover surrounded by those of household-name international authors, and later learned that in some publications, fudging of facts and fluffing of characters is considered quite routine for travel writing, I always—always!—feel a twinge of shame too.

You see, at least one person was hurt after all: me.

Since then, I have never told a lie in print. Well, not *knowingly*, anyway, which is not quite the same thing. I have believed sources and afterward wondered if I was too credulous. I have reconstructed the odd scene based on only one witness's account, and told myself that was okay because the other witnesses were hard to find, or because the way I described the scene made its source implicit.

And over the years, I have felt worse and worse about taking this kind of shortcut, even though I knew for sure that I was not alone in doing so. Other writers reconstructed scenes with loads of dialogue even though no one could possibly have remembered who said what, exactly. Or sliced, diced, mixed, and matched quotes for convenience's sake, much like "you" did with Harman Gow's "too many winters." And many editors (especially magazine editors) encourage this approach. Their goal is something known to literature scholars as *narrativity*—the quality of "well-toldness" in a good story. Since true life often lacks the narrativity of fiction, writers and editors play with the facts, just a teeny little bit, for the story's sake.

I don't, and won't, do it any more. If I've not made sure of the facts by means of evidentiary rigour, I will not report them, or, if I do, I will tell readers exactly what I know and what I am speculating about or what others say. I will paraphrase a quote if I have not written it down verbatim or recorded it on tape. I will introduce reconstructed scenes with lines such as, "What happened next, according to Joe Blow and his mates, went something like this…" If that lacks the smooth elegance of a narratively beautiful account, I'm okay with that. Truth trumps narrativity.

And that's a happy ending, right? Earnest but too-easily tempted reporter sees errors of his ways and reforms himself, and now lives a life as clean as fresh-fallen snow.

Not so much. Reporting no longer pays my rent: nowadays, I teach for a living, and write (occasionally) for the pleasure of it. That makes my scruples much more affordable.

Two-time Pulitzer Prize–winning writer of dramatic non-fiction Jon Franklin believes that he knows exactly what constitutes a good feature story:

> I went back and read how-to-write books from the '30s and '40s, and discovered complication-resolution form—the essential form of the short story of

old. I vowed to use that form to give shape to my newspaper stories. Within two years I was writing true short stories, complete with complications and resolutions—stories, as one puzzled newspaper editor put it, with "beginnings, middles, and ends." ...

I know, in short, what a story is ... and equally important, I know what a story *isn't*. As a result I can readily put my finger on a good yarn while my students undergo the tortures of the damned to find mediocre ones.

The straightforward definition of a story is as follows:

> *A story consists of a sequence of actions that occur when a sympathetic character encounters a complicating situation that he confronts and solves.*[8]

Franklin is an accomplished reporter and a fine writer, but he does not own the key to the writing universe. The fiction of authors like Henry James, Franz Kafka, James Joyce, Annie Proulx, and many others routinely breaks the rule that Franklin learned. Their stories may or may not centre on a "sympathetic" character, and the protagonist may or may not "resolve" the complications in his or her path, yet, they are nonetheless, unmistakeably, great stories. Nor does life on the planet earth follow this formula. Stephanie Nolen's story about the horrors taking place in Kenya, for instance, resolves nothing but shows much.

And Franklin's is not the only "rule" of narrative journalism that is worth a judicious second look. Take the "show, don't tell" rule. It's a pretty good rule, as rules go. We've referred to it several times in this book, and I bet you've heard it often before—a kind of journalistic equivalent to the prime directive on *Star Trek*, or Kant's categorical imperative, or the oath taken by doctors the world over: "First, do no harm." But a good starship captain knows when a rule stands in the way of what's good and necessary. Can you really live out your professional life showing, not telling?

I doubt it. A few weeks before writing this chapter, I read a revealing, complex, marvellously written profile in *The New Yorker* of Sabrina Harman, an American army reservist who, as a 26-year-old member of the military police, took the iconic pictures of detainees and guards at Abu Ghraib prison that later led to abuse charges against herself and others. The story depends for its readability and authenticity on vivid, detailed reconstruction and long quotations from letters home from Harman to her partner. So it certainly did a lot of "showing." But it could not have done justice to the complexities of her character and situation without some key interpretive ("telling") passages like these:

Nobody called Sabrina Harman Mother Teresa at the Abu Ghraib hard site. But even on the Military Intelligence block she retained her reputation as the blithe spirit of the unit, obviously not a leader and yet never a true follower, either—more like a tagalong, the soldier who should never have been a soldier. In her letters from those first nights, as she described her reactions to the prisoners' degradation and her part in it—ricocheting from childish mockery to casual swagger to sympathy to cruelty to titillation to self-justification to self-doubt to outrage to identification to despair—she managed to subtract herself from the scenes she sketched. By the end of her outpourings, she had repositioned herself as an outsider at Abu Ghraib, an observer and recorder, shaking her head, and in this way she preserved a sense of her own innocence.

Harman said that she had imagined herself producing an exposé—to "prove that the US is not what they think," as she wrote to Kelly. The idea was abstract, and she had only a vague notion of how to see it through or what its consequences might be. She said she intended to give the photographs to the press after she got home and out of the Army. But she did not pretend to be a whistle-blower-in-waiting; rather, she wished to unburden herself of complicity in conduct that she considered wrong, without ascribing blame or making trouble for anyone in particular. At the outset, when she photographed what was being done to prisoners, she did not include other soldiers in the pictures. In these images, the soldiers, or the order they serve, are the unseen hand in the prisoners' ordeal. As with crime-scene photographs, which show only victims, we are left to wonder: Who done it?[9]

In short, I believe there is only one categorical imperative for journalists, and it's a very simple one: try—try *hard*—to tell the truth. There are a lot of circumstances in which that rule must be juggled against the other duties and standards that pull at any human being, but matters of form (technique) should take second place to the pursuit of accuracy. When writers take a cavalier attitude toward truth, they are not committing journalism. Making a slight adjustment to the facts may seem harmless, but what's harmed, in my opinion, is the journalist's own attitude toward his or her job. Simply put, a journalist needs to work on becoming *obsessive* about finding, understanding, and communicating the truth.

In *The Elements of Journalism*, a book that every journalist should study, authors Bill Kovach and Tom Rosenstiel spelled out some almost indisputable principles of the practice of journalism. The first one reads: "Journalism's first obligation is to the truth." In a later chapter, the authors expand on what that obligation means in daily practice. Journalism's essence, they say, is "a discipline of verification."[10] For a model of this discipline, they and many others have looked to the history of the Peloponnesian War written by Thucydides two and a half millennia ago. That author explained:

> With reference to the narrative of events, far from permitting myself to derive it from the first source that came to hand, I did not even trust my own impressions, but it rests partly on what I saw myself, partly on what others saw for me, the accuracy of the report being always tried by the most severe and detailed tests possible. My conclusions have cost me some labour from the want of agreement by different eye-witnesses, arising sometimes from imperfect memory, sometimes from undue partiality for one side or the other.[11]

According to the Committee of Concerned Journalists, whose work was the precursor to *The Elements of Journalism*, the idea of a discipline of verification translates into five "intellectual principles of a science of reporting":

1. Never add anything that was not there.
2. Never deceive the audience.
3. Be as transparent as possible about your methods and motives.
4. Rely on your own original reporting.
5. Exercise humility.[12]

Of course, it's one thing to promise yourself to follow all these principles, but another to live up to them under the pressure of editors' demands, sources' reticence or unavailability, conflicting assignments and deadlines, and the crushing need to move on from one assignment to the next in order to pay the rent or assure your continued employment. The temptation to leave a fact unverified, tweak a quote, or compose a scene or character from elements drawn from a couple of different situations can be sharp.

Writers of the style of feature reporting variously known as docudrama, literary journalism, or narrative non-fiction, with its tendency to tell stories in a highly literary style, are especially at risk of taking shortcuts with the facts—"making stuff up." But one such writer, Mark Kramer, says that most of his peers agree that their contract with readers requires that writers "do what they appear to do, which is to get the reality as straight as they can manage, and not make it up." In what has become a classic essay on what he calls the "breakable rules" of literary journalism, Kramer writes:

> Some, of course, admit in private to moments of temptation, moments when they've realized that tweaking reality could sharpen the meaning or flow of a scene. If any writers have gone ahead and actually tweaked, however, they're

no longer chatting about it to friends, nor talking about it on panels. In recent years, a few literary journalists have drawn heavy fire for breaking trust with readers. It is not a subject about which readers are neutral.

Conventions literary journalists nowadays talk about following to keep things square with readers include: *no composite scenes, no misstated chronology, no falsification of the discernible drift or proportion of events, no invention of quotes, no attribution of thoughts to sources unless the sources have said they'd had those very thoughts,* and *no unacknowledged deals with subjects involving payment or editorial control.* Writers do occasionally pledge away use of actual names and identifying details in return for ongoing frank access, and notify readers they've done so. These conventions all add up to keeping faith. The genre makes less sense otherwise. Sticking to these conventions turns out to be straightforward.

Writers discover how to adhere to them and still structure essays creatively. There's no reason a writer can't place a Tuesday scene prior to a Monday scene, if the writer thinks readers should know how a situation turned out before knowing how it developed. It is easy to keep readers unconfused and undeceived, just by letting them know what you're doing. While narrating a scene, a literary journalist may wish to quote comments made elsewhere, or embed secondary scenes or personal memories; it is possible to do all these things faithfully, without blurring or misrepresenting what happened where and when, simply by explaining as you go along. Like other literary journalists, I've found that, in fact, annoying, inconsistent details that threaten to wreck a scene I'm writing are often signals that my working theories about events need more work, and don't quite explain what happened yet.

Not tweaking deepens understanding. And getting a slice of life down authentically takes flexibility and hard labor. Readers appreciate writing that does the job. It is not accidental that the rise of literary journalism has been accompanied by authors' nearly universal adherence to these conventions, which produce trustworthy, in-the-know texts and reliable company for readers.[13]

～～～

Does any of this mean that feature writers, and journalists in general, are supposed to be "objective"? Though the word has fallen out of favour in recent years, many journalists still hold themselves up to the standard of at least trying to place themselves at an emotional distance from the people and events about whom they write. Anthony DePalma, a former Canada correspondent for *The New York Times*, has written:

> The goal of objective reporting certainly remains real to those of us at the *Times*, at least in the news columns of the newspaper. The debate is not

whether objectivity is achievable. It certainly is, not just in journalism but in many other fields. We expect judges to put aside their personal preferences and to decide, according to written law or the Constitution, the cases in front of them. Likewise, we expect doctors, lawyers and even professors to put aside their personal likes and dislikes and approach their responsibilities with a high degree of professional balance.

In time, I came to think that the problem comes with the word objectivity, which carries so much baggage. It is only human for a correspondent who is covering a war, or insurrection, or even a local town council, to have personal feelings. But it is absolutely legitimate to expect that reporter to put aside those emotions and write dispassionately when it comes time to put the news article together.[14]

There is an alternative view: that the idea of objectivity, when applied to the goal of finding the meaning in and connection between events (that is, the "plot line" that explains the history of events) is an act not merely of subjectivity but of imagination, and journalists deceive themselves when they aspire to tell "truth" in the macro sense of the word. That view is commonly held, but I don't agree with it. I readily concede that journalists as individuals (as human beings) are never objective, and always somehow involved in the stories they are telling. But a journalist strives for a *method* that is objective.[15] As DePalma suggests, we expect judges to put instincts and beliefs on one side and judge cases according to the preponderance of facts and the parameters of law, and we expect chemists to use established standards to construct their experiments and then describe their methods in great detail in order so that others might replicate them. Why, then, should we not expect journalists to follow an objective and transparent evidentiary method?

Yes, the plot lines that we create to give meaning to events will always be products of our imaginations, but that should not stop us from seeking to report the events faithfully. Without methodological constraints aimed at maximum accuracy, we stop being journalists altogether. Which brings us back to the crucial point made by Kovach and Rosenstiel: independent verification of facts is the foundation of all journalism.

And, because intelligent readers expect to be able to evaluate the truth of your story, verification should be reasonably transparent. Facts should be attributed to their sources—though not necessarily in the lockstep forms of traditional news reporting ("according to Mr X, ..." or "Dr. So-and-so said ..."). If it's quite clear to the reader that a story is being told from a certain person's point of view, the attribution does not need to be drummed in at every turn. But a reader should know, or at least be able to guess with confidence, how you came up with and verified the story as a whole and the individual facts within it. Where a reader might be asking, "How can the writer know this?" you should be asking either the same question, or this one: "How can I tell this more clearly?"

It's that simple.

Not.

One reason why journalism's standards—verification, transparency, independence, originality, and others—are less than easy to implement is that every journalist lives in, and must live in, a dismaying web of conflicts of interest. I am not speaking here of the obvious occasional conflicts that should be avoided or at least disclosed—such as reporting on people you are entangled with, or companies in which you have an interest, or events in which you have played some part. I'm referring to conflicting obligations that inevitably and necessarily arise from the day-to-day realities of the trade.

It's obvious enough that journalists have obligations to their *readers*. Mostly, that obligation is a matter of telling the truth, of which much has already been said in these pages. But every journalist must marry that ethical duty with other obligations: to their employers (or clients, in the case of freelancers), to their sources, and to the subjects of their reporting.

To editors and publishers, a writer has several obligations. They include scrupulous originality, of course, since original content is what publishers promise their audiences and plagiarism (increasingly easy as it is to do, whether by intent or a mere slip of the mouse) breaks that contract. Obligations of truthfulness to your editor come in two forms: you must fully reveal any interests that might be seen to compromise your independence as a reporter, and you must reveal the breadth of what you find out in your reporting—even (or especially) when it contradicts what you have already reported or said to your editor in private. Finally, you are obliged to keep your promises, including the promise to deliver, on deadline, the story assigned.

All these obligations to the editor sound relatively obvious until they are laid side by side with the truthfulness you owe to your subjects, sources, and readers. Take, for instance, the promise to deliver the story that was assigned. Typically, a feature assignment is settled—the promise made—on the basis of a bare minimum of research. Then you start reporting the story, and life gets real on you.

I once was assigned to write a story for a national magazine about how homeless people fare when they move off the streets into homes. The story was my own idea, and my pitch started as follows:

Off the Street

She was homeless, and now the government has given her a home. Four walls.
A well-lit studio apartment in a brand-new mixed-use development in a safe
neighbourhood. Just one problem: the apartment's walls are yellow. Yellow
scares her. So she won't sleep there; she spends a few nights on the hallway
floor outside her front door, and when the neighbours complain, she moves
back to the street.

He was homeless, and now the government has given him a home. A room
in a suburban house shared with other down-and-formerly-outs. He has a
roof over his head now, and a social worker makes sure he eats. But he's still
a schizophrenic. After he breaks a few windows and spends a couple of nights
raging at his roommates, they insist on his eviction. So now he spends his
nights in shelters and his days on Yonge Street, like before.

She was homeless, and now the government has given her a home. And it
turns out, that's all she needed. She moves in, decorates her space, cleans up
her self, starts looking for a job, reaches out to her family, starts on the long
job of rescuing what's left of her life.

After years of public pressure fueled by many deaths, governments at all
levels have lately been spending money on anti-homelessness programs. In
Ontario, that means dollars for housing, and dollars for the social workers
who find people homes and help them settle in. But people don't get homeless merely because they can't pay the rent. And not everyone can make the
jump back to life under a roof.

The feature story I'd like to write for you would follow one mentally ill
homeless person from the street into her or his new life in supported housing.
It would show that fixing homelessness costs more than money....

That letter, which was based on a couple of interviews and a small amount
of background reading, contained an implicit promise that was key to the
resulting assignment. I would find a sympathetic central character, a homeless
person with whom readers might identify and about whom they would care,
and follow that person through the drama of reorienting from the street to
life within four walls. As things turned out, I couldn't deliver on that promise,
both for logistical reasons and because many of the homeless people I "audi-
tioned" for the story were considerably less than sympathetic. But there was
another implicit promise too, in the third paragraph of the pitch: the prospect
of a happy ending. Obviously I never guaranteed that the central person's
story would end well, but there was clearly the prospect of good outcomes in
the story. Somewhere, at least in the background, I had to show (not tell) how
some of these transfers might turn out well. But as I reported the story, settling
into a supported-housing operation and spending day after day observing life

there as a fly on the wall, it became clear that for various reasons—including that promise of hopeful outcomes—I could not deliver the story that the editor expected. Of course, I told the editor what I was finding, and was instructed to carry on. What I delivered in the end was, in the editor's words (if I remember the distressing phone call correctly), "gritty, believable, and vividly told"—but a more complicated and, frankly, depressing read than she believed her readers would be up for. So, my story was killed.

Luckily for me, the magazine was honourable enough to pay me a full fee for the story, since I had, in the editor's opinion, done my job in all respects. But no reporter is in the business of writing stories that will never see the light of day, and it was a depressing experience for everyone involved—for me, for the assigning editor, and for the staff and residents of the supported housing facility, who had given me much time over a period of several months and, more to the point, their trust.

Nor is this the unhappiest example I could have picked of how the assignment promise can break down in the reporting reality. In my time as an editor, I saw several cases when authors desperate to deliver on assignment expectations performed Olympian feats of writerly gymnastics to hide the fact that the truth did not measure up to the promise. Other authors disappeared for months of uncompensated research trying to find a story to match the assignment, and often failed.

Worse by far were the mercifully few cases of writers twisting, dodging, and weaving finely crafted webs of fudge. Sometimes, they even got away with it.

A few years ago, a young writer named Michael Finkel was turning out feature after magnificently written feature for America's leading magazines. His upward-spiralling career came to an abrupt halt after the publication of one story for *The New York Times Magazine*—a cover story about a Malian child labourer that was, like most of Finkel's earlier work for that and other magazines, expertly crafted and told in vivid, unrelenting detail. It was also a fake: the life story of a "composite" (that is, nonexistent) character. On being caught in February 2002, Finkel was fired, and vanished into obscurity.

Sadly, Finkel is not the first prominent journalist to be caught cheating and won't be the last. But what's compelling about the Finkel case is the set of circumstances behind this, his only known ethical lapse as a reporter. The story was born when the *Times* magazine received a charity's PR package on child slavery in Africa, and sent Finkel to write a narrative account centred on the slave business in Mali. When Finkel got there, he found (he later said) a more complicated situation than anyone had expected. The world's media, he decided, were being sold a slavery story while in reality children worked—willingly—as migrant labourers, seeking riches or at least money for a new pair of shoes. By his account, he returned to New York with a plan to write an exposé of media-manipulation, but his editor asked for something closer to the original concept: a narrative profile of one of the child migrants. Finkel had met no one on his travels who quite fit the bill, and the messy result is history.[16]

Finkel was, of course, quite wrong to file a pack of lies. But the story cannot be fully understood without taking account of how under-researched assignments can be, ensuing as they often do from presuppositions and secondary material rather than from original reporting. This kind of assignment can force a reporter to "find" a story that matches an agreed template, or, more likely, select, bend, and twist facts to match it rather than reflect the nuances of complicated truth.

Why didn't Finkel call his editor from Mali, describe the reality on the ground, and agree on new reporting directions? That's unarguably the best practice for a reporter in this situation, and Finkel has never fully explained his failure to do so. But he did write a poorly received book partially about the case, in which he described the conversation that took place after his return:

> There was some part of me that knew, right then, that I could not fulfill my editor's request. I should have said so immediately. But I sensed that my success as a writer was almost solely in [the editor's] hands, and I felt a powerful need to please her.[17]

This "powerful need" will ring a bell with many a reporter. In the vendor-purchaser relationship between feature writer and editor, the customer (rather than the reporter's sources or readers) must be right. In this case, Finkel had what he would in his book call "a job I had coveted almost all my life"—though not a job, really, but a tenuous freelance contract. Given the innate conflicts of interest that riddle the freelancer's job description, it's surprising that scandals don't come to light more often, and only a legion of skeptical editors, obsessive fact-checkers, and writers with both talent and discipline stand guard against the inevitably shaky consequences of a wobbly enterprise.[18]

My advice—any half-decent editor's advice—is that if (or rather, when) anything like this happens to you, you should come clean quickly and straightforwardly. Tell your editor: "I thought I would find X, but what I'm finding out is Y." It happens. Most likely, one of two things will happen next. Either you and the editor will decide to get out of the story before you're in too deep, or (quite likely) you will find in the reality a way to approach the story that is as good as, or better than, the assumptions you made when agreeing on the original assignment.

If, on the other hand, your editor puts pressure on you to distort your story to fit its shaky basis, that editor doesn't deserve his or her position of trust, and doesn't deserve to work with an honest writer like you.

Seen in the light of the politics and economics of assignment, then, the obligations of truthfulness to editor, reader, and source can come to seem quite fuzzy. And beyond truthfulness, there are other obligations that can conflict with one another. You want to avoid unjustifiable harm to the people about whom you write, but you want to deliver to your reader the truth in all its sometimes ugly reality. You want to provide your key source with the opportunity to comment on what you've turned up, but your deadline has arrived and she's on safari in central Africa without a satellite phone. You don't feel comfortable with trying to wheedle your way into a family's confidence at a time of vulnerability, but your editor smells a cover story, not a quotation from the Canadian Association of Journalists ethics code about respecting privacy "except when that right is superseded by the public good."[19]

Which brings us to another area of truthfulness—truthfulness with sources. In 1989, Janet Malcolm began a two-part feature story in *The New Yorker* with these now-famous words: "Every journalist who is not too stupid or too full of himself to notice what is going on knows that what he does is morally indefensible." The story she told was a compelling one: writer Joe McGinniss, eager to tell the full true-crime story of a brutal murder, had declared to the accused murderer a fervent belief in his innocence, and by this means secured access to the man himself, to his lawyers, and all the details he needed to write a vivid, compelling book that made the man's guilt as clear as day.[20]

Not all of Malcolm's peers agreed with the sweeping "every journalist" thesis that she had drawn from the account of how McGinniss got caught up in a relationship built on too hasty a faith in his subject's innocence. (Malcolm's thesis was unwittingly reinforced when her own integrity as a reporter was called into question by a messy lawsuit in 1991, but that's another story.) There's no doubt that sources often feel betrayed by reporters—and especially by feature writers, who, seeking to deliver a "good story" as described in textbooks like this one, find themselves placing on the story a "spin" that (however justified it may be by objectively observed facts) comes as an unpleasant surprise to the story's sources or subjects. But that's just a reality of the journalist's world: the truth can hurt.

Breaking promises is another matter. We journalists define ourselves as messengers of truth. "Trust us," we tell our audiences, "I am giving you the straight goods." But if we are untruthful in pursuing truth, who are we, and why should we trust even ourselves?

There are no easy answers to the questions raised throughout this chapter, but keeping promises seems a good start on the road to truthfulness. If, for instance, you tell a source that you will keep her identity secret, why not take a minute to be clear about what you mean. ("I'll veil your name and change identifying details in what I write," you might say, for example, "but if a court orders me to tell, I will. And if you lie to me, I won't protect you at all.") Sources have a right to be treated decently and with respect—for instance, by being told why we are asking questions and what kind of story we have in mind (especially if they are people who, unlike lawyers and politicians, for instance, may not understand how the media work.[21]) They also have a right to be quoted accurately, without distortions of meaning or context. And let's be especially protective of the welfare of children whose stories we tell, and of others who may not provide fully informed consent to what we're doing.

A long time ago, literary critics used to argue about the relationship between *res* (the thing, the matter or substance) and *verba* (the words or the form) in communicating, or about whether *utile* (usefulness) is more important than *dulce* (beauty). If those arguments seem old-fashioned today, that's because since the time of Cicero, it's become increasingly clear that the relationship is reciprocal: style provides force, momentum, and strength; but direction and purpose come from accuracy of observation and by substantive research and reflection.[22] Readers get enlightenment and edification through a proper balance of form and content. Some writers, especially young writers, are apt to forget this point when they hit the heights of inspiration and start whizzing down slopes of prose groomed by their brilliant style, but neither the best fiction nor the best non-fiction is powered solely by words. As Francis Bacon wrote disparagingly in 1605:

> [M]en began to hunt more after words than matter; more after the choiceness of the phrase, and the round and clean composition of the sentence, and the sweet falling of the clauses, and the varying and illustration of their works with tropes and figures, than after the weight of matter, worth of subject, soundness of argument, life of invention or depth of judgment.[23]

Journalism is not so much the fruit of creativity and imagination as of the hard slog involved in discovering facts, examining and testing them, interpreting their meaning, describing them clearly, and presenting them fairly. A work of journalism should be judged not only by the clarity and persuasiveness of its style but by the discipline and worth of its substance: its accuracy, independence, and contribution to society.

And its purpose? Its purpose is not just to add words or scenery to a world full of those things—its purpose is to tell the truth to a world in which truth-telling is an agonizingly scarce commodity.

To achieve that purpose in your feature writing will take stamina, self-discipline, and a passion for truth that includes a willingness to dig deep, listen carefully, watch piercingly, and think analytically. It will also take heart—an openness to let life touch you and move you. In the words of a Roman poet named Horace who lived two millennia ago: "If you want to move me to tears, you must first feel grief yourself."[24]

But most of all, perhaps, it will take grit: a readiness to work hard, to criticize yourself, to research until you get answers, to revise until you know you've achieved the best story you can write. It will take a willingness to try, and to risk failure. In that spirit, I will end this chapter and this book with a confession of my own failure in research. I have tried very hard to find a source for the following quote, passed on to me by my friend, the veteran editor, feature writer, and memoirist Ernest Hillen. Ernest had it written it down in a notebook but with no citation other than an attribution to the author Arnold Bennett, who died in 1931. As my friend wrote it down, and passed it on to me, it's now passed on to you: "No use sighing, 'If only I could be a better writer,'" he said. "You must feel more deeply and think more clearly."

Discussion Questions

1. Read "Into the Valley of Death" by Stephanie Nolen (pages 311–319). What is the central theme and purpose of Nolen's story?

2. What key choices did Nolen make in determining her approach to this story, and to what extent does the result deliver on the combination of narrative form and purposeful substance that you would like to achieve in your own feature writing?

3. Read or at least scan one of my feature stories, such as "The Ambulance Chaser" or "Once a Killer," at my website (IvorShapiro.ca). Have I been steadfastly true to the standards of transparency that I espouse here (by being clear about the sources of my facts)? How do you think the subjects of my stories felt about the way they were portrayed? What questions would you ask about my methods if you could meet me face to face?

Notes

1. Edith Wharton, *Ethan Frome* (New York: Penguin, 2005), pp. 1–3.
2. Stephanie Nolen, "Into the Valley of Death," *Globe and Mail*, January 26, 2008, A18.
3. Jeffrey Gettleman, "Ethnic Violence in Rift Valley Is Tearing Kenya Apart," *The New York Times*, January 27, 2008.
4. Northrop Frye, "Historical Criticism: Theory of Modes," in *Anatomy of Criticism: Four Essays* (Princeton, NJ: Princeton University Press, 1957). (Frye refers to the two levels as "fictional" and "thematic" aspects.)
5. See Cynthia Griffin Wolff, "Edith Wharton and the 'Visionary' Imagination," *Frontiers: A Journal of Women Studies* 2, no. 3 (Autumn 1977): 27–28.
6. See Hayden White, *The Content of the Form: Narrative Discourse and Historical Representation* (Baltimore: Johns Hopkins University Press, 1987), pp. 1–23.
7. Wharton, *Ethan Frome*, p. 4.
8. Jon Franklin, *Writing for Story: Craft Secrets of Dramatic Nonfiction by a Two-Time Pulitzer Prize Winner* (New York: Plume, 1994), p. 25 and p. 71.
9. Philip Gourevitch and Errol Morris, "Exposure: The Woman Behind the Camera at Abu Ghraib (Annals of War)," *The New Yorker*, March 24, 2008.
10. Bill Kovach and Tom Rosenstiel, *The Elements of Journalism: What News-people Should Know and What the Public Should Expect* (New York: Three Rivers Press, 2001).
11. Thucydides, *The Peloponnesian War*, ed. T.E. Wick (New York: McGraw-Hill, 1982), p. 13.
12. Kovach and Rosenstiel, *The Elements of Journalism*, p. 78.
13. Mark Kramer, "Breakable Rules for Literary Journalists," *Nieman Narrative Digest*, <http://www.nieman.harvard.edu/narrative/digest/essays/breakable-rules-kramer.html> (accessed February 20, 2008). Italics added.
14. Anthony DePalma, "Objectivity: Not Dead Yet," *J-Source.ca*, <http://www.j-source.ca/english_new/detail.php?id=605&pageid=151> (accessed June 10, 2008). DePalma is also the author of *The Man Who Invented Fidel* (New York: Public Affairs Books, 2006), an exploration of the objectivity or otherwise of controversial *New York Times* correspondent Herbert Matthews, who reported on the Cuban revolution a half-century ago.
15. Kovach and Rosenstiel, *The Elements of Journalism*, p. 74.
16. Jesse Sunenblick, "Straight Story, Curved Universe: Why Michael Finkel Is Not Jayson Blair," *Columbia Journalism Review* 44, no. 1 (May/June 2005), pp. 13–14.

17. Michael Finkel, *True Story: Murder, Memoir, Mea Culpa* (New York: Harper-Collins, 2005), p. 35.

18. See Ivor Shapiro, "Why They Lie: Probing The Explanations for Journalistic Cheating," *Canadian Journal of Communication* 31, no. 1 (January 2006).

19. "Canadian Association of Journalists Statement of Principles," <http://www.caj.ca/principles/principles-statement-2002.htm> (accessed February 21, 2008).

20. Janet Malcolm, "The Journalist and the Murderer," *The New Yorker*, March 20, 1989, 49–82.

21. For instance, most sources who are not media-savvy may expect to see a copy of the story before it's printed, and to have an opportunity to influence the way it comes out. Editors almost universally refuse to allow this, and certainly guard their prerogative to agree to such a request or not. Not all journalists agree with this long-standing tradition, and book authors (including me) have been known to show pages of manuscript to their sources as part of the fact-checking process.

22. See Marcus Tullius Cicero, *Cicero on the Ideal Orator*, trans. J.M. May and J. Wisse (New York: Oxford University Press, 2001), 3.142–143; Peter Dixon, *Rhetoric* (London: Methuen, 1971), pp. 17–19; Quintilian, *Institutio Oratoria (Institutes of Oratory)*, trans. H.E. Butler (Cambridge, MA: Loeb Classical Library, 1920), 8, pref. 21.

23. Francis Bacon, *Of the Advancement of Learning*, edited by G.W. Kitchin (London: Dent, 1973), <http://www.uoregon.edu/~rbear/adv1.htm> (accessed February 22, 2008), 1.4.2a.

24. Horace, *Ars Poetica*, trans. A.S. Kline, <http://www.tonykline.co.uk> (accessed March 11, 2008), line 102.

"Into the Valley of Death"

Anger at vote-rigging has worked to rip a thin scab off many years of frustration at poverty, corruption and inequitable land ownership

Stephanie Nolen, "Into the Valley of Death." *The Globe and Mail*, January 26, 2008, A18. Reprinted by permission of the author.

KIPKELION, KENYA—With the sun barely over the edge of the valley, the colours on the hills were muffled. The banana leaves were dull green, the sugar cane stalks pale yellow. And so the flames, when we saw them flare in first one house, then a second, then streets and streets on fire, were shocking, vivid orange, more alive than anything around.

I arrived in Mau Summit, a small town on a main road in Kenya's Great Rift Valley, just after dawn on Thursday morning. It had been burning for a couple of hours. At the sight of the flames, my driver, Mohammed AbuBakr, instinctively sped up. But in the centre of town, we found a police truck and a half-dozen officers and we stopped.

There were people all along the side of the road, but no one spoke. The only sound was the dull thud as they flipped over the fallen tin sheets that used to be roofs, looking for anything to salvage. The sight of the ruins seemed to stun people into silence.

I climbed through the rubble and held out a hand to a young man who stood in the smouldering remains of his small electronics shop. "*Pole, pole sana*," I said, Kiswahili for "very sorry," a phrase I had been using incessantly in the past few days. There was nothing to save, no trace of the 300,000 shillings—$4,350—that Jose Muiruri, 25, had saved up and invested. Next door was the shell of his family's house.

Then it got worse: Behind it, he found the body of a young woman. She was so badly burned that he could not tell who she was; her skirt and sweater were reduced to ash. But the baby, perhaps a year old, whom she clutched to her chest, small head tucked beneath her chin, was still discernible. Mr. Muiruri looked, and turned away. There was no one to help, nowhere to take their bodies. He needed to gather his family and get out.

"Last evening we heard noises, and we thought there was something planned, so we just stayed in the shop watching," he said. "But then a group came—so many, 20 in one group, 30 in another—and you could not recognize them, and they told us we must leave this place. So we turned and just ran for our life."

His family and many others ran to a gas station at the edge of town, where a few police officers had been posted in the convulsion of violence that has racked Kenya since a disputed presidential election on Dec. 27. The police called for reinforcements, but by the time they arrived an hour later, a mob of young men armed with bows and arrows and jerry cans of fuel had set the once-bustling town on fire.

Police tried to talk to the mob leaders, but the mob shot arrows, a traditional weapon of the Kalenjin, who are numerous in this area, toward the police and shop owners, most of them Kikuyu, and kept them at bay, until the shops and bars and the small hotels were all ablaze. Then they melted back into the valley.

"They were telling us to go, go," Mr. Muiruri said. "To go back where we are from." I asked where that was. He gave a bitter smile. "I was born just there," he said, pointing up the road. "But they say we are invaders and we have taken something of theirs."

It was a story I had heard a dozen times in the previous couple of days. Some 800 people are dead, 300,000 are displaced in Kenya now, and millions of dollars worth of property has been destroyed. And in nearly every case, the story is that anger over cheating in the presidential election has caused people who have lived side by side for decades to turn on each other in a vicious frenzy, shooting and beating and burning, and driving them from land and homes they have occupied for generations.

The Kenya I travelled through this week was not a country I recognized from more than a decade of travel here, the Kenya that was prospering and ambitious and dignified and peaceful. No one I have met seems able to believe that they have found themselves here—or able to imagine a way out.

This crisis is about much more than the election. Anger at vote-rigging has worked to rip a thin scab off many years of frustration at poverty, corruption and inequitable land ownership that dates from the colonial era. A handful of politicians have seized on ethnicity (Kenya has 37 different ethnic groups) as the most efficient way of mustering support, and incited people to "protect their own." There is evidence that some degree of ethnic-based violence was planned before the vote, that opposition supporters wanted revenge against government supporters if they won, and anarchy if they didn't.

Mr. Muiruri and his family are Kikuyu, whose "traditional" homeland is in the centre of the country. Thousands of Kikuyu came into the valley in the 1950s to work on the farms set up by white settlers, or to set up small businesses. The Kikuyu had the first contact with the British colonists, and were the first to learn to read. They parlayed their slim advantages into the purchase of modest parcels of land.

Independent Kenya's first independence president, Jomo Kenyatta, was a Kikuyu, and he encouraged his own people to move and take opportunities to prosper. He was succeeded by 27 years of dictatorship under Daniel arap Moi, a Kalenjin. By the end of his rule, Mr. Moi was despised by Kenyans in every tribe. In 2002, he was replaced by Mwai Kibaki, another Kikuyu, who won office in an election considered relatively fair.

Mr. Kibaki has presided over a growing economy, a flourishing civil society—and some profoundly corrupt dealings. Many of those in the political elite that surround him and who have grown rich in the past five years are also Kikuyu.

It is now clear that although both Mr. Kibaki's camp and that of opposition leader Raila Odinga cheated in the Dec. 27 vote, Mr. Kibaki's group inflated their tally more. Mr. Kibaki had himself instantly sworn in again, banned live media and called out security forces. Mr. Odinga's supporters, to whom all polls had given a narrow lead, reacted with rage.

Yet somehow the explosion of anger focused not on the abrogation of democracy, but on ethnicity. Marshals in Mr. Odinga's camp began to say that "the Kikuyu" had stolen their election, that Mr. Kibaki was intent on assuring that only Kikuyu, who make up 22 per cent of the population, would prosper, that they would never cede power. Marshals in Mr. Kibaki's camp told the Kikuyu that others resentful of their industry and prosperity were intent on destroying them, and only loyalty to the government would save what they had. Police, meanwhile, had shoot-to-kill orders, and unarmed protesters were shot in the back, further inflaming the opposition.

In an effort to understand this, how one of Africa's most stable countries could have gone so quickly up in flames, I set out from Nairobi for the Great Rift Valley. This area voted resoundingly—no rigging required, though some provided—for Mr. Odinga.

The area is dominated by non-Kikuyu tribes and has seen only limited economic development in the past 10 years. Where many white settlers made vast fortunes here and lived the gin-drinking, cricket-playing life of luxury immortalized in books and films such as *Out of Africa*, today it is home to smallholders and legions of young, unemployed people.

I had one destination in particular in mind: the Cistercian monastery in Kipkelion, where a mob of 1,500 people besieged the 600 or so of their neighbours sheltering there last weekend, vowing to kill them all. I wanted to talk to the people in the monastery, and I wanted to find some members of the mob to ask, "What's happened here?"

On the Road to Kipkelion

I arranged to travel with Mr. AbuBakr and his colleague from a community radio station in the Nairobi slum Kibera, Muchiri Kioi, a former reporter with the BBC Kiswahili service. Mr. Kioi is half Kikuyu, the group most targeted in the valley, and he was both curious and nervous about going there. He instructed us, grinning but serious, to call him Suleiman Salim—from now on, he was a Muslim opposition supporter.

From Nairobi, we drove to the regional capital of Nakuru and started to gather information about the safety of the roads. A local Kalenjin man, recommended by friends, would show us the route and talk us through military checkpoints on the way. We stocked up on food, water and cellphone air time, and set off.

Not long out of Nakuru, the road degenerated into a stone track, and I began to be deeply uneasy. There was no one. Not a woman with a bundle on her head, not a child in a school uniform, no men on bicycles, none outside the shops, all of which were locked tight. There was not a cow, a goat, a chicken.

Instead, all we passed were the hastily assembled roadblocks: boulders, felled electrical poles, piles of logs.

Two hours shuddering down that road and our truck suddenly slammed to a stop, engine dead. The men tinkered, with increasing anxiety. As the minutes ticked by, I tasted the flat metal of fear in my mouth. My cellphone rang: it was Father Dominic Nkoyoyo at the monastery. Armed youth were amassing in the road, he said, sealing it off. We should turn back as fast as we could.

The nearest town, Kipkelion, was ahead, so we began to push the truck, first up a hill, and then, fortunately, down. A vehicle stuffed to the roof with panicked refugees chugged by, and I pleaded my way on, hoping that in Kipkelion I might find help. We reached the town half an hour later and I began asking everyone I could find for a mechanic. The town was full of Kikuyu refugees, and there were several mechanics—but no one was willing to leave, not for any amount of shillings. When I asked, they simply held up their arms and mimed the action of shooting an arrow. I had given up in despair when Mr. AbuBakr and the others rolled the lifeless Land Cruiser into the town.

While they continued their efforts to repair it, I walked into the refugee camp that had sprung up around the police barracks. Some 800 people were sheltering there in improvised tents, many with nothing at all. I met Andrea Momonyi, 65, who had somehow contrived to keep his grey-and-white pinstripe blazer immaculate in the mud of the camp. Originally from the centre of the country, Mr. Momonyi came here in 1975, and bought his two-hectare farm from a settler. "I grew tomatoes, sugar cane, cabbage and maize," he said. "The children went to school, and I could grow our food and a bit extra to have some money. It was fine."

In the early evening of Dec. 30, just hours after the presidential results were announced, he looked out his front window to see a crowd so large he couldn't count the men in it. They carried bows and arrows. "They chased us, and we ran for our dear lives."

The mob set his house ablaze, and the granary full of maize, and all the fields. He ran, with his children, to the police station, and has been there since.

"We'd been co-existing happily together and I never expected this," he said, something person after person in the camp would tell me. "We were working together, living in the same places, going to the same drinking places."

And yet it was clear that Mr. Momonyi and everyone else knew the mobs that torched their houses contained their Kalenjin neighbours. And when pressed, they admitted they were not entirely caught off guard by recent events. I asked Mr. Momonyi about the land title documents for his farm—many suspect that one goal of the arson campaign is to get people off land, destroy their deeds and then move in and establish de facto ownership. But Mr. Momonyi still had his deed. In the early 1990s, when relations were tense and he thought the Kalenjin might come for his farm, he took the title documents out of the valley for safe-keeping. "We think it is a plot, hatched before the election," he said.

That thesis is now supported in most quarters. The violence that broke out in the Rift Valley hours after the results were announced was of a level of co-ordination and sophistication, such as trenches dug with tractors to keep security services off the roads, that it cannot have been spontaneous.

Which leaves Mr. Momonyi living under a sheet of grey plastic on damp earth at a police garrison. Could he go back home if the situation became more stable? He shook his head, and the crowd that had gathered to listen to our conversation chorused, "No!" We will never feel safe again, people said. But where will he go? At this, Mr. Momonyi twisted his cane in his hands. "I have only that piece of land."

When I walked out of the camp, I found our truck running at last. But already it was nearing dark, so we weren't leaving Kipkelion. A kind nun named Sister Anna Peter, who drives the mobile clinic for the Our Lady of Mercy mission, offered us narrow beds and blankets in the Catholic mission.

I wanted to know just who the refugees were so afraid of. So as night fell, we climbed the hill on the edge of town, looking for some Kalenjin. It didn't take long for a group of Kalenjin men to materialize out of the darkness. They said that the refugees such as Mr. Momonyi were liars. There had been no burning, no forced displacements. If the Kikuyu were seeking shelter from the police, it was because they had been killing Kalenjin and feared reprisal.

The men returned, over and over, to the topic of the election, the victory stolen from their candidate, whom they, like most Kenyans, call just Raila. "It's very painful to be deprived of this," said David Langaat, 58. He pointed to the local clinic, which he said lacked drugs and staff, and to the horrendous road. "It was our wish to have some change, some economic development."

Yet why should the theft of the election set neighbours against each other? They could not answer, shrugging silently. And so we went back down the hill—passing, on the way, a small group of young men carrying machetes, on their way to staff a roadblock.

Back at the mission, before we slept, Sister Anna Peter tried to answer that question. "When anger comes in, as with the election, people reflect on what else went on before," she said. "And the anger for ownership of land spills in. That anger has been a long time brewing. Everyone thinks of land; they want that one thing."

Before first light, we were back in the truck: We wanted to be well on the road before the roadblock militias had, as Mr. Kioi put it, "had some sleep and some tea and come out to work." For the first hour or so, as light crept into the valley, the roads were empty. And then we hit Mau Summit and the fire.

We did not loiter long. The police captain told us we were mad to proceed. But staying put wasn't appealing either. So on we went. Ten, 20, 30 kilometres, and things were fine.

And then, there it was, the scene I had been picturing, expecting around each bend. A row of vehicles stopped and trying to turn. A series of logs and rocks across the road. And on the other side, a crowd of perhaps 200 men, all of them clearly armed.

What I hadn't imagined was the next part: All the people attempting to get to Nakuru or Nairobi fell upon our truck. They had seen our vehicle, with the "International Press" signs taped to the windows. "Go, talk to them." The theory, it seemed, was that the chance to talk to someone, even a lone white reporter, might ease the tension of the gathering mob, and persuade them to open the road.

I stepped down from the car, and in an act of much greater bravery, so did Mr. Kioi. "Remember: Suleiman Salim," he hissed. I grabbed a notebook, camera, two pens, press card. He took his microphone. And we began to step over the logs and rocks toward the mob.

As we drew near the crowd of men, the buzz increased. I thought I might vomit. I walked into the middle of them and said loudly, "I work for a Canadian newspaper. I need to know who is in charge here. I would like to know what's going on." The crowd quieted slightly, moved back a little.

"No one is in charge," one man said. "We are all together." I noticed that every man carried a bow, made of yellow wood and almost his own height, and an arrow. It was hard to believe they were real weapons. A young man with a whole quiver of arrows, metal tips gleaming in the sunlight, jostled roughly against me. "Do you have a spokesman?" I asked, aware of my own absurdity. "No, no spokesman," came the angry response. "Well, what are you doing?" I asked desperately. "We are angry because they killed our people," one young man said. I held out my hand. "I'm Stephanie. I work for a newspaper in Canada called The Globe and Mail." He let my hand hang there, staring at me coldly. I waited, waited. Finally, Kenyan politesse outweighed his rage and he shook.

His name was Sammy Kirui and he was 30. He told me that in the night, some Kikuyu had come and torched a shop. When the alarm was raised, two young Kalenjin men, unarmed, had come from the hill to investigate. Police had shot them, he said. "We were preaching peace," he said. Until that night there had been no trouble in their town, Sachangwan. "But how can we always preach peace and they come and kill us?" The police chief is Kisi, a tribe from a different part of Kenya. "Instead of giving us backup, he is making matters worse."

These men spoke about their bitterness that Mr. Kibaki will not admit he rigged the vote. But what did that have to do with pointing bows and arrows at people in the road, I asked? With chasing Kikuyu out of town? "These people are very insulting," Mr. Kirui said. I asked him what he did for a living. "Nothing, I don't work," he said. "These people won't hire you for their business. There is nothing for … us."

While we were talking, the distraction had worked just as the crowd behind the roadblock had hoped. They had pulled back the logs and surged past us.

Now buses of travellers coming the other way pulled up, and the men with weapons began to pound the windows. "We need to go," Mr. Kioi said. Then he yelled it. Then he was running for the vehicle. I followed, pressing the shutter on my camera as I ran. The vehicle was moving when I got in. "They were saying," Mr. Kioi wheezed, "in their language that now they need to kill someone. That they should shoot someone through the window of the bus."

As we drove away, I realized that men with bows and arrows stood in lines on every ridge and along the road. A small group of police were standing, utterly ineffectual, at the edge of the mob. This part of Kenya, it seemed, was now lawless.

The next stretch of road was clear. And then, when it seemed we might actually be fine, we ran out of gas. There had been nowhere to refuel because every gas station had been torched. When the truck finally heaved to a stop, we were on the edge of Salgaa, a truck stop thick with bars and brothels. There had not been fuel there for weeks.

Mr. AbuBakr set off on the back of a motorbike with a jerry can, bound for a town five kilometres away rumoured to have fuel. An hour later, he returned empty-handed. The gas station would sell him none, convinced that he was bent on arson. But he had filled the tank of the motorbike, and now set about the laborious task of siphoning the gas into our truck.

As he worked, the town became choked with transport trucks, ranged four across the road as drivers debated whether it was safe to go on or safe to go back. When we rolled out, few were moving. Less than an hour after we left Salgaa, mobs set the town and many of the trucks alight.

Our nine litres of gas got us to Nakuru, and when we arrived there, there was no hint of trouble. Mothers took children in their best clothes out for lunch and a couple of tourists, brave or clueless, headed out to see the flamingos. The only sign of the trouble was at the fairgrounds, where several thousand refugees were sleeping in the buildings and on the playing fields. Dozens more were arriving, thinking they would be safe in Nakuru.

But on Thursday night, hours after we left, not long after Mr. Odinga said on national television that he is the "rightful president," the fighting spread here. Yesterday, Kikuyus began revenge attacks with machetes; local reporters described bodies lying in the streets, some with deep gashes, some studded with arrows.

In the afternoon, we left Nakuru for Nairobi, where former United Nations secretary-general Kofi Annan was performing frantic shuttle diplomacy between Mr. Kibaki and Mr. Odinga. He managed that day to get them in the same room for the first time since the vote. But Mr. Kibaki and his cabinet are entrenching their hold on power, while Mr. Odinga refuses to entertain any deal that doesn't name him president. It is difficult to imagine a compromise that Mr. Annan could broker.

And if he did, what impact would it have in Kipkelion? "It will take some time," Father Nkoyoyo said with priestly understatement, "because now people are wounded and the wounds can't be healed tomorrow. The people can't go back and rebuild somewhere where the neighbours tried to kill them. It is going to take more than some months or even years."

On the climb out of the valley from Nakuru to Nairobi, I asked Mr. Kioi and Mr. AbuBakr if anything we had seen surprised them. "That this is Kenya, and you cannot move from place to place," Mr. Kioi said, bitter wonderment in his voice. "That there is no control. That people are killing just like anything."

Index

J0677932

A

Void

the Size

of

the World

ALSO BY RACHELE ALPINE

You Throw Like a Girl

Operation Pucker Up

Best. Night. Ever.
(with coauthors)

A
Void
the Size
of
the World

RACHELE ALPINE

Simon Pulse

New York   London   Toronto   Sydney   New Delhi

For my sister, Amanda . . . your kindness and compassion
for others is inspiring. The world is so lucky to have you.

This book is a work of fiction. Any references to historical events, real people,
or real places are used fictitiously. Other names, characters, places, and events are products
of the author's imagination, and any resemblance to actual events or places or persons,
living or dead, is entirely coincidental.

SIMON PULSE

An imprint of Simon & Schuster Children's Publishing Division
1230 Avenue of the Americas, New York, New York 10020
First Simon Pulse paperback edition July 2018
Text copyright © 2017 by Rachele Alpine
Cover photographs copyright © 2017 by Chev Wilkinson (people);
copyright © 2017 by Thinkstock (clouds)
Also available in a Simon Pulse hardcover edition.
All rights reserved, including the right of reproduction in whole or in part in any form.
SIMON PULSE and colophon are registered trademarks of Simon & Schuster, Inc.
For information about special discounts for bulk purchases, please contact
Simon & Schuster Special Sales at 1-866-506-1949 or business@simonandschuster.com.
The Simon & Schuster Speakers Bureau can bring authors to your live event. For more
information or to book an event contact the Simon & Schuster Speakers Bureau
at 1-866-248-3049 or visit our website at www.simonspeakers.com.
Cover designed by Regina Flath
Interior designed by Steve Scott
The text of this book was set in Goudy Oldstyle.
Manufactured in the United States of America
2 4 6 8 10 9 7 5 3 1
Library of Congress Control Number 2016057313
ISBN 978-1-4814-8571-5 (hc)
ISBN 978-1-4814-8572-2 (pbk)
ISBN 978-1-4814-8573-9 (eBook)

Here

These violent delights have violent ends
and in their triumph die, like fire and powder
which, as they kiss, consume.
                    —William Shakespeare

1

I didn't mean to kiss my sister's boyfriend.

At least, not the first time.

The day it happened, thick gray clouds sagged and hung so low that it made you think you could reach out and brush your hand along the bottoms. The air blew fast and forced trees to bend toward the ground as their branches stretched for invisible objects. I kept an eye on the darkening sky as I headed home from my job where I scooped ice cream for sunburned kids, tired parents, and classmates. I snuck free cones even though my manager strictly forbade handouts. It wasn't the most glamorous job, but it was a paycheck. And a paycheck meant money that would get me out of this town one day.

I felt the rain on my back before I saw it; large blobs of water fell on my neck and covered the sidewalk in polka-dotted specks around me.

I was still a ways from my house, but only a block from

Morton Park. I ran and hoped I could make it there before it poured, because the only thing worse than being covered in ice cream was being soaking wet and covered in ice cream.

Most of the park wasn't anything special; it had the usual swings, slide, climbing gym, and seesaw. What made it different was that there was also a graveyard for half a dozen old construction tubes dumped in the grass by the city. They were pulled out of the street when it was repaved with asphalt. The tubes sat covered in graffiti and forgotten except as an alternative jungle gym for kids brave enough to scale their massive shapes.

My sister, Abby, and I used to beg Mom to take us here when we were little. Abby would quickly scurry to the top of some massive piece of equipment and I'd try to follow. I wanted to keep up with her, but instead, I'd slip back down and skin my knees. Abby would stand tall and proud, and the only way I could join her was when she reached out her hand to pull me up.

It was by those same tubes that I saw Tommy.

He had on the giant headphones he always wore, his head bobbing to the music. He moved farther and farther away from me, and I told myself to go over to him before he was gone. But I couldn't. These days it was impossible to be near him.

Because he wasn't mine.

A crack of thunder rattled the earth, and Tommy looked up and noticed me. But if he was surprised that I was in the park, he didn't show it.

"Rhylee!" He gestured at me to come toward him, but I remained rooted to my spot.

He hurried over instead and the air felt charged. It sizzled and crackled.

"Duck in here," he said and pointed at the construction tubes. "We'll be able to stay dry."

I followed, grabbed the top, and pulled myself through feet first until I was sitting on the bottom of the tube next to him. He placed his headphones around his shoulders, but didn't turn them off. The sound of piano music mixed with the rain that slapped the top of the tunnel, creating an angry symphony. I recognized the notes. It was a piece he wrote a few months ago. Whenever Tommy was working on composing music, he listened to it over and over again on a constant loop.

I sat with my back against the wall and feet stretched up on the other side. I pushed away some garbage and tried to slow my breathing.

I didn't belong here. I was an impostor, pretending to be comfortable this close to Tommy. The thought was ridiculous; we'd been best friends for years, but that had changed. I'd worked so hard these last few months to avoid him. And now here we were stuck together until the storm passed. It was as if the universe had decided play some cruel trick on me, to remind me of what I couldn't have.

Because he was my sister's boyfriend.

"What are you doing in the park?" I asked, not quite believing that chance had brought us to each other.

He ran his hand through his brown hair. It was wet, and the ends turned up in curls along the nape of his neck. He needed a haircut. "I was teaching a piano lesson. The family lives about a block away and I thought I could outrun the storm. What about you?"

"Serving Webster's World Famous Custard." I repeated the lame slogan plastered across my lime-green T-shirt and pretty much everything else at Webster's.

"World famous?" he asked, his eyebrow raised.

"Oh, yes." I nodded. "People flock from far off lands to sample our vanilla custard with rainbow sprinkles."

"I remember that cone you made for me a few weeks ago. You do put those sprinkles on perfectly. Not too much but not too little."

"What can I say? I've found my calling." And suddenly it was like old times again. The two of us talking and joking.

"I've missed you," he said.

It felt as if someone had knocked the breath right out of me. Those words were what I'd been dying to hear for so long, because I'd missed him too. After all, this was Tommy sitting next to me. The boy I grew up with; the two of us inseparable as we ran between our houses that sat side by side, only my family's field creating a separation.

"Yeah, well, things are different now," I said and wanted to say so much more, everything I'd held inside for so long.

"Different sucks."

"Whose fault is that?" I asked, not quite sure of the answer. I still didn't understand what had happened the night that changed everything. It confused the hell out of me, and no matter how much I tried to figure it out, I just went around

4

and around in circles, finding myself back where I started.

Tommy stared outside the tunnel. The rain warped everything and made it feel as if we were hiding in some kind of fantasy world.

He reached into his pocket, pulled out a cigarette and a lighter, then waved the two at me. "Is this okay?"

I started to tell him it wasn't, smoking was disgusting, but stopped.

"If you share," I said instead.

"You smoke now?" Tommy asked and tilted his head, as if what I said surprised him. As if I wasn't allowed to change anything he knew about me.

Tommy smoked with some of the other boys at school. They hid behind the baseball dugout, slipping away during lunch. My sister would never dream of smoking, because of running; she said it messed up your lungs. So this, this smoking, was something I could do that Abby wouldn't.

I shrugged as if it was no big deal. "I haven't in a while," I lied.

"Since Gina and Joe's wedding?" Tommy asked with the goofy lopsided smile I loved.

I narrowed my eyes at him and stuck out my chin. "I've smoked since then," I told him, which wasn't true at all. In seventh grade when his sister got married in their backyard, the party went into the night, and as our parents celebrated with an endless supply of alcohol, Tommy and I had slipped away with a beer hidden under his jacket and a pack of cigarettes we found abandoned on a table. We drank the beer, passing it back and forth, the foreign taste making our heads foggy and light at the same time. We lit cigarettes and pretended we knew what to do as we coughed our way through tiny puffs that made our eyes water. After, we lay in the field and watched the stars sparkle and shine in the inky blackness around us.

Abby caught us as we headed back, the smell a dead giveaway. She was hurt we left her behind. I felt bad and put an arm around her shoulder, pulling her into our group, but she shrugged it off and walked ahead of us. We tried to include her when she was around, but no matter what we did, it seemed that's how she always felt about Tommy's and my friendship. Left behind. Which was so different from what Abby was used to, because my sister was always the center of attention. Tommy had been the one thing that was mine and only mine, but Abby found a way to take him, too.

"We don't have anything better to do while we wait the storm out." Tommy interrupted my thoughts. He pressed on the lighter and held the cigarette against his lips. The end glowed bright as he took a breath in. He slowly blew the smoke out before he passed it to me.

I placed it in my mouth. I sucked in like he did, but the drag was too deep and my eyes watered. I fought the impulse to cough, even though my throat burned. Coughing was a sign of weakness.

"You haven't smoked again, have you." It wasn't a question but a statement. He knew me too well.

"There's a lot of things I haven't done," I told him. "But that doesn't mean I'm not good at them."

"Is that so?" Tommy asked in a slow, drawn-out way. He

6

reached for the cigarette and his fingers wrapped around mine, holding on for longer than a moment before he took the cigarette back.

"Something like that," I said, my voice caught in my throat. I stopped before I went too far. I was confused by what was going on. It sounded an awful lot like I was flirting with Tommy, and flirting definitely wasn't allowed with your sister's boyfriend. Especially when it felt as if he was flirting back.

The two of us sat so close our shoulders touched, the music from his headphones now a slow, sad song. He didn't mention Abby, and I wasn't about to bring her up. My sister had a way of taking over things. She'd gone with friends to a nearby lake earlier today. She had dropped me off at work on her way, her friends singing along to the radio, their hands trailing out the car windows as they drove away.

A flash illuminated the sky and the thunder that followed was so loud it seemed to shake the ground. I jumped and hit my head on the top of the tunnel.

"You okay?" Tommy touched the spot. His fingers wrapped around a piece of my hair and twirled it. We were so close I could feel the soft cotton of his shirt against my arm.

"I'm fine," I said, but I wasn't. I didn't feel fine at all. Instead, I was nervous and sad, but I definitely didn't want him to know any of that. I took the cigarette from his hand and placed it between my lips again. It was still wet from his mouth. I inhaled deeply, this time getting it right.

"Careful," Tommy said.

Thunder rumbled around us. I closed my eyes. My body hummed with electricity.

"I don't want to be careful," I said.

"Me either." He held my gaze, and I willed myself not to look away. His eyes revealed everything we weren't saying to each other, and I was dizzy with desire.

"I made a mistake," he said.

"I made a bigger one," I replied, and those words opened everything.

Because in this dark tunnel, with the rain pounding down around us, I felt different. Like I was the person Tommy was supposed to be with. I forgot about the night a few months ago when he tried to kiss me and I pushed him away, too scared of how things would change. I didn't think about the hurt on his face that changed to anger, because that wasn't the way he thought it would go. And I certainly didn't remember how I found him later that night, his arms wrapped around my sister as she kissed him in the way I should have.

Instead, I became the person I wish I'd been that night. The one who kissed Tommy back instead of running away scared.

I flicked the cigarette outside and watched it sizzle out in a puddle.

I couldn't wait any longer.

I made the first move, but Tommy didn't hesitate. We closed the space between us. I opened my mouth to let his air in. To let him in. His breath smelled sweet and smoky as his lips slid against mine and erased everything else in the world.

We didn't take things slow. There were no gentle kisses or hesitations. Instead, I kissed him with a furiousness that took my breath away. I pressed myself into him, trying to take everything that I could before I lost it all again.

And he let me.

He pulled me down so I was on top of him, and I would've traded my soul to the devil if we could've stayed like that forever. His skin burned against mine. I kissed him until my lips swelled and bruised, but still I wanted more more more.

Our kisses went beyond this moment. They held years of our friendship; scraped knees and mosquito bites we scratched until they bled, snowball fights on the way home from school, and Tommy crying next to me when a car hit his dog. It was him standing up to the boys who pushed me down in fifth grade, the two of us scaring ourselves silly over the horror movie we weren't supposed to watch, and me standing next to him and holding his hand at his grandma's wake when he was ten. It was the way things were always supposed to be.

He buried his face in my neck, my hair, against my mouth until it seemed as if neither of us could ever breathe again without the other. I don't know how much time went by; a minute, an hour, the entire night, our lifetime. It didn't matter.

Nothing mattered but us.

We kissed until his face was lit up in a flash of lightning. The thunder after was what shocked me back to reality and we paused to catch our breath.

"It was always supposed to be you and me," he said into my hair.

9

"Always," I answered back.

I put my hand on his chest and felt his heart racing through his shirt. He placed his hand on top of mine and this was us.

I thought about what he said. *You and me. You and me. You and me.* And what that would mean to my sister. His words took us to the edge of things that involved "deceit" and "destruction"—but for him, I was willing to jump.

2

I went straight to my room when I got home.

I walked past my eight-year-old brother, Collin, and Mom, who were making cookies in the kitchen, and crept past Abby's bedroom door, which was open enough for me to see that she was in there watching something on her laptop.

I searched through my music on my phone until I found the recording Tommy had made for me for my birthday last year. I'd asked him to record himself playing the piano, and he surprised me by sending a file of songs that sounded so good, you'd think you were sitting in one of those big fancy concert halls I've seen pictures of in New York City or Europe. But that was who Tommy was. He was music, and I had no doubt that one day he'd end up playing in those concert halls. We used to plan our future together. The two of us would go to college in New York City; Tommy would go to a fancy music school and I'd major in something artsy and creative. The two of us would page through old travel magazines and talk about exploring the world together. Tommy would wow audiences with his music, and I'd spend my days discovering places that tourists didn't know about, the hidden parts of the city that exist only for those willing to look.

I hadn't listened to his songs since he started dating Abby, but tonight, it was all I wanted to do. I put my headphones on and the notes poured over me. I thought about the two of us together in the concrete tube, about what didn't happen between us and now what had. I allowed myself once again to dream about a future that held the two of us.

I pulled out the shoe boxes I kept hidden in my closet. Three of them stacked on top of one another. When you opened each, a pair of shoes sat on top of tissue paper, but they were only a decoy. It was what was below that mattered.

They held stacks of papers full of the collages I made. My own secret worlds I had created since I was young. I held on to pieces of junk mail, scribbled doodles in notebook margins, and ripped pages out of magazines with places I longed to go, far off countries I fell asleep dreaming about. I used maps, newspaper articles, receipts, and other tossed-aside items to create backdrops for lives I wished to live. I pieced together letters and words to create poetry over my creations. And always, in the middle of every collage, I pasted an image of myself. Because here, I existed beyond my sister, outside of her shadow, and it seemed possible that if I created enough of these, I might be able to figure out exactly who that person was.

My fourth-grade teacher taught us that in China you go by

your last name first. Your family name is more important than your first name.

That's what life with my sister felt like. If you asked anyone in our town if they knew Abby, they'd tell you that they did. Even if they had never met her in person, they recognized her face. From the black-and-white grainy photos in the newspaper praising whatever race Abby had won that week or the highlights from the news during the sports segments. She was the track star. She was the pretty and smart one. She was the one Tommy was with. Abby was the chosen one.

And I was always Abby's sister, Rhylee. To teachers, friends of my parents, even classmates. Who I was, what I did, had never seemed important to anyone but Tommy, and then I'd lost that too.

But after today, that had all shifted. Tommy wanted me. Maybe I was a fool to believe it, but now that he had been mine for a moment, I didn't want to give him back.

Tonight, as Tommy's music washed over me and the burn of his kiss was still on my lips, I created a new collage. I layered pictures on top of one another to make a city landscape with an apartment in New York where the lights blazed against the ink black sky. And this time, it wasn't just me I placed in the center. I cut out a picture of Tommy so that we were together, and the line between fact and fiction blurred because maybe, just maybe, the images in front of me could be real.

3

I must have dozed off, because I woke up to a dark room and someone knocking on my door.

"Rhylee?" Abby called.

Shit.

I pushed my collages into the shoe boxes and shoved them under the bed. I'd put them away safely when I had the chance.

"Yeah?" I nervously answered, afraid she'd somehow found out. It was one thing to be with Tommy, it will be a completely different thing to admit to Abby what we've done.

"Mom wants to know if you're okay. We're having parmesan chicken for dinner; you never miss that."

I relaxed. She didn't know. She wouldn't be talking about dinner if she did.

"I'm okay, just tired from work," I replied. "Tell her I'll get some leftovers later if I'm hungry."

Abby left without saying anything more and the early

14

evening gave into night, and things remained the way they always had been. The TV turned on downstairs, and Dad and Collin cheered for the Cleveland Indians. Abby talked with her friends in the bedroom across from me, her laugh punctuated the air every once in a while, and Mom retreated to the bathroom to soak in the tub.

I hid in my room, not daring to come out for fear that everyone would notice I was different, because I sure felt different.

I fell asleep to Tommy's music on repeat; the familiar sound rushed over me and made it feel like everything was going to be okay.

I slept deeply until my phone beeped in the late hours of the night with a message from him. It was only five words, but five words was all it took to unhinge every last piece of me.

I'm breaking up with Abby.

I didn't respond right away. I understood what his words meant and what they'd do to Abby and me. We'd grown so far apart since she began to date Tommy. The cracks in our relationship were already there, and this, this would cause everything between us to crumble.

Was I ready for that?

I should write back and tell him that this couldn't happen. It was the right thing to do. But slowly, a tiny flash of hope began to unfurl.

I didn't want to leave Tommy to Abby anymore. I wanted that high-rise in NYC. I wanted to travel all over the world with him. I wanted to be a part of his life.

There was no way I could continue to pretend I didn't care that he and my sister were together. I'd lost him once; I wasn't going to make the same mistake a second time.

I want to be with you, I texted, and before I could stop myself, hit the send button.

I deleted both messages so Abby would never see them, the words burned into my heart. And in my ears, his music rose and fell in peaks and valleys, invading every part of me as if I was breathing in the sounds of him, absorbing them into my soul.

4

Three days passed and I didn't hear back from Tommy. I caught glimpses of him at school, but it was only for a quick moment and we never made contact. Our secret still seemed to be just that, a secret.

All around me, life too was paused. Fall would be here soon, and the world hung in a hazy suspension of denial. The kind where you suddenly felt like you needed to do everything you hadn't, but all you want to do is sit still and will the minutes not to rush forward.

I had grabbed the mail when I got home from school and now sat at the kitchen table sorting through the newest stack of college brochures. I saved the ones from the schools that I could see myself at and ripped out images from the schools that I wasn't interested in, to use in my collages.

These brochures had almost become an obsession. Ever since our guidance counselor talked to our sophomore class about "thinking ahead to our future" and told us how to request information, I couldn't get enough. The school had wanted to give all of us a push, try to boost their numbers of students who went to college, even though it was pointless; most of my classmates were fine with staying in Coffinberry their whole damn lives. But that wouldn't be me. I contacted all kinds of schools: big and small, universities in the middle of nowhere and others in big cities. It didn't matter. The only prerequisite was a school that didn't have a strong athletics program. My parents hadn't even gone to college, so it wasn't something they pushed on Abby and me, but the idea of living in a place that Abby didn't dominate was enough to motivate me to do whatever it took to get myself out of here.

Collin walked in and took a seat at the table. He waved his hands in front of the big fan that did nothing but stir the hot air around. It blew his blond hair straight back.

"Careful," I told him. "You'll chop your fingers off if they get stuck in there."

"They will not," Collin said.

I shrugged. "Maybe I'm wrong, but I sure wouldn't want to find out."

I handed a rolled-up piece of paper to him, and when he opened it, his eyes got huge.

"Another edition to your story," I told him. It was his own personal comic book. I'd been adding to it for months, ever since Collin wandered into my room one day when I was working on a collage.

"Can you create one of these for me?" he'd asked. "Something that gives me superpowers?"

And how could I say no? I made him a world where he was the hero. I created images where Collin leaped buildings, tamed tigers, and was cheered while up at bat by a baseball stadium packed with fans. I put him at the center of the universe in every picture, and he hung each one up over his bed. A quilt made from pictures where my brother ruled.

In today's collage, he soared through the solar system and raced alongside comets. I'd ripped pictures out of an old science textbook I'd found at the library's used book sale and created a sky peppered with stars.

"What do you think? Do you like it? I thought it was about time we got rid of you and sent you to the moon."

Collin stuck his tongue out at me but grinned. "I love it." He bent over and examined it up close.

"Good, I thought you would."

I grabbed a soda out of the fridge and headed outside to the porch to search for a breeze. The day was sweltering; even walking from room to room created a fine mist of sweat all over my body.

I sat on the old porch swing Dad had hung years ago and moved slowly back and forth, my bare feet scraping against the dusty wooden boards of our porch. In the distance, gray clouds sat lazily on the horizon and the sky flashed bright with lightning. In this heat, storms blew through daily, and today's would be here soon, stirring up the stale muggy air. My skin tingled as I remembered the park and the way

19

Tommy and I had kissed as if we couldn't get enough of each other.

The hum of a motor filled the air as Dad cut the field to the left of our house.

He sat on his old riding mower twice a week and followed the lines up and down in the early afternoon before he left for the night shift, attaching bumpers to the front of fancy cars we could never dream of affording. Bumpers that came in glossy colors with names like candy apple red and champagne bliss. He worked at the same car factory most of my classmates would end up at. The same one I'd end up at if I didn't get out of this town.

He mowed straight lines for Abby to run, and she ruled the field just as she ruled the cross-country team at our high school. Her long muscled legs raced the stretch along the woods, down the path Dad created, and up against the old wooden fence that separated our yard from Tommy's. Abby ran that trail every day. She never stopped moving, her blond hair shining in the sun, and I'd watch from the porch and wish I could be my sister.

I was born shortly after she turned a year old, and Mom would talk about how crazy those first two years were. We looked alike, but there wasn't anything twin-like about us. Her outgoing and confident personality was a foil to my quiet, introverted self. She was part of a team while I dreamed of leaving everyone behind and discovering a world that right now I was so small and insignificant in. She was the one teachers loved. They'd tell me over and over again that I was nothing like my sister. It was meant as a joke, but beneath, there was a sense of disappointment, exactly like the one I felt from my parents when I'd get a bad grade or they'd bug me to join a club at school, to get involved, as if it were so simple to find a place for myself when my world was so full of Abby.

Tommy was always the only thing I'd had that she didn't. And then she'd taken him, too.

But now I had him back.

And I liked that feeling.

My long hair stuck to the back of my neck in the heat. I twisted it around my hands and wished for a hair tie. Dad must be boiling out there without any shade. The rain would be welcomed, cooling us all.

The screen door creaked, and Abby came out and sat next to me. I stiffened. The ice in my glass clinked together as the swing moved back and forth from her weight.

"I swear, it's pretty much child abuse not to have air conditioning," Abby said and fanned her face with her hand. "It's cooler out here than it is inside."

"It feels like the whole world is on fire," I told her in a voice that didn't sound like my own. I was someone pretending everything was okay, and I was sure she could see through me, but she didn't.

"Your scrapbooking stuff is all over the table again," Abby said, and I relaxed a tiny bit. She wouldn't be complaining about that if Tommy had talked to her.

"It's not scrapbooking," I argued, even though it was pointless. Abby didn't get it. No one did. A few years ago I'd shown

21

my family a collage that had taken me hours to complete. It was on a giant piece of butcher paper, and I'd pieced together images and items from a family vacation. Abby thought it was hilarious that I'd spend that much time "playing with a glue stick," Dad hardly glanced at it, and Mom told me she thought it was "cute." It was stupid, really, to think they'd care. If it didn't have Abby's name attached to it, then forget about it. So now I kept that stuff private. They'd probably laugh me out of the house if I told them I actually thought I might like to do something with art for a living.

"Right, those pictures you make," she said in a way that made them feel so stupid and dumb. "Anyways, that's not why I'm here. I'm bored."

She held out a bottle of nail polish. It was pale pink, like the inside of a seashell. The same color she had on her nails.

"Give me your feet. I need something to do and it's too hot to run."

"I was about to work on some homework," I lied.

"Oh, please, homework can wait. I need someone to talk to, so stay out here and let me paint your toes," Abby ordered.

I did as she said, because I didn't have a better excuse. I stuck out my legs and laid them in her lap. They were even paler against her sun-colored legs, browned from days of running with the cross-country team. She slapped the bottle against the side of her hand and then bent over to draw the brush across my first toe. Her hair fell against my legs and tickled my skin.

"Don't move," she instructed when I wiggled.

22

The air shifted slightly as the storm drew closer; the loose pieces of hair twirled around my face. I wanted to be anywhere but here, but maybe this was my punishment for what I'd done. I was forced to face my sister straight on, and it sucked.

Abby concentrated as she painted each nail, the tip of her tongue sticking out the side of her mouth. The only noise was the buzzing of Dad's mower across the field and the low voices from some TV show Mom was watching inside. I studied my sister's face. The summer had stamped a constellation of freckles across her nose. It was odd to be this close to her when we'd grown so far apart. Tommy had pulled us away from each other, and it made me anxious to think about the secret I held inside.

When she finished the first foot, she pulled back and inspected her work.

"It looks good," I told her, and she nodded. She moved on to my second foot, dipping the brush into the bottle after each toe.

"Do you ever feel like something bad is going to happen?" she asked.

I closed my eyes and remembered Tommy's lips against mine. How we had betrayed her. "Bad things happen all the time. The news is nothing but gloom and doom."

She gazed across the field to Tommy's house. You could see the second-floor windows and roof from this far away. When I was younger, Tommy and I sent coded messages with flashlights. But that was so long ago. Now his light switched on and off as he lived a life separate from my own.

"Things aren't right," Abby said, and paused. A drop of

polish fell off the brush onto the porch. It spread out in a small puddle and sank into the wood.

I tried to brush it away with my thumb. Mom would kill us if she found it, but Abby didn't seem to care. She went back to painting my toes.

"I think Tommy's going to break up with me," she continued.

I jerked my foot away and a streak of polish smeared across the top of my foot.

"Jesus, Rhylee, look at what you did," Abby complained.

Far off, the sky grumbled as the sound of thunder reached us.

Shit. Did she know about the text message? Had Tommy said something?

"Here, give me your foot back so I can fix it before the polish dries."

I stayed still so she could finish and tried not to act as completely freaked out as I felt. She didn't know anything. She couldn't. Abby wasn't the type of person to play games, so if Tommy had told her about the park and the text message, she'd say something.

"Why do you think something is wrong?" I asked cautiously.

"He's being really strange, and he hasn't been over here in a few days. He keeps coming up with excuses that I know aren't true, because Mary Grace told me she saw him this morning at Otis's Diner when he said he had to help his dad with his truck."

She put the brush back into the bottle and rolled the polish back and forth in her hands. I'd never seen my sister this nervous before; she was the confident one. Even before a race, she was strangely cool and unaffected. So this seemed odd. Off. In a world where Abby was usually in control and the chosen one, the roles were suddenly reversed. This fear was something different, and even though I was the cause, I had to admit that I kind of liked it.

"He's probably busy," I said. "It's the end of the summer. I'm sure he's spending a lot of time helping his family out with the farm."

"No, it's not that. Something is going on." She sat straight up and tilted her head as if inspecting me. "You don't think he's cheating on me, do you?"

The soda I was taking a sip from went down the wrong way, and I coughed. I couldn't catch my breath and my eyes watered.

"Geez, what's your problem?" Abby pounded on my back as if that would help.

"Nothing," I said when I caught my breath. "I drank too much at once."

"What do you think?"

"About what?" I asked, done with the conversation. I didn't want to be out here anymore.

"About Tommy cheating on me."

"Tommy would tell you if something was going on; that's the type of person he is," I said, and thought of the text he'd sent me about breaking up with her.

"Yeah, I'm being stupid. Tommy and I are fine, right?"

I paused before answering. I remembered back to the

morning after the party when I had pushed him away from me and found them kissing. Abby had knocked on my bedroom door and climbed into bed with me, like we used to do when we were kids.

"Promise you won't get mad," she'd whispered, the two of us under the covers.

"Promise," I'd said, because how can you be mad at something you caused?

"Tommy kissed me last night."

I didn't tell her I already knew. That I had seen the two of them tangled around each other, and it had broken my heart.

"It's okay, right?" she asked. "You and Tommy aren't like that. . . ."

"No, of course we're not," I interrupted her, because what else could I do? I'd never told Abby how I felt about Tommy. And I'd had my chance with him, but I'd pushed him away. How could I stake my claim when it wasn't mine to stake?

But now, here, outside on our porch, I wanted to say the words I didn't all those months ago when Abby told me about the kiss she didn't know I saw. I could tell her I was in love with Tommy and had been for years. I could tell her how much it hurt to see the two of them together. I could confess the truth and maybe she'd understand.

But what if she didn't? Abby always got what she wanted.

So instead, I lied.

"I'm sure everything is fine." I looked off over our field

toward Tommy's house. The sky had darkened and the clouds raced in now. The storm would soon be here.

"You're right," Abby said. "I'm worrying about nothing."

"Exactly," I said. "Things will work out just the way they're supposed to."

5

Coffinberry, Ohio, is a pit. A town of about a thousand people, most of whom will never travel more than forty miles past its borders in their entire lives. A town so small we leave our back doors unlocked and if we aren't careful, we'll run out of people to kiss and have to start all over again at the beginning of the line. So when there isn't any fun to be had, we create our own. We walk through the fields and make fires deep enough in the woods that our parents turn a blind eye. The same woods they partied in when they were our age.

Saturday night began exactly like all the other nights where we hiked into the woods, carrying backpacks full of beer and scratchy wool blankets. It was the end of the summer. Fall loomed up behind us, and everyone was eager to let loose, ready to celebrate one of the last nights of warm weather.

I followed Abby and her friends across our field. It was

obvious our discussion yesterday hadn't worked. My sister was anxious and jumpy, talking and trailing off midsentence. I was anxious and jumpy too; I had no idea when Tommy was going to talk with her. I both dreaded and wanted it to happen.

Abby opened her purse and pulled out two of those miniature bottles of vodka. She dumped them into a water bottle of orange juice she'd poured in our kitchen while waiting for her friends Mary Grace and Erica to arrive.

"What are you doing?" I asked. This wasn't right. Abby never drank. Ever.

"Lighten up," she said and playfully tugged on the end of my ponytail. She pushed the cup at me. "I'm happy to share."

"I'm fine," I told her. Everything about this was off and made me uneasy.

"Suit yourself," she said.

We made our way through the woods to the bonfire. I soon fell a ways behind the girls, but it didn't matter because they pretty much acted as if I didn't even exist as they talked and joked with one another. I cursed myself for not agreeing to go with my best friend, Tessa, but she was getting a ride with her boyfriend, which pretty much meant being the third wheel to their nonstop PDA.

"We need to leave at eleven thirty," Abby reminded me. "Don't be late, or you can explain to Mom and Dad about why you missed curfew."

"I'll be here," I said, but Abby and her friends had already scattered, disappearing into the shadows as they made their way to the fire.

I followed behind. A mix of fear and excitement pulsed through my body as I thought about Tommy. Maybe tonight. Maybe it would happen tonight.

I spotted Tessa near the fire and waved.

"There you are, girl! I've been waiting forever for you to show up." She wrapped her arms around me and gave me a giant kiss on the cheek. One that probably left a bright red lipstick mark on me.

Leave it to Tessa to greet me in her usual dramatic fashion. Tessa was a hugger, and greeted everyone as if they were her long lost friend.

"Let me get a look at you." She put both hands on my shoulders and stepped back to inspect me. Her curly red hair was piled on top of her head in a messy bun and she had on jeans tucked into yellow rain boots. Ever since I'd met Tessa in kindergarten, when she'd colored her entire body in bright orange polka dots with a Sharpie marker from our teacher's desk, she did everything loud and big. She wanted to be on Broadway, and I had no doubt she'd make it there. Tessa had the confidence I wished I had and when she left a room, everyone remembered her.

I stood awkwardly as she took in my outfit of jeans and a tight black T-shirt that was cut just a little lower than I was comfortable with.

"You look hot!" she declared.

"You think?" I fiddled with the top of the shirt. She batted my hand away and pulled it even lower than before.

"I know so. Tommy will definitely notice you," she said and winked at me.

"Shhh," I hissed and looked around to see if anyone else heard. "Are you crazy?"

"Relax. Everyone here is either too drunk or too horny to care about you and your crush. Why don't you just tell him how you really feel already and get it on so I can stop listening to you moan about how in love you are with him?"

"Um, I think there's a little obstacle in the way called my sister," I said.

Tessa laughed. "Nah, your sister is a blip on the map. You're the one Tommy wants; you just have to let him know you're ready for him."

"The only thing I'm ready for is something to drink," I told her, so I wouldn't have to listen anymore. I was pretty sure Tessa's number one goal in life was to get Tommy and me together, regardless of what was in the way. I couldn't decide if I loved her optimism or wished she'd just let it go. One thing I did know was that she would go nuts when she found out that we'd kissed, and I hated keeping it from her, but I wanted to keep it to myself a little longer.

"And I'm going to get me some Jarrett." She pointed to where her boyfriend stood. She let out a wolf whistle and when he noticed, she blew a kiss his way.

"Keep it PG," I joked.

"I can't promise anything." She gave me a wave over her shoulder and skipped off toward him.

I stood near the fire for a moment and watched sticks pop and crackle in the flames. The night was loud and full of energy. Music played from a truck that had pioneered a road

31

through the woods. Kids from school ran past, their voices rising and falling in the muggy air.

Abby stood in front of the flames with Mary Grace. They looked like day and night together; Abby with her long blond hair next to Mary Grace with her tangle of dark curls. The two had their arms outstretched and faces turned up to the sky, spinning in circles. Abby moved so close to the fire that I half expected her to come out the other side, ablaze and streaming trails of light behind her.

I headed away from the fire. I told myself I was going the long way to get a drink, but in reality, I wanted to go back to where everyone parked to see if Tommy's truck was there.

When I reached the clearing in the woods, it wasn't only Tommy's truck I found, but Tommy himself. He sat inside with the headlights off. A country song played on the radio, the singer crooning about love gone wrong.

"Hey," he said to me out the window, and I felt shy, as if Tommy and I were strangers. I didn't know how to act around him now.

"Hey," I said back.

"Is your sister here?"

I tried not to look upset, but it was hard when the first thing he asked was about Abby. "She's over by the fire."

He didn't say anything, so I felt the need to keep talking. To fill in the silence. "She's been drinking. She never drinks."

"It's because of me," he said.

It was dark here. Shadows moved around his face so his features went in and out of focus. It warped who he was, and

I wondered if I looked different to him, too, because I sure as hell felt different.

"She's worried about you," I offered. "She asked me if I had any idea what was wrong."

"I'm pretty sure she knows what I'm planning to do." He climbed out of his truck so he was directly in front of me. "I never should've been with her in the first place," he said, and I let his words slip through me, fragile and thin.

"Then why were you?" I asked, because I had to. It wasn't like it was a one-time hook-up. They'd been dating for months. If he liked me, then why stay with her?

"That night—when you pushed me away, I was confused and hurt. I thought . . . I thought I was wrong. About everything. When Abby found me and kissed me, I didn't stop her."

"You could've ended things."

"I didn't know how. I tried to ignore how I felt and let myself believe Abby was right for me, but you can only pretend for so long."

"And I pretended like it didn't bother me," I said.

"But it did."

"It did," I confirmed, and a tremor of nervous excitement raced through my body. What was happening between us was real. I hadn't imagined it and however wrong it might be, Tommy felt the same.

If I were a good sister, I'd stop this from happening. I wouldn't want my sister to get hurt. But I wasn't good anymore. Not even close. Because I wanted to be with Tommy. I wanted him to be mine.

I reached out and touched his cheek. It was warm and smooth as if he'd just shaved. He placed his hand on top of mine, never once taking his eyes off me.

"I don't want the summer to end," someone at the fire shouted. "Screw school; I'm staying right here."

People cheered, and above them all, Abby shouted, "Tonight we're free!"

I wanted to be free too.

I pulled Tommy to me. He fell into me and his touch consumed me. He kissed me again as if it was what he'd been waiting for his entire life. His lips pressed against mine, and I took from Tommy until the sounds around me melted away. We kissed and we kissed.

"What are you *doing?*" A voice screamed and the two of us broke apart.

It was Abby.

"How could you?" she cried, and the pain on her face made it feel as if someone had punched me in the stomach and knocked the air right out of me.

I tried to say something, but I opened and closed my mouth, words useless. This wasn't supposed to be how she found out. This wasn't supposed to happen.

She turned and disappeared into the woods.

"Shit, shit, shit," Tommy muttered and backed away. "I need a flashlight."

I reached out to touch him, to calm him down so we could figure out what to do, how to make this right, but he pushed me away from him.

I stumbled and fell back to the ground. Pain shot through my wrist as I broke my fall, but it didn't hurt nearly as much as knowing how much I just hurt my sister.

"I need a goddamn flashlight," he yelled and rummaged around in the truck bed until he found one. He turned it on, raced into the woods, and vanished into the trees.

6

I went after Tommy and Abby.

The branches slapped and tore at my skin as I raced into the woods with only the light from my phone to guide me.

The party raged behind me. My classmates whooped and laughed, and their world seemed so separate from mine.

I found Abby before I found Tommy.

Her own phone's light winked as she ran through the trees.

"Abby," I yelled, and she stopped and turned toward me. Her face was a mess of tears, and pieces of her hair blew in front of her and stuck to her wet cheeks.

"Get away from me," she sobbed.

I reached out to touch her, to get her to look at me. She flinched as if I'd burned her, and I felt like a monster.

"No," she moaned as she walked backward.

"You need to come with me, it's not safe out here," I said. "Please, let's go back to the fire."

"I always knew," she said through her tears.

"What?"

"How Tommy felt about you. I ignored it, but it was there. Always."

I didn't know what to say; what could I say? It was true.

For once in my life, I was the chosen one. Tommy had wanted me instead of Abby.

And tonight, he'd chosen me again—but at what cost?

"Please," Abby begged. "You've done enough tonight. Leave me alone. Tell Tommy to do the same. I can't look at the two of you right now."

"Abby, wait." I tried to reach out to her again, but she'd already turned away from me. I touched nothing but thin air.

I tried to follow her, and got turned around. Everything was dark and confusing, as if I were running in a maze.

I wandered through the woods with only the light of my phone to guide me. I should've been terrified to be here alone at night, but I wasn't. I needed to find my sister and make right what I'd done.

Finally, a flash of light bounced off the trees and Tommy appeared in front of me.

"You haven't found her?" he asked.

"I tried to talk to her a few minutes ago, but she wouldn't listen. She told me to leave her alone and ran off. We need to find her and talk to her. We have to make this right."

Tommy nodded, and together we moved through the woods calling out and hoping to catch a glimpse of her as we shined the flashlight through the trees. We searched for more than an hour, but there was no sign of her.

"Do you think she went back to the fire?" Tommy asked.

"She's probably with Mary Grace and her other friends, telling them what I did."

"This wasn't the way it was supposed to happen," he whispered.

The wind rushed through the trees making a howling noise, and I shivered. This night was trying to swallow us whole.

7

We silently made our way out of the woods. I convinced myself that Abby would be okay. She'd find us back at the party. She'd be fine. She always was.

I walked close enough to Tommy that our shoulders touched. I breathed in his scent and began to believe he could be mine. Things hadn't happened in the best way—but they'd happened and opened up a world of possibility.

The clearing was still full of classmates and the bonfire blazed. I scanned the crowd to see if I could find Abby, but there was no sign of her.

I waited while Tommy walked through the group of people, weaving around classmates downing cans of beer.

"I bet she's already home," he said when he made it back to me, and I nodded.

Tommy and I walked to his truck, and even if someone

noticed us, it wasn't unusual. We were friends. We had been long before my sister staked her claim.

I stared into the woods as we drove home, and worried Abby was still in there, moving through the trees like one of those forest sprites that existed only in fairy tales. I studied the dark edges of the trees at a stop sign and imagined her there, reaching the end of the woods and turning around to be swallowed up again, as if afraid to enter back into our world. A world now full of betrayals and dishonesty.

8

Tommy didn't pull into my driveway. He stopped right before it, so we were half hidden under the canopy of an old oak tree.

The light was on in Abby's room, and I breathed a sigh of relief. She was home.

"Do you want to talk to her?" I asked as his headlights winked off.

"Not tonight."

"What do we tell her?"

"The truth."

Before we could say anything more, the front porch light switched on and I froze, expecting Abby to step outside. Instead, Dad opened the door and waved a hand in the air to us before closing it again.

"I think that's my cue to leave," I said.

"Life's going to suck for a while once everyone finds out

what we did, but this . . . this is us. This has always been us."

Tommy grabbed my hand and squeezed it. A calm settled over me. He was right. It would work out. How could it not after we had finally found our way back to each other?

I got out of the truck and watched him drive away. In the morning I'd have a lot of explaining to do, but for tonight, all I wanted to do was close my eyes and remember what it felt like when Tommy was mine.

Gone

What's done cannot be undone.
— William Shakespeare

1

I fully intended to hide from the morning as long as possible, because whatever faced me outside my door wasn't going to be pretty—even though I deserved it after what I'd done last night. What kind of awful person kissed her sister's boyfriend? Two separate times. I buried my face in my pillow and groaned. Not because I regretted what I'd done, but because I wanted to do it again.

I was surprised Abby hadn't stormed into my room yet. That was unlike her. She was always ready to make it known when she was pissed about something, whereas I was a pro at holding things inside, so it appeared as if everything was fine even if it wasn't. It was eerily quiet, which made the potential of what she was plotting a lot worse. We'd had our fair share of fights before, but I doubted they'd be anything like the one today.

I stayed in bed and tried to make sense of what had happened with Tommy. I hadn't set out to hurt my sister, but I did, and I had no idea how I'd even begin to make things right again. Especially if making it right meant not being with Tommy.

I reached for my phone on my night table, but couldn't find it. The drawer was open and as I searched for it in there, my hand landed on a piece of paper I'd hidden. I pulled out the picture of Tommy and me together in the made-up NYC apartment and thought about what I had wanted and what I did to my sister to get it.

I was granted twenty more minutes to myself until the floorboards creaked outside my room. I waited for the pounding I'd prepared myself for, but instead, the person knocked quickly and then tried to turn the knob.

"Rhylee, are you up? We need to talk." It was my dad, his voice hard and insistent.

Of course this was how it would go. Why would Abby take me on alone when she could pull Dad into it?

I crawled out of bed and had barely unlocked the door before he pushed it open and stepped into the room. He still had on pajamas; a pair of flannel pants that were a little too short and a worn white undershirt. It was rare to see Dad dressed like this, since he was usually getting home from his job when we were waking up. But it was Sunday, and that was the one day where Dad's nights and days weren't backward.

He surveyed my room.

"Is Abby here?"

"No," I said. His words were a glimmer of hope. Maybe I was safe for a little bit longer. Maybe she hadn't told Dad yet.

He certainly wasn't acting like someone who had any idea what I'd done.

"Have you seen her?"

"Not since last night at the bonfire."

"Didn't she come home with Tommy? His truck was outside."

"That was me," I said, afraid my voice would give too much away.

"Why wasn't she with the two of you? Why would he give you a ride home and not your sister?" he asked, and paced back and forth. That's when I knew for sure this wasn't about Tommy.

But I wasn't about to tell Dad the real reason why Abby didn't come home with us; he'd find out soon enough. "She was with her friends. I wanted to leave because I didn't feel good."

Dad stopped pacing, and I could tell what he was going to say even before the words came out. "She hasn't come home."

"I saw her light was on when I got home."

"Your mom thought she left the light on when she dropped off some of Abby's laundry. Her bed is still made with the clothes your mother washed piled up on it. She didn't sleep there and she's shut off her cell phone. We can't get in touch with her." Dad looked around my room one more time, as if he might find Abby. "Dress quickly and come downstairs. This isn't good."

2

I changed in record time and headed downstairs, where I found Collin in the family room watching TV and eating a big bowl of sugary cereal; the kind Mom never let us have but Dad always bought and snuck into the house. I ruffled his hair and went into the living room, where Mom sat on the couch, her shoulders hunched over and the rims of her eyes stained red. Usually on Sundays she was up early, dancing around to the radio that we keep on the kitchen table and making a big breakfast for us. Today she looked like a different person.

She stood when she saw me and I was sure she could see what I had done written all over my face.

"Why did you leave Abby last night?" Mom asked, her voice ragged and hoarse. She was barefoot in a pair of faded jeans and a wrinkled blue blouse that she wore to work. It was as if she'd grabbed whatever was nearby and threw it on.

"I didn't mean to," I told her. It was the truth. I didn't mean for any of this, not at all. "She was supposed to have a ride home. I'm sure she's at one of her friend's houses."

"Abby would've called. She wouldn't make us worry like this."

Mom was right, and it made me sick to think about. This was unlike Abby; she never missed curfew and she always checked in if she was going to be late.

But then again, she'd never had to come home to the person who had betrayed her.

"Calm down. This isn't Rhylee's fault," Dad said. "We need to focus and call as many of Abby's friends as we can think of."

He picked up a pad of paper and passed it to me. I glanced down and saw a list of names.

"What is this?" I asked him.

"We made a list of people to call. Are there any other names you can add? Who was she supposed to go home with?"

"We walked through the field with Mary Grace and Erica. I figured she'd go back with them."

"Okay, I'll call both girls."

I read through the names he'd already written down and saw everyone on the cross-country team Abby ran with, her friends from school, and, at the top of the list, Tommy.

"Have you talked to Tommy?" I asked.

Dad shook his head, and I held up my cell phone.

"I'll call him." I walked into the kitchen before they could object.

Tommy picked up on the first ring. "Hey, you," he said, and I swear I could hear the smile in his voice.

"Hey," I said back and then paused, unsure of what to say next.

"So how are things? You're still alive, huh?"

"Barely. And only because I haven't talked to Abby yet."

"Me either. Her phone is off. I'm surprised she hasn't busted down your door."

"She didn't come home last night," I told him, and saying the words out loud made me uneasy.

"What do you mean she didn't come home?" Tommy asked, and I could hear the same panicked sound in his voice that Dad had.

"She's not here."

"Have you called her friends?"

"My dad is doing that right now. I said I'd check with you and see if you had talked to her."

"I'll come over and help."

"Not right now. Things are too confusing. My parents are trying to track her down. I'll call you as soon as we find something out. Everything will be okay. I'm sure she'll be home any minute now," I said. But a heavy, deep feeling sat in my chest and I was afraid that wasn't the truth.

"Are you sure?" he asked.

"Positive. I'll talk to you later."

I hung up and walked back into the living room. Dad told the person he was talking with to wait.

"What did he say?" he asked.

Mom looked up expectantly, and I wished I had something to say to make everything better.

"He hasn't heard from her since we left," I said.

"I'll keep calling people," Dad said. "She probably overslept at one of her friend's houses."

Mom closed her eyes and took a deep breath. Abby never overslept. She was out running in the morning before any of us even thought about opening our eyes.

Dad and I went through each of the numbers on the list, but each reply was the same: No one had any idea where she was. All of these girls were safe at home with their families and my sister wasn't with them. Mary Grace told Dad that she tried to find Abby before she left and when she couldn't, she figured Abby was with Tommy.

But my sister wasn't with Tommy, and it was impossible to ignore the panic that was welling up inside; it fluttered like a bird that was trapped and couldn't get out.

A phone tree was set up, and in a town our size, that meant pretty much every person in Coffinberry received a message asking if they'd seen my sister.

Each and every reply was the same.

My sister was missing.

Dad moved on to another call. He spoke in a low hushed voice, but I could still tell that he was talking to the police.

Mom's shoulders shook as the tears she'd been holding inside escaped, and I stood helpless, drowning in guilt.

How had this gone so wrong?

3

The police showed up quietly. There were no flashing lights or sirens. Not that I expected cars to speed into our driveway and kick up dust as they screeched to a stop, like in the movies, but there should be something more to make this feel like a big deal. Because this had become a very big deal.

It was rare to need the police in our town. Disturbances were few and usually involved a noise outside that turned out to be a raccoon scavenging for food or a group of kids skinny-dipping at Black Willow Lake.

But this wasn't the first visit from a set of police officers at our house. The last time the police came to our door was a lot different. It was almost a year ago and late at night when the doorbell rang. Hound Dog had started a frenzy of barking that probably woke up everyone within a five-mile radius. I'd stumbled out of bed to the stairs, where I'd sat with Collin, hoping no one would notice and tell us to go back upstairs.

Abby had stood between the cops, dressed in black with smudges of thick dark paint under her eyes, a cross between a ninja and baseball player. She'd grinned at my parents and the cops had looked amused themselves, nothing like the gruff look they had when they walked up the bleachers during a football game and made sure no one was heading down the path of juvenile delinquency.

"Is everything all right?" Dad had asked. He'd stood in front of Mom with the door opened all the way so light snuck out and let anyone who was driving by know that the cops were at our house. "Is my daughter in some kind of trouble?"

The cops had exchanged a glance and then turned back to my parents. Hound Dog gave up his quest to sniff out their intentions and trotted up the steps to me. I'd grabbed his collar in my hand and scratched his ears the way that he loved, to get him to settle down.

"Well, she's not exactly in trouble," the bald cop had said. "We caught your daughter and a couple of other kids dropping off cards and flowers on people's doorsteps."

Mom had raised her eyebrows in confusion. "Cards and flowers? Why would Abby be delivering that?"

"Sympathy cards, Mom. To those on Bolton's team," she'd said, mentioning the cross-country team they'd be competing against at the meet in the morning. Abby had pulled an envelope out of her book bag and passed it to Mom.

"We wrote them out expressing the sadness we felt for the

other team's future loss tomorrow. We gave them flowers to let them know we're thinking of them in this time of great sorrow."

"You've got to be kidding," Dad had said, and tried to look angry for the cops' sake, but I could tell he'd wanted to laugh along with Abby.

"We don't think she was causing harm, but it's after curfew," one of the officers said.

"Yes, thank you, sir," Dad had said, acting serious. "We'll make sure to talk to her about this matter."

The cops had nodded and turned to leave, but the bald one had stopped. He crossed his arms across his chest and stared down Abby. "I think a fair punishment would be to win your race tomorrow."

"I can handle that," Abby had said, and patted the cop on the back as if he were an old friend, something I'd never dare to do.

Dad had waited until the door was closed to start laughing himself silly. "Really, Abby? Sympathy cards?"

Abby had shrugged. "Well, it wasn't as if we were going to congratulate them. We wanted to make the team feel better since we're going to destroy them tomorrow."

She'd grinned, and what could they do? It was the way Abby was.

And true to her word, Abby flew past the other team and reminded us on the car ride home that she had fulfilled her punishment.

Today, there were once again cops standing at our front door, but this time, Abby wasn't with them and no one was smiling.

4

The officers sat at our kitchen table, as if we were about to eat breakfast together. I half expected Mom to pull out one of her famous egg and sausage casseroles from the oven, but instead, she slouched in a chair and cried. I'd only seen Mom cry two times in my life: when Grandma died and on Collin's first day of preschool.

The kettle whistled on the stove as Dad made cups of tea. He moved back and forth across the kitchen, never settling for too long in one place. Collin sat wide-eyed, too enthralled by having real live cops in his kitchen to watch cartoons, and I avoided eye contact, as if they could see my truth just by looking at me.

"Are you here to bring Abby home?" Collin asked, and we fell quiet at the bluntness of his question.

"That's the plan," the older one, who'd introduced himself as Officer Donovan, said. He pulled a stick of gum out of his pocket and gave it to Collin. "You'll be fighting with your big sister again before you know it."

Collin grinned and unwrapped the gum while Officer Donovan focused on me.

"We need to get a statement from you about what happened last night."

"A statement?" I asked. My pulse quickened. That sounded official and important.

"No need to worry," he told me. "It's to help us get the events in order, so we can find your sister faster."

"Okay," I said. I twisted the bottom of my shirt around in my hands.

"When you left the bonfire, your sister was still there?" The second cop, Officer Scarano, asked, ready to note my every word on his pad of paper. He couldn't have been more than a few years older than me.

They sat on either side of me, and it felt as if I were trapped between them. I glanced from one to the other and neither of them relaxed the rigid look on their faces. They weren't messing around, and the seriousness of it scared me.

I hesitated.

If I let them know what really happened, maybe it would help. But I couldn't find the courage to do it, especially in front of the police. I'd told one story to my parents; what would happen if I changed it? They weren't going to care about why I kissed Tommy; all they'd listen to is the fact that I'd done this to my sister.

"Abby told me to leave, that she'd get a ride from her

56

friends," I said, which was the truth. I wasn't lying, I was simply leaving out the part about her saying it after she had caught me kissing her boyfriend and wanted me as far away from her as possible. My parents would hear all about it when she finally did return home. "Tommy dropped me off, and I went to bed."

"What time was that?" Officer Scarano asked.

"I don't know, around eleven? Dad saw us come home. He flashed the lights."

He nodded. "I thought it was the three of you coming home together."

"Is there additional information you can remember? Any little detail might help us figure out where she is," Officer Donovan added.

I paused, the truth dangling so close.

"Tell him something," Mom insisted, startling us all.

"Rhylee," Officer Scarano said, "time is important in helping us to bring your sister home. Any piece of information might help."

My mind flashed back to the look on Abby's face when she found Tommy and me together. She'd trusted me, and I betrayed her. I'd done this. There was no one to blame but myself.

"Help us find Abby," Mom shouted. She grabbed my upper arm. Her fingers dug into my skin. "Don't you understand? Something might have happened to her. We need to find her."

Mom's voice was close to hysterical. I looked at the floor, ashamed.

"I . . . that night, Tommy and I . . ." I wanted to tell. I really did, but the words wouldn't come out. How do you tell your parents that you kissed your sister's boyfriend? You couldn't. "I don't know. I don't have anything else to say that might help."

"That's not good enough," Mom snapped, and I wished I had the courage to say more.

"Rhylee's trying her best," Dad said to Mom. "Why don't you go see if you can find some pictures of Abby for the police to use?"

It was unnecessary; the entire town knew what Abby looked like. She was our star. They didn't need a photo of her.

"Can I go talk to Tommy?" I asked, and if anyone thought it was unusual, they didn't show it.

Officer Donovan nodded. "Tell him to come over here, if you don't mind. We need to get his statement too, and it'd be easier if we could stay here with your parents."

I agreed and ran toward Tommy's house. I needed him to tell me it was going to be okay.

5

I heard Tommy's music before I saw him.

The sound of notes from a song swelled and floated out the windows of his living room. He was hunched over the keys of his piano, and his fingers moved so fast they blurred. He played with a passion and talent that was unexpected. No one had any idea where it came from. He'd simply sat at their piano one day when he was little and plucked out a tune. His parents enrolled him in lessons, and to his teacher's amazement, he conquered pieces each week that usually took others a month to learn. He began to write his own songs when we were in middle school—silly ones at first that the two of us would make up words for, but now he created pieces that could make your chest swell with emotion. Tommy's music was one of the things I loved about him.

He was barefoot; he always played barefoot. He had on his usual jeans and one of the vintage T-shirts he searched for at the Goodwill a few towns over. The black ink of his tattoo peeked out from under the sleeve, a contradiction on someone who played the piano at the level Tommy did. But that's always been who he was: a contradiction in so many ways, including subverting everyone's expectations of the two of us ending up together when he began to date Abby.

I listened as he played, until his fingers rested on the keys.

I knocked on the window to get his attention and our eyes met. My body vibrated from the adrenaline. Neither one of us moved. It wasn't until a car flew around the corner, its brakes screeching, that I was startled out of his gaze.

"You're here," he said through the screen, and there was such genuine happiness on his face.

Happiness for me.

He still felt it, and my heart hurt for what I had to say next.

"The police are at our house," I told him through the screen. "Abby still isn't home and no one has seen her."

Tommy swung his legs over the side of the piano bench and jumped up. The front door opened and he came outside.

"Where is she?" he asked, his voice fast and frantic.

"I don't know. None of her friends remember seeing her when they left. And now the police are involved and they're asking questions and looking for pictures of her and they want you to come over so they can talk to you. . . ." My words hung in the air, their meaning heavy and serious.

He shook his head, but our denials couldn't erase what had happened. "We shouldn't have left without her."

"I tried get her to come with me," I said. But did I try hard enough? Did I really do everything I could have?

Tommy paced back and forth across his porch, his bare feet slapping against the old boards.

"This is my fault. I did this to my sister and now she's gone." My voice rose until I was yelling hysterically. I thought about the policemen in our living room and my parents and about the truth. Tommy and I had ignited all of this and now the repercussions of our actions were exploding around us. "I did this."

I backed away, but he grabbed me. He wrapped me in his arms and hugged my body against his.

"There's no 'I.' There's us. The two of us. You're not alone."

My knees buckled from the weight of it all, but he held tight. He refused to let me go.

"You're not alone," he repeated.

I gave up fighting and let him hold me.

"I did this," I sobbed, and continued to say the words over and over again into his chest.

6

Tommy and I walked side by side with just enough space between us that we didn't touch. No one knew what we'd done, and now, all of my hopes felt sour in the face of Abby's disappearance. The closer we got to my house, the more anxious I became, but I forced myself to go numb so my guilt wouldn't shine through and reveal everything to everyone.

I filled him in on what I told the cops. "I didn't say anything about the kiss. Or that Abby ran into the woods. They think I got sick and you took me home. I told them Abby was going to leave with Mary Grace." I said all of this in a hushed voice, like I was telling him a secret, and in a way, I was.

"We need to tell the truth," he said.

I shook my head quickly. "No, we can't. Think about how it would look if I change my story. Everything will be fine. Abby will come home, and we'll deal with it then."

I waited for him to argue, but he didn't.

"You're right. She'll be back in no time and everything will come out then," he said. But like me, he didn't sound convinced.

We slipped in through the back door and sat in the living room on the couch. Dad nodded at Tommy, and Mom gave him a sad half smile. I couldn't look at the two cops. I was pretty sure that if I did, they'd see the truth.

"I'm here to help," Tommy told my parents. "If there's anything I can do, let me know."

I put my elbows on my knees and bent forward, as my parents and the police went over and over the same facts about my sister, searching for a clue that would reveal itself in the information that seemed to play on a loop. I acted like things were fine. I pretended I hadn't just come from Tommy's house, where we'd held each other and worried about the role we'd played in all of this. I became a part of the group and focused on finding my sister. That's the way it had to be.

7

When Abby ran, some of her races would be so close that she'd go stride for stride with another runner. We'd hold our breaths as they neared the finish line and wait to see who'd pull forward in the end. Every single second counted and one misstep could cost her everything.

That's how I felt today when we searched for her.

I learned there was a certain protocol when someone goes missing. Things move fast, because the first twenty-four hours are the most crucial in bringing the person home okay. As time ticks away, so does the chance of a happy ending.

When it was clear that Abby wasn't staying at a friend's house, a call went out for volunteers, people who were willing to come over and help search for her. The police questioned everyone at the bonfire and talked with Johnson Franklin, an old Vietnam vet who lived in an army tent back in the woods about two miles from where the bonfire was. He was a fixture of our town and could be found every day pushing his shopping cart along our small main street, a handwritten sign hanging over the side, asking to please "Remember Those Who Served for You." He didn't take handouts, didn't want your money, and the only time he participated in a town event was during the Memorial Day parade, where he made sure to shake the hand of every man who served our nation. If you tried to offer him a place to stay, he'd tell you he "slept in the jungle during the war, and he can sure as hell survive in a forest in Ohio."

"He's been questioned in depth," Officer Scarano told my parents. "We're confident he isn't tied to Abby's disappearance."

"I'm relieved that he isn't a part of this," Dad said. "I only wish we had some answers. A way to bring Abby back to us."

"We all do, Mr. Towers. Believe me, we're looking."

Tommy's parents walked over with steaming carafes of coffee, and Tessa showed up with two giant pizzas from Calloos's, our go-to food when one of us was having a bad day.

"I have pepperoni pizza and cheesy bread with extra dipping sauce," she said as she presented the boxes to me.

"Thanks," I told her, even though I was pretty sure Collin would be the only one to eat the pizza. Food was the last thing on our minds.

"The more important question is, how are you?" she asked.

"I'm fine," I said, but I wasn't, not even close.

"That's bullshit," she said, always one to call me out on a lie.

"Okay, right. Things could be better."

Tessa rolled her eyes. "This is ridiculous. Your sister has

everyone worried. What a screwed-up way of sleeping off a hangover," she said, because years of friendship gave her the power to speak about Abby like that. She pulled a bag of M&M's from her purse and threw a few of them into her mouth. Tessa was always carrying some kind of candy; she devoured it as if her life depended on hourly sugar rushes.

"I'm not so sure it's a hangover," I said, and the words made me feel sick. "Let's go see what everyone is talking about." I pointed toward a large group that had gathered by the barn. Tommy stood at the edge, away from Abby's friends. He was alone, and Tessa headed toward him.

"Hey," he said to both of us. I tried not to look at him too long, afraid Tessa would be able to tell what we'd done just from the electricity that sparked in the air between us.

"This sucks, huh?" Tessa asked. "I told Rhylee it's going to be fine. Abby will come waltzing back home any minute now, and we'll laugh one day about how we overreacted."

"I hope so," Tommy said.

A man in a red polo shirt with a clipboard whistled loudly to get everyone's attention. He directed us to spread out in a line; our heels touched the road, our toes, the grass. We clasped hands and formed a giant chain.

"Okay, everyone," he said, "we need you to move slowly and keep your eyes on the ground. We're looking for clues. Something that might confirm that Abby was here. Don't rule anything out; a piece of paper, crumpled-up wrappers, things that may look like trash. Even if it doesn't seem like anything, it could be."

When we were ready, he gave the signal to move across the field. Tessa shook the rest of her M&M's into her mouth and held my hand tight. Tommy grabbed my other hand, and I flashed back to the day in the park in the tunnel and how badly I had wanted to be with him then. I tried to shake the memory out of my head. It wasn't right to be feeling things for him now, and I needed to focus on what we were doing.

The search reminded me of the game red rover we used to play on the playground with our classmates. We'd stand the same way, our hands clasped tightly as we yelled, "Red rover, red rover," inviting those who looked weak over. We'd tighten our grip, hot and sweaty, squeezing one another so the person from the other side couldn't break through. We stood strong and united, laughing when our human wall held the other side out.

I was part of a chain with thirty-six other searchers and we slowly moved across my family's field, walking the same path I'd walked with Abby and her friends the night before on the way to the bonfire. We took baby steps across the great expanse of our field that Abby could run in eleven minutes flat. Today it took almost an hour to cross. There was no running, no chanting, no laughing. We didn't want to keep anyone out of our wall. We wanted to find something.

Or someone.

We walked across the field slowly and kept our eyes to the ground, desperate for even the smallest clue.

"Hey, can we stop for a minute? This might be important," a man in a plaid shirt said and bent down. A murmur went through the group. People rushed to surround him. He held a gray sweatshirt high in the air as if it were a winning lottery ticket.

I recognized it. Abby had worn it the night before.

I let go of Tessa and Tommy's hands and pushed my way to the center of the circle where everyone was gathered. I stopped at the spot where the man found it. The ground was covered with brittle pieces of grass baked by the sun. Abby had been here. I bent down and pretended to tie my shoe, but instead, I grabbed a handful of grass and stuck it in my pocket, so I could somehow be close to her. I tried to convince myself that she'd dropped it on our walk to the bonfire, but as I stood, Tommy's face was full of fear, and mine reflected the same.

Officer Donovan took the sweatshirt and put it in a plastic bag. He didn't ask me if it was my sister's; he didn't even look at me. It was as if I wasn't even connected to her anymore. As if I wasn't even Abby's sister any longer. I was nobody.

We joined hands and continued our search. When we got to the woods, we walked as close to one another as we could, only breaking to go around trees. Step by step by step. We walked past the bonfire site to where Abby found Tommy and me, and continued to move through the trees. We didn't stop until we reached the edge of the river. No one talked, as if our words would change our worst fears into reality.

Officer Scarano and two other officers I didn't recognize walked a ways down, inspecting something in the dirt. One of them took out a camera and snapped some pictures.

"I'm going over there," I said.

"Maybe you shouldn't," Tessa told me, and Tommy nodded.

"Screw that, this is about my sister."

I let go of their hands and made my way over to the group. Officer Scarano spotted me, opened his mouth to say something, but then closed it. Whatever was out here couldn't be hidden from me. I'd find out. I was family.

But when I saw what they were inspecting, I wish I hadn't.

There were shoe prints in the dirt.

Fresh ones. There was no water gathered in them from the rains earlier this week, nor had the sun baked them dry. I put my shoe next to one of the prints. It was the same size as my own. The same size as Abby's.

I followed them until they stopped. The two officers were already scrutinizing them. They went right to the edge of the river. It looked as if one foot had gotten stuck deep in the mud, while the other foot streaked down and disappeared into the river.

It terrified me to think of Abby here, running along the river our parents had forbidden us to go near when we were younger. We stayed away from it, especially at this time of year when the bank was slippery and the water was high and fast from the heavy summer storms. It was to be avoided.

Except for last night, when Abby ran along the edge to get away from me.

Deep down inside of me, something shifted.

My sister was not okay.

And it was my fault.

8

Mom was waiting when I came back with the group from the fields. The police had told her it would be better to stay at home in case Abby returned, especially since Dad was driving around in his old Buick with some other men from the car factory, hoping to find her.

Mom saw Tessa and me, and she rubbed her hands against the sides of her jeans like she does when she's nervous. As we got closer, most of the group broke away and walked to their cars or the barn.

"Do you want me to stick around for a little bit?" Tessa asked. "Because I will. I'll stay all night if you need me to. Heck, I'll move in if it helps."

I wanted to smile, but it was impossible.

"Thanks," I said, and considered telling her everything.

Tessa was my best friend. She had been since we were six. We didn't keep secrets from each other. Ever. But now, it seemed as if all I did was hide things from people I cared about.

Things that made everything worse.

"Hang in there," Tessa said. "It'll be okay. Abby always lands on her feet."

I nodded, because it was easier to pretend things would work out than talk about how they might not.

"If you need me, all you have to do is text." She waved her phone in the air as she headed to her car.

It wasn't until she was gone that I became strongly aware that my hand was still gripping Tommy's. I took a deep breath and let myself hold on for a moment longer. I wanted to be connected to him, but this wasn't the right time. There might never be a right time again.

"I need to talk with my mom," I told him.

"I'll call you later," he said, but I shook my head.

"I don't think that's a good idea. I'll let you know the minute I hear something about Abby, but maybe it's best if we stayed away from each other."

His forehead creased in that way it does when he's upset. "We need each other."

"My *sister* needs me," I said.

He opened his mouth to say something, but I interrupted him. "I'll let you know if we hear anything, but for now, just give me space."

71

"Okay, if that's what you want," he said.

"It has to be what I want."

Above us, a helicopter made laps around the woods where Abby was last seen.

9

Abby didn't return for dinner.

She didn't return at all that night.

The police told my parents about her sweatshirt and foot-prints. Mom hadn't been able to stop crying since.

"Why is Mama so sad?" Collin asked, and it about broke me.

I bent down so we were on the same level.

"She misses Abby," I said. "We all miss Abby."

"Where is she?"

It was the first time I'd heard him ask, and I wondered what my parents had told him.

"She'll be back soon," I said, hoping he'd believe what even I couldn't.

"She's left us," he said firmly. When he fixed his gaze on me, his eyes were a dark blue like midnight. "She's gone."

"Don't be silly. Abby will be home before we know it, and

you'll wish she was gone again because she'll be bugging you so bad!"

My words got caught in my throat. It felt as if I was lying to Collin and that scared the hell out of me.

I threw one of the couch pillows at his head to distract him. He giggled and threw it back. I was about to send it over to him again when he spoke up.

"She visited me last night."

I froze, the pillow in my hands. "What do you mean?"

"When I was sleeping. I woke up and she was scratching on my window screen. She wanted to come in, but I couldn't get it open. Her hair was tangled with sticks and she was covered in mud."

I moved so I was real close to Collin. "Did you tell Mom and Dad that you saw her?"

He shook his head. "She told me not to. She said it was a secret."

"Why would she say that?"

"She didn't want anyone else to know she was out there."

"You were having a dream," I told Collin, but goose bumps covered my arms. "It was a bad dream."

"She was there," he insisted, and I didn't argue. I knew exactly how he felt. I wanted to believe she was out there too, because Abby haunted my every moment, and all I wanted was to see her again.

10

That night the wind blew wildly through my open bedroom window, moving the curtains like tissue paper ghosts.

I pressed my face against the screen and searched for Abby, while another storm rolled in over the field where she ran.

Lightning flashed and illuminated the corners of my room before it plunged into darkness again. But the storm was far off and never reached us.

I waited for her to come, and when sleep finally took hold, I yearned to see her in my dreams. I wanted Abby to appear, so I could tell her I was sorry, that I never meant for this to happen, but my dreams were empty.

There was nothing but black, black space.

11

The alarm went off the next morning, and I slammed my hand on the snooze button.

It went off three more times before I finally yanked the cord out of the wall.

I couldn't get out of bed.

I didn't want to get out of bed.

I didn't deserve to get out of bed.

A new day had come, even though I willed it not to. Abby was still missing. The secret burned hot within me, scorching my insides so it felt as if I might explode.

The sunlight grew brighter through my curtains, but all I wished for was a world of darkness where I could waste away as the blame burrowed deep within me.

The grass I had grabbed from the spot where Abby's sweatshirt was found was scattered across my dresser, a tangible reminder of the nightmare we were now living.

My family moved around the house, doors opened and closed, low voices, except for Collin's good-byes as he got onto the school bus.

At first I thought my parents were going to leave, forget that I still existed, my absence from breakfast not even something they noticed. It would make sense if they did. With Abby gone, I didn't know where I belonged.

But I was wrong. There was a knock on my door.

"Rhylee, are you awake?" Dad asked from the other side.

"I'm here," I told him. "You can come in."

"Hey, kiddo," he said, sitting on the edge of my bed. It felt weird to have him call me that, a term he hadn't used since I was young. "Not a good morning, huh?"

"The worst," I told him.

"I hear you. Do you want me to call you in sick from school?"

I nodded, afraid I'd cry if I spoke. He was being so nice to me, and I didn't deserve any of it. I owed him the truth, but it was the one thing I couldn't bring myself to give him. I was a coward.

When Collin got mad or upset, he'd put his fingers in his ears and sing real loud so he didn't have to listen to us. That's what I wanted to do right now, but I had a feeling that as much as I tried or no matter if I put my fingers in my ears and hummed and hummed and hummed, I wouldn't be able to escape the reality of what was happening.

"I'm going to head out to look for Abby, but your mom is downstairs. Are you okay here?"

77

"Yeah, I'm good."

"Give me a call if you need me." Dad placed a hand on my shoulder. "We're going to bring Abby home," he said with such certainty that I couldn't help but believe him.

I made myself get up and put my feet on the floor. I went into the bathroom, the door to Abby's room still closed tight. Usually the two of us fought over the tiny space. She'd dry her hair while the I tried to brush my teeth, or I'd want to shower and she'd be washing her face. It was a constant battle. Mom forbade us from locking each other out, but we never listened. It was pretty much inevitable that one of us would wake the rest of the house by pounding on the door for the other to get out.

I'd always wished for my own bathroom.

Just not like this.

Abby's toothbrush sat in its holder, ready for her to come use it. Her pale blue towel hung on the hook by the door and one of her hair ties sat on the sink with some golden hair wrapped around it. Everything waited for her to return.

I brushed my teeth and it felt strange to be doing something so normal when Abby wasn't here. The world moved on and we went through the motions, but none of it felt right. I examined my face in the mirror. I looked the same, but I didn't recognize myself. I was a stranger.

Dad was gone by the time I made it downstairs. I'm sure he was driving the streets in search of Abby. Hoping to find her among the other people in our town, as if it were a regular day and she'd only gone out for a run or to grab a doughnut at Otis's Diner.

I wondered where Tommy was. Did he go to school today? He'd left me alone like I asked, but last night he had gone out with Dad and a few other neighbors. They had searched the dirt roads that were used to access the hunting trails.

I'd picked up my phone a few times to text him, but I never sent them. As much as I missed Tommy and wanted to talk, I couldn't see how that would ever be possible again. Not after what we'd done to Abby.

The only thing I could think about was finding my sister, and as I finished eating a bagel, that's exactly what I set out to do. I didn't bother to leave a note; I figured my parents wouldn't be back until later, and if they did come home, they'd assume I was at school. I slipped out the door and headed into the field.

There wasn't a question about where I was heading. I took the same path Abby, Mary Grace, Erica, and I had walked on our way to the party. The ground was still wet from last night's storms, creating pockets of mud from the ruts where Dad's mower had gone. The grass brushed against the bottom of my legs, and a lazy breeze blew around me until I reached the woods. Once I entered the trees, the outside world was silenced. Except for the snapping of twigs and rustling of the leaves, it was only me.

I followed the trail into the woods and watched everything around me; my eyes scanned left and right as I hoped to catch a glimpse of my sister. It was eerie being here alone. The leaves on the trees created a canopy, so only bits of light escaped through the open spaces and reached the ground.

I caught a flash of movement out of the corner of my eye and froze. I prayed it was Abby, but when I crept forward for a closer look, I saw it was Johnson. He wore a blue thermal shirt that seemed too hot for this weather and clutched a pile of sticks against his chest.

The police had said that he wasn't a suspect, but how could he not be when he lived in the same woods my sister disappeared in? Had he seen her that night? Or heard her? Was he holding something back? I wanted to shout out to him, ask him what he knew, but I was alone in the woods that had swallowed my sister up; I was too scared to do anything more than wait for him to leave.

My hands were in fists. I relaxed them and continued along the path until I arrived at the bonfire site, now just a hole of black soot and charred logs. I kicked at one of the stones that lined the circle and when it didn't budge, a sharp lick of pain surged through my foot. But even that wasn't enough to numb all of my emotions. Abby had been here two days ago, twirling around the flames with her arms held out. How happy and carefree she had been.

I walked over to where the cars had been parked. There were tire tracks in the dirt filled with cloudy rainwater and crumpled-up beer cans. A reminder that people had been here.

Tommy and I had been here.

And Abby had found us.

I sank to the ground as thoughts spun around my head. They made me so dizzy it was hard to think straight.

What had I done to my sister?

Why hadn't I chased after *her*?

Why hadn't I *insisted* she come back with me when I saw her at the river?

Why hadn't I told her I was sorry?

Each *what-if* taunted me. There were so many things I could have done, but I didn't do any of them.

My mind flashed to Max Locke. He was in my class until last year, when his family moved away. He was supposed to stay home and watch his little brother one day, but instead he took his brother with him to the park so he could hang out with friends. When he wasn't watching, his brother wandered into the street, where a car hit him. He survived, but he was never, ever the same. I remember the way people at school treated Max. What they said to him and how they made him into some kind of monster. He never intended for that to happen to his brother. It was an accident, but it didn't matter. People would view me the same way if I told the truth about what happened.

I went in the direction Abby had when she ran away from Tommy and me. I moved through the woods quickly, as if it were that night again, and I was following her. I slapped tree branches out of the way and tripped over roots, but that didn't stop me. I moved faster and faster until I burst out into a clearing.

I was at the river.

The water moved swiftly. It churned and took anything in its way with it. A tree limb the size of a small car passed by me in an instant.

"Abby," I yelled, but the roar of the river was the only response.

I took a few small steps toward the river until my feet were at the edge of the embankment.

"Abby, please, you need to come home," I shouted into the empty spaces around me. "We need you."

I choked on my words.

"I need you."

I shifted my weight to take another step and slipped. My right foot slid down the muddy bank into the water. I grabbed at the roots that lined the edge and tried to pull myself up. I could feel the current tugging on me.

I clawed my way back, moving on all fours like an animal, struggling to get away from the angry water.

My pants got stuck on a rock, and it tore a hole through them, the cold water a shock to my bare skin. A bright red line of blood appeared, and I hurried to pull myself up all the way. I moved a few feet away from the river and fell to the ground.

I lay there, my chest heaving up and down, my heart punching against my skin. I'd almost gone into the water. I could've been swept away.

Panic set in as I imagined my sister too close to the edge so that with one misstep, the water could swallow her up.

The thought took my breath away, and it felt as if I were the one who was drowning.

12

I burst out of the woods and ran through our field as if an invisible demon was chasing me. I moved through the mowed lines my sister ran, and as I got close to our house, my parents and Officer Scarano rushed toward me.

"Rhylee, what's wrong?" Dad asked, alarmed.

I was a mess. My jeans were torn and bloody, my clothes were caked with dried mud, and my hands were scraped.

"Everything," I told him, and I choked back the fear that was threatening to smother me.

"Are you okay?" Mom asked. "Where have you been?"

"I tried to find her. I went back to the woods where the bonfire was. I searched by the river, but she wasn't there."

I broke down. I couldn't be strong any longer. I sank to the ground and brought my knees to my chest. I put my head down and sobbed, too ashamed to look at anyone.

Dad kneeled and pulled me to him. He rocked me like he had when I was young.

"You've been so strong, Rhylee. I know this is hard, but we have to believe she's going to find her way home." The stiff hairs from his beard rubbed against my cheek, and I wanted so badly to believe him.

But it wasn't true. I was by the river. I saw the footprints and how easy it was to be pulled into the water. Abby wasn't okay. She wasn't going to be okay. And if they had any idea what I'd done, no one would want to touch me anymore. No one would want to be near me.

"I need to ask you about that night again," Officer Scarano said when I let go of Dad.

I was suddenly on guard. What else did they want to know?

"I told you everything I know."

"It's about Tommy. You two are close, right?"

"We're friends," I said, and tried to be careful with my word choice because I had no idea where this was heading.

"Do you remember seeing him at the bonfire while you were there?"

"Yeah," I said cautiously.

"Do you remember if there was ever a point when you didn't see him around? Maybe for a little bit?"

"I don't know, maybe. He's my sister's boyfriend, not mine. I don't know what he's doing all the time. Why is that important?"

Mom and Dad exchanged glances. The two of them then

84

turned toward Officer Scarano. It made me nervous.

"What's going on?" I asked.

Officer Scarano cleared his throat before he spoke. "Tommy's being interviewed by some detectives right now."

"What for?"

"Rhylee, let's go inside. We can talk about this later," Dad said, placing a hand on my shoulder, but I shook it off.

"Tell me what's going on," I demanded.

"Some of your classmates came forward and said that they heard Abby yelling at someone near the bonfire. When one of them went to check on her, they saw Tommy push your sister down and then Abby and Tommy ran into the woods. We're trying to figure out what it was about." Officer Scarano said it as if it were no big deal. As if we were simply having casual conversation.

I sucked in my breath. I remembered how I'd reached out to Tommy to stop him. That wasn't my sister they saw, that was me.

"No," I said, not just to my parents and Officer Scarano but also to myself. "You're making a mistake. Tommy wouldn't hurt Abby."

"We're not saying that he did, but we need to check our leads."

"What leads?" I demanded. "Who's blaming him?"

When the officer wouldn't reply, Mom spoke up. "His shoe prints were found along the riverbank. Near where we found the ones that match Abby's shoe. But he said he never went near the water."

"I have to talk to him," I said, a sense of unease rising within me.

"You need to stay away from him," Mom said, surprising us all. She loved Tommy. She joked that she had four children, since he was over so much.

"You can't possibly believe he did something to Abby, can you, Mom? This is Tommy we're talking about," I said, mostly to convince her but also to silence the sliver of doubt that had edged into my mind.

Mom just stared at me. "Right now, all I know is that my daughter is missing and Tommy is the last person to have seen her," she finally said.

"He's not a suspect, is he?" I asked Officer Scarano, and when he didn't reply, Dad spoke up.

"We're trying to bring your sister home," he said. "That's what we need to focus on."

"Tommy didn't do anything to Abby," I said, but my words didn't sound so confident. And when the three of them said nothing, suddenly it wasn't only my sister I was afraid for, but also Tommy.

13

Tommy is not a suspect.

Tommy is not a suspect.

Tommy is not a suspect.

I sat in my room and wrote the words over and over again on notebook paper. I tried to make myself believe it was true. My pen pressed down so hard that it left an imprint on my desk.

Tommy was a good person. He'd never do anything to Abby.

But the police had planted a small doubt into me, and I wasn't sure I could shake it out of my mind. There were about thirty minutes between when Abby had run away from me and Tommy found me. What was he doing during that time?

I ripped a new sheet of paper out of my notebook and wrote a list of what might have gone on during those lost minutes:

1. Looking for Abby

2. Arguing with Abby

3. Trying to talk Abby into returning to the bonfire

4. Breaking up with Abby

5. Tommy did something to Abby

My pencil hovered over number five. I was scared to put down what the cops and my parents were thinking.

Tommy couldn't have done anything.

He wouldn't have done anything.

Right?

I crossed off five, then four, then three, then two. I pretended there were no other reasons or answers beyond Tommy searching the woods for my sister.

I grabbed a glue stick and created a new sort of collage. I pasted the scraps that proclaimed *Tommy is not a suspect* over my list. One on top of the other until the list disappeared and there was nothing but Tommy's innocence.

14

Mom might have forbidden me from talking to Tommy, but that was all the more reason I needed to. Forget about leads and what the police thought they'd found. I had to hear it from him that he didn't do anything.

I waited until my parents went to a community meeting to discuss efforts in the search for Abby. Collin was at a friend's house, so it was easy to slip away.

I walked alongside the road, not wanting to cut through the field. It didn't feel right when Abby wasn't here to run it every day.

It was dusk, that time of day when the bottom of the horizon seems to fade beneath the darkening sky. I wondered where Abby was and whether or not she saw the same sky.

Tommy's light was on in his room. His curtains were drawn, but a shadow moved in front of them. I pulled out my phone and dialed his number.

"I need to talk to you," I said when he answered. "I'm outside your window."

The curtains parted and Tommy appeared. The light behind him illuminated his face, and I felt the familiar pull toward him.

He held his index finger up, indicating that he needed a minute, the curtain dropped, and he disappeared again.

I waited for what felt like forever and almost thought he'd changed his mind when he walked out from the back of the house.

"Is something wrong?" he asked.

"The police questioned you," I said. "They said someone saw you running into the woods after Abby."

The light from his eyes faded.

"They're calling you a suspect," I continued.

"I'd never hurt Abby. You can't believe that," Tommy said.

I shook my head. "I don't know what to think, this is all so crazy."

Tommy sat on his front step and put his head in his hands. I reached out and my hand hovered over his back. In the life before Abby went missing, I never would've hesitated to offer support, but here, in our current reality, I pulled my hand back, unsure of what was right or wrong anymore.

Tommy finally raised his head. "I tried to find her. I looked for her everywhere. I went back to the woods after you had called and told me she hadn't come home. I searched through the trees, by the river. I wanted to bring her home, but I couldn't find her."

"You went to the river?" I asked.

"It was a dumb idea, all of it was. She'd run away the night before, but I had this strange feeling that something wasn't right. I didn't know what else to do."

"The police found your footprints there," I said, and it made sense. He'd gone back to find my sister.

"I told them I didn't hurt her. I was there because I tried to find her. I swear, I didn't hurt Abby."

"I believe you," I said with a certainty even I didn't understand. And this time I did rest my hand on his back.

"I told the police everything I could. About what happened at the bonfire. I told them Abby and I got in a fight because I planned to break up with her. I admitted to chasing after her, but told them I couldn't get her to come back with me. I didn't tell them you were there. They don't know you were involved. You're safe, Rhylee, and I'll make sure it stays that way."

Safe. I was safe. He couldn't know how much his words twisted inside of me. How could I ever be safe again after what I had done? Until Abby came home, I'd never feel safe again.

15

I stayed home from school again the next day and returned to the woods to look for Abby, but once I made it to the river, I couldn't move on.

I stood at the edge, because where did I go from here?

The water swirled and churned as if it waited for one wrong move to swallow me whole and claim me too. I stayed rooted to the edge, and my mind spun with reminders of how I'd betrayed my sister and the fear that no amount of searching would fix what I'd done.

16

My parents were waiting for me when I got home.

"We were hoping to meet with some of the neighboring cities' police officers to talk about ways to expand the search. Do you mind staying here until we get back?"

Translation, "We want someone here in case Abby returns," as if we needed to catch her and hold on to her so she doesn't run again.

"Sure," I told them, even though the idea of sitting in an empty house was the last thing I wanted to do.

"We're going to find her," Dad said, and I felt that familiar clutch in my stomach, the deep knot of fear, the whisper of doubt.

I turned on the TV after they left, because silence was impossible.

Mom had plastic bins full of pictures sitting on the dining room table. She'd been sorting through them and pulling out images of Abby to scan and upload onto a tribute page she created to help bring her home.

I grabbed a stack and laid each picture out, one after the other, until the whole table was covered. I moved each around and placed the images in chronological order the best that I could. My sister's life scene by scene.

I sorted through one of the stacks and found a picture of Tommy and me that I'd never seen before. We were on my front steps with Popsicles in our hands. There was purple juice from Tommy's Popsicle running down his hand and my lips were stained bright red. It was the summer before sixth grade, because I had Band-Aids on both my knees, my elbow, and my forehead. Tommy had dared me to climb the tree in his back-yard after his dad had been picking apples and left a ladder under it. The limbs were too high to get to from the ground, but the ladder made it the perfect climbing tree. At least it was until the branch I was on snapped and I slipped. The two of us had gotten in big trouble for going up in the tree, and for a week we weren't allowed to see each other. Abby and I had spent the days together, and I remember how upset she was when our parents got sick of Tommy and me whining and we were finally allowed to see each other again.

I'd chosen him over her, always. Nothing had changed. And now Abby was gone because of it.

I swiped my hand across the table and knocked the pictures on the floor. This was useless. It was all useless.

My thoughts were interrupted by a loud knock on the front door. For a second, a brief second, I thought it was Abby and she'd returned home, but that was silly. If it was her, she'd open the door and let herself in.

I tried to hide my disappointment when I saw it was Tessa.

"We missed you at school today," she said, and dropped the bag she carried so she could give me a hug. Her hair tickled my cheek as she wrapped her arms around me. I wanted so badly to be folded into her comfort. To take what she was offering. But how could I after what I'd done? I deserved none of it.

She let go and pulled a pile of mail from her bag. "Here, this was falling out of your mailbox."

"Checking the mail hasn't been our top priority these days," I said and took the stack. I noticed a bunch of college brochures on top. Texas A&M, Pepperdine, Boston University. I'd been so excited a few weeks ago about Boston University when I found out that they had a program where you could study art for an entire year in Europe. I'd imagined days filled with museums and evenings sitting at cafés and outdoor bars where I'd savor the memories of seeing the great works of art in person. I'd pictured myself there so easily, but now that felt like a lifetime ago.

Tessa followed me through the front hallway into the kitchen. I dumped the brochures in the trash. It was pointless. Who was I kidding? I wasn't getting out of this town. I wasn't going anywhere as long as Abby was missing.

We went into the family room, and even though the pictures were strewn all over the room, Tessa didn't say a word. Instead, we sat on opposite sides of the couch, our feet touching in the middle. The TV played in the background, some commercial about a sale at a furniture store.

"Have you heard anything else?" she asked.

"The cops think Tommy is a suspect," I said and hated the words on my tongue.

"Everyone at school is talking about it."

"He didn't do anything to Abby," I said, and wished I had the courage to tell her the real story about what happened.

"I never for a second thought he did," she said with a certainty that reminded me of how much I loved Tessa.

"Thank you," I told her.

When she spoke next, her voice was almost too soft to be heard over the television. "I'm worried about Abby."

"So am I."

"Where do you think she is?"

"I have to believe she's somewhere safe."

"We all do," she agreed. The mood in the room had shifted. The two of us focused on the television because what more could you say after that?

The afternoon news came back from commercials and Abby's face filled the screen. It was her school photo from last year. She wore a mint green shirt that made the blues of her eyes even more brilliant. Her hair was down and I remembered her braiding it the night before so the curls would be perfect. My sister smiled back at me from the television as a news anchor talked.

"Efforts are being made to help find a missing teen who disappeared this weekend. Abby Towers, a high school junior at Coffinberry High School, was last seen at a bonfire with classmates. A community-wide search is in effect, as everyone helps to locate her."

The woman went on to give a phone number for the police if anyone had tips or information, but I wasn't paying attention. Instead, I focused on the images that were on the screen.

It was Black Willow Lake, which was where the river flowed. The lake that was usually full of Coffinberry kids trying to find a place to cool off in the summer heat. Only in the images on the news, it wasn't full of my classmates but divers in black suits, sleek as seals.

I hit the mute button. I didn't want to hear what the newswoman had to say. I'd seen enough crime shows and movies to understand why someone would be diving in a lake.

They were searching for my sister.

Or more specifically, her *body*.

I jumped up from the couch, ran into the bathroom, and threw up. My hands gripped the sides of the toilet, unable to find absolution for what I'd done.

17

Officer Donovan showed up that evening as we sat around the dinner table. My parents had picked up a pizza on their way home, but Collin was the only one eating any of it. The poor kid pretty much subsisted on pizza or peanut butter and jelly these days. Next to him sat a stack of my collages that I'd made him.

"Can you make me another?" he asked me.

"I don't know, Collin . . . ," I said and trailed off, not quite sure how to tell him that wasn't going to happen anytime soon.

"Please? Something with Abby in it too. It's okay if she wants to share one of my pictures. The two of us could be doing something together. Like when she was here."

"I'll see what I can do," I told him, and the hope in his eyes made me feel even worse. It was as if someone had closed their fist around my heart.

Our doorbell rang, and Collin ran to the door.

"It's the police," he called to us. The police meant Abby, and we needed to be there for whatever it was they came here to tell us.

"Good evening, Mr. Towers," Officer Donovan said to Dad after he opened the door.

"Please, call me Will. Do you want me to make some coffee for you?" he asked. Never mind the fact that Dad didn't even drink coffee. He said even the smell of it made him sick.

"No, I think it's best that we go into the living room to talk." He gestured at Collin.

"Hey, buddy," Dad said to my brother. "I'm going to turn on some cartoons and you can stay in the kitchen. Does that sound okay?"

Collin nodded and I wished I could be like him, so easily swayed and made happy by having his favorite show turned on.

Mom, on the other hand, was the opposite. She shook her head like she was the one having a tantrum.

"I can't," she whispered. "I can't hear what you have to say."

Dad placed his hand on her shoulder, but she shook it off.

"What wrong, Mom?" Collin asked, now concerned with the conversation a second ago he couldn't care less about.

"Everything is okay," Dad said, and looked pointedly at Mom. "Rhylee, why don't you stay here with your brother?"

He gestured at me to take him upstairs.

"I'm coming with you," I said. "Abby is my sister; I need to hear what they have to say."

Dad looked from me to Collin, back and forth. I crossed my hands over my chest. I wasn't going to be left out of this conversation. He ran his fingers through his hair and sighed. "Fine. Collin, stay in the kitchen and watch your show."

Collin nodded, so we took the opportunity to move into the living room. Once we were all there, Officer Donovan spoke again.

"As you're aware, we had divers searching the lake today," he said, and I fought back a swell of bile that rose up from my stomach at the mention of the water. "We looked as much as we could, but the current was rough from the storms and visibility was near zero. The recent rains stirred everything up and debris and logs made it dangerous to search. However, the team found an item that belongs to your daughter."

"What is it?" Mom said in a voice louder than I'd heard her use in days.

Officer Donovan closed his eyes for a moment, as if what he had to say next was hard to get out.

"They found one of Abby's tennis shoes at the bottom of the lake. It was tangled in a bunch of weeds about halfway from shore."

"Are you sure it belongs to her?" Dad asked.

Officer Donovan eyes remained fixed on a spot beyond Dad's shoulder when he talked to us next. "It had her road ID on it."

I could picture the tag he was talking about in my mind.

It was metal and had Velcro so you could put it around the bottom of your laces. Her name and phone number were stamped on it in case something happened to her when she was out running. I'd made fun of her for wearing a tag like Hound Dog did. Now, it seemed, the tag had done exactly what it was supposed to do. Identify my sister.

"The footprints we found on the shore match the tennis shoe in the lake. It places Abby at the edge of the river," he continued. "Does she swim? Is there any reason she would've been in the lake?"

"No," Dad said. "Abby isn't the strongest swimmer. She stays away from the river. We've told her to since she was young."

Dad was right. Abby may have been the best runner our school had ever seen, but her athletic ability only existed on land. She was a terrible swimmer, usually opting to sit in the grass and tan while everyone else swam.

"She could have lost a shoe when she was in the woods," Mom said, her voice flat and hollow.

But that wasn't true.

People fool themselves into believing what they want to be real. They had found the proof. No amount of lies we told ourselves could undo the evidence the police had.

I had to get away. I couldn't hear Officer Donovan tell Mom she was wrong. That a person doesn't lose their shoe and then it ends up tangled at the bottom of a lake.

I slipped out of the room and went outside before he destroyed Mom's hopes.

I ran, even though I hated to run. I moved down the same stretch of earth that my sister's feet had followed so many times. I pushed myself even when my lungs ached for air. I went farther and farther and crossed the field into the entrance of the woods. The sun was nearly gone. The trees cast shadows everywhere, but still I raced forward until I was once again at the river's edge.

"I did this," I cried into the water, my words getting lost in the rush of the current. I yelled my guilt over and over again and prayed that wherever Abby was, she could hear me. I yelled until my voice became hoarse and raw, and it hurt to swallow.

I collapsed on the grass and crossed my hands over my chest. I tried to catch my breath, but it was thick and labored. My mind was tangled up with sins, about Tommy and me and how destructive love is.

This was it.

The end.

It had to be.

I could never, ever be with him again.

I made a promise to the universe.

"Tommy and I are nothing, just bring Abby home! Please!" I begged, my voice choked with sobs.

The river continued to rage. It taunted me for my foolishness, thinking that one could wish everything okay.

I closed my eyes and created a different ending to the story Officer Donovan just told us. In my version, when Abby fell into the water, she kicked off her shoes and striped off the clothes that were heavy and pulling her down. She swam to the surface and climbed out, running barefoot all the way back home to us, and I was there waiting. And Tommy never came between us again. There was only my sister and me, and everything was the way it used to be.

18

The police assumed the worst. They concentrated their efforts on the river, and even though nothing was said, there was a heavy feeling in the air that my sister's disappearance was now a recovery effort. Cadaver dogs were brought in to scour the woods, their noses kept low to the ground as they tried to catch a scent of Abby. The police would deny it if you asked them, and wanted to keep what they'd found in the water a secret, but I knew they were no longer looking for a missing person, but for a body.

The town wouldn't accept that my sister was gone from our lives forever. How does one come to terms with something like that? It was asking the impossible. So as day faded into night and night faded into day, we clung to the idea that she was still out there and would walk through our door at any moment.

A news conference was set up in front of our house, and my parents pled with everyone watching to come forward if they had any information to share. It interrupted the morning talk shows broadcast on every channel. I watched from the little TV in the kitchen, because there was no way I could hold it together enough to stand beside them on live TV. The news crew had put makeup on Mom, but it wasn't enough to hide the black circles under her eyes and the hollowness that sank deep into her cheeks. Everyone could see how broken she'd become as she and Dad spoke straight to the camera and begged Abby to come home.

I didn't go back to school that week. I stayed home and looked for my sister. How could I not? Abby was missing, and I needed to find her. No one said I couldn't, even on those mornings my parents were still in the house when I woke up. It was as if there was an unspoken rule that our lives would stay suspended until Abby returned.

I ignored Tommy's text messages. It was awful of me, but I was afraid if I read them, I'd answer them, and that could never, ever happen again. Tommy and I could never, ever happen again.

The thing about guilt is that it bites its teeth deep within you and doesn't let go. And why should it? Instead of getting easier, the days got heavier and heavier, weighing on my shoulders until I thought I'd explode. The moments when Mom would stare off into space and her eyes would gloss over, the lines on Dad's face that I don't remember existing a week ago, and Collin, who slept with the light on in his bedroom now and often woke up crying from nightmares he refused to tell us about.

105

I wanted to tell the truth, but at what cost? I practiced what I'd say to my parents, testing out words, but there was no right way.

I covered one wall in my room with Abby's missing person flyers. The picture had been taken at a picnic last summer. Abby was laughing at the camera, holding up a pinwheel. She and Collin had held them out of the car window on the way home, letting the breeze turn them around and around.

I hung each so it was perfectly aligned with the one next to it; her face smiled back at me over and over again. I hung up picture after picture of Abby, but no matter how many I added, they couldn't fill the space that she had left behind.

19

Dad opened my bedroom door Sunday morning and sat on the end of my bed. I was awake, but not ready to start another week without my sister.

"How are you doing, honey?" His voice was gentle, and it made me feel worse, because I didn't deserve it. Dad was doing his best to hold us together, to be the strong one, but it couldn't be easy not to fall apart in front of everyone.

"About as well as the rest of you are."

"Not good, then," Dad said, and I nodded.

"Not at all."

"This is hard for everyone." He nodded at the flyers I'd hung on the wall, but didn't say anything about them.

"It's pretty much impossible," I told him.

Dad took a deep breath and let it out. He looked exhausted. He never stopped moving. If he wasn't home trying to coordinate search efforts with others on the phone, then he was out himself with the groups trying to find Abby. I didn't know when he slept, but then again, maybe he didn't want to sleep. Nightmares clouded my dreams, and I wasn't sure what was better: what haunted me in my sleep or my reality.

He picked up a picture that was face-down on my desk, one of Tommy and me, and examined it. I'd gotten rid of everything else that reminded me of him, but I couldn't bring myself to throw away this image.

The picture was the two of us at the carnival that came to the nearby city every summer. We were standing in front of one of those rides that spins you around and around until you get sick. The two of us had huge grins on our faces, proud that we'd gone on it three times in a row.

"You know Tommy wouldn't hurt Abby, don't you?" I asked. "Mom thinks he did something to her."

He lowered the picture and walked over to my bed. "Your mom is trying to make sense of this."

"But how can she blame Tommy? Where's the sense in that?"

"No one is blaming Tommy. We're just trying to find answers so we can bring your sister home."

"Tommy isn't a part of this," I told Dad, and I needed him to believe me. "He'd never hurt her."

"I know that, honey." He pulled open my window shade and let the morning light flow in. "What do you think about going back to school tomorrow? You've already missed a week."

"I need to look for Abby."

"The FBI are bringing in a search team from out of state.

108

They'll look during the day, and we need to let them do their job. You can help when you get home, but I think it would be a good idea if you went back," he said in a way that told me this was an idea I couldn't turn down.

"I'm not sure I can handle being at school when she isn't."

"We need to keep moving," Dad said. "Try it for one day, and if it doesn't work, we'll talk again."

I nodded, but returning to school was the last thing I wanted to do. It didn't seem fair. It made me feel as if I were giving up on Abby; like I was going back to my normal life when she couldn't.

Dad placed his hand on my shoulder and squeezed. "Thanks for being so strong," he said, and I flinched.

I was anything but strong. I was weak and afraid I'd fall apart at any moment.

20

The next morning I got ready as if it were a regular school day. I showered, dried my hair, picked out an outfit, and even put a little lip gloss on. I had the radio on to the station I always listened to and had my usual breakfast of a piece of toast and a banana. I grabbed my bag and waited for the bus, and when it came, I climbed on and took a seat just like I always did. I forced myself to follow my usual routine, but it felt so very wrong. I shouldn't be allowed to do any of this, not after what I'd done.

I kept my eye on Tommy's house and wondered what he was doing. If it had been any other morning, Tommy would pull up, beep twice, and Abby would run out. He'd point to the middle seat if I was around and let me know I could squeeze in, but I never did. Life hurt a lot less when I didn't have to watch the two of them together.

Today, I stared at the screen on my phone to avoid the

stares of everyone around me. I searched "missing teens" on the Internet and read reports about others who had disappeared like Abby. There seemed to be hundreds of accounts about people who had vanished. I clicked on the image button at the top of the search engine and face after face appeared. I scrolled through and wondered what their stories were. Where did they go and had they returned?

The bus pulled up in front of the school and stopped with a giant lurch. I expected school to look different. I expected everything to be different now, because I was different. But everything was the way it always was, which made it even harder for me.

The chain-link fence that ringed the stadium had become a tribute to my sister. Styrofoam cups were stuck in between the links and spelled out ABBY COME HOME. My classmates used the fence to cheer on our sports teams or convince one another of who should be class president, but now it was a plea for my sister to come home to the place I'd once so desperately wanted to get away from.

I hid out in the bathroom before the first bell because there was no way I could talk to anyone and still hold it together. As I moved from class to class, it seemed as if my shame burned so bright that people must be blinded by it, but that wasn't the case. It was the opposite. People I never met before gave me sad half smiles and teachers spoke in low voices and asked if I needed anything. They told me not to worry about the lessons I had missed, that we'd figure out a way for me to catch up. The whole school treated me as if I was fragile and would break at any moment, which I might, but not for the reasons they believed.

I found myself searching for Abby in the halls. I prayed I'd spot her laughing with her friends or racing to get to class, her blond hair flashing as she dodged anyone in her way.

Friends of my sister walked around in a daze, a shocked look on their faces, as if someone had turned the light on in a dark room too fast. Her locker had become a shrine, notes were stuck through the slats, a pair of running shoes left below it, and a sheet of paper with the words WE MISS YOU taped to the front. She'd only been missing for a week, but Abby already haunted the halls, like she haunted my every second.

I hovered at the doorway to my art class. It had always been my favorite time of the day. I certainly wasn't talented enough at it in the way that Abby was with running, but art was one of those things I was really into. I loved that it was a time when I could forget about everything else and get lost in my work. However, the roar of silence in my mind that was usually so welcomed was the last thing I wanted today.

The bell rang, and the rush of students forced me to go through the door. I went to my cubby and pulled out the picture I'd been working on. My teacher had us doing a piece using contrast art, where the main image was blank and the background was full of colors or words. We took the negative space and used it to create a picture. I'd been working on a silhouette of me. In the middle of the page, my face was outlined. I'd begun to write words to fill the space around it.

Travel, Explore, Wanderlust, words that were so silly and insignificant now.

I erased them all, so I was left with nothing but blank space again. I pressed the pencil tip into the paper and wrote a new word.

Gone.

And then, *Lost*.

Where.

Are.

You.

I repeated the words until they filled the entire background of my picture. The words stretched and curved around the outline I'd made of my face. But when I stepped back to look at it from farther away, the silhouette created in the blank space of the picture didn't resemble me. It looked exactly like Abby.

21

The school day continued, even though it felt as if time should stand still. How do we keep moving forward when Abby isn't here? How do you exist when there's such a hole in your life? It didn't feel right. Why was I allowed to do such normal everyday things when my whole world was kicked off its axis and spun out of control?

Tessa found me in the lunch line. I'd grabbed a bunch of food to simply fill my tray, even though I had no appetite.

"Why haven't you answered my texts?" she asked. "I've been trying to talk to you for days."

"I haven't felt much like talking."

"I didn't know you were coming to school today."

I wished she'd stop talking. People around us were listening. I moved to the front of the line and gave the woman at the register my money.

"I didn't either," I said. "But right now I don't know what

the hell I'm supposed to be doing anymore."

My eyes filled with tears and Tessa wrapped her arms around me. My lunch tray jiggled in my hands. I pushed against her to get free and lost my grip. Everything fell to the floor, the silverware clanging as it hit.

I waited for the people around us to clap, like they always did when someone dropped something in the cafeteria, but instead the room got quiet. Abnormally silent for a cafeteria full of teenagers.

I hated it.

I hated that they didn't do anything because it was me. That even dropping my tray in the cafeteria wasn't normal anymore.

Tessa bent down to help pick up my things.

"I'm so sorry, Rhylee, I didn't mean to make that happen. . . ." She babbled on. It was so quiet; the whole room could hear her apologize. My cheeks burned with embarrassment, and I couldn't focus on anything but how much it hurt. A hand grabbed mine and jerked me forward.

"Follow me," Tommy whispered.

He pulled me out of the cafeteria. Some kids jumped out of the way, as if touching him might burn them, and a bunch of others looked at him with disgust.

Kyle Tanner, a boy on the cross-country team, shoved his shoulder into Tommy as we walked past. Tommy stumbled forward as he lost his balance. He grabbed on to a locker to steady himself.

"Watch it," Kyle called over his shoulder as we moved down the hallway.

"Asshole," Tommy said under his breath.

"This isn't right," I told him. "The way people are treating you. You don't deserve this."

"Just keep moving," Tommy muttered and elbowed his way forward. He walked in front of me and blocked everyone. We didn't stop until we reached the indoor pool, a contradiction to the rest of our run-down school. Some rich alum had donated the funds to build it over a decade ago and a swim team was created, those students arriving at class after early morning practices with wet clumps of hair, the smell of chlorine perpetually bouncing off them. He pushed opened the door and we slipped through. His hand still gripped mine as he led me up the steps to the observation deck.

"Hey, it's okay. You're okay," Tommy said, and I realized I was shaking. The water in the pool was still and blue, and I focused on that. The sun came through the windows above and created shadows in some sections and sparkles of light in others.

"It's not okay," I said. "I'm not okay, and *this* certainly isn't okay."

Tommy nodded, but didn't make a move to get up.

The bell rang, signaling the end of lunch period, and I could hear students outside in the hallway. Their voices rose and fell in conversation as they passed the entrance to the pool. The bell rang for the next period, and still, the two of us stayed. I thought about all the times I had wanted to be with Tommy. The daydreams I'd had of the two of us doing something exactly like this, slipping away during the school day, and it turned my stomach.

116

"What if something really has happened to her?" I finally asked.

"We can't think like that," Tommy said.

"But she was down by the water."

"Please," Tommy interrupted. "Stop."

"We can't be together," I said, and kept my voice monotone.

"Rhylee . . . ," Tommy said, but I wouldn't let him finish.

"I'm sorry. But this is the only way it can be. I owe it to my sister. We don't *deserve* to be with each other."

"We didn't mean to hurt her," Tommy said.

"But we did."

"We did," he agreed.

"I wasn't even sorry that I was taking you from her." My voice broke. Watching Abby and Tommy together had been impossible, but this was a hundred times worse. "We can't be together."

"Then what are we supposed to do?" Tommy asked.

"Survive," I told him, because really, that's all we had left.

22

Four more days passed without Abby.

Dad decided to go back to work on Monday. I heard him talking with Mom when they thought no one was around. His boss wanted him to take more time off, but he told Mom that we needed the money and he'd still be able to spend his days helping with the search. I thought about my own job at Webster's and how I never went back after Abby disappeared. I never even called to tell them, and they never called to see where I was. It was as if my family was given a pass to pause our lives, but for how long? And what were the consequences when everyone around us kept moving?

Life became an endless stream of hours, minutes, and seconds without my sister. We were essentially living, without really living. Our lives suspended, our breaths held, until she returned.

I began to create collages again, but not the ones Collin wanted and I didn't put myself into them. Instead, I invented new lives for Abby, reasons for why we hadn't heard from her. I placed her in islands with water so blue it hurt your eyes. I put her among crowds of thousands at rock concerts and alone on mountain peaks. She hiked through national forests and crossed sidewalks in cities congested with cars, people, and smog. She was everywhere, even though we couldn't find her anywhere.

We all wished for a miracle.

Even when each day ended and a miracle didn't come.

The time rushed by and still we hoped, because everyone seemed to know Abby, and even if they didn't, they pretended that they did because her disappearance was the biggest thing to happen in our town. Our own personal tragedy, and everyone loved to be connected to a tragedy, especially when it wasn't your family involved.

So it shouldn't have come as a surprise that the night the circles came, we didn't notice.

It was easy not to notice things these days, because we were so busy being consumed by just one thing.

Mom was the first to see them in the early hours of dawn when she opened the door to let Hound Dog out for his morning pee. She ran into Abby's room to get a better look.

"Will, come in here," she yelled, her voice high and insistent, also pulling Collin and me from our beds. We jostled into each other trying to get down the hall, tired, disoriented, and confused as to why Mom would be in Abby's room.

She stood in front of the window that faced the field. Dad hadn't mowed it since Abby went missing and the paths she had run through were thick with grass and weeds.

Except for the circles that were now cut into our field.

Crop circles in the middle of Coffinberry, Ohio.

They stretched about the size of a football field, and I counted four large circles and three small ones. *Seven circles. Abby's cross-country number.* But I told myself I was being silly.

The circles were attached, forming a pattern that seemed deliberate. The grass around the shapes pushed down. There were no paths outside of them. It was like someone had dropped something and pulled it back up to create the design, their feet never touching the ground. Like in one of those movies where aliens invaded. I half expected a little green creature to jump out of the weeds.

"What are those?" Collin asked as he rubbed sleep from his eyes. He clutched the teddy bear that Abby always slept with.

"Some kids' idea of a joke," Dad said, but Mom didn't think it was a joke. She squinted her eyes and studied them as if the reason for their appearance would suddenly show itself. I thought about my classmates, specifically the farm boys who drove their trucks to school, the backs full of feed and dirt. They sat in our parking lot before school blasting their country music, revving their engines. They were the type of kids who would do something like this; make a joke out of our family's tragedy for a laugh. I could picture the boys creeping into our yard last night, laughing and telling one another to stay quiet in hushed whispers. They'd be drunk, burping out breaths of stale beer and pissing in our grass.

I gazed out at the field my sister once ran and wondered how we didn't realize how lucky we were only weeks ago.

23

An hour later, Dad honked the horn of his car to get us to move.

While the circles were important, we had other things to do. Today was the first cross-country meet of the season, and they'd dedicated it to Abby. I had no idea how I was supposed to sit through the whole thing without breaking into tears. But there wasn't any way to get out of it, even if it would feel next to impossible to be there.

As hard as it was for me to go, it was even harder for Mom. Her bad days seemed to be outnumbering the good, and this morning even Dad couldn't convince her to come with us.

"I want to go," she had said when Dad tried to reason with her. "But I can't. I just can't do it."

I'd watched the two of them from the hallway. Dad had taken Mom into his arms and stroked her hair as if she were a little kid, rocking her back and forth.

Everyone says that the pain of grief lessens, but it was the opposite for us. The grief was elastic and continued to stretch further and further into everything around me, especially moments like that, when my family was so different than what we once had been.

Mom stood at the screen door as we backed out of the driveway. I willed the car to get a flat tire or break down, but no such luck.

I pressed my face against the window and watched the circles disappear from sight as we drove away.

It was a gorgeous day, the sky a blue so vivid it was as if you were living within a picture. It was the type of day where you wanted to stay outside and soak in all the sun you could.

Collin sat in the backseat and flipped through the pages of a comic book; something full of bangs, pows, and kabams with superheroes who saved the world in a single bound. They seemed the opposite from our reality where we had learned that a world where good prevailed and the bad guys perished seemed impossible.

"What planet do you think the circles came from?" Collin asked. "Mars? People say there's life on Mars."

Dad slowed for two kids walking across the street and glanced at Collin. "I don't know, buddy. Let's let the police figure that out."

"So you *do* think they came from outer space?"

Dad sighed. "They came from Earth. We'll find out exactly how, so you don't have to worry about it."

"It's weird," Collin continued. "Why didn't we hear anything? Hound Dog goes nuts when there's an animal in our backyard."

"It probably happened when we were sleeping," Dad said, and turned up the radio to try to stop the conversation, but Collin continued to push the topic.

"No, I bet it was because a human didn't make the circles."

"Collin," Dad said, "we're not talking about this anymore. We need to focus on what's happening today rather than the circles."

But today was the last thing in the world I wanted to focus on. It was Mary Grace who had suggested that the school dedicate the race to Abby. As a way to keep her in the town's mind. But it's not like she needed to; everything these days was about Abby. The school even named it the Abby Towers Hope Run.

A race named after my sister. She would've thought the whole town had gone nuts.

And maybe we had.

Dad, Collin, and I headed into the stadium so everyone could turn their gaze on us and give sad, pitying looks. I tried not to make eye contact, afraid they could see it all on my face. Mom was the one had stayed home, but I should have been the one who didn't go. After all, none of this would be happening if it wasn't for me and what I'd done.

You did this, I reminded myself. *And you weren't even sorry.*

My classmates stood on either side of the entrance with plastic bags in their hands. These were the same people who'd come to our house for pre-meet dinners where Mom would make pot after pot of spaghetti while they carbo-loaded for their races the next day. They all had the tall muscular look. Their legs long and arms lanky. The group ran together as a team, and I always thought they looked like one another after the first few weeks of the season. The girls with their hair held back in elastic bands and everyone in red track jackets with warm-up pants. Tessa and I called them the Cult of Coffinberry. I swear they'd run off a cliff like lemmings if the person in the front led them there.

"Hi, Mr. Towers," Amy, a senior who always wore her hair in a thick braid, said when we made our way to the girls. "It's good to see you." She dipped her hand into the bag. "Thanks for coming."

She pushed a purple bracelet into my hand with the words HOMEWARD BOUND printed on it. I twirled the bracelet around in my fingers. I didn't need to ask what it meant; they were the must-have accessory since Abby had disappeared. Purple was her favorite color, and the slogan was from one of the songs she'd played over and over. She loved old folk music: Crosby, Stills, & Nash; Bob Dylan; Neil Young—anyone who would go on and on about the world needing a' changing. We'd groan when she had control of the radio during a car trip. There was only so much rambling and sappy singing one could take. Dad would joke that it reminded him of his days in college lying in the grass and smoking a joint, and Mom would then elbow him or give him a look that made him apologize and quickly turn the joint into an ice-cream cone.

"We're glad you're doing this for Abby," Dad said.

I put my bracelet on even though it felt more like a shackle. They were supposed to show our solidarity, but it didn't mean anything. It wasn't going to bring back my sister. When they had first passed out the bracelets at school, I couldn't even look them, another constant reminder that Abby was gone and I was still here. I'd thrown mine into my locker, where it probably still sat.

Collin took his and slipped it over his wrist next to the four he was already wearing.

"Do you think Abby will be here?" he asked.

"I sure wish she was," I said. "Everyone is here because they really want her to come home." I wrapped my arms around him in a tight hug and tickled him to get him to smile.

"She's been gone long enough. She better come home soon," he said, and I wished I could promise him that.

My French teacher, Mademoiselle Lang, was the first to come up to us after we made our way into the stadium. She was short and dressed like she was going to some fancy cocktail event. She always wore pearls and pantyhose and heels, even when it was early in the school year and the days still blazed heat. Or at a cross-country meet on a Saturday morning when the rest of the world was looking like lazy bums in jeans and T-shirts.

Abby had urged me to sign up for French when I had to pick a foreign language.

"We'll both know a secret language that Mom and Dad can't understand," she'd said.

I chose it because Abby wanted me to, and while she

had picked up the language quickly and would walk around the house pointing at objects using the French word, it was obvious that I stunk. The words wouldn't come out right, no matter how much I rolled my tongue to make that stupid "r" sound that the rest of the class seemed masters at creating. Mademoiselle Lang would pucker up her face like she'd sucked a lemon when I tripped over my words. Once, when Mademoiselle Lang was particularly frustrated, she said, "I can't imagine how you can be so different from your sister. *Abby est magnifique avec le français.*"

Of course she was. Abby was always the better one. And now she was gone. How could I have ever thought to take her place—even just with Tommy? Would I have measured up to her in his eyes? And how would it be if things were reversed? If I was the one missing? Would people be as upset? Would the town hold out the same hope for me?

Mademoiselle Lang took Dad's hand, holding it between her own. "I'm so sorry to have to meet up with you under these circumstances, but it's good to see you here."

"The same to you," Dad said. He cleared his throat and spoke louder. "Thank you for coming to support my daughter."

"Abby was a wonderful girl," she said.

"Is," I corrected her.

"Pardon?" she asked, confused.

"You said Abby *was* a wonderful girl. She *is* a wonderful girl. There's no past tense to Abby." I said the words slow and steady, my voice firm.

Dad stepped in front of me, creating a blockade between

126

the two of us. "I'm sorry about that. This is hard for everyone."

Typical Dad, always trying to make things better. He was a master at pretending and apologizing for us. It was like he'd become some politically correct robot who only focused on facts and tried to please everyone. It was as if he followed the police's script, only repeating what we knew and not daring to talk about the things we feared.

I let him continue to make excuses and walked up the bleachers. Tessa was at the very top with her back against the press box.

She stood when she saw me and waved her hands in big sweeping motions. She looked like a bird about to take flight.

"Rhylee. Hey, Rhylee, over here."

I hurried up the rest of the steps to get to Tessa and silence her. There were enough people staring at me already. I didn't need her to create even more of a spectacle.

She had on a red Coffinberry High sweatshirt over black leggings and cowboy boots. Her hair was braided into two long pigtails and she had the bracelets for Abby all the way up both arms. She must have been sporting at least fifteen of them. I imagined Mary Grace's pursed lips when she saw how many Tessa had swiped.

Tessa threw herself at me when I finally reached her, wrapped me in a tight hug, and tried to pick me up off the ground.

"Okay, that's enough love from you," I said and swatted at her to get her to let me go.

"I want you to know that I'm sacrificing for you here."

"You are?"

She nodded and pointed to her red sweatshirt. "I wore my school pride even though my school pride clashes with my hair."

"I'm honored that you undertook such a great hardship for me."

"You should be."

She sat down and patted the spot next to her for me to do the same. I joined her and she pulled a bag of Swedish Fish out of her purse and offered them to me. I shook my head.

"I can't believe these people showed up today for Abby."

"Yeah, I know." I looked around the stadium. The place was packed, and most people had on the purple bracelets. A man a few rows down looked at me, nudged his wife, and pointed me out to her. "We're here on display so everyone can watch Abby's poor, sad family."

Tessa took a fish out of her bag and bit it in half. "They're here to *support* you."

I knew that. Logically. But still, I hated to be the center of attention and pretend everything was okay.

I scanned the crowd of my so-called supporters and found Dad and Collin on the sidelines of the field. Dad talked to the cross-country coach, Mr. Hoch, and Collin warmed up with some of the team as if he were going to run with them. My eyes continued to search the bleachers. There were kids who sat next to me in classes and never said a word to me and upperclassmen who didn't give a shit about cross-country. They wore a sea of purple, dressed to show their solidarity for

Abby's return. A stadium full of people who wouldn't be here if it wasn't for what I'd done.

It was in the very right hand corner near the top that I spotted Tommy. His feet were on the bleachers in front of him and he rested his elbows on his knees, his face in his hands and earphones around his shoulders. His foot bounced like he does when he's nervous. He was sitting alone, the seats around him empty, as if he were in his own personal VIP section. But there wasn't anything special about his seat. Tommy stared straight ahead and ignored everyone; his jaw muscle clenching and unclenching the only indication that the stares of those around him were affecting him. I thought back to how he pulled me out of the cafeteria when everyone was looking at me. And here I was, leaving him alone. It wasn't right.

"I should go sit by Tommy," I said. He'd do the same thing for me in an instant without even debating it. I couldn't leave him alone like that. Could I?

"You what?" Tessa asked.

"Nothing," I told her, because I couldn't go over there. Not after my promise to the universe. I could never sit near him again. "It's just that Tommy is over there alone and everyone is avoiding him like he's got some kind of deadly disease. He doesn't deserve that."

"They're looking for someone to blame. It's easier than not having an answer."

"It's bullshit," I said, my voice rising as I got madder and madder. I was the one they should be blaming for Abby missing from our lives. "Tommy didn't do anything, but everyone is acting like he did. Even my mom thinks he has something to do with Abby's disappearance."

"I know he didn't do it, and you do too. That's got to count for something," she said, and I was so happy she was my friend at the moment.

"I wish it did," I said. "The whole town believes he's the reason Abby is gone. It's like they're on some witch hunt to destroy him. Everyone's gone mad."

"Except you. Tommy has you," Tessa said, but that wasn't true. We hadn't talked since the day at the pool. He'd stayed away from me like I asked, but I couldn't help thinking I was abandoning him, when he was the one who was protecting me and letting everyone believe he was the reason Abby was gone.

But before I could do anything, Mary Grace stepped up to the microphone. The rest of the runners entered the field and stood in a line behind her, their hands linked. The crowd became quiet without her having to say anything.

"Thank you for joining us today. It's so important that we come together. Two weeks ago we lost someone very special to us," Mary Grace said.

"Lost?" I asked Tessa, my voice rising. "Why the hell is she talking as if Abby is dead? She can't really believe that, can she?"

In front of me, a woman turned and shushed me. Her face turned from a look of annoyance to one of recognition when she saw me.

"Sorry," she mouthed, and faced forward again.

Mary Grace went on. "Today we're here with Abby's family to send out prayers for her safe return."

The team let go of one another's hands and walked around Mary Grace, forming a semicircle.

"What the hell did they do? Choreograph this?" I asked, loud enough this time that a bunch of people turned around to look at me.

Tessa placed a hand on my knee. "Relax, it's going to be okay."

I pulled my leg back and tapped my foot against the bleachers. This was not going to bring Abby back, none of this would. As each day passed and Abby remained missing, the longing inside of me to see my sister again would destroy me.

Mary Grace turned to my family. "Mr. Towers, why don't you and Collin come stand with us?"

To give Dad some credit, he seemed a bit bewildered. His face froze in a look not much different than the one on animals who find themselves in the street with a car suddenly right in front of them. But Dad's expression quickly changed and he smiled at Mary Grace, ever the gracious community member, and stood, offering Collin his hand.

If Mary Grace was surprised that Mom or I were missing from the group, she didn't show it.

"Mr. Towers and Collin, I want you to know that every single person here is praying for Abby's safe return," Mary Grace said. "We miss her so much, and we need her to come home."

She wiped away tears and some of the girls on the team

stepped out of their formation to wrap their hands around her. I glanced at Tommy and locked eyes with him. Even across a crowd of people, he could still unnerve me.

I turned away, my attention on Dad instead as he stepped forward and took the microphone. Collin stood by his side, fidgeting with the pockets on his shorts. He looked confused and unsure of what to do, and I wished I could go swoop him up and take him away from everyone's prying eyes.

Dad searched the stands for a moment before he spoke. I slouched down and tried to hide from him. He finally gave up and talked to our community. "Thank you, everyone. I can't express how much your support means to us. My family owes you so much for your efforts and never-ending hope."

A few people in the crowd clapped. It got picked up by more and more people until the entire audience was applauding, and I swear it was so loud, Mom must have heard it all the way at our house.

But it didn't matter. It didn't help. Everyone was here for my family, but I never felt more alone. I couldn't tell the truth, and I couldn't be with Tommy. There was no end to any of this in sight, and I was afraid that if I stayed any longer, I'd break down in front of everyone.

I stood up. "I need to get out of here," I said.

"It's almost over," Tessa replied, but it wasn't. This wasn't close to being over.

"I *have* to get out of here."

I rushed down the steps of the bleachers, and almost lost

my balance and fell. My sandals made loud echoing slaps against the metal. I didn't look back at Tommy, Dad, or the crowd, all of whom were probably staring at the poor upset sister of Abby. I'd seen enough. My hand played with the bracelet Amy had given me when I entered.

I pulled it off and dropped it into the wastebasket outside the stadium.

24

I wasn't sure if Dad saw me leave the stadium, but it didn't matter. I needed to get away and calm down before anyone came to check on me.

The high school wasn't far from my house, but it also wasn't close enough that I'd ever willingly make the choice to walk home. I'd missed the bus last year and when my parents didn't answer their phones, I'd been forced to start the journey by foot. It was nasty and sweaty and everything nightmares were made of. My book bag had dug into my shoulder as cars whizzed past me, junior and senior boys leaning out with jeers and beeping the horn. When I'd finally made it home almost an hour and a half after leaving the school, I'd told myself that was never, ever going to happen again. I'd hitchhike if I had to, even if the guy who picked me up was in a big white van with no windows and had a creepy mustache.

But today was different. Heading home on foot didn't feel

like torture, but a necessity. My body hummed with adrenaline. I needed to get out of here before someone tried to find me, and I was pretty sure that I'd left a pair of tennis shoes in the car, which would make the walk home a lot easier.

I got to the car in the parking lot and opened the door. Just like the houses in Coffinberry, no one bothered to lock their cars. Besides, if anyone did break into my family's old Buick, all they'd find was empty bags from McDonald's, mountains of flyers with Abby's face on them, and wadded-up gas station receipts. Dad would probably thank them for stealing the stuff and cleaning out the mess.

I found the old pair of shoes that stank like gym class and put them on. My jeans weren't exactly workout-worthy clothes, but they'd do. I sent Dad a text that I was heading home on my own and not to worry.

My body vibrated. It was as if my thoughts were moving at a million miles per minute and I couldn't seem to get myself to calm down. Like the time Tessa and I each drank three energy drinks to stay up and study. We ended up staring at the clock as the hours passed, unable to focus on anything. That's what was happening to me now. It was too much, and I needed to leave it behind.

I picked up my pace to a jog. The road remained empty, even though I half expected Tessa to drive by and laugh at me. I didn't do jogging. Ever.

But today I was. And it wasn't hard.

In fact, before long, I was running. I kept waiting for my breath to catch in my throat or a cramp to start in my side, but it was easy. It was as if I'd been running my whole life.

I fell into a steady pace, chanting a word with each footfall.

"I . . . did . . . this," I said, the words beating a rhythm into my head.

I recalled a conversation I'd had with Abby last summer. I ran with her one afternoon, a brief flirtation with getting myself into shape, but after we got about six minutes away from the house, I stopped. My body yelled, fought, and revolted.

"That's what running is, Rhylee," Abby had said to me when I voiced my protests. She ran in place and spoke to me. "You run for that feeling."

"You run for the pain? Why would anyone want that?"

"You run because you can control the pain. You cause it and you can take it away. Running makes your body feel something. It makes you feel alive."

And she was right. Running was freeing. Today, it was as if Abby and I had switched roles, and I held on to that thought. I ran the rest of the way to my house as if I were my sister. As if I could fill the hole I'd created, and give back what I'd taken away.

25

Mom was in the kitchen when I walked through the door, sweaty and out of breath.

"What are you doing back so early?" she asked. She had a sandwich in front of her, but it was untouched. She'd always been thin, but now she looked especially frail. People had been dropping off casseroles and pasta dishes, but she rarely ate more than a few bites. Just the other day, Tommy's parents had brought one over. Dad had accepted it politely, but then made up an excuse about waiting for a phone call and quickly closed the door. Mom had watched them walk back down the road, and then promptly picked up the meal and dumped it into the wastebasket.

We'd lost so much more than my sister. My parents were shells of their former selves, and I don't remember the last time I'd seen either of them smile. They never went out, Mom stopped cooking, and Dad no longer joked with us. Instead, our house was a collection of hushed voices and quiet apologies as everyone tried to get through each day.

My parents used to be good friends with Tommy's too. The four of them would get together a few times a week, meeting for drinks after dinner or to play games, but now Mom wouldn't even acknowledge them. If I had to make a list of things that I'd ruined, I feared it would stretch on until infinity.

"I couldn't handle it," I explained. "It was too hard, so I left Dad and Collin there."

Mom didn't argue with that, because how could she? She'd used the same excuse earlier today.

"I'm going to take Hound Dog outside for a walk." I left her at the table, the circles in our field visible out the window behind her.

I called for Hound Dog, and he ran down from upstairs. He hung out in Abby's room more than the rest of the house; he'd been her pet, a present for her tenth birthday. A gift that surpassed anything I'd ever received. I'd asked for a pony when I was ten, but all I got was a new winter jacket. Abby had named him after Elvis. We'd protested the name, considering the fact that he was actually a big black poodle, but Abby insisted on calling him that.

Hound Dog endlessly searched for Abby. I'd find him whining in her room or sniffing around her shoes that sat waiting for her in the mud room. I was pretty sure I detected a bit of disappointment when I came home and he saw it was me and not Abby who walked inside.

But right now he was tail wags and wiggles, jumping up

and licking my face. I tried to push him off me and get him to sit, but he wouldn't stay.

"What's gotten into that dog?" Mom asked.

"I have no idea. Usually he couldn't care less about me."

"He's acting like he does when Abby comes home."

Mom was right. Hound Dog had now pressed himself against the side of my leg and stared up at me adoringly.

The two of us headed outside. He strained against his leash and pulled us toward the circles that spread throughout the fields. Dad wasn't here to stop me, so I followed Hound Dog's lead until we were standing right in the middle of one of the huge crop circles.

He ran with his nose pressed to the ground and whined, as if he picked up on a familiar scent. He darted back and forth between the sides of the path cut in the circle, and I pulled the leash tight, anxious from his pacing.

The grass crunched under my feet and the weeds were overtaking everything. In some places brambles, leaves, and vines twisted together, and thorns reached out, threatening to cut your legs if you tried to cross the field.

It hadn't rained since Abby went missing, and the weatherman didn't believe we'd have relief anytime soon.

I followed Hound Dog through the circles and felt a strange sort of unease. This was my house, my backyard, but it didn't seem right. A breeze lifted the tips of my hair and whistled past my ear as if it were trying to let me in on a secret.

Hound Dog froze and faced the woods. He barked three times, and then made a high-pitched whining sound. I expected to see something, but it remained dark and empty. The trees at the edge of the woods were still, but around me, the tall stalks of grass bent from some invisible wind that only seemed to be around us. He tugged to go farther, but I was done. This place was giving me the creeps.

"Let's go," I said, and pulled him in the other direction.

At first he balked. He sat back on his heels and refused to move, and for a minute I panicked. It was as if something was about to sneak up behind me and I wanted to get inside.

"Now," I said loudly and yanked him again. He gave up and followed me. I walked out of the circles quickly and then broke into a run as if I were being chased, and sprinted to my house.

26

I sat down with my lunch on Monday, and Tessa immediately turned to me with a serious expression on her face.

"We need to talk," she said, and I had a feeling this talk wasn't about last night's homework or what I wanted to do this weekend.

"I need you to explain the secret you've been hiding from me."

She pulled a newspaper out of her bag and shoved it at me.

"Why didn't you tell me about this?" she asked, and I detected a bit of hurt in her voice.

"Oh Jesus, you have to be kidding me," I said as I caught sight of the article.

"I could've come over and helped or something," Tessa said.

I put down my peanut butter and jelly sandwich and grabbed the paper. I took a deep breath before looking at it,

141

a habit I'd developed to prepare myself for whatever I'd see. It seemed like every morning I'd look at the paper lying on our kitchen table and see a picture, a story, a sentence about Abby. It had been almost three weeks since she'd disappeared and her face still smiled back from the front page of the paper pretty much every day.

I scanned the article and saw that it did in fact mention our name. But for the first time in what seemed like forever, it wasn't about Abby. There were no words on her cross-country accomplishments or disappearance. Today's article was about the circles.

"What's going on?" Tessa asked. She tapped her fluorescent yellow nails against the table. "You're not going to tell me aliens landed in your backyard, are you?"

I pushed the paper away from me. "The circles aren't from outer space; they just showed up Saturday. Dad went to the police, but no one made a fuss about them."

"Well, it seems as if they're a big deal now. My mom said every news station in the area is reporting on them. She drove by to try to see the circles and your yard is full of people."

I groaned. "Great, just what we need, another circus outside our front door."

"I'm coming home with you," she said, not bothering to ask me if it was okay. "You shouldn't have to deal with this alone."

I glanced over to where Tommy sat alone at a table in the corner of the cafeteria and wished that none of us had to deal with this alone.

27

Tessa was right. The circles had exploded into something huge. Cars were parked along my street and tall gray antennas jutted out of news vans and stood at attention against the blue sky. It was like the first days of Abby's disappearance all over again.

I spotted Collin with a group of his friends and Dad in the middle of a circle, arguing with a bunch of men. I wasn't surprised. Ever since the circles showed up, he'd been adamant about them not meaning anything. He wanted nothing more than to remove them, but the police had asked that he keep them until they determined who made them. What I couldn't believe was that Mom was also outside. Unless she was going with Dad to look for Abby, she hadn't stepped outside in the last couple weeks.

She stood off to the side, next to the big oak tree with the tire swing hanging from one of the branches.

Mom had come out for the circles.

Cameras swung toward Tessa and me as we walked up the driveway. I held my arm in front of my face and tried to conceal my pain, while Tessa put her head down and refused to look at anyone.

I dropped my book bag on the front porch and walked over to Mom.

"Rhylee," she said, with this strange half smile on her face.

"What's going on?" I asked.

There were news anchors positioned at different spots on the circles. I told myself they must be hard up for news to focus on some lame circles made as a prank in our yard.

Before Mom could answer, a heavily madeup reporter in a short dress began to talk. "We're standing outside the Towers residence, home of missing seventeen-year-old Coffinberry High School student Abby, where crop circles have mysteriously appeared in their field."

"This is ridiculous," Tessa said, and I was so glad to have someone who agreed with me, but deep down there was a twinge of fear. Everything was getting so big now; not only were the police involved, but so was the news. My destruction was taking over more and more lives, and I could only imagine what would happen when everyone found out that I was the cause of this.

People were interviewed and everyone speculated about where the circles came from. I tried to catch Dad's eye to get him to put an end to this craziness, but he was still with the same group of men and seemed as frustrated with them as I was with the group around me.

"Maybe it's a brain-slurping monster from space," Richie Fagan, one of Collin's friends, shouted. He was standing with a group of kids who nodded in agreement. They were actually speculating about it and from the sounds of things, it seemed as if they were trying to one up one another to see how absurd their guesses about the circles could get.

Another boy from the group spoke up and said, "I bet our town has been picked for some kind of extraterrestrial experiment where we'll be taken up to a spaceship."

A little girl with pigtails sticking straight out of both sides of her head shrieked and her mother wrapped an arm around her.

"Relax, there's some reasonable explanation for this," Officer Scarano said.

"It's some hillbilly's idea of fun," Jeff Vichaikul, our mailman, declared.

I wanted everyone to stop talking, to stop trying to figure out a reason for this madness, because the truth was, there were no answers. There was no way anyone could make sense out of what I'd done to Abby, and I hated that those around me thought they could.

"It's some high school kids' idea of a joke," Heather Tuck, the town's hairstylist, shouted at the camera. "How much grief can one family go through? Do you really think they deserve to be the punch line of some late-night trouble a group of kids decided to get into?"

"It's a sign of the Armageddon," a boy with a face full of freckles shouted. "I read it on the Internet. When things like this happen, it means the world is going to end. This is it.

Next thing you know, the whole state will be infested with zombies coming to track each of us down."

The little girl with the pigtails cried harder, and her mother shot the boy a dirty look.

Collin looked at me with panic in his eyes, and I shook my head no. "It's nothing. The police will figure out who did this, and then everything will go back to normal." He seemed to accept my words, but I knew better than to believe something as simple as that. Things wouldn't go back to normal. Life would never be normal until Abby came back. We were fools to believe otherwise.

"What if they have something to do with Abby?" One of our neighbors, Karin, spoke up.

I stared at her, incredulous. This had nothing to do with Abby, but before I could object, she elbowed her way to the front of the camera and continued to speak straight to the lens as if she were asking this question to everyone who might possibly be watching. "What if it's some kind of sign from Abby?"

"How is Abby a part of this? That's rubbish," Jeff said, and kicked the heel of his boot into the dirt. A cloud of dust wafted up between us. A few of the adults nodded in agreement.

"These are the fields she used to run," Karin insisted. "If she was going to return anywhere, it would be here. She disappeared in the woods, so she'd have to cross this field to get back home. She's trying to tell us something."

Was she for real? She didn't know us, and there was no reason she should act as if she did now.

"What is she thinking?" I asked Tessa.

"One of the things I liked about Abby," Karin continued, "is that she was always outside running her heart out. That girl loved to run, and it's true, it was this field that she always seemed to soar over."

"It would make sense that she'd return to it," Heather said, somehow won over easily by this awful reasoning. She wasn't the only one either. Other people's heads moved up and down as their thoughts filled with false optimism and imaginary ideas.

"No," I shouted, probably louder than I should have. The group turned toward me and a cameraman moved in closer, but I didn't care. "This isn't about Abby."

"But what if it is?" a voice asked. It was Mom. And for the first time in what felt like forever, her face turned into something that wasn't the expressionless wilt of her thin, chapped lips. Something moved behind her eyes that had long since been at a loss for expression.

The news reporters took the idea and ran with it. They connected our fields to Abby, and I could hear my sister's name now addressed to the camera. This would be the lead story on the news tonight, and I hated how they could talk about Abby so easily. They were using us, finding a way to put words to the nightmare of what was happening to our family.

But apparently, I was the only one who felt this way. All other discussions were stopped. The people in our yard had come to a conclusion: The circles had something to do with Abby.

28

I was on edge until the news trucks and reporters packed their gear and drove away when the sun went down.

Dad waited until the field was empty of people and then left for work. Collin sat in front of the living room windows with Abby's comforter wrapped around his shoulders to watch the circles. He'd pulled it off her bed, and when Mom didn't say anything he began to drag it around the house like a giant baby blanket. Collin was officially obsessed with the circles. After it was suggested that they might have something to do with Abby, he couldn't take his eyes off them.

Mom sat in front of the computer in our family room and signed into the missing person's page she had created for Abby. News about Abby had spread through word of mouth and there were now thousands of people who had liked the page and followed along to see how my sister's story would end.

Mom continued to upload pictures of Abby, driven by the

possibility that someone may have some kind of clue as to where she might be. She posted throughout the day, writing detailed posts full of updates and pleas for people to share any information that might help. And people were sharing. There were hundreds of messages from all over the United States, and it seemed as if everyone thought they had a clue to help.

Mom managed the page like it was her new full-time job. She pored over these messages as if they could bring Abby home. She had a notebook where she tracked each message. A column for the name of the person who posted, another for their location, and then a meticulous written record of any information they'd offered. She filled page after page with the so-called evidence she found here and studied it late into the night. She highlighted information, wrote her own notes on Post-its, and passed whatever she thought was important on to the police.

Mom was obsessed with this page and if she wasn't at the computer, she was on her phone, checking for new posts. I'd sneaked a look in her notebook to see if anyone had any ideas about Abby, but it all seemed so far-fetched. People said they saw Abby at the Brookline Hills subway stop near Boston or at Jensen Beach in Florida. Locations I'd never even heard of and couldn't believe Abby would be at. But Mom followed up on each clue, passing the information on to the police, poring over Google Maps and zooming in on the places, and sticking a pushpin in the location on the giant United States map she'd hung on the wall. Most people bought maps to mark off the places they've been; Mom used hers to mark the invisible world Abby was inhabiting. Cities, highways, and towns full of her, as if these people were haunted by her every moment.

Tonight she stuck a pin in a town about two hours away from us called Perry. It bordered Lake Erie, and I imagined Abby sitting on the shore watching the sun go down. Could she really be there? Maybe she was living the new life I so desperately wanted.

I ran my hand from one pin to another and created an imaginary path that Abby had run as she zigzagged across the whole United States. Even missing, she did the things I wanted to; these phantom sightings got her out of this damn town.

I moved to the window that overlooked the field.

"Dad should mow over the circles tomorrow," I told her. "It would keep everyone away from our house."

"Your father won't do that," she replied, her eyes going back and forth from the computer screen to her notebook.

"Of course he would."

"Those circles are important. They need to stay there."

"You're joking, right?" I half expected Mom to burst out laughing. She didn't.

"We don't know where they came from and what they mean. So until we figure it out, the circles stay."

"Isn't it obvious? Someone made them as a joke."

Mom finally looked up at me. "They stay, Rhylee."

There was no getting through to her. Dad would say to let her be. This was her way of coping. But I didn't understand how denial and forgetting about the rest of your family was the way a person coped. Although, what did I know? I wasn't dealing with this any better than Mom was, so I couldn't pretend to have the answers.

Outside, the fog rolled in over the field. Thick wisps like ghosts touched down for a brief moment and then swirled back up again. They'd do this dance over and over, rising and falling until they blew out of sight into the parts of the field where the light wouldn't touch.

I pictured the way Abby used to run across those fields; smooth and fast so if you squinted in the sun, you could almost pretend she was flying.

Where was she? Had she run so fast that she let the wind push her faster and faster, until she too was picked up and blown forever into the dark parts of the world that you weren't allowed to see?

29

In the deep hours of night, someone whispered my name.

I sat up in my bed. My eyes worked to adjust to the pitch black around me.

"Hello?" I asked, but there was no answer.

I stayed there, unmoving, for a few minutes and waited to see if I heard the voice again. Across the hallway, I could see a light glowing under Abby's bedroom door.

I squinted at the narrow strip and tried to remember if anyone had gone in there. Mom avoided it like the plague, but Collin went in from time to time. He took little items of Abby's. Her bear was first, then her comforter, and now it was stuffed animals. I noticed his bed was filled with Abby's old toys.

But it was too late for him to be in there right now. My clock said it was 3:41.

The air was hot and sticky, and my damp hair clung to the back of my neck.

I stared at the light in my sister's room and remembered all the times I'd listen to her move around in there as she got ready to go out with friends or when she came home from being out with Tommy. I took it for granted that she'd always be on the other side of the door.

A shadow flashed across the doorway and for a moment the hallway went dark before the light was back.

Someone was in her room.

I threw the covers off and walked to Abby's door, even though I was scared out of my mind. I put my hand on the doorknob and turned it.

It was locked.

Whoever was inside didn't want anyone else to get in.

I softly knocked. "Hello, Mom? Collin?"

When no one answered, I went to Collin's room. He was curled up in his bed, Abby's stuffed animals around him and his legs tucked against his chest. I peeked in the crack of the door to Mom's room, and she, too, was fast asleep.

The hairs on the back of my neck prickled. I told myself I was being silly. There was nothing to be afraid of.

I knocked again on Abby's door, but it was silent on the other side.

I grasped the doorknob and twisted it.

"Open up," I said. I didn't care who I woke. When nothing changed, I pounded on the door.

"Who's in there?" I yelled. I continued to beat on the wood, terrified about what was beyond, but I needed to know. I had to find out. I hit the door over and over again, until my hands throbbed and my voice was hoarse.

"What's wrong?" Mom rushed down the hallway, in nothing but a giant T-shirt.

"There's someone in here," I told Mom and pointed at Abby's room. But now the light was off. And when Mom tried the knob, the door swung open as if it had never been locked.

My sister's room was completely empty.

I told myself it had been a dream. It had to be a bad dream to add to the nightmare that was already our lives.

30

Mary Grace and Erica slid into the empty seats across from me at lunch the next day. I was flipping through biology note cards and cramming for a test I had that afternoon. Tessa was taking her time in the food line, probably trying to decide what would do the least amount of damage, a Salisbury steak or foot-long hot dog. I could've told her she was fighting a losing battle; both looked and tasted nasty.

"How are you holding up?" Mary Grace asked. She had a bag of mini carrots and took tiny bites out of each, unlike normal people who tossed the whole thing in their mouths. She probably also ate baby corn as if it were on the cob, one row after the other.

I shrugged, uncomfortable, and opened my bag of barbeque chips so I could shove a handful into my mouth to avoid answering. What was I supposed to say? *I kissed your best friend's boyfriend, and she caught us and ran into the woods. Where I left her. But I'm fine.*

"Can you believe Tommy is a suspect?" Erica asked.

"Tommy isn't a suspect," I told her.

"The police questioned him," Erica answered, as if she were an expert on the case of my sister's disappearance. Anger swirled inside of me.

"They didn't connect him to anything." I waited for Mary Grace to speak up and defend Tommy; she had hung out with him and Abby a lot, but she didn't say a word.

"Yeah, well, you never know," Erica told me. She acted like she was talking about some detective show on TV and not my sister. It made my food spoil in my stomach.

"Actually, I do," I snapped and wished she'd stop talking, but she seemed oblivious to the fact that I couldn't stand her right now.

"Have you found out any more about the circles?"

"No," I said, and it was the truth. It had been three days since the circles appeared, and I tried to ignore them, which wasn't easy considering that this morning the news stations had arrived again and continued their report in front of our house. More and more cars drove slowly down the stretch of road that usually had no more than five cars a day on it. Our house was now a tourist stop, a celebrity's home on a Hollywood bus tour.

"Everyone thinks they have something to do with Abby," said Erica.

"They don't have anything to do with Abby," I said, my voice a bit harsh. All of these people interested in the circles were nuts, and I wasn't about to feed into it.

"It's okay, Rhylee," Mary Grace spoke up. "I understand why you're angry. You're allowed to be mad. My mom says that sometimes people do that when they're hurting."

I swear she was about to reach out for my hand and stroke it. I pictured her pulling out some ginger ale and crackers from her lunch bag and offering them like Mom did when I was sick.

"It doesn't matter," Erica sighed. "We're not trying to fight with you." She pulled a purple bracelet out of her bag and put it in front of me. "You aren't wearing one. You can have mine."

"Why? It's not like it's going to bring her back," I snapped again.

Mary Grace spoke up. "We miss your sister. We don't want to forget her. A bracelet might help you feel like you're doing something."

Was she implying that I wasn't?

Maybe she was right. I felt so helpless about everything that was going on.

And what would she think if she knew the truth? She sure as heck wouldn't be sitting here, handing me a bracelet if she did. She and Erica would hate me, they'd shoot me dirty looks, trip me in the halls, and make it their mission to destroy me. Like everyone had with Max Locke. Like they were doing to Tommy.

I grabbed my lunch bag and stood. "Stop pretending that these things you're doing are going to help. Cross-country meets, prayers, and bracelets aren't going to bring my sister home."

"It's like you don't even want her to return," Mary Grace said, and her words sliced through me.

"How can you say I don't care?" I said.

"How can we not?" Erica replied.

"She's my sister. She's *my* sister, and she's gone." I squashed my lunch bag into a ball and made a fist around it, I was so upset. "I want her to return more than any of you. I *need* her to return."

"It doesn't seem like it," Erica said. "All you do is get mad at us when we try to help."

"Don't you get it? I can't act like I care. If I get caught up in all of this, it means she's gone. And she's not gone. She can't be," I yelled, and I didn't care that my classmates turned around in their seats to watch me. "I need to act like this because what's the alternative?"

And no one could reply because to admit any other alternative would be impossible.

31

I couldn't get away from Mary Grace and Erica fast enough. I blamed all the thoughts that clouded my head for why I wasn't thinking about where I was going. I'd been so careful about the corners I took at school, the hallways I walked down, and stairways I moved up, all so I could avoid Tommy.

Except today, I rushed away from Mary Grace and Erica and ran right into him.

"Sorry," I mumbled, and tried to calm myself so Tommy wouldn't see how upset I was. I focused on the floor where my biology index cards now lay. If I hadn't blown off studying last night, I'd leave them on the floor, spread out like confetti after ringing in the New Year. I bent to pick them up at the same time Tommy did.

"Let me help." He handed a few cards to me, and his arm brushed against mine. I paused, remembering what it felt like.

I shook my head to clear it and went back to collecting the cards.

Tommy handed a few to me. "Can you really not even stand to be near me?"

I held on to the stack of index cards so hard they cut into my palm. I reminded myself of the things that could never exist between us. Not now. Not ever. Not after what we'd done.

"I told you. I can't. We can't."

"We can still talk to each other," Tommy said, loud enough that people stopped to look.

"Quiet down," I told him. Most of my classmates walked right past on their way to class, but there were a few who had slowed and seemed to be waiting to see what exactly was happening between the two of us.

"You okay?" Kyle, the same boy who had shoved Tommy that day in the cafeteria, asked. "Is he giving you trouble?"

"We're fine," Tommy said.

"I wasn't talking to you," Kyle replied. He looked straight at me. "Everything good?"

"Everything is good," I said, my tone every bit as unfriendly as Tommy's was. It was obvious what Kyle was getting at, and I wasn't going to allow it.

Kyle nodded and headed back down the hallway, but shot one more look at Tommy over his shoulder.

"Asshole," Tommy said when Kyle was gone.

"It's my fault."

"Nothing is your fault."

"But it is. The way Kyle just treated you. It's because he thinks you had something to do with Abby."

"Don't worry about it," Tommy said.

"Are you kidding me? Don't *worry* about it?"

"I can handle it. Just ignore them."

I squeezed my eyes shut as if it would erase the awful feelings I had about myself and what Tommy was going through, but all it did was make things worse. "All I *do* is worry about it. You shouldn't have to be used to it."

"Rhylee, I'll be okay," Tommy said, but how could that be true? There was nothing okay about any of this.

32

Collin tackled me when I arrived home after school. His hair was messed up and he had smears of chocolate on his face. He must have had one of the pudding cups he was obsessed with. He dipped a spoon in peanut butter and then ate it with the pudding. It was absolutely brilliant; I'd be lying if I said I hadn't tried it myself. But Mom never let him do it. I wished I could believe she let him have it as a treat, but it was more likely she wasn't paying attention so he helped himself. Mom tuning out from the world seemed like the norm these days.

Our field was still full of people, but it looked as if the news trucks had backed off. It was mostly adults from our town. Officer Scarano stood off to the side. Dad had insisted that if we were going to keep these circles, the police needed to provide someone to keep a watch over things. But Scarano sure wasn't doing that great a job; he was on his phone more than he was keeping order.

Collin tugged at the bottom of my T-shirt. "What took you so long? I've been waiting for hours."

"More like half an hour. I know when your bus drops you off," I said and messed up his hair more. He pushed my hand away and made a face.

He dug around in his book bag and then shoved a pile of books at me. A few fell to the floor, but he left them there, too excited to show me the one still in his hand. He opened it to a page and shoved it in my face. "Look, Rhylee, look."

"What are these?" I grabbed the book out of his hands. The cover read *Urban Legends: Fact or Fiction*.

"The librarian helped me pick them out. They're research."

"Research?" I asked, giving him a look to let him know he wasn't fooling me.

"Hello—the crop circles. There's tons of information in these books." He pointed at a specific picture and jumped up and down, excited for me to look at it. "And this one looks like the ones we have. In 1976 Clayton Thorp discovered them in his cornfields."

"Clayton who?" This was getting a bit ridiculous.

"Thorp," Collin said and pointed at the grainy pictures of a field similar to my family's. A man with a long white beard stood in front of one of the circles, his lips set in a grim line like this was all very serious. "The circles showed up in his yard too. They came out of nowhere and then strange things began to happen."

"Like what?" I took the book out of his hand and glanced at the page, not wanting to encourage him, but they were interesting.

"Unusual stuff. His horses appeared in the road near his house even though he locked them in the stable at night, the leaves on his trees turned red and orange in the summer, and he'd find windows in his house wide open. It's like when Abby visited me. The circles are connected to her, I know it."

I thought about the other night with the light in Abby's room. *Stop it*, I told myself. *This is nuts*. I shook my head to clear it from any creepy ideas Collin's books were giving me. I refused to believe any of it. I closed his book and gave it back to him.

"The only strange thing about the ones in our yard is that a bunch of idiots find them important enough to stand around and stare at them for hours. Everyone needs to get a life."

I counted fourteen people in our field. They stood in the circles and faced the woods as if waiting for something. Something they had lost because of me. I yearned to tell them that the circles were useless, just like all the other things the town had tried to do to bring Abby back.

33

Later that night, while I was in the bathroom brushing my teeth, Mom called my name. I nearly choked on a mouthful of toothpaste when I realized she was in Abby's room. She hadn't been able to even walk by her room without crying.

"Are you okay?" I asked.

"Look outside." She sat on the desk chair, which she had pulled to the window. Her hand was draped over the back, lying against a purple sweater of my sister's that waited for her to return and put it on. "Tell me what you see."

I hesitated, afraid of what was out there, but when I looked, it wasn't any different from earlier that afternoon.

"A bunch of people," I told her.

"What do you think they're doing?"

"I have no idea." I pressed my face against the glass and tried to get a better look at the group that was outside in our field. I counted nine of them, six women and three men. They were older, maybe my parents' age, and wore thick-soled shoes better suited for being outside than the heels and shiny dress shoes the news crew had worn. I recognized a librarian from the children's room who always saved new books for me and a teacher from my elementary school. It was strange to see people from town hanging out in our yard. They walked in a line through the paths that cut into the circles.

I opened the window, half expecting one of them to notice me, but nobody did.

"Did you tell Dad?"

"He left for work before I saw them."

"They're saying something." I put my ear against the screen. I very faintly heard bits and pieces of their words. I turned back to Mom, puzzled. "It sounds as if they're praying."

We both fell silent, our heads tilted toward the outside. Mom's eyes grew dark and serious.

"They're praying for Abby," she said, and I listened again. When meaning was connected to the words, they became clear, and she was right; they were out there for Abby. I thought about all the prayers I had sent out to bring my sister home and how useless it seemed. I'd begged and pleaded with fate, willing to trade the world to have her back. I wondered how many more prayers would be sent up to Abby. And if anyone was listening.

34

I woke that evening to a light shining into my window.

Someone was in the woods behind our house.

The person stood there, unmoving, and held a flashlight with the bright beam pointed directly at my window.

It hit the wall where I hung Abby's missing person flyers, her face illuminated and then fading into the dark edges where the light didn't touch.

I placed my palms against the window screen and stared at the light. It was steady, held at the person's middle, and only wavered slightly every few seconds.

I ducked down onto my bed, as if whoever it was could see me, and counted to one hundred. When I came back up, they were still there. The light in the same position, the inky darkness swallowing up the edges.

It wasn't Abby.

It couldn't be Abby.

But a nervous thrill went through me.

What if it was Abby?

When my sister and I were younger, we used to play a game we called I Haunt You. We'd stand somewhere in the dark, usually a bedroom, the hallway, or the backyard, unmoving. Sometimes one of us was brave enough to walk up to the other person to see if that person was really there or if it was only shadows in the dark. Usually the game ended with the person jumping out and scaring the other or the light being flicked on. Tonight, as I watched the person with a flashlight, my mind went back to that game. What if Abby was waiting there for me? Maybe she was testing my courage to see if I'd come out and discover her.

I considered telling my parents, but they'd want to investigate, and I couldn't scare away whoever was there.

I needed to find out what was going on.

I threw on a sweatshirt over my pajamas and slipped out the door.

I tried not to be terrified, but I was.

The light pulled me toward it, as if I were connected to a string. I moved through the field; the dew-soaked grass clung to the bottom of my pants. With each step, I expected the person to leave or move, but they remained, and so each step brought me closer to whoever was out there.

The dark shadows of the woods played tricks on my eyes. They warped and changed so it looked as if people were hiding everywhere, a line of bodies at the edge of the forest.

This had to be a prank. Some kid from school messing with us like when the circles were created.

But what if it wasn't, a voice in my head kept saying.

"Abby?" I asked.

I took baby steps. One foot in front of each other. A wind stirred the leaves in the trees. It lifted the ends of my hair.

I continued to move forward, even though all I wanted to do was turn and run back to my room, lock the door, and hide under the covers until the morning light erased the night. But I couldn't run. I couldn't do that now, not if it really was Abby.

I was about ten feet away, but it was so dark, and the flashlight blinded me.

I stopped when I was close enough to reach out and touch the person. But I didn't touch them. Instead, I held my hands palm up, as if offering everything, even though I had nothing left to give. I'd lost it all.

I could hear their breathing. Deep and heavy and labored. As if it were impossible to take in air.

I took the final step toward the light and reached straight out. But as I touched skin, the flashlight went off.

I was plunged into darkness as whoever it was turned and ran away. I was left reaching out into the emptiness with the memory of brief contact with skin so cold it took my breath away.

35

A fight erupted between my parents the next morning at breakfast when Dad saw that a few people had spent the night in our field. I wondered if one of them had been the person who had stood at the edge of the woods. It had to be. There were no other explanations that didn't make me sound certifiably crazy.

"This has to stop," Dad argued with Mom. "I've put up with way too much this last week. I let the news crew come here and report for some ungodly reason, I allowed practically the entire town to converge here and hash out some insane conspiracy about how the circles had to do with our daughter, and said nothing when it was obvious some of the people here just had a sick curiosity to check out our tragedy. But this, this is where I draw the line. I'm not okay with a bunch of random people spending the night in our yard."

"They're not random," Mom said, the surprise advocate for

this strange group who had nothing better to do than hang out in our field. "We know every one of them. Jen, Gavin, a few parents from the kids' schools were there. No one is a threat."

Dad shook his head in frustration. "I didn't say they posed any threat. But our field does not have to be the gathering place in town."

"They're staying," Mom said with more force than I'd heard her use since Abby disappeared. "They're trying to help."

"Sitting in a field is not going to help anything," Dad shot back.

"No one knows what to do, and this is something. They're here for Abby. How could you be against that?"

Dad sighed and scratched his beard. "I'm not against it. I just don't like the idea of this."

"Nobody is hurting anyone," Mom said. "Let it be."

"I don't think that's a good idea . . . ," Dad said, the struggle apparent. Mom hadn't shown this much passion for anything since Abby left. But this. These people. It was all so strange.

"Please," Mom begged. "I'll talk with Officer Scarano. Check to see if he can patrol the house a few times a night. These people are doing good; they're praying for our daughter. How can we fault them in that?"

"We can't," Dad said and the decision was made. He'd allow these people to continue to search for some kind of meaning in a bunch of circles that were more than likely mowed into our fields by some of my asshole classmates with nothing better to do on a Friday night.

36

My parents weren't the only ones caught up in the circles. My classmates were fascinated too. The whole school talked about them. Not directly to me—that would be too awkward—but I'm sure they wanted to say something.

Two girls in my history class were whispering about them a little bit too loud when a student aide came in with a note. It was during the last class of the day, ten minutes before the bell rang, and all I wanted to do was get out of there.

"Rhylee, you need to go to the office," Mr. Scott said after he had read the piece of paper in his hand. "You can take your stuff, since class will probably be over before you get back."

I stood slowly. I was afraid. The office never called for me, and I hadn't done anything to earn a trip to see our principal. What if they had news about Abby?

What if it was bad news? Confirming what we were all afraid to say out loud.

My head spun with worries and fears as I made my way to the office. I wanted to walk past the door that led inside. I could keep going, right out of the building. I could go somewhere else, stay away from my house and live in perfect oblivion for a few more hours. But I couldn't do that. I had to face things no matter what the cost.

I relaxed a little when the secretary, Mrs. Hastings, smiled at me. I figured you couldn't tell someone bad news if you looked happy. At least I hoped that was the case.

Our principal, Mr. Ralston, walked out of the meeting room.

"Everything is okay, right?" I blurted out.

"Yes, yes, sorry about that, I didn't mean to make you nervous. Thanks for coming down." He shifted from the front of his feet to the back and looked uncomfortable.

"No problem," I mumbled, and prepared myself for a lecture. If this didn't have to do with Abby, I had a feeling it was about my grades and how bad they were. I wasn't a fool. I understood that I had to do well in school if I wanted any chance of going to college, especially since I wouldn't be able to pull it off without some sort of financial aid. But sitting down and studying wasn't exactly at the top of my list of things to do right now.

"Listen, I talked to your mother and we have some . . ." He paused for a moment and then spoke the last words quickly, ". . . possessions of your sister's. We gathered the stuff the police didn't take out of her locker, and when I talked to your mother, she said you could bring it home." He walked into a small room, and I stood there stunned. This was not what I'd expected when I got called down here. Was I supposed to follow him? I didn't want to. And I didn't want him to come out. I didn't want a bunch of Abby's stuff. Was Mom so clueless as to think I wouldn't mind bringing it home?

I couldn't believe they'd cleared out her locker as if to make way for someone else. It had only been three weeks. Something bitter bubbled up, and when I tried to push it back down, a sound that was half laugh and half cough popped out my mouth.

Mr. Ralston came back with a cardboard box. It had been used to ship something; the address blackened out with a thick marker. Pieces of masking tape stretched across the top to keep it closed, but you could still see inside if you wanted to look. I didn't.

I took the box as if it held a dead animal. It was surprisingly light, but too big to hide.

"Thanks," I muttered, and turned to leave.

"Of course. It's the least I can do to help." Mr. Ralston put his hand on my shoulder. "I heard about the circles. I was thinking of stopping by one of these nights."

I wanted to jam the box back into his hands and tell him that he could take the damn thing to my house then, but I simply nodded.

I left without saying a thing, the weight of Abby's items in my hands growing heavier with each step.

37

I stuffed the box into my book bag. The corners cut into my back and just knowing it was there made it feel as if it weighed a million pounds.

Instead of getting on the bus and having to give its contents to my parents, I went to the grocery store, since no one in my family remembered to buy food anymore. We grazed on the scraps around the kitchen: odds and ends, peanut butter and jelly or tomato soup for dinner, dry cereal for breakfast. We never seemed to run out of food, but we also never had the right food for a complete meal. Poor Collin had dined on a gourmet dinner of instant mashed potatoes and breakfast sausages last night.

I grabbed a basket and filled it with milk, fresh veggies, fruit, bread, some lunch meat, and two chocolate bars I planned to share with Collin.

On my way out, the bulletin board near the automatic

doors caught my eye. It had one of my sister's missing person flyers stuck on it.

Men in business suits rushed out with small bags of food and mothers walked in with sleepy babies in one hand and lists in the other. They moved past me without looking at the flyer, but I couldn't tear my eyes away from it.

I touched Abby's face. There were tabs at the bottom of the flyer with the police department's number to call if you had anything to report. Three of the tabs were ripped off. It reminded me of my collages, the images torn apart and pieced back together to create the reality I wanted. What if these tabs could do the same?

There was a slight twinge of excitement in my stomach. Usually when I saw these, they were intact, whole, but someone had touched this one. The numbers at the bottom were in someone's fist, pocket, purse, or sitting on top of a dresser. My mind spun. Did someone have knowledge about Abby? Could we be wrong about the river? The thought made me giddy with hope.

I pulled the flyer with the missing tabs off the board and stuffed it in my purse. This sheet of paper represented something to me. Maybe Abby was still out there and I needed to find her. If I could make sense of anything I'd done, it was that I shouldn't give up. I had to make things right.

38

Mom was at the living room table in front of the computer clicking away on Abby's tribute page when I got home. I waved the carton of milk at her as I tried to rush past, hoping she wasn't thinking about the box in my book bag. "Have no fear; we won't die of calcium depletion this week."

She looked up. "I didn't know we were out."

Of course not, I wanted to say. *You don't notice anything these days.*

I could create a whole list of things Mom didn't see these days, starting with the pile of unopened mail in our front hallway, the dust and dirt that collected on our floors, which hadn't been swept or mopped in weeks, and the fact that Collin got away with not taking a bath for almost a week before I noticed. My grades were falling so fast that I wasn't even sure if I could salvage them and Collin was practically a walking zombie from exhaustion, since Mom didn't enforce his bedtime anymore.

When I glanced back, she was already bent over her stupid notebook full of Abby sightings again, and frustration built inside of me. Her obsession with the messages on Abby's tribute page, Collin's obsession with aliens, the town's obsession with the circles—they were nothing. Nothing that would help.

But the flyer, I told myself, *that was something. That could mean something.* And the idea calmed me.

I put the groceries away and headed upstairs with the candy bars. I planned to unload the box of Abby's stuff and see if I could find some kind of connection to her. The box promised new ways to remember my sister.

I hesitated for only a second and considered handing it over to Mom or Dad. It would be the right thing to do, but this might be my only chance to see what was inside. If there was something in the box I could hold on to, I wanted to pull it out before one of my parents found it. Mom would probably set it on Abby's desk, another shrine to gather dust.

I locked the door to my room and dug my nails under the packing tape, not even bothering with scissors. The tape cut into my hands and twisted into tight ropes, so I broke it with my teeth. I yanked open the flaps at the top of the box and stuck my hand in.

The first thing I pulled out was a pair of her running shoes, held together with knots joining the bright purple shoelaces she loved to use. All of her shoes had purple laces; it was her trademark. I pictured her running ovals on the high school track during the school day. If you played a sport, you didn't have to take gym, so the period when Abby would've chased a

178

volleyball around or done enough jumping jacks to keep your heart rate up, she instead went out and ran. I could see her from the upstairs bathroom window of the school. Abby had a hypnotic effect on people. There were times when I'd let ten or fifteen minutes go by as I watched my sister, and then the bell would ring and break me out of my trance.

I tried her shoes on and they were the perfect fit. I stretched my legs in front of me, and it was as if Abby was sitting there. I pulled them off, because it didn't feel right. I stretched my own feet in front of me. The pink polish she had painted on my nails was chipped and almost all gone.

I dug back into the box and pulled out a half-empty bottle of the lemon-scented body spray she always doused herself with. I pumped the top of the bottle and caught the scent in the air, letting it settle around me.

There was a bunch of papers stacked on top of one another. I shifted through them and wished for a note, something personal, but they were all school papers, her slanted handwriting crowded together on each line, one word almost running into the next.

I found a pair of sunglasses that was missing one of its lenses and a hair tie, which I used to gather my hair into a ponytail. I pulled out her school-issued agenda that everyone was given the first day of school. I paged through it, but it was empty. I grabbed a pen from my desk and put a number one on the date she went missing. I numbered each day after it until I got to today. Day fourteen. I paged through the rest of the book and wondered how many other days would be empty of my sister. I couldn't think about it; she had to come home. I pushed the agenda aside and went back to the box.

There was a worn-out T-shirt folded neatly on the bottom. I recognized it immediately. I knew about the hole in the left corner and the blue stain on the backside without even looking. It was the shirt Abby had worn when she ran her first marathon on her sixteenth birthday. Most normal people would go for their driver's license, but not Abby. She'd wanted something more, so she'd set out to train months before, ignoring Dad's pestering that she should be practicing her driving skills. He'd made it more than obvious that he was counting the days until Abby got her license and could take over the job of chauffeuring Collin and me around.

"Why would I need wheels when I can run everywhere?" she'd asked, and it was true. Abby did run everywhere: to the store, friends' houses, and even school, which I didn't understand. I'd be a big sweaty mess if that was my means of transportation, but somehow Abby always managed to look as if she had taken a leisurely stroll.

"It's a goal, something to work toward," she'd told us when we teased her about the race.

"Nothing says celebration like a twenty-six-mile race," I'd joked, because even the idea of running that far made my legs ache.

"Twenty-six point two," she'd corrected me with a grin.

My family got up on the morning of her birthday not to watch her eat cake and open presents, but to watch her cross the finish line before coffee and cold air had fully woken us up. She'd ended the race with her hands held high in the air, and we'd wrapped our arms around her sweaty body, her T-shirt covered in messages we'd scrawled before the race.

I read the words on her shirt now and remembered when Abby had proclaimed, after running twenty-six point two miles, that she could now take on the world.

The last item in the box was a notebook with math problems written on the first few pages. I turned to the next page and a photograph fell out. It was of the two of us, hands slung around each other's shoulders with our heads tilted back as we were caught in mid-laugh. I couldn't remember when it was taken, but the happiness on both our faces was impossible to look at.

"I'm so sorry, Abby." I traced the outline of her face. "Please come home."

I flipped through the rest of the notebook and stopped when I found a page of her writing. It looked like the draft of a note, the words scratched out and written again.

A note written to Tommy.

I closed the notebook. It was private, not meant for me.

But what if I held a clue? I found the page again and read the words.

> Tommy,
> I don't know what I'd do without you. You saved me.
> You have no idea.

The note stopped there, and I imagined her writing it in class and having to turn the page when her teacher walked by or the bell rang.

You saved me. Saved her from what? What did he have no idea about? And if Tommy had saved my sister, what had *I* done to her?

"Destroyed her," I said out loud. "That's what you did."

I picked up the picture of the two of us and ripped it in half. I removed myself from the image because I didn't deserve to be with her. Not after what I'd done.

I hid the picture in my desk drawer. I couldn't bring myself to throw it away. I placed everything else back in the box.

I carried it to my parents' room and left it on their dresser. The scent of her perfume clung to my clothes, and if I closed my eyes, I could pretend that I wasn't standing here all alone.

39

I added the flyer I'd taken from the grocery store to the wall in my room.

Three missing tags.

Three chances to bring home Abby.

The paper was jagged where the tags had been ripped off, and I had to believe that they meant something.

If people were pulling off our number, then I was going to continue to plaster it all over town. I wouldn't be like Mom; I'd do something—something useful. I'd make sure the flyers were everywhere so no one could miss them.

"We need to hang more posters of Abby," I told Dad the next morning at breakfast.

"I think everyone did a pretty good job putting them around town, but I can talk with the police and see what they can do," Dad said, always the practical one, even when practicality was useless.

"No, that's not enough," I argued. "I want to go out and distribute them myself so we can make sure we have them everywhere."

It was probably pointless. I'm sure Dad was right about the town being blanketed in flyers, but what if more tabs were taken from some of them? What if all the tabs were taken from one and someone needed to take one? And I needed to get a new flyer up at the grocery store to replace the one I took. If I helped pass out the flyers, I'd know exactly where they were going, and I could keep track of them. If there was a chance Abby was still out there, I had to help.

"Please. We need to make sure the town is flooded with these posters," I insisted.

Dad must have realized how important this was to me, because he didn't even hesitate. "Sure, we can go this afternoon. I'll pick you up at school," he said.

"You can come too," I told Mom.

"I'd like that," she said, and I hoped she'd still be willing to go when the time came. It seemed as if her mornings were better than her afternoons. She got up, made us breakfast, and watched Collin leave for school. It was in the hours after that she seemed to forget about us. Something happened during the hours in between the morning and afternoon, so the Mom I said good-bye to in the morning was often different than the one I saw when I got home. She'd be sitting in front of the computer screen filling her notebook with name after name. The pins on the wall continued to multiply until it seemed as if Abby was everywhere.

"We need to keep her in everyone's mind," I said, as if anyone could think of anything but Abby. Her disappearance was a heavy weight, draped over us, dragging us down.

"What about me? I want to do something," Collin said.

"You can take care of Hound Dog for Abby. He misses her," I told him.

"Okay, the two of us will watch the circles," he said, and tried to coax the dog to the window.

Collin's obsession with the circles was getting worse.

Despite all of our conversations with him that there was nothing out of this world happening in our backyard, he wouldn't stop talking about it. If my parents were smart, they'd put blackout curtains on the windows so he couldn't stake out the field.

"The circles don't need anyone to watch over them," Dad said firmly.

"They mean something. These things don't appear without a reason," Collin insisted. He pulled sheets of paper out of his pockets. He laid images of circles all over our table. "The signs are here. The circles are from somewhere far away."

He talked fast, in an excited voice, as if someone might stop him. His finger traced one of the circles, moving around and around the intricate pattern. "This one was found in Michigan. That's not too far from here. And this field has a whole bunch just like our house. Maybe they're connected."

Dad shook his head and gathered the plates. "Collin, believe me, it's an awful joke. Nothing more. Don't get yourself worked up about something that doesn't mean a thing."

I nodded my agreement, but when I turned to Mom for her affirmation, she was bent over one of the pictures, studying it intently.

Collin saw the same thing and turned to her, speaking as if she were his singular audience. "This field had circles found it in it three times. They kept showing up." He continued to talk about the different pictures and Mom listened. She stared at the sheets that were spread out in front of her as if she was lost and was studying some map that would lead her back home.

cereal or
or le

40

"Where are we heading?" Dad asked when he picked me up after school with a backseat full of flyers for my sister. It was only the two of us. Dad apologized for Mom not "feeling up to joining us."

"The town square. I figure we can hit the stores on both sides of the street, and after, we can grab dinner."

"Now you're talking," Dad said. "I've been craving Deagan's."

"Maybe we could try something new?"

"Somewhere new? But you love eating at Deagan's."

"I used to love it. When we'd go together."

It was true. Deagan's was a family favorite. I craved their burgers, and Dad liked how they served breakfast whenever you wanted it. He was a firm believer that a person should eat a good breakfast at the start of their day, even if his day started in the evening because he worked the late shift. More often than not, he'd come home from work when we'd be eating

187

oast before school and he'd have a plate of spaghetti tover meat loaf. It frustrated Mom to no end, since she battled with Collin, who hated any type of breakfast food that wasn't a sugary cereal. Collin still didn't think it was fair that Dad got to eat the dinner leftovers while he was stuck gagging down Cheerios. We usually went to Deagan's once or twice a month, but since Abby disappeared, we hadn't been back. It didn't seem quite right. It was just another reminder of what I was able to do and Abby wasn't.

Dad placed his hand on my shoulder. "I hear you. We can go somewhere else."

I relaxed, relieved. "Thanks."

Dad and I went along the strip of stores that was Coffinberry's downtown. It wasn't a huge area, but the sidewalks were always crowded. People came here to get odds and ends, to listen to the weekly outdoor concert, or socialize. Our flyers would be seen.

I told Dad about the flyer at the grocery store.

"There were three phone numbers ripped off." I tried to hide the excitement in my voice. I'd been thinking of them and imagining scenarios that all ended with Abby coming home.

"That's three more numbers than we've seen in a long time," Dad said, which was true. "But I haven't heard anything new."

"Do you think someone knows something?"

"It was probably more likely a person interested in what was going on in our yard right now."

"I hope that's not the case," I said.

Dad was right about the flyers. There were piles of them in each store we stopped in, but I reminded myself of the three tabs. People were noticing, and I'd make sure there were enough flyers to do just that.

After we left the fifth shop, Dad suggested splitting up.

"How about you drop off flyers over there, and I'll get this side. Then we can meet for dinner at Otis's Diner when we're done."

"Sounds like a plan," I said.

He crossed the street, and I entered the first store, a little bakery that every bride in town ordered her wedding cake from. I refilled the stack of flyers. I hung another one on the bulletin board near the entrance of the coffee shop before I moved on to my next stop. I waved to Tessa's mom, who worked at the post office, and dropped a bunch off on the table they had set up near the stamp machine. I moved from store to store, making sure Abby's flyers were everywhere, so even if people wanted to keep her out of their minds, they couldn't.

I dropped off the rest of them at the little antique shop with a bell that rang when the door opened. The gray-haired woman who owned the place was working with some customers, so I put the papers near the register and felt a tiny bit better that at least I'd done something.

I was about to text Dad that I was done when Johnson appeared about a block in front of me. I studied him with a strange fascination.

He attempted to push his cart up a curb, the wheels not cooperating and the entire cart leaning to the left dangerously. People walked past without helping. A mom grabbed her daughter's hand and dragged her across the street, so the two of them wouldn't have pass him. It didn't take a genius to see that even though the police had cleared Johnson, the town wasn't letting him off that easily.

"Just like Tommy," I said to myself.

I joined the group of people who stopped and stared as Johnson tried to pick up the front of the cart and put it on the curb. There was this little voice in the back of my head that made me wonder if maybe, just maybe, he knew what happened to Abby.

A man in a Coffinberry High School football shirt walked up to Johnson and put a hand on his shoulder.

Johnson shook it off. "Hey, listen, no problems," he said and held his hands up in defense. "I want no trouble."

"How about you get out of here then," the man said in a way that made it clear it wasn't a question, but a statement.

"That's what I was trying to do," Johnson said.

I wanted to turn away, to leave all of this, but instead, like those around me, I stood glued to the spot, unable to move, and hated myself for the small bit of doubt about his innocence that had crept into my mind.

"Do it a little faster, asshole," the man said, and spat at Johnson. It hit him on the cheek, the wet blob dripping down.

Johnson made a fist and pulled his arm back as if he were

going to hit the guy. I tensed up, scared to see what would happen.

"Go ahead and hit me," the man said, and laughed. "It'll just prove to us that you had something to do with Abby's disappearance."

Johnson dropped his arm and pushed his cart forward, not even wiping the spit off his cheek. He moved down the street and the crowd dispersed, everyone going their separate ways as if nothing had happened.

I walked in the opposite direction, shocked. This must be how people viewed Tommy, too. It didn't matter that they were both officially cleared. When there wasn't an answer, the town needed to find one, and Johnson and Tommy were their targets. I was ashamed that I'd stopped like everyone else to watch what would happen with Johnson. How was that any different from the way people treated Tommy?

Things weren't going to change. I could scream the truth about Tommy, and people would not only go after him but me, too. Because we needed to find a reason that my sister wasn't here. And until Abby came home, the town wouldn't stop blaming people for taking her away.

My phone buzzed with a text from Dad. **Grabbed table at Otis's. Meet me when done.**

I headed to the restaurant and found Dad sitting near the back in a booth. I slid in across from him and he smiled.

"That was a good idea you had, putting up more flyers," he said.

"I feel like we need to keep doing things," I said, Johnson

still on my mind. "We need to bring Abby home, so we can end this nightmare."

A waitress came and took our orders, and Dad and I fell into an easy conversation with each other about school, the weather, and Hound Dog. Insignificant things.

I was halfway through my burger, dragging a French fry through some ketchup, when an older woman approached our table. She stopped in front of us.

"You don't know me, but I've been watching your family on the news," she said, as if it was perfectly okay to come up to people during dinner and interrupt them. "Every time I see a picture of your beautiful daughter, my heart breaks. And to think, that boy who she trusted might have hurt—"

I dropped my fork and it clattered against my dish. "He didn't do anything," I said.

She opened and closed her mouth as if she was trying to say something but didn't know quite what.

"Tommy," I clarified, just in case she didn't understand exactly what I was saying. "He isn't a suspect, so stop trying to make him one."

"Excuse me?" she said, confused, as if I were the one who crossed some kind of line at the moment.

"Rhylee, calm down," Dad said so loud that people at other tables turned to look. He apologized to the woman. "What she's trying to say is thank you."

"I was only trying to help," she said, pulling back.

"Of course, we appreciate your kind words," Dad said, and it took every ounce of control inside of me to stay quiet.

Dad pushed his plate away and leaned toward me. "Do you want to tell me what the hell that was about?"

"What? How she thought it was okay to interrupt us while we're eating to chat it up about Abby? How she accused Tommy, just like everyone else in this damn town?" I asked.

"You might not agree with her, but you need to respect her," Dad said.

It was the word "respect" that pushed me over the edge. I thought about the way everyone had treated Johnson, the way *I* had treated Johnson. How Tommy was now a target and about all the people in our yard, the endless news reports, the way my classmates stared at me with pity and Tommy with disgust. What was happening to our town had nothing to do with respect. It was about me and what I'd done and what I'd ruined. This, all of this, was my fault.

"How can I *respect* them when they treat Tommy like a criminal? Like he's the one who hurt my sister."

"The town is hurting," Dad said "Something like this makes people afraid—that this could happen to them, too."

"Then let them hurt," I shouted, not caring that I was causing people to look over at us. "But Tommy isn't the one they should blame."

"You're right, honey. It isn't fair, but we're trying to get through this. Everyone is searching for an answer in the nightmare that we're living now."

"I just want her home," I said, a truce to Dad. A signal that I was done fighting with him.

"We all do," he said. "There's nothing more that I want in the world than for your sister to come back to us."

It suddenly felt very important to tell him the full truth. If Dad was noticing a change in me, everyone else must be too. Abby was slipping further and further away from me; I couldn't do the same.

"What if I did something really bad; would you still love me?" I asked, terrified of his response. "Something that would be hard to forgive me for. Something awful."

"I'll always love you, no matter what," he said, and I wanted to believe that was true.

"I need to tell you something," I told him, and my heart sped up.

Dad leaned in, as if he could sense that this was important, but before I could confess, our waitress came over to our table.

"How are you two doing?" she asked.

"Great, we're great," Dad said.

"Are you thinking you want any dessert?"

I shook my head. I didn't have an appetite anymore. Not even for one of Otis's Diner's famous salted caramel sundaes.

"I think the bill is fine," he said.

She fished around in her pocket for a moment before pulling out a slip of paper. "Thanks so much. Have a great night."

Dad counted out a bunch of money and I waited in silence. My heart slowed and now that I had a few minutes to think, I realized how stupid I was to have tried to say something. I pictured Mom's face that first morning when Abby went missing. How she'd looked at me as if she hadn't recognized me.

How even though she tried to hide it, she blamed me for not coming home with my sister. Would admitting my role in all of this make things better or worse? Would it show that there was even more information Tommy was withholding or could it help him? I wasn't sure, but what I did know was that I didn't want to do anything that might possibly hurt Tommy even more. It had been selfish of me to want to shove the weight of my secret off my shoulders. What good would that do? Just so I could hear that my dad still loved me?

"What was it you wanted to tell me before I paid the bill?" Dad asked as he put his wallet back into his pocket.

"Nothing. It was nothing," I told him, even though it was really everything.

"You sure?" he asked, and I nodded.

"All right, ready to go?" Dad asked, standing up.

I slid out of the booth and followed him. He put his arm on my shoulder, and I wanted it to feel okay, but it didn't, not at all, because there was no way he could love me if he found out that my selfishness was what had made Abby run away.

41

Instead of going to lunch at school the next day, I walked over to the gym and stepped outside. There was a pay phone attached to a metal stand on the wall. Probably the only one left in America. It was covered in graffiti so thick with different colors that it looked like an abstract painting.

I grabbed the receiver and fished around for some change in the bottom of my purse. Pay phones were safe. Unlike cell phones, no one could identify the person on the other end.

I pulled out the magnet we'd gotten during homeroom when Abby first went missing. It had a list of phone numbers that "might be important during a time like this," said one of the crisis counselors they'd brought in to talk to us. Most of my classmates had rolled their eyes and stuck the magnets on the back of our metal seats or in the trash when they left the room. It did sound kind of crazy that anyone would actually call one of these numbers, but today I needed to talk to someone about what I had done. Anonymously, maybe, I could find some relief. I found the number I was looking for and punched it onto the keypad on the pay phone.

"National suicide prevention hotline," a female voice said. "Do you need an ambulance?"

I paused, taken aback. Nothing like expecting the worst right from the start.

I counted each breath to remind myself that I was still living. A boy wandered out of the gym, his eyes blinking in the sunlight. He walked toward me and I gripped the phone tightly against my ear. Not a lot of people used this phone anymore. It was once important to secure rides after practice or games, but now everyone had cell phones. The only people who still used it were probably kids who planned to call in bomb threats or make shady drug deals.

Regardless of what this kid wanted, he wasn't going to use the phone. I stared him down with a scowl on my face until he left.

"Do you need immediate medical attention?" the woman asked again, her voice firmer.

"No," I whispered at a level so quiet that I didn't think she could hear me. But she did.

"I'm glad you're okay, and I'm happy you called. My name is Kara." She sounded all soft, like butter left on the table, and I imagined her living this perfect life. I pictured her going home from her job, pulling on faded jeans, and ordering takeout with her boyfriend. They'd eat on the couch, and while they might fight over the remote, he always let her win.

"What's your name?" she asked.

"Abby," I said. That surprised me. I'm not sure why I gave her my sister's name.

"Abby, that's a nice name," she answered back, as if making a decision. As if she were picking out a dress to wear or deciding on a meal off a menu. "What has your day been like, Abby?"

"Awful," I said. I figured the direct route seemed to be the best way to go.

"Why is that? Sometimes it helps to talk."

"It's not fair," I told her.

"What isn't?"

"The fact that some people are here and some people aren't."

"What do you mean by 'here'?" She spoke in that same calm voice, and it made me want to talk more.

"Here. Earth. Living."

"Do you not want to be here?"

"No, the opposite. I'm missing someone really bad right now. So bad that it hurts to breathe when I think about it."

"Did someone you know pass away recently?"

"I don't know."

"You don't know?" Kara repeated after me, and I could tell that I was confusing her. I was confusing myself.

"That's why I'm calling," I said. "Someone disappeared, and I'm afraid she isn't coming back."

"Can you look for her?" Kara asked.

"We already have," I told her.

"Maybe you're not looking in the right spot," she said. "Maybe she's waiting to be found."

A door opened a ways down and a group of girls piled out with shorts and tennis rackets.

"I have to go," I told Kara.

"You don't," she said. "You can talk to me for as long as you like. I'm here for you."

"I know." I was impatient to finish the call before the girls made it to me. "I'm not going to hurt myself if that's what you think. I'm okay."

I hung up the phone before she could say anything more, and repeated the word "okay" over and over again until it didn't even sound like a word I was familiar with anymore.

42

On the second week of the circles, the police had to intervene because traffic had grown so heavy it blocked the intersection a quarter of a mile from our house. The light would change from green to yellow to red and no one would move because so many cars were trying to turn down our street. Officer Scarano directed those making the pilgrimage to our house to turn in to an empty field across the street from Tommy's front yard. The slam of car doors and engines turning on became part of the normal noise of the spectacle that had formed outside our house.

The school bus had begun dropping me off at the top of the street because it took forever just to get down my street. Today, I counted seven cars that passed me before I even made it to Tommy's house, and I was willing to bet that most of them were headed toward our field.

A beat-up Subaru pulled up alongside me, and a man

leaned out the window. He had a toothpick in his mouth that he chewed on.

"Excuse me, maybe you can help," he said. "Is this where the girl went missing?"

I didn't bother to answer. I continued to walk down the road. He followed me in his car.

"Did you hear me? I'm looking for the fields where the circles appeared. For the house where that family lives."

I turned toward him. "Why?"

"Why what?" he asked, confused.

"Why the hell do you care? What would seeing the house and the field do?"

He pulled the toothpick out and flicked it out the window. "Shit, I don't know. I thought it would be interesting. Something to do. You know what I mean?"

"No, I don't," I snapped.

"Aww, come on. It's all anyone is talking about. Most of these people are here for the same reason. You can't tell me you aren't curious."

It might have been the way he assumed I thought my family was a freak show. It might have been the way he joked with me as if what he was doing was perfectly normal. It might just have been that I was sick and tired of being on display. Whatever it was, I snapped. I was done being someone else's entertainment.

"Of course I'm curious. And do you want to know why? Because that's my house. That's my family and that's my sister missing. So how about you stop and think for a minute how *interesting* I find it that assholes like you drive all the way out here because they want to stare at someone else's tragedy."

"Well, I'll be . . . ," he said and instead of being apologetic for getting called out, he seized the opportunity to get a first-hand look at exactly what he had come here to find. His gaze felt unsettling and gross. "You're that girl's sister."

"And you're a pathetic human being," I said. I stepped in front of his car. Then I turned and continued down the middle of the street so that if he wanted to follow me, he'd have to run me over. It was nearly impossible not show how shaken up I was. But I did it. I walked all the way back to my house and never moved out of the road. He followed behind me at a slow speed. When I got there, I turned and stared him down. I placed my hands on my hips and made it clear I was not budging.

"Screw this," he finally said. "It isn't worth it."

He reversed his car into the grass along the side of the road, turned, and peeled out. There was a squeal of tires.

"Good riddance," I said. It might have only been one person I stopped, but it was one less person who made it to our house to use our family's heartbreak for their personal fun.

43

I wasn't the only one against the circles. Dad was fed up with them, and it had become a constant battle with him and Mom.

"This is ridiculous," he argued with her. "Our yard has become a circus."

But she wouldn't budge. She refused to destroy them.

"Why don't you go out there and mow them down?" I asked. "You can't tell me the police want you to keep them still. They've become nothing but a giant pain in the ass to everyone."

"I can't," he said. "I don't have the heart. Not when your mother finds some kind of solace in them."

And so the circles stayed and our family's misfortune continued to be Coffinberry's daily entertainment. We were our own morbid sideshow of loss, and people loved to gawk to see how we were holding up.

People brought food; picnic baskets with salads, cakes, and cold cuts to the field. They passed their plates around as they spoke about Abby and our field and faith. Everyone was praying for Abby. They wanted Abby home. I couldn't fault them too much because I wanted the same thing.

I slipped into the house after school one day without Mom or Collin stopping me to talk. Collin had parked himself in front of the window to watch the circles, and Mom sat at the dining room table uploading more pictures of Abby on the tribute site.

I should've been trying to catch up in my classes, since I seemed to be falling more and more behind, but it was impossible to concentrate on school. I had too much energy. The worry, the fear, the shame, everything was bottled up inside me, and it needed to get out. The urge to run surged through me, and I didn't think I could fight it.

I changed into shorts and an old T-shirt, but couldn't find my running shoes. I searched all over the house and they weren't in any of the usual places: near the door, outside in the garage, or hidden under the piles of clothes in my room. They were missing and I needed to run. It was as if my body craved the rush.

I remembered the pair that had been in the box from Abby's locker and ran upstairs to grab them. I laced up her shoes and slipped out of the house.

The sun began its slow crawl down, but people sat in the yard as if they'd never leave. There were twenty-three people out there now. They held hands and gazed at me as if I could give them some kind of answer to a question I didn't even understand.

I started with a slow jog, but then picked up my pace so I could leave them behind.

I ran the side roads of the neighborhoods, up streets that connected to the main road, and snaked my way through my city. I pushed myself so I breathed hard enough that there was no way I could think about anything else in my head.

Maybe that's why I ended up at Tommy's house. At least, I told myself it wasn't intentional.

The first thing I saw was his black pickup truck. He'd bought it himself, after saving up from his job stocking shelves at the grocery store. The day he got it, he'd picked me up and we drove around Coffinberry, savoring the feeling of being free. After Tommy and Abby began to date, she'd joke that he loved it more than her, and it wasn't unusual to see him outside cleaning it or doing god knows what under the hood. Tonight, though, he had a bucket of water and was scrubbing at the side of it. He rubbed the same area repeatedly.

"I think you got that spot clean," I yelled to him.

He spun around and stood with his back against the truck. "Yeah, it was dirty," he said. He played with the sponge in his hand, twisted it around.

I walked up the driveway toward him. He threw the sponge into the bucket of soapy water but didn't move.

I pointed to an invisible spot on the truck. "I think you missed a spot over here."

He moved to my side quickly. "Where?" He inspected the metal as if it were about to fall apart at any moment.

"Calm down. I was kidding. I don't get why guys are so into their trucks." I crossed back behind the truck and he hurried in front of me, blocking my path.

"What's going on?" I asked. "Why are you acting so strange?"

"I'm fine," he said, but he clearly wasn't.

He jumped into the truck bed and motioned for me to do the same. He reached out his hand and I climbed up. There were bags of grass clippings toward the back, and I sat against one. It made a soft hissing noise as the air escaped from it. I stretched my feet out in front of me. My calves burned from running, but it was that pain that I yearned for, just like Abby had told me.

Tommy pulled on one of my laces. He wrapped it around his finger and let it go. I'm sure he recognized Abby's purple laces.

"Why are you doing this?" he asked, and I couldn't tell if he was talking about the shoes or us.

"I have to," I said, and wasn't sure what I was talking about either.

We sat in silence and watched the clouds roll past overhead. I was too aware of how close he was and how just weeks ago I was willing to give it all to him. How I would've traded everything to be with him and how still, when it's the deep dark of night and I can't sleep, I think about those moments when I thought I finally had it all.

I jumped up. This was a bad idea. I shouldn't even be here.

"I'd better go. I'm not even sure why I ran past your house." I climbed down from the truck and walked around the side of it.

"Wait," Tommy said and tried to follow me, but it was too late. I found the reason why he was scrubbing his truck and why he didn't want me to walk around it. Written on the whole driver's side with red spray paint was the word "KILLER."

"Who did this?" I asked, sickened at the thought of Tommy walking to his car and finding this.

"It doesn't matter," he said. "It could've been anyone in Coffinberry."

"This isn't right. We need to do something about it."

"It's okay, Rhylee. I can handle this."

"You shouldn't have to. It's my fault. I can't let you carry this alone."

"I'm not alone," Tommy said, and I understood.

I stuck my hand in the bucket of soapy water and found the sponge. I brought it up to the letters and worked to scrub away the words that spelled out the sins of both of us. We rubbed the surface of his truck so much that little bits of paint chipped off. We scrubbed and scrubbed, but no matter how hard we rubbed, we couldn't get rid of that word.

44

It was late when I left Tommy's house. I ignored the people in my yard, their flashlights and candle flames waving back and forth. I opened the front door as silently as I could, easing it against the frame so it made no noise except for a small click.

Mom stepped out of the dark living room. "Where have you been?" she demanded. "Do you know how worried I've been?"

"I told you I was out running. I left a note."

"That was over two hours ago. It's dark outside; you could've been anywhere. Anything could've happened to you. Like your sister . . ." Mom's voice cracked and she swiped the back of her hand across her eyes. "You have to be careful."

She was right. It was stupid of me. Even though I'd left a note in the kitchen, I could only imagine Mom's fear.

"I'm sorry. I didn't realize I'd run as far as I did. By the time I turned around to come back, I was far from home."

I followed Mom into the living room. She took a seat on the couch, and I sat on the floor near her, my feet stretched out in front of me, my back against the chair Dad sat in.

She hummed an old lullaby she sang to us when we were young. A song she still sang to Collin on nights when storms rattled our windows and he was scared to go to sleep.

"I thought she'd come home," Mom said.

"Abby?" I asked, confused.

"I feel like she's everywhere. With the lights off, anyone could have mistaken you for her. You even smell like her," she said.

I thought about the perfume I'd found in Abby's box and wondered if the scent had found a way to creep onto me.

"Since when do you run?" she asked.

I shrugged, even though it was too dark for her to see me. What was I supposed to say? Now that Abby was gone I felt as if I had to do the things she couldn't do. That my penance was to live the life that I'd stolen from her. I couldn't very well tell her that one day I decided to run and found I could easily go for mile after mile. She'd never believe it. I couldn't believe it.

"I miss her so bad," Mom said.

Her words surprised me. She didn't speak like this, ever, and it was the first time she'd said anything like that since Abby disappeared. I moved closer and took her hand.

I figured she'd fight to let go, but instead, she let me hold on.

"I do too," I said. "And I miss you."

"I'm right here."

I gripped her hand tight. "It doesn't feel like it."

The words hung between the two of us.

She made a noise, and I couldn't tell if she was laughing or crying. "We're all still here, honey."

"Sometimes it feels as if I've lost you, too."

"You didn't lose me, honey," she said, but there was no comfort in her words because it was so hard to believe that was true.

45

When I untangled myself from my sheets and stepped out of bed the next morning, no one was awake. Yet the house already felt claustrophobic. I might not have been able to see the people in the field, but they were there and that made it even worse.

I was never a morning person before Abby disappeared. In fact, I despised the sound of the alarm and its insistence that it was time to get up.

But for running, I'd make an exception.

It was a few minutes before five a.m. Abby used to wake at this time every morning before any of us even hit the snooze alarm five million times. Her cross-country team appeared outside our house at precisely 5:11 a.m. every day. They were never late; keeping a close mark on their running time was essential to training. Even after Abby disappeared, they took the same route, moving as a group past our house. Maybe they hoped Abby would appear out of our front door and run with them.

Today, I wanted to be a part of their group. I had no clue how they'd react, but I planned to find out.

I didn't bother searching for my shoes. The team would run past at any minute, and I had to hurry. I grabbed Abby's pair and stepped outside. I imagined them moving in a pack, feet rising and falling together, ponytails bouncing in unison.

I waited on the porch, Abby's shoes tied tight on my feet. The team came into view and I jogged toward the sidewalk. I kept my eyes forward, so I wouldn't have to acknowledge those gathered in our field.

A few people on the team nodded or smiled, but most simply accepted me. They folded around me like sheep, so I was no longer a single person but part of the group. I moved in unison with them and pushed myself harder and harder until my heart thrummed against my chest.

My breath burst out in strong spurts and back in through thick gulps.

I realized why running was so important to me now. This was the pain Abby had been talking about. A feeling so real and sharp. I carried it like I carried my guilt, deep within me, so I felt it everywhere I went.

I ran to feel a pain so intense that it reminded me I was still here. I was still alive, and I hated myself for it.

46

Mom must have gotten something out of my words the night before, because she did start living, little by little. At least, her version of living, because after I got back from running, I found her dressed and ready to walk Collin outside to catch the bus.

"What are you doing?" I asked her.

"I wanted to talk to the people in the circles."

"No fair," Collin yelled and threw his book bag on the ground in protest.

"Collin, cool it," I said because Mom wouldn't.

"You won't let me go out there. Why are you allowed?" he shouted at her, which was true. He begged to go out almost every day but Dad refused. "What if you find something? What if the aliens come back?"

"There are no aliens," I told him firmly. I waited for him to explode, but instead, he gave up his fight with one final

213

rumble of frustration. Good, at least he was quiet. I turned to Mom. "You're going to hang out with the Miracle Seekers?"

"The what?" she asked, confused. I realized my mistake as soon as I called the group by their nickname.

Tessa and I had dubbed the group outside the Miracle Seekers because of their belief that standing in our yard praying could bring my sister back. It seemed like a contradiction because my family was never religious.

That's why I was surprised when Mom not only accepted the Miracle Seekers, but decided to go outside with them. Couldn't she see that she was substituting one obsession for another and neither would bring Abby home?

47

I crossed more days off in Abby's agenda. More days that we were lost without her.

Mom became friends with the people in our yard, Dad continued to alternate his time between work and search efforts, and Collin built forts inside our living room. Big elaborate ones with blankets and sheets. He covered the couch, table, and chairs and then lined them with pillows. It was a labyrinth of rooms with different sections, some narrowing so you had to crawl through them and others so wide and open that you could sit up.

He worked on them for hours, constructing his new hideout, and when completed, refused to sleep in his bed. Not that Mom even noticed, especially when I was the one changing our sheets since she had given up any type of household chores.

Dad hated the fort, and it would've been simple to pull the sheets down, but no one had the heart to do that.

"I need to be near the fields in case they come again," he told Dad.

"Oh for heaven's sake, there is no 'they,'" Dad said, no longer trying to soften the words.

"Something made those circles, and I'm not going to miss it when they touch down on Earth again," Collin insisted and crawled deeper into his fort. He made his way to the section against the large window facing our backyard. The sheet rustled and he was a bulge in the center. He wouldn't budge and no one wanted to crawl through those tunnels to try to get him to come out.

So Collin hung out under the blankets constantly and sure enough, that's where I found him when I came home from school. Today had been quiet; no one talked about the circles or my sister, but I'm sure that wouldn't last. I wasn't naive enough to think gossip just disappeared. It rose and fell like waves, some days crashing down on you so hard it was almost impossible to stay on your feet and other times a gentle lull that tricked you into believing everyone had moved on to something new. Tomorrow I'm sure my sister and those circles would again invade the lips of everyone in the school, much like they had invaded our backyard.

"Rhylee, come over here," Collin said from inside his fort, and I got on my hands and knees so I could see him.

"Where are you?"

"You need to come in all the way."

"Collin, I don't really . . ."

"Just do it," he said, and something in his voice made me

want to crawl toward him and wrap my hands around him. I moved carefully, so I wouldn't upset the city he'd created under the sheets. I found him on a pile of old blankets, the sheet above him dipped slightly in the center, so it brushed the top of his head.

"Welcome. I'm so glad you could make it," he said in the formal way that Mom had taught him to use when we had company. He nodded at my feet. "Please take off your shoes."

Collin pushed a plastic bowl toward me. "Would you like an appetizer?"

I smiled and took a handful of peanuts he must have swiped from the container that Dad kept next to his easy chair.

"I love what you've done to the place," I told him.

"Not everyone is allowed in here."

"I feel honored."

Collin turned so that he was low to the ground. He crawled toward a tunnel on his right and I followed, not knowing what else to do. He headed to the windows that faced out on the field. The space was now big enough to sit up in and was lit by the sunlight that streamed in from outside.

"This is where I keep watch," Collin said.

People milled around the field, and I thought for the millionth time how weird it was that strangers would want to hang in our yard. I couldn't stand being in my house anymore; how could these people make the choice to willingly be here?

"You watch everyone outside?" I asked him.

"No, I keep an eye out for the aliens."

"Collin, there's no such thing as aliens."

"There are too," he argued. "They made the circles and they took Abby."

"Aliens didn't take her," I told him, but it would have been as plausible as her simply vanishing.

"They did, Rhylee," Collin said, his voice calm and even. There was no convincing him otherwise; he spoke with the authority of one who might have seen it with his own eyes. "They took her from us, because everyone loves Abby. It was only a matter of time."

"She'll be back," I told Collin, but my words didn't sound as believable as I wanted them to.

48

I woke in the middle of the night to ice cold air. The scent of mud and earth filled the room.

Someone was here.

I couldn't see them, but I could feel their presence.

I remained still, and told myself I was disoriented. I counted to one hundred and when nothing happened, I convinced myself I must have been dreaming.

I burrowed under my sheets and had almost drifted off again, when my bed moved. Just a slight shift, but it was as if someone had sat on the edge.

"Collin?" I asked, but no one answered.

The curtains in my window stirred as if a wind was blowing.

Except, the windows were closed.

I didn't move. I couldn't move. I was terrified.

I pulled the sheets tight around me and told myself I only thought I felt something. I was in the room alone.

I don't know how long I stayed frozen, but I refused to budge or turn on the light, because I didn't want to see what the dark hid.

The bed shifted again.

I pulled the covers over my eyes and stayed buried underneath them until Dad's car pulled up when his work shift was over and the door slammed shut. I crawled out from under the sheets and glanced around my room. The morning light had fought its way through my window, and landed on Abby's running shoes that I wore when I ran.

The bottoms were covered in fresh mud, the purple laces wet and dirty.

And the missing person flyers and pictures of Abby lay on the ground. Every one of them ripped off of the wall and crumpled in a heap on the floor.

49

It was impossible to focus that day in school. Instead of listening to my teachers talk, my mind was stuck on what had happened the night before. It didn't make sense. None of this did. It was as if Abby was trying to get in touch with me, and the idea both excited and terrified me.

The thought that she was out there hiding from us seemed crazy; that wasn't who Abby was. And if she wasn't hiding, then what did it mean?

Tessa offered me a ride home from school. It was one of those rare days when she was able to use the car. Even though she'd had her license for a few months now, her mom usually drove the family's second car and Tessa and I were still doomed to take the bus forever.

"How'd you get permission to drive today?" I asked.

Tessa rolled her eyes. "My mom's having a bunch of friends from the neighborhood over this afternoon and she needed to

221

clean the house. They call it a book club, but they don't really talk about books. It's more like their monthly gossip session and excuse to drink way too much wine."

"Maybe we need to drive around so you're not subjected to that torture."

"I like the way you think," she said. "Let's stay away for a while."

And so we did. For the next hour, Tessa drove the stretch of road that bordered Coffinberry. She rolled the windows down and the air twisted through our hair as we passed farms and fields full of hay bales. She turned the radio up and sang along with the songs. When she opened the can of soda she had and it sprayed all over her, I busted out laughing. I quickly put my hand over my mouth. I hadn't laughed since Abby disappeared. It felt strange and unfamiliar.

"You're allowed to have fun," Tessa said, reading my mind.

"It sure doesn't feel like I should," I said.

"We're still here," Tessa said.

"And Abby isn't," I countered. The mood shifted in the car. I didn't want to live in a world where I existed and Abby didn't. I wanted us both to be able to laugh. At the dumb stupid things we used to joke about together. It shouldn't be about what I was allowed to do and not do.

"Abby wouldn't want you living this way," Tessa said, and I wanted to ask her what way that was, because ever since my sister had disappeared, I had no idea who I was. Who I was supposed to be.

Tessa turned down a side road, and I realized we were headed toward the part of the woods where Johnson Franklin lived.

"Slow down," I told her. She gave me a funny look, but did what I asked.

What if Johnson really did know something? The idea had been poking at the edge of my mind for some time now. Abby had run into the woods that night, and he had been there and could have some kind of clue.

I was fully aware that this was wishful thinking. If he knew something, he would've told the police. But I didn't have any other ideas, and I needed to bring my sister home.

A thin strip of smoke rose in the air from the woods. He was there.

"Can you stop for a minute?" I asked when she was parallel to the smoke.

"In the middle of the road? There's nothing here."

"There kind of is." I pointed toward the woods. "Johnson's tent is out there."

Tessa turned to look at me. "You're kidding, right?" But she pulled over anyway.

There was a small opening into the woods. When we were young, we'd dare one another to go in there and touch his tent when he walked the main road in town. I could find it again easily.

Before I could think it through, I opened the car door and jumped out. My feet raced across the field. Most of the town now avoided the woods like the plague. It had become a place full of monsters, goblins, and evil waiting to swallow you up. Parents forbade children to go inside and hunters carried their rifles a little closer to their bodies, but I couldn't let those fears rule me right now. I needed to take action. I needed to find Abby and set this right.

Tessa stood in the middle of the field and gestured at me to come back to her. I put my finger to my lips and moved to the opening to take a step in. I paused, waiting for something to happen; perhaps giant fingers would scoop me up and carry me away into the dark creepy places. But nothing stopped me. I stepped in farther.

Johnson didn't live too far from the entrance, and I imagined at night he could hear the same sounds Abby and I used to listen to. The cars and trains in the distance. We'd sit on the porch in the summer, when the heat was so hot it was almost suffocating in our house, and listen to the sounds of the night. Abby once told me that a train carried Abraham Lincoln across the U.S. and every time you heard a whistle late at night, it was the same ghost train carrying his spirit across the Earth, the whistle wailing the tears of the mourners. A few years back she even tried to run alongside a train, racing it as it sped through our town.

She was fearless. And now I had to be the same.

I smelled Johnson's fire before I saw it. The orange shimmered through the trees, the smoke twisted around the leaves. I crept closer but stayed hidden behind a bunch of trees. My clothes, a pair of jeans and navy blue shirt, weren't exactly camouflage, but at least they were dark.

I took a few more steps and there he was. He sat on a

bucket turned upside down, twirling a branch in his fingers. He mumbled something, but I was too far away to hear. His beard hung to his chest, and he wore a red wool hat that looked as if it had seen better days. Mom knitted hats for our city's food pantry to give out each Christmas and I wondered if he'd ever ended up with one.

His fire spat and snapped once in a while, but otherwise, it was silent. So silent that it seemed possible if Abby had come this way that night, Johnson would've heard her. I took a step forward. Things like being careful didn't matter now that Abby was gone. What mattered was finding her.

I held my breath as I moved. I didn't know what I'd do when I reached Johnson, but it seemed important to reach him. He kept poking at the fire until Tessa's voice rang out, spooking both of us.

"Rhylee, get out of there. I'm leaving," she yelled.

Johnson's head snapped up. He looked right at me and there was no turning back. I lifted my hand in a half wave and put it down.

He threw his stick into the fire and stood.

"What are you doing?" he yelled, and it wasn't in the welcoming way. "You have no business bothering me. Get the hell out of here."

I walked backward a few feet. I wasn't entirely afraid of him; I just didn't know how to act. He stood his ground and so did I.

"I wanted to talk to you. About my sister."

Tessa must have walked back to her car, because a horn

blasted through the air and a flock of birds flew from the trees, screeching at the sky.

"Get out." He took a few steps toward me; his patience had run thin. Tessa honked the horn in short bursts, and if I didn't get out of there soon, I'd have to walk home. I turned my back on Johnson and ran toward her car. This wasn't the last time I'd see him. I wouldn't let it be.

50

I woke the next morning to yelling in our back-yard. Collin ran into my bedroom.

"Something is going on in the circles," he said. "We need to get outside."

"Calm down. Let's wait and see what Mom says." I wasn't sure what had happened, and I didn't want to bring Collin out there if it was something bad.

"Please," he said. "We have to go."

"It's not a good idea," I said, but he wasn't listening. He ran down the stairs, so I rushed after him.

Light had begun to soften the dark edges of the woods into daylight and the dew had settled on the grass. Collin made his way to Mom, and she wrapped her arms around him. I kept my distance, not quite sure of what I was walking into.

"What's going on?" I asked.

"It's Abby. She was back near the woods."

"What?" I asked. A small flicker of hope ignited in me. "What do you mean?"

Mary Grace's mom stepped forward and spoke. "I saw her while everyone else was sleeping. I was reading my bible. Something moved over by the edge of the woods. I thought it was a large animal, a deer perhaps, but when it got closer, I realized it was Abby."

The group gathered together, and Mom stood in front of them, as Mary Grace's mom tried to recreate the image she claimed she'd never forget. "Abby was in her cross-country uniform, but it looked old, faded almost. It was foggy around her, so it was hard for me to see."

I thought about the mornings I ran with the team and the fog was sometimes so thick it was as if we were in the middle of the sky. The sound of our shoes slapping against the street would be the only way to tell there was someone else beside you. I knew exactly what Mary Grace's mom meant; that when the weather was like that, it was impossible to distinguish between what was real and what might not be.

Some of the Miracle Seekers stared at her, their heavy-lidded eyes fixed and unmoving, but others were more hysterical. A few went back to the edge of the woods where Abby was spotted and moved through the trees, trying to spot her again. A man near me held a rosary in his hands and prayed loudly, and a woman sat and rocked back and forth. Tears fell from her eyes.

My old piano teacher, Jodi Hunter, said, "She's telling the truth. I saw Abby too. I told myself it was a dream, so I went back to sleep. Abby was different. It was as if the fog followed her. Everything around me was clear as day, but she seemed transparent. She was there, but she wasn't."

Collin broke away from me and paced back and forth.

"I told you she was still here," he yelled to me. "She was out in our field, but no one would listen. Why did Mary Grace's mom let Abby leave? Why didn't she stop her?"

Collin buried his face into my arms and cried. I was jealous of him. He was still young enough to cry and yell and hurt openly, when that's all I wanted to do too. Honestly, I think it was all a lot of us wanted to do.

"You let her slip away," Mom said, and she wrapped her arms around herself. It was as if the cold had settled into everyone and no one could escape it.

"I wasn't thinking," Mary Grace's mom said. "All I could see was Abby. I couldn't take my eyes off of her."

But she wasn't really there, I wanted to shout. *This is all ridiculous. You're all ridiculous. How can you blame someone for something that didn't happen?*

Collin continued to sob. His heart was breaking, and I couldn't fix it.

"What does this mean?" Mary Grace's mom asked, standing beside me.

Everyone turned to one another searching for an answer, but like everything else in this mess, no one had a clue about what any of it meant.

51

I promised Collin I'd take him to the library to get some new books about the circles, which is how I found myself walking to our town's measly excuse for a library after school. It was one big room with the sections divided in each corner. I swear I read every picture book there at least five times each when I was younger.

I picked him up at his elementary school, and he practically dragged me the entire way. His eyes focused on every person we passed. He was looking for Abby. And how could I fault him? As ridiculous as it was, I did the same thing.

"We don't need to move as if we're being chased by a rabid dog," I told him. I carried both my bag and his on my shoulder, and the straps cut into my skin, making it impossible to keep up.

"What if there are no books left? What if someone else came and took them out?"

He had such panic in his eyes that I quickened my pace a bit to calm him down.

"I'm sure there'll be plenty of books for you to check out. I doubt there was a stampede to the library for books about aliens."

"You don't know that," Collin said, and I didn't argue. Who knew, he might be right. Everything I expected to be normal had flipped itself upside down these last few weeks; I wasn't sure what normal was anymore.

We were about to head inside the library when I saw Johnson.

Of course Johnson was here. I didn't need to creep into the woods to find him; he pushed his rusted-out shopping cart here every day.

He moved with his head down, but he didn't need to worry about making eye contact. Everyone around him still avoided him.

"Let's go, Rhylee." Collin drew out the last letters of my name into a high-pitched whine and tugged on my sleeve.

"Go ahead, I'll be right there," I said. He didn't have to be told twice. He raced into the library and I took a few steps forward so that I could have a clear view of Johnson. It was stupid and irresponsible of me to let Collin go into the library alone, but I was too focused on Johnson and what he might know about Abby. Besides, what could happen in the library? A stack of falling books crushing him?

I followed Johnson. I lagged behind, so I could keep my eye on where he was going and think about what I should do.

I doubted that he'd let me come up to him and ask a bunch of questions about my sister, but I didn't really know any other way to approach him.

I asked myself what Abby would do. She'd probably stop right in the middle of his path with a big smile on her face and introduce herself. So maybe that's what I should try. I ducked inside the small coffee shop that sat right next to the library. A few people glanced up from their newspapers for a second and one old woman gave me a sad smile, probably recognizing me, but no one tried to talk to me or offer me pitying words, thankfully.

"What can I get you?" a girl in a polka-dotted dress asked.

"Two coffees to go."

She took my order, and soon the hot cups were in my hands. I added cream and sugar to one and left the other black. I wasn't sure how Johnson took his coffee, and I didn't want to mess this up.

I couldn't find him when I stepped back out, but there was no way he could have gone too far. His cart kind of hindered a quick getaway. I headed in the direction I'd last seen him, and it wasn't long before I spotted him on a bench, his cart parked close to his side.

I closed my eyes, took a deep breath, and summoned every bit of Abby's courage I could find in myself. This was nuts, but it felt as if this was my only option. I owed it to Abby to talk to him. I sat at the other end of the bench and he shifted closer to his stuff as if I was going to steal his pile of junk. He kept his back turned to me, toward his cart, and didn't acknowledge that there was another person sitting next to him.

Great, this was a bit anticlimactic.

I scooted closer and caught a whiff of someone who definitely lived in the woods.

I moved even closer until we were almost touching. The coffee cups were warm against my hands, the heat radiating from them almost unbearable.

"I don't have anything for you to steal," he grumbled.

"I'm not planning to rob you," I said and thrust the coffee at him. "I brought you coffee."

"Coffee messes with my mind," he said.

"Good thing it's still early," I said and pushed both of the cups toward him. "Which do you want, black or cream and sugar?"

He turned to investigate me, a flicker of recognition on his face.

"Why are you bothering me, girl?"

"I want to . . ." I stopped and thought about how I'd phrase this. How could I get him to honestly listen to me? Because it seemed as if he was about to get up and leave. I decided to dive right in. "My sister was Abby. The girl who disappeared."

"Aww, shit. I had nothing to do with that." He stood and pushed his cart forward. "You have no right to—"

I jumped in front of him, banging my shin against his cart. "Wait, I don't think you did anything."

"Get out of my way," he said and tried to push his cart around me. I'm not sure exactly what happened next; his cart might have caught on a rock or something, but suddenly it tipped over on its side. He tried to right it, but the cart was too heavy and it crashed to the ground. "Son of a bitch. Look at what you did."

"I'm sorry." I bent to help him pick up his stuff. The coffee cups had flipped over on their sides and the liquid was making a slow descent toward the items in his cart that were strewn about the sidewalk. I handed him a flannel shirt and a garbage bag full of something soft and tried to stuff them back in the cart after he righted it.

"You don't know how to leave well enough alone. All of you. Messing in my business. Asking questions, looking at me like I'm some sort of criminal."

"I don't think you did anything. I'm just trying to find out if anyone saw anything. My sister . . . there's nothing . . . I was hoping maybe . . ." I spoke in disjointed sentences, but it wasn't making a difference. He wasn't listening to me.

"I told them what I knew. I've got nothing else."

"Rhylee," a voice yelled. Collin. I had forgotten about him. For a brief second it was as if two people had taken hold of each of my hands and were fighting over me, each person yanking me from side to side. I didn't know which way to go at first, but then turned toward my brother. How could I have forgotten him? I must have left him alone at the library for at least half an hour.

I stuffed the items in my hands in Johnson's cart. I didn't want Collin to see what I was doing, because he'd tell our parents.

"I gotta go. My brother is over there. I was only trying to find my sister. I didn't mean to bother you; I don't know what else to do."

Johnson continued to pick his things off the ground and acted as if I didn't exist.

"Collin!" I yelled and jogged over to him. I expected to see tears, but instead, he grabbed my hand and tugged me back toward the library.

"Come on. They're holding my books. They said you needed to check them out for me."

"Sounds like a plan," I told him and followed him up the steps of the library. "What kind of books did you find?"

"All different types. One of the ladies helped me. She got me a big huge stack. I'm going to be reading all night long, and Mom can't do anything to stop me."

"Of course she can't." I listened as he chattered on about his adventures at the library. I was glad he didn't think there was anything odd about finding me outside on the street talking to a homeless man with a shopping cart.

I followed him into the library shaken up about the whole conversation with Johnson. I repeated his words over and over again in my head, making sure I'd heard them right. He said he told the police everything he knew, but the police hadn't mentioned anything to my family. At least, nothing I heard about. That might mean there was something I didn't know, and I was determined to find out what that was. I owed it to Abby to find out.

52

The next day, I ran up and down roads looking for my sister. The real version, not the so-called ghost girl who haunted the town. I searched everywhere; through the center of town, past Webster's, the church we'd go to at Christmas and Easter, and the park where Tommy and I kissed. I moved faster and faster until I was afraid I was going to trip over my feet. Even then, I couldn't go fast enough.

I looped around the high school and into the stadium where they'd had the memorial for Abby. The cross-country team was doing timed runs on the track. I headed up the steps of the bleachers until I reached the top, and lay on my back so I could watch the sky. It was one of those days that warned you fall was creeping in. The kind where the clouds held on to the edge of the horizon and made everything look all doom and gloom, and if you squinted, you could picture the leaves on trees changing colors.

Someone yelled "10:13," calling out the time of a runner.

"That's pathetic!" a voice shouted back, and from the high-pitched whine, I recognized it as Erica's. "I bet Mr. Taylor could beat me in a race at that speed."

I laughed despite myself. Mr. Taylor was the seventy-six-year-old English teacher who seemed intent on teaching until he dropped dead.

Voices shouted back and forth below me, and I closed my eyes. I thought about how the world should be right now. Abby would be running on that track, and I'd still be aching for Tommy in secret. Collin would be annoying me by stealing stuff from my room, and my parents would be their normal boring selves, making small talk at dinner and writing our daily activities on the big calendar in the kitchen.

A whistle blew from the track and jarred me from my memories.

Someone walked up the bleachers, the clang of heels against metal. I peeked out through the slit of one eye. It was Tessa, looking ridiculous in jeans, cowboy boots, a plaid shirt, and a bandanna around her neck. Her hair was in two pigtails.

She nudged me with her foot.

"Last time I checked, cowboys don't live in Ohio," I said.

"Today was show choir practice," she told me, as if it were the most obvious thing in the world. "We're doing a medley of *Oklahoma* songs."

"Right, got it." I tried not to laugh at her outrageous outfit, but I couldn't hold it in.

"What's so funny? You're dressed in a costume too," she shot back.

I glanced at my shorts and tank top and then back at her. "What are you talking about? I went for a run."

"A run? And what's with your hair?" Tessa kept going.

I touched the French braid I'd put in earlier today. Abby always wore one when she ran, and I thought I'd give it a shot.

"Since when did you become an athlete?"

"Why does everyone find it so hard to believe that I could actually do something that involves physical activity?" I asked and then gestured toward the field. "I was thinking of joining the team."

"Sure you were," Tessa said, not buying a word of what I was saying. I had a hunch that even if she saw me running with the girls in the morning, she'd still think I was joking.

"What are *you* doing here?" I asked.

"I was leaving play practice when I spotted you here." She fished a box of Hot Tamales out of her bag and pushed it at me. I took a handful and jammed them into my mouth.

"Remember how Abby hated it when we watched her run?" I asked. "She never wanted to see us in the crowd before a race. She said it messed up her thinking."

Tessa laughed. "And you used to come up with the craziest costumes so she wouldn't know it was you."

"It always worked. We'd spend days inventing who we would be."

It became a joke in our family, what we could wear to throw off Abby. We tried to see how outrageous we could get with our costumes and still not have her notice us. Dad and I would go to the thrift store or garage sales and pick through racks of other people's discarded clothes. The two of us brought home hats, wigs, and oversize pieces of clothing to drape around ourselves. We stood next to families we knew at the away meets, and laughed because they didn't recognize us either. Abby acted as if she hated it when we crowded around her in running suits and sweatbands or wigs of long dark hair and sunglasses, but Mom would always pull something out of her purse for Abby to put on to become a part of our group instead of wearing her cross-country uniform, and she'd happily comply.

I realized Tessa was right about my outfit. I was in costume now, a costume that looked a lot like my sister. But was that so bad? Abby had always been the better one. Would it be so horrible if I disappeared and tried to bring her back in small ways? Especially when she's the one who should be here right now after what I did.

"Maybe Abby's hiding somewhere out there now, in her own costume, and we don't recognize her," Tessa said.

"I wish she was." The weight of my words hung between us.

"Listen." Tessa changed the subject for me. "If I ask you something, will you promise to think about it before you say no?"

"If you have to ask me that, I have a feeling I'm not going to like what you're about to say." I knew Tessa, and more often than not, her plans were a bit nuts.

She ignored me and launched into her idea, talking really fast so I wouldn't have time to interrupt.

"Jarrett and I are going to homecoming, and I think it would be good if you came along. We'll make it low key."

"How do you make a dance 'low key'?" I asked. It got crazy at school during homecoming and prom time. The girls talked about nothing but dresses and hair and nails and all that other stuff I didn't get involved in because I'd never been asked to a dance before. It was enough to make you want to crawl into a cave and hibernate until it was over.

"We won't make a big deal out of it. It'll be fun. We haven't done anything in forever, and you know how lame Jarrett is about dancing."

"I'm not sure this is such a good idea," I told Tessa, watching the team set up hurdles along the track. "It doesn't feel right to go to the dance with Abby gone."

"Your sister would want you to live your life," Tessa said. "Will you at least think about it?"

I sighed, a big heaving sigh mainly for her benefit. "Okay, I'll consider it for a minute or two, but that might be all the attention I give it."

"Perfect!" Tessa reached out her hand to me, and I grabbed it. She yanked me to my feet, and then draped her arm around me. "Let's get out of here."

I followed her as she clanked down in her cowboy boots. I watched the girls on the track and thought again about how Abby should be practicing with them. How she should be the one here.

53

I pushed the dance from my mind, but it was clear Tessa wasn't going to let it slide. I about jumped out of my skin two days later when she came up behind me and put her hands over my eyes as I was pulling books from my locker.

"God, freak out much?" She unwrapped one of the scarves from around her neck. She had at least four, and looked like a gypsy who'd escaped from the loony bin. "I've been looking for you everywhere."

"You have my schedule memorized; you couldn't have been looking too hard."

"But doesn't it sound more dramatic to think that I've been scouring the school from top to bottom for you?"

I pushed away the scarf that she now waved in my face. "You're nuts."

"Well, I have some news for you." Tessa got that look on her face I knew too well; the one where she gets a funny half smile, so you know she's up to no good. She does it when she's trying to figure out how to convince me to do things that'll probably end badly. Like the time she asked me to help dye her hair black and we ruined her parents' fancy towels after we used them to clean the countertops, or when we were in fourth grade and she thought it would be an adventure to hitchhike home. Our elementary school principal picked us up, and we had to listen to her lecture us about the dangers of taking rides from strangers the entire drive. Tessa was up to no good, there was no doubt about that. "We're set for Saturday, so you can't back out now."

"Saturday?" I said, playing dumb.

Tessa pulled an envelope out of her purse and passed it over to me. She shook her head back and forth as if I was a little child forgetting something. "The dance. I got us tickets, but you don't need to pay me back; it's no big deal. We just need to make sure you have a dress. Do you have a dress?"

"I didn't say I'd go. I told you I'd think about it."

"Come on, don't back out on me. You never do anything anymore, and Jarrett is excited that you're coming too."

"I find that hard to believe. No one likes a third wheel. What am I supposed to do during the slow songs, dance in between you two?"

"You won't be the third wheel; you know Jarrett hates to dance. That's why you have to come, and then I don't need to spend the entire night begging him to go out on the dance floor."

"There's no way I'm going to dance either," I tried to argue, but it was obvious Tessa wasn't going to let me out of this. We hadn't gone to last year's homecoming; most freshmen weren't brave enough to show up without a date, so instead, Tessa, Abby, and I had binge watched a new TV series while stuffing our faces full of ice cream and cookie dough. Tommy hadn't gone either. He'd told me we should go together as a joke to laugh at everyone dressed up in uncomfortable clothes. I pretended that would be funny, but I should've told him the truth. That I wanted to go with him and be one of those people dressed up.

I rubbed my temples. "I don't know, Tessa."

"What do you have to lose? Please, live a little," she said, and I could tell that she really did want me to go.

"Okay, but I don't think it's a good idea."

"It's a great idea," she said and hugged me.

The bell rang and our classmates scattered. As Tessa ran off down the hallway, I hoped she was right.

54

I lay awake that night staring at the ceiling. The air was still without a breeze. It hadn't rained since the day after Abby disappeared, and the weather stations had declared us officially in a draught. It had been weeks without more than a quick sprinkle, and people whispered their worries about the dangers of days with all sun and no relief in sight. September was almost over.

I had the curtains open to try to let some air in, and the faint strains of the Miracle Seekers' songs drifted above the whirl of the little fan I had on my night table.

There was a noise downstairs where Collin was sleeping in his blanket tent. He insisted on staying there since Mom refused to let him be out in the fields all night.

"Abby!" he yelled.

I lay still and waited for something to happen, almost as if my sister would answer.

"Abby!" he yelled again and began to cry. I jumped out of my bed and raced toward him.

He was curled in a ball, and his body shook.

"Hey, it's okay, Collin." I sat next to him and put my hand on his back. He had on his Spider-Man pajamas, the bottoms too short for his long legs. He climbed into my lap, even though he was too big to do that, and I let him because I needed it as much as he did.

The shaking stopped, but he continued to cry. "I missed you, Abby," he repeatedly said.

I hesitated. Did Collin really think I was Abby? *He's half asleep,* I told myself. *He doesn't know what he's saying. He probably won't even remember any of this.*

So I didn't correct him. Instead, I let him believe what we all wanted to believe.

"I miss you too," I told him and rubbed his back to calm him down.

He clung to me in the darkness and his body relaxed.

"I didn't think you were coming back," he said.

"I've always been here. I'm not going to leave you," I told him, because in the dark, you could pretend to be anyone you wanted to be.

55

I slept downstairs with Collin and didn't leave until I heard Dad pull up outside. I untangled from Collin carefully and headed upstairs to take a shower. It felt more important for me to stick around this morning than to go running.

Dad was frying bacon when I came back down, and Collin read the back of the cereal box. His hair stuck up in blond clumps and he swung his legs under the table as he hummed a song.

I slid into my usual seat at the table and nudged Collin with my elbow. He nudged me back and the two of us continued until he fell into a fit of laughter.

"Guess what?" Collin asked as he bent close to me.

"What?"

"Last night I saw Abby," Collin said, his eyes bright and shiny.

Dad turned from the stove so fast that he dropped the fork he was holding. He picked it up and walked over to Collin. "You did? Where did you see her?" he asked.

"She came right into the house and slept next to me all night long."

"Sounds like a wonderful dream," Dad said, and ruffled his hand through Collin's hair. Collin squirmed away from him.

"It wasn't a dream," he insisted, his happy mood vanished. "She's been visiting me at night. She sings me a lullaby when I can't sleep."

"You're pretty lucky she came to see you," I told him.

"It was even more special than those other people who saw her, because she stayed with me," he said. "She didn't run away. She really loves me. I just don't know why she didn't stay here and left again."

I leaned my head against the window next to the kitchen table. It was cool on my forehead, and I pulled back, blowing the glass to fog it up. I took my finger and drew a heart.

Collin smiled and drew his own heart encircling mine, reminding me how important family is.

56

Collin wasn't the only one who believed he'd seen Abby.

The Miracle Seekers kept a constant watch in our field for glimpses of her. They claimed she appeared more and more out of the blackness that leaked like ink through the field, but I wasn't buying it. It was always one person at a time who claimed to have spotted Abby, the rest left wondering how they could have missed her.

"How gullible are these people? Don't they find it odd that she's never been spotted by two people at the same time?" I told Dad before he left for work. He fought with Mom about the circles almost every day, but they'd gotten so big, it was next to impossible for him to put a stop to them anymore. "I mean, that's kind of a red flag that maybe these people are making it up."

"We're trying to believe in something right now," he said.

"But a ghost version of Abby?" I asked, my voice rising from frustration. "Abby isn't a ghost. This has to stop, Dad. It has to end. These people are ridiculous."

And they were. Especially since those who claimed to see her affirmed that she didn't just come at night, but during the day, too, in places that didn't even connect to our field.

"I was walking out of Calloos Pizzeria with my order and there she was," Jeannine Wilson said. "I spotted her across the street, bent over tying her shoe. I figured it was one of the high school girls, but when she stood, it was Abby. I yelled to her, but she moved too fast. I would've chased after her, but I had boxes of pizza in my hands."

"She was outside my bathroom window," Mr. Miller said. "I got out of the shower and glanced outside. She was cutting through my backyard. She climbed right over the chain-link fence, dropped down on the other side, and slipped through some bushes." He shook his head, as if he'd done something wrong. "I have no idea what she was doing there."

More people gathered in the field to try to catch a glimpse of my sister. Abby became some kind of urban legend. She was like the little girl in the story who appeared on the side of the road asking for a ride. When the man in the truck returned her to the house where she told him she lived, her parents said that she died over a year ago, and sure enough, she'd vanished from the front seat.

Abby sightings were the stories people told each other, like the ones we used to whisper around campfires or under blankets during sleepovers, the thrill of anticipation and fear running through us. But while people hung on to the idea that they really were seeing my sister as a ghost, I felt like she was moving further and further away. As everyone was looking for a ghost of Abby, I was terrified they were forgetting to find the real version of her.

57

Homecoming snuck up and tackled me before I could escape. I considered hiding when Tessa pulled into the driveway, but she'd track me down and drag me out like some Neanderthal caveman if she needed to.

I smoothed my sweaty hands on my dress. Correction, Abby's dress. It had hung in her closet forgotten after she went missing, the plastic bag around it and the price tag dangling from the back zipper. It had waited for her on a satin hanger that she had talked Mom into buying. The dress was pale yellow, like the glow under your chin when you hold a dandelion to it. It was strapless and dipped low in the front, different from anything I'd ever wear.

I tried it on last night because it was my only option. I didn't own anything nice enough for the dance, and I wasn't about to ask Mom to take me to the mall to get something to wear. The idea of Mom functioning anywhere beyond our house these days was a joke, so I didn't really have a choice but to wear it.

I'd waited until Collin was glued to some TV show, Dad was at work, and Mom was out in the field.

I'd slipped it on, jammed my feet into her shoes, and pretended for just a moment that I'd stepped into Abby's life.

I pushed that thought aside. Wasn't it this type of pretending that had ruined everything?

I'd practically ripped the dress off and hung it back up in the closet among Abby's other dresses, shirts, and pants that waited for her to come back and wear them again.

But with only thirty minutes until Tessa picked me up and no other options, that dress was going to have to work. I put it on in the downstairs bathroom so no one would see that I borrowed it.

I stood in front of the mirror, and felt like an impostor once again. Who did I think I was? What right did I have to wear my sister's dress to a dance she could no longer go to? And how was this any different than thinking it was okay to kiss her boyfriend? You don't just take things that don't belong to you, but that was exactly what I'd done and what I was about to do again. I reached back to unzip the dress. I needed to take it off. This wasn't right. Not the dress or going to the dance. But before I could, a horn blared from outside.

Tessa was here.

I ran barefoot to the car, out of my house before my parents found me in Abby's dress. I'd written a note earlier that I placed on the kitchen table for them to find when I was gone.

Abby's dress skimmed the ground and stirred up a fog of dust around the bottom. I was shorter than her and the dress wasn't quite the same on me.

Nothing was quite the same.

Tessa rolled down the window and whistled as I ran to the car. "Looking good, girl."

I put my finger to my lips and hoped she'd get the hint.

"Let's go," I said as I stepped into the car.

"What's the hurry? You're acting as if you robbed a bank."

"More like my sister's closet," I said. "This is her dress."

Tessa turned to me, and I waited for her to tell me I was crazy. Because really, who wears their missing sister's dress to a dance? The dress her sister didn't get to wear.

But Tessa didn't.

"It looks great on you," she said.

Her words made me feel even worse. I shouldn't look good in Abby's dress.

"There's only one problem," she said and reached over toward my armpit. She grabbed a tag that I hadn't even noticed and pulled it off in one quick yank. "There, you're ready."

I didn't like the finality of pulling off the tag. Of wearing something for the first time that didn't belong to me.

"Right now," I said as I buckled my seat belt, "I'd be happy to be just about anywhere other than this dance."

"Come on, Rhylee, tonight is going to be fun. Wait and see. You'll have a good time."

I wasn't sure that I wanted to. If I deserved to. I'd stolen Abby's boyfriend, her dress; could I steal her good time, too? What else would I take from her?

Tessa drove to Jarrett's house and honked the horn two times. When the lights above the front door flashed, she laid her hand on the horn and continued to announce her arrival.

"Uh, I think he knows you're here," I said.

"That's obvious, but Jarrett is worse than a girl. He'll take another ten minutes to get ready," Tessa complained. "If I keep beeping, he'll hurry so his mom doesn't get pissed."

I fluffed the fabric of my dress around me. It was as if I was sitting on a cloud, the skirt floating.

Jarrett came outside, his suit jacket flapping behind him half on and half off, and instead of opening the back door, he threw open the passenger side door. I held up my hand.

"Sorry, this seat is taken."

"No worries, I'll fit. I'd rather be here with you ladies." He slid in, the bones of his hips poking me as he pushed me against Tessa. "Nothing wrong with getting close to each other."

He laid the top half of his body against me in order to kiss Tessa. I grabbed a handful of the yellow dress fabric and yanked it out from under him. He positioned himself so he wasn't quite squashing me and ran his hands through his spiky black hair. I couldn't help but laugh at the baby blue suit he had put on with black and white two-tone shoes. As obnoxious as he was, Jarrett and Tessa were made for each other.

The ride went by way too fast. Before I knew it, we were at the high school.

"I don't know if I can do this," I told them when Tessa parked the car in the overflow lot by the football field. I played with the white sparkly bracelet I'd found in Abby's jewelry box. What was I thinking, agreeing to go to a dance that my sister couldn't go to in a dress she might never wear?

"Tough. I didn't want to shave my legs, but I did so I wouldn't hear Jarrett bitch about it later. We all have to do things we don't want to do."

"She's right," Jarrett said. "I like a woman with smooth legs." He reached over me again and tried to run his hand up Tessa's leg.

I stretched my body to the right and opened the passenger side door. Jarrett fell out.

"Hey, watch the merchandise," he joked before he walked over to talk to a group of guys standing around a truck.

"Tessa, really. I can't do this," I repeated. "I shouldn't be here. This was supposed to be Abby's dance."

What made me think it was okay to do this? I didn't go to dances or wear fancy dresses and makeup. Abby was the one who loved that kind of thing.

"Please, just take me home," I said, my words getting caught in my throat as I fought back tears.

"You can have a little fun," Tessa said and pointed at Abby's shoes on the floor of the car. "Put those on and let's give it a shot. If you're uncomfortable, we'll leave. I promise."

In the distance, people headed into the school. Couples held hands and groups of my classmates walked, laughed, and joked with one another. Three faint red dots glowed and then dimmed by the corner of the parking lot; the last cigarettes snuck before entering the gym.

I turned one of the shoes over, the bottoms black and scuffed, which was odd; I'd thought they were new shoes bought with the dress. I ran my fingers over the scratched soles and wondered when Abby had worn them. I slipped them on and before I could resist, Tessa grabbed my hand and yanked me out of the car and into the dance.

"Let's do this," she said, and reluctantly, I followed.

58

The dance theme was fire and ice. Lights shone down in a blue haze and cast a gray hue on everyone's faces, making them look like zombies. The corners had red strobe lights that flashed into the air, on and off.

The football team won last night, so everyone was in a good mood. The players strutted around and a good-size crowd of people jumped to the music on the dance floor. I could picture Abby among them. She had this way of dancing with giant movements that seemed to take over the space. She'd be right there in the middle of it with a huge smile on her face, not caring what anyone thought of her at all. I turned away from the dance floor, missing her.

Jarrett wandered over to the food table, where cookies in the shape of snowflakes and suns sat, and stuffed his face. Tessa grabbed my hand and tried to get me to the dance floor. I shook my head. I was here; she needed to be happy with that.

I found a table along one of the walls and planted myself in a chair, glad to be off my feet. I could count on one hand the number of times I'd worn heels. Tessa stayed near me, but moved to the music by herself. I rolled my eyes when a particularly fast song came on and she shook her head all around, her hair flashing in the lights so that it looked as if she was a part of the fire theme.

We stayed like that for a while, me sitting and Tessa rocking out until Jarrett came back and Tessa gave up dancing to make out with him. So much for sticking by me at the dance.

I wandered away from the spit fest that was now occurring and slipped through the crowd, not wanting to watch the two of them sucking face. I stood on the edge of the dance floor while everyone moved with the music. My classmates were dressed as fancy versions of themselves.

Someone grabbed my hand and yanked me into the crowd. It was one of Abby's teammates. She pulled me into the group she was dancing with. I slid through bodies slick with sweat that moved against me, threatening to swallow me up. I fell into the dark pulsating core. Those around me moved to the music, not caring who they bumped into, so I did the same. I danced with everyone the way Abby would have. I threw my arms up and moved with the crowd. I closed my eyes and the strobe lights darkened and brightened against my eyelids. The bass pumped deep into my chest so I wasn't sure if my heart was beating or if it was the music that kept me alive.

I allowed myself to be swept up in the group until a hand grabbed mine and pulled me out.

The person pulled me through the crowd, and it wasn't until we broke through that I saw it was Tommy.

My history teacher, Mr. Scott, stood guard near the door that led outside. His cell phone screen lit his face and he repeated the rules that he must have said a million times tonight without looking up. "No touching, no yelling, no running around, or you'll go back inside."

I couldn't make a scene. I couldn't do that to Tommy, so I let him pull me through.

He shoved his hands into the pockets of his black pants and looked at the ground. He wore a white dress shirt with the navy-blue tie he wore when he played the piano at weddings. His hair was slicked back and his sneakers were still in their perpetual state of being untied.

"Tessa told me you were coming tonight," he said. "I thought maybe we could talk. Maybe we—"

He was about to say more but paused as he noticed my dress. He reached out and touched a section of it. The fabric slipped through his fingers.

"Abby was supposed to wear this," he said. "She showed it to me after she bought it because she was so excited."

I was uncomfortable. Self-conscious. How could I explain to him why I was wearing Abby's dress? Why I'd tried it on?

"And you had her tennis shoes that day you were running," Tommy said. His voice was heavy with sadness.

We stood against the brick wall, our faces hidden in the

shadows. Inside, the music pulsed so deep that you could feel the beat in the ground, thumping through you. Red lights lit one corner of the courtyard. He took a step toward me, so I took a step back, the bottom of my dress swishing against my legs.

"At first I didn't know it was you," Tommy said. "On the dance floor, before. Maybe it was the lights or the music, but I thought . . ." He trailed off as if looking for the right words. Someone far off in the grass laughed. There was a flash of light, a match struck before a hand concealed it. "I thought you were Abby."

I touched the satin, cool in my sweaty hands. "I'll never be Abby."

But wasn't that what I was doing? Dressing like my sister? Going to the dance she was supposed to go to? I focused on my sister's shoes; clumps of dirt stuck to the heels. I had stepped into her life again, just like I had when I tried to make Tommy mine. I had taken so much away from Abby, and here I was doing it again.

"Why would you think I want you to be her?" Tommy asked, but wasn't the answer obvious? Abby had had Tommy.

"Everyone wants Abby," I told him.

Tommy ran his hand through his hair and paced back and forth, frustrated.

"I don't," he said, and my heart ached for what could never happen between us.

A large group of kids came out, laughing and pushing each other. The door stayed open, held by a boy who couldn't decide if he was going in or out. I knew that feeling. What it felt like to stand in between, not fitting on either side.

The outside door swung open again, and Tessa stepped out. She scanned the yard and stopped when she found me. She looked from me to Tommy, turned around, and headed back inside. She was giving me the chance to be with him, but she had it all wrong. I couldn't be with him.

I stepped away from Tommy and slipped through the doors before he could stop me.

59

I hid out in the bathroom for about half an hour, and when I came out, Tessa was back at the table with Jarrett, trying to get him to slow dance.

"I need to leave," I told the two of them. "Can we go?"

"What about Tommy?" Tessa asked. "I saw the two of you together."

"There is no Tommy," I said in a voice that made it very clear I wasn't going to talk about him.

"Yeah, sure, okay, let's go," Tessa said as she stood up. "We're ready, right?"

Jarrett nodded and followed the two of us out of the dance. I walked fast. I wanted to get out of there before Tommy found me again. I needed to stay away from him.

On the ride home, Tessa didn't mention anything about seeing us outside, and I wasn't about to volunteer any information. Instead, I turned the radio up loud enough to drown out any conversation we might have wanted to have.

When we got to my house, Tessa stepped out of the car and hugged me.

"I'm glad you came tonight," she said. "You know you can call me if you want to talk."

"Thanks for the ride," I said, not revealing anything else. I waved to Jarrett before heading inside.

I didn't see the Miracle Seekers at first. The group usually stayed in the field, so when one of them stepped out on our front walk, I jumped in surprise.

She stood in front of me in a sweater that went to her knees, her arms crossed.

"Sorry," I said. "I wasn't expecting anyone to be here." I reached into my purse for the house key. Since people now camped out in our fields, my parents had decided to keep the doors locked.

She took a step toward me and her sweater fell open. She wore a shirt with Abby's picture. Someone had taken an old photo from the sports section of our paper of her grinning and holding a medal and made piles of shirts for those searching for her. I didn't have to see the back of the shirt to know that the words "Homeward Bound" were written in bold purple letters.

"It must be nice to be able to go out and have fun when your sister isn't able to," she said.

"Excuse me?" I asked, stunned. I wasn't sure I heard her correctly. Usually the Miracle Seekers talked to my family with faces of concern and sadness, but this lady was looking at me with anger. I took a few steps closer to my door, now clutching the key I was holding tight in my fist in case I needed to use it. She made me nervous.

She moved forward so that she was right in front of me and blocked my path.

"You dressing up and having fun with your friends," she said, "when Abby can't. I sure wouldn't do something like that."

I stared at this woman, this stranger who knew nothing about my family beyond what she saw on the news or heard through gossip. This woman who had taken over my yard with her foolish optimism and acted as if my life was her business. I thought about the dance and how fun had nothing to do with it, but here she was judging me, as if I didn't already feel incredibly guilty for going.

"Screw you," I spat out with an anger I'd buried deep inside. I pushed her out of my way. She stumbled and threw her arms out, trying to gain her balance.

I didn't wait to see if she righted herself or fell. I jammed my key into the door and locked it behind me.

I went straight to Abby's room, kicked off her shoes, climbed onto the bed, and crawled under the sheets. I didn't even bother to take off her dress. I sobbed into her pillow until my eyes were swollen and aching.

That night I slept deeper than I had since Abby first disappeared. I swore I could smell her in the sheets, and it felt as if she was there with me.

60

Dad found me in the morning, cocooned under a pile of blankets, Abby's dress tangled around my legs.

"We need to talk," he said in a stern voice, and I was pretty sure he'd spoken to the Miracle Seeker who'd intercepted me at the door when I came home from the dance.

I followed him to the kitchen and poured the last of the box of cereal. It was stale and mostly crumbs, but I needed something to do with my hands, a way to keep my mouth shut.

Dad opened the curtains that covered the sliding door to our backyard, and for a second I was afraid that the woman would be out there. But only bright sunlight flooded the room.

"What happened last night? One of the women in the circle, she said her name was Mrs. Butler, stopped me when I went out to get the paper and told me you pushed her. Is this true?"

"Yeah," I told him. If he wanted the truth, I was going to give it to him. For once.

"First the woman at Otis's Diner and now this. What would possess you to do something like that?" He stared at me as if he didn't even recognize me.

I thought about apologizing, stepping down, but I didn't want to. The way that woman treated me wasn't fair. "Because of the way she was talking to me, like I did something bad. I went out last night to a school dance. Something pretty much everyone at my school did. I was just trying to get back to normal. She has no right to judge me. None at all."

"You're right. What she said wasn't appropriate, but that doesn't mean you can respond by pushing her. You do understand these people are here for your sister, don't you?" Dad asked.

"Abby is my sister. *Mine*. They act like they own her, but they don't. Not at all. This is happening to me, to you, to *our* family."

Dad sighed and rubbed his eyes. "I'll talk to her. This is hard for all of us, and she shouldn't have said what she said, but we raised you to be respectful."

Outside, Mom pulled into our driveway and stepped out of the car with boxes of doughnuts. She walked over to the group and passed them around to everyone.

"Mom shouldn't be out there. She cares about everyone in the field more than she does about her own family."

"That's not true—" Dad said, but it was. It couldn't be healthy. Mom blended in so well with the people outside that she was a part of them. Ever since that tiny step forward, the crop circles and Miracle Seekers had made her go a hundred steps back. She'd become a Miracle Seeker herself. She was so obsessed with those circles that she couldn't even see what was going on with her own family. Just the other day Collin wore pajama bottoms to school because he didn't have any clean pants. There was a pile of bills on the dining room table that were overdue, and I'd thrown away almost everything in our fridge last week because the food was rotten. We were a mess, and Mom refused to see that.

"Those people aren't right, Dad."

He shook his head. "They aren't hurting anyone."

"What about Mom? They're hurting her. She stands out there waiting for Abby to come home. Mom's looking for this ghost version of Abby, when she should be with us. Instead, she's in our field with a bunch of strangers."

"Your mother is trying to make sense of this, just like us."

"How can she, when she's pretty much forgotten the other three people in her family who are still here, because she's too busy with everyone outside filling her head with that bullshit? Abby might be gone, but we're still here and she doesn't even care."

"It's her way, Rhylee."

"Her way of what?"

Dad paused. "Grieving."

The clock in our kitchen ticked away the minutes and the voices outside rose and fell in peaks, valleys, growing loud, and then soft.

"We're grieving too," I finally said. "And right now Abby isn't the only one that I feel like I've lost."

61

"Did you hear about what happened when we left the dance on Saturday? Everyone is talking about the fight between Tommy and Kyle," Tessa said as soon as I got to school Monday morning.

"Tommy got in a fight?" I asked.

"I guess the two of them went at it in the middle of the dance floor. Mr. Ralston pulled them apart before much could happen, but people said that Kyle went nuts screaming at Tommy. He didn't mention it to you?"

"We don't really talk anymore," I said and hoped that would be enough to shut Tessa up. But things were never that easy.

"I saw the two of you were outside together at the dance," Tess pointed out.

"It wasn't like that," I said. I stayed on my knees in front of my locker and pretended to search through my books and papers. It was a lot easier to speak to the scratched metal and pile of books inside than to look at Tessa's face.

"The two of you were outside together in the dark. You're really going to try to tell me that isn't something?"

The bell rang, and I had no choice but to stand up. People slammed lockers around me and headed toward their classes. A book bag swung into me, and I almost became a casualty in the mad dash to avoid a tardy slip.

"Really, nothing happened."

"It's okay to spend time with Tommy," Tessa said. "No one says that there is anything wrong with talking to a person. You're allowed to be around him."

"I wish it were that simple."

"It is," she told me, and I couldn't believe we were arguing about whether it was okay to like my missing sister's boyfriend. Tessa had always supported me, but this, this seemed like too much.

"And what do I tell my sister when she returns?" I asked. "Sorry, Abby, I've been getting pretty close with your boyfriend while you disappeared."

"You can't stop living," Tessa said. "You're still here."

"But she isn't," I told her. "And until she is, I can't betray her." *Again*, I thought.

Tessa nodded as if she understood, but my words felt sour on my tongue.

The two of us headed to class, and the irony of worrying about betraying Abby made me sick. Can you betray a person a second time? Especially when the initial betrayal was enough to destroy them?

62

I ditched sixth period and called the suicide
hotline again. Tessa's words spun in my head. There was no
way I could ever be with Tommy. How could I after what we'd
done?

"Are you in immediate danger?" a woman's voice asked.

"No," I said. "I need someone to talk to."

"This is a great place do to that. I'm Laura. What's your
name?"

"Abby," I said again without thinking, then felt ashamed
to take something of my sister's once again.

"What's on your mind, Abby?" she asked, and there was a
rustling, as if she was eating something from a bag. I pictured
her lounging on the chair wherever the hotline was located,
her feet up on her desk, popping almonds into her mouth.

"I can't stop thinking about what I did." I decided to take
the confessional route. Laura might not be a priest, but it sure

felt good to burden someone else with my sins. I was afraid that if I carried these secrets around by myself much longer, I might collapse under their weight.

"What did you do? Was it something that could put you in danger?"

"It wasn't something I did to myself. It was my sister. I hurt her so bad she hasn't returned. I don't think she'll ever return."

"Did you hurt her physically?" Laura asked.

"No, no," I quickly said so she wouldn't try to trace my call and send the police for me. "I did something to her that I don't think she can ever forgive."

"I'm sure she doesn't feel that way."

"She can't feel anything," I said, my voice rising as I felt the bitter sting of my guilt. "She's gone, and I'm the one who should have disappeared."

"Oh, honey, nothing in this world is worth disappearing for."

I pressed the change return button repeatedly while scanning the area to make sure no one walked by. "I don't know what I'm allowed to feel anymore. It all seems wrong no matter what I choose."

"What do you want to feel?"

"Love," I said and thought about Tommy.

"Why don't you think you feel it?" Laura asked.

"I'm not allowed."

"Everyone is allowed to feel love," she answered, but she was wrong. There is no way that someone gets to love after what I did. Not a chance.

Of course she was going to tell me I was allowed to love; her job was to fill my head with positive thoughts and warm fuzzies so I didn't want to off myself, but she didn't know. How could she understand that it was impossible to love someone when loving them was what drove away the only other person you could possibly love more?

"Yeah, maybe you're right," I said to please her and make sure she believed I was okay. "Listen, I have to go. But thanks for listening."

I hung up the phone before she could say anything more. Maybe in her world you could feel love, but in mine, the love I felt was an impossible curse.

63

I stayed in the library until the bell rang for the end of the school day. I followed the crowd out the door to the buses, which was where Tommy caught up with me.

It was no use running from him; I'd make a scene doing that, so I slowed down, and he seized his chance to fall into step beside me.

"I need to talk to you," he said. I couldn't see his face—he had a hoodie pulled up over his head—but I could hear the urgency in his voice.

"We can't," I told him and fought to keep my voice firm, even though I was crumbling inside.

"Please, Rhylee," he begged. "This is important."

I relented and nodded. I reached out and touched his hoodie. "You don't have to hide from me. Tessa told me what happened."

"I don't want you to see me like this," he said, but pulled down the hood.

His left eye was puffy and swollen almost completely shut. A mess of yellow and purple tinged the edges and his face held a kaleidoscope of bruises.

"Oh my god," I breathed as I took in what Kyle had done to him.

"That's why I wanted to talk to you. I need to say good-bye."

"Good-bye?"

"I'm leaving," he said, his voice dull and empty.

"What are you talking about?" I asked in a voice loud enough that a few of my classmates turned around and stared at us. I lowered my voice. "Okay, we can talk, but not here. Where's your truck?"

He gestured to the right of the parking lot and the two of us headed toward it together. He unlocked the passenger door and grabbed a bunch of papers and junk from the front seat. "It's messy in here, sorry."

"I can handle it." I climbed in and pushed a few crumpled bags away with my feet. The truck smelled different from Tommy. A mixture of smoke and fresh grass. I remembered the last time I was in his truck, on the way home from the bonfire. Things were so different now. That night seemed like a dream.

"I'm sorry if I upset you at the dance," he said as he pulled out of the parking lot.

"I shouldn't have gone. It was a stupid idea."

"I don't know why I went either."

"No one knows what's right anymore," I said.

"That's why I have to get out of here for a while."

"What do you mean?"

"I need to get away. No one wants me here. My aunt said I could stay with her, which is a good thing. She's in upstate New York, so maybe I can work with a piano teacher, look into auditioning at some colleges in the city," he said, and it was as if the bottom dropped out from under me.

"You belong here," I told him, unable to hide the fear in my voice. Tommy couldn't leave; I wouldn't survive if both he and Abby were gone. And I was selfish enough to say it.

He gripped the steering wheel so tightly that his knuckles turned white. "They won't stop until they've gotten their revenge for what they think I did to Abby."

"You didn't do anything."

"But everyone thinks I did. They'll destroy me."

I wanted to tell him he was wrong. That people weren't like that, but Tommy was right; this was only the beginning. They wouldn't stop until Abby came home.

"I'll tell the truth." I pled with him, willing to do anything if it meant keeping him here. "About the two of us and what Abby saw. I'll let them know that you were with me the whole time. I'll make things right."

"It would only make it worse. Think about what they'll do to you if they find out you were a part of this. I won't let that happen."

"Maybe we should run away together," I said, only half joking.

"Remember when we tried to do that? What were we, in fourth or fifth grade?" Tommy smiled at the memory.

"I was mad at my parents because they wouldn't let me get my ears pierced."

"And you insisted on packing that giant blue suitcase that I had to carry."

"It was full of very important items," I said. I unrolled the window and let the air wrap itself around us.

"Oh yeah, you're right. We needed to bring your favorite books and a bathing suit."

"You never know when you might need to cool off. And don't forget I also packed the cookies you ate before we were even a few blocks from my house."

"Too bad you had to use the bathroom and we needed to turn around and come back."

"I guess I didn't plan for everything," I said and laughed, my body now relaxed. "I was so mad that our parents didn't even notice we had left."

"Now they'll be glad if I left," Tommy said, and reality shook me once again. The mood darkened in the truck.

"That's not true," I said, but I was lying. Mom didn't talk about Tommy to me, but she blamed him; everyone did. I'd heard her talk about him with the people in the circles, his name drifting through the open window.

"Believe me, it would be better for everyone if I was gone," he said.

"Not for me," I said, my words a betrayal of my sister and my promise.

"I have to get out of here," Tommy said.

"Don't leave me," I told him, unable to keep the fear out of my voice. "I've lost so much already. I can't lose you."

"You won't," Tommy said.

"Please," I begged.

Tommy didn't answer right away, but finally he sighed. "Okay, I'll stay for now. Until we find Abby. But I can't make any promises."

"I've made enough promises for the both of us," I said, and wished that wasn't true.

When he turned onto our street, I saw a large crowd of people in my yard.

"Do you go out there? To the circles?" Tommy asked.

"My mom keeps trying to get me to, but Tessa and I think they're a bit nuts."

"Yeah," Tommy said in a way that I couldn't tell if he was agreeing with me or not.

"You can park at your place. I'll walk the rest of the way."

"I don't mind dropping you off," Tommy said.

"I do," I said, the meaning of my words obvious.

I told myself it was because of the woman who yelled at me the night of the dance. If she flipped when I went to homecoming, what would she do if I showed up with Tommy? Would anyone understand why we were together in the truck? I didn't even know how to view it myself. But what I did know was that once again, I was a coward, unable to face the truth, especially when Tommy was willing to stay here for me and needed it the most.

64

Mom came into the kitchen that evening as I washed the dishes. They'd been sitting in dirty dishwater since yesterday, and we were out of silverware. The way Mom was these days, she probably hadn't even noticed them piled in the sink.

"I can do that," she said as she walked behind me.

Instead, I lifted my hands out of the water and pointed toward the towels. "You can dry."

She grabbed a towel and took each plate as I passed it to her. I could smell her rose-scented hand lotion. It was a smell I was familiar with, but hadn't been reminded of for weeks. I wasn't sure if it was because I hadn't been this close to her in such a long time or if she had stopped wearing it.

I dunked a plate underwater and scrubbed it.

"You should think about coming outside," Mom said. "Tomorrow night we're doing a prayer vigil."

"I've told you this before. There's nothing there for me." I picked at a piece of dried-on egg with my fingernail. I sounded like a broken record. I wished that we could just be together here instead of listening to her talk about the circles once again. It seemed as if those people invaded everything, stealing Mom away with their nonsense and pointless vigil.

She went on as if I hadn't spoken. "I can feel your sister when I'm out there. We all can. It's like she's at the edge of the woods waiting for us to find her," she said.

The truth in her words shocked me, and I dropped the plate I was holding. It shattered around my feet.

"I'm sorry," I said.

I bent down and picked up the pieces, holding them in my hands. A jagged section cut into my palm. I let go of it and a thin line of blood appeared.

A wave of dizziness washed over me. Mom pressed a cool wet towel into my palm. It was nice to have her take care of me, a feeling that seemed foreign to me now after we had been so consumed by bringing Abby home.

"Hold it tight, and don't let go. You need to put pressure against it. Go sit at the table, and I'll clean this up."

I didn't argue. I was woozy. I never could look at blood, mine or anybody else's. I wasn't even able to watch a TV character get a shot without feeling as if I was going to pass out.

Mom cleaned up the dish with a little broom and joined me at the table. My hand throbbed, but I didn't care, because Mom was here and for this brief moment, she was my old mom. I'd forgotten how much I missed just being with her.

"Would you at least think about coming outside?" she asked, and placed a hand on my arm. I caught the scent of her again, and it reminded me of what life was like before. I breathed her in and yearned for what we used to have.

"I'll think about it," I said. And maybe going outside would change things. Maybe it would be a good thing. I pressed the cloth harder into my hand, and the pain bit into my palm.

65

Collin was sitting on the front porch swing when I got home from school the next day. He broke into a run and met me as I got off the bus.

"Mom said I could go out into the fields tonight if you went out too. Will you do it? Please? Please?"

He tugged on my book bag and made it fall off my shoulder. I searched the yard for Mom, so I could tell her exactly how I felt about this little plan. Leave it to her to rope my brother into all of this. She knew there was no way I'd say no to Collin.

"You really want to be outside at night? There are bugs, and it's wet and cold. It's so much more comfortable inside."

"No, no way! Please say yes."

I remembered how he'd woken me in the middle of the night crying over Abby. He wasn't getting much attention, and it wouldn't be that big a deal to go outside for one night if it helped make him feel better.

"I'll go out for a little bit," I told him. "But don't think that I'm going to do this all the time."

"Yay!" He yelled and ran up the driveway, no doubt to find Mom so she could celebrate the victory.

I told him we had to wait until after dinner, and as soon as we cleared the dishes, he was waiting at the door.

Collin raced into the field, but I moved slowly, still skeptical about these people and their belief that they were doing the right thing to help bring Abby back.

I expected everyone to be in small groups in the backyard, kind of like high school where we sat in our cliques, not daring to cross over into a section that wasn't your territory, but it wasn't like that at all. It was one big group, as if they had become friends or family. Adults talked to teammates of my sister, neighbors sat next to teachers from my school, and the few classmates who were there seemed to be friends with one another.

I dragged Collin to Mom first. She was with our neighbor Karin, the one who suggested the circles had to do with Abby in the first place. The two of them were deep in conversation.

A woman with a pile of blankets tucked under one arm walked over to me and placed her hand on my shoulder.

"You must miss you sister very much," she said.

"Of course I do," I replied, immediately defensive, because is there any other way to feel?

"When I think about how much I miss her, I have to stop because it could never be as much as your family does."

I tilted my head to get a better look at this woman. Was she for real?

"How do you know Abby?" I asked.

"The same way most of these people do. She's a part of our town. I might not have known her personally, but I can feel the loss."

"Right," I said, wondering if the loss she felt hurt as much as the one I did.

She hiked the blankets higher and gave me one last smile. "Well, I wanted you to know that we're praying real hard for your family."

"Thanks," I mumbled and turned to Mom.

"Honey, you're here. Karin and I were just talking about how important these circles are."

"Oh, yes," Karin said. "I don't know what I'd do without them."

Um, how about go home and live your life, I thought to myself, because so far, the Miracle Seekers were pretty much exactly what I thought they'd be: a bunch of fakes who clung to Abby's disappearance to fill some hole in their own empty lives.

I didn't bother to answer her. Instead I turned to Mom. "I'm taking Collin over to Mary Grace, but we need to talk later."

She put on a fake smile and turned back to Karin. She knew exactly what I wanted to talk to her about, and I had a feeling she'd spend the night stuck to someone's side so the opportunity wouldn't happen.

I helped Collin spread out the blanket we had brought from inside and the two of us sat next to Mary Grace.

"Hi," I said, and wondered how I'd gotten to the point where I was outside sitting with her. She was surprisingly nice to me, considering the last time we'd spoken I wasn't exactly the most pleasant person in the world.

"I'm glad you're out here."

"Yeah, well, I didn't have much of a choice. It was either this or stay inside with Hound Dog. Since he stinks and needs a bath, coming out here won."

"I totally get your decision. I remember when he got sprayed by a skunk, and it took forever for you guys to get the stink off of him," she said. Her face grew serious. "Seriously, though, it's good to see you."

"Rhylee said we can come out here every night," Collin told her, settling onto the blanket I'd spread out next to Mary Grace.

"I said nothing of the sort," I told him.

"We'll see about that," he said and sounded exactly like Mom. He lay on his back and studied the sky. Stars peeked out among the inky blue backdrop, and he traced a path between each with his finger.

I pulled bits of grass out of the ground as a group of people came to stand by Mom and Karin. One of them rang a large cowbell.

"We're going to welcome in the evening with a song," he said, and those around me quieted down. The ladies drew together and sang something full of words about "god's glory" and "saving love."

The group passed around purple candles. I took one and

when Mary Grace lit her candle from the candle of a man sitting near us, I reached mine out and watched the flame catch. Collin stuck his candle in front of my face, and I helped him light it.

I stared at the flickering center as the sky grew darker and night fell.

"Why does everyone sing?" I asked Mary Grace.

"For Abby," she said.

"Abby doesn't like singing. She dropped out of choir freshmen year because she said it was boring."

"We don't sing because of the songs," Mary Grace said. She brought her candle close to her face. "It's so she can hear us. If she's out there somewhere, maybe she'll hear our voices and come home."

I almost laughed out loud at the ridiculousness of her response. Mary Grace was smart; she had to know that no amount of singing was going to bring Abby home. I turned to her to tell her as much, but what I saw made me keep my words to myself. She was holding her candle with both hands, staring into the flame that lit up the tears that ran down her face.

"I know this is all kind of stupid," she said, whispering the words that moments ago I'd been thinking.

"It's not," I told her, because I got it. I understood her sadness, because I felt it too. And maybe the circles were bullshit, but what we were missing wasn't.

66

When I got home from school the next day, I found Collin digging around in the guest room closet. We never had anyone stay over and use the room, so it had basically become a place to dump any random junk we had. Collin pulled out gift boxes, mittens that had no mates, and sports equipment I didn't even know we owned. He created a pile on the floor of so much stuff, you'd think the closet went on forever.

"What are you trying to find?" I asked him when a winter boot flew across the room and nearly hit me.

"My sleeping bag," he said.

"What for?" I asked, way too skeptical of his plans.

"The circles," he said, confirming what I already knew.

"Collin, last night was a one-time thing—"

"I don't care," he interrupted. "I'm going out there. You and Mom can't stop me."

"There isn't anything out there for us," I said, but he wasn't about to reason with me. Instead, he turned and began to dig through the closet again.

I sighed and pushed him aside. "Let me look. I think they're up top on the shelf, and you're not going to be able to reach them." I stood on my tiptoes and rooted around until my hand touched something soft and squishy. "Bingo!"

I pulled out a sleeping bag and dropped it down. We both stared at it, neither one of us making a move to touch it.

It was Abby's sleeping bag.

We each had our own color and Abby's was purple. I'd always been jealous Mom had let Abby pick her sleeping bag first and she got such a pretty color, while I was stuck with red.

Her bag well-worn from family campouts and sleepovers, especially the ones where we only ventured as far as the family room. It used to be a tradition to bring them out when a storm rolled in. We'd lie in our sleeping bags on the living room floor, open the curtains on our huge front windows, and watch the lightning flash across the sky. The four of us would fall asleep like that, lined up in a row listening to the weather rage outside, and wake to the bright sun filtering in. Mom acted as if we slept there to watch the storms, but she wasn't fooling us. They spooked her and she didn't want to sleep alone. We only did it when Dad was at work.

We stopped when Abby joined the cross-country team freshman year. We'd overslept one morning after an October storm shook most of the leaves off our trees. The team had stood outside, their hoodies zipped up and running in place to keep warm.

"Abby," Dad had said, still in his work uniform. "Your crew is on our driveway waiting for you."

She had scrambled up from her sleeping bag.

He'd opened the front door and waved. "Morning, everyone. Abby is just waking up. Do you want some breakfast while you wait? I bet you could give up a day of running for some of my blueberry pancakes."

Abby had pushed Dad aside, embarrassed, and waved the team away. "Go ahead without me. I'll catch up."

She'd closed the door before Dad could entice them in again with his pancakes and stomped up the steps.

We never slept in the living room after that. Abby had refused during the next storm, and it didn't feel the same to sleep beside Mom and Collin, so I'd stopped doing it too.

But tonight I stretched my hands back up to the top shelf and found Collin's green sleeping bag. I tossed it to him.

"Does this mean we can go outside?" Collin asked and jumped from one foot to the other, excited at the possibility.

"One more night," I told him.

"Yes!" he said, and made his way down the steps and toward the front door before I could get another word in. I reached into the closet to find my sleeping bag, but then thought better of it. Instead, I bent down, grabbed Abby's sleeping bag, and followed Collin.

67

It was nice to see Collin happy and excited about something, even if it was the circles. So as crazy as it sounded, I agreed to go outside for the third night in a row. I figured if spending a few hours out there helped him, I could grin and bear it.

I spent the time last night with Mary Grace again. The two of us traded stories about Abby. We told each other things about my sister that the other had never heard. And when you talked in the dark, it was easier to tell things we couldn't say to anyone else.

I told Mary Grace about how Abby would spread butter on Mom's meat loaf, a practice we found disgusting but one Abby assured us was delicious. Or how she left her tennis shoes in the hallway after a run and would have to find them from whatever hiding spot Hound Dog decided to drop them in after having a good chew.

Mary Grace shared the time she let Abby drive her parents' van before she got her license and she scratched it on a curb in the parking lot. She told her parents she did it so Abby wouldn't get in trouble. Or about the time when Abby tried to drink a whole gallon of milk after she heard it was impossible. Two-thirds of the way through, she found out the hard way why people couldn't do it.

I liked being with Mary Grace. Together, we brought parts of my sister back to life. If we were talking about her, it was as if she was still there, and we needed her with us so badly.

"Do you remember the duck eggs in the woods?" she asked.

I did, pale yellow and sitting in a nest of feathers. When I was younger, before there was Tommy, Abby and Mary Grace didn't allow me in on their secret adventures, even though I'd begged them. They'd run into the woods together, sometimes with me trailing after them, but they were always too fast. I'd fall behind and watch them disappear into the trees. I'd stand guard at the entrance until they reappeared, sweaty and flushed, laughing together.

The duck eggs, though, were a secret I became a part of. Abby and Mary Grace burst out of the woods one day, breathless. "Rhylee, come with us," Abby said.

At first, I suspected they were playing some trick on me, but Abby grabbed my hand and pulled me forward. "Hurry. You have to be quick or you'll miss it."

I blindly followed the two of them. They led me in twists and turns to some secret place.

"Where are we going?" I asked, surprised they were letting me join in.

"We need to be quiet or we won't be able to look," Abby said and pushed away branches and made her own path. We walked like this for about five minutes without breathing a word. Suddenly, Abby stopped. "Rhylee, look."

I turned to where she pointed and between the branches, near the edge of the riverbank, was a nest with seven fat eggs in it.

"It's her nest and that's the dad," Mary Grace said and pointed to a duck swimming in the water with another duck near the nest.

"When are they going to hatch?" I asked and kept my eye on the mother.

"Soon, I think. We've been visiting for about a week and she's always on the nest. Any day now there's going to be babies. We'll come back."

On the way home, and I couldn't stop thinking about those seven eggs and the fuzzy chicks that would hatch from them.

Abby and Mary Grace took me back every day. We made sure not to stay long if the mother was on the nest. She'd shift back and forth nervously and was bothered by our presence.

Until one day we got to the pond and she wasn't there.

Instead, there was only her nest with a single egg split in half. A long jagged crack down the center, the rest of the nest empty, the pond still.

"Abby, what do you think happened? Why are the eggs gone?" I'd asked.

She was scared. She walked around the nest and there were feathers all over. I thought about the coyotes we could hear howling at night.

"Do you think something—"

"Stop it," she interrupted. "Don't even say it." She'd turned and run away, leaving Mary Grace and me alone.

I shook my head, trying to get rid of the images of that day. We'd never talked about what happened to the eggs.

Just like we hadn't talked about what had happened with Tommy. She'd run away. And I'd never followed her.

Mary Grace poked me. "Earth to Rhylee. Are you still here?"

"Yeah, I'm here. I remember the eggs," I said.

"What do you think?" she asked.

"Think?"

"About them. Did they hatch? Or did something get to them?" She moved closer to my sleeping bag; the two of us huddled together.

"Of course they hatched," I said, because you couldn't think any other way. "And the mom took her babies away to an even bigger place so they could swim without bumping into one another."

"Me too," Mary Grace said. "I'm sure they survived."

68

A few days later, Tessa waited for me outside in the line of buses. From the way she stood with her hands on her hips, she wasn't looking for a casual conversation.

She took one long look at me as if I was a cow and she was appraising me for auction. "You look like crap."

"Don't even start with me," I grumbled. "I'm exhausted. I was outside in the field last night."

She placed both her hands on my shoulders so we were facing each other. "You, my friend, have turned cuckoo."

She walked around me, inspecting my head.

"What the heck are you doing?"

"Checking for a hole where they sucked your brains out. They've brainwashed you. I can't believe you're buying into the circles."

"Believe me, I'm not. Those people are still as crazy as they ever were. But if it helps Collin, I'm willing to do that,"

I told her. What I didn't tell her is that it helps me too.

"There are a million other things you can do to help your brother."

"Being out there isn't so bad. I usually spend the time talking with Mary Grace."

Tessa rolled her eyes. "Mary Grace? I thought she drove you nuts."

"She's not that bad. I actually kind of like her now."

"Whatever, do what you want, but it seems to me that your life is on pause right now."

"Shouldn't it be? My sister is missing."

"You're right, *she's* missing. But you aren't. Think about what you lose in the meantime. Do you really want to continue to spend the hours of your life suspended, waiting for Abby to return?"

"I can't let her go," I said.

"No one is asking for that. I miss her too, Rhylee. But I also miss you."

"I'm right here," I argued. I'd always been here.

"You're different," she said. "You're not the same anymore."

"How can I not be? My sister is missing."

"You don't think you've disappeared? What's the use of being here if you act as if you're gone too?" Tessa said. "You've let go of everything that you were, so it's almost as if you're a ghost too. We can't stop living. None of us."

And maybe she was right. Maybe I was gone. Maybe I was losing myself, little by little, until there was nothing left.

69

I wrote texts that I didn't send to Tessa. Words I wanted to say, explanations I tried to create, and excuses for the way I was acting. But I deleted them all, because nothing sounded right, especially when there was a hint of truth in her words and I didn't know what it meant. Was I losing myself? Was that even possible when I wasn't sure I ever knew who I was to begin with? I'd always been Abby's sister and that was enough. So now that she was gone, what did that make me? Who did I want to be?

I continued to take Collin outside to the circles, and the secrets Mary Grace and I traded grew darker, as if we needed each other to unleash those worries that were swirling around in our heads. I felt bad that I was confiding in her instead of Tessa, but she understood what I was going through.

"This morning I tried to remember what Abby looked like, but I couldn't picture her eyes," Mary Grace said. "It was as if her face was there, but her eyes were empty spaces. I couldn't even remember what color they were."

"A bluish-gray," I answered because I could see them clearly. Her eyes matched mine, and sometimes when I was looking in the mirror, I imagined it was Abby looking back at me. "And she had a tiny mole on her left cheek."

"You're right," Mary Grace said.

"Sometimes," I confessed, "I run downstairs because I think I hear the doorbell. I've thrown the front door open and there's nothing but the wind out there. The other day I stood in front of the open door for more than a half hour. I was convinced Abby had rung the bell and was out there."

"I call her phone to listen to her voice mail and look for her when I watch TV," Mary Grace said, understanding what I was talking about. "I search faces in the crowds on the news, thinking I'm going to find her."

"I haven't moved her stuff off the sink in the bathroom," I said. "Her towel is still hanging where she left it before we went to the bonfire and the cap is off on her lotion."

"Do you think—" Mary Grace started, and stopped. I didn't say anything because I knew, I just knew, this was it. We'd arrived at the place we'd been working to cross, and I needed her to step over it first.

She did.

"Do you think she's coming back?" Mary Grace asked.

"My mom does," I answered, even though that wasn't the response she was looking for.

"What about you?"

I felt the familiar sting of remorse before I answered. This conversation. These questions were because of me, and now, here was Mary Grace asking if I thought my own sister was going to return.

"I could hear her voice in my head when she first disappeared," I said. "It was so clear, but it's fading. It's like how I can't remember things about her. How I've forgotten what she sounds like, what she likes, who she was."

"I'm scared I'm not going to see her again," Mary Grace said. She filled in the spaces I left open. The real words I couldn't say yet.

Someone sang near us and more voices joined in. It was a song I'd heard Tessa sing before, the words from a musical that she was once in.

"Day by day, right?" I told Mary Grace.

"It's the only way to survive until she comes home," she agreed. And the two of us focused on the song because we didn't dare mention any of the fears we held deeper inside.

70

The next evening, the entire cross-country team was at the circles. They stayed for hours, some of them falling asleep, heads resting in one another's laps, music softly playing from a speaker someone brought. We talked about Abby, but we didn't focus on her the entire time. We also talked about other things, things that really weren't important but had once felt very important. We gossiped about certain classmates and complained about our teachers. We told one another funny stories and made plans for the following weekend.

As the sky grew darker, the team left, until it was only Mary Grace and me, the way it had been for the last few days. I told her about the time when Abby, Tommy, and I took Collin to the county fair and how Collin was stuck on top of the Ferris wheel with Tommy.

"It was one of the ones where the cage that you're in

swings around. Tommy spun it so fast that I swear you could hear them both screaming from miles away. I don't know who was more scared."

I remembered Abby and me at the bottom trying to record the two of them on her phone.

"I've never seen any two people more inseparable than you and Tommy," Mary Grace said.

"We *used* to be inseparable," I told her.

"Abby told me that Tommy was going to break up with her. Did you know that?"

"She what?" I asked, taken aback.

"He was different. She kept saying that something was going on."

I considered acting as if I had no clue what she was talking about, but it would've been a lie, and my lies were beginning to add up so high that they'd all topple down soon.

"It was because of me," I said. "I was the reason Tommy was going to break up with my sister."

And there, in the hours that come after the sky grows dark, that I told her what I hadn't been able to admit to anyone else.

"I kissed Tommy."

It was the first time I'd said the words to anyone. They came sliding out as if it was meant to be known.

I played with the zipper on my sleeping bag and waited for her to tell me how awful I was. For the sting of those words to finally get the reaction I deserved. But it never came.

"I'm not surprised. You two have always been close friends," she said, as if what I'd told her made perfect sense, as if it were only natural that Tommy and I would be together.

"No," I said, knowing I needed to correct her, but wishing I could leave it at that. Absolution doesn't work unless you dive all the way in, and the hardest part was still to come. "I don't mean . . . recently. I kissed him before Abby disappeared."

There was a silence before Mary Grace asked, "When they were together?"

"The night she disappeared," I whispered.

I paused and didn't say anything. Off to the right a group was singing and I swear that off in the distance, softly, so softly, I could hear Tommy playing the piano, the notes sliding over the night like a faint breeze.

"I'm the reason she's gone," I said, the words thick and substantial. "Tommy was going to break up with her that night. We kissed and Abby saw us. I'm the reason she ran into the woods."

My eyes stung with tears, and I willed myself not to cry, because I didn't deserve to feel bad about what I had done. But it was no use. Something in my chest was broken and it all fell out. Everything I'd kept hidden deep down seeped up like when you knock a glass over at the dinner table and it spreads out all over.

When we were little, Abby and I used to curl up and lie back to back. We'd pretend we were connected, that we were one person, pressed against each other. I moved onto my side and pulled my knees to my chest. I shut my eyes

300

tight and imagined Abby next to me. "And I wasn't even sorry I'd done it."

There it was. Everything. Out on the table. Exposed.

I waited again for Mary Grace to snap at me, to recoil in disgust. To shun me.

It didn't happen.

"Tommy's always liked you," Mary Grace finally said.

"What?" I asked. I could hardly believe that was her answer to my secret. That after everything . . . there was no shouting, no accusations, no shame.

"If we're telling secrets, I guess this one is worth a million." She paused, and then sat up, as if preparing herself for what she was about to reveal. "Abby was jealous of the way Tommy felt about you, even after they were together."

"That's ridiculous," I said, and it was. Abby had everything. Why would she be jealous of me?

"She told me once that she was afraid he'd realize he was with the wrong person and leave her."

That couldn't be true. Mary Grace had to be lying. Abby had never shown any indication that she was worried about my relationship with Tommy. But then I remembered Abby's words in the woods that night.

I always knew, she had said tearfully.

And there was the time when Tommy had come over to give Abby some notes she'd missed in class, but she wasn't home when he got to our house. Instead of heading back home, he'd sat on the porch steps with me. We were doing impersonations of people at our school and cracking up. It had been like old times, when we were still close. Tommy had me laughing so hard, I was bent over to catch my breath when Abby walked up.

"What's so funny?" she had asked, her hand on her hip.

"Nothing, just stupid stuff," I'd said, but when I'd looked at Tommy, the two of us fell into another fit of laughter.

"Really?" she'd asked.

"Your sister is hilarious," Tommy had said. He'd stood and grabbed my hand, pulling me up too. "Here's the papers. I'd better get going."

"You don't want to stay?" Abby had asked, pouting.

"I told my mom I'd help take some boxes into our shed. I need to get it done before it's dark," he'd said, and then turned to me and grinned. "I don't think I've laughed this hard in months. You're hilarious, Rhylee."

I'd taken a bow as Tommy waved good-bye to the two of us.

"He never laughs like that with me."

"What?"

"Tommy . . . the way he is with you. It's different." She had given me a look I couldn't quite place.

"What do you mean?"

"Nothing, it's stupid. Forget it. I need to go inside and study."

"Tommy's my friend," I'd said. I'd been angry. She had no right to get mad at me. "I'm allowed to talk to him. He was my friend long before you two were together."

"I know," Abby had said and sighed. "But sometimes it seems like he'd rather be with you than me."

"Believe me," I'd said, my voice low and serious. I'd remembered the night I had pushed him away. I'd pictured him kissing my sister. "You have nothing to worry about."

"I'm not worrying," Abby had said. Her voice had had a bit of an edge to it, as if she was angry that I'd have to reassure her of this.

"Abby used to say that it seemed so easy between the two of you. She worried about that," Mary Grace said.

"And then it happened," I said. "In the worst possible way."

"It's not your fault, Rhylee."

"How can it not be?" I remembered the look on Abby's face when she saw us. There was no way I could say that I hadn't caused that.

"You didn't know what was going to happen."

"No, but if it wasn't for us . . ."

"You can't think that way. No one caused Abby to disappear. It was an accident."

"Sometimes I believe that if I can find her, I can fix everything. I can tell her that it was a mistake, and Tommy and I will never, ever be together again. But most of all, I'd tell her how sorry I am."

"Are you?"

I turned to her. "Of course I'm sorry."

"But for what? Kissing Tommy? When she knew someday it would happen? When we all knew?" I couldn't see her face, but Mary Grace's voice got lower. "She didn't have to run away. She didn't have to run away from us."

Her words struck me hard in the chest. I'd never thought about it that way. About how maybe Abby had been just as much of a coward as me.

I gazed at the star-flecked sky and wished it was okay to believe Mary Grace.

71

I stayed outside all night with Mary Grace and the rest of the Miracle Seekers, and as soon as the light began to show in the sky I texted Tessa to call me.

"Seriously?" she grumbled when I picked up. "This is way too early to be awake, let alone trying to make conversation."

"Sorry, I needed to talk to you before you left for school. It's important."

Tessa yawned. "What's up?"

"Is there any way you could get your mom's car today? And then maybe cut school with me?"

"Whoa, rebel," she said. "Now you have my attention. What for?"

I thought about what she'd said about living and about what Mary Grace had said about Abby making the choice to run. We all made choices; those of us who chose to stay and those of us who ran.

What would it mean to move on? What would it feel like to live outside the shadow of my sister?

"I was thinking we could go somewhere. Somewhere far away. Somewhere Abby isn't the focus of everyone's attention," I said, and to Tessa's credit, she didn't argue with me.

"I've got this. Let me shower, and I'll be over in about an hour."

"Thanks," I told her, relieved that she understood.

I got dressed and made sure Collin was ready to catch the bus. When Tessa pulled up, I gave Mom a hug good-bye.

"I'm going to hang with Tessa after school," I told her in case she wondered where I was, which was silly. Mom was so consumed with these circles and the people inside of them that I could probably run away to Mexico and she wouldn't notice I was gone.

I climbed into the passenger seat and Tessa handed me a bag from my favorite doughnut shop.

"Here you go, vanilla custard with sprinkles," Tessa said and pointed at a cup of hot chocolate. This was the breakfast we used to grab together when Tessa had the car. Our morning sugar rush, she'd joke.

"You're wonderful," I said and sank my teeth into the glazed doughnut.

"Of course I am. That's why you love me," Tessa said. "Did you call in sick?"

"Yep, we're set." I faked a cough. "I have a very bad sore throat today, so I need to stay home."

"Perfect! Now let's road trip the hell out of today!"

I couldn't help but laugh. As guilty as I felt to admit it, it was nice to be with Tessa and just be ourselves. "Where are we heading?" I asked.

"That's for me to know and you to find out," she said, and I was okay with that. Life had been so much about doing what I thought I was supposed to be doing, that it was nice not to have to make a choice for once. So I settled into my seat and watched the streets that were so familiar to me disappear as Tessa did exactly what I'd asked her to do, drive us far far away from Coffinberry.

72

I must have fallen asleep, because it only felt like seconds later that the car was stopping and Tessa was declaring that we'd reach our destination.

I stretched and glanced at the clock. "I slept for two hours?"

"You needed it," she said. "I can't imagine you get the best sleep outside in those circles."

I didn't bother to argue with her, especially since she was probably right. I felt a million times better after that nap. My head wasn't foggy, and the world was clearer.

"Where are we?" Tessa had parked in a big parking lot packed with cars, so it was impossible to tell.

"Our future," she said. "We've fast-forwarded two years so you can see what's waiting for you.

I laughed. "I slept for a long time, but I don't think I slept that long."

She got out of the car, so I did the same.

"Trust me, this is where you want to be. And if it's not, we'll go somewhere else tomorrow until we figure out the perfect place for you."

She grabbed my hand and gave me a gentle pull. I followed her, curious about where we had ended up. She took me through the parking lot, along a sidewalk.

"Okay, keep your eyes on the ground until I tell you to," she said.

"Really?"

"Come on, Rhylee."

"Fine." I relented and let her lead me around the corner. We walked for a few minutes, and then she stopped.

"All right, open your eyes," she said, and when I did, a giant stone gate stood in front of me. It was the entrance way to a long path lined by old brick buildings. Boys and girls were all over the place, most with backpacks slung over their shoulders.

"We're at a college?"

"Not just any college, Westing College. One of your dream colleges!"

And she was right. I recognized the buildings from the brochures I pored over. We had a student who went there visit our study hall one day and talk with the class. The school sounded amazing. Tessa loved their musical theater department, and I thought the art therapy program sounded interesting. The girl talked about all the work-study programs they had to make it affordable, and the cost wasn't crazy expensive. The school actually seemed within my reach. But it was what they didn't have that had caught my attention: a strong athletic program, which meant that it was a school Abby would never consider. A school where I could go and be my own person.

"So here's the deal," Tessa said. "I'm going to go check out the theater department. Hopefully, they let me sit in on a few classes. And I think you should do the same. Sign up for a tour or walk around. Talk to some people about their majors. Walk through the art building. Figure out what the heck it is you want to do."

"Wait? Showing up here and taking a tour, is that the answer to figuring out my life?" I joked.

"Yep, I fully expect that you have a major figured out and a plan for your life," Tessa said.

"If I had only known it was that easy," I said.

"Don't be so serious. Have fun. You don't have to decide anything now, just check out college life." She paused and gestured toward a group of boys across the street. She let out a low whistle to show her appreciation. "And when I say college life, I mean *all* of it. Check it out from top to bottom."

"You're too much," I said, but laughed.

"We'll plan to meet up in a few hours. Give this a chance."

"I will," I said, but this was all a bit crazy to me. Westing College was the last place I had expected Tessa to take me today.

"Remember, you're still here. You've got to make the most of that." She opened the giant bag she was carrying and pulled a backpack out of it. "Here, put this on your shoulder. Now you look like an official college student."

"You're too much," I said, but slipped my arms through it.

"Perfect!" She waved her phone in the air. "Go explore. I'll text you in a little bit."

And like that, she was off as if we really were living our future and had simply made plans to meet after our classes. She headed down the path and the funny thing was, I could see our future happening for the first time in a long time. My future. All of this seemed more real than I could have ever imagined.

73

Across from the front gates was a small down-town area with a coffee shop, bookstore, post office, and bars lining the brick-paved road, so I headed toward that.

I ducked into the coffee shop first. I was starving. The doughnut felt like a lifetime ago. I ordered a Mediterranean bagel, with feta and fire-roasted red peppers. Foods that never existed in our house because Abby was such a boring eater.

"What do you want to drink?" the girl asked. She had thick dark curls and her nose was pierced. She chewed loudly on a piece of gum while she waited for my answer.

"How about a chai tea with almond milk," I said; the com-bination sounded foreign and exotic.

"You got it. Grab a seat and someone will bring it out when we're done."

I picked a booth right next to the window so I could see outside. The sidewalk was full of students. They walked in groups or alone; some talked on their phones, while others moved their heads to whatever song was playing through their headphones. Life moved on, people passed by, and not one of them noticed me.

And for once, I wasn't the sister of Abby the cross-country star or the girl whose sister disappeared. I didn't have to try to be like my sister or live the life I thought she should be living.

Here, I was nobody.

And it felt amazing.

I paged through a newspaper that was on the table. *The Westing Post*. It said it was student-produced under the title and each article had the author's name and graduation year on it. Many of them also included the author's major, but not all of them. It was the ones that didn't have the major that I read. These students wrote about rallies going on around campus, a project that was being done in a history class, and an opinion piece about the value of taking a public speaking course. I studied each of them. I tried to find hints of indecisiveness between the lines, but their words were strong and confident. Nothing in them told me they worried that they didn't know what they wanted to do yet. They didn't sound confused or lost. And maybe that wasn't the case at all. Maybe instead, it was freeing. They had the whole world in front of them and a lifetime to decide what to do.

I glanced around the coffee shop and wondered how many people here knew what they wanted to do. And for those that did, when did they decide? Was it something their parents had forced on them? Did they follow in the footsteps of someone else? Did their teachers push them toward something? Or were they like me and never felt they had the chance to even think about it, because their lives were spent living in the shadow of others? How many of them looked deep inside of themselves and chose what they loved? And were they happy with their decision? It was impossible to tell, but maybe that was the way it was with a lot of things. If there was anything I'd learned in the last few months, it's that you can never be certain of a single thing.

I finished my lunch and headed back to the front gate and the path Tessa had disappeared down earlier. I pretended I went here. There wasn't a soul who knew my story, so I created my own. I walked along the path as if I belonged. Students passed on either side and not one of them noticed me. I followed a group of girls into a building and took a seat behind them in a large lecture hall. The seats began to fill and there must have been over a hundred people in one single class.

A boy slipped into the seat next to me.

I waited for him to call me out, to tell me I didn't belong here, but instead, he pointed at his textbook.

"Did you do the reading last night?"

I shook my head and he nodded.

"Same here. I swear, Dr. Kohlings gives us more work than any of my other classes combined."

"Tell me about it," I agreed.

"Guess we'll have to just wing it. I won't tell if you won't," he said and winked at me.

"Deal," I said as a bubble of nervous excitement began to

form in my stomach. Was this boy flirting with me? A college student? But as quickly as the idea came, I pushed it back down. What would he think if he knew the truth about me and what I did to my own sister? And how was it fair that I was here and Abby wasn't?

You're allowed to live, I thought to myself, Tessa's words a mantra. But if that was the truth, why was it so hard to believe it?

A man I presumed to be Dr. Kohlings walked into the room and began to talk about an experiment that must have been a part of last night's reading. Something about rats being trained to do specific things in order to get a reward, even if it meant they'd harm themselves. Was that what it had been like with Tommy? Did I go after him even when if it would ruin everything? But what was the alternative? To be in the control group and never experience what it was I wanted? What would life have been like then? There was no right answer to this, only the consequences.

"So, I was wondering," the boy next to me whispered when class was over. "Since we both didn't do the homework, it might help us actually do the work if we had a way to remind each other."

"Remind each other?" I asked.

"Like if you texted me to see if I got it done, or I could text you," he talked fast and fidgeted.

"Are you asking me for my phone number?"

"Maybe . . . well, yeah," he said. "If that's okay. I mean, if you're dating someone, it's cool. Forget I said anything."

"No, no, I'm most definitely not dating anyone," I said.

"How about I give you mine," he said, his eyes lighting up. "That way, if you don't want to talk, no worries. I won't make it awkward."

I surrendered my phone to him and he typed in his number.

"I'm Dylan," he said. "In case you want to know who you're talking to."

I paused. Abby's name dangled on the tip of my tongue, because she's the one who caught boys' attention and got phone numbers. But that wasn't who I was. That wasn't who I was supposed to be. And maybe my world could be different.

"I'm Rhylee," I said and smiled.

"Rhylee," he repeated, and I liked the way my name sounded. "Hopefully, I'll get to talk with you soon."

He slipped out of the seats and followed the crowd out of the room. I stayed where I was until everyone was gone. The lecture hall stood empty. A room so big you could fit my graduating class in it, but I didn't feel alone. In fact, for the first time in forever, I felt as if I actually belonged. And not because I was Abby's sister, but because I was Rhylee.

74

Tessa didn't ask me how my day went, so I didn't say anything. I kept it deep inside of me so I wouldn't lose the magic that the day had held. When she dropped me off at my house, I reached across the front seat and gave her a hug that was so much like the infamous hugs she always gave me.

"What's that for?" she asked, surprised. She knew that wasn't my usual style.

"Today," I told her. "Thank you."

"It was pretty great, wasn't it?"

"The best," I said as I got out of the car.

Tessa leaned out her window. "You're pretty awesome, Rhylee. Don't forget that."

"I won't," I said and waved. Tessa blew me a kiss, and I laughed. The sound still felt unnatural, but I liked it.

I headed toward my house, where I lived surrounded by everything that was so familiar. But my view of the world had

317

changed. I'd moved out of my sister's shadow, if only for a minute, but it was that taste of freedom that I held on to and the thought that maybe one day I really could get out of here.

Today no one knew my sister or what I did.

I could leave and live my own life.

I could be myself.

75

That evening I stayed away from the fields. Instead, I opened my desk drawer and pulled out the two pieces of the picture I had found in Abby's notebook. I lined our faces back up next to each other and carefully placed a piece of tape down the middle to put them back together to make us whole.

The image was complete again, but you could still see the tears around the edges. It didn't fit perfectly together, but did it ever? Did we ever? And did we need to?

Abby was my sister, and I loved her, but we still had our flaws. We both made mistakes, we both fought, we both resented part of each other, but the important thing is that we also loved each other.

"I miss you," I whispered to the image. The pain of her loss consumed me. The void she had left behind was the size of the world.

"And I miss us," I said. "I miss us so bad."

But what did "us" mean?

I wasn't exactly sure of the answer, but what I did understand was that Abby and I were never meant to be the same person and I needed to figure out how to stand on my own. I wasn't my sister. I wasn't defined by her. And I didn't need to be. You could exist alongside a person without being that person. And maybe that could be enough.

76

The next morning, I'd just gotten out of the shower when I heard a rush of voices outside. I pulled back the window and saw everyone from the circle racing toward the woods.

The bathroom was hot with steam around me, and yet goose bumps appeared all over my skin.

I went to Abby's room and looked at our field. The Miracle Seekers were frantic, most running toward the edge of the woods, their belongings scattered as if a tornado had blown through. Mom and Collin were in the middle of the group, the two of them moving with the same urgency toward whatever caused the commotion.

I threw on some clothes and got myself out of there as fast as I could.

"What's going on?" I asked a neighbor who stood on the edge of the crowd.

"It's your sister. We saw her. She was beyond the trees over there."

"What are you talking about?" I turned to look where she pointed. I couldn't spot Mom anymore. Had she gone into the cluster of trees that guarded the edge of the field?

"She's here," my neighbor said. "We saw her before she went into the woods."

I searched the crowd again for Mom and instead found Collin. He was still in his Spider-Man pajamas and sat on Mary Grace, sobbing. As I got closer, I saw that his lip was bleeding. Mary Grace held a tissue against it as tears ran down Collin's cheeks.

"What happened here? Is he okay?"

"He tripped and fell when everyone was running. It doesn't look too serious; he's a bit shaken up, though."

"Where's my mom? Why isn't she with him?"

"She ran into the woods with the others."

Anger flashed through me. How could Mom let this happen? Did she really think it was okay to leave Collin here alone?

"Hey, buddy." I got down on his level. "You're being really brave right now."

He wrapped his arms around my neck and buried his face in my shoulder. I stroked his hair, trying to calm not only him but myself. This was ridiculous. The town was going mad and no one seemed to be the voice of reason.

Collin clung to me until his sobs turned into sniffles. He pulled his face away so he was facing me. "I saw her, Rhylee. She was here. Why did she run from me?"

"I don't know. I don't know what's going on." I untangled myself from Collin and held out to him one of the tissues Mary Grace passed to me. "How about you keep this against your lip to stop the bleeding?"

He placed it against his lip and looked up, his eyes two giant watery orbs.

"Do you think you're okay? Can you wait here so I can go and see if I can find Mom?"

He shook his head and his eyes filled back up with tears. "Don't leave me."

"How about you come with me?" I asked and bent down so he could climb onto my back, even though he was too old for that. The two of us hiked into the trees, Collin only letting go of his death grip around my neck to knock branches away from his face. We headed toward the voices.

We found everyone in the clearing where our bonfire had been the night Abby disappeared. The group didn't seem as frantic as the one outside of the woods. Instead, they sat around the burned wood and ashes, most people on logs but some right on the ground. They faced outward, everyone's back turned to the center.

As Collin and I stepped into the circle, a woman stood and shouted at us. "Oh my god, it's Abby. She's here!"

The group turned toward us. Collin climbed off my back and people rushed at me.

"Abby!" A woman said and sobbed.

A gray-haired woman moved toward me with her arms outstretched, as if she planned to embrace me. I took a few steps back and held out my hands to stop her, but she wrapped me into a hug. Her breath was hot on my neck.

People gathered around the two of us and reached out to touch me, as if they needed to make sure I was real. I broke free from them and tried to separate myself from the group.

"No, I'm Rhylee. Not Abby," I said and shook my head. It didn't even occur to me to try and pretend for them. I wasn't Abby. I wasn't.

A few stayed near me as if to make sure I was telling the truth, but most sat back down. I spotted Mom and stormed over to her.

"What are you doing here?" I yelled. I didn't care who saw me or what kind of scene I caused. "You left Collin in the field sobbing. He fell and cut his lip. He was bleeding."

Mom inspected his lip. "You're okay now, right? I had to follow everyone."

"It was your sister," a man prompted, and I shot him a disgusted look.

"That was not my sister," I said. "She's not out here."

"I don't get it," a woman yelled in frustration. "Why does Abby keep doing this to us? Doesn't she understand how much we want to see her? That we're waiting for her to return?"

"It's not right," another woman agreed. "Her running away from us. How can she hurt us like this?"

"Are you kidding me?" I shouted at the group as they argued about the unfairness of this all. "Abby isn't doing this. You're not seeing her. How can you be mad at someone who isn't even here?"

I tried to make them understand what I was saying, but it fell on deaf ears. Mom had already tuned out, and her eyes scanned the woods again. In fact, everyone had gone back to looking for a ghost that seemed more real to them than the lives they'd forgotten about.

77

Dad was getting out of his car when we all came out of the woods. Collin stayed close to my side, unnerved by everything that had happened, but when he saw Dad, he broke out into a run toward him.

"Hey, buddy," Dad said and hugged him. It wasn't until Collin pulled back that Dad noticed the blood all over him. "What's this blood from? Did something happen?"

Instead of responding, Collin broke out into sobs. He tried to tell Dad what had happened, but couldn't get the words out.

"Is he okay?" Dad asked me, and I shrugged.

"Physically, yeah, but those people are out of control. They all ran into the woods thinking they saw Abby. Mom followed too and left Collin all alone. Mary Grace found him on the ground; he had fallen and cut his lip open. It was bleeding all over, and Mom wasn't even here to take care of him."

Collin stuck his bottom lip out for Dad to inspect and wiped his nose with his sleeve.

"They saw Abby in the woods," he told Dad. "Why can't I see her?"

"That wasn't your sister. They made a mistake," Dad told him as he scanned the crowd of people. He found Mom and gestured to her to come over.

"What a morning, huh?" she asked.

"You could look at it that way," Dad replied. "Rhylee said you left Collin behind to run off into the woods. Is that true?"

"There was an Abby sighting. I had to go check it out. Collin was fine," Mom said.

"You call this fine?" Dad asked and pointed to Collin's bloodied shirt. "Your son was hurt and left alone. This is where I draw the line. I let these people stay in our yard, I didn't say a word when you went outside to join them. But this—this is too much. Collin is not to go out into the circles anymore."

"He's okay," Mom said at the same time Collin spoke up.

"That's not fair. I didn't do anything wrong," Collin said and another round of fresh tears began.

"That's the way it's going to be," Dad told him and looked Mom straight in the eyes. "That's the way you're going to make sure it is. No more encouraging him."

"If he wants to go outside—" Mom began, but Dad cut her off.

"Collin is not to hang out in them anymore. If that's too hard for everyone to understand, I'll make sure the circles simply get cut down, so it's no longer a problem."

"Will, the circles are good," Mom insisted.

"I didn't say you can't go out there, but I don't want my son out there. This isn't up for debate."

"This isn't fair. I'm not hurting anyone. I should be allowed in the circles," Collin argued.

"End of discussion," Dad said. "Or those circles will be gone by tomorrow."

Collin stormed away to the house and slammed the door so loud that we could hear it from where we stood across the yard.

"I meant what I said. I don't want Collin spending time out here anymore," Dad told Mom, but I wasn't sure she heard. Her eyes were focused on the patch of trees where Abby had been spotted, and I was pretty sure she was lost again in a world where real and make-believe merged.

78

Mary Grace was unusually quiet in school that day. She stared off in the distance with unfocused eyes.

When she wiped her sleeve across her eyes, I could tell something was going on.

"Is everything okay?"

She nodded, but she wasn't fooling me.

I put my hand on top of her arm and squeezed gently. "You're not okay," I said. I raised my hand and asked Mrs. Tetonis if we could go to the bathroom. As soon as the classroom door closed behind us, I turned to Mary Grace. "What's up?"

"It's stupid. It's so stupid," she said, and sank onto the floor, her back against a locker. I sat next to her.

"I'm sure it's not, if it's getting you upset," I said, and the irony didn't miss me. Here was the person who only weeks ago I couldn't stand. She'd oozed sympathy and all I'd wanted her to do was get the hell away from me. Now I was the one trying to help her. I understood the frustration she must have had with me when I refused to let her in. "It might help to talk about it."

Her eyes turned bright and wild. For a minute, I thought she was going to get up and run away. Instead, she said, "I'm so pissed off."

"At me?" I asked, confused. I tried to think if I had done anything to make her feel that way.

"No, Abby. I keep thinking about why she hasn't chosen me. What did I do wrong?"

"What are you talking about?"

"She's appeared to everyone but me. I've stayed up the last few nights hoping she'd run by. I don't get it. My mom has seen her. Complete strangers have seen her. Doesn't Abby know how bad I want her back? Doesn't she care?"

Mary Grace pulled her legs to her chest and wrapped her arms around them. She rested her head on her knees and her body shook with her sobs. You could probably fill an ocean with the amount of tears we'd cried over my sister. I stretched my feet out in front of me and stared at the lockers as I spoke.

"You can't be mad at her. It's not her fault she's gone," I said and thought back to my conversation with the Miracle Seekers in the woods. "That person they're seeing, she's not Abby."

"You don't know that for sure. What if it is? It's like what I said about her face. I can't remember what she looks like. What if she's standing right in front of me and I don't even know it's her?"

"It's the opposite for me. I'm afraid of seeing this vision of her and then knowing for sure it's not really her."

Mary Grace lifted her head. "I want to see her so bad."

"So do I, but not this way."

Mary Grace gave me the weakest of smiles and wiped at her eyes. "This ghost is what's been keeping me going. I search through the trees in every yard, look toward the woods and at sidewalks across the street."

"There isn't a moment that goes by when I'm not hoping she'll appear," I said, and wished there was a way to rewind our lives so we were back to the days when "missing" and "vanished" weren't even words in our vocabulary.

"It's my fault," she said.

"What do you mean? You didn't cause this."

"Not Abby. The circles. The way everyone is waiting for her to return," she said, but that didn't help. She wasn't making any sense.

"How are you to blame?"

"I have to tell you something, but I'm not sure what you're going to say."

When someone starts a sentence like that, you know it's going to be bad news. But Mary Grace didn't judge me when I told her about kissing Tommy, so how could I judge her?

"You can tell me," I said.

She took a deep breath and let it out before she spoke again. "I made the circles in your yard."

"You *what?*" I didn't know what I expected her to say, but I sure didn't think it would be anything like that.

The rest of her words came out in a rush. "The whole cross-country team did. The field where she'd run was overgrown and full of weeds. It killed us to see that. If Abby came home, we wanted it to be ready for her. So we cut it."

"How?" I asked, not quite believing her. "Those circles were huge. It would've taken hours."

"Some of the guys brought push mowers, because we didn't want to wake anyone. It was a tribute for her. Or at least, that's what we thought when we were doing it. The plan was to tell everyone what we'd done, but then the news came and reported on it and the police were looking for suspects, so we went along with everyone because suddenly it was a big deal."

"The cross-country team made the circles?" I asked, not willing to believe her confession.

Mary Grace looked like she was about to cry. "I swear, I wanted to say something, but the team promised to keep their mouths shut so we wouldn't get in trouble. We didn't think it would turn out this way. We honestly didn't know what to do."

"So you went along with everyone and let us believe they were made by my sister?"

"I wanted to believe they had something to do with her. We all did. I wanted to see your sister so badly. I began to fool myself, too."

"But the circles meant nothing," I said, and was surprised at how much it hurt to realize that the circles weren't, in fact, connected to Abby. "All those people out there every night, Collin, my *mom* . . . and they were just a hoax."

"But that's the thing, Rhylee. They started as a hoax, but it changed. They *did* mean something. Maybe your sister didn't make them, but the circles united us. They gave us hope."

"And now," I said slowly as the realization set in, "that hope is gone."

79

I didn't go back to class. I raced down the hall, my anger at her growing by the second. How could she do something like that? Those circles were our connection to Abby and now I find out it wasn't even real. How would Mom feel? And Collin? It would crush him.

I kicked a locker out of frustration; the noise echoed down the hallway. I yelped in surprise at the pain and tears gathered in my eyes. This was impossible. All of it.

I'd been so stupid to sit in that field and pretend we were connected. Pretend that Abby was closer to us because we were there. All of those things I confessed to Mary Grace in the dark, when she was the one who had fooled us to begin with by creating the circles.

Tears blinded me as I pulled out my phone and texted Tommy. I needed him, and I didn't care how it looked or what I was supposed to do or not do.

He rounded the corner less than two minutes later.

"Are you okay?" he asked. He reached out for me, but I pulled back. After weeks of avoiding any sort of contact, I still didn't feel right about him touching me. No matter how I was feeling.

Hurt flashed across his face, but was quickly covered by concern. "What's wrong?"

"What isn't wrong?" I asked and laughed, because it was the truth. How did I even begin to list everything? "I have no idea what's right anymore."

"I don't think any of us do," he said.

Before I could say anything more, the bell rang, and my classmates spilled out into the hallway.

"Hey, man," Kyle said, coming toward us. Two of his friends stood on either side like bookends, and all three of them looked at Tommy with disgust. "I told you nicely to stay away from Rhylee, but it looks like you didn't hear me."

Tommy stepped in front of me so I was hidden behind him. Protected. Other kids gathered around, as if sensing that something was going to happen.

"You can tell me whatever you want," Tommy said. "But I'm not going to listen to any of your bullshit."

"Kyle, really, it's fine," I said, trying to make peace between the two of them. "We're only talking."

It didn't work. He spoke to Tommy as if I wasn't even there. "You're not wanted here. In fact, you're not wanted anywhere."

"Go to your class," Tommy told me. "I'll take care of this."

"I'm not going anywhere," I told him. I was terrified, but if I left him, Kyle would do something worse than the black eye. I just knew it.

"Don't worry, I'll be fine."

"Listen to him," Kyle said. "It's better if you leave right now."

No. No more running away. No more being so stupid.

"I'm staying here," I said and crossed my arms over my chest. I tried to look tough, even though I was terrified.

Tommy shifted from foot to foot. He did not want me to stay, but I'd already backed away from so many other things and let him take the blame that I wasn't going to leave him alone now.

"Suit yourself," Kyle said. "If you want to watch me kick Tommy's ass, so be it. This is a school. Not a place for killers."

Tommy stiffened. He tried to let go of my hand, but I held on tighter.

"Forget about it," I whispered, but he couldn't. He broke free from my grasp and stepped up to Kyle so the two of them were almost touching chests.

"What did you say?" Tommy asked, his voice low and hard.

"You heard me. No one wants you here. Killer."

Kyle's fists went up, and I squeezed my eyes shut. There was a sickening crunch and Tommy groaned. When I opened my eyes, blood streamed out of his nose.

Kyle took another swing at Tommy, but Tommy ducked and landed a punch of his own. Kyle moved quickly, though, and drove his fist into Tommy's stomach. Tommy bent over and Kyle took the opportunity to push him to the ground. Tommy grabbed Kyle's ankle and yanked him down too. The two rolled around on the floor, a mess of hands, legs, and blood. Kyle got on top of Tommy and pinned him so that he was unable to fight back.

"Stop it!" I screamed as Kyle hit Tommy over and over again.

The crowd of students around us grew, and people held their phones out to record the fight as others cheered it on. And I hated them. Every single one of them.

Mr. Ralston and Mr. Scott pushed their way through the group, finally making it to the two boys.

"Break it up, both of you," Mr. Ralston said, but they wouldn't stop. Tommy wiggled out from under Kyle and curled up in a ball, and Kyle just kept hitting him.

"Please stop them," I yelled. "He's going to kill him!"

They were finally able to pull the two of them apart.

Tommy slowly sat up, his face covered in blood. He looked around at everyone, dazed.

Kyle coughed and wiped his mouth with the back of his hand. "Did you see the way he was hitting me?" he asked Mr. Scott. "He's psycho. No wonder the police think he killed Abby."

"Kyle's right," one of his friends said. "Tommy went after him. We were trying to go to class."

A few other boys nodded to confirm the story. I was amazed by how bold their lies were.

Tommy stood and backed away from everyone with his hands in the air. "I was only protecting myself."

"We'll discuss this in my office," Mr. Ralston said, and then faced the group of students gathered around. "I need all of you to go back to class. I'll take care of this. Mr. Scott, please escort Kyle to the bathroom to wash off. He can come to the office afterward to give his statement."

"Thanks," Kyle said. "I'm a little shaken up by all of this."

"Tommy didn't start it," I said, unable to contain myself. He was not going to take the fall for this. "You have it wrong."

"I need you go to go back to class too. I'm sure your parents wouldn't like it if they knew who you were hanging out with at school."

I tried to catch Tommy's eye, but he refused to look at me. His shirt was covered in blood and his left eye was starting to swell shut. I wanted to reach out and touch him, let him know it would be okay, but that was impossible. None of this was okay. Not at all. And no one was going to do a damn thing about it.

"No," I said, my voice sounding a lot stronger than I felt.

"Excuse me?" Mr. Scott asked.

"Miss Tower," Mr. Ralston warned, but I was done listening to him. He'd made it painfully clear whose side he was on, and I wasn't going to stand for it anymore.

"Tommy didn't do anything. He's innocent," I told the two of them and then faced the crowd. "You're the ones who should be ashamed of yourselves for what you've done to him."

"If he's so innocent, then why is he the police's number one suspect? You can't deny the obvious," Mike Connors, a football player in my grade, said. The group of students around us laughed.

"It's because of me!" I shouted to all of them, and there was no turning back. "It's because of me."

"Rhylee, no—" Tommy started, but I spoke over him.

"Do you want to know why my sister ran into the woods that night? It wasn't Tommy's fault. It was mine. I kissed him, and Abby saw it. She found the two of us together. That's why Tommy went into the woods. That's why he was muddy. He was trying to bring my sister back, because *I* betrayed her. So if you want to target someone, blame me. I did this. I made my sister disappear!" My voice broke as I battled the sobs that threatened to escape. I broke down, and I didn't care who the hell saw me.

Both Tommy and Mr. Ralston made their way to me, but I was done. I'd confessed. I ran past them before they could stop me, my feet flying across the floor as if I were Abby, racing to the finish line.

80

I ran all the way home, where I found Dad outside talking to Officer Scarano. They were next to his police cruiser, using it like a shield from the people in the field, who seemed to have moved a little bit closer, as if trying to figure out what was going on.

"What are you doing here?" I asked, because I was tired of not asking and not knowing.

"Afternoon, Rhylee," Officer Scarano said, ignoring my question. He turned back to Dad. "I'll talk with you tomorrow. We'll keep you up to date on everything."

"I appreciate that," Dad said and shook his hand.

Officer Scarano nodded at me once more before he left, but didn't make eye contact.

"Why was he here?" I asked Dad when the police car pulled away, kicking up gravel.

"He was checking in."

Dad headed inside, and I followed him. He was hiding something from me and after the day I'd had, I was done being nice to people. I was done with lies. Mine, and everyone else's. "What did he say?"

"He didn't have anything new to report," Dad said. He headed up the steps. "And I need to get ready for work now. I was already running late before he showed up."

"Why won't you talk to me about this?"

"There isn't anything to say."

"Stop, Dad. Please. Just stop!" He did. He turned to look at me, a little surprised. "We never talk anymore. If Abby did return, she wouldn't know where the hell she was. This isn't our home anymore. She'd never recognize this place; how could she when it feels so empty and cold?"

"That's enough," Dad said, and it really was. All of this was way too much. It was time to stop pretending. He paused and didn't say anything for a moment. Then he nodded.

"No, you're right," he said and his voice faltered. I wondered if he was going to cry. I'd never seen Dad cry.

"What's going on?" I asked.

Dad was quite for a moment. "The police think it's time we face the truth about what was found by the river."

His words hit me hard. Dad took a deep breath and let it out in one long sigh. My family had never, ever spoken those words out loud to one another. The policemen had talked in circles around what they had found at the river, both the shoe and the shoe prints, and what they might mean, but we'd never dared to connect the dots.

"They believe we should consider the facts," he said.

"I don't want to look at the facts," I told him, my body growing cold.

"None of us do," Dad said, his voice breaking again.

"Why now?" I asked him, fighting back my own tears.

"There haven't been any of leads or clues about what might have happened to Abby except what was found in the water. If there was some sign that said she could be somewhere else, the police would follow up on it, but there's nothing. They spoke to Johnson again and believe the river is the only place they can find answers. They plan to dredge the lake again and look for . . ." Dad's voice trailed off, and he didn't say it, but he didn't need to. I could finish the sentence with words I never thought we'd say.

"How can we just let go of hope?" I asked. "Won't that mean we're giving up on her?"

"It's been impossible to think of anything other than Abby coming home safely," he said, his voice thick with the same sorrow and regret. "I couldn't face any other possible truths, but I think we need to now."

I wanted to be mad at him. I wanted to yell and rage and strike out, but how could I? What he was saying made sense. I was an expert about not wanting to speak the truth—and how much damage that caused.

81

I didn't go back out to the circles. I couldn't. Everything I believed in wasn't true. Instead, I searched the house for my own sneakers. I was done wearing Abby's shoes.

I took off down the driveway and kept my eyes on the sky. The day had been filled with inconstant weather, and there was talk on the news that we'd finally get rain, providing relief to the drought that had plagued us for weeks. The sky grumbled and groaned echoes of thunder from the distance, moving closer to our house.

I ran with the clouds that raced in over our field and the wind that whipped around me so I had to strain to push forward.

I ran faster than I'd ever run before and left the crowd in the field.

I moved away from a family that was so busy trying to hold on to one person that they forgot about who was still there.

I ran and ran and ran, but it wasn't far enough. I couldn't lose myself in the pain.

Dad's words echoed in my mind. He'd mentioned Johnson. What had happened when the police talked to him again? Was he what made them so sure that the lake was where my sister was? I needed to get some answers, and Johnson was the one who might be able to give them to me.

I made it to the square, half expecting to find him waiting for me. Of course, it wasn't that simple. He wasn't there. I moved quickly, half running, half walking down the sidewalk. I dodged people as if they were an obstacle course. A friend of Mom's recognized me and waved. I could tell by the way she stopped in the middle of the sidewalk that she wanted me to slow down and talk, but I rushed past with a smile and a quick apology.

I finally found Johnson heading out of town, going back to the woods. A piece of blue ribbon tied around the edge of his cart flapped in the wind.

"Johnson," I yelled. He turned and I held my hands in the air, as if I were surrendering. I had nothing to hide. He was the only possibility for help, and I wanted him to see that I was there, open, free, and offering whatever I could to him. "I don't know what else to do. I feel as if what happened to my sister was my fault. I drove her away that night, and I need to make it better."

His shoulders lifted as he took a deep breath. "I can't help you."

"You were in the woods. She ran in your direction."

"Don't you know when to stop? There are some things not worth knowing."

"Like what?"

"You don't want to know." He turned from me and pushed his cart again.

I ran in front of him. "What do you mean? You can't just say something like that and then not finish it."

"Ask your father, little girl. I have no business saying anything else. You need to leave me alone."

I fell to the ground. I couldn't leave him alone. My knees gave out, and my jeans scraped against the concrete as the pressure of it all pulled me down. The sobs came fast and heavy. I missed Abby with an ache so strong that it scared me.

"Listen, you need to be quiet or half the town is going to be here circling the two of us. Come on, girl."

I swallowed and tried to silence everything that was swirling inside. "Please, I need to know the truth."

"I didn't see anything; that's what I told the police, and it's the truth. But I heard something. A scream. I don't mean when you kids are partying in the woods; I hear that all night long. This was different. It was high-pitched and long. It seemed to surround me; it went on and on. Then it stopped."

"What do you mean?" I asked, even though I wasn't sure I wanted to know.

Johnson paused. "I've heard that kind of scream before. In the war. It's primal. It's about survival."

I understood what he was telling me, even though I didn't want to believe him. My heart throbbed. I felt like I was dying

345

inside, but I stood up and stuck out my hand like I'd seen Dad do all the times we used to meet up with Johnson. "Thank you for letting me know."

He shook it, but didn't let go. Instead, he wrapped his rough fingers around mine. It seemed he was finally ready to confess too. "That's not the only thing I heard. There was a splash. A loud one. Usually I'll find a rotted-out tree trunk or a huge branch in the water. This time, when I went to check, there was nothing. At least in the water."

"But the shore . . . ," I said, still holding his hand.

"The shore," he repeated, and I was sure he was picturing the bank the way I'd seen it with the searchers. The footprints along the edge that slid into the water. He squeezed my hand and let go.

I felt numb. "Thank you," I told him, the words automatic on my lips.

"It's not easy to lose people. I couldn't tell you how many men I lost in combat, but what I do know is that it never got any easier."

His words definitely didn't help either. They pierced my chest. "No, sir, it doesn't," I said.

"You're a brave girl," he told me, and I sucked my breath in. Was I?

I could tell from the sadness in his eyes that in his mind, my sister wasn't going to return.

"I have to be," I said.

I left him there. I had found what I'd been searching for.

82

The rain caught up to me as I ran away from the center of town. Small drops at first, until the sky opened and poured.

I was soaked in a matter of minutes. I turned to head home. Lightning flashed in the sky and a few cars drove past. Their wipers made rapid movements to fight off the rain, and the water warped the faces of the drivers who peered out at me.

I ran through the grass on the edge of the road so a car wouldn't hit me, my feet squishing in the puddles of mud.

I stopped when I reached our field.

For the first time since the circles had appeared, the field was empty. There were no people, no candles, no singing, and no hope. The rain had driven them away. Now it was nothing but an empty field with the faint reminder of circles within circles carved into the grass. They were almost gone now that the grass had grown back, filling the empty spaces. The field looked a lot like our field again.

A normal field.

A field that didn't hold some kind of meaning or symbolism for our town.

A field that reminded me a lot of my old life.

My house was a blur in the distance; the lights in the windows were fuzzy in the slanting rain. Mom was probably in front of the computer, Collin in some tunnel deep in his sheets, and Dad at work.

Instead of joining them inside, I walked to the barn where the tools were kept. My clothes clung to me, my hair stuck against my face, and I was freezing. My hands shook as I picked up one of the tools. It was an old blade attached to a wooden stick. Dad called it a sickle and used it to create paths in the woods for Collin and his friends to explore. It was a bit rusty, but when I brought it down against a bale of hay, it cut right through.

I took it into the field.

I couldn't keep pretending Abby was going to return. It was time to stop believing the impossible. The police, Johnson, and Dad had all confirmed it. Abby wasn't coming home.

My body hummed with anticipation. As much as my family didn't want to admit it, we needed to move forward.

"Abby is gone!" I yelled into the storm. "She's gone and she isn't coming back!"

I brought the blade down against the middle of one of the circles.

"But we're still here! We're still living!"

I sliced again.

"And it's not my fault!"

I repeated this over and over as I sliced, the sickle moving back and forth.

It took me more than an hour to destroy the field.

I worked to cut the grass shorter and shorter, destroying any semblance of the circles that linked our town.

I hacked at the weeds, grass, and flowers in each of the centers, making it all the same length so you couldn't see any sort of shape.

I went from circle to circle doing the same thing. I chopped down everything until the field was only that, a field.

And the circles were gone.

I didn't stop. When the grass was sliced to the ground, I continued to cut. I hacked away at the field and the dirt and tried to uncover what used to lie beneath it.

I cut deeper and deeper and searched for the world that should've existed.

I cut until the field was nothing like what it used to be, until it was nothing but raw open earth.

Then I threw the blade down and headed toward my family.

83

My entire body ached so bad that it was almost impossible to climb the steps of our front porch. I kicked off my shoes and pulled off my wet socks. I was a mess of mud, sweat, rain, and tears.

Mom watched from the window. When she saw me, the curtain fell and she was gone.

What was she thinking, now that I'd destroyed the fields?

Our front porch was full of stuff from the Miracle Seekers: sleeping bags, baskets, lanterns, and other items that they must have stashed there when the skies opened. I pictured all of them coming back when the rain stopped and what they would think about the hacked-up field. Would they even return if the field didn't exist anymore? Was the field what had kept everyone together, or had it been something more?

To my surprise, Mom opened the front door and stood

with a towel. "I figured you'd need one of these."

I took it and wrapped it around my shoulders, the warmth welcome on my cold skin.

"I'm a mess," I said.

"I think," she said slowly, as if deliberating over each and every word, "we're all a bit of a mess."

"I can't keep living like this. We can't keep living like this."

"I know," she said and her voice was tired. Resigned.

"I miss who we used to be. We haven't just lost Abby. We've lost one another."

I waited for her to deny everything, to make up some excuse or say something about the circles, but she didn't. Instead, she looked ashamed. "I don't even know how I let this happen."

"We need to remember who we were. Please," I said, and it hurt that I was begging Mom to pay attention to me. But I needed her. I really did.

"We will," she said. "I promise."

I had to believe her. I needed to hold on to the belief that things would change.

I gestured toward the field. "I'm sorry I destroyed everything."

She shook her head. "We should've mowed down those fields when the circles first appeared."

"Not just the fields," I told her. "Everything. I did something awful."

"No, you didn't," Mom said, but she didn't understand.

"Tommy isn't the one you should blame for the night Abby disappeared. I am." I forced myself to meet her eyes. My sister deserved that. I wouldn't be a coward anymore. "When we were at the bonfire, Abby found Tommy and me together. We were kissing. She saw us, got upset, and ran into the woods. We chased after her, but she wouldn't listen."

"What are you talking about?" Mom asked. She reached out and brushed away a piece of hair that stuck to my wet face.

"She was so upset, and it's my fault. I did this to her. All this time you've been blaming Tommy, but it was me."

"Why didn't you tell me?" Mom asked, and I imagined the disappointment that I was so afraid was there. But I faced it.

"I was scared. I made her leave. How could I ever tell you and Dad that?"

"Oh, honey, you didn't make her leave," Mom said gently. "It was an accident."

"Abby isn't coming back," I said, and I wasn't sure if I was asking a question or making a statement. "What the police found at the river . . ."

"There's a good chance she isn't," Mom finished, so I didn't have to say anymore. It was the first time we'd acknowledged it to each other. The first time we'd tested out those words, and they felt strange and out of place, but also, they felt necessary.

Mom wrapped her arms around me, ignoring how dirty and wet I was. She tightened her grip and held on tight. "We can't forget who we are; Abby wouldn't want that."

"I feel like she's everywhere." I buried myself into Mom's

warmth. I smelled her. The familiar scent that seemed to be missing all this time. It made me remember how we used to be. I closed my eyes and tried to picture our lives before we lost Abby. I smelled all of us and summers sitting together on the porch, winters around the family room table, and life. Our life that was and the life I still had. The world I knew was still here, changed, but mine, and I clung to Mom and I clung to life.

84

I took a shower and changed into dry clothes. When I walked back downstairs, Mom was in the kitchen stirring something on the stove.

"I thought I'd make us some dinner."

I pulled the lid off a pot and a red sauce bubbled up.

"You're making actual food? That isn't delivery or from a box?"

"Hey, I can cook," Mom said defensively, one hand on her hip. "Maybe I took a break for a while, but it's about time to serve food to you and Collin that doesn't sit on the shelf for months."

Mom was right; it was nice to have something that wasn't from a can, and to eat it around the table together like we used to. Collin was so excited to have something this good for dinner that he had three helpings. I took my time, simply glad to be with my family.

After I did the dishes, I pulled on a hoodie and found

Mom in the living room. She was reading a magazine with the TV on low. Collin played on the floor with a bunch of his action heroes. The computer screen was dark.

"I need to go and talk to Tommy," I told her, and instead of fighting me like she usually did, she nodded.

The rain had stopped, but it was damp outside. The air was cool, the chill of fall settling in. The field sat raw, opened, and destroyed. I walked down the road slowly, not quite sure what I was going to say, but I had to see him.

He sat in his truck bed. Sparks blazed for a moment as he lit one match after another, letting each burn until he flicked it into the air and the flame fizzled out.

I climbed up with him. He moved over on the plaid blanket he'd spread out to make room for me, as if he'd been expecting me to join him.

I fought back tears as I took in what Kyle had done. Tommy's face was a mess. His eyes swollen, cheek battered and bruised. His lip was split and scabbed over.

"You didn't deserve this," I said. I reached out and gently touched a spot on his cheek that wasn't wounded.

"You can't change the way people think," he said.

"I couldn't walk away from you. Kyle was so angry, and what kind of person would—"

"It's okay, you don't have to explain," Tommy said. "Thank you. For everything."

"I told my mom the truth about that night. She said we'll have to talk to the police, but it wasn't our fault. What happened to Abby was an accident."

"She's right. We couldn't have predicted any of this."

Mom had said that no one had that kind of power, and it was true. We couldn't take things away, and we couldn't bring them back. No matter how much we searched or sat in the fields and wished for my sister to return, we'd never be able to make that happen. It was a cruel twist of fate the universe had played on us.

"How'd we get to this point?" I asked. I thought about everything between Tommy and me, from the night I didn't kiss him to the night that I did.

And here I was again with Tommy. My Tommy. The boy I grew up with and loved. The boy whose hands I'd clasped when I was young, the two of us shrieking as we jumped into the freezing cold swimming pool together. The boy who'd protected me on the playground when the other boys took my lunch box, and wrapped his T-shirt around my arm to stop it from bleeding when the dog down the street bit me. This was the boy who'd captured my heart and still held it. The boy I had to let go.

"I think if you want to go to New York, you should," I told him.

"I don't want to leave you alone," he said.

But I wasn't alone. I thought about Westing College and the day I'd spent there where I was able to be myself and nothing else. I thought about my future and where it might take me. What a world beyond my sister's shadow could mean.

"I'll be fine. I'm strong," I told him. "I'm Rhylee."

"You'll always be Rhylee," he said.

I let his words fill me and the two of us sat in the silence and instead of being afraid of what wasn't said in those moments, I felt at peace.

"She isn't coming home," I finally said.

Tommy nodded.

"I miss her so bad," I said.

"So do I," he answered softly.

"But we're still here," I told him.

His hand found mine, and I wrapped my fingers around his. The two of us sat there with nothing between us. Everything we wanted to say, everything we felt and our fears, right in front of us.

I thought about what I'd lost and what I still had.

I squeezed his hand and I was not Abby.

I was Rhylee and I was living and it was okay.

Author's Note

Rhylee called the suicide hotline as a way to cope with her sister's disappearance. If you are experiencing your own feelings of hopelessness or despair, know that there are people willing to listen and help. You are important.

National Suicide Prevention Lifeline

1-800-273-8255

suicidepreventionlifeline.org (to chat with someone online)

Acknowledgments

Writing often feels like a solitary thing, but the truth is, the help and support an author has is amazing. The list of people I could thank for helping to get this book on the shelves is pretty close to the size of the world. I may not be able to thank everyone individually, but you'd better believe that I've felt your love and encouragement.

This book started years ago as a tiny spark of a short story that demanded to be more. I couldn't shake it, the characters lingering inside of me and haunting my thoughts. Slowly, slowly, the story of Rhylee, Abby, and Tommy unfolded. So thank you to the NEOMFA Writing Program, specifically Prof. Rahman's Fiction Workshop class, where I first introduced the short story "Circles Within Circles." Your feedback, conversation, and ideas about that first version began to shape it into the book that it is now.

Thank you to my ever amazing, fabulous, and dedicated agent, Natalie Lakosil, who never, ever gave up on this book. You rock!

A thousand thanks to my editor, Alyson Heller. I can't even tell you how incredibly lucky I feel to have been able to work with you on this book. The story is so much better because of your insights, ideas, and enthusiasm. I'd like to "raise a glass" to you because you are "passionately smashing every expectation" for what an editor should be.

I am so appreciative of everything the brilliant team at Simon Pulse has done. Thank you to Regina Flath for designing the amazing cover, along with Rebecca Vitkus, Katherine Devendorf, Catherine Hayden, Carolyn Swerdloff, Steve Scott, and Faye Bi. Each and every one of you has put your magic touch on this book, and it's all the better for it.

The bond between sisters is one of the most important, loving, and complex relationships I've ever known. Thank you, Amanda, for being an incredible sister, best friend, and Auntie. We may have fought sometimes (okay, a lot of times!) growing up, but I want you to know I'm so lucky to have you in my life. Here's to years of stealing each other's clothes, visits from Michael Jackson and the Easter Bunny, crimping our Barbies' hair, The Shell Shop and Jensen Beach, Bobkittens, 303C Girls, Harborview, late-night Taco Bell, Wednesday visits, riding the choo-choo around the mall, and bowls of bone broth with Nonny!

Once upon a time, I met my Writing Soul Sister, Elle LaMarca, and life has never been the same. You're an amazing crit partner, cheerleader, and fellow Marnie-hater. WSS Book Tour, here we come! You bring the lipstick, and I'll bring the coffee!

Beta partners are the bomb-diggity, and I am eternally grateful for all my readers. Thank you to Nancy Skinner, Christina Lee, Marissa Marangoni, Colleen Clayton, Lisa Nowak, and Taryn Albright . . . you all rock!

Connecting with my readers is hands down my favorite part of writing. Thank you to all the book lovers out there. . . . I write for you.

A shout-out to what fueled this book: coffee, gummy candy, and some good old fashioned crying music (specifically, Coldplay, The National, Damien Rice, The Civil Wars, and The Swell Season...the melancholy in your words played on repeat as I wrote and revised this book). Thank you to Barnes and Noble in Mentor, Panera in Willoughby and Mentor, and the Willoughby Starbucks for providing a place to escape to when I needed to camp out somewhere and focus on nothing but writing. The amount of coffee I consumed writing this book may very well be able to fill an ocean.

Thank you to my family and friends who provide never-ending love and support for me to chase after my dreams. My colleagues (a special high-five to Jenny Hunter and librarian extraordinaire and future dog-walker Jodi Rzeszotarski) and students inspire me every day to want to write, write, write, and I'm so honored to have you are all on this journey with me. Especially to the NaNoWriMo Crew and Thursday After-noon Writers' Club; Sarah Estvanko, Fatima Martinez, Alexis Beckwith, David Vesey, Megan Carlson, Autumn Graham, and Chelsea Marino. You're all the next generation of writers, and I can't wait to see what amazing words you create!

And always, always, always, to Nolan . . . you will always be my greatest adventure and the best story I ever get to witness.

DISCOVER NEW YA READS

READ BOOKS FOR FREE

WIN NEW & UPCOMING RELEASES

RIVETED

YA FICTION **IS OUR ADDICTION**

JOIN THE COMMUNITY

DISCUSS WITH THE COMMUNITY

WRITE FOR THE COMMUNITY

CONNECT WITH US ON RIVETEDLIT.COM

AND @RIVETEDLIT

Seeds OF Peace

Seeds OF Peace

A Catalogue of Quotations
Compiled by
Jeanne Larson & Madge Micheels-Cyrus

new society publishers

Philadelphia, PA   Santa Cruz, CA

Phillips Memorial
Library
Providence College

JX
1937
L27
1987

Copyright © 1987 Jeanne Larson & Madge Micheels-Cyrus.
All rights reserved.
Inquiries regarding requests to republish all or part of *Seeds of Peace* should be addressed to: **New Society Publishers, 4527 Springfield Avenue, Philadelphia, PA 19143, USA.**

ISBN: 0-86571-098-8 Hardcover
0-86571-099-6 Paperback

Printed in the United States of America on partially recycled paper.

Cover graphic by Kathy Fox; Design by Mike Holderness.

This book was compiled as a project of **Waging Peace, PO Box 383, Hayward, WI 54843, USA.** A portion of the proceeds of this book goes to support the work of Waging Peace, a resource collective committed to creative peace education.

To order directly from the publisher, add $1.50 to the price for the first copy, 50¢ each additional. Send check or money order to: **New Society Publishers, PO Box 582, Santa Cruz, CA 95061, USA.**

New Society Publishers is a project of the New Society Educational Foundation, a nonprofit, tax-exempt, public foundation. Opinions expressed in this book do not necessarily represent positions of the New Society Educational Foundation.

Quotations from *Christ in a Poncho* by Adolfo Pérez Esquivel, © 1983 English translation. Reprinted by permission of Orbis Books.
Quotations from *Food First News* are reprinted with the permission of Ann Kelly, Publications Director of Food First, Institute for Food and Developmental Policy, San Francisco.
Quotations from *Johnny Got His Gun* by Dalton Trumbo, © 1969, Introduction Addendum copyright 1970. Reprinted by permission of Carole Stuart, Publisher, Lyle Stuart, Inc.
Quotations from *Meet Mr. Bomb: A Practical Guide to Nuclear Extinction*, © 1982, edited by Tony Hendra, published by Larry Durocher. Reprinted with permission of Larry Durocher, High Meadows Publishing, Inc.
Quotations from *Nuclear Winter* by Carl Sagan, © 1983. Reprinted by permission of Carl Sagan.
Quotations from *Cosmos* by Carl Sagan, © 1980. Published by Random House, Inc., NYC. Reprinted by permission of Carl Sagan.
Quotations from *Our Future at Stake: a Teenager's Guide to Stopping the Nuclear Arms Race*, © 1984 by Melinda Moore and Laurie Olson. Reprinted with the permission of the Citizens Policy Center Nuclear Action for Youth Project.
Quotations from *Please Save My World*, © 1984, edited by Bill Adler. Reprinted with the permission of Arbor House.
Quotations from *We Won't Go: Personal Accounts of War Objectors*, collected by Alice Lynd, © 1968 by Alice Lynd. Reprinted by permission of Beacon Press.
Quotations from the *Winter Soldier Archives*, an introduction to *The Short-Timer's Journal, Soldiering in Vietnam No. 1*, © 1980. Reprinted by permission of Clark Smith of the Winter Soldier Archive.

Contents

For our children
   (Jamila, Jay, Tamra, Tanya & Zachary);
      their children;
         their children's children;
            their children's children's children...

Preface

The words in this book contain a lot of *power*. It is the same kind of power that is found in a seed....Power that makes a small plant germ take hold on an inhospitable rock ledge and grow there into a sturdy tree....Power that causes tender green plants to rise up out of dark graves and break through a blacktop crust.

The words in this collection are powerful like that. We think that they deserve to be circulated widely. That is why we have created this resource, making over 1600 *seeds of peace*—quotations on war, peace, nonviolence and images of a peaceful world—available under one cover.

There are two main parts to the book: quotations on "Waging War" and quotations on "Waging Peace." Three smaller parts are found in the center section: "The Lighter Side of a Serious Subject"; "Patriotism"; and "Bumperstickers, Buttons, T-Shirts and Graffiti."

How to use the book

Like garden seed catalogues that serve both the committed and casual gardener, this catalogue of quotations has many uses. Those who write speeches, articles, sermons and newsletters will find "seed thoughts" in here. The user who wishes to find a quotation for a specific purpose will be aided by the book's 29 chapter headings and by the complete index. The purpose of the book is also served by a random sampling of the quotations. For every time a word about peace is read or spoken, a thought of peace stirred, or an image of peace created in the mind, we believe that activity alone brings peace a little closer. The quotation book will be "waging peace" every time it is used.

Within each chapter, the quotations are arranged to "tell a story." We found that persons who lived a century apart sometimes echoed one another's thoughts precisely. We have paired such quotations in the book. Sometimes it was the striking contrast between two perspectives that caught our attention and led us to put quotations together. In every case, we believe that the order of the quotations in the book will contribute to creative stirring of thought.

Direct sowing or composting?

Many of the quotations in the book are like seeds of peace that are suitable for "direct sowing." That is especially true of the quotations that are found in the "Waging Peace" section. Most of the quotations in

Part I, "Waging War," however, are of another variety. Those thoughts are not "plantable" so much as they are "compostable." These quotations first need to be composted in the thought process of the mind—where they can be decomposed, recycled and converted from death talk into ideas and images that support life.

What about sexist language?

In working on the seedbed of this project, we came across one big "rockpile." And that was what to do about the sexist language in many of the quotations. The more we worked on the book, the more aware we became of the power of words. (No wonder Edward Robert Bulwer-Lytton claimed that "the pen is mightier than the sword"!) What, then, to do about words that address everyone as male; words that exert their power in the direction of reinforcing sexism in society?

At first, there was no doubt in our minds. Where sexist language was used, we had to make what changes were necessary to make it inclusive language. Otherwise, we would be giving wider circulation to words that perpetuate the "power over" mentality that gives rise to a war and violence mentality. That would be defeating our purpose of waging peace by producing this book!

It was one thing to conclude that sexist language had no place in our book. Figuring out exactly what to do about it was another matter.

Should we change the sexist words to inclusive terms in the quotation with footnotes citing how it appeared in the original text? Should we italicize the sexist words (or put them in parentheses) to indicate that something is out of order there? Should we put the inclusive language term in parentheses alongside the sexist word used in the original text? Should we take the sexist language out of those quotations where it can be done so practically, and leave it in where it would require too much re-writing? Can we legitimately change a word, even if we do document the change? Should we do nothing in the text and urge the user to deal with the problem? Can we legitimately do nothing? How about offering two versions of each sexist quotation—the original and an inclusive language re-write—much like a bi-lingual text?

...We struggled!... What would you do, for example, with a quotation like this: "Can anything be more ridiculous than that a man has a right to kill me because he dwells on the other side of the water, and because his prince has a quarrel with mine, although I have none with him?" (Blaise Pascal, *Pensées*, IV)

We found that we could not address the sexist language word for word in quotations like this—be it with italics, parentheses, or footnotes—without unacceptably affecting the integrity and readability of the quotation.

We eventually reached our decision about what we would do with the recognition that there was no solution that would be 100% satisfactory—to us, or to every user of the book. To do nothing would insult readers whose patience with the use of sexist language has run out. To make changes of any kind would offend those whose literary and editorial ethics insist that no changes whatsoever of any kind for any reason can be made in an original text.

What we have done is this:
* Wherever an asterisk appears at the beginning of a quotation, we have determined that gender has been used in a sexist way in that quotation.

The asterisk is intended to serve as a "warning flag," encouraging the reader to be on the look-out for:
—gender-exclusivity in that quotation;
—the need for inclusive language adaptations whenever possible in the use of the quotation.

We found that there was one encouraging note about all the difficulty we had with the issue of sexist language. And that is that not many years ago, it would not have been an issue. That it was a problem for us now bears witness to the fact that basic cultural changes do take place. If our attitudes toward language can change, why not our attitudes about war and peace?

Sowing what you want to reap

...Finally, this book of seeds needs you, the sower, to become useful. We are confident that in your hands it will be a valuable tool for moving toward the harvest of peace that we all desire.

Jeanne Larson
Madge Micheels-Cyrus
October 1986

Acknowledgements

"...Did Beethoven do the dishes? Did Mozart sweep the floor?" These questions, posed in a folk song by Ginny Reilly and David Maloney, point to the reality of invisible support structures that make visible accomplishments possible.

Seeds of Peace clearly represents the efforts of more than two people.

It represents an accomplishment of Waging Peace, a unique support structure. We could not have composed this resource in our spare time alone. We had more than spare time to devote because peace work is our part-time wage work. We are hired by peers who want to see employment opportunities added to the volunteer work force in order to escalate the total peace effort. It is not only a lot of work that is represented here, but also a lot of *will*—will for peace on the part of the supporters of Waging Peace. The book in your hands is a testimony to that will and the power of what can be accomplished by it.

In addition, financial support has come from Jackie Rivet-River and Louis River, from the Division on Social Concerns of the Northwest Association and the Commission on Social Concerns—both of the Wisconsin Conference, United Church of Christ, and from the Church and Society Committee of the Presbytery of Northern Waters, Presbyterian Church (USA).

Others to be thanked for their help are our Waging Peace colleague Tom Hastings, who contributed prize quotes and picked up office chores, Sunshine Jones, Gerri Williams, Shelley Anderson and Jeanne Audrey Powers for their input on the problem of sexist language, Michael Skindrud for his clarification, Margaret and John Lintula for proofreading, Grandma and Grandpa Kanicky for helping out at home and with the youngest child, and Jack and Lynn whose support, literally, included washing dishes and sweeping floors.

Seeds of Peace is truly a collective accomplishment....May we propose a toast to us all?

Publisher's Note

Brief quotations and epigrams can have a powerful—and unpredictable—effect on our consciousness: often more powerful than whole books or even conversations. As someone who works with words, who is even unfashionably committed to the written word, I often have cause to wonder how often anyone's mind has ever been changed by reading. I suspect rarely: far more likely that reading something which is timely and sums up one's own part-formed thoughts will cause those thoughts to crystallize, to become active and powerful. This is, I hope, the potential of this book: among the almost overwhelming number of quotations here there may be one or two which will at a given time reach you personally, or which will reach audiences you are addressing. They may be phrases which remind us of the hope and beauty in the world, or those which remind us of what must be overcome.

When in the early Seventies I first came across the slogan *Nous sommes tous des juifs Allemands*: "We are all German Jews"—on a poster from the near-uprising in Paris of May 1968—I was disturbed and puzzled. The slogan made me stop and think. It was clearly a clever play on Kennedy's *Ich bin ein Berliner* (in which he unwittingly placed himself on a *Delikatessen* shelf—but that's another story). It seemed to be dramatising the *potential* for massive violence of the State, with its tanks at the ready on the outskirts of the city. But was it an irresponsible use of shock value? Did it trivialise the Holocaust?

In 1979, as I became immersed in the literature of Nagasaki and Hiroshima and cruise missiles, that slogan came back to me and made a great deal of sense—though perhaps not the sense that the presumed author, running off overnight posters on a silk-screen in some Paris basement, had in mind. We *are* all German Jews. We are *all* Communists and Gypsys and homosexuals. Sitting fearfully through the days after the bombing of Libya, startled by the flash of lightning or the wail of a ship's siren, feeling utterly powerless: is this how it felt in the Warsaw ghetto in 1941, in a Berlin hideout in 1937? Yet for me the image of that quotation is not—now—one of desperation. For opening ourselves to the depth of our predicament must be a part of changing it. When I am asked what I, as a pacifist, would have done against Hitler, I must answer: "Start earlier! Not start opposition when it was too late, in 1939 or 1941, but in 1920 or 1923..." We, in acting against a new Holocaust of all the earth's people, can start as soon as we like: now.

As much as this could be written about any quotation in this book. It may be that others will affect you in ways that their original authors, writing in other times, never imagined. It is probable that some quotations were not first uttered by those credited here; this is not an academic reference work. It *is* a "thought tool," a crystal seed for your thoughts and those of people around you.

Mike Holderness

1
Militarism

* Man has no right to kill his brother. It is no excuse that he does so in uniform; he only adds the infamy of servitude to the crime of murder.

Percy Bysshe Shelley

Soldiers are taught to consider arms as the only arbiters by which every dispute is to be decided....They are instructed implicitly to obey their commanders without enquiring into the justice of the cause they are engaged to support; hence it is, that they are ever to be dreaded as the ready engine of tyranny and oppression.

Joseph Warren, 1772

* Once a man enters the army, he is expected only to follow the heels ahead of him.

Carson McCullers

* A crew-cut captain greeted us with these words: "What does k-i-l-l spell?" "Kill," was the obvious, though not too loud, reply of most of the three hundred voices..."I can't hear you!" "Kill!" A deafening chant began: "Kill! Kill! Kill!..." I looked around me. Clerks, mechanics, teachers, college students, a few professional men, all were screaming, "Kill!" Who cares who? Just kill. Kill anyone that the President, the Congress, and the generals brand as "evil," "aggressors," "the enemy"....

As I look back, I cannot condemn these men, or those who went before or now follow them. Very few of these men are inherently cruel, depraved, or deranged. But fear, power, and hatred are the order of the day, and it is to these forces, so constantly presented to us both by demagogues and by those who should know better, that men submit without question. Good men do bad things because they are too benumbed to ask "Why?" or say "No!" Our society, but particularly the military, demands men who will follow without thinking.

Stephen Fortunato, Jr.
We Won't Go

If my soldiers began to think, not one would remain in the ranks.

Frederick the Great

If you would remain men be not soldiers; if you do not know how to digest humiliations, do not put on the uniform.

Jean Grave
Dying Society and Anarchy

* Humilities are piled on a soldier...so in order that he may, when the time comes, be not too resentful of the final humility—a meaningless and dirty death.

John Steinbeck
East of Eden

I can use up 25,000 men a month.

Napoleon Bonaparte, 1798

* The military has an almost metaphysical concept of its power and righteousness; the military demands that the individual abandon his reason and his conscience in a supreme and "patriotic" act of self-abnegation in order that he might proudly assume his niche in an invincible mass of manpower and machinery that will—to use military terms—"close with the enemy and destroy him."

Stephen Fortunato, Jr.
We Won't Go

* Man is the only Patriot. He sets himself apart in his own country, under his own flag, and sneers at the other nations, and keeps multitudinous uniformed assassins on hand at heavy expense to grab slices of other people's countries, and keep *them* from grabbing slices of *his*. And in the intervals between campaigns he washes the blood off his hands and works for "the universal brotherhood of man"—with his mouth.

Mark Twain

* Just as it would be stupid to plant weeds and try to harvest vegetables, so it would be stupid to encourage the lies, conscription, and murder of war, and hope to produce democracy, freedom, and brotherhood.

Dave Dellinger
on entering prison, 1943

Never think that war, no matter how necessary, nor how justified, is not a crime. Ask the infantry and ask the dead.

Ernest Hemingway

* Killing one man constitutes a crime and is punishable by death. Applying the same principle, the killing of ten men makes the crime ten times greater and ten times as punishable. Similarly, the killing of a hundred men increases the crime a hundred fold, and makes it that many times as punishable. All this the gentlemen of the world unanimously condemn and pronounce wrong. But when they come to judge the greatest of all wrongs—the invasion of one state by another—(which is 100,000,000 times more criminal than the killing of one innocent man) they cannot see that they should condemn it. On the contrary, they praise it and call it "right." Indeed, they do not know it is wrong.

Moh-tze
3rd Century B.C.
Courage in Both Hands

* Justice is as strictly due between neighbor nations as between neighbor citizens. A highwayman is as much a robber when he plunders in a gang as when single; and a nation that makes an unjust war is only a great gang.

Benjamin Franklin, 1785

* Can anything be more ridiculous than that a man has a right to kill me because he dwells on the other side of the water, and because his prince has a quarrel with mine, although I have none with him?

Blaise Pascal
Pensées, IV

It has been argued that, when killing is viewed as not only permissible but heroic behavior sanctioned by one's government or cause, the fine distinction between taking a human life and other forms of impermissible violence gets lost, and rape becomes an unfortunate but inevitable by-product of the necessary game called war.

Susan Brownmiller

I would no more teach children military training than teach them arson, robbery, or assassination.

Eugene V. Debs

* Now children are very pretty, very lovable, very affectionate creatures (sometimes); and a child can make nitro-glycerine or chloride of nitrogen as well as a man if it is taught to do so. We have sense enough not to teach it; but we do teach the grown-up children. We actually accompany that dangerous technical training with solemn moral lessons in which the most destructive use of these forces at the command of kings and capitalists is inculcated as heroism, patriotism, glory, and all the rest of it.

George Bernard Shaw

He had grown up in a country run by politicians who sent the pilots to man the bombers to kill the babies to make the world safe for children to grow up in.

Ursula K. LeGuin
The Lathe of Heaven

We've gained from the wars a lot of trouble and hatred and bitterness.... Women are for peace always. They are for peace by nature.

Jehan Sadat

Nowhere have women been more excluded from decision-making than in the military and foreign affairs. When it comes to the military and questions of nuclear disarmament, the gender gap becomes the gender gulf.

Eleanor Smeal
National Organization of Women

I'm certain that if a minority of women in every country would clearly express their convictions they would find that they spoke not for themselves alone but for those men for whom war has been a laceration—an abdication of the spirit.

Jane Addams
Nobel Peace Prize, 1931

War has shown that government by men only is not an appeal to reason, but an appeal to arms; that on women, without a voice to protest, must fall the burden. It is easier to die than to send a son to death.

Mary Roberts Rinehart
Kings, Queens, and Pawns

We have always borne part of the weight of war, and the major part....Men have made boomerangs, bows, swords, or guns with which to destroy one another: we have made the men who destroyed and were destroyed. We pay the first cost of all human life.

Olive Schreiner

As a woman, I can't go to war and I refuse to send anyone else...You can no more win a war than you can win an earthquake.

Jeannette Rankin
only Congressperson to vote against
US entrance into both World Wars

I want to stand by my country, but I cannot vote for war. I vote no...The world must finally understand that we cannot settle disputes by eliminating human beings.

Jeannette Rankin

It does not follow that if women will vote, they must fight, for war is not the natural state of the human family.

Elizabeth Cady Stanton

* It is sometimes said that war is a natural condition of man. As a military man, I do not believe it.

I do believe breathing, eating, loving, caring, are natural conditions of man. People don't make war, governments do.

And our governments appear willing to accept war, even nuclear war, as a natural event.

There is not one nation in the world where the people want war.

Rear Admiral Gene R. La Rocque
U.S. Navy (retired)

In peace, children inter their parents; war violates the order of nature and causes parents to inter their children.

Herodotus

Hear me, my chiefs, I am tired. My heart is sick and sad. From where the sun now stands I will fight no more forever.

Chief Joseph
Nez Percé, 1877

Revenge by young men is considered gain, even at the cost of their own lives, but old men who stay at home in times of war, and mothers who have sons to love, know better.

Chief Seattle, 1859

I am tired and sick of war. Its glory is all moonshine. It is only those who have neither fired a shot nor heard the shrieks and groans of the wounded who cry aloud for blood, more vengeance, more desolation. War is hell.

General William Tecumseh Sherman, 1879

There is many a boy here today who looks on war as all glory; but, boys, it is all hell. You can bear this warning voice to generations yet to come. I look upon war with horror.

General William Tecumseh Sherman, 1880

War is sweet to those who don't know it.

Desiderius Erasmus

* I have known war as few men now living know it. Its very destructiveness on both friend and foe has rendered it useless as a means of settling international disputes.

General Douglas MacArthur

War is, we have been forced to admit, even in the face of its huge place in our own civilization, an asocial trait...if we justify war, it is because all peoples always justify the traits of which they find themselves possessed, not because war will bear an objective examination of its merits.

Ruth Benedict
Patterns of Culture

As long as war is regarded as wicked it will always have its fascinations. When it is looked upon as vulgar, it will cease to be popular.

Oscar Wilde
Intentions

War, to me, is the greatest weakness of all.

Anaïs Nin

The guns and the bombs, the rockets and the warships, all are symbols of human failure.

Lyndon B. Johnson

Throughout history there has never been an evitable war. The greatest danger of war always lies in the wide-spread acceptance of its inevitability.

James P. Warburg

The possibility of a short and decisive war appears to be one of the most ancient and dangerous of human illusions.

Robert Lynd

* War has persisted because...men have made an exception of each particular war and gone out to mutual slaughter.

Jesse Wallace Hughan

Wars will cease when men refuse to fight—and women refuse to approve. Do not allow people to lead you to think for a moment that war is a necessary institution.

Jesse Wallace Hughan

General, your tank is a mighty machine. It shatters the forest and crushes a hundred men. But it has one defect: It needs a driver.

Bertolt Brecht

* The pioneers of a warless world are the young men who refuse military service.

Albert Einstein

War will exist until that distant day when the conscientious objector enjoys the same reputation and prestige that the warrior does today.

John F. Kennedy

* Weapons are instruments of fear; they are not a wise man's tools...
Peace and quiet are dear to his heart,
And victory no cause for rejoicing.
If you rejoice in victory, then you delight in killing;
If you delight in killing, you cannot fulfill yourself.

Lao Tsu
Tao Te Ching, **Thirty-One**

On happy occasions precedence is given to the left,
On sad occasions to the right.
In the army the general stands on the left,
The commander-in-chief on the right.
This means that war is conducted like a funeral.
When many people are being killed,
They should be mourned in heartfelt sorrow.
That is why a victory must be observed like a funeral.

Lao Tsu
Tao Te Ching, **Thirty-One**

To rejoice in conquest is to rejoice in murder.

Lao Tsu

The next dreadful thing to a battle lost is a battle won.

Wellington

* The problem after a war is with the victor. He thinks he has just proven that war and violence pay. Who will teach him a lesson?

A. J. Muste

After all, war isn't that effective. In every case, at least one side loses, which is only 50% effective, if you're lucky. The winner pays a very large price, as well.

Gene Sharp

There never was a good war or a bad peace.

Benjamin Franklin

Nothing is lost by peace; everything may be lost by war.

Pope Paul VI

We are ready to kill to keep our automobiles running. We're ready to kill to keep up our materialistic, wasteful economy...I am sick and tired of 18-year-olds being coerced into bearing the burden of the failure of politicians to face the tough economic choices needed to end our dependency on foreign oil.

Mark Hatfield
Senator, Oregon

I spent thirty-three years and four months in active military service....And during that period I spent most of my time being a high-class muscle man for big business, for Wall Street and for the bankers. In short, I was a racketeer, a gangster for capitalism...I helped make Mexico safe for American oil interests in 1914. I helped make Haiti and Cuba a decent place for the National City Bank boys to collect revenue in. I helped purify Nicaragua for the international banking house of Brown Brothers...I brought light to the Dominican Republic for American sugar interests in 1916. I helped make Honduras "right" for American fruit companies in 1903. Looking back on it, I might have given Al Capone a few hints.

Major General Smedley Butler, USMC
***New York Times* interview, August 1931**

When we were in Grenada, I really enjoyed myself. You were out there with your gun, shooting, taking prisoners, doing everything Marines are supposed to do.

Lance Corporal Gordon Brock

Patriots always talk of dying for their country, and never of killing for their country.

Bertrand Russell

The master class has always declared the wars; the subject class has always fought the battles.   **Eugene Debs**

Those who can't find anything to live for always invent something to die for. Then they want the rest of us to die for it, too.

Anonymous

* Government consists merely of professional politicians, a parasitical and anti-social class of men. They never sacrifice themselves for their country. They make all wars, but very few of them ever die in one.

H. L. Mencken

Militarism has been by far the commonest cause of the breakdown of civilization.

Arnold Toynbee

You can't say that civilizations don't advance, for in every war they kill you in a new way.

Will Rogers

Technological progress has merely provided us with more efficient means for going backwards.

Aldous Huxley

America has become a militaristic and aggressive nation...We have an immense and expensive military establishment, fueled by a gigantic defense industry, and millions of proud, patriotic, and frequently bellicose and militaristic citizens...Militarism in America is in full bloom and promises a future of vigorous self-pollination...unless the blight of Vietnam reveals that militarism is more a poisonous weed than a glorious blossom.

General David M. Shoup
Retired Marine Corps Commandant

Our whole social organism is riddled by the disease of militarism; and just as it seems that cancer can only be cured at the level of the organism as a whole, so we cannot hope to root out militarism without a similarly holistic therapy.

Rudolf Bahro

Show me who makes a profit from war, and I'll show you how to stop the war. **Henry Ford**

This country is in the early years of the most expensive military boom in history. The expansion in military science and technology is the most ominous component of a defense budget that is dense with the ghosts of past and future wars. **Emma Rothschild, MIT**
in the *New York Review of Books*

Profits are springing, like weeds, from the fields of the dead.

Rosa Luxemburg

The American military-industrial complex...was the real winner of World War II.   **David Dellinger**

...we will never have peace...so long as people go on manufacturing death and trying to sell it.
                                                          Edna St. Vincent Millay

The most disadvantageous peace is better than the most just war.
                                                          Desiderius Erasmus
                                                          Adagia

It is always immoral to start a war.

Diplomatic and other non-violent means should always be used to resolve conflicts and fend off aggression.

If non-violent methods fail, and one nation unjustly attacks another, the victim nation has as a last resort the right and duty to use violent means to defend itself within certain moral limits.

The military response to any attack may not exceed the limits of legitimate self-defense.

This means that the damage inflicted and the costs incurred must be proportionate to the good expected by the taking up of arms. The wholesale slaughter of civilians in large population centers is simply immoral, whether the destruction is intentional or unintentional, direct or indirect, no matter what weapons system is used.
                statement of the Catholic Bishops on the Just-War Theory

In the 1960's civilian and military deaths were about equal, but in the last decade civilian deaths rose sharply. The average in the later period is three civilian deaths to one battle death.

Weapons fired from great distances are more destructive and indiscriminate. Aided by mechanized equipment, conflicts fan out more rapidly, destroying crops and food supplies, causing floods of helpless refugees. Starvation takes many of them.
                                                          Ruth Leger Sivard

I am not proud of the fact that my son helped to bomb Vietnam....I would like to go up to each one of them [the Vietnamese people] and hold their hands in mine and say to them that I am sorry about the bombing of their country, and I am terribly sorry that Jim was part of it. It is not much, but what more can I say?
                                                          Virginia Warner
                                                          mother of a war prisoner
                                                          Winter Soldier Investigation
                                                          January 1971

The legacy of the Vietnam War is so sad, so riddled with frustration, anger, and guilt, that it is easy to fall into the complacent attitude that it is long over and best forgotten. But to forget that war has an immediate hazard. Forgetfulness and complacency help renew the forces that are still in place that originally caused the war. However painful the truth of the war might be, it is preferable to myths, illusions, and rationalizations and their manipulation by those planning the next conflict.

Winter Soldier Archive

A murder medal. They give you medals for killing people.

Stephen Gregory
Bronze Star recipient
while sentenced for taking hostages in a Maryland bank in 1977

They want to call us heroes for serving the country. They offer us recognition and honor, even a national monument. Heroes for serving a country that burned down villages and shot anything that moved. Recognition for being the agents and pawns of a ruthless death machine that systematically tortured and butchered civilians, that rained flaming jelly gasoline and poison chemical gas on old men, women, and children. Receiving a past due debt of honor for using the most advanced, blood-curdling, and flesh-tearing weapons of terror the world has ever known. A monument for being the tools of a modern imperialist army that vainly attempted for over ten years to crush, grind and pulverize the people and land of Vietnam into the Stone Age, an army that finally sank to a well-deserved defeat at the hands of a just and determined peoples' war.

statement from Vietnam era veterans

Some 110,000 veterans have died since their return from Vietnam, twice the official number that died in combat. Many were suicides. When a man dies in combat from "friendly fire," his death can be listed as accidental. Many veterans whose deaths are officially recorded as accidental were really suicides. If the actual number is uncertain, it is certain the suicides from depression and aggravation stemming from the Vietnam experience is significant and continuing.

Winter Soldier Archive

The official line on the Vietnam war is that it was a "mistake." (Oops, 55,000 dead, another 35,000 "accidentally" killed, 33,000 crippled, 330,000 wounded.)

Winter Soldier Archive

What is missing in American life is a sense of context...in our journalism the trivial displaces the momentous because we tend to measure events by how recently they happened....We've become so obsessed with facts we've lost all touch with truth.

Ted Koppel

Numbers have dehumanized us. Over breakfast coffee we read of 40,000 American dead in Vietnam. Instead of vomiting, we reach for the toast.

Our morning rush through crowded streets is not to cry murder but to hit that trough before somebody else gobbles our share.

Dalton Trumbo
addendum to Introduction—1970
Johnny Got His Gun

An equation: 40,000 dead young men is 3,000 tons of bone and flesh, 124,000 pounds of brain matter, 50,000 gallons of blood, 1,840,000 years of life that will never be lived, 100,000 children who will never be born. Do we scream in the night when it touches our dreams? No. We don't dream about it because we don't think about it; we don't think about it because we don't care about it. We are much more interested in law and order, so that American streets may be made safe while we transform those of Vietnam into flowing sewers of blood which we replenish each year by forcing our sons to choose between a prison cell here or a coffin there.

Dalton Trumbo
addendum to Introduction—1970
Johnny Got His Gun

If the dead mean nothing to us (except on Memorial Day weekend...), what of our 300,000 wounded? Does anyone know where they are? How they feel? How many arms, legs, ears, noses, mouths, faces, penises they've lost? How many are deaf or dumb or blind or all three? How many are single or double or triple or quadruple amputees? How many will remain immobile for the rest of their days?... The Library of Congress reports that the Army Office of the Surgeon General for Medical Statistics "Does not have figures on single or multiple amputees." ...in the words of a researcher for one of the national television networks "the military itself, while sure of how many tons of bombs it has dropped, is unsure of how many legs and arms its men have lost."

Dalton Trumbo
addendum to Introduction—1970
Johnny Got His Gun

Vietnam has given us eight times as many paralytics as World War II, three times as many totally disabled, 35% more amputees...But exactly how many hundreds or thousands of the dead-while-living does that give us? We don't know. We don't ask. We turn away from them. We avert the eyes, ears, nose, mouth, face. "Why should I look, it wasn't my fault was it?" It was, of course, but no matter.

Dalton Trumbo
addendum to Introduction—1970
Johnny Got His Gun

When we pay our army and navy estimates, let us set down—so much for killing, so much for maiming, so much for making widows and orphans....We shall by this means know what we have paid our money for.

Anna Laetitia Barbauld, 1739

...All right, so we don't buy war as a concept. It's worse—we buy it in reality. On April 15 we all sent in our tax dollars— "Here," we said to our administration, "spend it wisely for me—go to the market and purchase what I need to make my life better." But we didn't give them a marketing list. And so those busy little budgeters put their heads together. And here we go again. Sixty-five cents out of every dollar for war—past, present, and future. Sixty-five cents out of every dollar for death and destruction.

Bess Myerson
You Don't Have to Buy War, Mrs. Smith
Mothers Day, 1970

Leftist extremist groups say they're using terror for the liberation of the people. But with terror you liberate nothing. State terrorists say they're practicing terrorism because their backs are to the wall—they've been forced into this "dirty war," and they're only using the same methods to defend what they call "Western Christian civilization." But they're not defending a thing! They're defending themselves and their shabby little interests, that's all. They're not defending the dignity of the human person. They're not defending the people.

Adolfo Pérez Esquivel
1980 Nobel Peace Prize
Christ in a Poncho

Terrorism is a label applied to certain criminal acts when the state doesn't like the criminal's politics.

Martin Oppenheimer

The issue is not one of good versus evil as Reagan would have it, but of violence versus nonviolence. On this score, the President has no moral standing to judge others, for he has bloodied his hands in Nicaragua, Lebanon, Grenada, and El Salvador. His proposed solution to stop terrorism by escalating state violence will only water the roots of terrorism.

The Progressive
Editorial—August 1985

Violence now is mainly organized and governmental.

Bertrand Russell

We often arrogantly feel that we have some divine messianic mission to police the whole world; we are arrogant in not allowing young nations to go through the same growing pains, turbulence and revolution that characterized our history. Our arrogance can be our doom.

Martin Luther King, Jr.
March 1967

This peace loving nation has members of its armed forces stationed in 135 countries around the world—more than 100 troops in each of 25 countries. **Pentagon figures**

If democracy is so good, why do we have to go to other countries and try to jam it down their throats with a gun? Stay here and make democracy work. If it's good you don't have to force it on others, they'll steal it.

Dick Gregory

...the idea that honor is flung away in peace, and retained in war, we would point out that inevitably the price of war includes honor....Democracy cannot co-exist with militarism.

Tracy D. Mygatt

You can't defend freedom; you must extend it.

James Bevel

* Even in the public military service, or warlike expeditions by national authority, the law manifestly requires the soldier to think for himself, to consider before he acts in any war, whether the same be just, for, if it be otherwise, the Common Law of the kingdom will impute to him guilty of murder.

Granville Sharp, 1773

* According to the Biblical narrative Adam sinned against God, and then said that his wife told him to eat the apple, while his wife said she was tempted by the devil. God exonerated neither Adam nor Eve, but told them that because Adam listened to the voice of his wife he would be punished, and that his wife would be punished for listening to the serpent. And neither was excused, but both were punished. Will not God say the same to you also when you kill a man and say that your captain ordered you to do it?

Leo Tolstoy

* And no action is more opposed to the will of God than that of killing men. And therefore you cannot obey men if they order you to kill. If you obey, and kill, you do so only for the sake of your own advantage—to escape punishment. So that in killing by order of your commander you are a murderer as much as the thief who kills a rich man to rob him. He is tempted by money, and you by the desire not to be punished, or to receive a reward. Man is always responsible before God for his actions.

Leo Tolstoy

* Shameful is the position of the prostitute who is always ready to give her body to be defiled by any one her master indicates; but yet more shameful is the pcsition of a soldier always ready for the greatest of crimes—the murder of any man whom his commander indicates.... And therefore if you do indeed desire to act according to God's will you have only to do one thing—to throw off the shameful and ungodly calling of a soldier, and be ready to bear any sufferings which may be inflicted upon you for so doing.

Leo Tolstoy

What makes this inquest significant is that these prisoners represent sinister influences that will lurk in the world long after their bodies are returned to dust. They are living symbols of racial hatreds, of terrorism and violence, and of the arrogance and cruelty of power. They are symbols of fierce nationalisms and of militarism.

Nuremberg Trials for Nazi leaders

* Crimes against international law are committed by men, not by abstract entities such as states, and only by punishing individuals who commit such crimes can the provisions of international law be enforced.

That a soldier was ordered to kill or torture in violation of the international law of war has never been recognized as a defense for such acts of brutality....The true test, which is found in varying degrees in the criminal law of most nations, is not the existence of the order, but whether moral choice was in fact possible.

Nuremberg Tribunal judgment

* Hitler could not make aggressive war by himself. He had to have the cooperation of statesmen, military leaders, diplomats, and businessmen. When they, with knowledge of his aims, gave him their cooperation, they made themselves parties to the plan he had initiated....

To initiate a war of aggression is...not only an international crime; it is the supreme international crime....

Nuremberg Tribunal judgment

ADDITIONS:

2
Facts of the Arms Race

For a deterrence to Russia...we need enough nuclear power to kill 1/4–1/2 of its population and destroy 1/5–1/4 of its industry. That would take 400 nuclear bombs. We have over 30,000.

1968 study commissioned by Robert McNamara
Secretary of Defense

There are now more than 50,000 nuclear weapons, more than 13,000 megatons of yield, deployed in the arsenals of the United States and the Soviet Union—enough to obliterate a million Hiroshimas. But there are fewer than 3000 cities on the Earth with populations of 100,000 or more. You cannot find anything like a million Hiroshimas to obliterate.

Carl Sagan
The Nuclear Winter

The essential fact remains that neither of the two superpowers can attack the other without signing its own death warrant. The Americans have at their disposal 40 nuclear warheads for each Soviet city of 100,000 and above. By comparison, the Soviets only have 15. But only one warhead is sufficient to do the job. That is why the two superpowers are more partners than they are adversaries. And that is why Europe is alarmed about a *de facto* equilibrium in which European territory is a possible theatre of nuclear operations without jeopardizing the homeland "sanctuary" of its protector.

General George Buis
former French Army Chief of Staff

The explosive power of nuclear weapons equals three tons of TNT for every individual in the world.

Jan Martenson
Under Secretary-General
Department of Disarmament Affairs, UN

The total firepower of World War II was three megatons. Today we have 18,000 megatons or the firepower of 6,000 World War IIs. The United States and the Soviets share this firepower with approximately equal destructive capability.

Freeze It!
A Citizen's Guide to Reversing the Nuclear Arms Race

There are nuclear devices so powerful that the explosive power of one is more than has been used since the invention of gunpowder.

Jan Martenson
Under Secretary-General
Department of Disarmament Affairs, UN

A so-called "limited" nuclear war could kill 22.7 million Americans, more than 20 times the total number of American dead and wounded in

World War II and 10 times the total American dead and wounded in all the wars in our nation's history.

Jerry Elmer
American Friends Service Committee

One modern submarine equipped with nuclear missiles can carry more explosive power than was used during World War II.

Jan Martenson
Under Secretary-General
Department of Disarmament Affairs, UN

...just two U.S. Poseidon submarines which carry 320 nuclear weapons can destroy all the 200 major Soviet cities with the destructive potential of 1,000 Hiroshima-size weapons.

Rear Admiral Gene R. La Rocque
U.S. Navy (retired)

If the nation continues with its current nuclear retaliation policy, ELF is not needed because of the nature of submarine communications. Under a first strike policy, it is essential.

Gene R. La Rocque

Together, Project ELF and the Trident Fleet will transform the U.S. submarine force from a deterrence posture, into the ultimate first-strike weapon system.

Robert C. Aldridge
former design engineer for Trident missile system

[The D-5 (Trident II Missile) would give the United States] pre- emptive capability. [The missile would have the] yield and accuracy to go after very hard targets [such as missile silos, which are heavily protected.]

Dr. Richard DeLauer
Under Secretary of Defense for Engineering
October 1981

Trident submarines:
...can carry up to 408 super-accurate Trident II warheads on each sub with each warhead having *five* times the explosive power of the bombs we dropped on Japan.
...have a range of 4,000 miles.
...cost $1.5 billion a piece, without its missiles.
Our country is planning to build over twenty Trident submarines.

ELF, Trident and You

The capacity to destroy 408 different cities or targets is a lot of death and destruction to put under the control of one submarine commander.

Robert C. Aldridge

MX Missiles:
...an ICBM (intercontinental ballistic missile) called "MX" (for "Missile Experimental.")
...71 feet long, 7 1/2 feet in diameter.
...carry ten Mark 12-A warheads of about 350 kilotons apiece. (The Hiroshima bomb was 12.5 kilotons.)
...100 meter accuracy.
...a counterforce weapon to attack missile silos and other hardened targets in the Soviet Union. (A counterforce capability has no practical value except in a first strike—MX warheads would fall on empty silos unless used first.)
...originally planned to be mobile on tracks. Now to replace old missiles in silos.

American Friends Service Committee

Nuclear tipped missiles place all of us but 30 minutes from Armageddon—tonight, every night, every hour of every day. There is no spot on earth assured of safety from obliteration. The maximum warning time is measured in minutes.

Dwight D. Eisenhower

The people of Hiroshima are separated from us by 40 years and half the world. They are still dying from the effects of that "small" bomb. Each cruise missile is 15 times as lethal as the bomb that was dropped on Hiroshima.

Alice Cook and Gwyn Kirk
Greenham Women Everywhere

Cruise missiles:
...small, pilotless, subsonic surface-to-surface missiles designed to fly under Soviet radar.
...are about 21 feet long.
...travel at 550 m.p.h. with a range of 1,500 miles and accuracy within 100–300 feet.
...have warheads in the 10–50 kiloton range.
...are not verifiable.

Greenham Women Everywhere

Pershing II missiles:
...are a two stage, mobile, surface-to-surface, ballistic missile.
...are 33 feet long.
...have a range of 1,130 miles and accuracy within 65–130 feet.
...carry one airburst/surface burst 10–20 kiloton warhead.

Defense Monitor
1983

The 1,000 mile flight from a base in West Germany to Moscow would reportedly take the Pershing II missile 6 minutes.

Mark Hatfield
Senator, Oregon

During a 10-month period, North American Defense Command had 151 false alarms due to mechanical and human errors which could have resulted in a nuclear catastrophe.

Dr. James Muller

The Soviet Union has said they will put their missile system on launch-on-warning of attack. Experts say Soviet computers are 5 years behind ours.

Anonymous

Space weapons would create a situation in which any satellite malfunction could be misinterpreted as the beginning of war. As satellites become more complex and their numbers increase, malfunctions will continue to occur. And as the amount of "space trash" increases, so does the likelihood of a random object hitting a satellite—and the likelihood of miscalculation and catastrophe.

Union of Concerned Scientists, 1983

The President wants Americans to believe that space weapons will "shelter" the entire population of the United States from nuclear attack...despite the fact that the government's own scientific studies show that unless these weapons are 95% effective (an inconceivably high level of performance), a minimum of 100 million Americans will die instantly in a blazing firestorm in the event of all-out nuclear war.

Dr. Benjamin Spock

...an effective defense of our population is technologically unattainable because it can be so easily countered by the Soviets. In addition, any [space based] Ballistic Missile Defense (BMD) systems can be outflanked by using low-flying cruise missiles and short-range, submarine-launched weapons. Thus, it will encourage the construction of more offensive weapons, not less, and bring a new escalation of the arms race.

Union of Concerned Scientists

The projected cost of the BMD system is astounding. The Reagan Administration has asked Congress for twenty-five billion dollars merely to demonstrate the feasibility of the technology over the first five years. The total cost to develop and deploy the system has been estimated at half a trillion.

Union of Concerned Scientists

...such development [BMD] would require the United States to violate or to repudiate the 1972 Anti-Ballistic Missile Treaty. This would be the first such "abrogation" of an arms treaty by a superpower since the dawn of the nuclear age.

Union of Concerned Scientists

It is particularly important that [Star Wars] research be carried out in a manner fully consistent with the ABM Treaty. To ignore such treaty restraints would encourage Soviet disregard for it on a scale that would dwarf our current concerns about their compliance.

Elliot L. Richardson
former Secretary of Defense

There are those who would seek to raise false alarms—by saying for example, that the Soviet Union has more ships than we do. But the fact is, you do not compare numbers. You compare total firepower, you compare tonnage and combat capability—and you find we are on top.

Gerald Ford

There is too much pessimism about our current capability. I would not swap our present military capability with that of the Soviet Union, nor would I want to trade the broader problems each country faces.

General David Jones
Chairman, Joint Chiefs of Staff
February 1979

By most relevant measures, we remain the military equal or superior to the Soviet Union.

Harold Brown
former Secretary of Defense
February 1980

It is naive to believe that the Russians will play by our rules any more than we will accept theirs. It is naive to believe that they—any more than we—would willingly accept a position of second best in military strength.

Cyrus Vance
former Secretary of State
June 1980

In the central region of Europe, a rough numerical balance exists between the immediately available non-nuclear forces of NATO (including France) and those of the Warsaw Pact.

Harold Brown
former Secretary of Defense
January 1980

I can confirm in all responsibility that a rough parity in strategic nuclear arms, medium-range nuclear weapons, and conventional armaments exists between the Soviet Union and the United States, and between the Warsaw Treaty and NATO.

Dmitri Ustinov
former Defense Minister, USSR
November 1981

What's the difference whether we have 100 nuclear submarines or 200? I don't see what difference it makes. You can sink everything on the ocean several times over with the number we have and so can they.

Admiral Hyman G. Rickover
January 1982

The United States is the dominant military and economic power not only in that [Pacific] theater but also in every other theater in the world.

Admiral Robert Long
Commander in Chief U.S. Forces, Pacific
March 1982

The Soviets do not have, in my judgement, anything like strategic superiority in the sense of a militarily or politically usable advantage in strategic nuclear forces.

Harold Brown
former Defense Secretary
April 1982

Not in one single nuclear weapons category have the Soviets demonstrated technological superiority. We have more strategic nuclear weapons than the Soviet Union. But you never hear this because the myth of U.S. inferiority is being spread to try and panic the public.

Herbert Scoville
former Deputy Director for Research, CIA

On balance the Soviet Union does have a definite margin of superiority—enough so that there is a risk and there is what I have called, as you know several times, a window of vulnerability....the Soviet's great edge is one in which they could absorb our retaliatory blow and hit us again.

Ronald Reagan
March 1982

[When asked by Senator Charles Percy: "Would you rather have at your disposal the U.S. nuclear arsenal or the Soviet nuclear arsenal?"] I would not for a moment exchange anything, because we have an immense edge in technology.

Caspar Weinberger
Secretary of Defense, April 1982

The United States and the Soviet Union are roughly equal in strategic nuclear power.

Department of Defense
Annual Report, 1982

...we must remember that it has been we Americans who, at almost every step of the road, have taken the lead in the development of [nuclear] weaponry. It was we who first produced and tested such a device; we who were the first to raise its destructiveness to a new level with the hydrogen bomb; we who introduced the multiple warhead; we who have declined every proposal for the renunciation of the principle of "first use"; and we alone, so help us God, who have used the weapon in anger against others, and against tens of thousands of helpless noncombatants at that.

George Kennan
former US Ambassador to the USSR

About 30 countries have already begun installing nuclear reactors. In twenty years, 100 countries will possess the raw materials and the knowledge to produce nuclear weapons...a threat to the very existence of all nations.

Committee for Economic Development
***Nuclear Energy and National Security*, 1976**

Where military spending is concerned, billions of dollars are treated like loose pocket change—$226 billion in the defense budget for fiscal 1982, more than double the entire GNP of India. To portray graphically how much a billion dollars is, a billion one-dollar bills placed end to end would stretch from here to the moon—and back!... The Administration's blueprint for military spending calls for a total of $1.3– $1.5 *trillion* over the next five years. To reach $1.5 trillion we would have to stack up 15 piles of $1000 bills, each pile as tall as Mt. Everest, the world's tallest mountain.

Professor Robert Lee
***The Christian Century*, November 1981**

If one spent $1 million a day for 2000 years it would equal one-half of the Reagan Administration's proposed defense budget of 1.5 trillion for 1983 to 1988.

Anonymous

(Facts on military expenditures versus human needs can be found in Chapter 7—**Violence of Unused Weapons**—page 61.)

3
Mentality
of the Arms Race

* Someday science may have the existence of mankind in its power and the human race commit suicide by blowing up the world.

Henry Adams, 1862

We have now reached the age of unlimited power predicted nearly a century ago by Henry Adams: but we have neglected to heed his warning about the "effect of unlimited power on limited minds," and this farsighted anticipation of the madness of a nuclear arms race.

Sydney J. Harris
***Detroit Free Press*, April 1984**

* The greatest danger is the danger created by inventing weapons capable of destroying civilization faster than we produce men who can be trusted to use them wisely.

George Bernard Shaw

* We have guided missiles and misguided men.

Martin Luther King

We have grasped the mystery of the atom and rejected the Sermon on the Mount. Ours is a world of nuclear giants and ethical infants. We know more about war than we do about peace—more about killing than we do about living.

General Omar Bradley

We have made a great advance in technology without a corresponding advance in moral sense. We are capable of unbinding the forces which lie at the heart of creation and of destroying our civilization.

Archbishop of Canterbury
Anglican (Episcopal) Church, 1981

I should like to invent a substance or a machine with such terrible power of mass destruction that war would thereby be made impossible for ever.

Alfred Nobel

Perhaps my dynamite plants will put an end to war sooner than your [peace] congresses. On the day two army corps can annihilate each other in one second all civilized nations will recoil from war in horror.

Alfred Nobel

Once a weapon has been developed…it will be used.

Kurt Waldheim
Secretary-General, United Nations

I voiced to [Secretary of War Stimson] my grave misgivings...on the basis of my belief that Japan was already defeated and dropping the bomb was completely unnecessary...as a measure to save American lives.

Dwight D. Eisenhower

It is my opinion that the use of this barbarous weapon at Hiroshima and Nagasaki was of no material assistance in our war against Japan. The Japanese were already defeated and ready to surrender because of the effective sea blockade and the successful bombing with conventional weapons.

It was my reaction that the scientists and others wanted to make this test because of the vast sums that had been spent on the project.... My own feeling is that in being the first to use it, we had adopted an ethical standard common to the barbarians of the dark ages. I was not taught to make war in that fashion, and wars cannot be won by destroying women and children.

Admiral William D. Leahy
Chief of Staff under F.D.R. and Harry Truman

I confess that I cannot understand how we can plot, lie, cheat and commit murder abroad and remain humane, honorable, trustworthy and trusted at home.

Archibald Cox

* A poet can write about a man slaying the dragon, but not about a man pushing a button that releases a bomb.

W. H. Auden

In the thirty-six years since the atomic bombings of Hiroshima and Nagasaki, a new language has evolved....Nukespeak is the language of nuclear development....atrocities are rendered invisible by sterile words like "megadeaths," nuclear war is called a "nuclear exchange." Nuclear weapons accidents are called "broken arrows" and "bent spears." Plutonium is called a "potential nuclear explosive." The accident at Three Mile Island was called an "event," an "incident"...and a "normal aberration."...India called its nuclear bomb a "peaceful nuclear device."

Nukespeak: The Selling of Nuclear Technology in America

The nuclear arms race has nothing to do with defense, little to do with deterrence, and everything to do with a monopoly of U.S. intervention in other countries while blocking Soviet intervention.

Randall Forsberg

...the arms race is a system based on faith...faith that human nature works in the way that deterrence theorists say it does, faith that deterrence itself should be credited with preventing war, and faith that if deterrence prevented war in one generation then it can prevent war in the next despite radically changed technological and political circumstances.

Richard J. Barnet

Deterrence is like the old story of the man who fell off the skyscraper and shouted, as he plummeted past the tenth floor, "I'm doing all right so far."

Ed Snyder
Executive Secretary
Friends Committee on National Legislation

Europe's reluctance to have medium-range missiles on its soil results more than anything else from a growing suspicion—reinforced by careless White House utterances—that the Reagan Administration regards those missiles not as instruments of deterrence but as instruments of war.

George W. Ball
former Undersecretary of State

United States policy under seven presidents has never renounced the first use of nuclear weapons.

Melvin Price
Chairperson
House Armed Services Committee

From Secretaries of Defense...

...our basic defense policy is based on the use of atomic weapons in a major war and is based on the use of such atomic weapons as would be militarily feasible and usable in a smaller war, if such a war is forced upon us.

Charles Wilson
Secretary of Defense
1958

It would be our policy to use nuclear weapons wherever we felt it necessary to protect our forces and achieve our objectives.

Robert McNamara
Secretary of Defense
1961

If there were any hint from the U.S. government that we were to accept the blandishments of a few people in the arms control community or a few people on Capitol Hill that we would refrain from first use, that would have a devastating effect on NATO because NATO depends, in large degree, psychologically as well as in terms of force structure, on nuclear reinforcement of conventional capabilities, should that be necessary.

James R. Schlesinger
Secretary of Defense
1975

The United States has never ruled out a first use of nuclear weapons. If an enemy, whether by stealth and deception or by large-scale mobilization, should attempt to defeat U.S. and allied conventional forces, it is NATO and U.S. policy to take whatever action is necessary to restore the situation.... Accordingly, to the extent that a nuclear response may be required locally, theater nuclear forces have an indispensable function to perform in defense and deterrence.

Donald Rumsfeld
Secretary of Defense
1977

It is essential that we maintain the capability at all times to inflict an unacceptable level of damage on the Soviet Union, including destruction of a minimum of 200 major Soviet cities.

Harold Brown
Secretary of Defense
1978

When it comes to strategic thermonuclear war, I don't think there is such a thing as a number one or number two. In exchanging strategic nuclear weapons, the damage to both parties would be so great that there is no winner, and therefore no such thing as number one and number two.

Harold Brown
Secretary of Defense
1978

I think we need to have a counterforce capability. Over and above that, I think that we need to have a war-fighting capability.

Frank Carlucci
Deputy Secretary of Defense
1981

If conventional means are insufficient to ensure a satisfactory termination of war, the U.S. will prepare options for the use of nuclear weapons.

Department of Defense Guidance
1982

No matter what their original intent may have been, I cannot believe that any atomic power would accept defeat while withholding its best weapon....So eventually, even though it starts out to be nonatomic war, war between atomic powers, it seems to me, will inevitably be atomic war.

Donald A. Quarles
Secretary of the Air Force

The first use of U.S. tactical nuclear weapons would probably be in a defensive mode based on prepared defense plans. Later use could include nuclear support for offensive operations to destroy the enemy or regain lost territory.

Department of the Army
Operations Field Manual 100-5
1976

I have no faith in the so-called controlled use of atomic weapons. There is no dependable distinction between tactical and strategic situations. I would not recommend the use of any atomic weapon, no matter how small, when both sides have the power to destroy the world.

Admiral Charles R. Brown

[Regarding limited nuclear war remaining limited]: You could have a pessimistic outlook on it or an optimistic. I always tend to be optimistic.

Ronald Reagan
Boston Globe
November 1981

The image of an American president carefully and calmly discussing over the Hotline the "limited" nature of an American nuclear attack in progress with the leaders of the Kremlin would be comical if it were not so tragic.

Jerry Elmer
American Friends Service Committee

The Administration's belief that it can control its forces throughout a prolonged nuclear war is naive at best, foolhardy and dangerous at worst.

Defense Monitor
1983

Limiting nuclear war is like limiting the mission of a match thrown in a keg of gunpowder.

John Culver
former Senator, Iowa

Europeans, of course, ask themselves, "limited to what?" and the answer is clear: limited to Europe.

Dorothee Sölle
German theologian

Any use of nuclear weapons would run the risk of rapid escalation...

Harold Brown
former Secretary of Defense

We [scientists] know with the certainty of established truth, that if enough of these weapons are made by enough different states, some of them are going to blow up—through accident or folly or madness.

C. P. Snow
English physicist

Modern history offers no example of the cultivation by rival powers of armed force on a massive scale which did not end in an outbreak of hostilities.

George Kennan
former US Ambassador to the USSR

Some have said that the Soviet Union has already achieved superiority over the US. The truth is that we are second to none. The impulse and the passion for military superiority must be seen for what they are: unrealistic, simplistic, dangerous.

Harold Brown
former Secretary of Defense

* What difference does it make whether someone's first or sixth or ninth if he can destroy another nation eight or ten times over? Whether you're first or second is irrelevant, isn't it?   **Paul Newman**

The arms race is like two kids standing in a room full of gasoline up to their knees. Both are collecting matches and thinking that the more matches they collect, the more secure they will be.   **Anonymous**

The nuclear arms race is the strangest military competition in history. Before the nuclear age a nation could calculate its killing power, measure it against that of its enemy, and make a rational judgement whether to go to war.... But such a judgment is impossible in the world of the atomic bomb because there is no objective that is worth the destruction of your own society, and the risks of such destruction in what modern-day strategists blandly call a "nuclear exchange" are very great.

Richard J. Barnet

When I think of the ever escalating nuclear arms race, I think of alcoholics, who know that liquor is deadly, and who, nevertheless, can always find one more reason for one more drink.

William Sloane Coffin

Even the term "arms race" is misleading. It implies that the side with the most weapons will be the winner.

Parents and Teachers for Social Responsibility

Whoever does not understand that the danger lies not in the possibility that someone else might have more missiles and warheads than we do, but in the very existence of these unconscionable quantities of highly poisonous explosives, and their existence, above all, in hands as weak and shaky and undependable as those of ourselves or our adversaries or any other mere human beings; whoever does not understand these things is never going to guide us out of this increasingly dark and menacing forest of bewilderment into which we have all wandered.

George Kennan
former US Ambassador to the USSR
Albert Einstein Peace Prize recipient
1981

For if reality is not something we can fully understand, and if we can make errors, we must be certain we are not carrying hydrogen bombs when we stumble and bump into unexpected events.

David McReynolds

The simplest meaning of the nuclear arms race is that the world's most powerful nations are prepared to commit mass murder.

Jim Wallis
Sojourners

...we are rapidly getting to the point that no war can be *won*. War implies a contest; when you get to the point that contest is no longer involved and the outlook comes close to destruction of the enemy and suicide for ourselves—an outlook that neither side can ignore—then arguments as to the exact amount of available strength as compared to somebody else's are no longer the vital issues.

Dwight D. Eisenhower
April 1956

In the past, war has been accepted as the ultimate arbiter of disputes among nations. But in the nuclear era we can no longer think of war as merely a continuation of diplomacy by other means. Nuclear war cannot be measured by the archaic standards of victory and defeat.

Jimmy Carter

The danger of nuclear war lies largely within us. It lies in how we think about winning, in how we define success, and in our illusions of being able to impose results.

Roger Fisher

In a nuclear war there are no winners or losers. It's not like conventional war where armies fight, one side wins, the other loses and everybody goes home. Nuclear war is a mutual unleashing of genocidal forces...

Dr. Robert Jay Lifton
Yale University Medical School

We are quite literally a nation which is in the process of committing suicide in the hope that then the Russians will not be able to murder it.

Dorothy Day

War has become a Frankenstein to destroy both sides. No longer does it possess the chance of the winner of the duel—it contains rather the germ of double suicide.

General Douglas MacArthur
July 1961

The war planning process of the past has become totally obsolete. Attack is now suicide.

Thomas J. Watson, Jr.
President, IBM

The most monumental, dangerous illusion of our time is the belief that any nation can win an all-out war.

John Culver
former Senator, Iowa

...it is contrary to reason to hold that war is now a suitable way to restore rights that have been violated.

Pope John XXIII

Nuclear war is not a solution. It is worse than any problem it might "solve."

Roger Fisher
Professor of Law, Harvard

* It's very difficult and somewhat embarrassing for military men to accept the fact that we have no defense against Soviet missiles and that the Soviets have no defense against our missiles. We can destroy the Soviet Union even though they destroy us first. There are no *winners* in a nuclear war.

Rear Admiral Gene R. La Rocque
U.S. Navy (retired)

* The guy in the street is the smart guy, he knows you can't fight and win a nuclear war. It's only the generals who are brought up to fight who think you can survive.

Dr. Herbert Scoville, Jr.
former Deputy Director for Research
CIA

...will the Soviet Union and the U.S. destroy civilization to ensure that their economic system and their political philosophy dominate the world? The answer is clear. Both the United States and the Soviet Union are planning, training, arming, and practicing to destroy each other and all civilization. Neither side expects to win. Neither side can avoid losing.

**Rear Admiral Gene R. La Rocque
U.S. Navy (retired)
June 1983**

Within a month [in 1969] I had met the first of a small but not uninfluential community of people who violently opposed SALT for a simple reason: It might keep America from developing a first-strike capability against the Soviet Union. I'll never forget being lectured by an Air Force colonel about how we should have "nuked" the Soviets in the late 1940s before they got The Bomb. I was told that if SALT would go away, we'd soon have the capability to nuke them again—and this time we'd use it.

**Roger Molander
former nuclear strategist for
the White House's National Security Council
March 1982**

Sometime later in this decade, military plans which are being seriously discussed now by the military establishments on both sides would lead to...an immediate exchange...in a nuclear war of something between 10,000 and 20,000 megatons each...

**Dr. Bernard Feld
Professor, MIT**

Depending on certain assumptions, some estimates predict 10 million casualties on one side and 100 million on the other. But that is not the whole population.

**Eugene Rostow
former Chief U.S. Arms Negotiator**

The dangers of atomic war are overrated. It would be hard on little concentrated countries like England. In the United States we have lots of space.

Colonel Robert Rutherford McCormick

With greatly increased offensive and defensive preparations the United States could hold casualties in a nuclear war to 20 million, a level compatible with survival and recovery.

**Colin Gray
State Department Consultant**

A nuclear war could alleviate some of the factors leading to today's ecological disturbances that are due to current high-population concentrations and heavy industrial production.

U.S. Office of Civil Defense Official

To plan for nuclear wars in which tens of millions would die is to say that crimes against humanity are justifiable in the interests of national security.

Wes Michaelson
Sojourners
February 1977

We are dragging heaven into hell. Our nation and the Soviet Union are turning the vast reach of space into a battlefield for new and terrifying machines of destruction.

Union of Concerned Scientists

We will be doing in space all that we are doing in the atmosphere, on the ground and at sea. We are preparing to wage wars and to win them.

Major General John H. Starrie
U.S. Air Force Director for Space Affairs
speech to a House committee, 1983

We need not strain our imagination to see that the nation controlling space will also be the one controlling the world.

Edward Aldridge
Pentagon Undersecretary

I clearly recognize that defensive systems have limitations and raise certain problems and ambiguities. If paired with offensive systems, they can be viewed as fostering an aggressive policy.

Ronald Reagan
March 1983

I don't know of any country that has gotten into war by being too strong, unless it was an aggressive nation.

Ronald Reagan

The President says he is absolutely convinced that "Star Wars" will work...despite the fact that hundreds of today's most brilliant scientists have condemned proposals for a space-based weapons system as "illusions," "fantasies," and "totally science fiction."

Union of Concerned Scientists

The atomic bomb is a marvelous gift that was given to us by a wise God.

Phyllis Schlafly

People who believe absurdities will commit atrocities.

Anonymous

In the real world of real political leaders—whether here or in the Soviet Union—a decision that would bring even one hydrogen bomb on one city of one's own country would be recognized in advance as a catastrophic blunder; ten bombs on ten cities would be a disaster beyond history; and a hundred bombs on one hundred cities are unthinkable.

McGeorge Bundy
Advisor to President Kennedy

Nothing in human history is more obscene than the cool discussions of competing nuclear strategies by apocalyptic game-players. All sorts of scenarios are being put forward about the circumstances under which we would drop bombs on the Soviet Union and the Soviet Union would drop bombs on us, as though both countries were involved in nothing more than a super backgammon game. The strategists in both countries need to be reminded that they are not playing with poker chips but with human lives and the whole of the human future.

Norman Cousins
Saturday Review
December 1981

The unfortunate situation is that today we are moving—sliding down hill—toward the probability or the likelihood that a nuclear conflict will actually break out—and that somebody will use one of these nuclear weapons in a conflict or perhaps even by accident.

Herbert Scoville, Jr.
former Deputy Director for Research, CIA

Missiles will bring anti-missiles, and anti-missiles will bring anti-anti-missiles. But inevitably, this whole electronic house of cards will reach a point where it can be constructed no higher.

General Omar Bradley
November 1957

* We have gone on piling weapon upon weapon, missile upon missile, new levels of destructiveness upon old ones, helplessly, almost involuntarily, like victims of some sort of hypnotism, like men in a dream, like lemmings heading for the sea.

George Kennan
former US Ambassador to the USSR

However useless a defense concept, an argument to proceed is deemed conclusive on one of two grounds. Either the Russians are doing it and therefore we must do it in order to avoid falling behind, or the Russians are not doing it and therefore we must in order to stay ahead.

Patricia Schroeder
Congressperson, Colorado

The strongest argument in behalf of massive military spending is that the other side is spending at least as much or more. No one stops to inquire whether the other side may be spending its money wisely or whether, indeed, our own spending has anything to do with genuine safety. It is almost as though we can preserve our "manhood" only by superior foolishness.

Norman Cousins

Why then do the superpowers persist in the arms race?

The arms race has been self-propelling. Around the country thousands of scientists and engineers are developing weapons to counter weapons the Russians are expected to have eight to ten years from now. These people have a strong stake in continuing the arms race. So too have the Pentagon and the 22,000 prime contractors and 100,000 subcontractors who grow rich from military procurement. Others with an economic stake include the leadership of many unions whose members look to jobs from military production; academia which looks to research and development funds; the mayors and newspaper editors of cities who want defense contracts for investment in their areas; the "think tanks" that are paid large sums to devise a rationale for the arms race. Cementing together this military-industrial complex is the deliberately implanted thesis that "you cannot trust the Russians."

Sid Lens
"Launching the Arms Race"—*Mobilizer*, 1985

Defense contractors and their lobbyists argue that competition for defense business is an effective check on excessive profits.... But in fact there is little competition in defense work. Except for some common items such as food and clothing, most defense procurement is placed on a noncompetitive basis. Few firms can muster the financial, engineering, and manufacturing resources to perform multimillion-dollar defense contracts.... In fiscal year 1978 only about 8% of these contracts were awarded on a formally advertized, truly competitive basis.... The remaining 92% were either sole-source procurement or competitive-negotiated, where only a few firms can perform the work...

Admiral Hyman G. Rickover
March 1977

This conjunction of an immense military establishment and a large arms industry is new in the American experience.... We recognize the imperative need for this development. Yet we must not fail to comprehend its grave implications.... In the councils of government, we must guard against the acquisition of unwarranted influence, whether sought or unsought, by the military-industrial complex. The potential for the disastrous rise of misplaced power exists and will persist.

Dwight D. Eisenhower

We must admit that we are intoxicated with our science and technology (and) deeply committed to a Faustian bargain which is rapidly killing us spiritually and will soon kill us all physically.

Joseph Weizenbaum, MIT

You cannot simultaneously prevent and prepare for war.
Albert Einstein

There is an old Roman proverb that says: "If you would wish for peace, then prepare for war." *Rubbish!* If you would wish for peace, then offer alternatives to war!
Barbara Ward

The way to prevent war is to bend every energy towards preventing it, not to proceed by the dubious indirection of preparing for it.
Max Lerner

Arming in order to provide incentive to disarm has usually turned out to resemble growing obese in order to have incentive to diet and reduce. It only produces a fatter arsenal.
Clergy and Laity Concerned

It is quite strange, in fact, that as yet there is no such thing as a science of peace, since the science of war appears to be highly advanced....As a collective human phenomenon, however, even war involves a mystery, for all the people of the earth, who profess to be eager to banish war as the worst of scourges, are nonetheless the very ones who concur in the starting of wars and who willingly support armed combat.
Maria Montessori

* One of the most persistent ambiguities we face is that everybody talks about peace as a goal, but among the wielders of power peace is practically nobody's business. Many men cry "Peace! Peace!" but they refuse to do the things that make for peace.
  The large power blocs talk passionately of pursuing peace while expanding defense budgets that already bulge, enlarging already awesome armies and devising ever more devastating weapons. Call the roll of those who sing the glad tidings of peace and one's ears will be surprised by the responding sounds. The heads of all nations issue clarion calls for peace, yet they come to the peace table accompanied by bands of brigands each bearing unsheathed swords.
Martin Luther King, Jr.
Where Do We Go from Here: Chaos or Community?

It is startling to realize that nuclear war is no longer "unthinkable." It is not uncommon for people today to imagine, fear, even expect war. Few people imagine, anticipate, and expect peace. It is not war but world peace that has become "unthinkable."
Waging Peace
Statement of Purpose

Peace, to many, has become a fighting word.   **Anonymous**

I don't think about it, there's nothing I can do about it.

Classic Nonsequitur

On a global scale, members of the human family are acting like many victims of domestic violence. They appear ready to passively accept their "beating," believing somehow that it is "deserved" or, in any case, that there is no way out.

Waging Peace
Statement of Purpose

My fellow Americans, I am pleased to tell you I just signed legislation which outlaws Russia forever. The bombing begins in five minutes.

Ronald Reagan
August 1984

I was wondering if people really know what war is. It's not like kids— they just fight. We could have a nuclear war and kill off the whole world; it's not just a fist fight.

Anonymous 6th Grader

* My suggestion is quite simple. Put the codes that are needed to fire nuclear weapons in a little capsule, and then implant that capsule right next to the heart of a volunteer. The volunteer would carry with him a big, heavy butcher knife as he accompanied the President. If ever the President wanted to fire nuclear weapons, the only way he could do so would be for him to first, with his own hands, kill one human being. The President says, "George, I'm sorry but tens of millions must die." He has to look at someone and realize what death is—what an innocent death is. Blood on the White House carpet. It's really brought home.

When I suggested this to friends in the Pentagon they said, "My God, that's terrible. Having to kill someone would distort the President's judgement. He might never push the button."

Roger Fisher
co-founder, Harvard Negotiation Project
Evolutionary Blues

A nuclear explosion is many times more powerful than a TNT explosion, and you shouldn't have much trouble recognizing one.... Count the number of seconds between the flash of light and the bang (explosion). If you are in charge or alone, submit this information as an NBC 1 report. Stay calm, check for injury, check your weapon and equipment for damage, check your buddies, and get ready to go on with your mission.

U.S. Army Field Manual
FM 21-41

Dig a hole, cover it with a couple of doors, and then throw three feet of dirt on top. It's the dirt that does it.... Everybody's going to make it if there are enough shovels to go around. Dirt is the thing that protects you from the blast and the radiation—Dirt is just great stuff.

T. K. Jones
Deputy Undersecretary of Defense for Strategic Nuclear Forces
January 1982

Following a nuclear attack on the United States, the U.S. Postal Service plans to distribute Emergency Change of Address Cards.

Executive Order 11490
Federal Emergency Management Agency
1969

You will be allowed three pounds of meat, six eggs, seven pints of milk, four pounds of cereal, and one-half pound of fats and oils per week.

Executive Order 11490
FEMA
1969

Be sure to carry your credit cards, cash, checks, stocks, insurance policies, and will. Every effort will be made to clear trans– nuclear attack checks, including those drawn on destroyed banks. You will be encouraged to buy U.S. Savings Bonds.

Executive Order 11490
FEMA
1969

If the attack happens on July 1, say some people have paid withholding and some people have paid nothing, but you have to forgive and forget on both sides.

Executive Order 11490
FEMA
1969

Dear Mr. President,
    Please tell me how I can be a leader. I heard you are going to save the leaders in the nuclear war. Me and my dog want to be leaders.

Love,
Lisa
P.S. Please make Amy and her dog leaders too.

If we reach, or when we reach, Heaven's scenes, we truly will find it guarded by United States Marines.

Ronald Reagan
June 1985
from the Marine Corps Hymn

...many...have grown tired of just watching as the leaders of the superpowers behave like teenagers playing chicken on the highway to catastrophe.

Ellen Goodman
The Boston Globe
November 1981

...we will no longer be led only by that half of the population whose socialization, through toys, games, values, and expectations, sanctions violence as the final assertion of manhood, synonymous with nationhood.
Wilma Scott Heide

* Every man will fall who, born a man, proudly presumes to be a superman.
Sophocles

[Speaking of males] Of course his attempt to make himself Lord has kept him, in fact, a child.

Barbara Deming
Love Has Been Exploited Labor

Out of our posturing and game-playing comes the growing and dangerous tendency to think of nuclear weapons as political symbols, as message bearers. But we cannot count on them remaining just political symbols. They're becoming all the more deadly and more vulnerable. And that increases the risk that a nuclear war will start out of panic. There is an easier way to send a message—and that is through communication.

Paul Warnke
Chief SALT II Negotiator

Project ELF is not communication. Communication is meeting people, talking with people, working for peace.

Women's Peace Presence

* We profess that we in the "free world" put a special value upon men's lives. This is supposedly precisely what differentiates us from our antagonists. It is in the name of this difference, in fact, that—by a queer logic—we profess our willingness to risk the continued existence of mankind.

Barbara Deming

[National interest] involves making the Soviets an offer for the sake of our nation which they find too attractive to refuse. [National advantage] involves making the Soviets an offer they cannot accept in order to keep or attain an advantage which we desire.

Wisconsin Clergy and Laity Concerned
Newsletter
August 1984

A phenomenon noticeable throughout history regardless of place or period is the pursuit of governments of policies contrary to their own interest.

Barbara W. Tuchman
The March of Folly

"In God We Trust." That is on our coins. We in America pretend to believe that. We do not. We trust only in weapons and bribes and treaties and admonitions—as does our adversary. The old, old history—the history of death.

Taylor Caldwell
The Listener

ADDITIONS:

4
Insanity of Warmaking

We are healthy only to the extent that our ideas are humane.
                                                   Kurt Vonnegut, Jr.

* A psychiatrist found Eichmann "perfectly sane".... Sanity is no longer
a value or an end itself. The "sanity" of modern man is about as useful
to him as the huge bulk and muscles of the dinosaur. If he were a little
less sane, a little more doubtful, a little more aware of his absurdities
and contradictions, perhaps there might be a possibility of survival.
                                                   Thomas Merton

* War has always seemed to me "the ultimate insanity." Violence and war
as the maximum demonstration of man's capacity for inhumanity to man
were against my religious beliefs, my sense of morality, and my common
sense.
                                                   Dag Hammarskjöld

* Have you ever thought that war is a madhouse and that everyone in the
war is a patient? Tell me, how can a normal man get up in the morning
knowing that in an hour or a minute he may no longer be there? How
can he walk through heaps of decomposing corpses and then sit down
at the table and calmly eat a roll? How can he defy nightmare-risks and
then be ashamed of panicking for a moment?
                                                   Oriana Fallaci
                                                   Nothing **and** *So Be It*

We have to have armies! We have to have military power! We
have to have police forces, whether it's police in a great city or
police in an international scale to keep those madmen from taking
over the world and robbing the world of its liberties.
                                                   Billy Graham
                                                   1965

The people of the United States want peace. The people of China
want peace. The people of the Soviet Union want peace. Why
can't we have peace? We don't realize the proliferation of these
weapons and the arms race of $400 billion that we're spending on
arms in the world—insanity, madness!
                                                   Billy Graham, 1979

Soldiers with fingers on nuclear triggers are regularly tested for "sanity."
Sanity in this case is defined as willingness to calmly obey orders. These
orders might include the destruction of cities.
                                                   Anonymous

Thus the greatest anomaly of all in our time is the imitation of madness.
Society has devised a phrase that stifles the moral indignation, paralyzes
the rational intelligence, and produces unreasoning acquiescence. The
phrase is "national security." It is not necessary for those who invoke

this magical phrase to demonstrate exactly how the national security will be served by any of the cataclysmic terrors that now inhabit the arsenals. All that is necessary is to point to the Russians. And, in this world of mirror images, all that is necessary for the Russians is to point to the Americans. The madness is reciprocal, inexorable, inexcusable.

Norman Cousins

The dynamic of the arms race is the manufacture of fear. In the name of shoring up deterrence, proponents of the arms race on one side fuel the fears of those on the other, and then on it goes in a self-perpetuating spiral. The peace movement's target has to be the arms-racers' symbiotic paranoia.

Todd Gitlin

* The arms race is a race with one's own shadow. No matter how fast you go, the other guy's going to keep up with you and stay connected with you; in fact, he's a part of you. He is the projection of yourself—of your dark side. No one will win the arms race, nor will anyone drop out. We can never out-distance the fear of those parts of ourselves that we have projected on others: Americans on Russians, Jews on Arabs, Protestants on Catholics, whites on blacks. Making the bomb the issue and disarmament the goal shields us only briefly from the realization that it is we ourselves—we human beings—that are the source of the danger. We must understand why we are afraid of our "shadow." What is the origin of the fear of the "other," and how can we deal with it? Why do we project on other societies qualities we have within ourselves, and then maintain that they are bad guys and we are the good? They are, of course, doing the same thing with us.

Robert Fuller

If American nuclear power is to support U.S. foreign policy objectives, the United States must possess the ability to wage nuclear war rationally.

Colin S. Gray and Keith Payne
Victory is Possible

We are dealing here with nothing less than the logic of madness...

Robert Jay Lifton and Richard Falk
Indefensible Weapons

This entire preoccupation with nuclear war, which appears to hold most of our government in its grasp, is a form of illness.

George Kennan
former US Ambassador to the USSR

It can be taken as an axiom that if the human race is mad enough to construct the means of its own destruction, it contains within itself the madness to use those means.

David McReynolds

To try to win a war, to set victory as an aim, is pure madness, since total war with nuclear weapons will be fatal to both sides.

B. H. Liddell Hart
Defense or Deterrence, **1962**

We prepare for our extinction in order to insure our survival...

Jonathan Schell
The Fate of the Earth

Shelters are fine except for three things: getting to them, staying in them, and getting out of them. It's a dangerous illusion to tell the American public that shelters will protect them.

Robert Jay Lifton
Professor, Yale University

[Regarding civil defense preparations for nuclear war] When such a fantasy structure becomes fixed, we call it a delusion. This fantasy or delusion is a product not of individual but of social madness. We thus encounter the kind of situation in which individual people who are psychologically "normal" (in the sense of being functional in a given society) can collude in forms of thought structure that are unreal in the extreme...

Robert Jay Lifton
Richard Falk
Indefensible Weapons

The Supreme Trick of mass insanity is that it persuades you that the only abnormal person is the one who refuses to join in the madness of others, the one who tries vainly to resist. **Eugène Ionesco**

The unseen madness is to live life as usual under the threat of nuclear holocaust. **Interhelp**

But there are some things in our social system to which all of us ought to be maladjusted....I never intend to become adjusted to the madness of militarism and the self-defeating method of physical violence.

Martin Luther King, Jr.

...to be unemotional about the end of the earth approaching, is mentally sick. To feel no feelings about it, to be uninvolved is inappropriate, to be psychologically comfortable today, absolutely inappropriate.

Dr. Helen Caldicott
Physicians for Social Responsibility

Lack of emotionalism in discussions about nuclear war is not a sign of reason, but of a sick passivity.

Alice Cook
British Journalist

...the worst insanity is to be totally without anxiety, totally sane.

Thomas Merton

When life itself seems lunatic, who knows where madness lies?...To surrender dreams...this may be madness....Too much sanity may be madness and, the maddest of all, to see life as it is and not as it should be.

Don Quixote in
Man of La Mancha

Where does one go from a world of insanity? Somewhere on the other side of despair.

T. S. Eliot

ADDITIONS:

ADDITIONS:

5
Insecurity of
Nuclear Weapons

As our military strength approaches infinity, our security approaches zero.

Speak Truth to Power
American Friends Service Committee

Our security is the total product of our economic, intellectual, moral, and military strengths.... There is no way in which a country can satisfy the craving for absolute security—but it can easily bankrupt itself, morally and economically, in attempting to reach that illusory goal through arms alone.

Dwight D. Eisenhower

The weakness of the United States is not caused by insufficient arms but by insufficient wisdom. Our judgements are out of balance and out of touch with reality. They lack a feeling for history and principle. They have been angry, impulsive, and irrational—unguided by any sound policy. Its military spending is indiscriminate. It buys fat as well as muscle—insecurity as well as security.

Adlai Stevenson
former Senator, Illinois

Reliance on weapons and brute force for strength has come to a dead end. The road to peace via competition for military superiority has not led to safety but to greater insecurity and danger.

Women's Peace Presence

The biggest threat to our security is the arms race itself.

I. F. Stone

Grownups can't be trusted with guns and bombs.

Cynthia G.
Milwaukee
Age 8
Please Save My World

* ...I doubt that any columnist...is concerning himself with what is the true security problem of the day. That problem is not merely man against man or nation against nation. It is man against war.

Dwight D. Eisenhower
April 1956

There are powerful voices around the world who still give credence to the old Roman concept—if you desire peace, prepare for war. This is absolute nuclear nonsense and I repeat—it is a disastrous misconception to believe that by increasing the total uncertainty one increases one's own certainty.

Lord Mountbatten
August 1979

As a military man who has given half a century of active service I say in all sincerity that the nuclear arms race has no military purpose. Wars cannot be fought with nuclear weapons. Their existence only adds to our perils because of the illusions which they have generated.

Lord Mountbatten
August 1979

The human tragedy reaches its climax in the fact that after all the exertions and sacrifices of hundreds of millions of people…we have still not found peace or security and that we lie in the grip of even worse perils than those we have surmounted.

Winston Churchill

Today there is a growing awareness that the long reliance on violence has now produced a real danger of human extinction.

Anonymous

You do need one thing, security of life. Life is the greatest truth. And now you are being told, "If we build huge nukes, an arsenal and the whole thing, then we will have security." You will have only one security; you will be evaporated. We don't need that.

Yogi Bhajan

There is no presumption more terrifying than that of those who would blow up the world on the basis of their personal judgement of a transient situation.

George F. Kennan
former US Ambassador to the USSR

What's most frightening, however, is that we have not matured beyond this mindless historical game. And we now play this ancient game with what may be the world's last weapon, the ultimate silencer.

Rusty Schweickart
Apollo astronaut

It gets harder for any of us to rest comfortably on a king-sized bed of missiles.

Ellen Goodman
The Boston Globe, **November 1981**

The term "national security" has a built-in contradiction: in the atomic age, no *national* security is possible. Either we have a workable world security system or we have nothing. The efforts of the individual nations to achieve military supremacy or even adequacy are actually competitive and provocative in their effect.

Norman Cousins

We cannot make our end of the boat safer by making the Soviet end more likely to capsize. We cannot improve our security by making nuclear war more likely for them.

Roger Fisher

The global balance of terror, pioneered by the United States and the Soviet Union, holds hostage the citizens of the Earth.

Carl Sagan
Cosmos

Even though the "balance of terror" has been able to avoid the worst and may do so for some time more, to think that the arms race can thus go on indefinitely, without causing a catastrophe, would be a tragic illusion.

Pope Paul VI

...the security of the global community cannot forever rest on a balance of terror.

Jimmy Carter

The worst to be feared and the best to be expected can be simply stated. The *worst* is atomic war. The *best* would be this: a life of perpetual tension; a burden of arms draining the wealth and labor of all peoples; a wasting of strength that defies the American system or the Soviet system or any system to achieve true abundance of happiness for the peoples of this earth.

Dwight D. Eisenhower

Security as the good of a nation is incompatible with the insecurity of the people.

Brazilian Bishops
Christian Exigencies of a Political Order, 37
February 1977

I'm not really sure who is ahead in the arms race and I don't think it really matters. I mean, it doesn't make me happy to think that we're ahead, or sad to think that maybe the Russians are ahead. We both have enough bombs to kill each other, and if someone drops the bomb, no matter who, we all suffer. I would only feel secure if the U.S. got rid of its nuclear bombs.

Debra Britt
Age 15
Our Future at Stake

Dear Astronaut,
    Please take the nuclear bombs to the moon on your next space flight and leave them there.

Your friend,
Rachel L.
Chicago, Age 9
Please Save My World

In a nuclear war, the best defense is not to have an offense.

David Hoffman

This poses a terrible problem, because we at that point, particularly with the MX, would have a clear first-strike capability against their ICBMs, which would be devastating to them. They would have to consider a U.S. first strike whether we think we would do that or not.

General Lew Allen
US Air Force Chief of Staff
Senate Appropriations Committee Hearing
May 1981

From a security point of view we would be in a more dangerous position if both countries had systems which could threaten the other's ICBMs than if the Soviets alone had them. Having a missile which can threaten a major part of the Soviet deterrent is only asking the Soviets to launch a pre-emptive strike or put its missiles on launch on warning.

Herbert Scoville, Jr.
former CIA Deputy Director for Research
March 1982

Every government defends its participation in the arms race as necessary to guard its national security. But this is an illusion. What makes the arms race a global folly is that all countries are now buying greater and greater insecurity at higher and higher costs.

Alva Myrdal
Nobel Peace Prize Winner

The belief that it is possible to achieve security through armaments on a national scale is a disastrous illusion—in the last analysis the peaceful coexistence of peoples is primarily dependent upon mutual trust.

Albert Einstein

One of the questions which we have to ask ourselves as a country is— what in the name of God is strategic superiority? What is the significance of it—politically, militarily, operationally—at these levels of numbers? What do we do with it?

Henry Kissinger
1974

Nuclear superiority does no good.

I. F. Stone

Nuclear superiority is unattainable.

Paul Warnke
former chief SALT II negotiator
October 1980

Neither Communism nor anti-Communism can be built on mountains of human corpses.

Bertrand Russell

Fear at either end of the rifle only tends to pull the trigger.

Ned Richards
Courage in Both Hands

Only when we have alternatives to violence and the threat of violence for settling conflicts will we be truly secure.

Women's Peace Presence

ADDITIONS:

6
Consequences
of Nuclear War

We turned the switch, we saw the flashes, we watched them for about ten minutes—and then we switched everything off and went home. That night I knew that the world was headed for sorrow.

Leo Szilard
experimenting with nuclear fission
March 1939

If I knew then what I know now, I never would have helped to develop the bomb.

George Kistiakowsky
Manhattan Project scientist

In some sort of crude sense which no vulgarity, no humor, no overstatement can quite extinguish, the physicists have known sin; and this is a knowledge which they cannot lose.

J. Robert Oppenheimer
head of Manhattan Project

Updrafts became so violent that sheets of zinc roofing were hurled aloft....Disposing of the dead was a minor problem, but to clean the rooms and corridors of urine, feces, and vomit was impossible....The sight of them was most unbearable. Their faces and hands were burnt and swollen...their flesh was wet and mushy...their ears had melted off....I saw fire reservoirs filled to the brim with dead people who looked as though they had been burned alive...none of the patients had any appetite and were dying so fast I had begun to accept death as a matter of course...bloody diarrhea was increasing...sanitation teams were cremating the remains of people who had been killed. Looking out, I could discern numerous fires about the city....White chips of blistered paint and mortar settled over us like falling cherry blossoms....What a dismal view...the shabby figure of a dog trudging along with his hips bent, tail down, and hair gone.

Dr. Michihiko Hachiya
Hiroshima Diary

When I arrived, some were still alive. They were unable to move their bodies. The strongest were so weak that they were slumped over on the ground. I talked with them and they thought they would be O.K., but all of them would die within a week. I cannot forget the way their eyes looked at me and their voices spoke to me, forever.

Michito Ichimaru

...regaining consciousness, I found myself lying on the ground covered with pieces of wood. When I stood up in a frantic effort to look around, there was darkness. Terribly frightened, I thought I was alone in a world of death, and groped for any light.

Haruko Ogasawara

When the darkness began to fade, I found that there was nothing around me. My house, the next door neighbor's house, and the next had all vanished. I was standing amid the ruins of my house. No one was around. It was quiet, very quiet.

Haruko Ogasawara

* The bomb that fell on Hiroshima fell on America, too.
It fell on no city, no munition plants, no docks.
It erased no church, vaporized no public buildings,
    reduced no man to his atomic elements.
But it fell, it fell.
It burst. It shook the land.
God have mercy on our children.
God have mercy on America.

Hermann Hagerdorn
The Bomb That Fell on America

I'm not proud of the part I've played in it [the development of nuclear power]. That's why I'm such a strong proponent of stopping this whole nonsense of war. The lesson of history is that when a war starts, every nation will ultimately use whatever weapon has been available....we must expect that if another war...breaks out, we will use nuclear energy in some form. That's due to the imperfection of human beings....I think we'll probably destroy ourselves.

Admiral Hyman Rickover
January 1982

...if the inventory of East-West nuclear warheads and delivery systems were used in war it would kill hundreds of millions of persons, carry radioactive injury and death to many of the world's nations, profoundly damage the environment of the earth we live and depend on, and unhinge and devastate the target nations so effectively that they would no longer function as modern industrial states.

Union of Concerned Scientists

Immediate deaths—20–160 million.
Middle-term effects—Enormous economic destruction and disruption. If immediate deaths are in low range, more tens of millions may die subsequently because economy is unable to support them. Major question about whether economic viability can be restored. Unpredictable psychological effects.
Long-term effects—Cancer deaths and genetic damage in the millions; relatively insignificant in attacked areas, but quite significant elsewhere in the world.

Office of Technology Assessment
U.S. Congress
The Effects of Nuclear War

Neither they, nor we, could survive a thermonuclear war; that's the nature of a thermonuclear war, that devastation is so great that even good defenses don't suffice.

Harold Brown
Secretary of Defense
1977

I think that one is talking, when one talks about a full thermonuclear exchange, about damage to both countries so great that afterwards it would be hard to tell what recovery meant.

Harold Brown

...a war which, though regarded as a "limited war" by the superpowers, would be no less than a war of annihilation for the countries of the battlefield.

Helmut Schmidt
Chancellor of West Germany

Those leaders who speak of "winning" or surviving limited nuclear war can't be aware of the medical facts.

Dr. Howard Hiatt
Dean, Harvard School of Public Health

People are getting toughened about death. They do not realize the prolonged suffering of nuclear attacks, with hundreds of people taking weeks to die, screaming to be shot, with no medical help available. Our whole concept of a civilized response to a tragedy is totally inapplicable.

D. Thomas Chalmers
Mount Sinai Medical School
March 1981

If nuclear war begins, there will be no hospitals, no doctors, nothing to eat, no government. This will be the peace, the complete peace of the graveyard.

Shri R. S. Mishra, M.D.

Currently, U.S. defense preparedness planning expects some 40 to 60 million prompt fatalities after a nuclear explosion....It's not without interest that 20 years ago when a committee organized by the President studied the problem of providing health care in the post-attack era, their recommendation simply was to stock-pile opium to make it a little easier for people to get over into the other world. That still is our primary response to a nuclear attack—our opium and morphine stockpiles.

William Kincade

* It is my belief that any physician who even takes part in so-called emergency medical disaster planning—specifically to meet the problem of nuclear attack—is committing a profoundly unethical act. He is

deluding himself or herself, colleagues, and by implication the public at large, into the false belief that mechanisms of survival in any meaningful social sense are possible.

D. H. Jack Geiger
Physicians for Social Responsibility

Nuclear war would be the last epidemic our civilization would ever know.

Dr. Howard Hiatt
Dean, Harvard School of Public Health

War must be dealt with as an untreatable epidemic for which there is only one approach—that of prevention.

Dr. Howard Hiatt
Dean, Harvard School of Public Health

Scientists initially underestimated the effects of fall-out, were amazed that nuclear explosions in space disabled distant satellites, had no idea that the fireballs from high-yield thermonuclear explosions could deplete the ozone layer and missed altogether the possible climatic effects of nuclear dust and smoke.

Carl Sagan
The Nuclear Winter

Our results have been carefully scrutinized by more than 100 scientists in the United States, Europe, and the Soviet Union...the overall conclusion seems to be agreed upon: there are severe and previously unanticipated global consequences of nuclear war—sub-freezing temperatures in a twilit radioactive gloom lasting for months or longer.

Carl Sagan
The Nuclear Winter

Vast numbers of surviving humans would starve to death. The delicate ecological relations that bind together organisms on Earth in a fabric of mutual dependency would be torn, perhaps irreparably. There is little question that our global civilization would be destroyed. The human population would be reduced to prehistoric levels, or less. Life for any survivors would be extremely hard. And there seems to be a real possibility of the extinction of the human species.

...the heating of the vast quantities of atmospheric dust and soot in northern latitudes will transport these fine particles towards and across the Equator. The Southern Hemisphere would experience effects that, while less severe than in the Northern Hemisphere, are nevertheless extremely ominous. The illusion with which some people in the Northern Hemisphere reassure themselves—catching an Air New Zealand flight in a time of serious international crisis, or the like—is now much less tenable, even on the narrow issue of personal survival for those with the price of a ticket.

Carl Sagan
The Nuclear Winter

But what if nuclear war can be contained, and much less than 5000 megatons is detonated? Perhaps the greatest surprise in our work was that even small nuclear wars can have devastating climatic effects. We considered a war in which a mere 100 megatons were exploded, less than one percent of the world arsenals, and only in low-yield airbursts over cities. This scenario, we found, would ignite thousands of fires, and the smoke from these fires alone would be enough to generate an epoch of cold and dark almost as severe as in the 5000 megaton case. The threshold for what Richard Turco has called the Nuclear Winter is very low.

Carl Sagan
The Nuclear Winter

[I speak]...as one who has witnessed the horror and the lingering sadness of war—as one who knows that another war could utterly destroy this civilization which has been so slowly and painfully built over thousands of years.

Dwight D. Eisenhower

A nuclear Holocaust would silence life on our planet forever. It would not only be the death of human life and plants, but the death of music and painting and books. The silence is total and eternal. The earth only a rock spinning forever alone. It would be the death of life and the death of death itself.

Jonathan Schell and Helen Caldicott

The Stone Age may return on the gleaming wings of science.

Winston Churchill

ADDITIONS:

7
Violence of
Unused Weapons

A. Economic Implications

B. Health and Environmental Effects

C. Spiritual and Psychological Distress

Nuclear weapons in existence at this time have the potential to destroy life on this planet. In addition, these weapons kill without being used. The radiation-related diseases of uranium miners, the consumption of valuable natural resources, and the elimination of vital services for the poor and needy are aspects of the present effects of these murderous devices.

An Open Letter on the Nuclear Arms Race
from the Presbyterian Peace Fellowship, 1981

This world in arms is not spending money alone. It is spending the sweat of its laborers, the genius of its scientists, the hopes of its children.

Dwight D. Eisenhower
April 1953

A. Economic Implications

Were the money which it has cost to gain, at the close of a long war, a little territory...expended in improving what they already possess, in making roads, opening rivers, building ports, improving the arts and finding employment for the idle poor, it would render them [the nations] much stronger, healthier and happier. This I hope will be our wisdom.

Thomas Jefferson

It cost $200,000 to kill a single enemy in World War II, $500,000 per kill in Vietnam.

Franklin Pollard

It is a tragic mixup when the United States spends $500,000 for every enemy soldier killed, and only $53 annually on the victims of poverty.

Martin Luther King, Jr.
October 1967

Rockets and armies are poised to destroy the work of human hands and the creation of God, while each day warless violence kills by hunger and the withholding of necessities.

International Fellowship of Reconciliation

Every gun that is made, every warship launched, every rocket fired signifies, in the final sense, a theft from those who hunger and are not fed, those who are cold and are not clothed.

Dwight D. Eisenhower
April 1953

The arms race is one of the greatest curses on the human race; it is to be condemned as a danger, an act of aggression against the poor, and a folly which does not provide the security it promises.

Vatican Statement to the United Nations, 1976

In the long run, no country can advance intellectually and in terms of its culture and well-being if it has to devote everything to military buildup. I do not see much hope for a world engaged in this all-out effort on military buildup, military technology, and tremendous attempts at secrecy.

Dwight D. Eisenhower

A process of technical, industrial, and human deterioration has been set in motion within American society. The competence of the industrial system is being eroded at its base. Entire industries are falling into technical disrepair and there is a massive loss of productive employment because of inability to hold even domestic markets against foreign competition....The same basic depletion operates as an unseen hand restricting America's relations with the rest of the world, limiting foreign policy moves primarily to military-based initiatives. This deterioration is the result of an unprecedented concentration of America's technical talent and fresh capital on military production.

Seymour Melman
Our Depleted Society

* The old imperialism—exploitation of raw materials and of colonies—has been replaced by a new kind of imperialism: the pentagonist mother country exploits her own people in order to insure the aims of an economy permanently geared to war. The people are exploited as a source of labor and of taxes, which in turn assure that men and war material will be wasted in an endless cycle which profits only the military-industrial complex.

Dr. Juan Bosch
Pentagonism...a Substitute for Imperialism

The only solution to the current balance of terror is for the USA and the Soviet Union to wind down the arms race together....Military spending is by far the largest single expenditure from the federal government's general tax revenues and the largest contribution to the federal debt....Yet, this inflationary spending creates fewer jobs than the federal spending in the civilian economy.

William Winpisinger
President, International Association
of Machinists and Aerospace Workers
1979

World military expenditure equals the entire collective income of the poorest half of the world's population.

Housmans Peace Diary 1985

Developing countries are encouraged to spend five times as much money on importing arms as on buying agricultural equipment.

Housmans Peace Diary 1985

While so many people are going hungry, while so many families are suffering destitution, while so many people spend their lives submerged in the darkness of ignorance, while so many schools, hospitals, homes worthy of the name, are needed, every public or private squandering...every financially depleting arms race...all these we say become a scandalous and intolerable crime. The most serious obligation enjoined on us demands that we openly denounce it.

Pope Paul VI

Our weapons are our greatest danger. The superpowers hold 10 to 12 tons of TNT equivalent for every man, woman and child on the face of the earth. We are not only endangered from without, but from within—as the size of the Pentagon budget determines what is left for our human needs.

Ron Dellums
Representative, California

The arms race can kill, though the weapons themselves may never be used....by their cost alone, armaments kill the poor by causing them to starve.

Vatican Statement to the United Nations, 1976

Unused weapons are no less murderous—these require human energy and resources which are therefore not available to relieve desperate human needs. While a million dollars a minute is spent on the arms race, millions of people suffer malnutrition.

International Fellowship of Reconciliation

Today there is more tonnage of explosives in the world than tonnage of food.

Anonymous

Thirty children a minute are dying from hunger. If 10% of the world's military budget was converted to meet the needs of the hungry in the world, hunger could be obliterated.

World Bank

Today, about 27,000 people died from starvation and malnutrition-related diseases. Starvation could have been prevented for only 50 cents per person per day, or $13,500.
Today, the world spent over $2.2 billion on military expenditures.

Hunger Action Coalition

The money required to provide adequate food, water, education, health and housing for everyone in the world has been estimated at $17 billion a year. It is a huge sum of money...about as much as the world spends on arms every two weeks.

Anonymous

Today the United States and Russia have enough nuclear weapons to kill each person in the world 12 times.

Before we decide that we should cut back on health research in order to add to the nuclear overkill, I would ask you to do one thing. *Tomorrow at breakfast, take a look across the table* and ask yourself whether the security of the person you see is going to be more enhanced over the next 10 years by better heart research, better cancer research, better arthritis research or by an extra MX missile.

David Obey
Representative, Wisconsin
April 1986

The federal government is paying more attention to housing missiles than providing housing for people...

Richard Hatcher
Mayor of Gary, Indiana

Two-thirds of all governments spend more to guard their populations against military attack than against all the enemies of good health, while according to some estimates 70% of people die from preventable diseases.

Housmans Peace Diary 1985

Redirecting seven hours' worth of world military expenditure could eradicate malaria from the face of the world.

Housmans Peace Diary 1985

The cost of a single new nuclear submarine is the equivalent of total education spending in 23 low-income countries with 160 million school-age children.

Housmans Peace Diary 1985

We plan to build about 226 missiles at about $110,000,000 each. For each missile we cancel, we could eliminate poverty in 101,000 female-headed families for a year. If we cancelled the whole program, we could eliminate poverty for all children in the United States twice over and have enough left to send all female heads of low-income families to college for a year.

Marian Wright Edelman
President, Children's Defense Fund

The world spends eight times as much money developing new weapons as on researching new energy sources.

Housmans Peace Diary 1985

In an oil-short world, new tanks consume 1.9 gallons of petrol [gasoline] each mile.

Housmans Peace Diary 1985

Global arms spending is 2400 times higher than expenditures on international peacekeeping.

Housmans Peace Diary 1985

B. Health and Environmental Effects

Thousands of Americans have already been killed by nuclear weapons— our own.

from *Radiation: The Human Cost*
SANE

...[there are] estimates that up to two million Americans were present at [atomic bomb] tests potentially exposing them to some degree of low level radiation.

Malcolm W. Browne

The evidence mounts that, within the range of exposure levels encountered by radiation workers, there is no threshold, i.e., a level which can be assumed as safe in an absolute sense...any amount of radiation has a finite probability of inducing a health effect, e.g., cancer.

Robert Minoque and Karl Goller
Nuclear Regulatory Commission
September 1978

Nuclear fission is the most profound and dangerous tinkering ever introduced into the environment by human beings. Nuclear fission represents an incredible, incomparable and unique hazard for human life. People whose business it is to judge hazards, the insurance companies, refuse to insure nuclear power stations anywhere in the world.

E. F. Schumacher
Small Is Beautiful

From uranium mining to waste disposal, nuclear technology is at war with life.

Waging Peace

The problem faced by the atomic industry and the Federal government is simple to state: they have got millions of tons of deadly radioactive waste that has been accumulating for over 40 years, with no known safe way to dispose of it. Worse, the pile of waste is growing at an increasing pace because new uranium mines are opening, new nuclear power plants are being built, and more nuclear weapons are being produced.

Anonymous

* Whole empires have risen and fallen in a fraction of the time that Strontium and Cesium will have to remain sealed away. Neanderthal man appeared only about 75,000 years ago compared to the 250,000 years Plutonium needs to be guarded.

Friends for a Nonviolent World
Twin Cities Northern Sun Alliance
Want Not, Waste Not

* No degree of prosperity could justify the accumulation of large amounts of highly toxic substances which nobody knows how to make "safe" and which remain an incalculable danger to the whole of creation for historical or even geological ages. To do such a thing is a transgression against life itself.... It means conducting the economic affairs of man as if people (and creation) really did not matter at all.

E. F. Schumacher

Radioactive waste becomes a threat only if it escapes into the bio-system.

Nuclear waste is buried in eleven major sites in trenches that government officials assured us would contain the wastes safely for hundreds of years. In less than 10 years, 6 of them leaked.

Friends for a Nonviolent World
Twin Cities Northern Sun Alliance
Want Not, Waste Not

Testimony given at U.S. Department of Energy hearing on siting of a national high-level nuclear waste repository:

I don't care where they build it, it is too close to our children.
woman elder of Menominee (anonymous)

I will not have my son used in an experiment.
father of a 4-month-old son (anonymous)

If I had a patient who was in the process of creating a virtually permanent toxin, and who admitted this toxin could really not be contained or stored, but wanted to go ahead and make lots of this toxin anyway, I would have that person hospitalized and treated for obvious suicidal ideation.
Neil Nathan, M.D.

My grandmother told me to tell you that we could go indefinitely without nuclear power; we could go only about a week without water.

Anonymous

As a physician, I contend that nuclear technology threatens life on our planet with extinction. If present trends continue, the air we breathe, the food we eat, and the water we drink will soon be contaminated with enough radioactive pollutants to pose a potential health hazard far greater than any plague humanity has ever experienced.

Dr. Helen Caldicott
Physicians for Social Responsibility

For me this [the nuclear freeze] is a family issue and a medical issue. I took the Hippocratic Oath of healing seriously and the nuclear freeze is the ultimate medical issue.

Dr. Helen Caldicott
November 1983

Our nuclear program was built in the name of national security—protecting the lives of Americans. One can't help but wonder, who was protected and at whose expense?

Pat Schroeder
Representative, Colorado
sponsor, Citizens' Hearings for Radiation Victims

The existence of nuclear weapons is killing us. Their production contaminates our environment, destroys our natural resources, and depletes our human energy and creativity. But the most critical danger they represent is to life itself. Sickness, accidents, genetic damage and death, these are the real products of the nuclear arms race. We say no to the threat of global holocaust, no to the arms race, no to death. We say yes to a world where people, animals, plants and the earth itself are respected and valued.

Women's Encampment for a Future of Peace and Justice
Seneca Army Depot, New York
July 1983

C. Spiritual and Psychological Distress

Child abuse consists not only of violent acts toward children but also of threats of violence. The existence of nuclear weapons in our world represents global child abuse for those weapons threaten children with hideous personal injury and death.

As a result of this nuclear threat, mental health professionals are documenting disturbing children's behaviors of: terror, anger, despair, avoidance of involvement in personal relationships, and a gnawing fear they will never grow up. As adults, we have a responsibility to remove this threat.

Patrick Gannon

When we talk to today's children, they wonder if they have a future, and I think we have to wonder what we are doing. Our priorities are on the military and not on our nation's health.

Carol Nadelson
American Psychiatric Association

How are we supposed to start our lives with death looking over our shoulders?

Jessica
Age 17
In the Nuclear Shadow: What Can the Children Tell Us?

Sometimes it occurs to me that I might not grow up.

Anthony
Age 11
In the Nuclear Shadow: What Can the Children Tell Us?

Dear God,
    Adam was the first man on earth. I hope I'm not the last.

Billy K.
Chicago
Age 7
Please Save My World

I was on a camping trip in the fifth grade, and one kid started telling me that there were these bombs that could just wipe us all out. I felt sick. Ever since then I've been aware of things on TV, things people say, and it will pop up all of a sudden, on a nice day or when I'm having fun—I'll remember that it could all end in a minute.

Caedmon Fujimoto
Age 16
Our Future at Stake

The effects of nuclear weapons lie in our heads as well as in radioactive fallout. The damage that is being done *now* to people's vision of the future and their faith in future generations is incalculable.

Alice Cook and Gwyn Kirk
Greenham Women Everywhere

Young people are trying to find their way in a troubled and complex society. But hopeful signs are few, and the participants feel relatively powerless to influence events.

Stanley Elam
"Educators and the Nuclear Threat"
Phi Delta Kappan

When young people are deprived of an opportunity to give their lives a meaning, and when they have lost their last glimmer of hope, they fall victims to drugs and crime.

Declaration of the International
Meeting of Latin American Bishops
November/December 1977

* Men have brought their powers of subduing the forces of nature to such a pitch that by using them, they could now very easily exterminate one another to the last man. They know this—hence arises a great part of their current unrest, their dejection, their mood of apprehension.

Sigmund Freud
Civilization and Its Discontents

I am a child psychologist and author of books on how children's intelligence develops. Lately I have been doing some research on the effects of the nuclear threat on children's thinking, and it worries me greatly...

Mary Ann Pulaski

I worry too much about nuclear war and I'm too young to worry.

Billy C.
Las Vegas
Age 7
Please Save My World

I don't want to be the last person on earth because then I will have nobody to play with.

Laura R.
Buffalo
Age 6
Please Save My World

If everybody in the world says that they want peace how can we still have nuclear bombs? Somebody in the world must be lying.

Joan G.
Brooklyn
Age 10
Please Save My World

Since I learned about the bomb I don't smile so much any more.

Judith K.
Nashville
Age 7
Please Save My World

Depression is not sobbing and crying and giving vent. It is plain and simple reduction of feeling.

Judith Guest
Ordinary People

Given the social taboo against crying out [over the threat of nuclear annihilation] people distance themselves from each other as do the families and friends of the terminally ill.

Harvey Cox

You can't love someone if you don't think you will have them long.
teenage girl
In the Nuclear Shadow: What Can the Children Tell Us?

We are a society caught between a sense of impending apocalypse and an inability to acknowledge it. The refusal of feeling takes a heavy toll. The toll is not only an impoverishment of emotional and sensory life—the flowers dimmer and less fragrant, loves less ecstatic. This psychic numbing also impedes the capacity to process and respond to information. The energy expended in pushing down despair is diverted from more creative uses. We erect an invisible screen, selectively filtering out anxiety-provoking data. In a world where organisms require feedback in order to adapt and survive, this is suicidal.

Joanna Macy

...I am often too scared or depressed to want to meet this issue head on...

Kay Copenhauer

The schools I went to never talked about nuclear weapons or Hiroshima or the arms race. I think maybe teachers were afraid to talk about it. It made me think it just wasn't a big deal to them, or it wasn't important, or they were afraid. But that seemed strange to me....It's not like we don't hear about nuclear weapons. It's on the news, it's in the papers, it's on television. But people act like we aren't supposed to talk about it.

Ursell Austin
Age 16
Our Future at Stake

Other kids should know that if we don't do something soon, terrible things will happen. They should know about the dangers of nuclear weapons and also that there are things we can do to prevent a nuclear war....At first I was scared to bring it up, but now I do it. Sometimes I try to talk to people but they don't want to hear it. I think they are scared to face reality. That makes me really sad.

Regina Hunter
Age 15
Our Future at Stake

The Americans are forcing even their friends into becoming their enemies. It is curious that the Americans, who calculate so carefully on the possibilities of military victory, do not realize that in the process they are incurring deep psychological and political defeat. The image of America will never again be the image of revolution, freedom, and democracy, but the image of violence and militarism.

Martin Luther King, Jr.

The problem in defense is how far you can go without destroying from within what you are trying to defend from without.

Dwight D. Eisenhower

A nation that continues to spend more money on military defense than on programs of social uplift is approaching spiritual death.

Martin Luther King, Jr.

ADDITIONS:

8
The Lighter Side
of a Serious Subject

You ask if we need anything—Ann wants an elephant, Nancy and I would like a Xerox machine, and I'll take a piano. Also if you could spread some farm animals around the lawn so the rooster alarm clock can function I'll feel right at home....We want a bouquet of wildflowers, world peace, and 27 people to go over the ELF fence....If you are unable to fulfill all these wishes, we'll take a watermelon instead.

Kathy Kelly
letter from Ashland County jail
July 1985

I am for a nuclear freeze. Even in the summertime.

Andy K.
Seattle, Age 8
Please Save My World

Dear Mr. President,
    Please wear mittens in the White House so you won't be able to put your finger on the button.

Andy S.
San Francisco, Age 9
Please Save My World

Received at Disneyland—a letter from the Selective Service System addressed to Mickey M. Mouse and opening with these words: "Dear Registrant: Our records indicate you have not responded to our initial request for necessary date of birth information..."

The Progressive

Some white folks I just can't understand. They're more concerned about busing a kid to school than they are about shipping a kid to Vietnam....That's like worrying about dandruff when you've got cancer of the eyeballs.

Dick Gregory
Write Me In

Being a pacifist between wars is as easy as being a vegetarian between meals.

Ammon Hennacy

"Peace" is that period of cheating between battles.

Ambrose Bierce
The Devil's Dictionary

Two things I am afraid of—the bomb and the dentist.

Holly G.
Seattle, Age 7
Please Save My World

Advertisement before a nuclear attack:
RUN FOR YOUR LIFE!
You've always been careful when it comes to your health.
You've jogged.
You've done the marathon in under three.
You're a leader. A winner. A survivor. A runner.
So when your life depends on it you'll want running shoes that give you
blast-off capability equal to the situation.
NUKES
The *Nuke* running shoe has a unique deep-waffle sole that gives you that
extra spring you need to go from Ground Zero to Mile 20 in just five
seconds. Break in a pair of *Nukes* today. You might be there to be glad
you did.

Meet Mr. Bomb
A Practical Guide to Nuclear Extinction

Depending on your distance from ground zero, you could experience
temperatures of up to 4000 degrees Centigrade. Why not prepare for this
by spending 10 to 15 minutes a day in your clothes dryer?

Meet Mr. Bomb
A Practical Guide to Nuclear Extinction

Blast is actually no worse than if a 500,000-ton baseball, hit on a line
drive, were to strike your home.

Meet Mr. Bomb
A Practical Guide to Nuclear Extinction

An effective shelter should be strong enough to withstand a direct hit by
a five-megaton warhead....The new super material developed by NASA
for use in the space shuttle is the only building material that can meet
this requirement. Two-by-four panels of the metal can be purchased from
most aerospace manufacturers....A typical 2000 square foot residence
can be made bomb-proof with about 5000 panels at a cost of $3.4 million.
Most banks will be happy to give you a home improvement loan to
finance your new shielding...

Meet Mr. Bomb
A Practical Guide to Nuclear Extinction

For more information write INSANE, Washington D.C. INSANE
(Interested Non-seditious Americans for a Nuclear Event) is a prominent
anti-freeze group.

Meet Mr. Bomb
A Practical Guide to Nuclear Extinction

I am not very keen for doves or hawks. I think we need more owls.

George Aiken

Dear God:
Please save the world. Even if you're not crazy about it.

Lionel T.
Hershey, Age 8
Please Save My World

How I Would Save the World
First, I would take all the generals and put them in a big boat in the middle of the ocean. Then I would forget to pick them up.

Robert Stuart
Age 9
Please Save My World

Reporter: Mr. Gandhi, what do you think of Western Civilization?
Mr. Gandhi: I think it would be a good idea!

---

* More than any other time in history, mankind faces the crossroads...one path leads to despair and utter hopelessness, the other to total extinction. I pray we have the wisdom to choose wisely.

Woody Allen

Pray for the dead, and fight like hell for the living.

Mary Harris "Mother" Jones

The thing about peace work is the hours are long...but the pay is really lousy.

Barb Katt

We pray for peace every Sunday at Church. Everybody at Church prays for peace. Even the people who are sleeping.

Eric W.
New York, Age 9
Please Save My World

My hometown is the hotbed of social rest.

Anonymous

Well, you lose some...and you lose some.

Sister Marjorie Tuite

We should lock up all the bombs in a bank then nobody could get them because nobody can get into a bank.

Annie G.
Baldwin, Age 7
Please Save My World

The trouble with good ideas is that they quickly degenerate into hard work.

Anonymous

Little children and animals don't want war. Only grownups and crocodiles.

Anthony R.
Atlanta, Age 10
Please Save My World

SMILE! We're one day closer to World Disarmament—and a real big party.

Anonymous

ADDITIONS:

ADDITIONS:

9
National Ideals

The people we call our "founders" are often referred to as "rebels," "radicals," "patriots," or "revolutionaries."

Voices of the American Revolution

* We hold these truths to be self-evident, that all men are created equal; that they are endowed by their Creator with certain unalienable rights; that among these are life, liberty, and the pursuit of happiness. That, to secure these rights, governments are instituted among men, deriving their just powers from the consent of the governed; that, whenever any form of government becomes destructive of these ends, it is the right of the people to alter or to abolish it, and to institute a new government, laying its foundation on such principles, and organizing its powers in such form, as to them shall seem most likely to effect their safety and happiness...experience hath shown, that mankind are more disposed to suffer...than to right themselves by abolishing the forms to which they are accustomed...it is their right, it is their duty, to throw off such government, and to provide new guards for their future security.

Declaration of Independence
July 1776

The care of life and happiness, and not their destruction, is the first and only legitimate object of good government.

Thomas Jefferson

Some boast of being friends to government; I am a friend to righteous government founded upon the principles of reason and justice; but I glory in publicly avowing my eternal enmity to tyranny.

John Hancock
1774

...may [our] country itself become a vast and splendid monument, not of oppression and terror, but of wisdom, of peace, and of liberty...

Daniel Webster

Those who are desirous of enjoying all the advantages of liberty themselves, should be willing to extend personal liberties to others.

Rhode Island Assembly
1774

* I have always strenuously supported the right of every man to his opinion, however different that opinion might be to mine. He who denies to another this right, makes a slave of himself to his present opinion, because he precludes himself the right of changing it.

Thomas Paine

The government of the United States of America is not in any sense founded on the Christian religion.

George Washington

When shall it be said in any country of the world, my poor are happy; neither ignorance or distress is to be found among them; my jails are empty of prisoners, my streets of beggars; the aged are not in want, the taxes are not oppressive; the rational world is my friend, because I am the friend of its happiness; when these things can be said, then may that country boast of its constitution and government.

Thomas Paine

True patriotism hates injustice in its own land more than anywhere else.

Clarence Darrow

* What has commonly been called rebellion has more often been nothing but a glorious struggle in opposition to the lawless power of rebellious kings and princes.

Sam Adams, 1776

The American war is over; but this is far from the case with the American Revolution. On the contrary, nothing but the first act of the great drama is closed.

Benjamin Rush, 1787

God forbid we should ever be twenty years without a rebellion.

Thomas Jefferson, 1787

A sanguine confidence in the future has been a hallmark of the American character and a source of national pride.

Joanna Rogers Macy

ADDITIONS:

ADDITIONS:

10
Forsaken Ideals

To sleep, perchance to dream, aye, there's the rub.
To fight, perchance to win, aye, there's the rub.
For victory brings power and prestige
And the children of the children of the fighters take all for granted and
in turn oppress.

Pete Seeger

There is no other measure by which to validate government save for its
contribution to life. The government that fails by this standard has
violated its troth. It is illegitimate. It is a threat to the people.

Terry Herndon
Teacher

Rulers have no authority from God to do mischief.

Jonathan Mayhew, 1750

* Civil tyranny is usually small in its beginning, like the "drop in the
bucket," till at length, like a mighty torrent of raging waves of the sea,
it bears down all before it and deluges whole countries and
empires....Tyranny brings ignorance and brutality along with it. It
degrades men from their just rank into the class of brutes. It dampens
their spirits. It suppresses arts. It extinguishes every spark of noble ardor
and generosity in the breasts of those who are enslaved by it. It makes
naturally strong and great minds feeble and little and triumphs over the
ruins of virtue and humanity. This is true of tyranny in every shape.
There can be nothing great and good where its influence reaches.

Jonathan Mayhew, 1750

I believe there are more instances of the abridgement of the freedom of
the people by gradual and silent encroachments of those in power than
by violent and sudden usurpations.

James Madison

When an act injurious to freedom has once been done, and the people
bear it, the repetition of it is most likely to meet with submission. For
as the mischief of the one was found to be tolerable, they will hope that
of the second will prove so too; and they will not regard the infamy of
the last, because they are stained with that of the first.

John Dickinson, 1768

* If the liberties of America are ever completely ruined it will in all
probability be the consequence of a mistaken notion of prudence, which
leads men to acquiesce in measures of the most destructive tendency for
the sake of present ease. When designs are formed to raze the very
foundation of a free government, those few who are to erect their grandeur
and fortunes upon the general ruin will employ every art to soothe the
devoted people into a state of indolence, inattention and security, which
is forever the forerunner of slavery....And it has been an old game played

over and over again to hold up the men who would rouse their fellow citizens and countrymen...as "pretended patriots," "intemperate politicians," "rash, hot-headed men," "wretched desperados."

Sam Adams, 1771

If once the people become inattentive to the public affairs, you and I and Congress and assemblies, judges and governors, shall all become wolves.

Thomas Jefferson, 1787

* All pretenders to government which have not ultimately the good of the governed in view and do not afford, or endeavor to afford, protection to those over whom they pretend such claims, should, instead of the respects due to legislatures, courts and the like, be esteemed and treated as enemies to society and the rights of mankind.

Ethan Allen, 1780

Tyranny and oppression are just as possible under democratic forms as under any other. We are slow to realize that democracy is a life and involves continual struggle.

Robert M. La Follette

...if totalitarianism comes to this country, it will surely do so in the guise of 100% Americanism.

Huey Long

When fascism comes to the United States, it'll be because the people voted it in.

Irving Wallace
The R Amendment

We despise totalitarianism so much that we are willing to become totalitarian to destroy it.

American Friends Service Committee
Speak Truth to Power

The House Un-American Activities Committee is the most un-American thing in America.

Harry S. Truman

* As soon as men decide that all means are permitted to fight an evil, then their good becomes indistinguishable from the evil that they set out to destroy.

Christopher Dawson
The Judgement of Nations

ADDITIONS:

11
Military Might

The great oppressors of the earth were entrusted with power by the people to defend them from the little oppressors. The sword of justice was put into their hands, but behold they soon turned it into a sword of oppression.

Samuel Webster, 1777

Though it has been said that a standing army is necessary for the dignity and safety of America, freedom revolts at the idea. Standing armies have been the nursery of vice and the bane of liberty from the Roman Legions to the planting of British cohorts in the capitals of America.

Mercy Warren, 1788

The spirit of this country is totally adverse to a large military force.

Thomas Jefferson, 1807

Tyrants always support themselves with standing armies!

Samuel Webster, 1777

Nothing can be more aggravated than for the shepherds to mislead and butcher the flock they were set to defend and feed.

Samuel Webster, 1777

If there be one principle more deeply rooted than any other in the mind of every American, it is that we should have nothing to do with conquest.

Thomas Jefferson

Observe good faith and justice towards all nations; cultivate peace and harmony with all.

George Washington
Farewell Address
1796

ADDITIONS:

12
Freedom of the Press

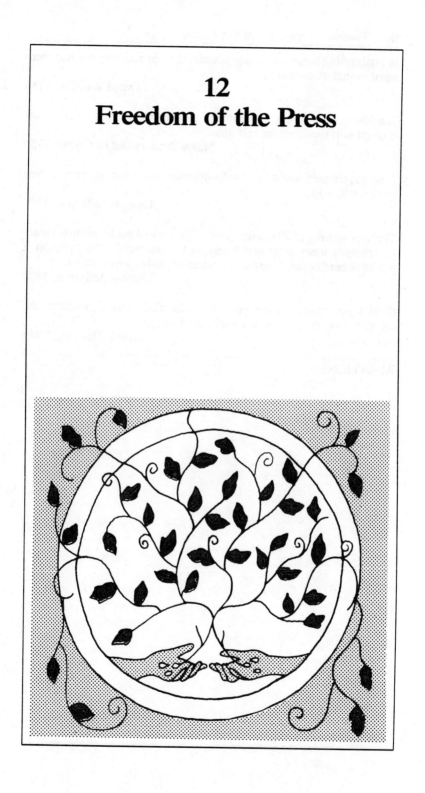

In establishing American independence, the pen and the press had merit equal to that of the sword.

David Ramsay, 1783

The liberty of the press is essential to the security of freedom in a state. It ought not, therefore, be restrained.

Massachusetts Bill of Rights, 1780

...no government ought to be without critics and where the press is free no one ever will.

Thomas Jefferson, 1791

The only security of all is a free press. The force of public opinion cannot be resisted, when permitted freely to be expressed. The agitation it produces must be submitted to. It is necessary to keep the waters pure.

Thomas Jefferson, 1823

Should the liberty of the press be once destroyed, farewell to the remainder of our invaluable rights and privileges.

Isaiah Thomas, 1700s

ADDITIONS:

13
Informed Citizens

Enlighten the people generally, and tyranny and oppressions of body and mind will vanish like evil spirits at the dawn of day.

Thomas Jefferson, 1816

* ...it is the practice of the new world, America, to make men as wise as possible, so that their knowledge being complete, they may be rationally governed.

Tom Paine, 1778

Liberty cannot be preserved without a general knowledge among the people.

John Adams, 1767

It is a shame, a scandal to civilized society, that part only of the citizens should be sent to colleges and universities, to learn to cheat the rest of their liberties.

Robert Coram, 1791

Neither piety, virtue, or liberty can long flourish in a community where the education of youth is neglected.

Samuel Cooper, 1780

If science produces no better fruits than tyranny, murder, rapine and destitution of national morality, I would rather wish our country to remain ignorant.

Thomas Jefferson

Where learning is confined to a few people, we always find monarchy, aristocracy and slavery.

Benjamin Rush, 1786

ADDITIONS:

14
Big Business

I hope we shall crush in its birth the aristocracy of our moneyed corporations, which dare already to challenge our government to a trial of strength and bid defiance to the laws of our country.

Thomas Jefferson, 1814

* Experience declares that man is the only animal which devours his own kind, for I can apply no milder term...to the general prey of the rich on the poor.

Thomas Jefferson, 1787

[Monopolies are] odious, contrary to the principles of a free government, and the principles of commerce.

Maryland Revolutionary Constitution, 1776

* Government is instituted for the protection, safety, and happiness of the people, and not for the profit, honour, or private interest of any man, family, or class of men.

Mercy Warren, 1788

Harmony, and a liberal intercourse with all nations, are recommended by policy, humanity, and interest. But even our commercial policy should hold an equal and impartial hand; neither seeking or granting exclusive favors or preferences; consulting the natural course of things; diffusing and diversifying, by gentle means, the streams of commerce, but forcing nothing...

George Washington
Farewell Address, 1796

* The protection of a man's person is more sacred than the protection of property.

Tom Paine
***The Rights of Man*, 1792**

ADDITIONS:

15
False Patriotism

Guard against the postures of pretended patriotism.

George Washington
1796

I venture to suggest that patriotism is not a short and frenzied outburst of emotion, but the tranquil and steady dedication of a lifetime.

Adlai E. Stevenson

* Let the history of the Federal Government instruct mankind that the mask of patriotism may be worn to conceal the foulest designs against the liberties of the people.

Benjamin Bache
1798

Patriotism is the finest flower of western civilization as well as the refuge of the scoundrel.

Leonard Woolf

* Patriotism is not, as sentimentalists like to assert, one of the profoundest of man's noblest instincts.

Ida Alexa Ross Wylie

Patriotism is the last refuge of a scoundrel.

Samuel Johnson

Christian faith makes uncritical patriotism impossible.

Peter Monkres

A people living under the perpetual menace of war and invasion is very easy to govern. It demands no social reforms. It does not haggle over expenditures on armaments and military equipment. It pays without discussion, it ruins itself, and that is an excellent thing for the syndicates of financiers and manufacturers for whom patriotic terrors are an abundant source of gain.

Anatole France

* I am persuaded that there is absolutely no limit in the absurdities that can, by government action, come to be generally believed. Give me an adequate army, with power to provide it with more pay and better food than falls to the lot of the average man, and I will undertake, within thirty years, to make the majority of the population believe that two and two are three, that water freezes when it gets hot and boils when it gets cold, or any other nonsense that might seem to serve the interest of the State. Of course, even when these beliefs had been generated, people would not put the kettle in the refrigerator when they wanted it to boil. That cold makes water boil would be a Sunday truth, sacred and mystical, to be professed in awed tones, but not to be acted on in daily life. What would happen would be that any verbal denial of the mystic doctrine

would be made illegal, and obstinate heretics would be "frozen" at the stake. No person who did not enthusiastically accept the official doctrine would be allowed to teach or to have any position of power. Only the very highest officials, in their cups, would whisper to each other what rubbish it all is; then they would laugh and drink again.

Bertrand Russell
Unpopular Essays
1950

* Why of course the people don't want war. Why should some poor slob on a farm want to risk his life in a war when the best he can get out of it is to come back to his farm in one piece? Naturally the common people don't want war: Neither in Russia, nor in England, nor for that matter in Germany. That is understood. But after all, it is the leaders of the country who determine the policy and it is always a simple matter to drag the people along, whether it is a democracy, or a fascist dictatorship, or a parliament, or a communist dictatorship. Voice or no voice, the people can always be brought to the bidding of the leaders. That is easy. All you have to do is tell them they are being attacked, and denounce the pacifists for lack of patriotism and exposing the country to danger. It works the same in any country.

Hermann Goering
Hitler's Deputy

ADDITIONS:

ADDITIONS:

16
Love It and Change It

Our country, right or wrong. When right, to be kept right; when wrong, to be put right.

Carl Schurz
famous German immigrant

* Truth is great and will prevail if left to herself...she is the proper and sufficient antagonist to error, and has nothing to fear from the conflict unless by human interposition disarmed of her natural weapons, free argument and debate.

Thomas Jefferson

The origin of all power is in the people, and...they have an incontestible right to check the creatures of their own creation.

Mercy Warren
1788

Sir, I would rather be right than be President.

Henry Clay

The real patriots are those who love America as she is, but who want the beloved to be more lovable. This is not treachery. This, as every parent, every teacher, every friend must know, is the truest and noblest affection.

Adlai E. Stevenson

It is un-American *not* to criticize your country when it does wrong.

Clergy and Laity Concerned

Criticism is more than a right; it is an act of patriotism—a higher form of patriotism, I believe, than the familiar ritual of national adulation. All of us have the responsibility to act upon the higher patriotism which is to love our country less for what it is than for what we would like it to be.

William Fulbright
former Senator, Arkansas

* The real patriot is the person who is not afraid to criticize the defective policies of the country which he loves.

Joseph J. Fahey

* It is the duty of every good citizen to point out what he thinks erroneous in the commonwealth.

James Otis
1764

I can't see how not wanting to blow up the world is un-American.

William Winpisinger
President
International Association of Machinists and Aerospace Workers

If it is un-American to be against arms build-ups that are created primarily to give more power to the military and more hefty profits to arms manufacturers, then yes, we are un-American.

Clergy and Laity Concerned

I should like to be able to love my country and still love justice.

Albert Camus

The love of one's country is a splendid thing. But why should love stop at the border?

Pablo Casals

If we are to be leaders—Number 1—let it be as an example of a government concerned with the dignity and growth of people everywhere.

Madge Micheels-Cyrus

America is great because America is good and if America ever ceases to be good, America will cease to be great.

Alexis de Tocqueville

America must choose one of three courses after this war: narrow nationalism, which inevitably means the ultimate loss of our own liberty; international imperialism, which means the sacrifice of some other nation's liberty; or the creation of a world in which there shall be an equality of opportunity for every race and every nation.

Wendell L. Wilkie, 1940s

Nothing less than a global patriotism is demanded in the 3rd century of the U.S.....*all* people are created equal. Any "more perfect union" must involve the whole human family. Our quest for "domestic tranquility" must recognize the globe as our common domicile.

Philip Scharper
The Patriot's Bible

ADDITIONS:

Phillips Memorial
Library
Providence College

ADDITIONS:

17
Bumperstickers,
Buttons,
T-Shirts,
and Graffiti

Nuclear weapons
May They Rust in Peace

Bread Not Bombs

If the people lead,
eventually the leaders will follow.

Stop the Arms Race
Not the Human Race

Military Intelligence
is a contradiction in terms.

Think Globally
Act Locally

Uranium
Leave It In The Ground

Plutonium
is Forever

We don't want nuclear waste here;
So don't make it anywhere.

Better Active Today
Than Radioactive Tomorrow

Split Wood
Not Atoms

Solar Employs
Nuclear Destroys

No Nukes is
Good Nukes

Wearing Buttons
Is Not Enough

War is not healthy for children and other living things.
Another Mother for Peace

Child Care
Not Warfare

You can't hug your kids with nuclear arms.

Arms Are For Linking

Arms Are For Embracing

I Want To Grow Up
Not Blow Up

Give Children Dreams
Not Nuclear Nightmares

Bombs Scare Bears

This House Has No Fallout Shelter
Peace Is Our Only Security

There Is No Silver Lining
In A Mushroom Cloud

Nuclear war is bad for peace of mind
Nuclear war is bad for war veterans
Nuclear war is bad for international relations
Nuclear war is bad for real estate
Nuclear war is good for nothing
The Hundredth Monkey

In Every War
There's A Hiroshima
Waiting To Happen

Hands off Outer Space
Star Wars "Defense"
An Offensive, Deadly Lie

Peace on earth
and in space

Military Solutions Are Problems

El Salvador is Spanish for Vietnam.

Join the Army;
travel to exotic, distant lands;
meet exciting, unusual people—and kill them.

Don't Register
For World War III
The War Without Winners

Support Your Local
Draft Resister

They can jail the resister,
but not the resistance.

Why do we kill people who kill people
to prove that killing people is wrong?

America: Love it or leave it.

America: Love it and change it.

Peace is Patriotic

Peace is growing

Civil Disobedience
is Civil Defense

Peace In The World
Or The World In Pieces

Be All You Can Be
Work For Peace

The Moral Majority Is Neither

No One Is Right
If No One Is Left

WAR doesn't decide who's right
—only who's left.

Minds are like parachutes; they only function when they are open.

Kites rise highest
against the wind.

Help Cure America's
Military-Industrial Complex

> The government says 140,000,000 deaths are acceptable in a
> nuclear war. The question is, is the government acceptable?
> **Minnesota Nuclear Freeze Campaign**

Nuclear war can spoil
your whole day.

* God made heaven and earth in six days.
Man can destroy it in six minutes.

I haven't learned to live with the bomb.

War Is Costly
Peace Is Priceless

Teach peace.

Legalize peace.

Feed The Cities
Not The Pentagon

Save the Nukes
No Whales

Extinct is Forever

Live Simply
That Others May
Simply Live

Violence Ends
Where Love Begins

The Meek
Are Getting Ready

"Meek" Ain't Weak

Be Realistic
Demand The Impossible

Peace is Possible.

Create Peace

World War III
Cancelled by Popular Demand

                                        Vision Or Fission

Save The World?
...You Bet!

        Without World Disarmament...Who Will Have Grandchildren?
        Women's International League For Peace And Freedom

Hope springs maternal.
Another Mother for Peace

ADDITIONS:

18
Earth As One

* No man is an island, entire of itself....any man's death diminishes me, because I am involved in mankind; and therefore never send to know for whom the bell tolls; it tolls for thee.

John Donne

I am one with this planet.
I am one with all people.
I am one with all life.

Rusty Schweickart
Apollo Astronaut

* There is a destiny that makes us brothers;
    None goes his way alone;
  All that we send into the lives of others
    Comes back into our own.

Edwin Markham

* We were born to unite with our fellow men, and to join in community with the human race.

Cicero
Definibus, **IV**

* Don't become your brother's keeper, be your brother's brother.

Jesse Jackson

Something broke for me Wednesday, a thunderstorm of the heart, when we were at the gate early, keening. Fingering the barbed wire along the top of the fence, I felt all the fences that separate us humans, all the barbs of ignorance and violence...culminating in our casual consideration of blowing up our planet-home. There was a great healing then in my sobbing on that poisoned land, at seeing the tears of the women around me spill down with my own.

Andi Scott
Women's Peace Encampment, Seneca Falls, NY
1983

It is "isolation" that is critical to war. You can't be abusive when you realize your connectedness.

David Kadlec

Peace is inclusive.

Madge Micheels-Cyrus

No peace which is not peace for all, no rest till all has been fulfilled.

Dag Hammarskjöld

We are all members of one family, yesterday, today, and tomorrow. We know we shall find peace only where we find justice—only where we find respect for all human beings, only where all human beings have the right to a decent living for themselves and their families.

The "Snarlers" of the Perús Cement Company
Brazil, 1974
Christ in a Poncho

We have learned that we cannot live alone, at peace; that our own well-being is dependent upon the well-being of other nations, far away.

Franklin Delano Roosevelt

Especially important it is to realize that there can be no assured peace and tranquility for any one nation except as it is achieved for all. So long as want, frustration and a sense of injustice prevail among significant sections of the earth, no other section can be wholly released from fear.

Dwight D. Eisenhower

The social progress, order, security and peace of each country are necessarily connected with the social progress, order, security and peace of all other countries.

Pope John XXIII

Injustice anywhere is a threat to justice everywhere. We are caught in an inescapable network of mutuality, tied in a single garment of destiny.

Martin Luther King, Jr.
Letter from a Birmingham Jail

* You can only protect your liberties in this world by protecting the other man's freedom. You can only be free if I am free.

Clarence Darrow

...while there is a lower class, I am in it; while there is a criminal element, I am of it; while there is a soul in prison, I am not free.

Eugene Debs

The good we secure for ourselves is precarious and uncertain...until it is secured for all of us and incorporated into our common life.

Jane Addams
Nobel Peace Prize, 1931

Where nature makes natural allies of us all, we can demonstrate that beneficial relations are possible even with those with whom we most deeply disagree, and this must someday be the basis of world peace and world law.

John F. Kennedy

If we cannot end our differences, at least we can help make the world safe for diversity. For, in the final analysis, our most basic common link is that we all inhabit this small planet. We all breathe the same air. We all cherish our children's future. And we are all mortal.

John F. Kennedy

* The wave of the future is not the conquest of the world by a single dogmatic creed but the liberation of the diverse energies of free nations and free men.

John F. Kennedy

* All your strength is in your union.
All your danger is in discord.
Therefore be at peace henceforward.
And as brothers live together.

Henry Wadsworth Longfellow
The Song of Hiawatha

* One of the most moving letters in the New Testament was the Apostle Paul's letter to the churches at Galatia, in which he wrote:
There is neither Jew nor Greek.
There is neither slave nor free.
There is neither male nor female.
You are all one.
And we add there is neither Russian nor American, for all are one. "All are Abraham's offspring. All are heirs, according to the promise."

Philip Zwerling

There are no Communist babies. There are no Capitalist babies.

Jackie Rivet-River

No ideological or political doctrine should be considered more important than life and love of our fellow human beings. Without ideological and political doctrines we can still live in peace, but without respect for life, the world will be destroyed.

Thich Thien Minh

The basic problem is not political, it is apolitical and human. One of the most important things to do is to keep cutting deliberately through political lines and barriers and emphasizing that these are largely fabrications and that there is a genuine reality: the human dimension.

Thomas Merton

From her father, Jane learned that "the things that make us alike are stronger than the things that make us different."   **Dorothy Nathan**
Women of Courage
written about Jane Addams

It is we human beings who have made pigmentation a leprosy in our lives instead of a gift.   **Anonymous**

Our lives extend beyond our skins, in radical interdependence with the rest of the world.

Joanna Rogers Macy

Though I am different from you, we were born involved in one another.

T'ao Chien

We cannot live for ourselves alone. Our lives are connected by a thousand invisible threads, and along these sympathetic fibers, our actions run as causes and return to us as results...

Herman Melville

When we try to pick out something by itself, we find it hitched to everything else in the Universe.

John Muir

We are one, after all, you and I; together we suffer, together exist, and forever will recreate each other.

Teilhard de Chardin

I would like us to be interventionists everywhere in the world. I would like to intervene everywhere with whatever benefits we've had from living in this land—health care, education, housing. We also need to learn from those people, learn how their cultures have prospered in the past, learn from their mistakes and their successes. We ought to be actively involved everywhere in the world all the time, but not militarily.

Rear Admiral Gene R. La Rocque
U.S. Navy (retired)

* In every man there is something wherein I may learn of him, and in that I am his pupil.

Ralph Waldo Emerson

Let us unite, let us hold each other tightly, let us merge our hearts, let us create for Earth a brain and a heart, let us give a human meaning to the superhuman struggle.

Nikos Kazantzakis

The moment we cease to hold each other,
The moment we break faith with one another,
The sea engulfs us and the light goes out.

Anonymous

We have a long, long way to go. So let us hasten along the road, the roads of human tenderness and generosity. Groping, we may find one another's hands in the dark.

Emily Greene Balch

We're all part of the Great Holy mystery—all of us—and so we can't hate each other or we are hating ourselves.

Anonymous

The supreme reality of our time is our indivisibility as children of God and the common vulnerability of our planet.

John F. Kennedy

We travel together, passengers on a little spaceship, dependent on its vulnerable reserves of air and soil; all committed for our safety to its security and peace; preserved from annihilation only by the care, the work, and the love we give our fragile craft, and, I may say, each other.

Adlai E. Stevenson
his last speech

Nuclear holocaust is five minutes away. But maybe those minutes are the graced moment in which God is speaking to all of humanity. We have no option but to go the way of peace. Maybe God is using this threat to give us the opportunity to recognize our common humanity, to bring us into the one world, the one community, the one family of God.

Bishop Walter Sullivan
Sojourners
January 1982

Therefore if you insist upon fighting to protect me, or "our" country, let it be understood, soberly and rationally between us, that you are fighting to gratify a sex instinct which I cannot share; to procure benefits which I have not shared and probably will not share; but not to gratify my instincts, or to protect either myself or my country. For...in fact, as a woman, I have no country. As a woman, I want no country. As a woman, my country is the whole world.

Virginia Woolf
Three Guineas

People who develop the habit of thinking of themselves as world citizens are fulfilling the first requirement of sanity in our time.

Norman Cousins

* Our country is the world, our countrymen are all mankind.

William Lloyd Garrison

I'm not into isms and asms. There isn't a Catholic moon and a Baptist sun. I know the universal God is universal....I feel that the same God-force that is the mother and father of the Pope is also the mother and father of the loneliest wino on the planet.

Dick Gregory

We appeal, as human beings to human beings: Remember your humanity, and forget the rest.

in a statement signed by
Bertrand Russell, Albert Einstein, and others

ADDITIONS:

ADDITIONS:

19
Earth Keeping

...peace, not conflict, is the prevailing mode of life in nature: 95 percent of all living beings die naturally of old age or sickness (without human interference), and violence causes only 5 percent of all deaths.

Sydney J. Harris

Peace on and with the earth. For all its children.

The Second Biennial Conference on the Fate of the Earth

* The earth-mother had many children other than men: the stem of long wild grass that developed into a stalk of maize, the lofty spruce, all the birds of the air, the beasts of the plain and forest, the insect and the ant. They too had equal rights to life.

Hopi Legend
Frank Waters
The American Indian Speaks

A weed is nothing more than a flower in disguise.

Jane Russell Lowell

Treat the earth well...it was not given to you by your parents....It was lent to you by your children.

Kenyan Proverb

In our every deliberation, we must consider the impact of our decisions on the next seven generations...on those faces that are yet beneath the ground.

The Great Law of the Six Nations Iroquois Confederacy

* We seek a renewed stirring of love for the earth. We urge that what man is capable of doing to the earth is not always what he ought to do, and we plead that all people, here, now determine that a wide, spacious untrammeled freedom shall remain as living testimony that this generation, *our own*, had *love* for the next.

David Brower

...we need to preserve a few places, a few samples of primeval country so that when the pace gets too fast we can look at it, think about it, contemplate it, and somehow restore equanimity to our souls.

Sigurd Olson

So many major structures of belief have arisen at least in part from experiences in wilderness....Moses, Jesus and Mohammed in the desert mountains, Siddhartha in the jungle...the five year wilderness voyage of a Victorian amateur naturalist named Charles Darwin. There evidently is more to wilderness than meets the eye...psychic raw materials from which every age has cut, dammed or quarried an invisible civilization....

David Rains Wallace
The Klamath Knot

We face the question whether a still higher "standard of living" is worth its cost in things natural, wild and free. For us of the minority, the opportunity to see geese is more important than television, and the chance to find a pasque-flower is a right as inalienable as free speech.

Aldo Leopold

We sang songs that carried in their melodies all the sounds of nature—the running of waters, the sighing of winds, and the calls of the animals. Teach these to your children that they may come to love nature as we love it.

Grand Council Fire of American Indians
to the Mayor of Chicago
December 1927

To us peple the woods and the big hills and the Northern lights and the sunsets are all alive and we live with these things and live in the spirit of the woods like no white person can do. The big lakes we travel on, the little lonely lakes we set our beaver traps on with a ring of big black pines standin in rows lookin always north, like they were watchin for somethin that never comes, same as the Injun, they are real to us and when we are alone we speak to them and are not lonesome, only thinkin always of the long ago days and the old men. So we live in the past and the rest of the world keeps goin by. For all their modern inventions they cant live the way we do and they die if they try because they cant read the sunset and hear the old men talk in the wind.

Anaquoness
Ojibway, wounded while serving in France in WWI
February 1918

* The smallest mosquito is more wonderful than anything man will ever produce. So man must never lose his sense of the marvelousness of the world around and inside him—a world which he has not made and which, assuredly, has not made itself. Such an attitude engenders a spirit of nonviolence...

E. F. Schumacher

I never kill a bird or other animal without feeling bad inside. All true hunters must have that feeling that prevents them from killing just for killing's sake. There is no fun in just destroying life, and the Great Spirit puts that shadow in your heart when you destroy his creatures.

Joe Friday
Woods Cree Indian

With riches has come inexcusable waste. We have squandered a great part of what we might have used and have not stopped to conserve the exceeding bounty of nature, without which our genius for enterprise would have been worthless and impotent.

Woodrow Wilson

Garbage is not something you throw away. There is no such place as away. Disposal is a myth...

Nancy Cosper
Knowing Home

Every now and then I am impressed with the thinking of the non-Indian. I was in Cleveland...talking with a non-Indian about American history. He said that he was really sorry about what had happened to Indians, but that there was good reason for it. The continent had to be developed and he felt that Indians had stood in the way and thus had to be removed. "After all," he remarked, "what did you do with the land when you had it?" I didn't understand him until later when I discovered that the Cayahoga River running through Cleveland is inflammable. So many combustible pollutants are dumped into the river that the inhabitants have to take special precautions during the summer to avoid accidentally setting it on fire. After reviewing the argument of my non-Indian friend I decided that he was probably correct. Whites had made better use of the land. How many Indians could have thought of creating an inflammable river?

Vine Deloria, Jr.
We Talk, You Listen

Our honeymoon with the planet earth is over. We must take our marriage with the earth seriously. We cannot divorce it, but it can divorce us!

Grandon Harris

* How can the spirit of the earth like the white man?...Everywhere the white man has touched it, it is sore.

Wintu woman
Touch the Earth

We have probed the earth, excavated it, burned it, ripped things from it, buried things in it, chopped down its forests, leveled its hills, muddied its waters and dirtied its air. That does not fit my definition of a good tenant. If we were here on a month to month basis, we would have been evicted long ago.

Rose Bird
Chief Justice
California Supreme Court

An environmental setting developed over millions of years must be considered to have some merit. Anything so complicated as a planet, inhabited by more than a million and a half species of plants and animals, all of them living together in a more or less balanced equilibrium in which they continually use and reuse the same molecules of the soil and air, cannot be improved by aimless and uninformed tinkering.

E. F. Schumacher
Small Is Beautiful

* [According to the Bible] man was created in God's own image and divinely commanded to subdue the earth....We have so denuded the grasslands and forested mountains that the topsoil is washing down the drain into the sea. The underground water level is lowering so rapidly that we are being forced to develop means for purifying sea water for our use. The very air we breathe is becoming dangerously toxic in all our cities, and radioactive fallout from our latest technological triumph is laying wide swaths around the whole planet.

Yet it is not enough to have subdued a continent and exhausted its natural resources. There still remains a vast domain of untouched nature in the universe—the other planets in outer space.

Frank Waters
The American Indian Speaks

When you have pollution in one place, it spreads all over. It spreads just as arthritis or cancer spreads in the body. The earth is sick now because the earth is being mistreated, and some of the problems that may occur, some of the natural disasters that might happen in the near future, are only the natural adjustments that have to take place to throw off the sickness.

Rolling Thunder
modern medicine man

* Man did not make the earth, and though he had a natural right to occupy it, he had no right to locate as his property in perpetuity, any part of it.

Tom Paine
1796

* The earth was created by the assistance of the sun, and it should be left as it was...the country was made without lines of demarcation and it is no man's business to divide it....I never said the land was mine to do with it as I chose. The one who has the right to dispose of it is the one who created it. I claim a right to live on my land, and accord you the privilege to live on yours.

Chief Joseph
Nez Percé

* Some of our chiefs make the claim that the land belongs to us. It is not what the Great Spirit told me. He told me that the lands belong to Him, that no people owns the land; that I was not to forget to tell this to the white people when I met them in council.

Kannekuk
Kickapoo prophet
1827
I Have Spoken

How can you buy or sell the sky, the warmth of the land? If we do not own the freshness of the air and the sparkle of the water, how can you buy them?

> **Chief Seattle**
> **1854**

The land was not tangible property to be owned, divided, and alienated at will. It was their Mother Earth from which they were born, on whose breast they were suckled, and to whose womb they were returned in a prenatal posture at death.

> **Hopi Legend**
> **Frank Waters**
> *The American Indian Speaks*

The earth is part of my body, and I never gave up the earth.

> **Toohulhulsote**
> **a Nez Percé prophet**

Too many people don't know that when they harm the earth they harm themselves, nor do they realize that when they harm themselves, they harm the earth.

> **Rolling Thunder**
> **a modern medicine man**

* This we know. The earth does not belong to man; man belongs to the earth. This we know. All things are connected. Whatever befalls the earth befalls the sons of the earth. Man did not weave the web of life. He is merely a strand in it. Whatever he does to the web, he does to himself.

> **Chief Seattle**
> **1854**

* Man was not created apart from nature...but out of nature whose unconscious forces and instinctual drives still swayed him. So we, the white, while subduing nature, also tried to subdue the aspect of nature within ourself....Our own minds and bodies became the battleground of man against nature, man against God, and man against himself, divided into two warring selves: reason and instinct, the conscious and the unconscious....They had cut themselves off from the roots of life.

> **Frank Waters**
> *The American Indian Speaks*

* A man's heart away from nature becomes hard...lack of respect for growing, living things soon leads to lack of respect for humans too.

> **Lakota Belief**
> *Touch the Earth*

When we see land as a community to which we belong, we may begin to use it with love and respect.

Aldo Leopold

...understanding begins with love and respect. It begins with respect for the Great Spirit, and the Great Spirit is the life that is in all things—all the creatures and the plants and even the rocks and the mineral....Such respect is not a feeling or an attitude only. It's a way of life. Such respect means that we never stop realizing and never neglect to carry out our obligation to ourselves and our environment.

Rolling Thunder
a modern medicine man

* Man must recognize the necessity of co-operating with nature. He must temper his demands and use and conserve the natural living resources of this earth in a manner that alone can provide for the continuation of his civilization.

Fairfield Osborn

When we deal gently with the earth—even when we have thoughtlessly damaged it—we can repair our friendship with it.

René Dubos

* Nature is sovereign and man's inner nature is sovereign. Nature is to be respected. All life and every single living being is to be respected. That's the only answer.

Rolling Thunder
a modern medicine man

The nuclear peril is usually seen in isolation from the threats to other forms of life and their ecosystems, but in fact should be seen as the very center of the ecological crisis....Both the effort to preserve the environment and the effort to save the species from extinction by nuclear arms would be strengthened by this recognition. The nuclear question, which now stands in eerie seclusion from the rest of life, would gain a context, and the ecological movement...would gain the humanistic intent that should stand at the heart of its concern.

Jonathan Schell
The Fate of the Earth

* If, in a nuclear holocaust, anyone hid himself deep enough under the earth and stayed there long enough to survive, he would emerge into a dying natural environment. The vulnerability of the environment is the last word in the argument against the usefulness of shelters: there is no hole big enough to hide all of nature in.

Jonathan Schell

If animals could vote they would be against nuclear war.

Mark M.
Los Angeles, Age 7
Please Save My World

If we don't stop the bomb who will take care of the flowers?

Neil J.
Seattle, Age 9
Please Save My World

We are the curators of life on earth. We hold it in the palm of our hands. And it is our ultimate responsibility as spiritual, and moral, feeling human beings, and not as scientists, to save this planet.

Dr. Helen Caldicott

If we do not speak for Earth, who will? If we are not committed to our own survival, who will be?

Carl Sagan
Cosmos

* The frog does not drink up the pond in which he lives.

Native American proverb

Any scientist can testify that a dead ocean means a dead planet....No national law, no national precautions can save the planet. The ocean, more than any other part of our planet,...is a classic example of the absolute need for international, global action.

Thor Heyerdahl

I pledge allegiance to the world,
To cherish every living thing,
To care for earth and sea and air,
With peace and freedom everywhere.

Lillian Genser
Women's International League for Peace and Freedom

ADDITIONS:

20
Social Justice

Peace is not just the absence of war but the presence of justice.

Anonymous

If you want peace, work for justice.   Pope Paul VI

Only justice ends war.   Anonymous

There is something within the human spirit that cries for and demands to be treated with basic fairness and justice. When such is violated, peace is undermined. Seeking justice for others is a way to peace.

Myron R. Chartier

The best defence of peace is not power, but the removal of the causes of war...

Lester B. Pearson
former Prime Minister, Canada

The simple repression of subversion can never be a lasting remedy, for it fails to take account of the causes of subversion. Most of the causes reside in our situations of institutionalized violence. Thus the radical remedy for subversion is the radical suppression of social inequalities...

Declaration of the International Meeting
of Latin American Bishops
Nonviolence: A Power for Liberation
November/December 1977

We live in a whole climate of violence. There is violence in the area of economics by reason of acute fiscal crises, the repeated devaluation of our currencies, unemployment, and soaring taxes— the burden of which ultimately falls on the poor and helpless. There is violence at the political level, as our people in varying degrees are deprived of their right of self-expression and self-determination and of the exercise of their civil rights. Still more grave in many countries are human-rights violations in the form of torture, kidnappings, and murder. Violence also makes its appearance in various forms of delinquency, in drug abuse as an escape from reality, in the mistreatment of women—all tragic expressions of frustration and of the spiritual and cultural decadence of a people losing their hope in tomorrow.

Declaration of the International Meeting
of Latin American Bishops
November/December 1977

It is organized violence on top which creates individual violence at the bottom.

Emma Goldman

There are two different sorts of violence: violence of assault and violence of defense. There are those who seek "conflict at any price" and there are those who seek "peace at any price." The price in both cases is violence....We reject both brands of violence. And we call for the radical elimination, not of the enemy, surely, but of the root cause of the enmity.

Chilean Bishops
The Gospel and Peace
September 1975

We realize conflicts may not cease. But we know that increasing the size and capabilities of the military is like increasing the size of a band-aid when a disorder is internal.

Healing will take place only as we understand and treat the root causes of instability within and between nations.

Women's Peace Presence

Peace cannot suddenly descend from the heavens. It can only come when the root-causes of trouble are removed.

Jawaharlal Nehru

...since justice is indivisible, injustice anywhere is an affront to justice everywhere.

Martin Luther King, Jr.

If a free society cannot help the many who are poor, it cannot save the few who are rich.

John F. Kennedy

We know that a peaceful world cannot long exist one-third rich and two-thirds hungry.

Jimmy Carter
1977

We cannot build a secure world upon a foundation of human misery.

Robert McNamara

Development is the new word for peace.

Anonymous

...those who defend the ideal of liberating the underdeveloped lands from the slavery of communism should learn from Paul VI that poverty also is a slavery, and that freedom is an empty word...absolutely meaningless for the two-thirds of humanity who are slaves to hunger, disease, ignorance and colonialism.

Archbishop Dom Helder Camara

...their politics are confined to bread.

Mahatma Gandhi

Poverty is the worst form of violence.   **Mahatma Gandhi**

Hunger and poverty are no accidents. They are the fruits of social injustice.

Clergy and Laity Concerned

...statistics suggest that the world hunger problem is not one of inadequate food, but one of unequal distribution of the available resources—food, sanitation, education.

Hamilton, Whitney, and Sizer
Nutrition, Concepts and Controversies

The myths that hunger results from overpopulation or insufficient production have been exploded. The planet has the productive capacity and technology to feed the population. Hunger is the product of unjust policies and economic structures, of consumerism and materialism, of greed and avarice.

Moises Sandoval

It is often argued that poverty is caused by people's having too many children, but persuasive statistics from many sources reveal that this is not the cause of their poverty. Rather, the poverty is the cause of their having so many children: hunger is one of the prime causes of the population explosion.

Hamilton, Whitney, and Sizer
Nutrition, Concepts and Controversies

There is enough food for everyone. But not everyone has enough food. Too much food produced by the poor feeds the animals eaten by the rich. Too much land in developing countries produces cash crops for the industrialized world. When some people go hungry, it is not food that's in short supply—it's justice.

Food First **newsletter**

I worked on the hacienda over there, and I would have to feed the dogs bowls of meat or bowls of milk every morning, and I could never put those on the table for my own children. When my children were ill, they died with a nod of sympathy from the landlord. But when the dogs were ill, I took them to the veterinarian in Suchitoto.

You will never understand violence or nonviolence until you understand the violence to the spirit that happens from watching your children die of malnutrition.

a peasant in El Salvador
Witness to War

Half of Central America's agricultural land produces food for export, while in several of its countries the poorest 50 percent of the population eat only half the protein they need. (The richest 5 percent, on the other hand, consume two to three times more than they need.)

Frances Moore Lappé and J. Collins
Food First: Beyond the Myth of Scarcity

Mexico now supplies the United States with over half of its supply of several winter and early spring vegetables, while infant deaths associated with poor nutrition are common.

Frances Moore Lappé and J. Collins
Food First: Beyond the Myth of Scarcity

We see dramatic news footage of South African police shooting randomly into crowds. We hear daily reports of more deaths caused by violence. But what many people do not know is that apartheid kills in other ways. Many more black South Africans die from hunger than from police violence—some 50,000 black children die from hunger every year.

Food First newsletter

Apartheid means starvation in a land of plenty. South Africa is among the top seven food exporters in the world. Every year it exports more than a billion dollars worth of beef, grain, vegetables and fruit.

Yet every day 136 black children die from hunger.

The problem is not a lack of food but a lack of justice. It is apartheid—South Africa's system of racial domination—that keeps the black majority hungry. There can be no end to hunger in South Africa without an end to apartheid.

Food First newsletter

Africa is a net exporter of barley, beans, peanuts, fresh vegetables, and cattle (not to mention luxury crop exports such as coffee and cocoa), yet it has a higher incidence of protein-calorie malnutrition among young children than any other continent.

Frances Moore Lappé and J. Collins
Food First: Beyond the Myth of Scarcity

...if we compare the sums we receive from abroad in the form of investments with the money returning there, we see that we, the poor, the underdeveloped are helping the developed countries. This is shocking! It's unbelievable!

Archbishop Dom Helder Camara

The tragic scenario unfolds this way. Large landowners and multinational corporations control the best farmlands, and they use them mainly to grow crops that can be exported at considerable profit. Native persons work for below-subsistence wages and are forced onto marginal lands to do their own farming. The poor work hard, but they are cultivating crops for other people, rather than for themselves. The money they earn is not enough even to buy the products they help produce. The result is that the foods they export—bananas, beef, cocoa, coconuts, coffee, pineapples, sugar, tea, winter tomatoes, and others fill our grocery stores, while the poor who grow these foods, have even less food than before. Countless examples can be cited to illustrate how natural resources are diverted from producing food for domestic consumption to producing luxury crops for those who can afford them.

Hamilton, Whitney, and Sizer
Nutrition, Concepts and Controversies

Paying for a worldwide military presence is part of this nation's hidden cost...for relatively low-cost bananas, clothes, gasoline and aluminum foil.

Russell Herman

The primary reason for hunger in Ethiopia is that the government in power is essentially a military government, with military priorities.

Joe Collins
Institute for Food and Development Policy

Peace we want because there is another war to fight against poverty, disease and ignorance. We have promises to keep to our people of work, food, clothing and shelter, health and education.

Indira Gandhi

We must abandon our Edsel policy of building ever more devastating bombs and win the important competition to produce better lives and economies in the Third World. Americans must join to take the management of the American enterprise away from the experts who produced the Edsel.

William E. Colby
former Director, CIA

Stop looking at nations by who their leaders are allies with and start looking at leaders and how they meet the needs of their people.

Anonymous

Our nation cannot call for respect for human rights when it lacks the moral courage to save its own cities, its own poor, its own minorities whose rights are trampled upon.

Vernon Jordan

The mark of a civilized society is that people are fed and clothed and housed.

Madge Micheels-Cyrus

Someone has described this country as having socialism for the rich and capitalism for the poor.

Anonymous

The pathos of it all is that the America which is to be protected by a huge military force is not the America of the people, but that of the privileged class; the class which robs and exploits the masses, and controls their lives from the cradle to the grave.

Emma Goldman

The arms race is the welfare program of the sun belt and the upper class.

I. F. Stone

Without "industrial disarmament"—that is, an absolute reduction in global demand for raw materials and energy, and a corresponding technological transformation—it will be possible neither to attain a genuine military disarmament nor to restore the ability of poor Southern Hemisphere countries to provide themselves with adequate means of subsistence. The voracity of our giant industrial machinery cannot do without rapid deployment forces and neocolonial production branches.

Rudolf Bahro

We consume arms, we consume useless products, we consume everything in sight. And we end up by consuming human beings themselves.

Adolfo Pérez Esquivel
1980 Nobel Peace Prize
Christ in a Poncho

No one has the right to create an economy at the expense of the world's poor.

Adolfo Pérez Esquivel
1980 Nobel Peace Prize
Christ in a Poncho

* I sit on a man's back choking him and making him carry me, and yet assure myself and others that I am sorry for him and wish to lighten his load by all possible means—except by getting off his back.

Leo Tolstoy

No world settlement that affords nations only a place on relief rolls will provide the basis for a just and durable peace.

William O. Douglas

Capitalism and communism are both imperialisms that provide only half answers. They make the human being an object....We want something besides capitalism or communism, something on the order of self-management and sharing.

Adolfo Pérez Esquivel
1980 Nobel Peace Prize
Christ in a Poncho

What good is culture, philosophy, or science if men and women become objects instead of subjects?

Adolfo Pérez Esquivel
1980 Nobel Peace Prize
Christ in a Poncho

There are two ways to get enough. One is to continue to accumulate more and more. The other is to desire less.

G. K. Chesterton

Find out how much God has given you, and from it take what you need; the remainder is needed by others. The superfluities of the rich are the necessities of the poor. Those who retain what is superfluous possess the goods of others.

St. Augustine

There is an important task of education facing us, especially with our youth, lest they too be dragged into the consumer society we have created for ourselves. We must help them find life values, life's essential values. They must learn that a more just and humane world is possible only if...we live with our sisters and brothers in understanding, in sharing, and in communion.

Adolfo Pérez Esquivel
1980 Nobel Peace Prize
Christ in a Poncho

I am a man of peace. God knows how I love peace. But I hope I shall never be such a coward as to mistake oppression for peace.

Lajos Kossuth

All oppression creates a state of war.

Simone de Beauvoir

* The man who has got everything he wants is all in favour of peace and order.

Jawaharlal Nehru

Nothing is so hard for those who abound in riches as to conceive how others can be in want.

Jonathan Swift

Those who make peaceful change impossible, make violent revolution inevitable.

John F. Kennedy
Address to Latin American Ambassadors
1963

Whatever the apparent cause of any riots may be, the real one is always want of happiness. It shows that something is wrong in the system of government that injures the felicity by which society is to be preserved.

Thomas Paine
1792

* For the social revolution means nothing if it is not a battle for humanity against all that is inhuman and unworthy of man. That is why we have always asserted that the more there is of real revolution, the less there is of violence; the more violence, the less of revolution.

Barthelemy de Ligt

There can be no beauty if it is paid for by human injustice, nor truth that passes over injustice in silence, nor moral virtue that condones it.

Tadeusz Borowski
This Way for the Gas, Ladies and Gentlemen

Some things you must always be unable to bear....Injustice and outrage and dishonor and shame. No matter how young you are or how old you have got....Just refuse to bear them.

William Faulkner

They made us many promises, more than I can remember, but they never kept but one; they promised to take our land, and they took it.

Anonymous Native American

Red power means we want power over our own lives....We do not wish power over anyone. We are only half a million Indians. We simply want the power, the political and economic power, to run our own lives in our own way.

Vine Deloria
National Congress of American Indians
1966

Power should not be concentrated in the hands of so few and powerlessness in the hands of so many.

Maggie Kuhn

In South Africa:
- Blacks are 70% of the population but can own land in just 13% of the country.
- Blacks can own no more than 4 acres of land, while white farms average 3,000 acres.
- Black workers earn as little as $30 per month, and unemployment is over 25 percent.
- Blacks are denied basic rights such as voting and deciding where to live.

Institute for Food and Development Policy

Those who invest in South Africa are here for what they get out of our cheap and abundant labor. They are buttressing one of the most vicious systems.

Bishop Desmond Tutu
1984 Nobel Peace Laureate

Women constitute half the world's population, perform nearly two-thirds of its work hours, receive one-tenth of the world's income and own less than one-hundredth of the world's property.

United Nations Report
1980

Individuals can resist injustice, but only a community can do justice.

Jim Corbett
sanctuary worker

But if by some miracle, and all our struggle, the Earth is spared, only justice to every living thing (and everything is alive) will save humankind.

Alice Walker

We move from the quicksands of social injustice to the solid rock of human dignity.

Martin Luther King, Jr.

All we ask, Oh Lord, is to be safe from the rain, just warm enough in winter to watch the snow with a smile, enough to eat so that our hunger will not turn us to angry beasts, and sanity enough to make a justice that will not kill our love of life.

Joseph Pintauro

Although the world is very full of suffering, it is also full of the overcoming of it.

Helen Keller

ADDITIONS:

21
By and About the Soviets

A bad compromise is better than a good battle.

Russian proverb

In recent times a complete change has come about. Today, Russia possesses in reality, and not simply on paper, an army which is always prepared for battle and which can quickly be concentrated at a given location....We believe that the conquest of Europe [by Russia] will be easy in the future if the social order of Europe continues to deteriorate and if the governments continue to grow weaker...and particularly if France is completely debilitated politically by an increasing republicanization or by socialistic-communistic revolutions.

Baron August von Haxthausen
1852

No nation in the history of battle ever suffered more than the Soviet Union suffered in the course of the Second World War. At least 20 million lost their lives. Countless millions of homes and farms were burned or sacked. A third of the nation's territory, including nearly two-thirds of its industrial base, was turned into a wasteland—a loss equivalent to the devastation of this country east of Chicago.

John F. Kennedy
June 1963

Soviet War Deaths—WWI and WWII: 31,700,000
American War Deaths—Civil War through Vietnam: . . . 1,000,000

Defense Monitor
Center for Defense Information

They [Soviets] don't want nuclear war any more than we do. In fact, in many ways they—this generation has been through hell. They lost 20 million people. They talk to you about it all the time. They don't want to see their children go through the hell they went through. And anybody that thinks they want to bring war to their territory just doesn't understand this generation of Russian leaders.

Averell Harriman
former US Ambassador to the USSR

I find the view of the Soviet Union that prevails today in our government and journalistic establishments so extreme, so subjective, so far removed from what any sober scrutiny of external reality would reveal, that it is not only ineffective, but dangerous as a guide to political action. This endless series of distortions and over-simplifications; this systematic dehumanization of the leadership of another great country; this routine exaggeration of Moscow's military capabilities and of the supposed inequity of its intentions; this daily misrepresentation of the nature and the attitudes of another great people...this reckless application of the double standard to the judgment of Soviet conduct and our own; this failure to recognize the commonality of many of their problems and ours as we both move inexorably into the modern technological age...these, believe me, are not the marks of the maturity and realism one expects of the diplomacy of a great power.

George Kennan
former US Ambassador to the USSR

Our anti-communism has become so totally a national obsession that it colors and dominates all our thinking, all our planning, and all our name-calling. We no longer give much thought to what is better for America, but rather what is worse for Russia. The most effective argument in official debate or personal argument is the assertion that communists favor a course of action someone is opposing.

The Progressive
October 1951

The Nation which indulges toward another an habitual hatred or an habitual fondness is in some degree a slave. It is a slave to its animosity or to its affection, either of which is sufficient to lead it astray from its duty and its interest.

George Washington

* Fear of Communism has more often than not poisoned us to our roots. Fear of Communism degraded us by murdering Sacco and Vanzetti. Fear of Communism caused countless deaths and mutilations in the Labor Movement in the years before World War II. This terrible fear, inflamed by Senator Joe McCarthy, turned friend against friend, wife against husband, brother against brother and ruined the lives and reputations of hundreds of innocent men and women, thirty years ago. Most catastrophic of all, encouraged by industrial profiteers, our fear has led us into wars in places we never belonged; wars whose dismal outcome can show little or no gain, moral or physical, for the fact of our participation. Hideous and bloody stalemates like Korea, or far worse, Vietnam, where thousands and thousands died utterly futile deaths, or returned home maimed and brutalized in body and spirit.

William Styron
author, Duke University speech

We have been opposed to any social change that carried the taint of the political left, especially any change that could be labeled "communistic." We have supported fascists, dictators, and military juntas—anyone who professes "anti-communism"—no matter how oppressive and reactionary, no matter how they retard the legitimate aspirations of the people, as long as they served the perceived temporary self-interests of the United States. We have become the caretakers of the status quo.

Anti-communism is an inadequate substitute for a rational and humanitarian foreign policy; we should express a concern for people and not their ideology....The world of the "good guys and the bad guys" may be less complex, less troublesome, and problems seem to be more easily resolved, but it simply does not exist.

Dale E. Noyd
Air Force officer who refused to go to Vietnam
We Won't Go

No government or social system is so evil that its people must be considered as lacking in virtue. As Americans, we find communism profoundly repugnant as a negation of personal freedom and dignity. But we can still hail the Russian people for their many achievements....Both the United States and its allies, and the Soviet Union and its allies have a mutually deep interest in a just and genuine peace and in halting the arms race.

John F. Kennedy

We use a word like "Communist." POW! That person vanishes. We have all kinds of emotional content in that word Communist. I want you to know that I went to the Communist bloc countries to share some of our knowledge, and do you know what I found? (And don't let it get out.) They're people just like you...did you know that? They don't have tails, 'cause I looked. And they don't have horns, because I felt. But they do cry just like you do, and they do care about their kids just the way you do, and they do feel lonely sometimes and they do feel great joy sometimes and sometimes they dance in the street and sing happy songs, just like you. Isn't that incredible? "Communist." POW! Just the word alone is enough for us to get a gun and go kill 'em. The horror of words!

Leo Buscaglia

I've been called naive and stupid because I say the Russians cannot be all evil and let's go and get acquainted, but the idea of talking with Communists does not strike me with shaking palsy....Here are two populous and intelligent but poorly communicating masses of people, living far from each other, speaking different languages, seldom seeing each other, and really having nothing tangible to quarrel about, who are poised ready to attack each other.... I say, for the love of God and humanity and Earth and all the goodness—yes, and all of the sorrows— let us not deliberately continue carelessly this eye-for-an-eye and tooth-for-a-tooth behavior.

Dr. Karl Menninger

If we insist on demonizing these Soviet leaders—on viewing them as total and incorrigible enemies, consumed only with their fear or hatred of us and dedicated to nothing other than our destruction—that, in the end, is the way we shall assuredly have them, if for no other reason than that our view of them allows for nothing else, either for us or for them.

George Kennan
former US Ambassador to the USSR

Psychologists tell us that we always project our most loathsome and vile features onto the enemy.

Rusty Schweickart
Apollo Astronaut

I'd like to have a world with peace because I could make friends with the Russian people and have even more friends than what I have now.

6th Grader

Many fear that we cannot work with the Russians. The truth is that we already are doing so.   **William Ury**

The problems presented by the Soviet Union are serious. But stereotypes do not provide us with an adequate basis for responding intelligently.

Marshall D. Shulman
former State Department employee

Americans should know the people of the Soviet Union—their hopes and fears and the facts of their lives...people-to-people initiatives...will help break down stereotypes, build friendships, and, frankly, provide alternatives to propaganda.

Ronald Reagan
November 1985

One superpower is noted for its advocacy of "political" human rights, the other for its attention to "economic" human rights—yet both blocs are notorious for rights they neglect or ignore.

International Fellowship of Reconciliation

Human Rights! New York is where you should look for violations. There, the people have to sleep on the sidewalks and sift through garbage cans.

Andrei Gromyko
May 1984

Either we have to learn to live with the Russians or we and the Russians will die at about the same time. And I am all for living.

George Kistiakowsky
scientist, Manhattan Project

The Soviet Union is not our enemy, nuclear weapons are the enemy. We're going to have to learn to live with the Russians or we and the Russians are going to die at about the same time.

Rear Admiral Gene R. La Rocque
U.S. Navy (retired)

The communist threat grows strong when there are prospects for weapons contracts but diminishes as opportunities to market American goods in Russia present themselves.   **Robert Aldridge**

Unfortunately, we've tended to think of arms control as being some sort of favor that we're doing for the Soviet Union. So when the Soviet Union misbehaves, we cancel the arms control negotiations. That makes no sense.

Paul Warnke
U.S. negotiator for SALT II

The Soviet buildup is not a sudden surge. It has been a long-range program. I don't necessarily think that buildup is for adventures around the world. It is my feeling that they are doing it because they feel it is necessary for their own security.

Gerald Ford
January 1977

The Soviets learn their lessons well, but in many cases too well, and they may find themselves doomed to repeat history by paying too much attention to it. Virtually every major characteristic of the Soviet groundforce structure and every attendant tactic is a result of a lesson learned (usually at great cost) during World War II.

Edward A. Miller
Assistant Secretary of the Army for Research and Development
and Lt. General Howard H. Cooksey
Deputy Army Chief of Staff for
Research, Development, and Acquisition

The Soviets are upgrading and expanding the ballistic missile defense system at Moscow but are thus far remaining within the limits of the treaty.

General John A. Wickham, Jr.
Army Chief of Staff
on Soviet Anti-Ballistic Missile Treaty compliance
1984

The 100-missile interceptor defense projected for the ongoing Moscow upgrade would quickly be exhausted in a large-scale attack....The available evidence does not indicate with any certainty whether the Soviets are making preparations for deployments beyond the limits of the ABM Treaty.

General Charles A. Gabriel
Air Force Chief of Staff
1984

As you know, with the subs and missiles, they have pretty well conformed to SALT II. There may have been some cheating on the margins, but they have pretty well stuck to the numbers requirements in SALT I and II, and we can see that as they dismantle their subs and whatnot.

General Charles A. Gabriel

New missiles, bombers and aircraft carriers are being churned out in some kind of pathological obsession. The present U.S. Administration is thinking in terms of war and acting accordingly.

Andrei Gromyko
January 1984

Militarism, hostility and war hysteria are exported together with those missiles. As a result, the world is pushed closer and closer to a nuclear abyss.

Dmitri Ustinov
March 1984

There are some who would like to turn space into an arena of aggression and war, as is clear from the plans announced in the United States.

Konstantin Chernenko
May 1984

It is a long time since the American capital has seen such a noisy militaristic orgy, arranged by the Reagan Administration on the occasion of the burial of the Unknown Soldier.

TASS (Soviet press agency)
May 1984

[The Reagan Administration] has chosen terrorism as a method of conducting affairs with other states and peoples.

Konstantin Chernenko
June 1984

The Americans and the Soviets are literally scaring each other to death...

George McGovern
August 1985

We must make sure that we don't allow ourselves to get involved in a lot of senseless competition with the West over military spending....We must be prepared to strike back against our enemy, but we must also ask, "Where is the end of this spiraling competition?"

Nikita Khrushchev

There is no illusion more dangerous than the idea that nuclear war can still serve as an instrument of policy, that one can attain political aims by using nuclear weapons and at the same time get off scot-free oneself, or that acceptable forms of nuclear war can be found.

N. A. Talenski
Soviet Major General

The first time one of those things is fired in anger, everything is lost. The warring nations would never be able to put matters back together.

Leonid Brezhnev

Above all, nuclear powers must avert those confrontations which bring an adversary to a choice of either a humiliating retreat or a nuclear war. To adopt that kind of course would be evidence only of the bankruptcy of our policy—or a collective death wish for the world.

John F. Kennedy

In a nuclear war, the survivors would envy the dead.

Nikita Khrushchev

Today, when the danger is looming large, when several minutes is enough for millions of people in any part of the planet to get annihilated in a nuclear conflagration, we must rally still closer the ranks of those who struggle for peace, against the threat of a nuclear catastrophe, so as to preserve life on Earth, and save our children's future.

Using concerted efforts, we should seek to make the new negotiations between our countries to be held on questions of nuclear and outer space armaments, constructive, just, and having as their basis the principle of equality and equal security.

K. Proskurnikova
Vice-President
Soviet Women's Committee
January 1985

* When you reach America again...tell them that here we are full of joy and love, we are not afraid. Tell them that our life, the life of the church, is a miracle. Tell them that the Church is alive. We can see and feel here the presence of the kingdom of God, and tell them that we must pray for each other, and for the peace of the whole world.

Mrs. Voskrenenia
Russian hostess for visiting American Christians

Better to turn back than lose your way.

Russian proverb

ADDITIONS:

(See also quotes in Chapter 2—**Facts of the Arms Race**—especially page 23 by Dimitri Ustinov.)

22
Spirituality of Peace

A. Inner Peace

B. Love

C. Moral Condemnation of Violence and War

D. Spiritual Teachings

E. The Bible on Peace

    1. The Old Testament

    2. The New Testament

F. Religion and Politics

What we have experienced and are still experiencing must surely convince us that the spirit is everything and that institutions count for very little....The best planned improvements in the organization of our society cannot help us at all until we have become at the same time capable of imparting a new spirit to our age.

Albert Schweitzer
The Decay and Restoration of Civilization
1923

* I do not believe the greatest threat to our future is from bombs or guided missiles. I don't think our civilization will die that way. I think it will die when we no longer care—when the spiritual forces that make us wish to be right and noble die in the hearts of men. Arnold Toynbee has pointed out that 19 of 21 civilizations have died from within and not conquest from without. There were no bands playing and flags waving when these civilizations decayed. It happened slowly, in the quiet and the dark when no one was aware.

Lawrence Gould
former President
Carleton College

* With the phenomenal rise and spread of Western civilization we have now become the richest materialistic nation that ever existed on this planet, and we have created untold benefits for all mankind. The monstrous paradox is that we have impoverished ourselves spiritually in the process.

Frank Waters
The American Indian Speaks

* You white men will soon be crushed under your machines, rotting in the endless swamp of your materialism. You have lost the essence of man; the impulse toward something that is more than yourselves.

Nikos Kazantzakis

* Admittedly it may take an all-out fatal shock treatment, close to catastrophe, to break the hold of civilized man's chronic psychosis. Even such a belated awakening would be a miracle. But with the diagnosis so grave and the prognosis so unfavorable, one must fall back on miracles—above all, the miracle of life itself, that past master of the unexpected, the unpredictable, the all-but-impossible.

Lewis Mumford
The Origins of War

People usually consider walking on water or in thin air a miracle. But I think the real miracle is not to walk either on water or in thin air, but to walk on earth.

Thich Nhat Hanh

* The world needs a revolution in feeling, in sensitivity, in orientation, in the spirit of man.

A. J. Muste

A. Inner Peace

There never was a war that was not inward; I must fight till I have conquered in myself what causes war...

Marianne Moore

...your ideas form your private and mass reality. You want to examine the universe from the outside, to examine your societies from the outside. You still think that the interior world is somehow symbolic and the exterior world is real. That wars, for example, are fought by themselves or with bombs. All of the time, the psychological reality is the primary one, that forms all of your events.   (Seth) Jane Roberts
The Individual and the Nature of Mass Events

When we do not find peace within ourselves, it is vain to seek for it elsewhere.

Duc François de La Rochefoucauld

He had so much security inside that he could afford to go without any outside.

said about Kagawa, a Japanese pacifist
Courage in Both Hands

To me the only answer to all our problems, whether they're political, economic, personal or whatever, is to act from the center of ourselves. Act, not react. Acting from the wholeness that we are, which is our soul level...and when we contact that we're not defensive or on the defensive or offensive or anything else because we're secure in what we are. We know who we are. We know we're part of the whole.

Dorothy Maclean
founder of Findhorn

I make myself rich by making my wants few.

Henry David Thoreau

B. Love

* Free love? As if love is anything but free! Man has bought brains, but all the millions in the world have failed to buy love. Man has subdued bodies, but all the power on earth has been unable to subdue love. Man has conquered whole nations, but his armies could not conquer love.

Emma Goldman

We believe the spiritual force capable of both changing us and stopping the arms race is that of *agape*: the love of God operating in the human heart.

Jim Douglass
Sojourners
February 1984

Love, as revealed and interpreted in the life and death of Jesus Christ, involves more than we have yet seen, and is the only power by which evil can be overthrown and the only sufficient basis for human society.

International Fellowship of Reconciliation

Peace is the work of justice indirectly, in so far as justice removes the obstacles to peace; but it is the work of charity (love) directly, since charity, according to its very notion, causes peace.

Thomas Aquinas
Summa Theologica

All the good that you will do will come not from you but from the fact that you have allowed yourself, in the obedience of faith, to be used by God's love. Think of this more and gradually you will be free from the need to prove yourself, and you can be more open to the power that will work through you without your knowing it.

Thomas Merton

Love alone is capable of uniting living beings in such a way as to complete and fulfill them, for it alone takes them and joins them by what is deepest in themselves.

Teilhard de Chardin

Conspire, in its literal sense, means "to breathe together." Pierre Teilhard de Chardin urged "a conspiracy of love."

Marilyn Ferguson
The Aquarian Conspiracy

* Fear, a more or less reflexive response that we share with other species, drives each of us, as an individual, to save himself in the face of danger. Fear cannot distinguish between a fire in one's own house and a nuclear holocaust—between one's own death and the end of the world—and is therefore useless even to begin to suggest to us the meaning of the nuclear peril. Its meaning can be grasped only to the extent that we feel the precise opposite of fear, which is a sense of responsibility, or devotion, or love, for other people, including those who have not yet been born. In Germany, the Peace movement has inverted the traditional Biblical admonition "Fear not" to say "You must fear." But the original version was the right one, for nuclear matters as for others. Fear isolates. Love

connects. Only insofar as the latter is strong in us are we likely to find the resolve to prevent our extinction.

Jonathan Schell

The only real security in the end is the love we have given and the love we have received.

Friends Journal, **May 1980**

"Cogito, ergo sum," said Descartes. "I think, therefore I am." Nonsense! Amo, ergo sum—I love, therefore I am.

William Sloane Coffin

...to love human beings is still the only thing worth living for...without that love, you really do not live.

Søren Kierkegaard

The ultimate miracle of love is this...that love is given to us to give to one another.

Anonymous

...it is not how much we do, but how much love we put in the action that we do.

Mother Teresa
Nobel Peace Prize Speech

All works of love are works of peace.

Mother Teresa

(See also Chapter 23, **Nonviolence**—pages 161–180)

C. Moral Condemnation of Violence and War

* I saw prevailing throughout the Christian world a license in making war of which even barbarous nations would have been ashamed; recourse was had to arms for slight reason or for no reason; and when arms were once taken up, all reverence for divine and human law was thrown away; just as if all men were thence forth authorized to commit crimes without restraint.

Hugo Grotius
1625

There is perhaps no phenomenon which conveys so much destructive feeling as moral indignation, which permits envy or hate to be acted out under the guise of virtue.

Erich Fromm

Christian values are never defended by murder, torture, or repression. Sad indeed would be those "humanistic, Christian values" that require violence for their maintenance.

Declaration of the International
Meeting of Latin American Bishops
November/December 1977

War is the greatest plague that can afflict humanity; it destroys religion, it destroys states, it destroys families. Any scourge is preferable to it.

Martin Luther

War and preparation for war must be judged in moral perspective, perspective derived from centuries of collective experience and expressed in our great religious traditions. These traditions agree with striking similarity and clarity that we must neither contemplate nor prepare for the killing of innocent persons. The killing of innocent people is an inevitable characteristic of warfare. The rejection of war is the conclusion of morality seriously applied to politics.

Fellowship of Reconciliation

[When warfare] involves such an extension of evil that it entirely escapes from human control, its use must be rejected as immoral....The pure and simple annihilation of all human life is not permitted for any reason whatsoever.

Pope Pius XII

The God of peace is never glorified by human violence.

Thomas Merton

Nothing can be politically right, that is morally wrong; and no necessity can ever sanctify a law, that is contrary to equity.

Benjamin Rush
1786

Our sole safeguard against the very real danger of a reversion to barbarianism is the kind of morality which compels the individual conscience, be the group right or wrong. The individual conscience against the atom bomb? Yes. There is no other way.

Life
August 1945

Sensitivity to the immense needs of humanity brings with it a spontaneous rejection of the arms race, which is incompatible with the all out struggle against hunger, sickness, under- development and illiteracy.

Pope John Paul II

We as concerned citizens recognize...Billions are being spent on arms, while people's basic needs, such as food, housing, health care and education are underfunded, that to be able to kill and to be killed many times over in the name of defense is an evil waste of world resources.

United Church of Christ
Reversing the Arms Race
a Pronouncement of the General Synod 12
1979

The armaments race...is to be condemned unreservedly. Even when motivated by a concern for legitimate defense, it is in fact...an injustice. The obvious contradiction between the waste involved in the overproduction of military devices and the extent of unsatisfied vital needs...is in itself an act of aggression against those who are victims of it. It is an act of aggression which amounts to a crime, for even when they are not used, by their costs alone armaments kill the poor by causing them to starve.

Vatican statement
to the United Nations on Disarmament
1976

As Christians we believe that armaments and military force are inconsistent with the ways of Jesus Christ and the biblical hope of justice and peace.

American Baptist Churches
Resolution on Disarmament
adopted by the General Board
1978

The nuclear arms race may well be regarded as the penultimate subject of our time. There is no greater affront to the Lord and Giver of life, no more convincing evidence of human enslavement to the dark powers of this age, and no more urgent cause for the church's prophetic witness and action....The nuclear arms race is first and foremost a false religion. It is, to be sure, also bad politics, bad economics, bad science, and bad war. It can and should be opposed on all these fronts.

Reformed Church in America
Christian Faith and the Nuclear Arms Race: A Reformed Perspective
1980

The use of the modern technology of war is the most striking example of corporate sin and the prostitution of God's gifts.

Church of England Bishops
1978

...In every age God's people have identified sin and called its servants to repentance. Now it is our turn. It is not good enough to condemn only the sins which everyone agrees are evil and uncivil. We will have to see the idolatry of our time and identify the false god of nuclear weaponry. To topple this idol may leave our neighbors, both within and without the church, feeling momentarily insecure and afraid. But with the death grip of a false security weakened, they may find true hope in the Giver of Life....We believe that the concept of nuclear deterrence, which involves a trust in nuclear weapons, is a form of idolatry.

Mennonite Central Committee
1978

The taproot of violence in our society today is our intention to use nuclear weapons. Once we have agreed to that, all other evil is minor in comparison. Until we squarely face the question of our consent to use nuclear weapons, any hope of large scale improvement of public morality is doomed to failure.

Richard McSorley

In a recent radio broadcast Mr. Reagan urged that schools include the teaching of morality in the classroom along with content. The present moment, then, appears to be the appropriate time to discuss the morality of war, the morality of stockpiling nuclear weapons, and the morality of peace since these are among the greatest issues of our times.

Grandmothers For Peace Newsletter
Fall 1985

* Nuclear war is politically irrational and morally an indefensible and hideous atrocity, whoever perpetrates it. Preparation for such war is also politically irrational, and since there is no guarantee that the preparation will lead to anything but war, the preparation itself is an atrocity and a degradation of mankind.

A. J. Muste

It's a sin to build a nuclear weapon.

Richard McSorley

Even the possession of weapons which cannot be morally used is wrong. They are a threat to peace and might even be the cause of nuclear war. The nuclear weapons of communists may destroy our bodies. But our intent to use nuclear weapons destroys our souls. Our possession of them is a proximate occasion of sin.

Richard McSorley

Nuclear weapons aren't weapons—they're an obscenity.

Dr. Marvin Goldberger
President
California Institute of Technology

All the missiles that ELF can trigger are centered on the heart of Christ.

Michael Miles
Poppy Seed Six

God made heaven and earth in 7 days and the bomb can ruin it all in two seconds. That isn't fair to God.

Rachel M.
Baltimore
Age 6
Please Save My World

* We are now living in the shadow of an arms race more intense, more costly, more widespread and more dangerous than the world has ever known. Never before has the human race been as close as it is now to total self-destruction. Today's arms race is an unparalleled waste of human and material resources; it threatens to turn the whole world into an armed camp; it aids repression and violates human rights; it promotes violence and insecurity in place of the security in whose name it is undertaken; it frustrates humanity's aspirations for justice and peace; it has no part in God's design for His world; it is demonic.

World Council of Churches
Conference on Disarmament
April 1978

D. Spiritual Teachings on Peacemaking

Peace is more than the absence of war, more than a precarious balance of powers. Peace is the intended order of the world with life abundant for all God's children.

United Presbyterian Church in the USA
General Assembly, 1980

* The Great Spirit who has made us all has given us different complexions and different customs. Why may we not conclude that he has given us different religions, according to our understanding?

Red Jacket
Seneca Indian
1792

I have given you lands to hunt in,
I have given you streams to fish in,
I have given you bear and bison,
I have given you roe and reindeer,
I have given you brant and beaver,
Filled the marshes full of wild fowl,
Filled the rivers full of fishes;
Why then are you not contented?
Why then will you hunt each other?

Gitche Manitou in
Song of Hiawatha
Henry Wadsworth Longfellow

* Our fathers came to this western area to establish a base from which to carry the gospel of peace to the people of the earth. It is ironic, and a denial of the very essence of that gospel, that in this same general area there should be constructed a mammoth weapons system potentially capable of destroying much of civilization.

> **The Church of Jesus Christ of Latter-Day Saints (Mormons)**
> **on the MX missile**
> **1981**

We express profound concern about the danger of a precarious balancing of humanity on the brink of nuclear catastrophe. We know that still more terrible weapons are being developed which can only lead to greater fear and suspicion and thus to a still more feverish arms race. Against this we say with one voice—NO! In the name of God, NO!...Thus the Lord has set before us again life and death, blessing and curse: Therefore, choose life that you and your descendants may live.

> **Christ is Our Peace**
> **joint communiqué issued by the Metropolitan Juvenaly**
> **(Russian Orthodox Church)**
> **and Dr. Claire Randall**
> **National Council of Churches**
> **1980**

Biblical imperatives call us to fie to our idolatrous sense of security in the arms race, our profiteering in weapons of death, and our infatuation with violence, and to become alive to the good news of peace, the ministry of reconciliation, the way of suffering love, and resurrection faith in the Kingdom coming.

> **New Call to Peacemaking**
> **Second National Conference**
> **1980**

Only by moving with the Tao, or the Way, or the will of God, can we hope to bring peace on earth.

> **Anonymous**

From Taoism we learn that religion is a mode of connectedness with the creative force of life. When one is thus connected one's actions are responsive to the needs of life; when one is truly part of the body of humankind, then a hurt in one part of the body will trigger remedial action in the other parts.

> **Anonymous**

Lord, make me an instrument of Your peace; where there is hatred, let me sow love; where there is injury, pardon; where there is discord, union;

where there is doubt, faith; where there is despair, hope; where there is darkness, light; and where there is sadness, joy.

O Divine Master, grant that I may not so much seek to be consoled as to console, to be understood as to understand, to be loved as to love; for it is in giving that we receive, it is in pardoning that we are pardoned, and it is in dying that we are born to eternal life.

St. Francis of Assisi

We find our security in God, not in weapons, and would point those around us to that security.

Church of the Brethren
resolution adopted at the Annual Conference
1980

* We humans are not misbegotten progeny, children of the curse. We need not rape and kill—one another, mother earth, earthly father, anyone. Born as we are, helpless, vulnerable, weaponless, we need not become subjects of the new biology of violence....We are the disarmed daughters and sons of a disarmed God, who in Christ, bares Himself, body and blood, to deterrent powers of this world. And so disarms death itself.

Daniel Berrigan

The servants of the All-Merciful are those who go about the earth with gentleness, and when the foolish ones address them, they answer, "Peace!"

Koran 25:63

O humankind! Behold We created you male and female and We made you into nations and tribes so that you might come to know one another.

Koran 49:13

If you are not for you who will be? If you are only for you what's the purpose?

Rabbi Hillel

...the truest and greatest power is the strength of Peace...because Peace is the Will of the Great Spirit...

Hopi Declaration of Peace

...we've got to admit—it feels good, when someone has wronged us, to "get 'em back." If they've done wrong to someone—they should have a taste of their own medicine. Right? Fair is fair.

It makes sense to me...but not...to my Lord.

According to Matthew and Luke, Jesus said: "You have heard it was said: An eye for an eye, and a tooth for a tooth. But now I tell you—do not take revenge on someone who wrongs you. If someone slaps you on the right cheek, let them slap you on the left as well."

Lynn S. Larson

An eye for an eye. A Hiroshima for a Pearl Harbor. A Hanoi for a Saigon. A contra-force for a revolution. Twelve executions in Florida and Texas for twelve murders in Florida and Texas. A warhead for a warhead. An El Salvador for an Afghanistan. A cussing out for a costly mistake. A rude look for a cold shoulder.

An eye for an eye and a tooth for a tooth: We've learned it too well!

Jesus said: "You've heard an eye for an eye and a tooth for a tooth...but I'll tell you a better way."

Lynn S. Larson

There is no rigid distinction between peace among nations, economic justice, bodily health and a spiritually right relationship with God.

Wes Granberg-Michaelson
Reformed Church in America

Peace is not simply the absence of war, a nuclear stalemate or combination of uneasy cease-fires. It is that emerging dynamic reality envisioned by prophets where spears and swords give way to implements of peace (Isaiah 2:1–4); where historic antagonists dwell together in trust (Isaiah 11:4–11); and where righteousness and justice prevail. There will be no peace with justice until unselfish and informed love are structured into political processes and international arrangements.

The United Methodist Church and Peace
adopted by the General Conference
1980

We spoke of our oneness in Christ with Russian believers and the fragile bridge that our churches are building between East and West. We promised to remain as one with our Russian sisters and brothers in Christ, no matter what our governments may do.

As we spoke, we saw human faces like our own—heads nodding in assent, eyes filled with tears, smiles of hope. Then we walked through the congregation. Hands reached out to touch us. And the people greeted us in Russian with words that have a deeper meaning for us now: "Christ is risen!" and "Peace!"

Robert White
A Holiday in the Soviet Union

Peacemaking is fundamentally a spiritual struggle, a battle for the soul of humanity.

Richard Barnet
a founder of World Peacemakers

E. The Bible on Peace
1. The Old Testament

Thou shalt not kill.

Exodus 20:13
King James Version

...you shall demolish their altars, smash their sacred pillars and cut down their sacred poles. You shall not prostrate yourselves to any other god.

Exodus 34:13
The New English Bible

I have set before you life and death, blessing and curse; therefore choose life, that you and your descendants may live...

Deuteronomy 30:19
Revised Standard Version

Do you want long life and happiness?...strive for peace with all your heart.

Psalm 34:12,14
Today's English Version

* How beautiful upon the mountains are the feet of him who brings good tidings, who publishes peace...

Isaiah 52:7
RSV

Take away from me the noise of your songs; to the melody of your harps I will not listen. But let justice roll down like waters, and righteousness like an ever-flowing stream.

Amos 5:23–24
RSV

(See also Chapter 29—Visions of Peace—pages 261–275.)

2. The New Testament

> The teachings of Christ are becoming subversive again—as they were in the days of the Roman Empire.
>
> I. F. Stone

Blessed are the peacemakers: for they shall be called the children of God.

Matthew 5:9
KJV

* You have heard that it was said, "An eye for an eye, and a tooth for a tooth." But now I tell you: do not take revenge on someone who wrongs

you. If anyone slaps you on the right cheek, let him slap your left cheek too.
Matthew 5:38
TEV

You have heard that it was said, "Love your friends, hate your enemies." But now I tell you: love your enemies and pray for those who persecute you...
Matthew 5:43
TEV

* What good will it be for a man if he gains the whole world, yet forfeits his soul?
Matthew 16:26a
New International Version

* Glory to God in the highest, and on earth peace, good will toward men.
Luke 2:14
KJV

Would that even today you knew the things that make for peace.
Luke 19:42
RSV

Let us therefore follow after the things which make for peace...
Romans 14:19
KJV

* Be not deceived; God is not mocked: for whatsoever a man soweth, that shall he also reap.
Galatians 6:7
KJV

But the wisdom from above is pure, first of all; it is also peaceful, gentle, and friendly; it is full of compassion and produces a harvest of good deeds; it is free from prejudice and hypocrisy. And goodness is the harvest that is produced from the seeds the peacemakers plant in peace.
James 3:17, 18
TEV

There is no fear in love; perfect love drives out all fear.
1 John 4:18a
TEV

* If someone says, "I love God," but hates his brother, he is a liar. For he cannot love God, whom he has not seen, if he does not love his brother, whom he has seen. This, then, is the command that Christ gave us: he who loves God must love his brother also.   **1 John 4:20,21**
TEV

F. Religion and Politics

To see the universal and all-pervading Spirit of Truth face to face, one must be able to love the meanest creature as oneself. Whoever aspires after that cannot keep out of any field of life...those who say that religion has nothing to do with politics do not know what religion means.

Mahatma Gandhi

* The straightforward course, and the one that would serve the Church best in the long run, would be to close our professedly Christian Churches the moment war is declared by us, and reopen them only on the signing of the treaty of peace. No doubt to many of us the privation thus imposed would be far worse than the privation of the prosaic inconveniences of war. But would it be worse than the privation of faith, and the horror of the soul, wrought by the spectacle of nations praying to their common Father to assist them in blowing one another to pieces with explosives that are also corrosives, and of the Church organizing this monstrous paradox instead of protesting against it?

George Bernard Shaw

If all the Churches of Europe closed their doors until the drums ceased rolling they would act as a most powerful reminder that though the glory of war is a famous and ancient glory, it is not the final glory of God.

George Bernard Shaw
Common Sense about the War
1914

The biblical insight that violence against others imperils our relationship to all creation finds a startling expression in the nuclear threat....Abolishing nuclear weapons, eliminating hunger and saving the ozone layer are all part of a biblical call to earthkeeping, and should be addressed by the church not as individual political issues, but as indivisible dimensions of our response to God's love.

Wes Granberg-Michaelson
Reformed Church in America

* As Christians we recognize a demonic element in the complexity of our world, but we also affirm our belief in the good will and purpose and Providence of God for his whole creation. This requires us to work for a world characterized not by fear, but by mutual trust and justice.

Episcopal Church
Christian Attitudes to War in a Nuclear Age
1981

The present insanity of the global arms race, if continued, will lead inevitably to a conflagration so great that Auschwitz will seem like a minor rehearsal....The nuclear issue is not just a political issue—it is a moral and spiritual issue as well.... I believe that the Christian especially has a responsibility to work for peace in our world....We must seek the good of the whole human race, and not just the good of any one nation or race.

Billy Graham

...for it is God and God alone who is justified in using the credo "Peace Through Strength."

Peter Monkres

The church that bows before the altar of national pride and militarism leaves the gospel there.

Mernie King
Sojourners Fellowship

From the vantage point of history, we can view the churches of the past and accuse them of social and political captivity. They are easy enough to recognize. Our favorites are the German national church that bowed before Nazism and deserted its Lord for a new lord, and the white church of the South that worshipped at the altars of racial superiority and forgot its Lord. What can be said of the captivity of an American church that has for 30 years largely supported a government that plans nuclear war?

Mernie King
Sojourners Fellowship

* We must win clear of the tendency to associate religion and spirituality with withdrawal from the world and the field of action. The Goddess is ourselves *and* the world—to link with Her is to engage actively with the world and all its problems.

Starhawk
The Spiral Dance

ADDITIONS:

23
Nonviolence

The natives were good people, for when they saw I would not remain, they supposed I was afraid of their bows and arrows, and taking the arrows they broke them into pieces and threw them into the fire.

Henry Hudson
of the people he found along the river later named for him
1609

* A good end cannot sanctify evil means; nor must we ever do evil, that good may come of it. We are too ready to retaliate, rather than forgive or gain by love and information....Force may subdue, but love gains. And he that forgives first, wins the laurel.

William Penn

There is no greater fallacy than the belief that aims and purposes are one thing, while methods and tactics are another.

Emma Goldman

The means is the end in the process of becoming.

Jacques Maritain
Catholic philosopher

The means are the seeds that bud into flower and come to fruition. The fruit will always be of the nature of the seed planted.

19th century American pacifist

All who affirm the use of violence admit it is only a means to achieve justice and peace. But peace and justice *are* nonviolence...the final end of history. Those who abandon nonviolence have no sense of history. Rather they are bypassing history, freezing history, betraying history.

André Trocmé

The method of nonviolent resistance is effective in that it has a way of disarming opponents. It exposes their moral defenses, weakens their morale and at the same time works on their conscience. It makes it possible for the individual to struggle for moral ends through moral means.

Martin Luther King, Jr.

If one takes care of the means, the end will take care of itself....We have always control over the means and never of the ends.

Mahatma Gandhi

His fundamental trust was that the most effective way of defending those for whom he was responsible was to keep on using the right means.

speaking of Ned Richards
Courage in Both Hands

You will understand, if you are a practicing idealist, that you cannot kill in the name of peace. For if you do so your methods will automatically undermine your ideal. The sacredness of life and spirit are one and the same....The end does not justify the means. If you learn that lesson, then your good intent will allow you to act effectively and creatively in your private experience and in your relationships with others. Your changed beliefs will affect the mental atmosphere of your nation and of the world.

(Seth) Jane Roberts
The Individual and the Nature of Mass Events

If it were proved to me that in making war, my ideal had a chance of being realized, I would still say "No" to war. For one does not create a *human society* on mounds of corpses.

Louis Lecoin
French pacifist leader

I would say that I'm a nonviolent soldier. In place of weapons of violence, you have to use your mind, your heart, your sense of humor, every faculty available to you...because no one has the right to take the life of another human being.

Joan Baez

* If we kill man, with whom are we to live?

Thich Nhat Hanh
Vietnamese pacifist

I shall die, but that is all that I shall do for Death.

Edna St. Vincent Millay
Wine from These Grapes

I am prepared to die but there is no cause for which I am prepared to kill.

Mahatma Gandhi

* The greatest heroes of the world are not men who kill other men in war. They are quiet heroes who are brave in other ways.

Rufus Jones
Quaker

Patriotism is not enough, I must have no hatred or bitterness for anyone.

Edith Cavell
nurse killed by German firing squad during WWI

Don't ever let them pull you down so low as to hate them.

Booker T. Washington

Hate is too great a burden to share.

Martin Luther King, Jr.

Hatred is like rain in the desert—it is of no use to anybody.
African saying

The price of hating other human beings is loving oneself less.
Eldridge Cleaver

* Hatred, which could destroy so much, never failed to destroy the man who hated and this is an immutable law.
James Baldwin

Anger is an acid that can do more harm to the vessel in which it stands than to anything on which it's poured.
Anonymous

When you clench your fist, no one can put anything in your hand, nor can your hand pick up anything.
Alex Haley
Roots

...we cannot sow seeds with clenched fists. To sow we must open our hands.
Adolfo Pérez Esquivel
1980 Nobel Peace Prize
Christ in a Poncho

Interior presence—cannot occupy the human soul at the same time that it is occupied by hatred.
Ann Fairbairn
Five Smooth Stones

We must find an alternative to violence. The eye-for-an-eye philosophy leaves everybody blind.
Martin Luther King, Jr.

An eye for an eye and a tooth for a tooth—that way everyone in the world will soon be blind and toothless.
Fiddler on the Roof

Imagine the vanity of thinking that your enemy can do you more damage than your enmity.
St. Augustine

Never in the world can hatred be stilled by hatred; it will be stilled only by non-hatred—this is the law eternal.
Buddha

Christ knew also, just as all reasonable human beings must know, that the employment of violence is incompatible with love, which is the fundamental law of life.

Leo Tolstoy
September 1910

We know too that one evil cannot be cured by another. Evils don't cancel each other out. They total up.

Adolfo Pérez Esquivel
1980 Nobel Peace Prize
Christ in a Poncho

The ultimate weakness of violence is that it is a descending spiral, begetting the very thing it seeks to destroy. Instead of diminishing evil, it multiplies it. Through violence you murder the hater, but you do not murder hate. In fact, violence merely increases hate....Returning violence for violence multiplies violence, adding deeper darkness to a night already devoid of stars. Darkness cannot drive out darkness; only light can do that.

Martin Luther King, Jr.

We must meet hate with creative love.   **Martin Luther King, Jr.**

Hatred and bitterness can never cure the disease of fear, only love can do that. Hatred paralyzes life; love releases it. Hatred confuses life; love harmonizes it. Hatred darkens life; love illumines it.

Martin Luther King, Jr.

Our truth is an ancient one: that love endures and overcomes; that hatred destroys; that what is obtained by love is retained, but what is obtained by hatred proves a burden.

American Friends Service Committee
Speak Truth to Power

Many waters cannot quench love, neither can the floods drown it.

Song of Solomon

If a single person achieves the highest kind of love it will be sufficient to neutralize the hate of millions.

Mahatma Gandhi

Only one individual is necessary to spread the leavening influence of *ahimsa* [non-violence] in an office, school, institution or country.

Mahatma Gandhi

Love is the most durable power in the world....Love is the only force capable of transforming an enemy into a friend.

Martin Luther King, Jr.

When the power of love overcomes the love of power, then there will be true peace.

Sri Chin Moi Gosh

* ...there is only one thing that has power completely, and that is love; because when a man loves he seeks no power, and therefore he has power.

Alan Paton
Cry, the Beloved Country

* Military power is as corrupting to the man who possesses it as it is pitiless to its victims. It is just as devastating to its employer as it is to those who suffer under it.

American Friends Service Committee
Speak Truth to Power

Power in our society is seen as "power over" and that's an addictive drug that you have to keep taking over and over again. It doesn't last. You have to continue to dominate other people in order to still feel powerful.

If you feel proud of who you are and strong with who you are, then you realize there is not a scarcity of power; that if one person has power then another person can have it also, can have their power....That's sharing of power.

Geof Morgan

The theory and practice of nonviolence are roughly at the same stage of development today as those of electricity in the early days of Marconi and Edison.

David Dellinger

Nonviolence is a mighty opportunity for Christians today and all men and women of goodwill. Now they have a way to strike a blow for a society whose goal will be victory over all forms of domination.

Declaration of the International
Meeting of Latin American Bishops
November/December 1977

In nonviolence, the masses have a weapon which enables a child, a woman, or even a decrepit old man to resist the mightiest government successfully. If your spirit is strong, mere lack of physical strength ceases to be a handicap.

Mahatma Gandhi

No longer can any liberation movement anywhere in the world truly claim that "revolutionary" violence is the only path open to them to effect change. For the overthrow of Marcos, like the overthrow of the former Shah of Iran, shows without question that even late in the twentieth century, it is still possible for an unarmed but mobilized population to overthrow a conscienceless, technologically sophisticated, dictatorial regime, backed by the most powerful military power in the history of the world, through recourse to the tactics and strategies of *nonviolent action*.

David H. Albert
People Power: Applying Nonviolence Theory

* First, it must be emphasized that nonviolent resistance is not a method for cowards; it does resist. If one uses this method because he is afraid or merely because he lacks the instruments of violence, he is not truly nonviolent.

Martin Luther King, Jr.

Practice nonviolence not because of weakness, practice nonviolence being conscious of strength and power; no training in arms is required for realization of strength.

Mahatma Gandhi

There is nothing so strong as gentleness; nothing so gentle as real strength.

Anonymous

[In response to then-President Marcos' continued attacks on her lack of political experience] I concede that I cannot match Mr. Marcos when it comes to experience. I admit that I have no experience in cheating, stealing, lying or assassinating political opponents.

Corazon Aquino
Time, February 3, 1986

Gandhi once declared that it was his wife who unwittingly taught him the effectiveness of nonviolence. Who better than women should know that battles can be won without resort to physical strength? Who better than we should know all the power that resides in noncooperation?

Barbara Deming
Revolution and Equilibrium

World peace through nonviolent means is neither absurd nor unattainable. All other methods have failed. Thus we must begin anew.

Martin Luther King, Jr.

The choice is no longer between violence and nonviolence. It is between nonviolence and nonexistence.

Martin Luther King, Jr.

* For perhaps the first time in history reflective men have had to grapple with the pacifists' question: "Can national interests and human values really be served by waging a war with atomic and hydrogen weapons?"

James Reston
New York Times column

Some of you will ask a further question: If we abandon reliance upon military force—before international agreements have been signed— upon what alternative power can our country rely? The answer, I would say, is clearly the power of nonviolent resistance.

Barbara Deming
Revolution and Equilibrium

There is no escape from the impending doom save through a bold unconditional acceptance of the nonviolent method. Democracy and violence go ill together. The states that today are nominally democratic have either to become frankly totalitarian or, if they are to become truly democratic, they must become courageously nonviolent.

Mahatma Gandhi

No sovereign people defending its land can be subjugated from without. If a people is destroyed, it first destroys itself from within. It becomes flaccid, loses contact with the land, which is turned into property, and with its own powers, which are delegated to the state. It becomes, in short, like the peoples of nuclear-bearing powers, who are not only at the mercy of their weapons, but so sapped in strength and resolve that they can scarcely imagine an alternative to them. If a modern nation, by contrast, ever became accomplished in non-violence, it could resist an aggressor without weaponry and through active non-cooperation and other means of non-violent resistance.

Joel Kovel

The abolition of war does not require anti-war, anti-military lobbies or demonstrations and protest, but the development of effective nonviolent alternatives to military struggle.

Gene Sharp

The only effective defense at this point in history is social defense—the organized nonviolent resistance of a whole population to an invader.

former West German General Gerd Bastian
1983

In dozens and hundreds of significant conflicts, including international ones...nonviolent struggle has already taken the place of military violence.

Gene Sharp

...in nonviolent combat what we do is just exactly what nice players aren't supposed to do. We refuse to play by one of the rules the system tries to foist on us: the rule that says you have to counter violence with violence. If your opponents can get you to swallow that idea, then they can unleash still greater violence on you. The essential thing in nonviolent combat is for us to render these tactics inoperative by refusing to play by the rules and by imposing our own conditions instead.

Adolfo Pérez Esquivel
1980 Nobel Peace Prize
Christ in a Poncho

You can make tyranny helpless by refusing cooperation with it.

Gene Sharp

...if, as revolutionaries, we will wage battle without violence, we can remain very much more in control—of our own selves, of the responses to us which our adversaries make, of the battle as it proceeds and of the future we hope will issue from it.

Barbara Deming

Nonviolent resistance is the only type of defense which, from beginning to end, yields to the enemy not even a prospect of any of the usual rewards of invasion: prestige, glory, indemnity, subject people, trade or military advantages, available territory, triumph of ideas.

Jesse Wallace Hughan
1942

First, something seems wrong to most people engaged in struggle when they see more people hurt on their own side than on the other side. They are used to reading this as an indication of defeat, and a complete mental readjustment is required of them....Vengeance is not the point; change is.

Barbara Deming
Revolution and Equilibrium

Victory can be achieved by various means. It can be gained with tanks and missiles, but I think that one wins better with truth, honesty and logic....This is a new weapon.

Lech Walesa
November 1982

...Nonviolence is a weapon fabricated of love. It is a sword that heals. Our nonviolent direct action program has as its objective not the creation of tensions, but the surfacing of tensions already present. We set out to precipitate a crisis situation that must open the door to negotiation. I am not afraid of the words "crisis" and "tension." I deeply oppose violence, but constructive crisis and tension are necessary for growth. Innate in all life, and all growth, is tension. Only in death is there an absence of tension.

Martin Luther King, Jr.

Non-violent direct action seeks to create such a crisis and establish such creative tension that a community that has constantly refused to negotiate is forced to confront the issue.

Martin Luther King, Jr.

Conflict there will still be between one nation, one class, one group, and another. Let those who have faith in the justice of their cause demonstrate their conviction by self-suffering, not by attempting to coerce or to destroy the "enemy."

Mahatma Gandhi

* Nonviolence is the answer to the crucial political and moral questions of our time; the need for man to overcome oppression and violence without resorting to oppression and violence.

Man must evolve for all human conflict a method which rejects revenge, aggression and retaliation. The foundation of such a method is love.

Martin Luther King, Jr.

I believe that unarmed truth and unconditional love will have the final word in reality. That is why right, temporarily defeated, is stronger than evil triumphant.

Martin Luther King, Jr.

Nonviolence is not a garment to be put on and off at will. Its seat is in the heart, and it must be an inseparable part of our being.

Mahatma Gandhi

Nonviolence, which is a quality of the heart, cannot come by an appeal to the brain.

Mahatma Gandhi

Nonviolence is a plant of slow growth. It grows imperceptibly, but surely.

Mahatma Gandhi

* All I claim is that every experiment of mine has deepened my faith in nonviolence as the greatest force at the disposal of mankind.

Mahatma Gandhi

Resistance and nonviolence are not in themselves good. There is another element in our struggle that then makes our resistance and nonviolence truly meaningful. That element is reconciliation. The tactics of nonviolence without the spirit of nonviolence may become a new kind of violence.

Martin Luther King, Jr.

* Nonviolence means avoiding not only external physical violence but also internal violence of spirit. You not only refuse to shoot a man, but you refuse to hate him.   **Martin Luther King, Jr.**

We should be innocent not only of violence but of all enmity, however slight, for it is the mystery of peace.

St. John Chrysostom

Peacemaking aims at transformation and reconciliation. We are engaged in transforming relations. We are not seeking to make people accept the results of a long history of enmity but rather to recognize enmity, to discover its causes, to find the human face beneath the enemy image, and to struggle with every gift we have to heal division and brokenness.

Jim Forest
International Fellowship of Reconciliation

Satyagraha was a term I coined because I did not like the term "passive resistance"....Its root meaning is "holding on to truth," hence "force of righteousness." I have also called it love force or soul force....the mighty power of truth to be set against the evil of falsehood.

Mahatma Gandhi

We try to act in truth. This is what gives our movement its security: the truth—respect for the human person. Respect for the human person generates constancy and steadfastness. And constancy and steadfastness generate an attack on evil and the possibility of altering the structures of injustice.

Adolfo Pérez Esquivel
1980 Nobel Peace Prize
Christ in a Poncho

Once people understand the strength of nonviolence—the force it generates, the love it creates, the response it brings from the total community—they will not easily abandon it.

Cesar Chavez

Nonviolence is the constant awareness of the dignity and humanity of oneself and others; it seeks truth and justice; it renounces violence both in method and in attitude; it is a courageous acceptance of active love and goodwill as the instrument with which to overcome evil and transform both oneself and others. It is the willingness to undergo suffering rather than inflict it. It excludes retaliation and flight.

Wally Nelson
conscientious objector and tax resister

Nobody was born nonviolent. No one was born charitable. None of us comes to these things by nature but only by conversion. The first duty of the nonviolent community is helping its members work upon themselves and come to conversion.

Lanza del Vasto

The nonviolent revolution begins in your mind. You must first redefine yourself. When people redefine themselves, slavery is dead. Then the power structure makes a motion, but doesn't get a second.

James Bevel

The first step toward liberation occurs when a human being comes aware that he or she is a person.

Adolfo Pérez Esquivel
1980 Nobel Peace Prize
Christ in a Poncho

...The important thing is to awaken a critical consciousness in the basic communities, so they can find their own solutions to their problems.

Adolfo Pérez Esquivel
1980 Nobel Peace Prize
Christ in a Poncho

The basic community has some unique characteristics: It enables each member to find himself or herself as a person. It develops a sense of solidarity, a sense of a community of brothers and sisters....Here is a mighty force for changing the structures of injustice that mark our society.

Adolfo Pérez Esquivel
1980 Nobel Peace Prize
Christ in a Poncho

Be what you want to become. Thus, if you want to have free elections, begin by freely electing someone; if you want to have free speech, speak freely; if you want to have a trade union, found a trade union. The Poles discovered that if enough people act in this way, the very foundation of the unwanted government begins to dissolve even while it retains the monopoly on the means of violence.

Solidarność

But nonviolent defense requires not only willingness to risk one's life (as any good soldier, rich or poor, will do). It requires renunciation of all claims to special privileges and power at the expense of other people.

David Dellinger

The major advances in nonviolence have not come from people who have approached nonviolence as an end in itself, but from persons who were passionately striving to free themselves from social injustice.

David Dellinger

The first thing to be disrupted by our commitment to nonviolence will be not the system but our own lives.

Jim Douglass

To change the world for the better you must begin by changing your own life. There is no other way. You begin by accepting your own worth as a part of the universe and by granting every other being that same recognition. You begin by honoring life in all of its forms. You begin by changing your thoughts toward your contemporaries, your country, your family, your working companions. If the ideal of loving your neighbor like yourself seems remote, you will at least absolutely refrain from killing your neighbor. And your neighbor is any other person on the face of the planet. You cannot love your neighbor, in fact, until you love yourself, and if you believe that it is wrong to love yourself, then you are indeed unable to love anyone else.

(Seth) Jane Roberts
The Individual and the Nature of Mass Events

For a start you will acknowledge your existence in the framework of nature, and to do that you must recognize the vast cooperative processes that connect each species with each other one. If you truly use your prerogatives as an individual in your country, then you can exert far more power in normal daily living than you do now. Every time you affirm the rightness of your own existence, you help others. Your mental states are part of the planet's psychic atmosphere.

(Seth) Jane Roberts

Hopefully you will see...as something of your mission, a mission of peace and prosperity...a mission of love—of love that not only extends to one's enemies. You know, I've had a lot of experience loving my enemies—I've been thrown in jail and beaten up and I never lost my temper with the Ku Klux Klan. The problem is that I have lost my temper with my wife, I have lost my temper with my mother, I have lost my temper with my 12-year-old son—but ultimately the problems that we talk about on a macroeconomic level or on a global level, all come back to that human level where we begin to learn to love one another at home, and in families and in one-to-one relationships; where we begin to appreciate those differences, where we begin to develop partnerships...

Andrew Young
Boston College commencement speech
June 1985

...nonviolent actions are by their nature androgynous. In them the two impulses that have long been treated as distinct, "masculine" and "feminine," the impulse of self assertion and the impulse of sympathy, are clearly joined; the very genius of nonviolence, in fact, is that it demonstrates them to be indivisible....One asserts one's rights as a human being, but...asserts them...as rights belonging to another person.

Barbara Deming
Two Perspectives on Women's Struggle

* The nonviolent approach does not immediately change the heart of the oppressor. It first does something to the hearts and souls of those committed to it. It gives them new self-respect; it calls up resources of strength and courage that they did not know they had. Finally, it reaches

the opponent and so stirs his conscience that reconciliation becomes a reality.

Martin Luther King, Jr.

As long as people accept exploitation, exploiter and exploited will be entangled in injustice. But once the exploited refuses to accept the relationship, refuses to cooperate with it, they are already free.

Mahatma Gandhi

A nonviolent person will not oppress another person; nor will they be oppressed.

Madge Micheels-Cyrus

A liberation movement that is nonviolent sets the oppressor free as well as the oppressed.

Barbara Deming

The question isn't who is the enemy, but what is the enemy?

American Friends Service Committee
Speak Truth to Power

One must never confuse error with the person that errs.

Pope John XXIII

Let's show the world we know a way to grow, inwardly as human beings. Let's show them how they can win a fight without hatred or under-handedness. A person can grow as a human being by defending truth or justice. A person can grow as a human being by learning to distinguish between people and their acts.

The "Snarlers" of the Perús Cement Company
Brazil, 1974
Christ in a Poncho

* Nonviolence is a method of achieving change. Nonviolent action is a way of confronting someone who's responsible for a wrong with the facts of his evil and the respect for his personhood.

American Friends Service Committee
Speak Truth to Power

Many oppressors are also oppressed. Nonviolent confrontation is the only confrontation that allows us to respond realistically to such complexity.

Jane Meyerding
Reclaiming Nonviolence

Nonviolence has the unique ability to simultaneously accept and reject— to acknowledge and connect us with that which is valuable in a person at the same time as it resists and challenges that person's oppressive attitude or behavior.

Jane Meyerding
Reclaiming Nonviolence

* Passive resistance is an all-sided sword, it can be used anyhow; it blesses him who uses it and him against whom it is used.

Mahatma Gandhi

* It has always been a mystery to me how men can feel themselves honoured by the humiliation of their fellow beings.

Mahatma Gandhi

I always prefer to believe the best of everybody—it saves so much trouble.

Rudyard Kipling

* We have to remember that God loves all men, that God wills all men to be saved, that all men are brothers. We must love the jailor as well as the one in prison. We must do that seemingly utterly impossible thing: love our enemy.

Dorothy Day

Help me to know that my love's not complete until I have loved the oppressor.

Lee Domann
from the song "Peace with Justice"

* Heretic, rebel, a thing to flout,
They drew a circle that shut him out.
But love and I had the wit to win,
We drew a circle that took them in.

Edwin Markham

---

* Senator: Mr. President, I believe that enemies should be destroyed.
President Lincoln: I agree with you sir, and the best way to destroy an enemy is to make him a friend.

Truth has given me the trail of peace, honoring all, fearing none.
Eddie Benton-Banai

We will match your capacity to inflict suffering with our capacity to endure suffering. We will meet your physical force with soul force. We will not hate you, but we cannot in good conscience obey your unjust laws....And in winning our freedom, we will win you in the process.
Martin Luther King, Jr.

If you want to see the brave, look at those who can forgive. If you want to see the heroic, look at those who can love in return for hatred.

from the Bhagavad Gita

It can't be measured on the Richter Scale, but can you fathom the power of the words from the cross: "Forgive them...they know not what they do."

Lynn S. Larson

Those who discovered the law of nonviolence in the midst of violence were greater geniuses than Newton.

Mahatma Gandhi

Nonviolence is really tough. You don't practice nonviolence by attending conferences—you practice it on the picket lines.

Cesar Chavez

I knew someone had to take the first step and I made up my mind not to move.

Rosa Parks
refused to move to the back of the bus
Montgomery, Alabama
December 1955

Yes, the challenge of those who believe in nonviolent struggle is to learn to be aggressive enough.

Barbara Deming

Nonviolence doesn't always work—but violence never does.

Madge Micheels-Cyrus

Violence is rejection as well as attack, a denial of needs, a reduction of persons to the status of objects, to be broken, manipulated or ignored. Violence is any human act or social process that deprives, debases, or exploits people. Violence is any sword that diminishes people by dividing them from one another, from themselves, from what they have made, from what they can become, from the world around them.

American Friends Service Committee

Violence leaves society in monologue rather than dialogue.

Martin Luther King, Jr.

Violence is resourcelessness.

Jo Vellacott
Women, Peace and Power

I love my country with my conscience. It would be a sort of treason to use arms to defend what is so precious.

Philippe Vernier
French pastor, WWII

The "peace" won by violence proves only to be a pause between wars, with each war more disastrous than the one before.

International Fellowship of Reconciliation

We have always questioned armed liberation movements—for today's oppressed will become tomorrow's oppressors.

Adolfo Pérez Esquivel
1980 Nobel Peace Prize
Christ in a Poncho

I despair to see so many radicals turn to violence as a proof of their militancy and commitment. It is heart-breaking to see all the old mistakes being made all over again. The usual pattern seems to be that people give nonviolence two weeks to solve their problem...and then decide it has "failed." Then they go on with violence for the next hundred years...and it seems never to "fail" and be rejected.

Ted Roszak

Once the connection between conflict and violence is broken, it can be a very creative experience.

Thomas Fehsenfeld

Nonviolence offers no guarantees. But the curious thing is that people who do violence don't receive any guarantees either. Statistics show that you have a better chance of coming out alive in a nonviolent battle.

Joan Baez

Violent changes are, in effect, limited to the sphere of technology. They are simply power shifts or power reversals which cannot even pretend to attempt the abolition of hierarchical (i.e., oppressive) practices. Violence can be an effective method for reform, but it cannot effect radical change.

Jane Meyerding
Reclaiming Nonviolence

I do not believe in violence...hatred...or armed insurrection. They take place too quickly. They change the circumstances of people's lives without giving them time to adapt to the changes. It is useless to dream of reforming socio-economic structures...without a corresponding deep change in our inner lives.

Archbishop Dom Helder Camara

...it is absurd to talk of revolution without nonviolence, because all violence is reactionary, causing the exact conditions it intends to destroy.

Ira Sandperl

A violent revolution is no revolution at all. It only perpetuates the old conditions.

James Bevel

There is a contradiction in the term "violent revolutionary" because revolution means change, and violence is a reversion to a former pattern.

Joan Baez

Nonviolence is the most revolutionary method for social change.

Anonymous

The only thing that's been a worse flop than the organization of nonviolence has been the organization of violence.

Joan Baez

* I think also that deep down somewhere in me, and in all men at all times, there is a realization that the pattern of violence meeting violence makes no sense, and that war violates something central in the human heart— "that of God" as we Quakers sometimes say.

Albert Bigelow

In the evolution of civilization, if it is to survive, all men and women cannot fail eventually to adopt Gandhi's belief that the process of mass applications of force to resolve contentious issues is fundamentally not only wrong, but contains within itself the germs of self-destruction.

General Douglas MacArthur

What makes the neglect of this particular idea [that worldwide knowledge of nonviolent tactics could avert bloodshed] so odd is that most people, if they are asked, say that they don't much believe in killing. It's not bloodlust that perpetuates violence so much as a lack of imagination, an unwillingness to reconsider. As a result, most of us specialize in rebutting new ideas so that we can quickly forget about them.

The New Yorker
December 1983

* But when I note the reluctance with which men today go to war even when obviously hostile armies and navies are arrayed against them and they naturally believe that if they do not kill they will be killed, I find no good reason for supposing that any army could be gotten to invade a people which flatly renounced war.

A. J. Muste

The pen is mightier than the sword.

Edward Robert Bulwer-Lytton
Governor-General of India
1875-1880

An army of principles will penetrate where an army of soldiers cannot.

Thomas Paine
1795

No army can withstand the strength of an idea whose time has come.

Victor Hugo

An invasion of armies can be resisted; an invasion of ideas cannot be resisted.

Victor Hugo
1877

There is one thing stronger than all the armies in the world, and that is an idea whose time has come.

The Nation
April 1943

No force is as great as an idea whose time has come.

Pierre Teilhard de Chardin

Suddenly knowledge and wisdom from our social and behavioral sciences is coalescing into a whole new field of nonviolent conflict management...and there is new hope.

Milton C. Mapes, Jr.
former Executive Director
National Peace Academy Campaign

ADDITIONS:

ADDITIONS:

24
Civil Disobedience

Resist much. Obey little.

Walt Whitman

It is through disobedience that progress is made.

Oscar Wilde

* I'd say that civil disobedience is...based on the idea that you break small laws—like defying lunchcounter segregation laws, or antistrike laws, or laws about draft files, or nineteenth-century laws forbidding you to shelter runaway slaves—to point out the existence of higher laws, like the brotherhood of man or the atrocity of war, which society seems to have forgotten about.

Francine Du Plessix Gray
March 1971

* Laws and conditions that tend to debase human personality—a God-given force—be they brought about by the State or individuals, must be relentlessly opposed in the spirit of defiance shown by St. Peter when he said to the rulers of his day: "Shall we obey God or man?"

Chief Albert Luthuli

* If civil authorities legislate for or allow anything that is contrary to the will of God, neither the laws made nor the authorizations granted can be binding on the consciences of the citizens, since God has more right to be obeyed than men.

Pope John XXIII

* Must the citizen even for a moment, or in the last degree, resign his conscience to the legislator? Why has every man a conscience, then? I think that we should be men first, and subjects afterward. It is not desirable to cultivate a respect for law, so much as for the right. The only obligation I have a right to assume, is to do at any time what I think right.

Henry David Thoreau
On the Duty of Civil Disobedience

Noncooperation in military matters should be an essential moral principle for all true scientists.

Albert Einstein

* The mass of men serve the state...not as men, mainly, but as machines, with their bodies....A very few—as heroes, patriots, martyrs, reformers in the great sense, and *men*—serve the state with their consciences also, and so necessarily resist it for the most part; and they are commonly treated as enemies by it.

Henry David Thoreau
On Civil Disobedience
1849

Disobedience to be civil, must be sincere, respectful, restrained, never defiant, must be based upon some well-understood principle, must not be capricious, and above all, must have no ill-will or hatred behind it.

Mahatma Gandhi

First, never kill,
Second, never hurt,
Third, commit yourself incessantly and with perseverance,
Fourth, remain always united,
Fifth, disobey the orders of the authorities that violate or destroy us.

**Principles of the peasants of Alagamar, Brazil
in their nonviolent land struggle**

In a society which exalts property rights above human rights, it is sometimes necessary to damage or destroy property, both because property has no intrinsic value except insofar as it contributes to human welfare, and also in order to challenge people to discover a new sense of priorities.

David Dellinger
Revolutionary Nonviolence

I came to this act because of moral imperatives. This so-called property [a missile silo] has no right to exist because it is violent and imposes indiscriminate destruction. We are in an historic moment of drastic confrontational policy in our government and economic system. No serious efforts have been made to contain this madness, much less to dismantle it. We keep making more missiles and warheads every day for greater stockpiles.

Some of us cannot stand by and let this happen without shouting and acting, "Not in my name."

Father Paul Kabat

...the United States is signatory to...the Nuremberg Principles, which outlaw weaponry of mass and indiscriminate destruction, as well as preparing for using those weapons. I come to ELF to dismantle a small portion of the nuclear death machine in the hope that this will be but a small part of the growing race amongst the peoples of the Earth to personally and collectively disarm directly, with our own hands, this illegal and immoral global oven under construction.

**Tom Hastings
cut down an Extra-Low Frequency communications (ELF) pole
May 1985**

It is time to make a stand for sanity, to be responsible and accountable. I choose life and I choose to go on record in that position.

Tom Hastings

The risks are great. The risks I take today are puny compared to the risks we take collectively in allowing this madness to continue unchecked.

Tom Hastings
May 1985

And so I act today in accordance with the teachings of the great spiritual teachers in history—Gandhi, Christ, the Indians—and in accordance with the basic moral underpinnings of humanity as expressed in the various world religions....These teachings find expression in various international laws to which the United States is a party—most notably the Nuremberg principles and the various Hague and Geneva Conventions. All speak of the basic respect for all life and of our responsibility to protect all life from harm. In order to fulfill this responsibility, I act here today to begin the disarming of Wisconsin ELF.

Jeff Leys
on notching an ELF pole
August 1985

Our primary duty and responsibility is to the children—to create a safe and secure future for them. I dedicate this action to those children who constantly remind me of this and who are a source of great strength to me.

Jeff Leys

As I ponder over the punishment to be meted out to these two people who were attempting to unbuild weapons of mass destruction, we must ask ourselves:...Why are we so fascinated by a power so great that we cannot comprehend its magnitude? What is so sacred about a bomb, so romantic about a missile?

...The anomaly of this situation here...is that I am called upon to punish two individuals who are charged with having caused damage to the property of a corporation in the amount of $33,000. It is this self-same corporation which only a few months ago was before me, accused of having wrongfully embezzled from the United States Government the sum of $3.6 million.

It is also difficult for me to equate the sentence I here give you for destroying $33,000 worth of property, because you have been charged—with those who stole $3.6 million worth of property but were not charged, demoted or in any way punished.

My duty is done, my conscience is clear.

U.S. District Judge Miles Lord
on sentencing two protesters to six months' probation
for damaging computer components at Sperry Corp.
November 1984

...our primary goal was to call attention to the idolatrous militarism and artifacts of our present-day society, our modern "golden calf" located in the fields, the hills, the valleys of our Mother Earth.

Father Carl Kabat

Your honor, I am the mother of three children, and it's my understanding that the parenthood of every generation, from the day the earth began, carries its responsibilities. And I believe that the responsibilities of parenthood change from generation to generation, as our world changes.

And I truly believe, deep down in my heart, that one of the responsibilities this generation has is to protect our children from the fear of holocaust....I have three children...and I don't want them to burn to death, like the children of Hiroshima....It was for that reason that I blockaded.

Barbara Bannon
blocked entrance to the
Livermore National Weapons Lab
June 1983

* Under a government which imprisons any unjustly, the true place for a just man is also a prison.

Henry David Thoreau

I do not feel I stand here today as a criminal. I feel this court is dealing in trivia by making this charge against us, while those who are the real criminals (those who deal in our deaths) continue their conspiracy against humankind.

Greenham Common woman's statement
Magistrate's Court—Newbury, England
April 1982

I still maintain hope for acquittal—slim as it is, I still have that hope. What is life worth after all if we don't have faith and hope in our brothers and sisters to act for Justice, for Peace, for Truth?

And if it should be a "guilty" verdict? I'll joyfully continue my witness wherever I'm sent in the prison system and continue to celebrate life. The government may do whatever it pleases with our bodies, but it can't touch our spirits!

Jeff Leys
written from jail while awaiting trial
September 1985

I disagree with those who think that "doing time" is necessarily wasting time...[we can compromise] our basic beliefs or so restrict our activities that we have, in effect, imprisoned ourselves out of prison.

Dave Dellinger
Revolutionary Nonviolence

I may be arrested. I may be tried and thrown into jail, but I will never be silent.

Emma Goldman

By our refusal to cooperate, we keep reminding them of our dissent, refusing to allow them the godlike sense that their will alone exists.
Barbara Deming

Your Honor, that's the problem with these people. They keep coming back!
the prosecutor in the Trident Nein case

* ...to compel a man to furnish contributions of money for the propagation of opinions he disbelieves and abhors, is sinful and tyrannical.
Thomas Jefferson
Virginia bill for Establishing Religious Freedom
1779

* If a thousand men were not to pay their tax bill this year, that would not be as violent and bloody a measure as it would be to pay them and enable the State to commit violence and shed innocent blood.
Henry David Thoreau

Ralph: What are you doing in jail?
Henry: What are you doing out of jail?
Ralph Waldo Emerson to Thoreau
while imprisoned for refusal to pay taxes for the Mexican War

Conscription

The most distasteful task of all for the objector to war conscription is to object. One does not live to become an objector but to create a society where such disagreeable conduct will not be necessary.
Evan Thomas
Conscience in Action

1. Historical Opposition

* A free government with an uncontrolled power for military conscription is the most ridiculous and abominable contradiction and nonsense that ever entered into the head of man. Where is it written in the Constitution, in what article or section is it contained, that you may take children from their parents and parents from their children, and compel them to fight the battle in any war in which the folly or wickedness of the government may engage itself.
Daniel Webster
1812

Much as I dislike to believe it, yet I am convinced that most of the propaganda in favor of selective conscription is founded not so much upon a desire to win the war as it is to accustom the people to this method of raising armies and thereby to establish it as a permanent system in this country. Let us not pay Prussian militarism, which we are seeking to destroy, the compliment of adopting the most hateful and baneful of its institutions.

Carl Hayden
Arizona Congressperson
1917

The claim that the draft is democratic, is the very antithesis of the truth. The draft is not democratic, it is autocratic; it is not republican, it is despotic; it is not American, it is Prussian. Its essential feature is that of involuntary servitude.

James A. Reed
Senator, Missouri
1917

Opposition to compulsory military service is characteristic of every government fit to be called a democracy....Democracies abhor that principle of compulsory service, the exercise of which menaces and may destroy their liberties....We are now told that compulsory military service is democratic. Mr. President, that is a libel and a reproach upon the name of democracy. It is as repugnant to democracy as any despotic principle which can be conceived.

Charles F. Thomas
Senator, Colorado
1917

* All our history gives confirmation to the view that liberty of conscience has a moral and social value which makes it worthy of preservation at the hands of the state. So deep is its significance and vital, indeed, is it to the integrity of man's moral and spiritual nature that nothing short of the self-preservation of the state should warrant its violation; and it may well be questioned whether the state which preserves its life by a settled policy of violation of the conscience of the individual will not in fact ultimately lose it by the process.

future Chief Justice Harlan F. Stone
The Conscientious Objector
1919

I regard the vote upon the pending measure to be the most important vote I shall ever be called upon to cast in this body. Upon the result of this vote hinges the ultimate destiny of this Republic. The question, plainly and bluntly put, is simply this: Shall we abandon the time-honored traditions of a peace-loving, liberty-loving people for that of a military despotism? That is the question in a nutshell.

Senator Billow
South Dakota
on the return of conscription, 1940

I believe that...in this bill...we are asked to vote on the adoption of compulsory selective military training and service as a permanent policy for the United States of America and to do it under the impulsion of an "emergency."

Jerry Voorhis
California Congressperson
1940

It is said that a compulsory draft is a democratic system. I deny that it has anything to do with democracy. It is neither democratic nor undemocratic. It is far more typical of totalitarian nations than of democratic nations. The theory behind it leads directly to totalitarianism. It is absolutely opposed to the principles of individual liberty which have always been considered a part of American democracy.

Robert Taft
Senator, Ohio
1948

The great mass of 18-year-olds...are given no choice. Thus...the older generation immolates the younger, on the altar of Moloch. What God, centuries ago, forbade Abraham to do even to his own son,—"Lay not thy hand upon the lad, neither do thou anything unto him"—this we do by decree to the entire youth of a nation.

A. J. Muste
Of Holy Disobedience
1952

I believe that conscription is good for our country—It's a great teacher of democracy.

Colonel Daniel O. Omer
Deputy Director
Selective Service
1967

Ultimately we should end the draft. Except for brief periods during the Civil War and World War I, conscription was foreign to the American experience until the 1940s.

Richard Nixon
1969

---

2. Vietnam Resisters

I knew I had arrived at conscientious objection. I was opposed in body and soul to the organized, budgeted, and officially sanctified use of violence called war. I was opposed to the compulsory and regimented aberration from the laws of God and reason, called conscription. I could no longer, in conscience, bear arms.

Stephen Fortunato, Jr.
while a U.S. marine
We Won't Go

I came to conscientious objection over a somewhat circuitous route—via the Marine Corps....With all the passion and exuberance of youth I became a trained killer. I went to classes where I learned how to rip a man's jugular vein out with my teeth. I growled like a tiger when I was told to growl like a tiger.

I was told that the Ten Commandments, however worthy they might be in civilian life, had to be suspended in the name of national interest. I was greatly impressed to see that an act perpetrated by the enemy was *ipso facto* vicious and deceitful, whereas the self-same act perpetrated by the United States was just and praiseworthy.

Stephen Fortunato, Jr.
We Won't Go

I am possibly confronted with fighting in a war that I believe to be unjust, immoral, and which makes a mockery of both our Constitution and the Charter of the United Nations—and the human values which they represent.

Apart from the moral and ethical issues and speaking only from the point of view of the super-patriot, it is a stupid war and pernicious to the self-interest of the United States....Although I am cognizant that an open society may have its disadvantages in an ideological war with a totalitarian system, I do not believe that the best defense of our freedoms is an emulation of that system.

Dale E. Noyd
Air Force Officer
refused to serve in Vietnam
became a Conscientious Objector after 11 years of honorable service
We Won't Go

* I think the Army does make an effort to deaden—to kill a man's sensitivities and make of him a conditioned response. Identity is destroyed effectively at basic training and patterns are drilled in hour after hour. No mind is called for, no thought process cultivated. Just do, do, do—to learn to do without thought—and, as the need arises, without resistance. It power-houses its way over any urge to resist, and when it destroys a man's natural tendency to resist when pushed, it has a soldier.

James M. Taylor
resisted while in Army
served two years of a three-year sentence
We Won't Go

* The best soldier, the Armed Forces teach us—contrary to our Christian tradition of values—is the most efficient murderer. The feeble voice of humanity's "Thou shalt not kill," is drowned out by the sergeant's roaring "Thou shalt kill and kill well!"

"All men are brothers," we learn in our Sunday Schools. But the Army teaches, "The best soldier is the one who makes the clearest distinction between the 'good guys' [and 'bad guys']." The best soldier realizes soonest that all men are brothers except the "Japs," the "Krauts," the "Commies," the "VC."

The best soldier ignores religion, God, and his conscience and learns to "follow orders." The best soldier can kill without thinking twice about it because he realizes that it is "his job" to do so.

These are the values that our society has decided to instill into the minds, hearts and reflexes of its youth. These are the values that I must reject. These are the values that are contrary to the "national interest." This is why draft resistance is work in "the national interest," and in the interest of all humanity.

> **Richard Boardman**
> **letter to the Selective Service**
> **gave up Conscientious Objection deferment to be a resister**
> **April 1967**

* One would think (from the human perspective) that our society would demand that its young men should show cause why they *can* become soldiers—and if need be, to kill—in all good conscience. Instead, from the military perspective of our society, we insist that a young man must show cause why he should be allowed *to refuse* to kill, to refuse to participate in the Army.

> **Richard Boardman**
> **letter to the Selective Service**
> **April 1967**

* I have tried my best to arrange a compromise—only to discover that by compromising my adherence to very basic, human, ethical principles—I defeat myself and do a disservice to mankind's best interests.

> **Richard Boardman**
> **letter to the Selective Service**
> **April 1967**

* A truly free man would not support a totalitarian system to defend freedom;...No, I came to believe that a free man preserves his freedom by acting freely and not by following those who would herd men into regiments or send people scurrying like moles into bomb shelters. Most important of all, the free man must remain free not to kill or to support killing.

> **Stephen Fortunato, Jr.**
> ***We Won't Go***

3. Draft Registration

The word "registration" to young people is code for "draft," an idea that evokes painful memories of Vietnam for many and an idea that has always seemed alien in a democratic society.

Ronald Reagan
1980 Campaign

* Registration cannot be separated from a draft; it's all part of the same program. The peacetime draft is more characteristic of a totalitarian system than a free society...[a] system of involuntary servitude. If we had not had the draft, we would never have been at war for the length of time we were in Vietnam. As long as each President had that unlimited supply of manpower, he could sustain that policy without a Congressional declaration of war.

Mark Hatfield
Senator, Oregon

To refuse military service when the time has come for it to be necessary, is to act after the time to combat the evil has run out.

Mahatma Gandhi

Though growing unemployment figures represent a major problem, they may act to improve our recruiting and retention [in the armed forces].

Secretary of Defense Harold Brown
June 1980

It all revolves around unemployment, you know, the economic thing. You know, it is ironic that most of the brothers I met in the army were in the infantry, in combat units, you know—the ones who would be doing the fighting and dying. Most of them, I found out, were just like myself, they didn't have any money, jobs were tight and they had to survive, so they joined the Army. And then— BANG—Vietnam....I noticed that most of the brothers who did go into the jungle returned to walk around in a kind of mindless stare. They did not know what they were doing out there, they did not want to go back out there, but most importantly they really began to realize, that for the most part, their commanding officers, and the army itself, considered them expendable. Racism was rampant in Vietnam. My advice to black people, or any people of color, is to stay out of the military.

Al Ceasar
Black Vietnam-era Veteran

When the time comes for you to march against the draft, think of me in this wheel chair. I thought I was fighting for the American dream. I know now I was cheated and tricked and lost three-fourths of my body for nothing [in Vietnam]. Now, the audacity, the madness, they want to brutalize another generation. Well, I say if they try to bring back the draft, they'll reap a rebellion like they've never seen.

Ron Kovic
paralyzed from the chest down
at an anti-draft rally on the Capitol steps, April 1979

Registering for the draft is like lining up for Kool Aid in Jonestown.

Daniel Ellsberg

We will not cooperate with military registration...noncooperation is the best way to demonstrate our opposition to the return of the draft and militarism....We do not take this position lightly. Prison, exile or the underground is hell, but war is worse.

Rick Stryker and Mark Furman

There is no purpose for registration and a draft except as a machinery to make interventionist wars possible abroad. Those of us who lived through the horror of Vietnam and the abuses of the draft that made it possible, know the hard choices ahead for America's young people. Those choices last time split a nation, jailed thousands, sent hundreds of thousands into exile or underground, separated families and ruined lives, disrupted and destroyed the promise of a generation.

Central Committee on Conscientious Objection (CCCO)

The revival of draft registration is being used to threaten war....Refusing the call to arms is based on the fundamental moral reality that there is no longer any threat greater than war itself....The members of Sojourners Fellowship have determined to refuse the call to arms at every point, including registration for the draft. Further, we advocate that others likewise refuse. Specifically, we encourage young men and women to refuse to register for the draft and support them in that decision.

Jim Wallis
***Sojourners*, March 1980**

Registration for a military draft is a major step toward war...as leaders of religious and academic communities...we oppose registration and will work to stop it. We believe that many young men (and women) will refuse to register....Some of us will resist the draft by wearing arm bands during any registration, by picketing places of registration, or by refusing to pay federal taxes for the draft...we hope to share some of the terrible burden put upon our young people by a compulsory registration and draft system that threatens once again to send them to far parts of the world to kill and be killed.

Call to Conscience
signed by key religious and academic leaders
issued by the Fellowship of Reconciliation, April 1980

The National Resistance Committee is confident that a strategy of concerted resistance can bring conscription to a halt. The draft, like all forms of tyranny, depends on the compliance of people who become victims through their tacit obedience to immoral laws. By withholding our cooperation, boycotting registration, and standing in solidarity with thousands of other resisters, the Selective Service System law will be made inoperative and unenforceable.

National Resistance Committee
Spring 1980

Compulsory military registration and service prior to congressional approval of war are unwarranted, dangerous and possibly illegal...

Equally as troubling is the extent to which the draft facilitates involvement in foreign conflicts. As the Vietnam War again illustrates, the burden of stopping an undeclared war through congressional action is exceptionally difficult, no matter how wrong the war, and the burden is rightfully and constitutionally placed on the President to demonstrate to Congress the need for a draft at time of war...

We are equally as opposed to a system of universal registration for military service in the future as we are to the actual draft. The registration system facilitates actual conscription, and we believe that it is being offered as a first step in that direction...

Congressional Black Caucus
June 1979

Sisterhood is international—it does not stop at international borders. If we embrace militarism and conscription as part of equality we will be declaring our sisters as enemies. That is something we as women and as feminists *will never* do. We must refuse the mad rush toward military confrontation. Sisterhood is powerful. Say NO to registration; say NO to the draft.

Women's International League for Peace and Freedom
January 1980

I can well understand that you, a young man full of life, loving and loved by your mother, friends, perhaps a young woman, think with a natural terror about what awaits you if you refuse conscription; and perhaps you will not feel strong enough to bear the consequences of refusal, and knowing your weakness, will submit and become a soldier. I understand completely, and I do not for a moment allow myself to blame you, knowing very well that in your place I might perhaps do the same thing. Only do not say that you did it because it was useful or because everyone does it. If you did it, know that you did wrong.

Leo Tolstoy

The first responsibility of a person conscientiously opposed to a particular institution is to refuse to cooperate with—or be a part of—that institution....What I am advocating is draft *resistance*, not draft *evasion*. People who oppose the draft because of deeply held moral or religious reasons—because they believe that war is a crime against humanity—should *publicly* refuse to register.

Refusing to register is the most *effective* way to manifest opposition to the current nature and direction of American foreign policy. I advocate this even though I realize that in so doing I may be violating the Selective Service law.

Jerry Elmer
Field Secretary, Rhode Island
American Friends Service Committee

If Congress votes for registration, War Resisters League supports all those who refuse to register. If one person refuses, the State will jail that person as an example. If a hundred refuse, the State will arrest them as a warning. If a thousand refuse to register, the State will arrest them as a threat to public order. But if a hundred thousand openly refuse to register, the President cannot enforce the law and no arrests will occur.

War Resisters League
Spring 1980

The issue is not equal treatment under compulsion, but freedom from compulsion.

American Friends Service Committee

I hold sacred all life and try to live in that spirit which removes all suffering. Because of my beliefs I must in all conscience work to defeat registration, the draft and the militarization of all society.

Glenda Poole
peace and social activist
mother of two sons

If these efforts should prove fruitless and our government reinstitutes draft registration, I shall, with the assistance of God, encourage, aid and abet all young persons to become nonregistrants. I shall advise these same young people on the evils of compliance with a system of militarization designed to maim and kill other people because of disputes which our leaders are either incapable of or unwilling to solve.

Glenda Poole
peace and social activist

They will tell you to register and be a man. Don't confuse manhood with machoism. A man is a mature person. A mature person recognizes the need for creative, not destructive acts. Your father and I have tried to teach you that no person is your enemy. Hunger, disease, servitude, fear of the unknown are enemies. They are the things a man should want to conquer, not people or nations....War is destructive...to destroy is not manly.

Madge Micheels-Cyrus
A Mother's Letter to Her Son...on Reaching Draft Age

Your father and I have tried to teach you that violence brings violence. It is courageous to love, to care for life, because it means a constant vigilance against any person or any government which dishonors life. War dishonors life.

Madge Micheels-Cyrus
A Mother's Letter to Her Son...on Reaching Draft Age

There are people across the United States who say "YES" to those who say "NO."

Anonymous

(See also Chapter 1—**Militarism**—page 10.)

ADDITIONS:

ADDITIONS:

25
Challenge to Make Peace

A. Facing the Nuclear Reality
B. Silence and Conformity
C. Challenge to the Individual
D. Challenge to the Collective Conscience
E. Challenge to the Nation

A. Facing the Nuclear Reality

* If atomic bombs are to be added as new weapons to the arsenals of a warring world, or to the arsenals of nations preparing for war, then the time will come when mankind will curse the names of Los Alamos and Hiroshima.

J. Robert Oppenheimer
headed the Manhattan Project
which built the atom bomb

What the world is dealing with, then, is not a problem of machines, but of the mind. And the mind has had a very odd relationship with the bomb from the moment it conceived it....The mind made the bomb, the mind denied it, and the mind can stop it cold. If that should sound impossible, consider how impossible nuclear fission must have seemed at the start, or how impossible the Holocaust, or how impossible to the children of Hiroshima that August 6, 1945, would turn out to be anything but another summer day.

It is time to see the bomb as a real weapon again, and not as an amorphous threat or a political lever. It is time to look straight at its drab snout and recall quite clearly what it once did and still can do.

Roger Rosenblatt
Time
July 1981

We've become immersed in dehumanized technicalities and statistics and as a result we have lost the elementary fundamental sense of horror and anguish that is needed to make us see the truth...we can reach back—and we should—through the years to the bombing of Hiroshima and Nagasaki and recover many things we would rather forget.

John Culver
former Senator, Iowa

Here I was, a young physician with good medical training behind me, a chest of all the best medicines then known to science, and I was powerless to help these atomic bomb victims in any way. This was true horror...

I do not want physicians ever again to have to face a landscape of six inches of black ashes, twisted metal beams, severe leukemia, and sizzled bone marrow—and know that they can do nothing.

Nuclear war has been called unthinkable, but our governments continue to prepare for it. To me, what is unthinkable is not to speak out.

Charles S. Stevenson
first American physician in
Nagasaki after the atomic bombing
Physicians for Social Responsibility

Some of what I...describe is horrifying. I know, because it horrifies me. There is a tendency—psychiatrists call it "denial"—to put it out of our minds, not to think about it. But if we are to deal intelligently, wisely, with the nuclear arms race, then we must steel ourselves to contemplate the horrors of nuclear war.

Carl Sagan
The Nuclear Winter

After a nuclear exchange not even the most ardent ideologue is going to be able to tell the ashes of communism from the ashes of free enterprise.

John Kenneth Galbraith

Since nuclear armaments here and in the Soviet Union have created a world in which the whole can nowhere be protected against its parts, our own national security has reached the zero point. The issue is no longer the survival of one nation against another. We stand now in mortal danger of global human incineration.

Episcopal House of Bishops
Pastoral Letter
1980

No one wants to kill another family's child, or another child's family. Yet we prepare to do so.

Karol Schulkin

The last major childhood disease remains and it's the worst of them all: nuclear war.

Beverly Sills
opera star

Human rights, civil rights, women's rights are meaningless before the greatest issue of all—nuclear war and our survival.
Brigadier-General B. K. Gorwitz

Women's rights, men's rights—human rights—all are threatened by the ever-present spectre of war so destructive now of human material and moral values as to render victory indistinguishable from defeat.

Rosika Schwimmer

Nuclear weapons threaten the most basic of human rights—the right to life.
Anonymous

Nuclear war. It's deadly. And it could affect more children than have ever suffered in the whole history of the world. Two hundred million. Eight hundred million. Nobody knows.... This is the only issue I've ever worked for. I believe, right now, it is the only issue.

Sally Field, actress

Superintendents and curriculum specialists place "nuclear disarmament" on a par with "pollution of the earth's environment" as the social issue most significant for humankind.

Stanley M. Elam
"Educators and the Nuclear Threat"
Phi Delta Kappan

I share your sense that all other current issues pale into footnotes to history in comparison with issues of nuclear war.

Nannerl O. Koehone
President, Wellesley College

This is not an issue. This is survival! It should not be political or partisan. Nor for Democrats or Republicans. It's survival. Period. Both countries have gone past any sensible assessment of the problem...if this problem is not solved soon I really have little faith that the world can continue.

Joanne Woodward
actress

There is no issue more important than the avoidance of nuclear war. Whatever your interests, passions or goals, they and you are threatened fundamentally by the prospect of nuclear war. We have achieved the capability for the certain destruction of our civilization and perhaps of our species as well. I find it incredible that any thinking person would not be concerned in the deepest way about this issue.

...The Earth is an anomaly; in all the Solar System it is, so far as we know, the only inhabited planet. I look at the fossil record and I see that after flourishing for 180 million years the dinosaurs were extinguished. Every last one. There are none left. No species is guaranteed its tenure on this planet. And we've been here for only about a million years, we, the first species that has devised the means for its self-destruction. We are rare and precious because we are alive, because we can think. We are privileged to live, to influence and control our future. I believe we have an obligation to fight for that life, to struggle not just for ourselves, but for all those creatures who came before us, and to whom we are beholden, and for all those who, if we are wise enough, will come after us. There is no cause more urgent, no dedication more fitting for us, than to strive to eliminate the threat of nuclear war. No social convention, no political system, no economic hypothesis, no religious dogma is more important.

Carl Sagan
To Preserve a World Graced by Life

We are all in a great big huge emergency room and we have no doctors to heal us but ourselves.

Barbara Bialick
A Planetary Healing Crisis

We are going to have to find a way to immunize people against the kind of thinking that leads to self-devastation. In effect, we are the malignant virus that is capable of self-destruction.

Jonas Salk

This is the only time in history where humans have the capacity to destroy the world completely. And it could be done by mistake.

Eloy Alfaro
assistant rector, University of Peace

* Mankind faces extinction either through a nuclear or an environmental catastrophe unless humanity changes its ways.

19 Nobel Prize winners and leaders
of about 100 of the country's
environmental and arms control groups

In fact, I think we are in a really close race between our ability to change and our capacity to self-destruct.

Rusty Schweickart
Apollo astronaut

We are reaching a point where more armaments are making the world less safe from a nuclear holocaust. This could be our last chance to say no to the next batch of weaponry.

Owen Chamberlain
Nobel Laureate

Before it is too late, we must narrow the gaping chasm between our proclamations of peace and our lowly deeds which precipitate and perpetuate war. We are called upon to look up from the quagmire of military programs and defense commitments and read the warnings on history's signposts.

One day we must come to see that peace is not merely a distant goal that we seek but a means by which we arrive at that goal. We must pursue peaceful ends through peaceful means. How much longer must we play at deadly war games before we heed the plaintive pleas of the unnumbered dead and maimed of past wars?

Martin Luther King, Jr.

The insistent awareness of absurdity gives us the incentive for radical new approaches and at the same time energizes even the more limited methodical efforts. It is when we lose our sense of nuclear absurdity that we surrender to the forces of annihilation and cease to imagine the real.

Robert Jay Lifton and Richard Falk
Indefensible Weapons

* Unconditional war can no longer lead to unconditional victory. It can no longer serve to settle disputes. It can no longer be of concern to great powers alone. For a nuclear disaster, spread by the winds and waters of fear, could well engulf the great and the small, the rich and the poor, the committed and the uncommitted alike. Mankind must put an end to war or war will put an end to mankind.

John F. Kennedy

* Almost imperceptibly, over the last four decades, every nation and every human being has lost ultimate control over their life and death. For all of us, it is a small group of men and machines in cities far away who can decide our fate. Every day we remain alive is a day of grace, as if mankind as a whole were a prisoner in the death cell awaiting the uncertain moment of execution....A halt to the nuclear arms race is at the present moment imperative.

The Delhi Declaration
signed by the heads of state of Argentina,
Greece, India, Mexico, Sweden and Tanzania

We are confronted here, my friends, with two courses. At the end of the one lies hope—faint hope, if you will—uncertain hope, hope surrounded with dangers, if you insist. At the end of the other lies, so far as I am able to see, no hope at all.

George Kennan
former US Ambassador to the USSR

Behind the black portent of the new atomic age lies a hope which, seized upon with faith, can work out salvation....Let us not deceive ourselves; we must elect world peace or world destruction.

Bernard Baruch
speech to the UN Atomic Energy Commission
August 1946

Science has made unrestricted national sovereignty incompatible with human survival. The only possibilities are now world government or death.

Bertrand Russell

* Through the release of atomic energy, our generation brought into the world the most revolutionary force since prehistoric man's discovery of fire. This basic power of the universe cannot be fitted into the outmoded concept of narrow nationalisms. For there is no secret and there is no defense, there is no possibility of control except through the aroused understanding and insistence of the peoples of the world.

Albert Einstein

Only when American citizens understand that the threat of nuclear war is not something "over there"—in Europe, in the Soviet Union, or in some remote desert factory, but right here at home, no farther away than the next truck on the freeway, might they take the action necessary to end the arms race.

Samuel H. Day, Jr.
The Progressive, **November 1984**

The growing controversy surrounding nuclear fission is the most important issue the American society and the world has ever faced. A national and international debate on this subject is long overdue, and the participation of each individual will determine its outcome. We must begin today by first of all learning as much as we can about the critical issues involved, because what we don't know may kill us. We need new creative initiatives to avoid nuclear catastrophe, and they must begin with awareness, concern and action on the part of the individual.

Dr. Helen Caldicott
founder and past president
Physicians for Social Responsibility

American political and military leaders should publicly acknowledge that there is no realistic prospect for a successful population defense, certainly for many decades, and probably never.

Harold Brown
former Secretary of Defense

Being an ingenious people, Americans find it hard to believe there is no forseeable defense against atomic bombs. But this is a basic fact. Scientists do not even know of any field which promises us any hope of adequate defense.

Albert Einstein

There is no civil defense against nuclear war except prevention of nuclear war.

Paul Warnke
SALT II negotiator

The nuclear bomb is an equal opportunity destroyer.

Ron Dellums
Congressperson, California

The Story of The Bomb: No place to hide.

Randy L.
Boston
Age 8
Please Save My World

...just as the sun shines on the godly and the ungodly alike, so does nuclear radiation. And with this knowledge it becomes increasingly difficult to embrace the thought of extinction purely for the assumed satisfaction of—from the grave—achieving revenge. Or even of accepting our demise as a planet as a simple and just preventive medicine administered to the universe. Life is better than death, I believe, if only because it is less boring, and because it has fresh peaches in it.

Alice Walker
author

Everybody knows there will always be wars, right? Wrong! Everybody knows there will always be *conflict*. For a growing number of nations possessing nuclear weapons, attempting to settle conflict with war isn't an option anymore.

Jeanne Larson

When we get to the point, as we one day will, that both sides know that in any outbreak of general hostilities, regardless of the element of surprise, destruction will be both reciprocal and complete, possibly we will have sense enough to meet at the conference table with the understanding that the era of armaments has ended and the human race must conform its actions to this truth or die.

Dwight D. Eisenhower
April 1956

* We must remold the relationships of all men, of all nations in such a way that these men do not wish, or dare, to fall upon each other for the sake of vulgar, outdated ambition or for passionate differences in ideologies, and that international bodies by supreme authority may give peace on earth and justice among men.

Winston Churchill
House of Commons
August 1945

But this very triumph of scientific annihilation—this very success of invention—has destroyed the possibility of war's being a medium for the practical settlement of international differences. The enormous destruction to both sides of closely matched opponents makes it impossible for even the winner to translate it into anything but his own disaster.

General Douglas MacArthur
July 1961

There is no political reason on earth that can morally justify the continued uncontrolled existence of these weapons.   **Christine Cassel**
Physicians for Social Responsibility

There is nothing, except a tragic death wish, to prevent us from re-ordering our priorities, so that the pursuit of peace will take precedence over the pursuit of war.

Martin Luther King, Jr.

We recognize that once a civilization has invented nuclear weapons, the only alternative to self-destruction is to invent peace. War has been made obsolete.

Women's Peace Presence

All war must be declared obsolete in the nuclear age.   **Irene Brown**

Peace is the one condition of survival in this nuclear age.

Adlai E. Stevenson

The way to win an atomic war is to make certain it never starts.

General Omar Bradley

The hydrogen bomb is history's exclamation point. It ends an age-long sentence of manifest violence.

Marshall McLuhan

I think both the Soviets and the U.S. are very dangerous governments building up very dangerous weapons. I don't care who is ahead, because if there is a nuclear war we'll all be wiped out. We're past the point of it making any sense who is ahead.

Zafra Epstein
Age 13
Our Future at Stake

The arms race is just silly to me, and it's gone on for so long. One government thinks "If I stop now, the other countries will hurt me," but the building up just increases all of our chances of mistakes or someone using them. Communication and understanding would work much better than threats, and it could not be more expensive or take more effort than the arms race does, could it? We should all at least just stop now for a breather and think for a while. Even just a one-year breather in the arms race would give us a chance to be more rational about it.

Wenonah Elms
Age 13
Our Future at Stake

I have this image of what this missile stuff is all about and that is that somehow these nations were big boys or brothers fighting in the alley and waiting for a parent to come out and break them up....It started dawning on me that there weren't any parents to break them up—all there was was just kids,...the whole world was just kids.

Paul Paulos

We must raise the question with utmost urgency: are nuclear arsenals poised to destroy entire civilizations realistic methods of keeping us from harm?

Fellowship of Reconciliation

[Referring to nuclear weapons and the direct disarmament movement]
They're going to get us or we're going to get them.
Philip Berrigan

We will have "Star Wars" or arms control. We can't have both.
Clark Clifford
former Secretary of Defense

As few as 100 nuclear weapons on each side, half of one per cent of the
current arsenals, could devastate the US and the USSR beyond any
historical experience and perhaps beyond recovery as industrial societies.
To end the danger of nuclear war the nations must not merely freeze
nuclear weapons but abolish them.
Randall Forsberg
Scientific American, **November 1982**

The end of further experiments with atom bombs would be like the early
sunrays of hope which suffering humanity is longing for.
Albert Schweitzer

For while unilateral disarmament poses a *risk*, the paranoid-technocratic
confrontation between superpowers poses a *certainty*: extermination
through nuclear holocaust.
Joel Kovel

We balance the risks of an unarmed world against one with nuclear
weapons and we know that while capitalism and communism as they
now exist would not survive disarmament, humanity would.
David McReynolds

Many more nations have been brought to destruction by fear of change
than by love of it.
Bertrand Russell

Death can never be overcome without danger.   **Greek wisdom**

If the human race wishes to have a prolonged and indefinite period of
material prosperity, they have only got to behave in a peaceful and helpful
way toward one another.   **Winston Churchill**

* We, the citizens of Hiroshima, ever mindful of this cruel experience,
clearly foresee the extinction of mankind and an end to civilization should
the world drift into a nuclear war. Therefore, we have vowed to set aside
our griefs and grudges and continuously plead before the peoples of the
world to abolish weapons and renounce war so that we may never again
repeat the tragedy of Hiroshima.   **Takeshi Araki**
Mayor of Hiroshima
August 1976

B. Silence and Conformity

Time changes; truth is altered. We must perceive and react from what we understand at this moment in time.

Henry Ibsen

At present, most of us do nothing. We look away. We remain calm. We are silent.

Jonathan Schell
The Fate of the Earth

Most of us build prisons for ourselves, and after we occupy them for a period of time we become accustomed to their walls and accept the false premise that we are incarcerated for life. As soon as that belief takes hold of us we abandon hope of ever doing more with our lives and of ever giving our dreams a chance to be fulfilled. We begin to suffer living deaths; one of a herd heading for destruction in a grey mass of mediocrity.

Barb Katt
on being sentenced for destroying
a war-related computer at Sperry Corp.

Why weren't there Germans blockading the tracks to Auschwitz?

Daniel Ellsberg

I have often wondered what I would have done if I were a German in the '40s watching the boxcars of people pass through my town. Would I have left it to someone else to step forward, to raise the question, to try to stop the trains?

Karol Schulkin
reflecting on nuclear weapons
the equivalent of nuclear ovens
Ground Zero, Spring 1983

In Germany they first came for the Communists and I didn't speak up because I wasn't a Communist. Then they came for the Jews, and I didn't speak up because I wasn't a Jew. Then they came for the trade unionists, and I didn't speak up because I wasn't a trade unionist. Then they came for the Catholics, and I didn't speak up because I was a Protestant. Then they came for me—and by that time no one was left to speak up.

Pastor Martin Niemöller

"Good Germans" is the phrase historians use to describe a people who silently go along with their government's grand plans for military adventures. If the madness of World War III really is upon us, perhaps this is the era of Good Americans.   **Colman McCarthy**
1980

The violence is here; it is a fact. Injustice exists; this is reality. As Christians we may not abide this. We may not allow ourselves to grow accustomed to evil, least of all to an evil that is daily and constant. We may not keep silent, especially when people try to intimidate us with threats, campaigns of vilification, and reprisals.

Declaration of the International
Meeting of Latin American Bishops
November/December 1977

It may well be that the greatest tragedy of this period of social transition is not the glaring noisiness of the so-called bad people, but the appalling silence of the so-called good people.

Martin Luther King, Jr.

The sin of omission—the refusal to get involved—is one of the worst things in the world.

Adolfo Pérez Esquivel
1980 Nobel Peace Prize
Christ in a Poncho

The hottest places in hell are reserved for those who, in time of great moral crisis, maintain their neutrality.

Dante

We know what happens to people who stay in the middle of the road. They get run over.

Aneurin Bevan

Nothing will ever be attempted if all possible objections must be first overcome.

Samuel Johnson

All we need for the triumph of evil is that good people do nothing.

Edmund Burke

* I have thought for a long time now that if, someday, the increasing efficiency of the technique of destruction finally causes our species to disappear from the earth, it will not be cruelty that will be responsible for our extinction and still less, of course, the indignation that cruelty awakens and the reprisals and vengeance that it brings upon itself...but the docility, the lack of responsibility of the modern man, his base subservient acceptance of every common decree. The horrors which we have seen, the still greater horrors we shall presently see, are not signs that rebels, insubordinate, untameable men, are increasing in number throughout the world, but rather that there is a constant increase, a stupendously rapid increase, in the number of obedient, docile men.

Georges Bernanos
French writer

We will never understand totalitarianism if we do not understand that people rarely have the strength to be uncommon...

Eugène Ionesco

[Children should be taught] to resist unjust or ridiculous authority....The worst thing...is how easily people can be led by any kind of authority figure, or even the most minimal signs of authority....We put up a sign on the road "Delaware closed today." Motorists didn't question it. Instead they asked,"Is Jersey open?"

Allen Funt
Candid Camera
May 1985

The evils of government are directly proportional to the tolerance of the people.

Frank Kent

The limits of tyrants are prescribed by the endurance of those whom they oppress.

Frederick Douglass

There is no slavery where there are no willing slaves.

Jose Riza
Filipino patriot

The essence of power is not in military might but in the people. They are ruled by the state to the degree that they cooperate with the state. The state loses its power to the degree that the people withdraw or sever their cooperation.

Gene Sharp

* The land of propaganda is built on unanimity. If one man says "NO," the spell is broken and public order is endangered.

Ignazio Silone
Bread and Wine

There must have been a time, near the beginning, when we could have said "No."

Tom Stoppard
Rosencrantz and Guildenstern Are Dead
(A play taking off from the plot of *Hamlet*)

They that give up essential liberty to obtain a little temporary safety deserve neither liberty nor safety.

Benjamin Franklin

* To sin by silence when they should protest makes cowards of men.

Abraham Lincoln

Cowards die many times before their deaths, the valiant never taste of death but once.

William Shakespeare
Julius Caesar

Something we were withholding made us weak. Until we found it was ourselves.

Robert Frost

Far more violence to human beings in history has been done in obeying the law than in breaking the law.

Howard Zenn
Lovejoy's Nuclear War

Conforming has killed more people—though perhaps more slowly—than rebelling; and especially the millions, in all countries, who conventionally tramped off to wars that accomplished nothing except keeping the map-makers busy.

Anonymous

A common and natural result of an undue respect for law is, that you may see a file of soldiers, colonel, captain, corporal, privates, powder-monkeys, and all, marching in admirable order over hill and dale to the wars, against their wills, ay, against their common sense and consciences, which makes it very steep marching indeed, and produces a palpitation of the heart. They have no doubt that it is a damnable business in which they are concerned; they are all peaceably inclined...

Henry David Thoreau

When great changes occur in history, when great principles are involved, as a rule the majority are wrong.

Eugene Debs

A very great historic change that has been based upon nonconformity, has been bought either with the blood or with the reputation of nonconformists.

Ben Shahn

The moment we begin to fear the opinions of others and hesitate to tell the truth that is in us, and from motives of policy are silent when we should speak, the divine floods of light and life flow no longer into our souls....Every truth we see is ours to give the world, not to keep to ourselves alone, for in doing so we cheat humanity out of their rights and check our own development.

Elizabeth Cady Stanton

* The reasonable man adapts himself to the world; the unreasonable one persists in trying to adapt the world to himself. Therefore, all progress depends on the unreasonable man.

George Bernard Shaw

Liberation is an awakening of the consciousness, a change of mentality for ways of thinking so that the person no longer thinks what their present society wants him/her to think but rather learns to think and act for him/herself in dialogue with others in order to create a new world in which it is easier to love.

Magaly Rodriguez O'Hearn

C. Challenge to the Individual

* We have seen the enemy, and he is us.

Walt Kelly
Pogo

Knowing is terrifying
Not knowing is terrifying
But not knowing is hopeless
And knowing may save us.

high school student
Brookline, Massachusetts

On Hiroshima/Nagasaki: To know and not to act is not yet to know.

Anonymous

Extinction is not something to contemplate; it is something to rebel against.

Jonathan Schell
The Fate of the Earth

I will act as if what I do makes a difference.

William James

For it isn't enough to talk about peace. One must believe in it. And it isn't enough to believe in it. One must work at it.

Eleanor Roosevelt

We can begin anywhere—everywhere. "Let there be peace" says a bumper sticker, "and let it begin with me"....Let there be transformation, and let it begin with me.

Marilyn Ferguson

Peace if it is to be mine and shared with the world must begin in me; a personal peace.   **Alex Birkholz**
7th Grader

It is not yours to finish the task, but neither are you free to take no part in it.

from the Jewish *Wisdom of the Fathers*

Everything now, we must assume, is in our hands; we have no right to assume otherwise.

James Baldwin

It is time for us to raise our voices. No one of us can do everything—but each of us can do something. We can demand a government that embraces life.

Terry Herndon
teacher

Each of us is an expert with the full passion and resources to change the world. We should activate ourselves and not wait for the male experts, but follow the love and the passion in our hearts and our minds to bring about the kind of transformation so our children can live.

Patricia Ellsberg

We should say to each of them: Do you know what you are? You are a marvel. You are unique. In all the world there is no other child exactly like you. In the millions of years that have passed, there has never been a child like you...and when you grow up, can you then harm another who is, like you, a marvel? You must cherish one another. You must work—we must all work—to make this world worthy of its children.

Pablo Casals

There are no sidelines in life. We must enter in and live.

Swami Satchedananda

When somebody says, "Well, there's nothing I can do," I know they're not awake. When you're awake you could use a hundred other people to help you.

Anonymous

No one has a right to sit down and feel hopeless. There's too much work to do.

Dorothy Day

* He who stands for nothing will fall for anything.   **Anonymous**

* If a man doesn't find something to die for he probably hasn't anything to live for.

James Bevel

One has to speak out and stand up for one's convictions. Inaction at a time of conflagration is inexcusable.

Mahatma Gandhi

The ultimate measure of a person is not where they stand in moments of comfort and convenience, but where they stand at times of challenge and controversy.

Martin Luther King, Jr.

Moderation in temper is always a virtue, but moderation in principle is always a vice.

Thomas Paine

It isn't just a question of gender and gaps, of motherhood and morality. It isn't a question of men versus women, but of citizens who do and don't participate. At the core, the arms debate isn't a matter of statistics but of values and choices and that's a language anybody can learn.

Ellen Goodman
columnist

Every person is the right person to act. Every moment is the right moment to begin.

Jonathan Schell
The Fate of the Earth

I am only one, but still I am one. I cannot do everything, but still I can do something; and because I cannot do everything I will not refuse to do the something that I can do.

Edward Everett Hale

I wondered why somebody didn't do something for peace....Then I realized that I am somebody.

Anonymous

Kids know, better than grownups, what we do is more important than what we say.

Pete Seeger

Each one of us has inside a piece of peace that must emerge and live outside us.

Anonymous

It is in each of us that the peace of the world is cast...from there it must spread out to the limits of the universe.

Leo Cardinal Suenens

What I want to bring out is how a pebble cast into a pond causes ripples that spread in all directions. And each one of our thoughts, words and deeds is like that.

Dorothy Day

Putting our money where our hearts are is one more, potentially very powerful way to integrate our lives and work for peace—and a sustainable future.

Susan Meeker-Lowry
co-editor, *Good Money: A Newsletter of Social Investing*

Against the ruin of the world, there is only one defense—the creative act.

Kenneth Rexroth

...You must be a practicing idealist if you are to remain a true idealist for long. You must take small practical steps, often when you would prefer to take giant ones—but you must move in the direction of your ideals through action. Otherwise you will feel disillusioned, or powerless, or sure, again, that only drastic, highly unideal methods will ever bring about the achievement of a given ideal state or situation.

(Seth) Jane Roberts
The Individual and the Nature of Mass Events

The journey of a thousand miles begins with one step.

Lao-tse

The journey of a thousand leagues begins with a single step. So we must never neglect any work of peace within our reach, however small.

Adlai E. Stevenson

Every citizen who loves this country, its freedom and good life; every parent whose children yearn for their day in the sun; every American who believes our national heritage still represents "the last, best hope of earth," must become earnestly engaged in the active quest for peace.

Frank Church
former Senator, Idaho

Ask not what your country can do for you, but rather what you can do for your country.

John F. Kennedy
quoting Seneca

In light of my faith, I am prepared to live without nuclear weapons in my country.

Fellowship of Reconciliation

I have an 8-month-old daughter and I'm very concerned about a nuclear war. I look at my baby girl and wonder what, if any, kind of future she will have. I feel that everyone has a responsibility to do what they can...I couldn't live with myself if I didn't try to do something. I love my daughter too much.

Debra J. Elslager

I don't want my children coming up to me and saying, now what did you do, and me saying I didn't know.

Dorothee Sölle

* Every thoughtful citizen who despairs of war and wishes to bring peace should begin by looking inward, by examining his own attitudes toward the possibilities of peace, toward the Soviet Union, toward the course of the cold war, and toward freedom and peace here at home.

John F. Kennedy

* Let us examine our attitude toward peace itself. Too many of us think it is impossible. Too many think it unreal. But that is a dangerous, defeatist belief. It leads to the conclusion that war is inevitable, that mankind is doomed, that we are gripped by forces we cannot control.

John F. Kennedy

* Our problems are man made. Therefore, they can be solved by man. And man can be as big as he wants. No problem of human destiny is beyond human beings. Man's reason and spirit have often solved the seemingly unsolvable, and we believe they can do it again.

John F. Kennedy

* Samantha couldn't accept man's inhumanity to man. She stood fast in the belief that peace can be achieved and maintained by mankind.

Samantha Smith
13-year-old peace activist
as described by her mother
after Samantha's death in a plane crash
1985

* For without belittling the courage with which men have died, we should not forget those acts of courage with which men...have lived....A man does that which he must—in spite of personal consequences, in spite of obstacles and dangers and pressures—and that is the basis of all human morality.

John F. Kennedy

Each time a person stands for an ideal, or acts to improve the lot of others, or strikes out against injustice, he or she sends forth a tiny ripple of hope. And crossing each other from a million different centers of energy and daring, those ripples build a current that can sweep down the mightiest walls of oppression and resistance. Few are willing to brave the disapproval of their fellows, the censure of their colleagues, the wrath of their society. Moral courage is a rarer commodity than bravery in battle or great intelligence. Yet it is the one essential vital quality for those who seek to change a world that yields most painfully to change.

Robert F. Kennedy

We may be frightened of taking risks, not knowing what will happen to us, of standing out by making a personal statement, of being embarrassed in public...of losing security...or the respect of people we had thought were friends.

Greenham Women Everywhere

Every public reform was once a private opinion.

Ralph Waldo Emerson

It is no dishonor to be in a minority in the cause of liberty and virtue.

Sam Adams
1771

The probability that we may fail in the struggle ought not to deter us from the support of a cause we believe to be just.

Abraham Lincoln

* The men who try to do something and fail are infinitely better than those who try nothing and succeed.

Lloyd Jones

People do not lack strength, they lack will.

Victor Hugo

I realize suddenly that it is not a question of faith, but of will. I *will* life to go on.
    We have collectively created the death cults. We can collectively create a culture of life.
    But to do so, we must be willing to step out of line, to forgo the comfort of leaving decisions up to somebody else. To will is to make our own decisions, guide our own lives, commit ourselves, our time, our work, our energy, to act in the service of life. To will is to reclaim our power, our power to reclaim the future.

Starhawk
The Spiral Dance

I've been to demonstrations, and the big surprise was that they were fun. Being there with so many people who are there for a sense of purpose makes you feel energy and power.

Caedmon Fujimoto
Age 16
Our Future at Stake

* I have been to demonstrations before and they were fun. I try to think about it like an adventure and then it's not scary. The one thing that really scares me, though, about civil disobedience is what about if I get arrested by a racist police officer and he decides to take it out on me...I

want to try it though...I need to try all kinds of ways to protest the arms race, but I'm a little scared.

Ursell Austin
Age 16
Our Future at Stake

I feel that getting involved and trying to do something about nuclear bombs has made me feel much better—a lot less depressed. I'm glad I'm one more person trying to do something about it. It seems to me like this age, 15 years old, is when you really start thinking about things, thinking about your life, and it's good to feel you can do something about the things you don't agree with.

Regina Hunter
Age 15
Our Future at Stake

I think any action is worth doing. Demonstrations make me feel happy and exhilarated. People focus on love of life rather than death or fear. It's great.

Max Friedman
Age 16
Our Future at Stake

I don't think there is any single most effective way to stop this craziness. Everyone has their own way. When people learn about the arms race and get active, each one finds something to do that feels right to them— wearing buttons, praying, writing letters, getting arrested, demonstrating. It all adds up, every little thing we do touches someone. Putting your body on the line may be more dramatic or get more attention from the media, but it's not necessarily more effective than some smaller or quiet things that touch people. Whatever people do is good. But everyone has to do something.

Zafra Epstein
Age 13
Our Future at Stake

As you come to know the seriousness of our situation—the war, the racism, the poverty in the world—you come to realize it is not going to be changed just by words or demonstrations. It's a question of risking your life. It's a question of living your life in drastically different ways.

Dorothy Day

People say to me "What a sacrifice you've made! How brave you are! How much you gave up!" And it makes me want to laugh because I have given up nothing. Nothing. Nothing except irrelevance.

Jane Fonda
actress

The most powerful antinuclear weapon in the world is YOU!
Nuclear Times
March 1983

Nothing could be worse than the fear that one had given up too soon and left one unexpended effort which might have saved the world.
Jane Addams

They were told "No" a thousand times and after the final "No" there was a "Yes" that saved the world.
Wallace Stevens

D. Challenge to the Collective Conscience

Can one generation bind another and all others in succession forever? I think not. The Creator made the earth for the living not the dead.
Thomas Jefferson
1781

We must never relax our efforts to arouse in the people of the world, and especially in their governments, an awareness of the unprecedented disaster which they are absolutely certain to bring on themselves unless there is a fundamental change in their attitudes toward one another as well as in their concept of the future.
Albert Einstein

* The unleashed power of the atom has changed everything save our modes of thinking, and thus we drift toward unparalleled catastrophe. We shall require a substantially new manner of thinking if mankind is to survive.
Albert Einstein

This generation has, quite humbly, the final responsibility and the last chance to turn terror into hope.   **Albert Einstein**

Increasingly, it is evident that our generation has arrived at a turning point. Will we indeed fulfill the theory that our species is fatally flawed because it is incapable of controlling its aggressive tendencies and is, therefore, destined for extinction or will we move in a fresh direction toward a disarmed world?   **Fellowship of Reconciliation**

If you put a frog into a pot of boiling water, the frog will jump out. However, if you put a frog in a pot of cold water and slowly raise the temperature, the frog will boil to death.
     When it comes to the military preparations going on around us, do we recognize the rise in temperature?
Rosalie Bertell
biostatistician

The overwhelming priority to do away with nuclear arms has not penetrated the collective consciousness or conscience of the general public....Nuclear arms must not just be limited, they must be eliminated.

Reverend Maurice McCrackin
Community Church of Cincinnati

Probably every generation sees itself as charged with remaking the world. Mine, however, knows it will not remake the world. Its task is even greater: to keep the world from destroying itself.

Albert Camus

We who are about to die demand a miracle.

W. H. Auden

* Shall we put an end to the human race or shall man renounce war?

Albert Einstein

We still have a choice today: non-violent co-existence or violent co-annihilation. We must move past indecision to action. Now let us begin. Now let us rededicate ourselves to the long and bitter—but beautiful— struggle for a new world...The choice is ours, and though we might prefer it otherwise, we must choose in this crucial moment of human history.

Martin Luther King, Jr.

* Removing the threat of a world war—a nuclear war—is the most acute and urgent task of the present day. Mankind is confronted with a choice: we must halt the arms race and proceed to disarmament or face annihilation.

Final Document
U.N. Special Session on Disarmament
1978

For with the advent of atomic weapons we have come either to the last page of war, at any rate on the major international scale we have known in the past, or to the last page of history.

B. H. Liddell Hart
Why Don't We Learn from History?

* We must learn to live together as brothers or we are going to perish together as fools.

Martin Luther King, Jr.

We can look at it now in one of two ways. This is the end and we might as well get over it...or this is the hard birth of the new age.

Ram Dass

If we let it, the Bomb can provide us with the necessary stress…to create the unity which [could bring forth] the new age.

Joanna Rogers Macy

For, although it is true that fear and despair can overwhelm us, hope cannot be purchased with the refusal to feel.

Susan Griffin

Nuclear war is inevitable, says the pessimist;
Nuclear war is impossible, says the optimist;
Nuclear war is inevitable unless we make it impossible, says the realist.

Sydney J. Harris
columnist

* These are the times for real choices and not false ones. We are at the moment when our lives must be placed on the line if our nation is to survive its own folly. Everyone of humane convictions must decide on the protest that best suits his convictions, but we all must protest.

Martin Luther King, Jr.

For the love of God, your children and the civilization to which you belong, cease the madness. You have a duty not just to the generation of the present: you have a duty to civilizations past, which you threaten to render meaningless, and to its future, which you threaten to render nonexistent.

George Kennan
former US Ambassador to the USSR

We are faced with the fact that tomorrow is today. We are confronted with the fierce urgency of now. In this unfolding conundrum of life and history there is such a thing as being too late. Procrastination is still the thief of time.

Martin Luther King, Jr.

If we are to survive on this planet, the arms race must be slowed, stopped, and reversed. The time to start is now.

Rear Admiral Gene R. La Rocque
US Navy (retired)

There is no time left for anything but to make peace work a dimension of our every waking activity.

Elise Boulding

* …Today we have achieved—we and the Russians together—in the creation of these devices and their means of delivery, levels of redundancy of such grotesque dimensions as to defy rational understanding. What a confession of intellectual poverty it would be,

what a bankruptcy of intelligent statesmanship, if we had to admit that such blind, senseless acts of destruction were the best we could do.

George Kennan
former US Ambassador to the USSR

Wars can be prevented just as surely as they can be provoked, and we who fail to prevent them must share in the guilt for the dead.

General Omar Bradley

War is not created by basic human aggressiveness, war is organized! Peace has to be organized even more effectively!

The Great Peace Journey
Swedish brochure
1985

...because we want peace with half a heart and half a life and will, the war, of course, continues because the waging of war, by its nature, is total—but the waging of peace, by our own cowardice, is partial. So a whole will and a whole heart and a whole national life bent toward war prevail over the [mere desire for] peace...

Daniel Berrigan

Events have proved the futility of war, but war still rules the world because its uncompromising opponents are too few.

Jesse Wallace Hughan

There is no peace because there are no peacemakers, there are no peacemakers because the making of peace is at least as costly as the making of war.

Daniel Berrigan

We cannot have peace if we are only concerned with peace. War is not an accident. It is the logical outcome of a certain way of life. If we want to attack war, we have to attack that way of life.

A. J. Muste

Very few people chose war. They chose selfishness and the result was war. Each of us, individually and nationally, must choose: total love or total war.

Dave Dellinger
statement on entering prison
1943

Destructive power inherent in matter must be controlled by the idealism of the spirit and the wisdom of the mind. They alone stand between us and a lifeless planet.

John Foster Dulles

Two thousand years ago a Roman noble said: "If you would have peace, prepare for war." For two thousand years men have been preparing for war—and fighting wars. Women know we are preparing for a war right now. This time a nuclear war in which there will be no winner. We realize that we must begin to prepare for peace if we want a future for our children.

Joanne Woodward
actress

The lessons of Hiroshima and Nagasaki go unnoticed as governments continue to develop nuclear arms and nuclear power....Primarily it is women who are involved in the struggle to sustain and maintain life....Women are speaking and struggling toward rebirth for the life of the planet and the children.

Linda Hagan
Chickasaw Nation

It has been a woman's task throughout history to go on believing in life when there was almost no hope. If we are united, we may be able to produce a world in which our children and other people's children can be safe.

Margaret Mead
anthropologist

* An earth fit for growing children is what every woman should work for.

Lillian Smith

I, too, believe that one of our greatest hopes lies in mobilizing the passion we have as women for the survival of our children.

Patricia Ellsberg

If we want to survive we must love our children more than we hate and fear our enemies.

Irene Brown
Michigan activist

We must have the strength to recall to our fellow Americans that to be loyal to this country does Not, Not, Not compel us to be disloyal to the human species, to all life on the planet.   **Daniel Ellsberg**

Those nuclear weapons are aimed at you and me, our friends, our neighbors, our kids. We have to aim back with our votes, with our petitions, with our voices, to tell the people in Congress, in the White House, in the Pentagon, here and in the Soviet Union, and all over the world, that people want to live.

Bella Abzug
former Congressperson,
New York

We have the obligation to create a world order in which we neither have
to kill or be killed.

A Human Manifesto by Planetary Citizens

World peace starts right here. I will not raise my child to kill your child.

Barbara Choo

If we are to reach real peace in this world and if we are to carry on a
real war against war, we shall have to begin with the children.

Mahatma Gandhi

If we really acquire this will to peace, we will gradually impart it to our
children, but we will have to give them something to take the place of
the adventure and excitement of war. We will have to go even further
and devise something to take the place of the sacrifice which is so great
an element in patriotism and which no matter how selfish youth may be,
is the element in their nature which drives them to deeds of heroism and
to heights of unselfish devotion which they would be incapable of except
in times when they feel the call to be somewhat greater than they really
are....This challenge to organize a new social order not in one place,
but all over the world, has possibilities of adventure and excitement, a
society which of itself should take the place of the old glamour
surrounding war. Only women and the youth of any country can initiate
this change.

Eleanor Roosevelt

If peace...only had the music and pageantry of war, there'd be no more
wars.

Sophie Kerr

I have decided for what remains of my life to be an activist....And I ask
you to join all of us out here who want to see—for you and your
children—a survival, a solution—to find the dignity of peace.

Stanley Kramer
film maker

The signers of this declaration pledge to commit ourselves to work
unceasingly to establish a just peace, to reverse the "arms race" both
nuclear and conventional, and to completely dismantle all nuclear
weapons, that the children of the world may be free of the threat of
nuclear war and may share in a beneficent and bountiful future.

Hiroshima/Nagasaki Committee
Washington, D.C.
1985

Let's be in peace with each other and not in pieces with each other.

Nicholas Lorberter
5th Grader

* Somehow we must transform the dynamics of the world power struggle from the negative nuclear arms race, which no one can win, to a positive contest to harness man's creative genius for the purpose of making peace and prosperity a reality for all nations of the world.

Martin Luther King, Jr.

We need not only a moral equivalent to war, as William James called for, but also a politically effective substitute....Those of us who oppose the violence of the status quo and reject the violence of armed revolt and class hatred bear a heavy responsibility to struggle existentially to provide nonviolent alternatives.

Dave Dellinger
Revolutionary Nonviolence

We have it in our power to begin the world again.

Thomas Paine

Future people will wonder why we endured so many evils which we had the power to change.

Ashleigh Brilliant

The ultimate power is always in people—in their will to resist.

Ralph Templin
Democracy and Nonviolence

This revolution is not being made through military power. It is people power!

Fidel Ramos
Philippine Deputy Armed Forces Chief
February 1986

* The joke told and retold all over was about a meeting of Marcos strategists in Manila. One strategist told Marcos: "Mr. President, we will win. We can't lose at all. The Batasan members are ours, the governors are ours, the mayors are ours, the village heads are ours, the military are ours, the judges are ours, the poll chairmen are ours, the Comelec [Commission on Elections] are ours. How can we lose?" To which one meek soul spoke faintly just above a whisper, "But Mr. President, the people are not ours."

Eliezer D. Mapanao
President, Southern Christian College
Philippines

True the elephant is stronger. But the ants...well, there are more of them.

Adolfo Pérez Esquivel
1980 Nobel Peace Prize
Christ in a Poncho

Histories are *written* by intellectuals, who generally give undue credit to other intellectuals for making history. But history is *made* by people who commit themselves, their lives, and their energies to the struggle.

Dave Dellinger
Revolutionary Nonviolence

We must remember that one determined person can make a significant difference, and that a small group of determined people can change the course of history.

Sonia Johnson

We are malign enough, twisted enough, to bring creation to a smoking ruin;
—we have the instruments.
—we have the myths.
—we even have the blueprints.
They are stashed away in some war room, in some hollowed out mountain. Who will confront this crime?...I think it is only the resisting people. Those who confront weapons, weapons-makers and their immaculate guardian—the law. If a God exists, these are God's people.

Daniel Berrigan
Book of Uncommon Prayer

I know of no safe repository of the ultimate power of society but people. And if we think them not enlightened enough, the remedy is not to take the power from them, but to inform them by education.

Thomas Jefferson
1820

Establishing lasting peace is the work of education; all politics can do is keep us out of war.

Maria Montessori

The facts about nuclear energy must be taken to the village square and from there a decision made about its future.

Albert Einstein

...women all over the country can get to know the facts...so they can stand up and ask the hard questions and say, "We want to be involved in the details of our own protection, rather than trusting it to the same old craziness."

Pat Schroeder
Congressperson, Colorado

By exerting electoral pressure, an aroused citizenry can still move its government to the side of morality and common sense. In fact, the momentum for movement in this direction can only originate in the heart and mind of the individual citizen.

Dr. Helen Caldicott
founder and past president
Physicians for Social Responsibility

No social advance rolls in on the wheels of inevitability. It comes through the tireless efforts and persistent work of dedicated individuals.

Martin Luther King, Jr.

Those who profess to favor freedom and yet depreciate agitation, are people who want crops without ploughing the ground; they want rain without thunder and lightning; they want the ocean without the roar of its many waters. The struggle may be a moral one, or it may be a physical one, or it may be both. But it must be a struggle. Power concedes nothing without a demand; it never has and it never will.

Frederick Douglass
1857

The power of an aroused public is unbeatable. Vietnam and Watergate proved that. It must be demonstrated again. It is not yet too late, for while there is life there is hope. There is no cause for pessimism, for already I have seen great obstacles surmounted. Nor need we be afraid, for I have seen democracy work.

Dr. Helen Caldicott
founder and past president
Physicians for Social Responsibility

While the people retain their virtue and vigilance, no administration, by any extreme of wickedness or folly, can very seriously injure the government in the short space of four years.

Abraham Lincoln

It is a superstition and ungodly thing to believe that an act of a majority binds a minority. Many examples can be given in which acts of majorities will be found to have been wrong and those of minorities to have been right. All reforms owe their origin to the initiation of minorities in opposition to majorities.

Mahatma Gandhi

War is much too serious a matter to be entrusted to the military.

Georges Clemenceau

We need to make sure the decision-makers know that for us there are limits to this absurd stockpiling of nuclear weapons, and for us as believers there is an alternative to mutual nuclear suicide.

John Cardinal Krol
The Churches and Nuclear War, September 1979

We do not have to wait for our political leaders. Mass consciousness regulates behavior far more than the formal laws and controls by which societies attempt to regulate it from the top. This consciousness changes, when it does, by a lot of people changing their minds, sometimes only a little. Such a change in mass consciousness has been the driving force for all the great social transformations in history. Thus, as the word spreads that peace is possible, world consciousness can shift.

Willis W. Harman

There is another major shift in consciousness taking place in the 1980s...the synthesis of personal and planetary concerns—a wedding of psychological, spiritual and political dimensions into a unified approach to change.

Kevin McVeigh
Interhelp

There is a shift at a level below politics which could be more significant than any negotiations taking place in Geneva.

E. P. Thompson

I like to believe that people in the long run are going to do more to promote peace than are governments. Indeed, I think that people want peace so much that one of these days governments had better get out of their way and let them have it.

Dwight D. Eisenhower

* Controlled, universal disarmament is the imperative of our time. The demand for it by the hundreds of millions whose chief concern is the long future of themselves and their children will, I hope, become so universal and so insistent that no man, no government anywhere, can withstand it.

Dwight D. Eisenhower

If we do not change our direction, we are likely to end up where we are headed.

Ancient Chinese proverb

My generation has failed to stop the arms race. But it's really the men who have failed. Now it's up to the women, and I believe they can do it.

Rear Admiral Gene R. La Rocque
U.S. Navy (retired)

Women, if the soul of the nation is to be saved, I believe that you must become its soul.

Coretta Scott King

The will to peace will have to start with women and they will have to want peace sufficiently to be crusaders. It's up to the women.

Eleanor Roosevelt

An aroused woman is unstoppable. We've got the babies.

Dr. Helen Caldicott
founder and past president
Physicians for Social Responsibility

If we are ever going to eliminate the threat of nuclear war, it is going to take the untapped power of American women to help bring it about.

Grace Kennan Warnecke
Business Executives for National Security

What is the arms race and the cold war but the combination of male competitiveness and aggression into the inhuman sphere of computer-run institutions? If women are to cease producing cannon-fodder for the final holocaust, they must rescue men from the perversities of their own polarization.

Germaine Greer
The Female Eunuch

Without new ideas, new leadership and new action by women, men will go on preparing for the next war because they have always prepared for war.

But women know that the next war will be the end of us, our children and our fragile, beautiful planet....

Our only hope is to prevent that war and the decision on how to do that is too important to be left to the men alone.

Joanne Woodward
actress

How will nuclear disarmament conferences be different when the dress code no longer requires suits and ties? Above all, women have the capacity to look afresh at the many problems we face today. Because we have been so totally excluded from decision making in the realm of foreign and national security affairs, we do not have to be defensive about present dead-end policies.

The bright, eager young men—the best and the brightest in David Halberstam's phrase, once so confident as they thought up such things as our triad of strategic forces, by which we divide our nuclear weapons launchers among airplanes, submarines and groundbased systems—these same young men are less cocky, less sure about their creations....A newcomer, who doesn't need to be defensive about past policies because he or she had no part in formulating them, can point out that the triad is not the Holy Trinity.

Dr. Anne H. Cahn

This is a war about which women were never consulted. And because we were never consulted we have no need to defend the decisions or ideas that have produced over 50,000 nuclear warheads. We say "no" to this obscenity. And we say "yes" to the fresh ideas and alternatives that people all over the world are coming up with. New ideas that will pull us away from the abyss we are all poised on.

Joanne Woodward
actress

No longer is woman's moral reasoning viewed as simply a different style; it has become a political necessity for the preservation of the world.

Dr. Dorothy Austin

It is women who can bring empathy, tolerance, insight, patience and persistence to government—the qualities we naturally have or have had to develop...women of a nation mold its morals, its religion, and its politics by the lives they live. At present, our country needs women's idealism and determination, perhaps more in politics than anywhere else.

Shirley Chisholm
former Congressperson, New York

As women, we must suggest the solutions which men haven't faced or dared to implement. We must arrive at convincing strategies to start women and men thinking in terms of peace and thus strategies to achieve lasting peace.

Lucinda Mundor^c

We'll turn this thing around yet!

Jane Alexander
actress

For centuries, men have left home to go to war, now women are leaving home for peace.

Greenham Women

...In the name of womanhood and of humanity, I earnestly ask that a general congress of women without limit of nationality may be appointed and held at some place deemed most convenient and at the earliest period consistent with its objects, to promote the alliance of the different nationalities, the amicable settlement of international questions, the great and general interests of peace.

Julia Ward Howe
Boston
1870

Arise, then, women of this day!
Arise all women who have hearts, whether your baptism be that of water or of tears!
Say firmly: "We will not have great questions decided by irrelevant agencies, our husbands shall not come to us, reeking with carnage, for caresses and applause,
Our sons shall not be taken from us to unlearn all that we have been able to teach them of charity, mercy and patience,
We women of one country will be too tender of those of another country to allow our sons to be trained to injure theirs."
From the bosom of the devastated earth a voice goes up with our own. It says "Disarm, Disarm!"
The sword of murder is not the balance of justice! Blood does not wipe out dishonor nor violence indicate possession. As men have often forsaken the plow and the anvil at the summons of war, let women now leave all that may be left of home for a great and earnest day of counsel.

Julia Ward Howe

Don't mourn—Organize!

Joe Hill

Don't agonize. Organize.

Florynce Kennedy

The future depends on what we do in the present.

Mahatma Gandhi

Think through the problem to take back control of your future from those who are only concerned with their present.   **David Durenberger**
Senator, Minnesota
speech to high school students

We cannot wait for the world to turn, for times to change that we might change with them, for the revolution to come and carry us around in its new course. We ourselves are the future. We are the revolution.

Beatrice Bruteau
philosopher

Peace is our work....To everyone, Christians, believers, and men and women of good will, I say: do not be afraid to take a chance on peace, to teach peace....Peace will be the last word of history.

Pope John Paul II

Peace is positive, and it has to be waged with all our thought, energy, and courage and with the conviction that war is not inevitable.

Dean Acheson
former Secretary of State

The major task that good persons should set themselves to is to teach others to say no.

Pierre J. Proudhon
1858

We have seen how the vicious circle of the war system feeds on itself: distrust breeds distrust; hostility generates (and seems to justify) hostility. We forget that the benign circle of building real security is far more potent. The explosive chain reaction of peacemaking is something we rarely consider, yet I believe it will happen. Only when we see it happening will we look back and say, "If only we had known then that it was possible."

Wendy Mogey

It is the depth of the crisis that empowers hope. The power of turning, that radically changes the situation, never reveals itself outside of crisis.

Martin Buber

Ronald Reagan says we have a "window of vulnerability" and need more nuclear weapons. I see the Nuclear Freeze campaign as a "window of opportunity."

James Oberstar
Congressperson, Minnesota

* If men can develop weapons that are so terrifying as to make the thought of global war include almost a sentence for suicide, you would think that man's intelligence and his comprehension...would include also his ability to find a peaceful solution.

Dwight D. Eisenhower

* What has been spoiled through men's fault can be made good again through men's work.

I Ching

War is an invention of the human mind. The human mind can invent peace with justice.

Norman Cousins

* Since war begins in the minds of men, it is in the minds of men that peace must be constructed.

UNESCO Constitution

It was a thought that built this whole portentous war establishment, and a thought shall melt it away.

Ralph Waldo Emerson

Take an ecologically fragile planet with scarce resources and a growing population and we have a recipe for human conflict. Add conventional weapons—a recipe for war. Add nuclear weapons—a recipe for holocaust. This is our challenge as a species. But we are not without resources. Add human intelligence, knowledge, ingenuity, problem-solving skills. Add a deep value commitment to peace, to the common good. Add the spiritual tradition of humanity. We are equal to the task. But we must prepare, educate and train ourselves to be peacemakers.

Northland College
Peace Studies Department

...We have extraordinary mental equipment for the task [of evolving past nuclear weapons]—equipment we are only beginning to mobilize on behalf of the...individual and collective change required for survival.

Robert Jay Lifton and Richard Falk
Indefensible Weapons

The possibilities for tomorrow are usually beyond our expectations.

Anonymous

Can we eliminate the institution of war? The institutions of war and slavery entered history at about the same point as agricultural societies were emerging. They need to leave history at about the same point.

Yvonne V. Delk
Office for Church in Society
United Church of Christ

Many people justify war because the Bible says there will be wars and rumors of war. The Bible also talks about slavery. But we have abolished slavery. The new abolitionists will abolish war and poverty.

Anonymous

It is human will, operating under social forces, that has abolished slavery, infanticide, duelling, and a score of other social enormities. Why should it not do the same for war?

John Haynes Holmes

Though previous generations were also inspired by the fervent will to improve the world, they failed because they did not call a final halt to the forces of destruction. To do this is precisely the task of the present generation...

Queen Juliana
of the Netherlands

The basic terms of the nuclear arms race were set down 40 years ago, and since then the debate has barely changed. Generations of political leaders have failed to come to terms with the fundamental issues of nuclear terror. Today things are changing. With the example and encouragement of groups such as Physicians for Social Responsibility, citizens are becoming willing to assert their own expertise and power over nuclear questions. This is essential for the future of all of us, and of all of tomorrow's children.

Anthony S. Earl
Governor, Wisconsin

The Roman Catholic Bishops' pastoral letter on war and peace is a prophetic statement which challenges current nuclear policies and directions and democratizes the nuclear debate. It may well mark a turning point toward Einstein's new way of thinking, the paradigm shift which turns us from the prospect of nuclear holocaust to a safer world.

Major General Kermit D. Johnson
retired Army Chief of Chaplains

We are not haunted so much by events as by our beliefs about them, the crippling self-image we take with us. We can transform the present and future by reawakening the powerful past, with its recurrent message of defeat. We can face the crossroads again. We can rechoose. In a similar spirit, we can respond differently to the tragedies of modern history. Our past is not our potential. In any hour, with all the stubborn teachers and healers of history who called us to our best selves, we can liberate the future. One by one, we can re-choose—to awaken. To leave the prison of our conditioning, to love, to turn homeward. To conspire with and for each other. Awakening brings its own assignments, unique to each of us, chosen by each of us. Whatever you may think about yourself and however long you may have thought it, you are not just you. You are a seed, a silent promise. You are the conspiracy.

Marilyn Ferguson
The Aquarian Conspiracy

Before water turns to ice, it looks just the same as before. Then a few crystals form, and suddenly the whole system undergoes cataclysmic change.

Joanna Rogers Macy

Where there is a will for peace, there is a way for us working together to have it.

Jeanne Larson

If I could have 3 wishes, world peace would be all three.

Marlia Moore
8th Grader

* In the face of the man-made calamity that every war is, one must affirm and reaffirm, again and again, that the waging of war is *not* inevitable or unchangeable. Humanity is not destined to self destruction. Clashes of ideologies, aspirations and needs can and must be settled and resolved by means other than war and violence.

Pope John Paul II

I would guess there is at least an 85 percent certainty that humanity will wipe itself out in the reasonably near future—but I put my faith in the remaining 15 percent.

Leo Szilard
early atomic scientist

I have to cast my lot with those who age after age, with no extraordinary power, reconstitute the world.

Adrienne Rich

In the final analysis, the best guarantee that a thing should happen is that it appears to us as vitally necessary.

Pierre Teilhard de Chardin

It is necessary; therefore, it is possible.

G. A. Borghese

It is absolutely realistic in that we have to do it. We have to learn to resolve conflict without war or die, along with the rest of life on the planet. It is the people who still believe war is still an alternative who are dealing in fantasy.

Regina Roney
Beyond War Project

Nonviolent action, seeking just structures and also a conversion of attitude involving the entire human society...is a practical way of choosing life over death.

International Fellowship of Reconciliation

* The brontosaurus became extinct, but it wasn't its fault, so to speak. If we become extinct, it will be our fault....in order to survive, man has to evolve.

And to evolve, we need a new kind of thinking and a new kind of behavior, a new ethic and a new morality. It will be that of the evolution of everyone rather than the survival of the fittest.

In terms of evolutionary behavior, that means choosing at each moment to adopt the attitudes and values—cooperation, caring, loving, forgiving—that are absolutely essential if we are not to destroy ourselves.

It's not easy, but it's worth every difficulty.

There is nothing mushy, vague or soft-headed about loving and forgiving. In fact, the end result would be to release the power in the nucleus of each individual—a power much greater in its positive effects than atomic power is in its negative.

Jonas Salk
Parade
November 1984

We will love one another or we will die.

Jehan Sadat

We must erase the lines that keep us from peace.

Erin Troy
4th Grader

If we would see peace flowering in the world tomorrow we must plant the seeds of love today.

Anonymous

We have continuously to repeat, although it is a voice that cries in the desert, "No to violence, yes to peace."

Bishop Oscar Romero
El Salvador

E. Challenge to the Nation

Dear Mr. President:

Please don't have a war even if you get mad at the Russians. My mother always tells me that if I get mad at somebody I should count to ten first.

Bennett K.
Cincinnati, Age 9
Please Save My World

A wiser rule would be to make up your mind soberly what you want, peace or war, and then to get ready for what you want; for what we prepare for is what we shall get.

William Graham Sumner
War

If the State wishes that its citizens respect human life, then the State should stop killing.

Clarence Darrow

There mustn't be any more war. It disturbs too many people.

French peasant woman

* Will allegiance to the fatal ideal of national sovereignty be transferred to the ideal of world government in time to save mankind from self-destruction?

Arnold Toynbee

I think arms control and the United Nations are good ideas, but I don't think they can work unless the governments want them to work. And I don't think governments want them to work.

Lena Flores
Age 17
Our Future at Stake

Business people who succeed know that when the survival of their enterprise is threatened, they must change course. As influential shareholders in our national enterprise, business leaders must mandate our management—our employees in government—to stop and reverse the nuclear arms race. We must tell them: Find a way. Come up with a plan. It can be done. It must be done. Do it.

Harold Willens
business executive

...the only way to handle the enormous problems of the arms race is to get on with the job of disarmament itself.

Arthur Lall

I hear some people say that it would take a miracle to put peace in the world, but it wouldn't. If the two presidents would talk together, it would work out all right.

6th Grader

Bombs can't tell anybody how they're feeling, they'll have to talk themselves, not war it.

6th Grader

...I wish Reagan and Andropov could just sit down and talk without TV cameras and without interpreters and just talk like two human beings.

Wenonah Elms
Age 13
Our Future at Stake

When I went to preschool the teachers told me to always talk a problem out with a friend instead of fighting. I've often thought of that when people speak of war. I don't see why people have to fight like they do.

Heather Prior
7th Grader

I mean, if we could be friends by just getting to know each other better, then what are our countries really arguing about? Nothing could be more important than not having a war if a war would kill everything.

Samantha Smith
Age 10
letter to Andropov on returning
from the Soviet Union at his invitation

If nations could overcome the mutual fear and distrust whose somber shadow is now thrown over the world, and could meet with confidence and good will to settle their possible differences, they would easily be able to establish a lasting peace.

Fridtjof Nansen

...Down the long lane of history yet to be written America knows that this world of ours, ever growing smaller, must avoid becoming a community of dreadful fear and hate, and be, instead, a proud confederation of mutual trust and respect....Disarmament, with mutual honor and confidence, is a continuing imperative. Together we must learn how to compose differences, not with arms, but with intellect and decent purpose.

Dwight D. Eisenhower

More than an end to war, we want an end to the beginnings of all wars—yes, an end to this brutal, inhuman and thoroughly impractical method of settling the differences between governments.

Franklin Delano Roosevelt

If they want peace, nations should avoid the pin-pricks that precede cannon-shots.

Napoleon Bonaparte

Why do we invest all our skills and resources in a contest for armed superiority which can never be attained for long enough to make it worth having, rather than in an effort to find a *modus vivendi* with our antagonist—that is to say, a way of living, not dying?

Barbara Tuchman
The March of Folly—From Troy to Vietnam

The time has come when we must ask our leaders to find new ways to settle conflicts. If we put as much time, energy and money into peace as we do into weapons of destruction, there is no question but that we would find new solutions.

Betty Bumpers
founder of Peace Links

They are talking about basing modes instead of basics. Why does the arms race go on? Why, if we can negotiate a wheat deal, can't we negotiate a reduction in nuclear weapons? If we don't, we could end up in a world where there will be nobody to grow the wheat and nobody to eat the bread.

Mary McGrory
October 1981

There is no practical problem existing between nations whose importance is in any proportion to the tremendous losses which must be expected in an atomic war.

Albert Schweitzer
Teaching of Reverence for Life, 1965

If peace is the overriding concern of the human race, we ought to be willing to bend our best energies and intellect to a consideration of how the ethical insights of each nation are translated into a charter of peace for all nations.

Earl Warren
former Chief Justice
U.S. Supreme Court

Is it too much to hope that what is made possible for just a couple of days by the occurrence of common holidays, may soon prove feasible for a longer period by the new commitments that peace requires, so that an atmosphere may be created which is necessary for meaningful talks to be held in the quest for a peaceful solution?

U Thant
former Secretary-General, UN

Let us never negotiate out of fear, but let us never fear to negotiate.

John F. Kennedy

I have said time and again there is no place on this earth to which I would not travel; there is no chore I would not undertake if I had any faintest hope that, by so doing, I would promote the general cause of world peace.

Dwight D. Eisenhower

* Never have the nations of the world had so much to lose or so much to gain. Together we shall save our planet or together we shall perish in its flames. Save it we can and save it we must, and then shall we earn the eternal thanks of mankind and, as peacemakers, the eternal blessing of God.

John F. Kennedy

Let us take the risks of peace upon our lives, not impose the risks of war upon the world.

Quaker proverb

We call upon governments to accept risks of peace rather than to impose upon us and our children the certainties that grow out of massive preparations for war.

Fellowship of Reconciliation

To break this mad cycle we call for bold and creative initiatives such as a unilateral decision by our government to terminate all nuclear tests and the production of all nuclear weapons and their delivery systems. In turn, we appeal to the Soviet Union to reciprocate in order to halt the rush toward a nuclear holocaust.

Church of the Brethren
Annual Conference resolution, 1980

The U.S. having led in the development of nuclear power should also lead in its effective utilization and control...

**Episcopal Church
General Convention resolution
1976**

* The country that adopts a policy of total disarmament, without waiting for its neighbors, will be able to lead the world away from hatred, fear, and mistrust towards the true community, the harmony of man.

Mahatma Gandhi

The world waits for a great nation that has the common sense, the imagination, and the faith to devote to the science and practice of nonviolence so much as a tenth of the money, brains, skill and devotion which it now devotes to the madness of war preparation. What is that nation waiting for before it undertakes its mission?

A. J. Muste

The greatest honor history can bestow is the title of peacemaker. This honor now beckons America....This is our summons to greatness.

Richard M. Nixon

God and the politicians willing, the United States can declare peace upon the world, and win it.

Ely Culbertson

ADDITIONS:

ADDITIONS:

26
Peace Conversion

The Defense Department cannot and should not assume responsibility for creating or maintaining levels of economic activity.

Policy Declarations
U.S. Chamber of Commerce
1975

We know too that vast armaments are arising on every side and that the work of creating them employs men and women by the millions. It is natural, however, for us to conclude that such employment is false employment, that it builds no permanent structures and creates no consumers' goods for the maintenance of a lasting prosperity. We know that nations guilty of these follies inevitably face the day when either their weapons of destruction must be used against their neighbors or when an unsound economy like a house of cards will fall apart.

Franklin D. Roosevelt
December 1936

The idea of planned economic conversion means a redirection of the scientific and technical talent now concentrated in military production. There are many who attribute the faltering U.S. economy to the fact that nearly half of all our scientists and engineers are employed in the defense sector. If their numbers were redeployed to research and development in the civilian sector, the United States could regain its once dynamic role in the world economy.

Anonymous

Next spring, almost one-third of the bright young engineers graduating from the Massachusetts Institute of Technology will take jobs designing weapons.

Rick Atkinson and Fred Hiatt

I wonder what the engineers, technicians, and workers who make weapons all day long for killing their neighbor can possibly be thinking of. They're not working for a living; they're working for dying.

Adolfo Pérez Esquivel
1980 Nobel Peace Prize
Christ in a Poncho

We can no longer afford—socially or financially—to support irresponsible companies that endanger the very future we are investing for.

Susan Meeker-Lowry
co-editor, *Good Money: A Newsletter of Social Investing*

More and more people are beginning to "put their money where their heart is," which is the basic premise behind what is called social or ethical investing.

Susan Meeker-Lowry
co-editor, *Good Money: A Newsletter of Social Investing*

If the goal is to provide jobs and employment opportunities, then almost any category of non-military employment will produce more work for one billion dollars than does defense production.

U.S. Department of Labor

Many people assume that military spending is necessary to create jobs. In fact, however, defense production is one of the least effective means of providing employment. As military production has become more capital intensive and automated, the volume of employment has dropped. Military spending also accelerates inflation and hinders the development of civilian technology.

Anonymous

We know that the roller coaster cycle of defense production does not provide us with economic and job security....Planned economic conversion is the humane way, the sensible way, the only way to get workers, communities, and even entire states off the dependency hook.

William Winpisinger
President, International Association
of Machinists and Aerospace Workers

* I think it is a terrible thing for a human being to feel that his security and the well-being of his family hinge upon a continuation of the insanity of the arms race. We have to give these people greater economic security in terms of the rewarding purposes of peace.

Walter Reuther
labor leader
1969

We believe we can convert our industries to meet human needs....We do not have to choose between protecting our jobs and protecting our lives!

Women's Peace Presence

...we call upon the President...and Congress...to seek seriously the development of peaceful ways to resolve conflicts between nations and to plan expeditiously for conversion to a healthy economy based on production for nonmilitary purposes.

The Christian Church
(Disciples of Christ)
resolution "Concerning Ending the Arms Race"
1979

We are all too familiar with community outcries when a military base is threatened with closure. Yet forty-eight bases which have been closed now house seven four-year colleges, twenty-six technical institutes, six vocational schools, and a variety of other educational centers with a total student enrollment of 62,000.

Anonymous

The nuclear industry has developed to become an industry of narrow specialists, each promoting and refining a fragment of the technology, with little comprehension of the total impact on our world system....We [resigned] because we could no longer justify devoting our life energies to the continued development and expansion of nuclear fission power—a system we believe to be so dangerous that it now threatens the very existence of life on this planet.

Dale Bridenbaugh, Richard Hubbard and Gregory Minor
Nuclear Engineers, General Electric Company

My reason for leaving G.E. is a deep conviction that nuclear reactors and nuclear weapons now present a serious danger for the future of all life on this planet. I am convinced that the reactors, the nuclear fuel cycle, and waste storage systems are not safe.

Gregory Minor
former Manager, Advanced Control, G.E.

I do not want you or anyone to be put out of work. That would not be peace. Peace is where people can work in similar jobs but no one will have to do work connected to nuclear weapons or military communications.

Jeanne Larson
to engineer at ELF facility

We want our country's use of money and minds *redirected* from inventing ways to destroy one another to learning how to *live* together.

Women's Peace Presence

We make a living by what we get, but we make a life by what we give.

Winston Churchill

Our life is more than our work; our work is more than our jobs.

Charlie King
from the song "More Than Our Work"

The highest reward for toil is not what you get for it but what you become by it.

John Ruskin

27
Encouragement for
Peace Workers

Every noble work is at first impossible.

Thomas Carlyle

All truth passes through three stages.
First, it is ridiculed.
Second, it is violently opposed.
Third, it is accepted as being self-evident.

Schopenhauer

Beware of:
   Justification of procrastination
   Paralysis of analysis.

Martin Luther King, Jr.

It is better to have inadequate answers to relevant questions rather than sophisticated answers to obsolete questions.

Action Linkage

We sometimes fall into the delusion that power is elsewhere, that it belongs to a different group, that we are unable to find access to it. Nothing could be further from the truth. The universe oozes with power, waiting for anyone who wishes to embrace it. But because the powers of cosmic dynamics are invisible, we need to remind ourselves of their universal presence. Who reminds us? The rivers, plains, galaxies, hurricanes, lightning branches and all our living companions.

Brian Swimme
The Universe Is a Green Dragon

* He who molds public sentiment goes deeper than he who enacts statutes or pronounces decisions. He makes statutes or decisions possible or impossible to make.

Abraham Lincoln

Caring about the world doesn't begin with fear or morbidity but with fascination.

Garrison Keillor

Nothing in life is to be feared, it is only to be understood.

Marie Curie

Survivalists arm and retreat—they will only die. We are the survivalists—those of us who disarm and reach out our arms to others.

Anonymous

* Of every invention, of every organization, of every fresh political or economic proposal, we must dare to demand: Has it been conceived in love and does it further the long-term purposes of man? Much that we do would not survive such a question. But much that is still open to

man's creative acts of self-transformation would at last become possible. Not power but power directed by love into the forms of beauty and truth is what we need for our survival, to say nothing of our further development. Only when love takes the lead will the earth, and life on earth, be safe again. And not until then.

Lewis Mumford
The Opening Future

They call us radicals but there is nothing more radical than nuclear war. In fact, we are the conservatives bent on saving the planet.

Anonymous

The job of the peacemaker is to stop war, to purify the world, to get it saved from poverty and riches, to heal the sick, to comfort the sad, to wake up those who have not yet found God, to create beauty and joy wherever you go, to find God in everything and everybody.

Muriel Lester

To find the way to make peace with ourselves and to offer it to others, both spiritually and politically, is the most important kind of learning. To accept our abilities and limitations, and the differences of others; this is the contentment that gives life its highest value. It frees us to grow without restraint and to settle without pressure.

Wendy C. Schwartz

* ..there is a pervasive form of contemporary violence to which the idealist fighting for peace by nonviolent methods most easily succumbs: activism and overwork. The rush and pressure of modern life are a form, perhaps the most common form, of its innate violence. To allow oneself to be carried away by a multitude of conflicting concerns, to surrender to too many demands, to commit oneself to too many projects, to want to help everyone in everything is to succumb to violence. More than that, it is cooperation in violence. The frenzy of the activist neutralizes his work for peace. It destroys his own inner capacity for peace. It destroys the fruitfulness of his own work, because it kills the root of inner wisdom which makes work fruitful.

Thomas Merton

* He who attempts to act and do things for others or for the world without deepening his own self-understanding, freedom, integrity and capacity to love, will not have anything to give others. He will communicate to them nothing but the contagion of his own obsessions, his aggressiveness, his ego-centered ambitions, his delusions about ends and means, his doctrinaire prejudices and ideas.

Thomas Merton

We must have a flaming moral purpose so that greed, oppression and exploitation shrivel before the fire within you.

graffito in South Minneapolis
Indian neighborhood

Bull Connor would next say, "Turn the fire hoses on." And as I said before, Bull Connor didn't know history. He knew a kind of physics that somehow didn't relate to the transphysics that we were about. And that was the fact that there was a certain kind of fire no water could put out.

Martin Luther King, Jr.

* Liberty lies in the hearts of men; when it dies there, no law, no jury, no judge can save it.

Judge Learned Hand

* Liberty lies in the hearts of men; when it exists there, no law, no jury, no judge can destroy it.

David Samas
Fort Hood Three
We Won't Go

To avoid burnout (a state of mental distress or apathy, not to be confused with simply getting tired):
1) We must not take ourselves too seriously (although the things we care about are serious issues),
2) We must recognize we can only do as well as we can and no more, and
3) Laugh a lot—at yourself, the world and with others.

Madge Micheels-Cyrus

Let me tell you the secret that has led me to my goal. My strength lies solely in my tenacity.

Louis Pasteur

The fight must go on. The cause of civil liberty must not be surrendered at the end of one or even one hundred defeats.

Abraham Lincoln

People say, what is the sense of our small effort. They cannot see that we must lay one brick at a time, take one step at a time.

Dorothy Day

* When nothing seems to help, I go and look at a stonecutter hammering away at his rock perhaps a hundred times without as much as a crack showing in it. Yet at the hundred and first blow it will split in two, and I know it was not that blow that did it—but all that had gone before.

Jacob Riis

The power of ideals is incalculable. We see no power in a drop of water. But let it get into a crack in the rock and be turned to ice, and it splits the rock.

Albert Schweitzer

* When you begin a great work you can't expect to finish it all at once; therefore, do you and your brothers press on, and let nothing discourage you...

Teedyuscung
Delaware Tribe
1758

When you get into a tight place and everything goes against you, till it seems as though you could not hold on a minute longer, never give up then, for that is just the place and time that the tide will turn.

Harriet Beecher Stowe

I still believe that we shall overcome. This faith can give us courage to face the uncertainties of the future. It will give our tired feet new strength as we continue our forward stride toward the city of freedom. When our days become dreary with low-hovering clouds and our nights become darker than a thousand midnights, we will know that we are living in the creative turmoil of a genuine civilization struggling to be born...

Martin Luther King, Jr.
on receiving the Nobel Peace Prize

Courage is the price that life exacts for granting peace.

Amelia Earhart

Civic courage, as we call it in time of peace, is the kind of valor to which the monuments of nations should most of all be raised.

William James

A rabbi (who lived and preached a life of virtue while his congregation ignored him and went on with their selfish ways) was asked: "Rabbi, why do you bother? Nobody listens. You're not changing anything." And the rabbi replied: "But you misunderstand. I don't do it to change them. I do it to keep them from changing me."

Anonymous

I'm not trying to change the world. I'm trying to keep the world from changing me.

Ammon Hennacy

In other words we have to push against the walls to find out where they really are. The other reason we have to push is that if we do not push them out, they push us in.

John Holt

* There are moments when things go well and one feels encouraged. There are difficult moments and one feels overwhelmed. But it's senseless to speak of optimism or pessimism. The only important thing is to know that if one works well in a potato field, the potatoes will grow. If one works well among men, they will grow—that's reality. The rest is smoke. It's important to know that words don't move mountains. Work, exacting work, moves mountains.

Danilo Dolci

Perhaps it is an idle task to judge in times when action counts.

Albert Einstein

Actions are clearly effective when those involved in them experience their capabilities and their strength. That exciting feeling of empowerment is something that cannot be taken away. It becomes part of how we think about ourselves, as purposeful, effective people who can express ourselves clearly on an issue of vital importance.

Greenham Women Everywhere

Jesus asks us to speak for peace whether or not it is effective in the worldly sense. The whole question is the question of faithfulness, and not just the question of change....So in the middle of this world we need to say "no" to war even when we don't see immediate results. In the Second World War when the Jews were all being gassed, lots of us didn't do or say anything, because we said we couldn't do anything about it. But those who did speak and act, without success, are still celebrated as people who gave history hope.

Henri Nouwen

* We who lived in concentration camps can remember the men who walked through the huts comforting others, giving away their last piece of bread. They may have been few in number, but they offer sufficient proof that everything can be taken from a man but one thing: the last of the human freedoms—to choose one's attitude in any given set of circumstances— to choose one's own way.

Viktor Frankl

* God has not called me to be successful. He has called me to be faithful.

Mother Teresa

An act of love that fails is just as much a part of the divine life as an act of love that succeeds, for love is measured by its own fullness not by its reception.

Harold Loukes

We must approach the job of creating a peaceful world with the discipline and patience of a fine gardener. We make our plans, we break the ground and prepare it to receive our seeds. We work with the cycles of growth and weather. At times we work hard, sweating in teams; at other times we quietly repair our tools in solitude. Some of our crops are fast-growing and nourish us sooner than other ones will. The flowers give us beauty and joy throughout the season. We do a little every day, and we know that after a long period of tending and growth, a lovely harvest is coming.

Mary Hayes-Grieco

...for every gardener knows that after the digging, after the planting, after the long season of tending and growth, the harvest comes.

Marge Piercy
The Influence Coming into Play: The Seven of Pentacles

In the struggle rewards are few
In fact I know of only two
Loving friends and living dreams
These rewards are not so few it seems

Anonymous

I have no political analysis of resistance to offer that justifies hope. We have to expect the worst, for a while. But I know from the tradition that sustains the struggling and suffering people...that terror will not have the last word.

Dorothee Sölle

Hope is not the lucky gift of circumstance or disposition, but a virtue like faith and love, to be practiced whether or not we find it easy or even natural, because it is necessary to our survival as human beings.

Clara Park
The Siege

Hope is a waking dream.

Anonymous

Hope is that thing with feathers that perches in the soul and sings the tune without the words and never stops at all.

Emily Dickinson

No peace lies in the future which is not hidden in the present instant.
Take peace.
The gloom of the world is but a shadow;
Behind it, yet within reach, is joy.
Take joy.

Fra Giovani
1513

If I can't dance...I don't want to be part of your revolution.

Emma Goldman

A movement is when people do all the things they sing about.

James Bevel

I'd rather vote for something I want and not get it than vote for something I don't want, and get it.

Eugene V. Debs

Say I was a drum major for justice, I was a drum major for peace, I was a drum major for righteousness, say that I left a committed life behind...

Martin Luther King, Jr.

The future does not belong to those who are content with today. Rather it will belong to those who can blend vision, reason and courage in a personal commitment.

Robert F. Kennedy

The fabric of the new society will be made of nothing more or less than the threads woven in today's interactions.

Pam McAllister
Reweaving the Web of Life

They never die, who have the future in them.

Meridel Le Sueur

ADDITIONS:

28
Role of Imaging in Peace Work

A mind that is stretched by a new idea can never go back to its original dimensions.

Oliver Wendell Holmes

You may say I'm a dreamer, but I'm not the only one.

John Lennon

A person without dreams is standing still. A state without dreams is standing still. A nation without dreams is standing still.

Paul Simon
Senator, Illinois

Where there is no vision, the people perish.

Proverbs 29:18a
King James Version

With compass, the mariner is able to navigate regardless of the nature of the craft or the conditions of the weather. With a theory that lets us see—we can perceive what is at work in us, through us, and for us in this planet-time. It helps us to stay steady and sure. Without it, we risk the extremes of being locked in numbness or swept away by panic as we open to the magnitude of the dangers confronting us.

Joanna Rogers Macy
Despair and Personal Power in the Nuclear Age

Twentieth century humans have lost their capacity to visualize a future different from the present, and that only by reconstituting our visioning capacity can we make any meaningful future possible for the human race.

Fred Polak
Image of the Future

I believe that focussing on what the social order might look like if we handled conflict without weapons is a critical part of the task of imaging any future at all.

Elise Boulding

We have actually forgotten that every civilization has had its vision of the world as a peaceable garden, with abundance for all, a garden without weapons....That vision is the oldest and most persistently recurring vision in human experience. And yet today we cannot even visualize what a disarmed world would look like.

Elise Boulding
1981

In our striving for peace in the 1980s, we have looked too much to Washington, Moscow, Geneva, Vienna...and too little to *ourselves*. It is not only a failure of arms control negotiations that keeps peace from being a reality in our time but also a failure of our *own imaginations*.

Waging Peace

I am not proposing a static utopian depiction for the peace movement. I am suggesting that we return to a long forgotten tradition of visualizing the good society and exploring what the visualizations themselves might teach us about strategies for the present.

Elise Boulding

Only when we can in some sense visualize a world without weapons can we find the path to it....What happens as the result of this kind of work is that we perceive connections that we normally do not see. We develop images of strategies we have never thought of.

Elise Boulding

The images just are. Let them come to you. See where they will take you into a world without war. This is adventure, this is journey, this is discovery.

Warren Ziegler

Fantasies are more than substitutes for unpleasant reality; they are also dress rehearsals, plans. All acts performed in the world begin in the imagination.

Barbara Harrison

Imagination is more important than knowledge.

Albert Einstein

* Nothing ever built arose to touch the skies unless some man dreamed that it should, some man believed that it could, and some man willed that it must.

Charles Kettering
past President
General Motors Research Corporation

In planning for a future of peace, there are no experts to lead us. There are no colleges to train us. The inventions will arise from our deep longing, our imagination, our hopes, our common sense. We can start building a peaceful future by first creating images of it in our minds.

Women's Peace Presence

* Anything that a man can dream, a man can do.

John Lily
Center of the Cyclone

What you can imagine, you can create.

Anonymous

For tomorrow is what we make it, and it will be ours.

> **The Mothers of the Plaza de Mayo**
> **Argentina, July 1980**
> *Christ in a Poncho*

...The wild dream is the first step to reality by which we set our highest goals and discern our highest selves.

> **Norman Cousins**

Most advocates of realism in this world are hopelessly unrealistic.

> **Jawaharlal Nehru**

* I refuse to accept the idea that the "isness" of man's present nature makes him morally incapable of reaching up for the "oughtness" that forever confronts him.

> **Martin Luther King, Jr.**

Other people see things and say why—but I dream things that never were and say why not?

> **George Bernard Shaw**

* Some men see things as they are and ask why. I dream things that never were and ask why not.

> **Robert F. Kennedy**

Beware what you set your heart upon for it surely shall be yours.

> **Ralph Waldo Emerson**

What we call non-existent is what we do not desire enough.

> **Nikos Kazantzakis**

What you can do, or dream you can, begin it. Boldness has genius, power, and magic in it.

> **Goethe**

Societies generate images of the possible and then draw their behavior from those images.

> **Elise Boulding**

The paradigm of the *Aquarian Conspiracy* sees humankind embedded in nature. It promotes the autonomous individual in a decentralized society. It sees us as stewards of all our resources, inner and outer. It says that we are not victims, not pawns, not limited by conditions or conditioning. Heirs to evolutionary riches, we are capable of imagination, invention, and experience we have only glimpsed.

> **Marilyn Ferguson**
> *The Aquarian Conspiracy*

...by asking our help you recognize that connection; and...we are reminded of other connections that lie far deeper than the facts on the surface...to discuss with you the capacity of the human spirit to overflow boundaries and make unity out of multiplicity. But that would be to dream—to dream the recurring dream that has haunted the human mind since the beginning of time; the dream of peace, the dream of freedom. But with the sound of guns in your ears you have not asked us to dream. You have not asked us what peace is; you have asked us to prevent war...not by repeating your words and following your methods but by finding new words and creating new methods.

Virginia Woolf
Three Guineas

The future is not a result of choices among alternative paths offered by the present, but a place that is created—created first in the mind and will, created next in activity. The future is not some place we are going to but one we are creating. The paths are not to be found, but made, and the activity of making them changes both the maker and the destination.

John Schaar

We cannot discover new oceans unless we have the courage to lose sight of the shore.

Anonymous

Think about the kind of world you want to live and work in. What do you need to know to build the world? Demand that your teachers teach you that.

Kropotkin

Imagine, imagine, that whatever you see can come true...
Imagine, imagine—just as long as what you see you do!

Susan Savell

You are never given a wish without also being given the power to make it true. You may have to work for it, however.

Richard Bach

In hope against all human hope...Faith, mighty faith, the promise sees and looks to that alone; laughs at impossibilities. And cries, "It shall be done."

Anonymous

It's fun to do the impossible.

Walt Disney

I ask myself, is it just a wild flight of imagination to conceive of a world without war...but someone must try...

Julia Grace Wales

One of the things in which women are vitally interested to-day is the abolition of war as a means of settling disputes between nations, and I feel that this is particularly a question which is up to the women...The will to peace will have to start with women and they will have to want peace sufficiently to be crusaders on the subject. Joan of Arc, who was only a simple peasant girl, had a vision of how she could lead her country through victorious war to freedom. The women of to-day must have a vision of how to lead the world to peace.

Eleanor Roosevelt
1933

It is a peculiar fact of life for those of us alive today...that without a near-future breakthrough into a true realization of our familyhood, there will be no future generations. Let us envision utopia, and thus bring it into existence. There is no reasonable alternative.

Dr. Willis Harman
regent, University of California

What we want to change is immense. It's not just getting rid of nuclear weapons, it's getting rid of the whole structure that created the possibility of nuclear weapons in the first place. If we don't use imagination nothing will change. Without change we will destroy the planet. It's as simple as that.

Lesley Boulton
Greenham Common
1982

ADDITIONS:

29
Visions of Peace

A.   Peace Is/Is Not

B.   Old Testament Images of Peace

C.   Peace Is Possible

D.   Images of Government
     in a Peaceful World

E.   Beyond War

Let the people take heart and hope everywhere, for the cross is bending,
the midnight is passing, and joy cometh with the morning.

Eugene Debs

We grow toward the light, not toward darkness.

Ashley Montagu

The dark night is over and dawn has begun,
Rise, hope of the ages arise like the sun!
All speech flow to music, all hearts beat as one.

John Greenleaf Whittier

No war, or battle's sound
Was heard the world around.
The idle spear and shield were high up hung.

John Milton
On the Morning of Christ's Nativity

A. Peace Is/Is Not

There is no way to peace, peace is the way.

A. J. Muste

Peace is a spirit, and not an intellectual abstraction: it is a life, not a theory.

Eliliu Burritt
1846

Peace is like a plant, growing with the care of a human being.

Lance Schellin
9th Grader

Peace is like a newborn baby, waiting to be noticed by the world.

Melissa Naumann
9th Grader

...peace is neither the absence of war nor the presence of a disarmament
agreement. Peace is a change of heart.

Richard D. Lamm
Governor, Colorado

Peace is people talking together with a heart in between them.

Child
Age 8

Peace is the countries of the world coming together to be one in friendship.

Katie Hisrich
7th Grader

Go down to the foot of the mountain; throw away your gun, your ammunition, your provisions, and your clothing; wash yourself in the stream which flows there, and you will then be prepared to stand before the Master of Life.

Pontiac
Ottawa
1763

The thickness of your skin will be seven spans, for you will be proof against anger, offensive action, and criticism. With endless patience you shall carry out your duty, and your firmness shall be tempered with compassion for your people. Neither anger nor fear shall find lodgement in your mind, and all your words and actions will be tempered with calm deliberation. In all your official acts, self-interest shall be cast aside. You shall look and listen to the welfare of the whole people, and have always in view, not only the present but the coming generations—the unborn of the future Nation.

Dekanawidah
to leaders of the Iroquois Confederation

Peace is a maze, winding and twisting to find a way out of confusion and blackness.

Andy Hagan
9th Grader

Lead me from death to life, from falsehood to truth.
Lead me from despair to hope, from fear to trust.
Lead me from hate to love, from war to peace.
Let peace fill our heart, our world, our universe.

World Peace Prayer

Peace is not an absence of war, it is a virtue, a state of mind, a disposition for benevolence, confidence, justice.

Benedict Spinoza

We realize that the peace we enjoy is the absence of war, rather than the presence of confidence, understanding and generous conduct.

Raymond G. Swing

We are changing because we must. Historically, peace efforts have been aimed at ending or preventing wars. Just as we have defined health in negative terms, as the absence of disease, we have defined peace as non-conflict. But peace is more fundamental than that. Peace is a state of mind, not a state of the nation. Without personal transformation, the people of the world will be forever locked in conflict. If we limit ourselves to the old-paradigm concept of averting war, we are trying to overpower darkness rather than switching on the light. If we reframe the problem—if we think of fostering community health, innovation, self-discovery, purpose—we are already engaged in waging peace. In a rich, creative, meaningful environment there is no room for hostility. War is unthinkable in a society of autonomous people who have discovered the connectedness of all humanity, who are unafraid of alien ideas and alien cultures, who know that all revolutions begin within and that you cannot impose your brand of enlightenment on anyone else.

Marilyn Ferguson
The Aquarian Conspiracy

Consider the history of America closely. Never has America lost a war....But name, if you can, the last peace the United States won. Victory yes, but this country has never made a successful peace because peace requires exchanging ideas, concepts, thoughts, and recognizing the fact that two distinct systems of life can exist together without conflict...

Vine Deloria, Jr.
I Have Spoken
1969

It must be peace without victory.. .Victory would mean peace forced upon the loser, a victor's terms imposed upon the vanquished. It would be accepted in humiliation, under duress, at an intolerable sacrifice, and would leave a sting, a resentment, a bitter memory upon which terms of peace would rest, not permanently, but only as upon quicksand. Only a peace between equals can last.

Woodrow Wilson

We are living in a pre-war and not a post-war world.
Eugene Rostow
former member, US Arms Control and Disarmament Agency
June 1976

This is not peace time but a pre-war period.
Anonymous

Peace cannot be kept by force. It can only be achieved by understanding.
Albert Einstein

Peace is not only better than war, but infinitely more arduous.
George Bernard Shaw

Peace is not fighting because the world may die.
Alisa
Age 8

And is not peace, in the last analysis, basically a matter of human rights—the right to live out our lives without fear of devastation, the right to breathe air as nature provided it, the right of future generations to a healthy existence.

John F. Kennedy
1963

Peace is knowing that someone cares about me.

Kim Harshman
8th Grader

Peace is
Everyone trusting
And
Caring for
Each other.

Rachel Minshall
8th Grader

* True peace is not merely the absence of tension but is the presence of justice and brotherhood.

Martin Luther King, Jr.

* The outpouring of good sense and reason will cause men to reconsider their ways. Then, as peace settles over this earth, it is hoped people everywhere can celebrate life without fear of deadly weapons, to love instead of hate, the right to health, to earn a living, to be happy in a decent home, all things that bring about dignity.

Cleo Darmon

Peace begins when the hungry are fed.

Anonymous

They have not wanted Peace at all; they have wanted to be spared war—as though the absence of war was the same as peace. Peace is not the absence of war. Peace is a positive condition—the rule of law.

Dorothy Thompson

Peace is not the absence of conflict but the presence of creative alternatives for responding to conflict—alternatives to passive or aggressive responses, alternatives to violence.

Jeanne Larson

It is crucial that we begin to understand peace to mean, not only an end to war, but an end to all the ways we do violence to ourselves, each other, the animals, the earth.

Pam McAllister
Reweaving the Web of Life

Peace is everything living together in harmony.

Rachel Liegel
7th Grader

Peace is a chorus singing in harmony.

Jamie Hovey
9th Grader

B. Old Testament Images of Peace

...and they shall beat their swords into plowshares, and their spears into pruning hooks; nation shall not lift up sword against nation, neither shall they learn war any more.

Isaiah 2:4
RSV

The wolf shall dwell with the lamb, and the leopard shall lie down with the kid, and the calf and the lion and the fatling together, and a little child shall lead them. The cow and the bear shall feed; their young shall lie down together; and the lion shall eat straw like the ox.

Isaiah 11:6–7
RSV

And the effect of righteousness will be peace, and the result of righteousness, quietness and trust for ever. My people will abide in a peaceful habitation, in secure dwellings, and in quiet resting places.

Isaiah 32:17–18
RSV

And I will make for you a covenant on that day with the beasts of the field, the birds of the air, and the creeping things of the ground; and I will abolish the bow, the sword, and war from the land; and I will make you lie down in safety.

Hosea 2:18
RSV

C. Peace Is Possible

My song is the song of peace. We have had many war songs in my country but we have thrown them all away....I heard the voices of my ancestors crying to me in a voice of love, "My grandson, my grandson, restrain your anger; think of the living; rescue them from the fire and the knife."

Kiosaton, Iroquois Chief
1645
I Have Spoken

It seemed to me that the spirit of [my son] Hirohisa, his friends of the First Middle School who died with him, and the countless people of Hiroshima who died that day, have all gone up to the heavens and turned to stardust, and are softly looking down at us every night, so that such a catastrophe will never be repeated on earth.

Toshie Fujino

I still believe that people are really good at heart. I simply can't build up my hopes on a foundation consisting of confusion, misery and death. I see the world gradually being turned into a wilderness, I hear the ever approaching thunder, which will destroy us too. I can feel the sufferings of millions and yet, if I look up into the heavens, I think it will all come right, that this cruelty too will end, and that peace and tranquility will return again.

Anne Frank
July 1944

We will break through the layers of our denials, put aside our fainthearted excuses, and rise up to cleanse the earth of nuclear weapons.

Jonathan Schell

We shall hew out of the mountain of despair, a stone of hope.

Martin Luther King, Jr.

If someone with courage and vision can rise to lead in nonviolent action, the winter of despair can in the twinkling of an eye be turned into the summer of hope.

Mahatma Gandhi

If we all can persevere, if we can in every land and office look beyond our own shores and ambitions, then surely the age will dawn in which the strong are just and the weak secure and the peace preserved.

John F. Kennedy

I believe without a shadow of doubt that science and peace will finally triumph over ignorance and war, and that the nations of earth will ultimately agree not to destroy, but to build up.

Louis Pasteur

War is on its last legs; and a universal peace is as sure as the prevalence of civilization over barbarism, of liberal governments over feudal forms. The question for us is only—How soon?

Ralph Waldo Emerson

* When shall all men's good be each man's rule, and universal peace be like a shaft of light across the land?

Alfred Lord Tennyson

What if they gave a war and nobody came...?

Anonymous

It is possible to live in peace.

Mahatma Gandhi

* All of us—great and small, belligerents and neutrals—we must not close our ears to the dire warning of this hour, the threat of such unthinkable horrors. Peace is at hand! As a thought, a desire, a suggestion, as a power working in silence, it is everywhere, in every heart. If each one of us opens his heart to it, if each one of us firmly resolves to serve the cause of peace, to communicate his thoughts and intimations of peace—if every man of good will decides to devote himself exclusively for a little while to clearing away the obstacles, the barriers to peace, then we shall have peace.

Hermann Hesse
Shall There Be Peace?

Peace is in the air everybody can have it nobody can steal it we all can share it in the world. Peace is a special thought or a special love or light or spark that we all share within ourselves. If there was peace there would be no wars or fights just a special love all over the world.

Joel
Age 11

D. Images of Government in a Peaceful World

We, the people of the United States, in order to form a more perfect union, establish justice, insure domestic tranquility, provide for the common defense, promote the general welfare, and secure the blessings of liberty to ourselves and our posterity, do ordain and establish this Constitution for the United States of America.

Preamble to the U.S. Constitution

* We, the peoples of the United Nations, determined to save succeeding generations from the scourge of war, which twice in our lifetime has brought untold sorrow to mankind, and to reaffirm faith in fundamental human rights, in the dignity and worth of the human person, in the equal rights of men and women and of nations large and small...And for these ends to practice tolerance and live together in peace with one another as good neighbors...Have resolved to combine our efforts to accomplish these aims.

United Nations Charter

The future is international.

Anonymous

* The art of democratic government has grown from its seed in the tiny city-states of Greece to become the political mode of half the world. So let us dream of a world in which all states, great and small, work together for the peaceful flowering of the republic of man.

Adlai E. Stevenson

I am convinced that the Great Framer of the World will so develop it that it becomes one nation, so that armies and navies are no longer necessary.

Ulysses S. Grant

* We shall soon enter upon the continuing period of peace, a period when there will be no more war, when disputes between nations will be settled by the application of man's power of reason, by international law.

Linus Pauling

There must be, not a balance of power, but a community of power; not organized rivalries, but an organized common peace.

Woodrow Wilson

There is no salvation for civilization, or even the human race, other than the creation of a world government.

Albert Einstein

Is there a doubt whether a common government can embrace so large a sphere? Let experience solve it....It is well worth a fair and full experiment.

George Washington

* World federalists hold before us the vision of a unified mankind living in peace under a just world order....The heart of their program—a world under law—is realistic and attainable.   **U Thant**
former Secretary-General, United Nations

When Kansas and Colorado have a quarrel over the water in the Arkansas River they don't call out the National Guard in each state and go to war over it. They bring suit in the Supreme Court of the United States and abide by the decision. There isn't a reason in the world why we cannot do that internationally.

Harry S. Truman

It will be just as easy for nations to get along in a republic of the world as it is for you to get along in the republic of the United States.

Harry S. Truman

The question is not one of "surrendering" national sovereignty. The problem is not negative and does not involve giving up something we already have. The problem is positive—creating something we lack...but...imperatively need...—the extension of law and order into another field of human association which heretofore has remained unregulated and in anarchy.

Emery Reves
The Anatomy of Peace

Internationalism does not mean the end of individual nations. Orchestras don't mean the end of violins.

Golda Meir

The tough-minded...respect difference. Their goal is a world made safe for differences, where the United States may be American to the hilt without threatening the peace of the world, and France may be France, and Japan may be Japan on the same conditions.

Ruth Fulton Benedict

We have a vision that our land and our people will once again be strong in ways that make us proud.

Women's Peace Presence

* If a nation were willing to risk destruction for peace and truth, man as a human being rather than a brute would have reasserted himself. Humanity as a spiritual reality would live. Truth, decency, honor, courage would still live on earth in the midst of madness. In time, civilization could be rebuilt on firmer and more beautiful lines than ever. In a profound sense all the suffering and the travail of men might be redeemed.

A. J. Muste

I refuse to accept the cynical notion that nation after nation must spiral down a militaristic stairway into the hell of thermonuclear destruction.

Martin Luther King, Jr.

* We dip into the future, far as human eye can see,
See the vision of the world and all the wonder that shall be,
Hear the war-drum throb no longer, see the battle flags all furled
In the parliament of man, the federation of the world.

Alfred Lord Tennyson

E. Beyond War

In hundreds of ways, we are killing this planet. The bomb is just the easiest way. We have a dream, Katya and I, a dream that we might stop killing things and preparing to kill each other. A dream that we might start...preparing for life, the life of those who will come and live on this planet.

from the play *Peace Child*

The broad ultimate requirements of survival...are in essence...global disarmament, both nuclear and conventional, and the invention of political means by which the world can peacefully settle the issues that throughout history it has settled by war.

Jonathan Schell
The Fate of the Earth

...ideological differences and vested interests must be dealt with in nonmilitary terms.

New Frontiers Center Newsletter
Fall, Winter 1983

We cannot expect to dispose of armaments until we have a plan for the common safety.

Norman Cousins

The world, in freeing itself of one burden, the peril of extinction, must inevitably shoulder another: it must assume full responsibility for settling human differences peacefully.

Jonathan Schell
The Fate of the Earth

We need an Academy of Peace, not to do away with conflict, but to learn and teach how to creatively "manage" conflict.

Theodore M. Hesburgh

* What do I now see as the way out for the underdeveloped world? Not violence. Today established violence keeps millions of people in a subhuman situation. For the third world to turn to violence would be to declare that no alternative exists....I dream about the day when there will dawn for mankind a new civilization with justice and peace recognized as the essential values. For me that dream has validity because I believe in the power of truth and love. I believe in the work of God, who will not allow falsehood and hate to prevail among men for all time. So I shall continue my attempts to carry out concrete action looking toward justice and peace, confident that those values will prevail— perhaps tomorrow, perhaps the day after tomorrow.

Archbishop Dom Helder Camara

Our earth is but a small star in the great universe, yet of it we can make, if we choose, a planet unvexed by war, untroubled by hunger or fear, undivided by senseless distinctions of race, color or theory.

Stephen Vincent Benét

I have a dream...deeply rooted in the American dream...that my four little children will one day live in a nation where they will not be judged by the color of their skin but by the content of their character...that little black boys and black girls will be able to join hands with little white boys and white girls and walk together as sisters and brothers.

Martin Luther King, Jr.
August 1963

* I have the audacity to believe that people everywhere can have three meals a day for their bodies, education and culture for their minds, and dignity, equality and freedom for their spirits. I believe that what self-centered men have torn down men other-centered can build up. I still believe that one day mankind will bow before the altars of God and be crowned triumphant over war and bloodshed, and nonviolent redemptive goodwill proclaim the rule of the land.

Martin Luther King, Jr.
on receiving the Nobel Peace Prize

We envision a world where children face the future without the threat of nuclear war. We imagine nations cooperating to feed people with the money now spent on weapons. We seek reconciliation between ourselves and our Mother, the Earth. We want our national forests used to shelter *life* rather than ELF transmitters that signal submarines with nuclear missiles. We believe that a world at Peace is within our common reach.

Women's Peace Presence

* The great question is: Can global war now be outlawed from the world? If so, it would mark the greatest advance in civilization since the Sermon on the Mount. It would lift at one stroke the darkest shadow which has engulfed mankind from the beginning. It would not only remove fear and bring security—it would not only create new moral and spiritual values—it would produce an economic wave of prosperity that would raise the world's standard of living beyond anything ever dreamed of by man.

General Douglas MacArthur
1961

If I heard all the nuclear weapons were being dismantled, I'd feel so relieved and so happy. I'd do 200 cartwheels in a row.

Katy
Age 9
In the Nuclear Shadow: What Can the Children Tell Us?

It will be a great day when our schools get all the money they need and the air force has to hold a bake sale to buy a bomber.
Women's International League for Peace and Freedom

It'll be a great day when our day care centers have all the money they need and the navy has to hold a bake sale to buy battleships.
Anonymous

If we can change our priorities, achieve balance and understanding in our roles as human beings in a complete world, the coming era can well be that of a richer civilization, not its end.

Sigurd Olson

A federation of all humanity, together with a sufficient measure of social justice to ensure health, education, and a rough equality of opportunity, would mean such a release and increase of human energy as to open a new phase in human history.

H. G. Wells
The Outline of History

Why believe that we in 2010 have come to a "lasting peace"? Perhaps it is the conviction that there comes a time when the time has come, when what we human beings could not previously do we now can do, should do, must do. Paul Tillich called such historical moments a *kairos*, from the Greek meaning when the time is ripe. Such a *kairos* came during the nineteenth century with the abolition of slavery. Since then the world has not looked back. Ten years ago, in the year 2000, the joint resolution on world peace, signed by every member of the General Assembly of the United Nations, noted that "disagreement is inevitable but war is unacceptable." Today, no one is interested in looking back.

J. Edward Barrett
Peace 2010
Christian Science Monitor

I dream of giving birth to a child who will ask: "Mother, what was war?"

Eve Merriam

May there always be sunshine,
May there always be blue skies,
May there always be Mama,
May there always be me.

Russian boy
Age 5

When the voices of children are heard on the green
And laughing is heard on the hill,
My heart is at rest within my breast
And everything is still.

William Blake
Nurse's Song

Peace. The choice of a new generation.

Matt Bell
7th Grader

I can't wait for peace, can you?

Faunia Fox
Age 6

Ring out old shapes of foul disease,
Ring out the narrowing lust of gold;
Ring out the thousand wars of old,
Ring in the thousand years of peace.

Alfred Lord Tennyson

...Some day, men and women will rise, they will reach the mountain peak, they will meet big and strong and free, ready to receive, to partake, and to bask in the golden rays of love. What fancy, what imagination, what poetic genius can foresee even approximately the potentialities of such a force in the life of men and women.

Emma Goldman

* Someday, after we have mastered the winds, the waves, the tides and gravity, we shall harness for God the energies of love. Then for the second time in the history of the world, man will have discovered fire.

Pierre Teilhard de Chardin

ADDITIONS:

Author Index

DEMCO, INC. 38-2931

Beauregard the Cat

SUGARBUSH ELEMENTARY
48400 Sugarbush Road
Chesterfield Twp., Michigan 48047

Beauregard the Cat

BY

ROBERTA PANTAL RHODES

ILLUSTRATED BY

JOHN T. WARD

For Norman—R.P.R.
Special thanks to Rebecca Webb, and to Shelley Harwayne, Principal; Sharon
Taberski, second grade teacher; and the children of The Manhattan New School,
as well as to my husband Norman.

To Jane, Liam, and Dazy—J.T.W.

Text copyright © 1997 by Roberta Pantal Rhodes
Illustrations copyright © 1997 by John T. Ward

All rights reserved.
No part of this publication may be reproduced, except in the case
of quotation for articles or reviews, or stored in any retrieval system,
or transmitted in any form or by any means, electronic, mechanical, photocopying,
recording, or otherwise, without written permission
from the publisher. For information contact: Mondo Publishing,
One Plaza Road, Greenvale, New York 11548.

Printed in Hong Kong by South China Printing Co. (1988) Ltd.
00 01   9 8 7 6 5 4

Designed by Becky Terhune
Production by Our House

Library of Congress Cataloging-in-Publication Data
Rhodes, Roberta Pantal.
Beauregard the cat / by Roberta Pantal Rhodes ; illustrated by John T. Ward.
p.   cm.
Summary: Beauregard the cat loves Rebecca more than anyone else in the whole wide world.
ISBN 1-57255-219-0 (pbk.)
[1. Cats—Fiction.   2. Pets—Fiction.]   I. Ward, John T. (John Thomas), 1957- ill.   II. Title.
PZ7.R34768Be   1996
[Fic]—dc20   96-1254
CIP   AC

Contents

Being Close

In the middle of the night, Beauregard
the cat howled and howled. He longed
for Rebecca.

Beauregard loved to curl up under the covers next to Rebecca. He liked to sleep beside her.

Rebecca loved having Beauregard's soft fur next to her. And she liked to hear him purr. He was like a little motor that sang her to sleep.

But no matter how close Beauregard got
to Rebecca, it was never close enough.

First he put his paw on her shoulder.

Then he tickled her with his tail.

And finally he rested his face next to her
cheek and fell fast asleep.

Beauregard loved Rebecca more than
anyone else in the whole wide world.

Happiness

Early in the morning, Beauregard sat
quietly outside the bathroom door. He
was waiting for Rebecca.

But as soon as Rebecca opened the
door, Beauregard howled and howled
with delight.

Rebecca went into her bedroom and curled up on the bed. She began to brush her shiny black hair.

Beauregard followed. He jumped up on the bed, still howling, and sat next to Rebecca.

Beauregard looked into Rebecca's eyes.
And then, the way cats do, he blinked a long
slow blink.

"What is it?" Rebecca asked. "What do you want?"

Beauregard toppled over next to Rebecca and lay on his side, still howling.

"Okay, okay," Rebecca said. She got up, went to the dresser, and opened a drawer.

Rebecca sat back down on the bed and began brushing Beauregard with his special steel-toothed brush made especially for cats.

With each stroke of the brush, Beauregard purred and purred.

He closed his eyes, still purring, and soon fell fast asleep.

Beauregard loved Rebecca more than anyone else in the whole wide world.

Contentment

Beauregard sat by his dish and waited and
waited for his dinner.

Rebecca opened a can of cat food and
emptied it into Beauregard's dish.

Beauregard looked at the food, took one
sniff, and quickly walked away.

He strutted into the bathroom and howled
and howled. Beauregard was not happy.

Neighbors throughout the apartment building where Rebecca and Beauregard lived opened their windows to see who was making all that noise.

They opened their doors and looked in
the halls. They even knocked on Rebecca's
door to make sure everything was all right.

Rebecca went into the bathroom where Beauregard was still howling.

"Stop making so much noise," she scolded, shaking her finger.

Beauregard gave Rebecca a long hard stare. Then he shut his eyes, the way cats do, for ever so long.

"Come with me," Rebecca said. "I have something for you."

Beauregard quickly followed Rebecca into the kitchen. He watched her put a bowl on the floor, next to the table.

In the bowl was spaghetti with tomato sauce. Beauregard began licking the sauce. Then he noisily slurped the individual strands of spaghetti into his mouth.

When he was finished eating, Beauregard cleaned himself, licking his legs and his paws. Then he washed his face the way cats do after they eat.

Finally content, Beauregard jumped up
onto Rebecca's lap and fell fast asleep.
Beauregard loved Rebecca more than
anyone else in the whole wide world.

A New Neighbor

Rebecca sometimes let Beauregard wander in the hall between apartments. She thought he was lonely and liked to visit the neighbors.

Sometimes when he meowed people opened their doors and gave him cat treats.

One day, while Beauregard was roaming the halls, he heard a meow. Curious, he walked over to the door where the meow had come from.

Beauregard sniffed at the door. Then he saw a black and white paw squeeze under the door. He sniffed the stranger's paw.

Suddenly the door opened. A beautiful black and white cat with greenish eyes and a pink nose was standing there. Mrs. Wilson, who always had cat treats for Beauregard, introduced Samantha.

Samantha strutted back and forth, rubbing against Beauregard, the way cats often do.

Beauregard licked Samantha's face, her ears, and her neck.

"Beauregard, it's time for you to go now," Mrs. Wilson said after a short while. "But you can come back tomorrow to see Samantha." Then Mrs. Wilson closed the door.

Beauregard continued to sit outside the closed door, howling and howling. He was in love.

That night Beauregard couldn't sleep. He sat next to Rebecca's door all night, waiting to visit Samantha.

The next morning Beauregard couldn't eat. He was still sitting next to the door, waiting to visit Samantha.

Finally Rebecca opened the door and let Beauregard out. He ran to Mrs. Wilson's and howled and howled until she opened the door.

There was Samantha, looking as beautiful as ever with her pink bow, waiting for Beauregard.

"I have a surprise for you," Mrs. Wilson said to Beauregard. "I am moving to a place that doesn't allow pets. But Rebecca said Samantha could live with you from now on."

That night, Beauregard let Samantha eat first. He even let her lie in his favorite spot next to Rebecca.

But when it came time to go to sleep, Samantha slept next to Beauregard. And Beauregard slept next to Rebecca because he still loved Rebecca more than anyone else in the whole wide world.

YOU SHOULD MEET Ruth Bader Ginsburg

by Laurie Calkhoven

illustrated by Elizabet Vukovic

Ready-to-Read

Simon Spotlight

New York   London   Toronto   Sydney   New Delhi

SIMON SPOTLIGHT

An imprint of Simon & Schuster Children's Publishing Division

1230 Avenue of the Americas, New York, New York 10020

This Simon Spotlight edition August 2019

Text copyright © 2019 by Simon & Schuster, Inc.

Illustrations copyright © 2019 by Elizabet Vukovic

All rights reserved, including the right of reproduction in whole or part in any form.

SIMON SPOTLIGHT, READY-TO-READ, and colophon are registered trademarks of Simon & Schuster, Inc.

For information about special discounts for bulk purchases, please contact Simon & Schuster Special Sales at 1-866-506-1949 or business@simonandschuster.com.

Manufactured in the United States of America 0719 LAK

2 4 6 8 10 9 7 5 3 1

Library of Congress Cataloging-in-Publication Data

Names: Calkhoven, Laurie, author. | Vukovic, Elizabet, illustrator.

Title: Ruth Bader Ginsburg / by Laurie Calkhoven ; illustrated by Elizabet Vukovic.

Description: First edition. | New York : Simon Spotlight, [2019] | Series: You should meet | Audience: 6–8. |

Identifiers: LCCN 2019011438 (print) | LCCN 2019011747 (eBook) | ISBN 9781534448599 (eBook) |

ISBN 9781534448582 (hardcover) | ISBN 9781534448575 (paperback)

Subjects: LCSH: Ginsburg, Ruth Bader—Juvenile literature. | Women judges—United States—Biography—

Juvenile literature. | Women lawyers—United States—Biography—Juvenile literature. | Women's rights—

United States—Juvenile literature.

Classification: LCC KF8745.G56 (eBook) | LCC KF8745.G56 C35 2019 (print) |

DDC 347.73/2634 [B]—dc23

LC record available at https://lccn.loc.gov/2019011438

CONTENTS

Introduction

Have you ever wanted to make the world a better place? Or seen people being treated unfairly and wanted to help? If so, then you should meet Ruth Bader Ginsburg.

In 1993, Ruth Bader Ginsburg became the second female Supreme Court justice in American history. But before that, she had to fight to become a lawyer at a time when many people believed it was a job only men should do.

As a lawyer, Ruth argued legal cases to make sure women were treated equally in the courts and in the workplace.

Over the years she became such a strong voice for what she believed in that people started calling her the "Notorious R.B.G.," after a rap and hip-hop artist (the Notorious B.I.G.) who was also from Brooklyn. **Notorious** means "widely known," sometimes for something bad. In Ruth's case, it's because she fights for what she believes in.

Once you meet Ruth Bader Ginsburg, you'll understand why!

Chapter 1
Brooklyn Born

Ruth Bader was born on March 15, 1933, in Brooklyn, New York. Her parents, who were both Jewish, came from families that had left Europe to escape anti-Jewish persecution.

Ruth's father, Nathan, was a furrier. He never finished high school. Her mother, Celia, earned top grades. She would have liked to go to college. Celia's family didn't think it was necessary to educate girls. At that time, most girls got married and raised children and didn't work outside the home. Instead of going to college herself, Celia went to work to help pay for her brother's education.

Ruth's mother never forgot how much she had wanted to go to college. She encouraged Ruth to get as much education as she could. She told her daughter stories about taking part in suffrage parades twenty years before. The word **suffrage** means "the right to vote in political elections." Suffrage parades were marches

to win women the right to vote. She
wanted Ruth to have more opportunities
than she'd had.

Celia loved to read, and she passed on
that love to her daughter. Every week, she
dropped Ruth off at the local library. Ruth
liked to read books about mythology. She
also enjoyed Nancy Drew novels and wanted
to be brave and adventurous like Nancy.

Ruth was a top student in high school. She liked to keep busy! Ruth edited the school newspaper, twirled a baton, and learned to play cello. She loved music, especially opera.

Those activities kept Ruth busy. However, things were sad at home. Her mother had cancer and was very sick. Ruth often did homework at her mother's bedside. That made her mother happy.

Ruth was chosen to make a speech at her high school graduation. Sadly, her mother died the night before. Instead of walking across the stage to accept her

diploma, Ruth planned a funeral with her father.

As sad as she was, Ruth knew her mother wanted her to go to college. She had earned a scholarship to Cornell University. In September 1950, she set off to fulfill her and her mother's dream of getting a college education.

College girls weren't encouraged to work hard. But Ruth wanted to study! She learned where all the women's bathrooms were on campus and often snuck inside one to study unseen. But studying didn't stop her from making friends and going on dates.

Ruth was still a freshman when she went on a blind date with Martin "Marty" Ginsburg. Marty, Ruth said later, was the first boy "who cared that I had a brain."

The two made a good team. Ruth was shy and quiet; Marty was outgoing. They both decided to be lawyers. Ruth wanted to use the law to help people.

The couple was married a few days after Ruth graduated from Cornell with a degree in government in 1954. Marty had just finished his first year at Harvard Law School. Ruth planned to join him there in September. Then Marty got drafted into the army, and the couple's law school plans were postponed. In the meantime, they had a daughter named Jane. Finally, in the fall of 1956, Ruth entered Harvard Law School. Ruth was one of just nine women in a class of five hundred students.

One night, the **dean** invited those nine women to his house for dinner. (The dean is the head of the law school.) He went around the table and made each woman tell him why she deserved a place at the law school when that spot could have gone to a man. He made the women feel as if he

really didn't want them there. Ruth didn't know how to answer. She knew in those days it wasn't considered feminine to want to work outside the home. She told the dean that she wanted to be able to discuss her husband's work with him during dinner when he came home at the end of the day.

That wasn't the only time Ruth felt unwelcome at law school. Once, she needed an article from a certain room in the law library. A guard wouldn't allow her in. He said the room was only open to men.

Ruth remembered her mother's advice and didn't give in to anger. She earned good grades. She kept that up even in her second year when Marty was diagnosed with cancer. She took care of Marty and their daughter, Jane, and made sure Marty got notes from all his classes. He graduated because of Ruth's help. When Marty's health improved, he got a job in New York City. Ruth transferred to Columbia Law School and tied for first in her class.

There was just one problem. Once again, no one wanted to hire her because she was a woman.

Chapter 3
Professor Ginsburg

Ruth had graduated at the top of her law school class, but not one law firm in New York City wanted to hire her. The men who ran the law firms didn't believe that a woman, especially a mother, could do the job as well as a man.

One of Ruth's professors tried to get her a job as a law clerk. A law clerk is an assistant to a judge. A clerk's responsibility is to do legal research and provide general assistance. Two judges turned him down because they didn't want to hire a woman. The third one said yes. Ruth turned out to be one of his best clerks ever. Her research was always very thorough, and she met every deadline.

Ruth later went on to become a professor at Rutgers Law School. When she learned that she was pregnant with her second child, her son, James, she kept it a secret by wearing baggier clothes. At the time, pregnant women were discouraged from working. Many were fired.

Women across the country were getting tired of being treated unfairly by the law

and by their employers. They wanted the same chances to succeed that men had. They wanted to earn the same money that men did for doing the same jobs.

Ruth worked with the American Civil Liberties Union (ACLU) to start the Women's Rights Project. Ruth was going to fight for women's rights in the courts.

Chapter 4
The Women's Rights Project

Ruth chose her cases for the Women's Rights Project very carefully. She looked for cases that would prove to the courts that laws that treated men and women unequally were bad for everyone. Because those cases challenged laws that had been in effect for a long time, many of them ended up at the Supreme Court—the highest court in the United States.

In January 1973, Ruth argued her first case before the nine male justices of the Supreme Court. Ruth was so nervous, she didn't eat lunch that day! Wearing her mother's earrings and circle pin for luck, she argued that laws treating men and women differently were unfair.

RUTH BADER GINSBURG
FIGHTS FOR WOMEN

GINSBURG

GINSBURG WINS CASE
FOR EQUAL RIGHTS

In her argument, Ruth quoted Sarah
Grimké, a woman who'd fought hard to
win the right to vote. "All I ask of our
brethren," Ruth quoted, "is that they

take their feet off our necks." In other words, Ruth wanted men to stop holding women back.

Ruth won her case! She went on to argue five more legal cases before the Supreme Court, wearing her mother's circle pin and earrings each time. She won four of the cases. She also helped write the arguments for many other successful cases. Her family was so proud of her, especially her children.

EQUAL RIGHTS CASE HITS HOME FOR RUTH BADER GINSBURG

Ruth's children weren't the only ones who were impressed by their mother's thinking. President Jimmy Carter also heard about Ruth's keen legal mind. He asked Ruth to be a judge on the US Court of Appeals, the second-highest court in the United States. She soon had a reputation for being fair-minded. Thirteen years later, in 1993, when there was an opening on the Supreme Court, President Bill Clinton turned to Ruth and nominated her for the position.

She would become the second woman in history, and the first Jewish woman, to sit on the highest court in the United States. (In 1981, Sandra Day O'Connor was the first woman appointed to the Supreme Court.)

Chapter 5
You Can't Spell "Truth" without Ruth!

Ruth stood next to President Clinton in the Rose Garden of the White House to accept the nomination to the Supreme Court in 1993. She was wearing her mother's circle pin and earrings.

In more than twenty-five years on the Supreme Court, Ruth earned a reputation as a brilliant legal mind. She's also known for her famous friendships with people who don't always agree with her. More recently, though, she has become known for her **dissents**.

In order to win a Supreme Court case, five or more of the nine justices have to agree. They are the **majority**. Those that disagree with the majority—the **minority**—have an opportunity to explain why they disagree. These are called dissents.

After President George W. Bush appointed two new justices to the bench in

the 2000s, Ruth often found herself in the minority. More and more often, she could be heard saying, "I dissent."

People began to love Ruth for her dissents. That's when people started calling her the Notorious R.B.G. Other people took up the slogan "You Can't Spell 'Truth' without Ruth."

Ruth is also known for the fancy collars she wears with her black robes. People who follow the Supreme Court know that if she is wearing the collar with the gold trim and charms, she's part of the majority opinion. She wears her glass-beaded velvet collar for dissents. And she has many other collars to wear when listening to legal arguments.

Ruth has battled cancer three times. After the first time, she started exercising to stay strong. During her treatments, she rarely missed a day's work. Many people have asked Ruth, who turned eighty-six

in 2019, when she will retire. Her answer is always the same. As long as she can still do her job, she will remain on the Supreme Court.

The Notorious R.B.G. will never stop fighting to make the world a better place. Now that you've met her, don't you want to do the same?

BUT WAIT...

THERE'S MORE!

Turn the page to learn more about Ruth Bader Ginsburg's life and the Supreme Court.

Did You Know?

Ruth thinks it's important to maintain a healthy workout routine. She is in her eighties and works out with a personal trainer twice a week and can do up to twenty push-ups!

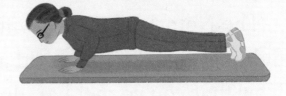

Ruth loves listening to opera music. One of her all-time favorite operas is called *The Marriage of Figaro* composed by Mozart.

Ruth learned Swedish to coauthor a book, *Civil Procedure in Sweden*, with Anders Bruzelius. Ruth learned Swedish because she didn't want anything she said in the book to be incorrectly translated. The book is about civil legal procedure in Sweden.

The Supreme Court

The Supreme Court is the highest court in the United States. The court's job is to uphold the laws of the nation.

The president of the United States nominates Supreme Court justices, and the Senate confirms them. Once they are accepted, they hold their office for life.

The Supreme Court's motto is "Equal Justice Under Law."

To date, only four women have served as justices on the Supreme Court of the United States (SCOTUS): Sandra Day O'Connor, Sonia Sotomayor, Ruth Bader Ginsburg, and Elena Kagan.

Women on the Supreme Court

Currently there are three women on the Supreme Court: Ruth Bader Ginsburg, Sonia Sotomayor, and Elena Kagan. You've already read about Ruth; now read a little bit about the other two amazing women currently on our Supreme Court!

Justice Sonia Sotomayor

Sonia was born in the Bronx in New York. She was nominated to the Supreme Court by President Barack Obama on May 26, 2009, and became the first Latina Supreme Court justice in US history. She attended Princeton University and initially felt overwhelmed and

received a low grade on her first midterm paper. This only made her more determined to study harder and do better, and her hard work paid off in the end. She graduated summa cum laude (with highest distinction) from Princeton in 1976. She was also awarded the Pyne Prize, which is the highest academic award given to Princeton undergraduate students. Sonia has become well-known for her legal battles against discrimination, and for demanding equal rights and representation for all.

Justice Elena Kagan

Elena was born in New York City, New York. She was nominated by President Barack Obama to the Supreme Court on May 10, 2010. Elena was introduced to the practice of law at an early age, as her dad was a partner at the law firm Kagan & Lubic. She attended Princeton University; the University of Oxford in Oxford, England; and Harvard Law School, where she graduated magna cum laude (with great distinction) in 1986. Before her nomination to the Supreme Court, President Obama chose Elena for the role of solicitor general. The United  States solicitor general is the fourth-highest-ranking official in the US Department of Justice. Elena was confirmed by the US Senate on March 19, 2009, and became the first woman to serve as solicitor general of the United States. A little over a year later, she took her seat on the Supreme Court on August 7, 2010.

By the Numbers

The Supreme Court began with only six justices.

As of 2019, there are now eight associate justices on the court and one chief justice. Currently six are men and three are women.

The court receives more than seven thousand cases to review each year. They typically agree to hear about eighty cases during the year.

The longest-serving justice on the Supreme Court was William O. Douglas, who served thirty-six years, seven months, and eight days in office.

Martin Ginsburg

Martin "Marty" Ginsburg was Ruth's husband. They were married from June 23, 1954, until his death on June 27, 2010. That's fifty-six years!

They had two children together: Jane Carol Ginsburg and James Steven Ginsburg.

Marty had a major impact on Ruth's life and work. When Ruth started arguing cases before the Supreme Court, Marty took over at home. After tasting Ruth's awful tuna noodle casserole early in their marriage, he realized that he had better learn to cook! Many years later, Ruth's daughter, Jane, joked, "My father did the cooking, and my mother did the thinking!"

Ruth once wrote of Marty: "I betray no secret in reporting that, without him, I would not have gained a seat on the Supreme Court."

She also said, "I have had more than a little bit of luck in life, but nothing equals in magnitude my marriage to Martin D. Ginsburg. I do not have words adequate to describe my supersmart, exuberant, ever-loving spouse."

Now that you've met Ruth, what have you learned?

1. How many Supreme Court justices serve on the court today?
a. nine   b. six   c. seven   d. ten

2. Ruth wears her gold-trimmed collar when she opposes a decision on the court.
a. true   b. false

3. What advice did Ruth's mother give her?
a. to get as much education as she desired
b. to never give in to anger or jealousy
c. to be independent
d. all of the above

4. What type of entertainment does Ruth enjoy the most?
a. theater   b. opera   c. piano concerts   d. movies

5. When was Ruth appointed as a Supreme Court justice?
a. 1972   b. 1954   c. 1993   d. 1965

6. Where did Ruth study?
a. Harvard Law School   b. Cornell University
c. Rutgers Law School   d. A and B

7. Which president nominated Ruth to the Supreme Court?
a. Bill Clinton   b. George W. Bush
c. Barack Obama   d. Jimmy Carter

8. Ruth Bader Ginsburg was the first woman to serve on the Supreme Court.
a. true   b. false

9. Why did Ruth choose her cases carefully?
a. She wanted to show how smart she was.
b. She wanted to prove men and women should be treated equally.
c. She wanted to be famous.
d. She wanted people to like her.

10. What is Ruth known for wearing?
a. a lucky bracelet   b. her mother's necklace
c. fancy collars   d. ruby earrings

Answers: 1.a 2.b 3.d 4.b 5.c 6.d 7.a 8.b 9.b 10.c

REPRODUCIBLE